Scale 1:250,000

CONTOUR INTERVAL 100 FEET

THE TUSCARAWAS VALLEY

IN

INDIAN DAYS

1750-1797

THE TUSCARAWAS VALLEY

IN

INDIAN DAYS

1750-1797

Original Journals
&
Old Maps

with
Analysis
by

Russell H. Booth, Jr.

Gomber House Press
Cambridge, Ohio

Copyright © 1994 by Russell H. Booth, Jr.
All rights reserved

Fourth Printing, May 2000

Publisher's Cataloging in Publication

The Tuscarawas Valley in Indian Days, 1750-1797: original
  journals & old maps / with analysis by Russell H. Booth, Jr.
  p. cm.
  Includes bibliographical references and index.
  Preassigned LCCN: 94-75795.
  ISBN 0-9640634-6-8

  1. Tuscarawas River Valley (Ohio)--History. 2. Ohio--History--
To 1787. 3. Ohio--History--1787-1865. I. Booth, Russell H.

  F497.T93T93 1994   977.1'66'01
                                        QBI94-583

This Gomber House Press book is printed on acid-free paper, and meets
the guidelines for permanence and durability of the Committee on
Production Guidelines for Book Longevity of the Council on
Library Resources

Printed in the United States of America

ACKNOWLEDGMENTS

The person to whom, unquestionbly, I owe the greatest debt for most of what is new in this book is Mr. Richard H. Schorr, an Assistant Auditor in the Land Office of the Auditor of State at Columbus. On my several visits to that office, he has very enthusiastically provided me with all the assistance I needed to find copies of the Original Survey maps, as well as other old maps of the period. It can easily be seen from the great number of these maps that appear in this book the extent of the value of his services to the enlargement of our knowledge of the Tuscarawas Valley in Indian Days. Through his assistance, we now know the locations of Muskingum, Bouquet's 16th Encampment, White Eyes Town, more about Three Legs, and the list could go on and on. I am deeply appreciative of his help in increasing our knowledge of the area.

That this book ever got launched at all is due to Marcia Grodsky, the Librarian at the Darlington Memorial Library in Pittsburgh. I had hesitated to start the actual writing of the book for I knew there was still at least one journal I had not been able to locate, and I did not want to write this book unless I felt that I had included all of the journals the existence of which I knew at the time. Through her efforts, however, I was able to learn that there was a misprint in the Darlington Edition of the Christopher Gist Journals, and the David *Mellouse* mentioned in that book as having preached in Newcomerstown in 1772 should have read David *McClure*. There was, therefore, no further need to try to locate the journal of a David *Mellouse*, for it, and he, did not exist. I already had the *McClure* journal and so I could go ahead with the writing of the book. She was also helpful on several other occasions in locating rather obscure, old books. My wife and I enjoyed our visits to the Darlington Library and our meetings with her.

Earl Olmstead, of New Philadelphia, Ohio, very graciously lent me his copies of translations of the Moravian Diaries from which much information can be obtained that is simply not available from any other source. I am very grateful for his assistance in this regard and have enjoyed our numerous conversations concerning events and people in the valley during the 1700s.

Robert Richardson, the Bookman of Tiltonsville, Ohio, has been very helpful in locating many of the hard-to-find books of the period, and I have been able to build up a rather extensive library through his efforts. I have also very much appreciated his personal interest in this book.

Ruth Norton, the Historian at Roscoe Village, near Coshocton, gave me copies of the Survey Route of Bouquet's Road in 1764, thus enabling me to establish the location of Bouquet's 16th Encampment survey point and confirming my previous opinion as to the location of the Indian town of Muskingum (within one mile of the Roscoe Village Visitor Center). I appreciate very much her assistance in this regard.

To our son, Rick, I am indebted for his relentless pursuit of the comma, and other errata, while proofreading the book, and to our daughter, Sally, goes my appreciation for her enthusiastic promotion of this book among the attorneys and judges of eastern Ohio, (she's a court reporter), even before I had taken it to the printer.

And finally, to my wife Ruth Anne and our son Robbie, I wish to extend my appreciation for the many evenings they had to spend alone while I was at the office putting these pages into the computer. My wife has been especially supportive and has made many valuable suggestions throughout the preparation of this book.

CONTENTS

LIST OF MAPS
(Maps follow page numbers shown below)

MAJOR TOWNS VISITED

Wakatomika

McKee, 1762	61
Zeisberger, 1772	130
Heckewelder, 1773	149
Thomas, 1774	157

Coshocton area

Gist, 1750	2
Trent, 1752	11
DeLery, 1755	13
Stuart, 1755	23
Le Roy, 1758–9	26
Gibson, 1758–9	31
Bouquet, 1764	66
Croghan, 1767	93
Wood, 1775	166
Cresswell, 1775	170
Butler, 1775	177
Zeisberger, 1776	181
Wilson, 1776	182
Heckewelder, 1778	187
Brodhead, 1781	197

Walhonding towns

Gist, 1751	2
Smith, 1755	17
Cresswell, 1775	170
Butler, 1775	177
Wilson, 1776	182
Zeisberger, 1781	199

Newcomerstown

Beatty, 1766	79
Zeisberger, 1771	95
Zeisberger, 1772	100
Ettwein, 1772	105
McClure, 1772	112
Zeisberger, 1772	130
Jones, 1773	140
Heckewelder, 1773	149

Lacey, 1773	151
Parrish, 1773	154
Wood, 1775	166
Cresswell, 1775	170
Butler, 1775	177
Brodhead, 1781	197

Gnadenhutten

Ettwein, 1772	105
Jones, 1773	140
Lacey, 1773	151
Parrish, 1773	154
Wood, 1775	166
Cresswell, 1775	170
Rose, 1782	210
Heckewelder, 1793	218
Heckewelder, 1797	219

Schoenbrunn

Zeisberger, 1772	100
Ettwein, 1772	105
Parrish, 1773	154
Cresswell, 1775	170
Butler, 1775	177

Tuscarawas

Croghan, 1760–1	41
Rogers, 1761	43
Croghan, 1761	46
Kenny, 1761–2	47
Heckewelder, 1762	50
McKee, 1762	61
Trent, 1763	63
Bouquet, 1764	66
Beatty, 1766	79
Cresswell, 1775	170
Butler, 1775	177
McCully, 1783	212
Steiner, 1789	214
Brickell, 1791	217

SOURCES

Primary sources have been used whenever possible throughout this book. There is no substitute for the eyewitness account. It is as though you were listening to that person, himself, describing his recent trip into the valley. Accordingly, the major part of this book consists of those first person accounts that have previously been published. In all cases, the source is cited.

Much of what is new, however, in this book has been derived from an analysis of these journals and the maps of the period, especially the Original Survey maps of 1797 (some of them may have actually been made in 1798, but I have simply referred to the entire survey as being the 1797 survey). On several of these maps the vestiges of Indian towns mentioned in the journals are shown. In some cases, even the length of these towns, or the location of old fields near the towns, are mentioned. Indian trails are also occasionally shown. These maps are found in the Land Office of the Auditor of State in Columbus. The modern topographic maps showing the same locations as they are today can be purchased from the U. S. Geological Survey and the Ohio Division of Geological Survey, Department of Natural Resources, at Columbus.

Of special importance are the diaries kept by the Moravian missionaries. These are in the Archives of the Moravian Church at Bethlehem, Pennsylvania. It is to be hoped that someday they would all be translated and printed, making access to this wealth of information more readily available. A card index to the diaries, which index alone contains much valuable information, has been prepared. It is known as the Fliegel Index, and is available through Research Publications, Woodbridge, Connecticut, which also has available on microfilm all of the Moravian Diaries relating to the period. Most of them, however, are still in German although portions of the Schoenbrunn and Gnadenhutten Diaries have been translated and are on the microfilm in English.

Although I have tried to put into this one book all of the eyewitness accounts of which I am aware, there is one exception to this. Three accounts have been written of the removal of the Moravian Indians to the Sandusky towns in 1781—Zeisberger in his Diary, written shortly after it happened; Heckewelder in his *Narrative...*, written over forty years later, and Heckewelder in a document entitled "Captivity and Murder", written some time after the event and quoted extensively in Wallace's *Thirty Thousand Miles With John Heckewelder*. To avoid considerable duplication I have chosen to use the Zeisberger account simply because it was written so soon after the events described therein. Both of the other accounts are extremely interesting, however, and persons wanting to learn more of what took place at that time are advised to read those accounts as well.

No attempt has been made to tell the entire story of what was happening in the valley in the 1700s, for to do so would be to have to rely to a large extent on secondhand accounts, with a corresponding loss of reliability. There are numerous frontier history books, many of which are cited in my Bibliography, in which these other accounts can be read. No doubt there is much truth in them. But to have included them in this book would be to have gone beyond my stated objective, that being to set forth in the words of the participants themselves, through their journals, the happenings in the valley. I consider this to be the most accurate way of telling their story—let them speak for themselves.

FOREWORD

In compiling a book of this nature, consisting primarily of the journals and diaries of persons who came into the Tuscarawas Valley in Indian days, two problems immediately become apparent—punctuation and spelling!

Most of these accounts were published many years ago, usually preserving the spelling and punctuation as used by the particular writer. While this is probably the most intellectually honest way of presenting this material, it can make for rather difficult reading at times. I have, therefore, occasionally inserted marks where I felt it would make the reading easier. The primary purpose of this book is to tell the story of what was going on in the valley in those days, and if the absence of punctuation marks got in the way of telling the story, I felt justified in putting them where they belonged, at least occasionally.

Spelling is also a problem—in two ways. First, for example, some people in those days would leave out an "l" in some words; "could" becomes "coud", "would" becomes "woud", etc. In those cases, I have usually left the text alone, for it soon becomes obvious that throughout that particular journal, that is the way it is going to be spelled, and the reader gets used to it. Other misspellings are also rampant throughout many of these journals but, again, you get used to it. For the most part, then, I have let the journalist spell it in his own way.

The second spelling problem concerns the names of the Indians. Since the Indians had no written language of their own, the spelling of a particular Indian's name depended entirely upon the skill of the listener, both as to the accuracy of his hearing and the ability to put in writing what he had heard. Even a person's nationality complicates the process. A German may spell what he hears differently than a Frenchman or an Englishman. Some listeners were quite literate, other's almost illiterate. The result is a real hodgepodge of the spelling of some Indian names, each of which could refer to the same Indian. (I believe that this difficulty could even be appreciated by the Indians, themselves, in their relations with the white man and is perhaps one reason that so many Indians also had white men's names—so that that particular Indian could be more easily identified. It was a lot easier to say, and spell, White Eyes than Koquethagachton.)

As a general rule, then, if a particular name appears to be close enough to another to be referring to the same Indian, it is fairly safe to assume that they really are the same person. Thus, Bisquettam and Pisquetomen are simply two different spellings of the name of a brother of Beaver and Shingas. (In the *Gibson* captivity narrative, he is called Bisquettam and is said to be a brother of Beaver and Shingas, but since *Gibson* refers to him as accompanying Post on his mission to the Indians mentioned in the introduction to the *Kenny* journal, and since it is a well known fact that Pisquetomen is the more common way of spelling the name of the brother of Beaver and Shingas who accompanied Post, it is virtually certain that they are the same Indian.)

Throughout this book, then, there will be many apparently misspelled words, but they are misspelled because that's the way the writer wrote it. Only in the most flagrant cases has any attempt been made to "correct" a spelling.

In no case, however, has the text been changed or altered in any other way.

PREFACE

The Tuscarawas Valley in east central Ohio is unique among the river systems of the state with respect to its Indian history. There's a lot of it available. It's just a matter of finding it.

This book is the result of many years of looking for this history. I have tried to put into it all of the journals and diaries that I could find (excepting only a few that will be mentioned later), with a view to enabling the reader to see the valley as those early travelers saw it, expressed in their own words. Other than, perhaps, a photograph (and there was no photography in the 1700s) there is no better way to capture the flavor of those times than through the words of the participants themselves.

What made the valley of the Tuscarawas so unique?

First, its location. Ohio has three river systems that are rich in Indian history; the Muskingum–Cuyahoga, the Scioto–Sandusky and the Miami–Maumee, with portages connecting the principal rivers in each system. The Tuscarawas River, known in those days as the Upper Muskingum or more often, simply, the Muskingum, is in the easternmost of these systems and was the closest to the white settlements. It was, therefore, the most accessible.

Second, since the Indians in the Tuscarawas Valley were so near to the settlements, they tried to maintain a state of neutrality during the Revolutionary War, neither helping the British at Detroit, nor the Americans at Fort Pitt. This enabled some whites to venture into the Indian country for a longer period of time than they otherwise could have, had the Indians been hostile from the start.

Third, and probably most important of all, is the fact that during the 1770s and early 1780s, the Moravians had established several mission towns in the valley and their ministers maintained a frequent correspondence with the authorities at Fort Pitt, as well as keeping daily diaries of the activities in their towns. They would also occasionally be called upon to serve as translators and write letters from the Indian chiefs at Newcomerstown and Coshocton to the civil or military officials at Pittsburgh. No other river system in Ohio had such an extended period of diary-keeping and letter-writing by whites who were actually living in the Indian lands.

Since the Moravians did keep their diaries on a daily basis, however, each of the diaries would be a book unto itself, and those diaries, therefore, are not reprinted here. Excerpts will, however, occasionally be quoted as they help to "fit in" with another journal that is contained in this book.

Also not reprinted here are the orderly books of the two military expeditions into the valley, Bouquet's Expedition in 1764 and the McIntosh Campaign to Fort Laurens in 1778. Mostly, these books consist of the orders for the next day, the countersigns, the duty officers, etc., and are not descriptive of the valley itself. Portions of them that do include something of particular interest are included, however.

With the above exceptions (and also those referred to on page x), I have tried to include in this book all of the journals that I am aware of. Some of them are very detailed and contain much of interest—descriptions of the Indian towns, houses, council meetings, dances, rum frolics, and just plain conversations with the Indians on a variety of subjects. Other journals are not very interesting and contain little of detail. Even so, they are included for the sake of completeness. I would hope, therefore, that this book will serve as a convenient one-volume reference for anyone desiring to see as much of the valley as possible through the eyes of those who were here in Indian days.

It will probably come as a surprise to many readers to see just how much activity was going on here in the 1700s. Traders were constantly coming and going, land speculators were scouting out the good land for their companies to purchase when it would become available for settlement, ministers of various faiths came to preach to the Indians, captives were brought to the towns, and, on several occasions, military expeditions came into the area. It was a very busy place.

With the reading of these journals another fact becomes apparent that may also come as a surprise to many. The whites and the Indians were not always at war with each other. Often, for years at a time, there was peace on the border and people could travel into the Indian country in absolute, or at least comparative, safety. Indians traveled with their families to Fort Pitt, a few went as far as Philadelphia, and, more rarely, some chiefs had even gone to England to see the Great King over the water. Many Indians became good friends of certain whites, sometimes even taking their names or the name of someone among the whites that they admired. Thus, we have Sir William Johnson, William Henry, John Lewis, Simon Girty—and many others—all of them Indians.

These periods of peace were not permanent, however, and for one reason or another troubles would break out and a full-fledged Indian war would be the result. At such times as this, the usual consequences of Indian–white warfare would then take place in all their fury—killing, scalping, torturing, and carrying into captivity on the part of the Indians, and raids against the Indian towns by white militia or soldiers. Eventually, though, things would settle back down and peace would once again come to the border. So it went throughout the latter half of the 1700s.

Finally, these accounts will probably change the preconceived notion that some persons have of an Indian as a savage, with a tomahawk in one hand and a bloody scalp in the other. It was not always so. More often, this same Indian was peacefully living out his life, helping to raise his children, hunting for fur to trade for the white man's goods, and treating everyone with whom he came in contact, white or Indian, in a perfectly proper and friendly manner.

It is my hope, then, that after reading these journals the reader will almost feel he has actually known the Killbucks, White Eyes, Netawatwees, Jo Peepe, the young Englishman, Nicholas Cresswell, the courageous Moravian missionaries, Zeisberger and Heckewelder, and the many other people who lived in or came into the area in the 1700s—known them as the real people that they were and not just as characters in a book.

HISTORICAL BACKGROUND

Before late 1600s   Ohio largely uninhabited by Indians.

Late 1600s   Dispossessed Indians from the east begin to move into the Ohio area. French fur traders establish posts.

Late 1720s   A few English fur traders come into the area.

1730s & 1740s   Rivalry between French and English fur traders intensifies.

1750   The Ohio Company of Virginia sends Christopher Gist into the region for the purpose of land speculation, giving us our earliest detailed look at the country to the west of the mountains. His is the first journal in this book.

1753   Washington is sent by Governor Dinwiddie of Virginia to the newly-constructed French forts near Erie, Pennsylvania, asking the French to leave the area. Christopher Gist is his guide.

1754   The French construct Fort DuQuesne at the Forks of the Ohio (now Pittsburgh) and the French and Indian War breaks out.

July 9, 1755   General Braddock is defeated by the French and Indians along the Monongahela near Fort DuQuesne, suffering nearly 1,000 casualties out of about 1,400 engaged.

1758   General Forbes captures Fort DuQuesne. It was rebuilt as Fort Pitt. Delaware Indians living along the Beaver River in western Pennsylvania move into Ohio along the Upper Muskingum (Tuscarawas) and Cuyahoga rivers.

1760   Fort Detroit is captured by the British. French influence in the area wanes.

1761   Christian Frederick Post tries to establish a mission at Beaver's Town, also called Tuscarawas, near Bolivar.

1763   Pontiac's War breaks out. Delawares move their towns from the Upper Muskingum and Cuyahoga to the Hocking, the Walhonding, and the Tuscarawas near Newcomerstown. Many white persons are prisoners in these towns.

1764   Col. Bouquet enters the Tuscarawas Valley with 1,500 men and proceeds to the vicinity of Coshocton. He enters into treaties of peace with the Indians and takes back over 200 of the white captives.

1772	Schoenbrunn (originally called Welhik Thuppeek), the first of the Moravian towns in the Tuscarawas Valley, is established. Gnadenhutten is also begun a few months later.
1774	Dunmore's War breaks out between the Shawnees, living mostly in the Scioto area, and the Virginians. (Dunmore was the Governor of Virginia.) Delawares along the Tuscarawas are not directly affected, but the Shawnee towns at Wakatomika (near Dresden) are destroyed by an expedition from Wheeling commanded by Maj. Angus McDonald.
1775	Revolutionary War begins. Delawares remain neutral. Netawatwees, also called Newcomer, moves his town from Newcomerstown to Coshocton.
1776	Netawatwees dies. Gelelemend (also called John Killbuck Jr.) is his designated successor, but White Eyes, a friend of the Americans, becomes their most influential leader.
1778	Fort Laurens, at Bolivar, is built by the Americans, but is abandoned the next year. White Eyes dies, attributed at the time to smallpox, but later is said to have been murdered by American militiamen. His death is a great loss to the American cause.
1781	Most of the Delawares openly enter the war on the side of the British. A few, including Gelelemend, remain friendly to the Americans. Colonel Brodhead destroys Coshocton. Later that year, the Christian Indians are forcibly removed, by the Indians who were supporting the British, from their towns along the Tuscarawas to the Upper Sandusky area.
1782	The Gnadenhutten Massacre occurs when 90 of the Christian Indians who had gone back to harvest the crops left behind when they had to leave their towns the year before are killed by American militiamen.
1795	The Battle of Fallen Timbers, in the northwestern part of the state, ends the Indian hostilities in Ohio and opens the territory for settlement.
1797	Lands given to the Moravian Church by the federal government, as recognition of the services performed by the Moravian missionaries in secretly aiding the Americans during the Revolutionary War, are surveyed. Heckewelder assists in locating these tracts. His is the last journal in this book.

INTRODUCTION

The Political Background

The journals in this book cover the years from 1750 to 1797. During this period of time, the Indian villages in the Tuscarawas Valley changed from Wyandot and Ottawa to Delaware, and the Indian-white contacts from French to English. In reading these journals, therefore, the political situation of that era must be kept in mind.

Long before the English had penetrated the Allegheny barrier, the French had established an active fur trade among the Ohio Indians. With the establishment of Fort Niagara in 1678 and Fort Ponchartrain at Detroit in 1701, they had bases from which their traders could go into the Indian towns, taking all manner of goods desired by the Indians in exchange for furs for the European market. The French had a monopoly on this trade until the late 1720s when a few English traders, primarily from Pennsylvania, began to cross the mountains. Gradually these newcomers made inroads upon the earlier traders, for they could sell their goods to the Indians for a cheaper price than that charged by the French. The resulting competition between France and England for the control of the fur trade of the Ohio Valley culminated in the last, and greatest, of the French wars of the eighteenth century, now called the French and Indian War. With the signing of the Treaty of Paris in 1763, control of all of this part of the North American continent, including even Canada, passed to the English.

The Delaware Indians had fought against the British in that war and were deeply alarmed when the French abandoned Fort Duquesne in 1758. They had been residing in western Pennsylvania along the Beaver and Allegheny rivers, but after the British took over Fort DuQuesne, renaming it Fort Pitt, they moved their towns farther west, fearing reprisals for their conduct in the war. They went first to the Cuyahoga and Upper Muskingum area, near Bolivar, later moving to other parts of the state but eventually settling in the vicinity of Newcomerstown. Most of the Indians in this book, therefore, are Delawares, and most of the towns are located along what is now called the Tuscarawas River, from Coshocton to Bolivar.

There were, of course, other Indians in Ohio. The Shawnee settlements closest to the Delawares were a few towns along the Lower Muskingum near Dresden, collectively called Wakatomika. These towns were also sometimes referred to as the Upper Shawnee Town (or Towns). The main Shawnee town, however, was known as the Lower Shawnee Town, originally along the Ohio just west of the mouth of the Scioto, and later the name was given to a collection of towns on the Pickaway Plains between Circleville and Chillicothe. To the north, along the Sandusky River, were the Wyandots, also called Hurons or Dellamatenos (some of them, the "over the lakes" Indians, were in Canada, near Detroit), and further west, the Miamis, sometimes known as Picts or Twightwees. In addition, there were a few Mingos, originally along the Ohio River near Steubenville and, later, on the Muskingum at Wakatomika.

Having thus indicated generally where the Indian towns and tribes were located in the late 1700s, it should be said that there was sometimes considerable overlapping of these tribal areas. There were Delaware towns in the vicinity of Zanesville and Duncan Falls, also near Lancaster on the Hocking River, and even on the Scioto near Columbus. Most of the Delawares, however, were along the Tuscarawas River and the Walhonding.

In 1763 an Indian uprising occured, sometimes referred to as Pontiac's War. All of the British forts west of the mountains except those at Detroit and Pittsburgh were destroyed, and hundreds of people, including many Indian traders, were killed. At that time the Delawares were living along the Cuyahoga and Upper Muskingum. Since the Indian trail from Fort Pitt to Detroit passed through this area, they were afraid that they would be caught between the contending parties. They accordingly sent a message to the authorities at Fort Pitt telling them about the uprising among the tribes to the west of them and ending with the following words:

> Brother: We thought your king had made peace with us and all the Western Nations of Indians, for our part we joined it heartily and desired to hold it always good, and you may depend upon it we will take care not to be readily cheated or drawn into a war again, but as we are settled between you and these nations who have taken up the hatchet against you we desire you will send no warriors this way till we are removed from this, which we will do as soon as we conveniently can; when we will permit you to pass without taking notice, till then we desire they may go by the first road you went.
>
> (Source: *Trent's* journal of 1763)

This is the Indian way of saying that they would be moving their towns in order to get out of the way of the coming war between the British at Fort Pitt and the Indians to the west of them. It was at this time, therefore, that the next migration of the Delawares took place.

The chief of the Turkey tribe, Beaver, moved his town to the Hocking River area; the chief of the Wolf tribe, Custaloga, moved his town to the Walhonding (he may have done this somewhat earlier); and the chief of the Turtle tribe, Netawatwees, moved his town at first to the Scioto but eventually to the Tuscarawas in the vicinity of Newcomerstown. (This assertion that the Turtles went first to the Scioto may be in error, but is based upon certain inferences that I have drawn from the *McCullough* captivity narrative which will be discussed more fully in another section of this book.)

The Tuscarawas Valley in Indian Days

Since the head chief of the Turtle tribe, Netawatwees (also called Newcomer by the whites), had apparently become the spokesman for all three tribes in their dealings with the whites, he was often referred to as "King Newcomer", and his town, Newcomerstown, was thought of as the principal town of the Delaware "Nation". For this reason, and also because it was probably the largest of the Delaware towns, it was to Newcomerstown that most of the travelers came when they visited with the Delawares. It was in existence as the primary town of their nation from the autumn of 1764 (again, inferred from the *McCullough* narrative) until 1775 when Netawatwees moved to the Coshocton area. Under the influence of Netawatwees and, after his death in 1776, Whites Eyes, the Delawares had remained neutral during the Revolutionary War, but after White Eyes died in 1778, they eventually came into the war on the side of the British. Colonel Brodhead then destroyed Coshocton in the spring of 1781, and the Delaware occupation of the valley came to an end.

A Glossary of Names

Rivers

Tuscarawas	called Elk's Eye Creek by *Gist* in 1750.
	called Naguerre Konnan by *DeLery* in 1755.
	called Muskingum by the rest of the travelers.
Walhonding	called White Woman's Creek by *Gist* in 1751.
	called Conchake by *DeLery* in 1755.
	called Walhanding by the rest of the travelers.
Sugar Creek	usually called Margaret's Creek.
Stillwater	usually called Gekelemukpechunk Creek.

The "Forks of the Muskingum" refers to the junction of the Walhonding and Tuscarawas rivers at Coshocton.

[Note: Since most of the journalists refer to the Tuscarawas River as the Muskingum, I find that it is usually easier, and less confusing, to also refer to it as the Muskingum in my notes and special studies.]

Principal Towns

Tuscarawas	at the crossing place of the Muskingum just above Bolivar, on the west side of the river. Called Beaver's Town in early journals.
Newcomerstown	at Newcomerstown. Also known as Gekelemukpechünk, Gekelemukpehong, Kekalemahpehoong, Kighalampegha and probably even by other spellings.
White Eyes Town	Two miles east of West Lafayette, on the south side of the river.
Muskingum	sometimes spelled Moschkingo. In 1750, this was a town of the Wyandots, on the Tuscarawas near the northeastern part of the town of Coshocton (mostly on the north side of the river, however) and approximately two miles upstream from the junction with the Walhonding. Called Conchake by *DeLery* in 1755. It was decimated by disease in 1751 or 1752 and there were only two houses in it in 1755. By 1758, however, Bisquettam's Delawares had moved to the vicinity according to the captivity narratives of *Hugh Gibson* and *Marie Le Roy*. When Bouquet came into the area in 1764, however, it had again been abandoned.
Coshocton	at Coshocton. Also sometimes spelled Coashoking, Coashoskin, Coashoskis or Cooshasking. Probably even other spellings. Newcomer moved here in 1775. Destroyed by Brodhead in 1781.
Wakatomika	near Dresden, on the west side of the Muskingum. Sometimes spelled Wappatomika. A collection of Shawnee towns. Destroyed in 1774 by McDonald's Expedition during Dunmore's War.
Schoenbrunn	near New Philadelphia, on the east side of the Tuscarawas. Originally called Welhik Thuppeek. Also sometimes called the upper Moravian town. The first of the mission towns, founded in May of 1772.

Gnadenhutten   at Gnadenhutten. Also sometimes spelled Kanaughtonhead or Kanantohead. Occasionally called the lower Moravian town, but after Lichtenau was founded, then referred to as the middle Moravian town. The second of the mission towns, founded in October of 1772. Site of the massacre of Christian Indians in 1782. The Christian Indians who settled here originally started to build their town on the west side of the Tuscarawas near the mouth of Stone Creek, but after a few weeks they were told by the Indian chiefs at Newcomerstown to locate their town at the site of Beaver's old town, at Gnadenhutten.

Lichtenau   about two miles below the Forks of the Muskingum at Coshocton, on the east side of the river, established on the site of the old Indian town known as Mowheysinck. The third of the mission towns, founded in April of 1776. Abandoned in 1780. Delawares then moved there and it was destroyed by Brodhead in 1781.

New Schoenbrunn   one mile west of Schoenbrunn on the west side of the river. Usually called simply Schoenbrunn. The fourth of the mission towns, founded in December of 1779.

Salem   about one and one-half miles southwest of Port Washington, on the north side of the Tuscarawas. The last of the mission towns, founded in April of 1780.

There were many other towns, mostly small, scattered throughout the area—Tulllhas, Custaloga's Town, Pipe's Town, Wingenund's Town, Old Hundy and New Hundy, all along the Walhonding or its tributaries; Tom's Town, Snake's Town, and the Vomit Town, along the Lower Muskingum; and several un-named villages on the Tuscarawas between Coshocton and Gnadenhutten. Some of the above towns may be at the same locations as earlier towns that would have had a different name. For instance, Custaloga, Pipe, and Wingenund may all, at different times, have lived at the same town site along the Walhonding, and while they lived there, the town would have been known by their name. Naming a town is one thing, however—finding it is something else, and it is often very difficult to determine the exact location of a particular town. In the absence of visible vestiges of a town when the region was surveyed in 1797 (fortunately the remains of a few towns were still visible at that time and were noted by the surveyors), about the best that can be done is simply to approximate a town's location using whatever evidence is available in the journals of the period.

Notable Indians

Netawatwees

A Delaware chief of the Turtle lineage, also called Newcomer, and, in some of the journals, Netatwhelman or Nettautwaleman. After the death of Beaver, he seems to have become the principal spokesman, or "King", of all three lineages of the Delawares, i. e., the Turtle, Turkey, and Wolf tribes. He was living in western Pennsylvania along the Beaver Creek in the 1750s, took part in the French and Indian War on the side of the French, and moved to the Cuyahoga after the British captured Fort DuQuesne in 1758. He was still there in 1762 when Heckewelder first came into the area but moved to the southward at the outbreak of Pontiac's War in 1763, eventually settling at Newcomerstown in 1764. He was a friend of the Moravians and was instrumental in inviting the Christian Indians to the Tuscarawas Valley. He tried to maintain the neutrality of the Delawares during the Revolution and died at a very advanced age (nearly 90) at Pittsburgh on October 31, 1776, while attending a treaty.

Killbuck

The popular name of a well-known Delaware family.

Killbuck, Sr. was of the Wolf lineage and was one of their principal warriors during the French and Indian War, fighting on the side of the French. His Indian name was Bemineo. He was one of Netawatwees' principal counsellors, was favorable to the American cause during the Revolutionary war, but was somewhat cool towards the Moravian presence in the Tuscarawas Valley. According to Heckewelder, he spoke "good English". He became blind in his old age and died in 1779 or 1780.

Killbuck, Jr., also called John Killbuck, Jr., Capt. Killbuck, and Gelelemend, with various spellings of the last name, was the son of Killbuck, Sr. and was of the Turtle lineage. Upon the death of Netawatwees, as his designated successor, he became chief of the Turtle tribe, although it is not clear that he was ever actually elected to the position. He was friendly to the American cause during the Revolution and tried to maintain the neutrality of the Delawares. Eventually, however, in the spring of 1781, the more warlike elements of the Delawares, primarily under Capt. Pipe of the Wolf tribe, gained the ascendency, and most of the Delawares entered the war on the side of the British. By that time, Killbuck, Jr. had taken the name of William Henry, obtained a commission in the American army, and, after Brodhead's Expedition to Coshocton in 1781, moved to Pittsburgh for his own safety. He later joined the Christian

Indians and died at Goshen in 1811. He is buried beside David Zeisberger in the mission cemetery.

In reading these journals, it is often very difficult to tell which Killbuck a particular diarist is talking about if all he uses is the name "Killbuck".

White Eyes

A war chief and one of the principal counsellors of the Delaware nation, belonging to the Turkey lineage. After the death of Netawatwees, he seems to have become the principal spokesman for all of the Delawares and was a firm friend of the Americans during the Revolutionary War. He had travelled all of the way down the Mississippi and taken a ship to the Eastern seaboard. Consequently, he was aware of the great strength and power of the whites and of the inevitable spread of their culture across the Allegheny Mountains. He tried to prepare the Delawares for some type of accomodation with the whites but died in 1778 before anything could be accomplished. His death, at the time, was attributed to smallpox, but later evidence suggests he was murdered by American militiamen. After his death, Killbuck, Jr. was simply not a strong enough leader to keep the Delawares neutral and they eventually entered the war on the side of the British.

Captain Pipe

A Delaware chief of the Wolf lineage. He was pro-British during the Revolutionary War and was one of the principal Indians who caused the removal of the Christian Indians from their towns to the Upper Sandusky area in 1781.

Beaver

A Delaware chief of the Turkey lineage, sometimes called King Beaver. In 1761 he was living at Tuscarawas, near Bolivar. During Pontiac's War in 1763 he moved to the Hocking, but when he died in 1769 he was living on the site of Gnadenhutten.

Shingas

One of Beaver's brothers (according to the *Gibson* captivity narrative there were seven of them altogether—a distinguished family). As a war chief he fought so ferociously against the English in the French and Indian War that he was known as "Shingas the Terrible" and a price was put upon his head. He was living at Tuscarawas in 1762, was well liked by Hecke-welder, who was one of the attendants at his wife's funeral, and is believed to have died in the winter of 1763–64. He was sometimes called King Shingas.

Pisquetomen

Another of Beaver's brothers, called Bisquetam in the *Gibson* narrative. Mason and Dixon met him in 1767 during their famous survey and stated, at page 175 of their published journal, that he was 86 years of age, "spoke very good English", and that "his face is deeply furrowed with time".

Joseph Peepy A Delaware Indian often used as a guide and translator by whites who came into the area, especially preachers. His wife, Hannah, his daughter-in-law (the wife of his son, Anton), and several of his grandchildren would die in the Gnadenhutten Massacre. He died in about 1782, "being upwards of 90 years old." (Heckewelder, in *Transactions...*, p. 386.)

Getting To The Valley

Travelers to the valley from Fort Pitt would customarily cross the Allegheny River at Pittsburgh and proceed along the north side of the Ohio, cross the Beaver, and then, depending upon where they were going, choose from a variety of routes.

1. They could proceed on down the Ohio to the vicinity of Crow's Town (Mingo Junction now), below Steubenville, and then head westerly towards the Gnadenhutten area. *McClure* apparently came into the valley this way.

2. After crossing the Beaver, they could head west on the Tuscarawas path for a number of miles, then southwesterly towards the Gnadenhutten area on what Hutchins had called the Muskingum path. (In 1763 when Hutchins was describing the Indian paths, Gnadenhutten had not yet been founded, but since the path went on to the Forks of the Muskingum he called it the Muskingum path.) *Stuart, Beatty* (returning), *Lacey, Parrish* and *Wood* used this route.

3. They could stay on the Tuscarawas path to the vicinity of Magnolia. At that point they could proceed southwesterly towards the Tuscarawas at Zoarville, cross it there and go down the Tuscarawas to Stone Creek, then follow it and Evans Creek to the Tuscarawas again near Orange (*DeLery* did this heading east), or, if they had digressed from Evans Creek above Bakersville and continued to head southwest they would hit the Tuscarawas near the mouth of White Eyes Creek (*Gist's* route).

4. If they did not leave the Tuscarawas path at Magnolia, they could stay on it until reaching the famous "crossing place of the Muskingum" at Bolivar, known then as Tuscarawas. After crossing the "Muskingum" at Tuscarawas and proceeding on to Margaret's Creek (Sugar Creek now), they could then head either south towards Newcomerstown (*Beatty* did this), or southwest towards Coshocton (*Bouquet's* route).

The entire journey took several days.

On Indian Place Names

It is often difficult to tell what is meant when an event is described as happening at a certain place. For instance, if something in 1761 is said to have occured at "Muskingum", what is actually meant by that?—the town of Muskingum mentioned by *Gist* in 1750?—the area around the Forks of the Muskingum at Coshocton?—or some other place along the river itself, which could include as far north as above Bolivar? (*Steiner* referred to even that part of the river as the Muskingum in 1789.) Is "Tuscarawas" a town, an area, or a river? If it's a river, just where does it begin and end? (*Steiner*, with Heckewelder present, even calls the Sandy the Tuscarawi, refers to the two plains near Malvern as the Tuscarawi plains, and calls the river it runs into, near Bolivar, the Muskingum.) Zeisberger, in 1772, seems to call the Sandy and even part of the river below Bolivar the Tuscarawi, and only later mentions that they finally came to the Muskingum. Where? Near Zoarville, after the Connotton joins it, or near Dover at the junction of Sugar Creek, or someplace else?

With regard to the naming of towns, that seems to be more the white man's doing than the Indians'. Attaching a name to the town itself was probably a meaningless act to an Indian. To the Indian, it was just a collection of houses at a particular place. If the *place* had a name (such as the Forks of the Muskingum at Coshocton being thought of simply as "Muskingum"), then perhaps the "town" would be called by its place name. Or, where a prominent chief resided might be thought of as *his* "town", such as Newcomer's Town or Custaloga's Town. This way of designating a "town", however, could also be used to describe any place in which a particular Indian lived, prominent chief or not—just use his name. All you are doing is saying that that is the place where so-and-so lives.

The purpose of this discussion, then, is simply to let the reader be aware of these problems as he reads the journals. Don't be too quick to jump to a conclusion as to a place name. You could be wrong. Of course, this applies equally to me as I have prepared this book. Perhaps I have come up with some wrong conclusions, myself, and still do not realize it.

Lineage

Delaware society was matrilineal. By that it is meant that it was through the mother's bloodline that kinship was determined.

The Delawares seem to have been divided into three divisions, originally based on geographical areas of residence in New Jersey and eastern Pennsylvania. These divisions were known as the Unami, the Unalachtigo, and the Minsi (or Monsey), popularly called the Turtle, the Turkey, and the Wolf Tribes. The dialect of the Unami and the Unalachtigo was very similar and eventually the smaller Unalachtigo began to be thought of as simply a part of the larger Unami tribe and the tripartite division of the nation became somewhat blurred.

Presumably for genetic reasons, marriages were supposed to be between persons of different tribes. Thus a Turkey man would be expected to marry a Turtle or Wolf woman.

Their children would be of whatever tribe the mother was. If she was a Turtle, all of her children would also be Turtles. These children would marry either a Turkey or a Wolf, and their offspring would be of the same lineage as *their* mother, etc.

Within any particular Indian town, then, there would be a significant mixture of tribes. Thus, Newcomerstown, named for Netawatwees, the chief of the Turtle Tribe who resided there, did not consist of just Turtles. Even Netawatwees' wife was either a Turkey or a Wolf. His children were, therefore, either Turkeys or Wolfs, and they had to marry outside of their tribe, as well. So it can be seen that just because a chief in a Town was of a particular tribe, it did not mean that all of the Indians living there were also of that same tribe.

This concept of lineage determined to a great degree the question of who was qualified to succeed a particular chief when he died or otherwise left his office. The matter of succession was supposed to stay in the bloodline of the chief. For example, since Netawatwees was a Turtle, he had to be succeeded by a Turtle of his bloodline. His own sons were not eligible, for they were not Turtles. They would be of whatever tribe their mother was. A chief would, therefore, usually be succeeded by his brother (who would, of course, be of the same tribe and bloodline as the chief, since they had the same mother), or a nephew who was the son of a sister of the chief (the sister also having the same mother as the chief would be of her lineage and her children, both sons and daughters, would also, therefore, be of that same lineage).

Chiefs, Counsellors and Captains

A chief presides at council meetings and is responsible for the good order and well-being of his tribe. Although the Indians have no formal laws, the decisions arrived at by the chief and his counsellors, after mature deliberation, are obeyed without further question. Council meetings are conducted with great solemnity and decorum, each person who wishes to speak being allowed to do so without interruption until he is done—then another may speak.

The counsellors are the captains and the older men of the village who, by the respect they have earned through the years, are looked upon by the people as persons whose advice and wisdom should be sought in matters of importance to the tribe or village.

The captains are men of very great influence in the tribe. If a person who leads a group of men on a raid has been fortunate on six or seven occasions and has captured prisoners and taken scalps without losing any of his own men, he is entitled to be considered as a captain. If he does lose a man, he is expected to bring back a prisoner in his place. Only through merit can an Indian be considered to have earned the rank of captain. Captains decide on questions of war or peace. If war is declared, the principal captain replaces the tribal chief in the management of the tribe until such time as peace is later declared by the chief, at which time the chief resumes his place as leader of the tribe.

Indian–White Warfare in the 18th Century

The manner in which Indian–white warfare was conducted in the latter half of the 18th century was far different from the manner of that conducted between the English and the French, or, later, the British and the Americans. That difference was cultural.

As the whites moved over the mountains into the Ohio valley, the fact that there were Indians already living, or hunting, on that land seemed irrelevant. From the white point of view, Indian habitations were so flimsy, and the Indian lifestyle so transient, that they could simply be brushed aside. It seemed to the whites that the Indians could simply move farther west, since the land in that direction seemed limitless.

To the Indian, however, the land was not limitless. Other Indian tribes already occupied or claimed as their hunting grounds the land to the west, and those Indians did not want to have to give up some of what they already had, not even to other Indians.

Therefore, the Indians fought back. It was very rare for the Indians to attack an entire town or a fort. Usually, they used terror tactics on a small scale, attacking individual homesteads, sometimes killing the entire family but, often, taking the women and children prisoners. They would then rush back to their towns as rapidly as possible, knowing that they were being pursued by the whites who were hoping to recapture the prisoners. If someone, even a small child, could not keep up with the fast pace, he was killed. After reaching the Indian towns, the children would usually be adopted into an Indian family and raised like one of their own children. The women would sometimes eventually marry an Indian and possibly live the rest of their lives with them. If men had been taken prisoner, they were often, but not always, killed when the Indians arrived at their towns. Occasionally, they, too, were adopted into the tribe. (This was the case with Daniel Boone.) The taking of prisoners and adopting of them into the tribe helped to increase the population of the tribe and to replace those who had already been killed by the whites, or had otherwise died. From the Indian point of view, then, their objective was to frighten the whites to the point where they would move back over the mountains and leave the Indians in possession of their lands.

The whites, on the other hand, had no use for prisoners at all. When they fought with the Indians, therefore, they simply killed them. There was no point in capturing them, for what would you do with them then? It seems harsh, now, to realize that, just as the Indians killed most male prisoners that they took, so, too, did the whites kill Indian prisoners that happened to fall into their hands, including occasionally even women and children. (Indian boys would grow into Indian warriors.) But that was simply a fact of life in the 18th century manner of warfare between the races.

The whites, in initiating a raid into the Indian country, did not directly go after the Indian warriors, for it would have been virtually impossible to locate them in sufficient numbers to bring them to battle. Rather, they tried to destroy the towns in which the Indians lived, thus driving them from the land and making it more difficult for them to continue their raids against the white settlements. In 1774, Maj. McDonald destroyed the Upper Shawnee Towns at Wakatomika and in 1781 Col. Brodhead destroyed the Delaware towns of Coshocton and Lichtenau. In the Wakatomika campaign, most of the Indians had already fled from the towns and there was just a small skirmish with the few that remained, but the towns were destroyed and the objective of the mission was attained. In the Coshocton campaign, although many of the Indians had already left the town before Brodhead arrived, there were still a few there who were captured by Brodhead. (There does not seem to have been a battle, for no whites were killed or wounded at all.) After capturing the Indians, Brodhead apparently executed the warriors and destroyed the town, along with Lichtenau, two miles south of Coshocton. He then returned, having accomplished his mission—not the killing of some Indians, but the destruction of the Delaware towns.

That, then, was the way that the Indians and the whites fought in the 18th century.

By the 19th century, the whites realized that the land to the west was not limitless, and the reservation system for the Indians came into existence. The Indians did not simply have to be killed, but rather could be subdued and placed on these reservations.

For the Indians of the earlier times, however, it was kill or be killed.

The Indians

The following comments regarding the Indians and their habitations are taken from "David Zeisberger's History of the Northern American Indians" as published in the *Ohio Archaeological and Historical Society Publications,* Volume XIX:

p. 17   Houses of the Indians were formerly only huts and for the most part remain such humble structures, particularly in regions far removed from the habitation of whites. These huts are built either of bast (tree-bark peeled off in the summer) or the walls are made of boards covered with bast. They are low structures. Fire is made in the middle of the hut under an opening whence the smoke escapes. Among the Mingoes and the Six Nations one rarely sees houses other than such huts built entirely of bast, which, however, are frequently very long, having at least from two to four fire-places, the families being related. Among the Delawares each family prefers to have its own house, hence they are small. The Mingoes make a rounded, arched roof, the Delawares on the contrary, a high pitched, peaked roof. The latter, coming much in contact with the whites, as they do not live more than a hundred miles from Pittsburg, have learned to build block houses or have hired whites to build them. Christian Indians generally build proper and comfortable houses and the savages who seek to follow their example in work and household arrangement learn much from them.

p. 17   Their britchen [bunks], made of boards and arranged about the fire, serve as table, bench and bedstead. The underbedding upon which they lie, is either an untanned deer or bear skin or a mat of rushes, which grow in ponds or stagnant water; these the women are clever enough to decorate in red, black or other colors, finding the materials for the latter in the forest. These mats they also fasten about the walls of their lodges, keeping out the cold of winter as well as for ornamentation. Blankets worn during the day as part of the clothing serve at night as covering.

p. 86   Their houses are fairly clean, some being superior in this respect and affording a comfortable night's lodging for a European. In case a guest is expected, especially if it be a white person, they prepare as comfortable a bed as possible. They sweep the bunk, that serves as seat and table in the daytime and as bed at night, and spread a mat with one or more deer or bear skins upon it. Though usually a comfortable couch in summer time it may be made very uncomfortable by the fleas brought in by dogs. Their kettles, dishes and spoons are not kept in good order; sometimes they are only licked by the dogs in lieu of washing. Dishes and spoons they make themselves of wood, sometimes of tree knots or growths, often very neatly. The spoons are generally large and round shaped. Occasionally, a spoon will be used by several people, turn about, at a meal. Brass kettles, to be found in most houses because very necessary for sugar boiling, are bought from the whites.

p. 12   The North American Indians are of middle size, well built, straight, light-footed, well adapted for travel through the forest, much of which is due to the fact that they do no heavy work, but support themselves by the chase. Their color is brown, but of different shades. Some are light brown, hardly to be distinguished from a brown European, did not their eyes and hair betray them. Again, others are so dark that they differ little from mulattoes. Their hair is jet-black and coarse, almost like the hair of a horse's mane. Their heads become gray or even white in old age, otherwise they are without exception, black. The men rarely let the hair grow long, and it is common practice among them, though the custom is obsolescent, that they root out the hair from the forehead backward so that the head is bald up to the crown and only a hand-breadth of it in circular form is suffered to remain, whence in the case of savages generally depend long braids, one on either side, closely plaited and bound by bracelets of coral, some, also, hanging silver upon them. It is a very common [sic] that they wear a plume of feathers on the middle of the head, rising straight up or hanging downward. They frequently cut the helix of the ear, leaving the upper and lower ends intact and then hang bits of lead to it so that it is stretched. Then this curved border of the auricle is bound with brass wire, distending it considerably, and decorated with silver ornaments. Among Indians who have come in contact with whites this is less often done. They, also, pierce the nose and adorn it with silver. The beard is rooted out as soon as it begins to grow. The men tattoo their bodies in arm, leg or face with all manner of figures, serpents, birds or other animals, which are marked out by pricking the skin with a needle, powder or soot being afterward rubbed into the punctures. Occasionally, the women mark their bodies thus. The women let the hair grow long, so that it sometimes reaches to the knees; they do not braid it but tie a cloth around it. The Mingoes, Shawano and

Wiondatoo women have a long braid reaching the hips, bound in cloth and red ribbon, in the case of the rich, being further adorned with silver clasps of considerable weight from top to bottom. The Delawares, also, do this, though not so generally. The women wear earrings of wampum, coral or silver.

p. 15   Their dress is light; they do not hang much clothing upon themselves. If an Indian has a Match-coat, that is a blanket of the smaller sort, a shirt and brich clout and a pair of leggins, he thinks himself well dressed. In place of a blanket, those who are in comfortable circumstances and wish to be well dressed, wear a strowd, i.e., two yards of blue, red or black cloth which they throw lightly over themselves and arrange much as they would a Match-coat. Trousers they do not wear; but their hose, reaching considerably above the knee and held together by a piece of strowd and extending only to the feet, to some extent supply the place of trousers. If they desire to go in state, they wear such hose with a silken stripe extending from top to bottom and bordered with white coral. Their shoes are made of deer skin, which they prepare themselves, the women being particularly skilled in doing this and in working all manner of designs; Mingoe women excel all others in this particular. Some wear hats or caps secured in trading with the whites; others do not cover themselves but go bare-headed.

Women are distinguished in dress only in this respect, that instead of a coat they wear a strowd over the hips bound about the body next the skin, removed neither day nor night and extending but little beyond the knees. They anoint the hair liberally with bear's fat, so that it shines. Their adornment consists in hanging much wampum, coral and silver about their necks and it is not unusual for them to have great belts of wampum depending from the neck. Their shirts and strowds they adorn with many silver buckles. It is also customary for them to sew red, yellow or black ribbon on their coats from top to bottom, being very fond of bright things.

Men as well as women wear silver bracelets, and the latter also arrange silver clasps in their hair or wear a band about the head with as many silver ornaments on it as it will hold.

p. 86   The Indians are lovers of finery and dress, the women more than the men; the latter take care that the women adorn themselves in proper manner. The men clothe themselves rather meanly, regarding it as a disgrace to be better appareled than their wives. The dress which particularly distinguishes the women is a petticoat or strowd, blue, red or black, made of a piece of cloth about two yards long, adorned with red, blue or yellow bands laid double and bound about the body. Many women wear a white shirt over the strowd, decorated with silver buckles, the more the better. Red or blue leggings are worn, made of fine cloth joined by a broad band of silk bordered with coral. These leggings reach only to the feet. Shoes are made very neatly. Over the first strowd they may wear another, not decorated with ribbons, which if it inconveniences them in their movements may be easily laid aside. Thus clad a woman is well dressed. In place of the white shirts, blue linen or cotton may be worn. When they wear a white shirt, which is preferably of fine linen, it is often dyed red with cinnabar about the neck. Such a shirt may be worn unwashed until it is torn. More careful women, however wash their clothing. Men and women paint their faces almost daily, especially if they go out to a dance in the evening. Men, particularly, think it is proper to paint and often their whole head is colored vermillion. Here and there black spots may be introduced, or they paint one-half of their head and face black, the other red. Figures are added according to taste. Indian women never paint their faces with a variety of figures, but rather make a round red spot upon each cheek and redden the eyelids, the tops of their heads and, in some cases, the rims of the ears and the temples. Older women adorn themselves but rarely, usually appearing in old cast-off garments. Even if the husband of such a woman provides new clothing, she will rarely put it on, especially if she has a daughter to whom she gives the new clothing in exchange for old garments.

p. 116   When a guest comes into a house, food is placed before him; that comes before anything else. If the guests are from a distance and very good friends, the whole kettle of food is set before them, they are given dishes and spoons and allowed to help themselves first to as much as they wish. The guests having partaken of the food, pass the kettle back to the people of the house. They live very simply. Meat, corn, gruel, corn-bread, are the principal articles of diet. In lieu of meat, various dishes are prepared with corn, or Sopan, milk and butter are used. They like to discuss affairs of state and communicate their opinions. In fact they are more ready to discuss such matters in course of visits than in the Council House, for there they prefer to let the older people speak. Occasionally visits are made with the purpose of discovering the opinions of others; in a chief's home all manner of reports, true and false, furnish material for discussion. The women speak of their work, their plantations, the pouches, bags, baskets, carrying bands they have made, many of them though not all smoking tobacco. Stories are carried by women from house to house; they are so often manufactured that if men, having listened attentively to some tale, hear that it originated with a woman they will give it no credit until confirmed by some more reliable authority.[!]

On this rather droll note, let us now go back in time over 200 years, to a place where roads, as we know them, do not exist, where the loudest noise is the barking of dogs and the shouts of children at play, where the only light at night is firelight or moonlight, and where time is measured in days rather than minutes and seconds.

The year is 1750.

THE JOURNALS

Within the journals, brackets [ ] and parentheses ( ) are as in sources.
Braces { } are my comments.

Documents in shaded boxes, unless clearly indicated
otherwise, are direct quotations from sources cited.

Christopher Gist
1750-1

1750 was a watershed year in our history, in both a figurative and a literal sense, for it was in that year that Dr. Thomas Walker set out from North Carolina to explore the lands west of the mountains, known as Kentucky, for purposes of future settlement, and, a little later that same year, on October 31st, Christopher Gist left Thomas Cresap's house at Old Town along the Potomac on a similar journey whose sole purpose, also, was to seek out and explore lands west of the mountains, in the watersheds of the Ohio and Mississippi rivers, for purposes of future settlement. No longer would the English be confined to a comparatively narrow strip of land along the Atlantic seaboard. Manifest Destiny—18th century style—had arrived.

It would not happen soon. Both the French and the Indians and, eventually, even the British had to be reckoned with (two wars and a revolution later), but it was a beginning.

This journal is the first detailed description that we have of places and events in the Ohio country. Because of its importance to our history, Mr. Gist's instructions and that portion of his journey from Old Town on the Potomac to his arrival in the area of the Scioto River is included in this book.

Old Town was about fifteen miles southeast of Cumberland, Maryland, on the north side of the Potomac River. There was no direct Indian trail from Old Town to the Forks of the Ohio and so Gist headed north along the Warrior's Path until he struck the trail used by traders going into the Ohio country from Harris' Ferry (now Harrisburg), Pennsylvania. He reached this trail about eight miles east of Bedford and then headed west toward Shannopin's Town.

Shannopin's Town is where Pittsburgh now stands, the Indian town being about four miles up the Allegheny from its junction with the Monongahela at what is known as the Forks of the Ohio.

Logstown, a trading center on the north side of the Ohio, was about eighteen miles downstream from the Forks and was often used as the place at which the whites would hold councils with the Indians. Washington was here in 1753 on his way to the French forts near Lake Erie. Many of the journalists in this book mention passing through Logstown on their way to the Tuscarawas Valley.

The town of the Ottaways on Elk's Eye Creek was, I believe, in the vicinity of Zoarville, but on the west side of the Tuscarawas.

George Croghan's name looms large in the history of the Ohio country in the 1750s–1760s. He was the best known of the Indian traders and was often used in treaty negotiations with the Indian tribes. The Indians knew and trusted him.

Andrew Montour, likewise, is a person often met with in the journals of those times.

He was frequently used as an interpreter in negotiations with the Indians.

The other men mentioned in the journal were Indian traders. Thomas Burney would later die at Braddock's defeat in 1755.

After leaving the Tuscarawas Valley, Gist proceeded to the Lower Shawnee Town at the mouth of the Scioto, then to the Twigtwee town near Piqua, after which he returned to the Lower Shawnee Town by a more southerly route. He then crossed the Ohio and returned to his home in North Carolina. Two years later he accompanied George Washington to the French forts and still later served as a guide with Braddock. He died in 1759.

Notable features of the journal are his mention of the size of the town of Muskingum, the English flags flying over the Indian town, the Christmas Day religious service, the killing on the next day of a captive, and his meeting with Mary Harris, the white woman for whom the creek (now the Walhonding) was named.

Note: Gist's compass courses and distances traveled are to be read as follows:

Oct. 31 – "N 30 E" means a course of 30° toward the east from due North. (N 45 E means northeast.)

Nov. 1 – "N 1 Mile N 30 E 3 M" means north for one mile, then 30° toward the east of due North for 3 miles.

Etc.

INSTRUCTIONS GIVEN MR. CHRISTOPHER GIST BY THE COMMITTEE OF THE OHIO COMPANY THE 11TH DAY OF SEPTEMBER, 1750

You are to go out as soon as possible to the Westward of the great Mountains, and carry with you such a Number of Men, as You think necessary, in Order to search out and discover the Lands upon the River Ohio, & other adjoining Branches of the Mississippi down as low as the great Falls thereof: You are particularly to observe the Ways & Passes thro all the Mountains you cross, & take an exact Account of the Soil, Quality, & Product of the Land, and the Wideness and Deepness of the Rivers, & the several Falls belonging to them, together with the Courses & Bearings of the Rivers & Mountains as near as you conveniently can: You are also to observe what Nations of Indians inhabit there, their Strength & Numbers, who they trade with, & in what Comodities they deal.

When you find a large Quantity of good, level Land, such as you think will suit the Company, You are to measure the Breadth of it, in three or four different Places, & take the Courses of the River and Mountains on which it binds in Order to judge the Quantity: You are to fix the Beginning & Bounds in such a Manner that they may be easily found again by your Description; the nearer in the Land lies, the better, provided it be good & level, but we had rather go quite down the Mississippi than take mean broken Land. After finding a large Body of good level Land, you are not to stop, but proceed farther, as low as the Falls of the Ohio, that We may be informed of that Navigation; And You are to take an exact Account of all the large Bodies of good level Land, in the same Manner as above directed, that the Company may the better judge where it will be most convenient for them to take their Land.

You are to note all the Bodies of good Land as you go along, tho there is not a sufficient Quantity for the Company's Grant, but You need not be so particular in the Mensuration of that, as in the larger Bodies of Land.

You are to draw as good a Plan as you can of the Country You pass thro: You are to take an exact and particular Journal of all your Proceedings, and make a true Report thereof to the Ohio Company.

1750. — In Complyance with my Instructions from the Committee of the Ohio Company bearing Date the 11th Day of September 1750

Wednesday Octr 31. — Set out from Col. Thomas Cresap's at the old Town on Potomack River in Maryland, and went along an old Indian Path N 30 E about 11 miles.

Thursday Nov 1. — Then N 1 Mile N 30 E 3 M here I was taken sick and stayed all Night.

Friday 2. — N 30 E 6 M, here I was so bad that I was not able to proceed any farther that Night, but grew better in the Morning.

Saturday 3. — N 8 M to Juniatta, a large Branch of Susquehannah, where I stayed all Night.

Sunday 4. — Crossed Juniatta and went up it S 55 W about 16 M.

Monday 5. — Continued the same Course S 55 W 6 M to the Top of a large Mountain called the Allegany Mountain, here our Path turned, & we went N 45 W 6 M here we encamped.

Tuesday 6 Wednesday 7 and Thursday 8. — Had Snow and such bad Weather that We coud not travel for three Days; but I killed a young Bear so that we had Provision enough.

Friday 9. — Set out N 70 W about 8 M here I crossed a Creek of Susquehannah and it raining hard, I went into an old Indian Cabbin where I stay'd all Night.

Saturday 10. — Rain and Snow all Day but cleared away in the Evening.

Sunday 11. — Set out late in the Morning N 70 W 6 M crossing two Forks of a Creek of Susquehannah, here the Way being bad, We encamped and I killed a Turkey.

Monday 12. — Set out N 45 W 8 M crossed a great Laurel Mountain.

Tuesday 13. — Rain and Snow.

Wednesday 14. — Set out N 45 W 6 M to Loylhannan an old Indian Town on a Creek of Ohio called Kiscominatis, then N 1 M NW 1 M to an Indian's Camp on the said Creek.

Thursday 15. — The Weather being bad and I unwell I stayed here all day: The Indian to whom this Camp belonged spoke good English and directed Me the Way to his Town, which is called Shannopini Town: He said it was about 60 M and a pretty good Way.

Friday 16. — Set out S70 W 10 M.

Saturday 17. — The same Course (S70 W) 15 M to an old Indian's Camp.

Sunday 18. — I was very sick, and sweated myself according to the Indian Custom in a Sweat-House, which gave Me Ease, and my Fever abated.

Monday 19. — Set out early in the Morning the same Course (S 70 W) travelled very hard about 20 M to a small Indian Town of the Delawares called Shannopin on the SE Side of the River Ohio, where We rested and got Corn for our Horses.

Tuesday 20 Wednesday 21 Thursday 22 and Friday 23. — I was unwell and stayed in this Town to recover myself; While I was here I took an Opportunity to set my Compass privately, & took the Distance across the River, for I understood it was dangerous to let a Compass be seen among these Indians: The River Ohio is 76

Poles wide at Shannopin Town: There are about twenty Families in this Town: The Land in general from Potomack to this Place is mean stony and broken, here and there good Spots upon the Creeks and Branches but no Body of it.

Saturday 24. — Set out from Shannopin's Town, and swam our Horses across the River Ohio, & went down the River S 75 W 4 M, N 75 W 7 M W 2 M, all the Land from Shannopin's Town is good along the River, but the Bottoms not broad; At a Distance from the River good Land for Farming, covered with small white and red Oaks and tolerable level; fine Runs for Mills &c.

Sunday Nov 25. — Down the River W 3 M, NW 5 M to Loggs Town; the Lands these last 8 M very rich the Bottoms above a Mile wide, but on the SE side, scarce a Mile wide, the Hills high and steep. In the Loggs Town, I found scarce any Body but a Parcel of reprobate Indian Traders, the Chiefs of the Indians being out a hunting: here I was informed that George Croghan & Andrew Montour who were sent upon an Embassy from Pennsylvania to the Indians, were passed about a Week before me. The People in this Town, began to enquire my Business, and because I did not readily inform them, they began to suspect me, and said I was come to settle the Indian's Lands and they knew I should never go Home again safe; I found this Discourse was like to be of ill Consequence to me, so I pretended to speak very slightingly of what they had said to me, and enquired for Croghan (who is a meer Idol among his Countrymen the Irish Traders) and Andrew Montour the Interpreter for Pennsylvania, and told them I had a Message to deliver the Indians from the King, by Order of the President of Virginia, & for that Reason wanted to see M. Montour: This made them all pretty easy (being afraid to interrupt the King's Message) and obtained me Quiet and Respect among them, otherwise I doubt not they would have contrived some Evil against me — I immediately wrote to M Croghan, by one of the Trader's People.

Monday 26. — Tho I was unwell, I preferred the Woods to such Company & set out from the Loggs Town down the River NW 6 M to great Beaver Creek where I met one Barny Curran a Trader for the Ohio Company, and we continued together as far as Muskingum. The

Bottoms upon the River below the Loggs's Town very rich but narrow, the high Land pretty good but not very rich, the Land upon Beaver Creek the same kind; From this Place We left the River Ohio to the SE & travelled across the Country.

Tuesday 27. — Set out from E side of Beaver Creek NW 6 M, W 4 M; up these two last Courses very good high Land, not very broken, fit for farming.

Wednesday 28. — Rained, We could not travel.

Thursday 29. — W 6 M thro good Land, the same Course continued 6 M farther thro very broken Land; here I found myself pretty well recovered, & being in Want of Provision, I went out and killed a Deer.

Friday 30. — Set out S 45 W 12 M crossed the last Branch of Beaver Creek where one of Curran's Men & myself killed 12 Turkeys.

Saturday Dec' 1. — N 45 W 10 M the Land high and tolerable good.

NOTE; by Mr. Gist's Plat he makes these 2 Courses N 45 W 10 M, & N 45 W 8 M, to be W 8 M and N 45W 6 M.

Sunday 2. — N 45 W 8 M the same Sort of Land, but near the Creeks bushy and very full of Thorns.

Monday 3. — Killed a Deer, and stayed in our Camp all Day.

Tuesday 4. — Set out late S 45 W about 4 M here I killed three fine fat Deer, so that tho we were eleven in Company, We had great Plenty of Provision.

Wednesday 5. — Set out down the Side of a Creek called Elk's Eye Creek S 70 W 6 M, good Land, but void of Timber, Meadows upon the Creek, fine Runs for Mills.

Thursday 6. — Rained all Day so that we were obliged to continue in our Camp.

Friday 7. — Set out SW 8 M crossing the said Elk's Eye Creek to a Town of the Ottaways, a Nation of French Indians; an old French Man (named Mark Coonce) who had married an Indian Woman of the six Nations lived here; the Indians were all out a hunting; the old Man was very civil to me, but after I was gone to my Camp, upon his understanding I came from Virginia, he called Me the Big Knife. There are not above six or eight Families belonging to this Town.

Saturday 8. — Stayed in the Town. [See Note at the end of the journal as to the location of this town.]

Sunday 9. — Set out down the said Elk's Eye Creek S 45 W 6 M to Margarets Creek a Branch of the said Elk's Eye Creek.

Monday Dec 10. — The same Course (S 45 W) 2 M to a large Creek.

Tuesday 11. — The same Course 12 M killed 2 Deer.

Wednesday 12. — The same Course 8 M encamped by the Side of Elk's Eye Creek.

Thursday 13. — Rained all Day.

Friday 14. — Set out W 5 M to Muskingum a Town of the Wyendotts. The Land upon Elk's Eye Creek is in general very broken, the Bottoms narrow. Thw Wyendotts or little Mingoes are divided between the French and English, one half of them adhere to the first, and the other half are firmly attached to the latter. The Town of Muskingum consists of about one hundred Families. When We came within Sight of the Town, We perceived English Colours hoisted on the King's House, and at George Croghan's; upon enquiring the Reason I was informed that the French had lately taken several English Traders, and that Mr. Croghan had ordered all the White Men to come into this Town, and had sent Expresses to the Traders of the lower Towns, and among the Pickweylinees; and the Indians had sent to their People to come to Council about it.

Saturday 15 & Sunday 16. — Nothing remarkable happened.

Monday 17. — Came into Town two Traders belonging to M Croghan, and informed Us that two of his People were taken by 40 French Men, & twenty French Indians who had carried them with seven Horse Loads of Skins to a new Fort that the French were building on one of the Branches of Lake Erie.

Tuesday 18. — I acquainted Mr. Croghan and Andrew Montour with my Business with the Indians, & talked much of a Regulation of Trade with which they were much pleased, and treated Me very kindly.

From Wednesday 19 to Monday 24. — Nothing remarkable.

Tuesday 25. — This being Christmass Day, I intended to read Prayers, but after inviting some of the White Men, they informed each other of my Intentions, and being of several different Persuasions, and few of them inclined to hear any Good, they refused to come. But one Thomas Burney a Black Smith who is settled there went about and talked to them, & then several of them came; and Andrew Montour invited several of the well disposed Indians, who came freely; by this Time the Morning was spent and I had given over all Thoughts of them, but seeing Them come, to oblige All, and offend None, I stood up and said, Gentlemen, I have no Design or Intention to give Offence to any particular Sectary or Religion, but as our King indulges Us all in a Liberty of Conscience and hinders none of You in the Exercise of your religious Worship, so it would be unjust in You, to endeavour to stop the Propagation of His; The Doctrine of Salvation Faith, and good Works, is what I only propose to treat of, as I find it extracted from the Homilies of the Church of England, which I then read them in the best Manner I coud, and after I had done the Interpreter told the Indians what I had read, and that it was the true Faith which the great King and His Church recommended to his Children: the Indians seemed well pleased, and came up to Me and returned Me their Thanks; and then invited Me to live among Them, and gave Me a Name in their Language Annosannah: the Interpreter told Me this was a Name of a good Man that had formerly lived among them, and their King said that must be always my Name, for which I returned them Thanks; but as to living among them I excused myself by saying I did not know whether the Governor woud give Me Leave, and if he did the French woud come and carry me away as they had done the English Traders, to which they answered I might bring great Guns and make a Fort, that they had now left the French, and were very desirous of being instructed in the Principles of Christianity; that they liked Me very well and wanted Me to marry Them after the Christian Manner, and baptize their Children; and then they said they woud never desire to return to the French, or suffer them or their Priests to come near them more, for they loved the English, but had seen little Religion among them: and some of their great Men came and wanted Me to baptize their Children; for as I had read to Them and appeared to talk about Religion they took Me to be a Minister of the Gospel; Upon which I desired Mr. Montour (the Interpreter) to tell Them, that no Minister coul venture to baptize any Children, until those that were to be Sureties for Them, were well instructed in the Faith themselves, and that this was according to the great King's Religion, in which He desired his Children shoud be instructed & We dare not do it in any other Way, than was by Law established, but I hoped if I coud not be admitted to live among them, that the great King woud send Them proper Ministers to exercise that Office among them, at which they seemed well pleased; and one of Them went and brought Me his Book (which was a Kind contrived for Them by the French in which the Days of the Week were so marked that by moving a Pin every Morning they kept a pretty exact Account of the Time) to shew Me that He understood Me, and that He and his Family always observed the Sabbath Day.

Wednesday Dec' 26. — This Day a Woman, who had been a long Time a Prisoner, and had deserted, & been retaken, and brought into the Town on Christmass Eve, was put to Death in the following manner: They carried her without the Town, & let her loose, and when she attempted to run away, the Persons appointed for that Purpose pursued her, & struck Her on the Ear, on the right Side of her Head, which beat her flat on her Face on the Ground; they then stuck her several Times, thro the Back with a Dart, to the Heart, scalped Her, & threw the Scalp in the Air, and another cut off her Head: There the dismal Spectacle lay till the Evening, & then Barny Curran Desired Leave to bury Her, which He, and his Men, and some of the Indians did just at Dark.

From Thursday Dec' 27 to Thursday Jan' 3 1751. — Nothing remarkable happened in the Town.

Friday Jan 4. — One Teafe (an Indian Trader) came to Town from near Lake Erie, & informed Us, that the Wyendott Indians had advised Him to keep clear of the Ottaways (these are a Nation of Indians firmly attached to the French, & inhabit near the Lakes) & told Him that the Branches of the Lakes are claimed by the French; but that all the Branches of Ohio belonged to Them, and their Brothers the English, and that the French had no Business there, & that it was expected that the other Part of the Wyendott Nation woud desert the French and come over to the English Interest, & join their Brethren on the Elk's Eye Creek, & build a strong Fort and Town there.

From Saturday 5 to Tuesday 8. — The Weather still continuing bad, I stayed in the Town to recruit my Horses, and tho Corn was very dear among the Indians, I was obliged to feed them well, or run the Risque of losing them as I had a great Way to travel.

Wednesday 9. — The Wind Southerly, and the Weather something warmer: this Day came into Town two Traders from among the Pickwaylinees (these are a Tribe of the Twigtwees) and brought News that another English Trader was taken prisoner by the French, and that three French Soldiers had deserted and come over to the English, and surrendered themselves to some of the Traders of the Pick Town, & that the Indians woud have put them to Death, to revenge their taking our Traders, but as the French Prisoners had surrendered themselves, the English woud not let the Indians hurt them, but had ordered them to be sent under the Care of three of our Traders and delivered at this Town, to George Croghan.

Thursday 10. — Wind still at South and warm.

Friday 11. — This Day came into Town an Indian from over the Lakes & confirmed the News we had heard.

Saturday 12. — We sent away our People towards the lower Town intending to follow them the next Morning, and this Evening We went into Council in the Wyendott's King's House — The Council had been put off a long Time expecting some of their great Men in, but few of them came, & this Evening some of the King's Council being a little disordered with Liquor, no Business coud be done, but We were desired to come next Day.

Sunday Jan' 13. — No Business done.

Monday 14. — This day George Croghan, by the Assistance of Andrew Montour, acquainted the King and Council of this Nation (by presenting them four Strings of Wampum) that the great King over the Water, their Roggony [Father] had sent under the Care of the Governor of Virginia, their Brother, a large Present of Goods which was now landed safe in Virginia, & the Governor had sent Me to invite Them to come and see Him, & partake of their Father's Charity to all his Children on the Branches of Ohio. In Answer to which one of the Chiefs stood up and said, "That their King and all of Them thanked their Brother the Governor of Virginia for his Care, and Me for bringing them the News, but they coud not give Me an Answer untill they had a full or general Council of the several Nations of Indians which coud not be till next Spring"; & so the King and Council shaking Hands with Us, We took our Leave.

Tuesday 15. — We left Muskingum, and went W 5 M, to the White Woman's Creek, on which is a small Town; this White Woman was taken away from New England, when she was not above ten years old, by the French Indians; She is now upwards of fifty, and has an Indian Husband and several Children — Her name is Mary Harris, she still remembers they used to be very religious in New England, and wonders how the White Men can be so wicked as she has seen them in these Woods.

Wednesday 16. — Set out SW 25 M to Licking Creek — The Land from Muskingum to this Place rich but broken — Upon the N Side of Licking Creek about 6 M from the Mouth, are several Salt Licks, or Ponds, formed by little Streams or Dreins of Water, clear but of a blueish Colour, & salt Taste the Traders and Indians boil their Meat in this Water, which (if proper Care be not taken) will sometimes make it too salt to eat.

Thursday 17. — Set out W 5 M, SW 15 M, to a great Swamp.

Friday 18. — Set out from the great Swamp SW 15 M.

Saturday 19. — W 15 M to Hockhockin a small Town with only four or five Delaware Families.

Sunday 20. — The Snow began to grow thin, and the Weather warmer; Set out from Hockhockin S 5 M, then W 5 M, then SW 5 M, to the Maguck a little Delaware Town of about ten Families by the N Side of a plain or clear Field about 5 M in Length NE & SW & 2 M broad, with a small Rising in the Middle, which gives a fine Prospect over the whole Plain, and a large Creek on the N Side of it called Sciodoe Creek. All the Way from Licking Creek to this Place is fine rich level Land, with large Meadows, fine Clover Bottoms & spacious Plains covered with wild Rye: the Wood chiefly large Walnuts and Hickory here and there mixed with Poplars Cherry Trees and Sugar Trees.

From Monday 21 to Wednesday 23 — Stayed in the Maguck Town.

Thursday 24. — Set out from the Maguck Town S about 15 M, thro fine rich level Land to a small Town called Harrickintoms consisting of about five or six Delaware Families, on the SW Siodoe Creek.

Source: Gist, *Christopher Gist's Journals,* pp. 31–42

Note

Every writer who has ever annotated Gist's route states that the "Town of the Ottaways" was at the crossing place of the Muskingum just above Bolivar, the place later known as Tuscarawas.

I disagree. I think Gist struck the Muskingum near Zoarville, about six miles southeast of Bolivar.

I base my opinion upon the following:

1. Gist's course for Wednesday, December 5th, was S70W 6 M "down the Side of a Creek called Elk's Eye Creek." This would be the Sandy, and his camp that night would have been about one mile northeast of Magnolia. It rained the next day and he did not travel. On the 7th, he "Set out SW 8 M crossing the said Elk's Eye Creek to a Town of the Ottaways." Proceeding SW from Magnolia takes one to Zoarville, not Bolivar. Bolivar is west of Magnolia, not southwest.

2. Gist does not call it Tuscarawas, just a "Town of the Ottaways" and a small one at that—"not above six or eight Families".

3. Two days later, when he left the town, he says he "Set out *down the said Elk's Eye Creek* [emphasis added] S45W 6 M to Margaret's Creek." If he was starting from Bolivar, a course of S45W would *not* take him "down the said Elk's Eye Creek". He would be going away from it, for the Muskingum runs southeast from Bolivar to Zoarville, not southwest. That same course from Zoarville, however, *does* follow the Creek, and at 6 miles, you do come to Margaret's Creek, just as Gist says.

4. The next day, he says he proceeded the same course (S45W) 2 M to a large creek. While the course is actually more southerly than that (if you follow the Muskingum), at about two miles from Margaret's Creek, you do come to the mouth of Stone Creek. If, however, he had been proceeding from Bolivar, although he would have struck Margaret's Creek about six miles from Bolivar on the first day's travel, he would not have struck a large creek the next day two miles further along the same southwest course.

5. Proceeding up Stone Creek to Evans Creek, then down Evans Creek to about a mile north of Bakersville, and then continuing on a southwesterly course over several ridges to the mouth of White Eyes Creek at its junction with the Muskingum, the total distance is just about exactly the 20 miles that Gist states he traveled over the next two days.

6. At the end of that second day (the 12th), if the starting place for the last few days had been from Bolivar, he would not have struck the Muskingum at all that day. He would still have been about 5 miles north of it, above Canal Lewisville.

7. His last course of W 5 M to Muskingum is very close to the 5½ miles it actually is from White Eyes Creek to the Town site of Muskingum.

8. If Gist had followed these same courses and distances from Bolivar instead of Zoarville, his last course to the town of Muskingum would have been almost straight south rather than west.

In view of all of the above, I cannot subscribe to the generally accepted belief that the "Town of the Ottaways" was at the location of Tuscarawas. I see no compelling reason to consider it so, for the courses and distances are much better suited to the Zoarville route than the Bolivar one. Just because in the 1760s there was a well-known town near Bolivar called Tuscarawas does not mean that there was a town there in 1750. There could just as easily have been a town near Zoarville and none at Bolivar, or perhaps there could have been towns at both places. Even so, the only way you can leave that town, whichever it is, heading southwest, and at the same time be proceeding along the Muskingum is if the town you are starting from is near Zoarville, not Bolivar. Furthermore, DeLery came over this same route five years later, heading in the opposite direction, and he passed through the Zoarville area, rather than going on up to Bolivar. If DeLery could use this route, why not Gist as well? DeLery makes no mention of a town when he crossed the Muskingum near Zoarville, so probably the Ottaways had moved on by then.

Further evidence that Gist did not pass through Tuscarawas is furnished by the map of his route on the next page. Although the map does show a town called Tuscarawas, the map was made in 1752, and the town may or may not have been there in 1750.

Indian Opinions of Whites in the Woods

The Indians say, that when the white people encamp in the woods they are sure to lose something; that when they are gone, something or another is always found which they have lost, such as a knife, flints, bullets, and sometimes even money. They also observe that the whites are not so attentive as they are to choosing an open dry spot for their encampment; that they will at once set themselves down in any dirty and wet place, provided they are under large trees; that they never look about to see which way the wind blows, so as to be able to lay the wood for their fires in such a position that the smoke may not blow on them; neither do they look up the trees to see whether there are not dead limbs that may fall on them while they are asleep; that any wood will do for them to lay on their fires, whether it be dry or wet, and half rotten, so that they are involved during the whole night in a cloud of smoke; or they take such wood as young green oak, walnut, cherry, chestnut, &c., which throws sparks out to a great distance, so that their blankets and clothes get holes burned in them, and sometimes their whole camp takes fire. They also remark that the whites hang their kettles and pots over a fire just kindled, and before the great body of smoke has passed away.

Source: Heckewelder's *History...*, p. 191

Map 1 – The John Mercer Map of 1752

Map 1

The John Mercer Map of 1752

Although Gist's plat of his route cannot now be located, his route is set forth on a map known as the John Mercer map of Ohio Company land, made before November 6, 1752. A copy of this map is in the Darlington Memorial Library at the University of Pittsburgh, and is shown on the facing page. Gist's route is the dotted line, barely visible, running northwesterly from Loggstown, crossing the Little Beaver Creek, and then proceeding on to Muskingum. You will notice that although he shows a town known as Tuscarawas on the map, the dotted line does not show him as passing through it.

It should also be noted, however, that although he shows the White woman's town on the map and we know from his journal that he visited it, the dotted line does not pass through it, either. I believe, however, that there is an explanation for this. From the John Patten map of 1752 [Map 14] shown in the special article on Three Legs, it appears that the usual trader's route after leaving Muskingum was to go out the White Woman Creek to her town *and then return to the forks of the Muskingum* before proceeding on to the Scioto towns. Probably there was no direct trail leading from the White woman's town to the Scioto towns, but there evidently was a trail from Muskingum to those towns. I believe, therefore, that Gist simply took a day to go out to the White woman's town and return to Muskingum before proceeding the next day with his journey. The route as shown on the map does not, therefore, show this one-day digression from his overall route even though he obviously did go there.

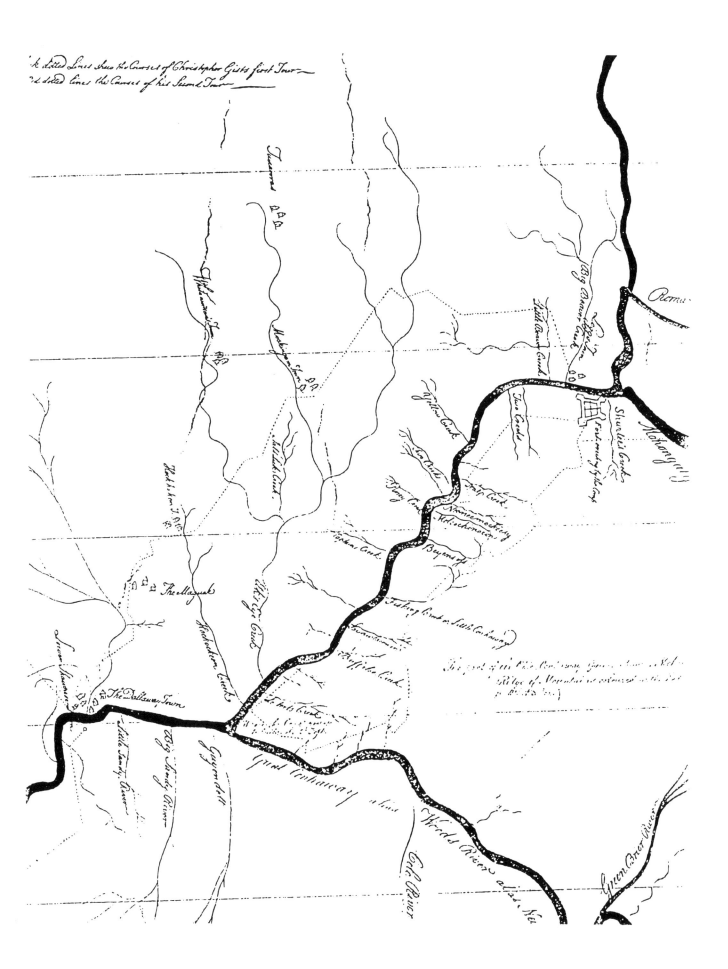

When we came within Sight of the Town, We perceived English Colours hoisted on the King's House, and at George Croghan's.

Christopher Gist   December 14, 1750

William Trent
1752

William Trent was an Indian trader and land speculator. The purpose of his journey to the Ohio country was to deliver a "present" from the governor of Virginia to the Miami (Twightwee) Indians at Pickawillany, near Piqua. They had recently broken away from the French and were transferring their allegiance to the English. At a treaty held at Logstown earlier in the year, "presents" had been given to the other tribes who were in the English interest and it was hoped that the delivery of these goods to the Miamis might further help to bring them to the English side. The French and their Indian allies, however, had struck back and virtually destroyed Pickawillany before Trent got there. As he proceeded through the Tuscarawas Valley on his way to the "Pick Town", he was receiving the alarming news of what had been happening further west. The "Hockhocken" mentioned in the journal is the name often given to the Indian town on the site of Lancaster. It was also sometimes called the "Standing Stone", referring to the large rock outcropping known as Mt. Pleasant. Hockhocking was the Indian name of the Hocking River along which the town was situated.

He continued his journey, first to the Shawnee town on the Scioto and then to Pickawillany, but it was deserted by the time he got there. Later, while back at the Shawnee town, some of the Twightees arrived and he was able to deliver the present to them at that time.

His journal is probably the least descriptive of all of the journals in this book as to the Indian towns in the Tuscarawas Valley, but it does tell us that there evidently still was a town at Muskingum in 1752. Unfortunately, he says nothing about it's size.

As the Note following the journal shows, however, in February of 1754, there were only about 30 men in the town. When Gist was there in 1750, he estimated about 100 families, which would have meant probably at least 150 warriors. Something had caused a large drop in the town's population. Hanna states that the Indians in Ohio were stricken with a smallpox epidemic in 1751 and 1752 and our next journalist, Delery, states that "120 of them died in one summer", so that is the most likely explanation of the drop in population.

Trent's letter to Washington brings out very vividly the extreme threat to the lives of the English traders in Ohio. The 200 Indians who were in the French interest had come to the area and wanted to kill the whites at Muskingum but, even though there were only 30 Wyandot men in the town, they presumably were able to save their lives.

Washington's letter, written in June of the same year, tells us that apparently there were still some Wyandots at Muskingum at that time. By the time that our next journalist visited the area, however, the Wyandots were gone.

11

June the 21st, 1752.   We left the Logstown.

25th. We met a white man who had been thirteen days from the Pick town; he informed us that the French Indians had been there, and that twenty-five families of the Picks or Twightwees had gone back with them to the French.

27th. We met a Mingoe man called Powell, who had been then just twenty days from Fort D'Troit, and ten days before he left the fort three hundred French and Indians had set off, either to persuade the Twightwees back to the French, else to cut them off.

29th. We got to Muskingum, 150 miles from the Logstown, where we met some white menfrom Hockhocken, who told us the town was taken and all the white men killed, the young Shawanees king having made his escape and brought the news.

July the 2d. We reached Hockhocken where we met with William Ives, who passed by the Twightwee town in the night. He informed us that the white men's houses were all on fire, and that he heard no noise in the fort, only one gun fired, and two or three hollows.

Source: Trent, *Journal of Captain William Trent,* p. 84

Note

In a letter to George Washington dated February 19, 1754, and written from Yaughyaughgany big Bottom, [which letter has not been found but the information in which was in the *Maryland Gazette* (Annapolis), 14 Mar. 1754] William Trent stated that he had been informed by the Indians that "200 Ottaways and Chipawas came to Mushingum and demanded the White People there, and shewed them the French Hatchet; the Wayondotts, tho' not above 30 Men, refused to let them kill them in their Town; but they expected every Day to hear they had cut off the Whites and likewise the Wayondotts."

A few months later, Washington, in a letter to Governor Dinwiddie written from Fort Necessity on June 3rd, 1754, stated at the end of the letter "since writing the above there has arriv'd two Indians from Moskingam who inform that the Wyendotts &ca are ready to strike so soon as they hear the 6 Nation's and English have."

Source: Abbot, *The Papers of George Washington,* Vol. 1, pp. 68, 125.

Lieutenant Joseph DeLery
1755

The French occupied the Forks of the Ohio in 1754 and immediately began the construction of Fort DuQuesne at the junction of the Allegheny and Monongahela rivers. In March of 1755, Lt. Joseph DeLery, an officer of engineers in the French army, was ordered to proceed from Detroit to Fort DuQuesne to assist in the laying out and construction of improvements to the fort. He proceeded from Detroit to Sandusky and then on to Fort DuQuesne by a somewhat circuitous route—down the Mohican to the Walhonding (he calls it the Conchake), down the Conchake (crossing Killbuck creek) to within about a mile of the Forks of the Muskingum (he called the Muskingum the Naguerre Konnan), then striking cross-country to the town of Conchake (Gist had called it Muskingum). Most of its inhabitants had either died or moved on. Only two cabins were inhabited. He then proceeded along the north side of the Tuscarawas to Evans Creek, thence northeasterly to Stone Creek, down Stone Creek to the Tuscarawas near Dover, crossed the Tuscarawas near Zoarville and proceeded out of the valley to the northeast.

His journal establishes the fact that the town of Muskingum, flourishing as of 1750, had virtually disappeared by 1755.

The French measurements mentioned by DeLery have their English equivalents as follows: an arpent is 191.85 feet; a toise is 2.1 yards and a French league is just under two and one-half miles.

{March} 26th, Wednesday. At 8 o'clock we started {from somewhere north of Mansfied.} At 6 o'clock we camped. Our bearing was southeast. We made many detours to avoid bad pieces of country. We traveled eight leagues {just under 20 miles}. At noon we passed a river flowing eastward. It is six toises {12 yards} wide and the water is two feet deep. In the afternoon, we passed several small ones. We saw the dung of Illinois buffaloes. I think we passed the height of land in the morning and that the river we crossed at noon is the Conchake. Fine weather all day.

27th, Thursday. We started at 8h. 15m.

At 11 o'clock we came upon the main road leading to Conchake. We had traveled in a southeasterly direction. At 2 o'clock we came upon a branch of the Conchake River, which we followed until 5h. 15m. when we camped. At 4h. 14m. we passed a place on the bank of the said river where some Hurons [Wyandots] had taken refuge after the treacherous deed they committed at Detroit. It is called the Fugitive's Camp.

After we struck the road at 11h. 15m. we traveled S. by S.E. This branch of the river is from seven to eight toises {14 to 17 yards} wide, and canoes can go down it. The weather was cloudy all day; a little rain fell also; it began at

13

half-past six and lasted all night, falling heavily. We had traveled eight leagues {20 miles}.

28th, Friday. The rain stopped at 7 o'clock. At eight we started. At eleven we again followed the river. Until then we had passed many mountains. At 4h. 45m. we arrived at Quiouhiahinse, which means "boiling water" in the Huron language.

At 3 o'clock we passed a steep declivity beside the river, where the road through the rocks was very narrow and dangerous for a distance of two arpents {384 feet}. From noon until we were two leagues {5 miles} from Tourieuse, we ascended and descended many mountains and rocky places. Tourieuse is a place wither the Huron [Wyandot] fugitives had withdrawn. At that spot is a river that falls into the Conchake {this would be the junction of the Mohican with the Walhonding}. It is fully twenty toises {42 yards} wide; and that of Conchake as many. Our route was S.S.E. and we traveled 8 1/4 leagues {20.6 miles}. The rain fell in showers during a portion of the afternoon.

29th, Saturday. We started at 8 o'clock and at once crossed the branch of the Konchake River, the water being up to our waists. At 3 o'clock we crossed a second branch [Killbuck Creek?] of the Konchake, not so wide as the first, but deeper. We were benumbed with cold, all the more so that hail and sleet fell all day, with a heavy north wind. At 5 o'clock we came to a small branch of the Conchake {Mill Creek?}, across which we waded, the water being up to our knees. Its width is four toises {8.4 yards}. At half-past five we left the Conchake River and at 6 o'clock we reached the village of Conchake. During the day we passed many mountains and steep declivities along the said Conchake River, which we followed nearly all the time. It may be from twenty to twenty-five toises {42 to 52.5 yards} wide. The rain had caused its waters to rise; it is rather rapid. Our route was nearly always S.E. and we traveled at least seven or eight leagues {17.5 to 20 miles}. We noticed that the buds were beginning to come out on the sassafras trees.

30th, Sunday. Easter Sunday. At half-past eight we started; and camped at half-past five. At noon we left the Riviere de Naguerreconnon and followed a stream {Evans Creek? – see Note at end of the journal} until 4

o'clock when we ascended a high mountain, after which we followed a stream running east by northeast. The one we left at 4 o'clock follows the same direction, but we were going up it while we were descending the last one. Our route was nearly always E. by N.E. I calculate that we traveled 8 1/4 leagues {20.6 miles}. We had snow and hail all day. The sun did not come out. Nevertheless we marched on.

Conchake is a place where the Hurons [Wyandots] took refuge during the war [1747-48]; 120 of them died in one summer. One can still see the graves and the vestiges of the village that stood there then. At present there are only two cabins, one of which is occupied by a Christian savage from Sault St. Louis who has been there a long while. The other belongs to the Five Nations. Tegana-Koissin lent me a horse for my journey to Fort Duquesne without specifying any price. He was to send for it in a month. Weather cold; strong north wind.

31st, Monday. I was unable to start before half-past eight, because the horse lent me by the savage at Conchake had run away. We looked for him but in vain, so that I had again to use my legs for the journey and was much disgusted at not having the horse. At 11 o'clock we came to the River Naguerreconnan. At noon we passed two Huron winter cabins. We had followed the stream of the previous day which falls into the river. At 11h. 30m. we followed the said River until 4 o'clock, when we waded across it, the water being up to our waists. It may be thirty toises {63 yards} wide. Until 12 o'clock we had traveled E. by N.E.; from noon to 5h. 15m., N.E. by N. At 5h. 15m. we camped. We found mineral coal on the mountains and below. The distance we traveled was 7 1/4 leagues {18 miles}.

1st April, Tuesday. We started at half-past seven and camped at half-past four; we traveled about 7 1/4 to 7 3/4 leagues {18 to 19 miles}; we ascended and descended two high mountains, going in a northerly direction for this. At 8h. 45m. we crossed a branch of the River Naguerre Konnan. The water runs north at that place. We passed four prairies, the largest being a league {2.5 miles} in extent. After passing the two mountains at 9h. 45m. we went E.N.E. until noon and east from noon to half-past four. During the day we passed several small mountains. Weather fine; wind E.N.E. It began to rain at 7 o'clock and lasted until midnight.

2nd, Wednesday. It rained from midnight until 9 o'clock, when we started. At 1h. 15m. the rain began again and we camped. We traveled two leagues {5 miles} in an easterly direction. At 10 o'clock we crossed the branch of the River Naguerre Konnan, ascended and descended a mountain, nearly always following the same branch, which is three toises {6.3 yards} wide, on the bank of which we slept. I estimated that we were eighty leagues {200 miles} from Lake Dosandoske according to my calculation of each day's journey. As on the previous day, I found the country very fine and very suitable for settlement.

3rd, Thursday. It snowed at night and the weather was very cold, as it was also during the day. We started at 10 o'clock when the wind stopped. At 4h. 30m. we camped, having travelled seven leagues {17.5 miles}. We followed the branch of the River Naguerrekonnan until it was only two feet wide. We ascended and descended a mountain. We came to a small stream which we followed. At half-past one we crossed the road leading to Cachelacheki {Kuskuskies}. It seems to run N.N.E. At 3h. 15m. we crossed a River which is a branch of the Kenten Raiatanion [the West Fork of Little Beaver Creek]. This is the same which, in 1739, I called Riviere au Portrait, because, at the spot where it enters the Belle Riviere {the Ohio River}, there are many marks and figures of men and animals cut out on the rocks, as if with chisels. It is three toises {6.3 yards} wide; the depth of the water is one foot six inches, and it flows southward where we crossed it. At 4 o'clock we again came to the said river. We followed it until 4h. 10m., when we left it. We passed many mountains. Our direction was E. by N.E.

4th, Friday. We started at 7h. 15m. At 9h. 45m. we crossed a River fifteen toises {31.5 feet} wide, the water being two feet deep. It flows southward. Between our starting point and the said River we crossed two streams at equal distances. At noon we crossed a River similar to that which we crossed at 9h. 45m. It flows southward and eastward like the other branch of the River Outstinragayatonyon {Little Beaver}, a branch of which we passed on the previous day. At 2h. 30m. we came to a small

stream that falls into the River Chininque [Big Beaver River]. At 5h. 15m. we camped. I estimate that we traveled today ten leagues {25 miles} E. by N. E. At 6 o'clock it began to rain and it lasted all night. Fine country with open woods. In the evening we heard cries, which my savages recognized as those of panthers, of which they have a great dread. To protect ourselves during the night we made a strong shelter, because they say those animals can climb. We put our arms in order and one of us remained on guard. We heard the same cries in the distance throughout the night.

5th, Saturday. I started at a quarter past seven in the morning. At 8h. 45m. we came to the Riviere de Chininque, two leagues {5 miles} from the spot where we slept. We passed some high mountains. That River is about thirty-five toises {73.5 yards} wide; the water is four and one-half feet deep. It runs north and south from the place where we crossed it to the Belle Riviere, into which it falls from twelve to fifteen arpents {about ½ mile} lower down. The route we followed to reach it was E. by southeast. At 10h. 15m. we came to the Belle Riviere which I had not seen for sixteen years, when I scaled it on my way to the Thicachats [Chickasaws] in 1739. We followed it to the Little Chaouanon Village [the new Logstown] where we arrived half an hour after noon. It is four leagues {10 miles} distant from the River Chininque. Half way is a house in which a French officer [La Force] spent the winter in 1754.

At half-past two I started on horseback for Fort Duquesne, which I reached at half-past eight. For one-half the distance one goes through woods along the Oyo River; then one goes on the beach for two leagues {5 miles} and then enters the woods, where the road is good. The beach is followed only when the water is low, to avoid the mountains and rocky ravines on the road through the woods. The Petit Rocher [now known as McKee's Rock] is on the side opposite to the road.

Source: Hanna, *Wilderness Trail,* Vol. 2, pp. 176–80

Note

Hanna in his *Wilderness Trail* states that DeLery left the Muskingum by way of White Eyes Creek, then followed Sugar Creek to its intersection with the Muskingum again near Dover. I don't agree with this assertion, however. I believe that DeLery proceeded northeast on Evans Creek, then continued to proceed down Stone Creek to the Muskingum just a mile or two below Dover. My reasons for choosing the Evans Creek route rather than the White Eyes Creek one are as follows:

1.   He left Conchake at 8:30 and left the Muskingum at noon. At 2½ miles per hour (which was the average speed that he was traveling the day before, coming down the Conchake), he could have travelled about 8½ miles. The distance from Conchake to White Eyes Creek is only 5½ miles but to Evans Creek is almost exactly 8½ miles. Distance wise, therefore, he would easily have been able to go as far as Evans Creek in 3½ hours of travel.

2.   DeLery's map shows an island in the Muskingum, where he turned north. The original survey maps of 1797 also show an island at Evans Creek, but not at White Eyes Creek.

3.   DeLery emphasizes that the stream he followed when he left the Muskingum led to another stream, heading in the same compass direction but *flowing* in the opposite direction. This description *exactly* describes Evans Creek and Stone Creek. It does *not* describe White Eyes Creek and Sugar Creek.

4.   The direction of the creeks as set forth by DeLery, E by NE, better describes Evans Creek than White Eyes Creek, which is more northerly.

5.   DeLery's map, after striking the Muskingum again, clearly shows him *crossing* a large stream coming in from his left. That would be Sugar Creek.

6.   DeLery crossed the Muskingum again where it turns NW (heading upstream) near Zoarville. The time from when he struck the Muskingum, south of Dover, to Zoarville is 5 hours. The distance is 8 miles. He could easily have traversed this distance in that time.

Map 2

DeLery's Route

These two maps are taken from the *DeLery* journal set forth in Hanna's *Wilderness Trail,* Vol 2, p. 178.

The upper map has been turned upside-down to align north towards the top of the page. The stream coming in from the upper left is the Conchake (Walhonding) and the small "house" between the streams represents the town of Conchake. The dotted line then shows his route along the Muskingum until he turned off to the northeast on what I believe is Evans Creek. He then followed it to Stone Creek which flowed the opposite way but in the same compass direction that he had already been heading. Notice the small island in the Muskingum at the point where DeLery left it. There was no such island at the mouth of White Eyes Creek in the 1700s, but *there was an island at the mouth of Evans Creek.* That fact, and the constant compass direction of the two creeks is why I believe DeLery went up Evans Creek and not White Eyes Creek, as stated by Hanna.

The other map on the facing page is further confirmation of my belief in this regard. It shows DeLery's path, from left to right, as he struck the Muskingum again near Dover. Notice that a large stream comes in from the north and DeLery *crossed* it. That stream is obviously Sugar Creek, about two miles above the mouth of Stone Creek. I believe that Hanna is simply mistaken when he says DeLery came *down* Sugar Creek to the Muskingum, for the map clearly shows him *crossing* it, not coming down it. He then went along the Muskingum for about six miles until it turned to the northwest at Zoarville, crossed it at that place, and continued to head to the northeast.

B. No 59

B. n. 40.

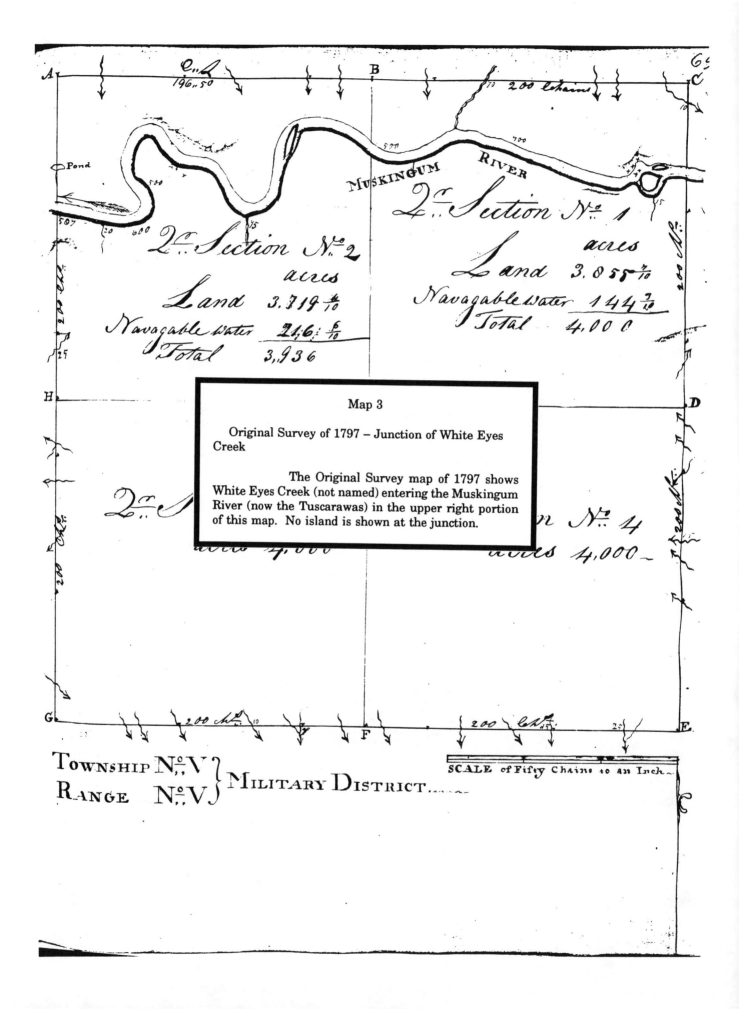

A
℄... 𝒜
196"50
B
70 200 chains
C
6⁹
Pond
500
587 20 600
75
MUSKINGUM   RIVER
2ᵈ Section Nᵒ 2
acres
Land 3.719 ⁷⁄₁₀
Navagable Water 21,6: ⁶⁄₁₀
Total 3,936
2ᵈ Section Nᵒ 1
acres
Land 3.055 ⁷⁄₁₀
Navagable Water 144 ³⁄₁₀
Total 4,000
200 chᵈ

H
D

Map 3

Original Survey of 1797 – Junction of White Eyes Creek

The Original Survey map of 1797 shows White Eyes Creek (not named) entering the Muskingum River (now the Tuscarawas) in the upper right portion of this map. No island is shown at the junction.

2ᵈ
Nᵒ 4
acres 4,000
acres 4,000

G
200 chᵈ 10
F
200 chᵈ 15
25
E

TOWNSHIP Nᵒ V } MILITARY DISTRICT
RANGE Nᵒ VI }

SCALE of Fifty Chains to an Inch

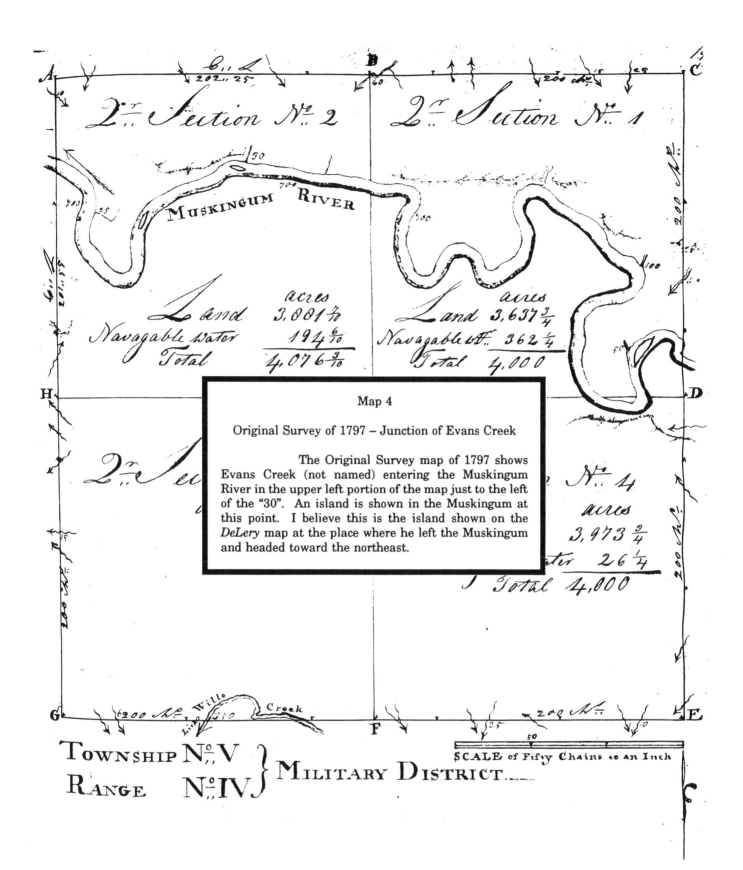

2ⁿ Section Nᵒ 2   2ⁿ Section Nᵒ 1

MUSKINGUM RIVER

Land   acres 3,881 ⁷⁄₁₀
Navagable water   194 ⁶⁄₁₀
Total   4,076 ³⁄₁₀

Land   acres 3,637 ³⁄₄
Navagable Wr.   362 ¼
Total   4,000

Map 4

Original Survey of 1797 – Junction of Evans Creek

     The Original Survey map of 1797 shows Evans Creek (not named) entering the Muskingum River in the upper left portion of the map just to the left of the "30". An island is shown in the Muskingum at this point. I believe this is the island shown on the *DeLery* map at the place where he left the Muskingum and headed toward the northeast.

2ⁿ Sec...   Nᵒ 4
acres
3,973 ²⁄₄
ter 26 ¼
Total 4,000

Willo Creek

TOWNSHIP Nᵒ V }
RANGE   Nᵒ IV } MILITARY DISTRICT...

SCALE of Fifty Chains to an Inch

I asked him if I had done anything that had offended the Indians, which caused them to treat me so unmercifully? [running the gauntlet]. He said no, it was only an old custom the Indians had, and it was like how do you do.

James Smith   Summer, 1755

James Smith
1755

The captivity narrative of James Smith is of interest in several respects. He was a prisoner at Fort DuQuesne as the English General Braddock approached, and his description of the events of July 9, 1755, as seen from the French and Indian perspective—the Indians grabbing arms and ammunition and hurrying off to meet the British, and, later in the day, returning triumphantly with hundreds of bloody scalps and other booty from the field of battle—brings a sense of realism to that tragic event which a mere recital of the facts of the battle itself could never achieve. Also, the descriptions of running the gauntlet and his adoption into the Indian tribe are equally colorful.

During his several years of captivity he frequently moved from one location to another, spending only about two months in the Tuscarawas Valley (more accurately, along the Walhonding), from August, 1755 to October, 1755. In July of 1759, while residing with the Indians near Montreal, he escaped to the French, was soon after exchanged with other English prisoners, and returned to Pennsylvania.

Since he did spend some time in the Tuscarawas Valley, even if only as a prisoner passing through, his narrative is included in this book as being typical of the experiences of many persons who were captured by the Indians.

In May 1755, the province of Pennsylvania, agreed to send out three hundred men, in order to cut a waggon road from Fort Loudon, to join Braddock's road, near the Turkey Foot, or three forks of Yohogania. My brother-in-law, William Smith esq. of Conococheague, was appointed commissioner, to have the oversight of these road-cutters.

Though I was at that time only eighteen years of age, I had fallen violently in love with a young lady, whom I apprehended was possessed of a large share of both beauty and virtue; — but being born between Venus and Mars, I concluded I must also leave my dear fair one, and go out with this company of road-cutters, to see the event of this campaign; but still expecting that some time in the course of this summer, I should again return to the arms of my beloved.

We went on with the road, without interruption, until near the Allegheny Mountain; when I was sent back, in order to hurry up some provisions waggons, that were on the way after us; I proceeded down the road as far as the crossings of Juniata, where, finding the waggons were coming on as fast as possible, I returned up the road again towards the Allegheny Mountain, in company with one Arnold Vigoras. About four or five miles above Bedford, three Indians had made a blind of bushes, stuck in the ground, as though they grew naturally, where they concealed themselves, about fifteen yards from the road. When we came opposite to them, they fired upon us, at this short distance, and killed my fellow traveller, yet their bullets did not touch me; but my horse making a violent start, threw me, and the Indians immediately ran up, and took me prisoner. The one that laid hold on me was a Canasatauga, the other two were Delawares. One of them could speak English, and asked me if there were any more white men coming after? I told them not any near, that I knew of. Two of these Indians stood by me, whilst the other scalped my conrade: they then set off and ran at a smart rate, through the woods, for about fifteen miles, and that night we slept on the Alegheny Mountain, without fire.

The next morning they divided the last of their provision which they had brought from Fort DuQuesne, and gave me an equal share, which was about two or three ounces of mouldy biscuit — this and a young Ground-Hog, about as large as a Rabbit, roasted, and also equally divided, was all the provision we had until we came to the Loyal-Hannan, which was about fifty miles; and a great part of the way we came through exceeding rocky Laurel-thickets, without any path. When we came to the West side of Laurel-Hill, they gave the scalp halloo, as usual, which is a long yell or halloo, for every scalp or prisoner they have in possession; the last of these scalp halloos were followed with quick and sudden shrill shouts of joy and triumph. On their performing this, we were answered by the firing of a number of guns on the Loyal-Hannan, one after another, quicker than one could count, by another party of Indians, who were encamped near where Ligoneer now stands. As we advanced near this party, they increased with repeated shouts of joy and triumph; but I did not share with them in their excessive mirth. When we came to this camp, we found they had plenty of Turkeys and other meat, there; and though I never before eat venison without bread or salt, yet as I was hungry, it relished very well. There we lay that night, and the next morning the whole of us marched on our way for Fort DuQuesne. The night after we joined another camp of Indians, with nearly the same ceremony, attended with great noise, and apparent joy, among all, except one. The next morning we continued our march, and in the afternoon we came in full view of the fort, which stood on the point, near where Fort Pitt now stands. We then made a halt on the bank of the Alegheny, and repeated the scalp halloo, which was answered by the firing of all the firelocks in the hands of both Indians and French who were in and about the fort, in the aforesaid manner, and also the great guns, which were followed by the continued

shouts and yells of the different savage tribes who were then collected there.

As I was at this time unacquainted with this mode of firing and yelling of the savages, I concluded that there were thousands of Indians there, ready to receive General Braddock; but what added to my surprize, I saw numbers running towards me, stripped naked, excepting breech-clouts, and painted in the most hideous manner, of various colours, though the principal color was vermillion, or a bright red; yet there was annexed to this, black, brown, blue, &c. As they approached, they formed themselves into two long ranks, about two or three rods apart. I was told by an Indian that could speak English, that I must run betwixt these ranks, and that they would flog me all the way, as I ran, and if I ran quick, it would be so much the better, as they would quit when I got to the end of the ranks. There appeared to be a general rejoicing around me, yet, I could find nothing like joy in my breast; but I started to the race with all the resolution and vigor I was capable of exerting, and found that it was as I had been told, for I was flogged the whole way. When I had got near the end of the lines, I was struck with something that appeared to me to be a stick, or the handle of a tommahawk, which caused me to fall to the ground. On my recovering my senses, I endeavored to renew my race: but as I arose, some one cast sand in my eyes, which blinded me so, that I could not see where to run. They continued beating me most intolerably, until I was at length insensible; but before I lost my senses, I remember my wishing them to strike the fatal blow, for I thought they intended killing me, but apprehended they were too long about it.

The first thing I remember was my being in the fort, amidst the French and Indians, and a French doctor standing by me, who had opened a vein in my left arm: after which, the interpreter asked me how I did, I told him I felt much pain; the doctor then washed my wounds, and the bruised places of my body, with French brandy. As I felt faint, and the brandy smelt well, I asked for some inwardly, but the doctor told me, by the interpreter, that it did not suit my case.

When they found I could speak, a number of Indians came around me, and examined me, with threats of cruel death, if I did not tell the truth. The first question they asked me, was, how many men were there in the party that were coming from Pennsylvania, to join Braddock? I told them the truth, that there were three hundred. The next question was, were they well armed? I told them they were all well armed, (meaning the arm of flesh) for they had only about thirty guns among the whole of them; which, if the Indians had known, they would certainly have gone and cut them all off; therefore, I could not in conscience let them know the defenceless situation of these road-cutters. I was then sent to the hospital, and carefully attended by the doctors, and recovered quicker than what I expected.

Some time after I was there, I was visited by the Delaware Indian already mentioned, who was at the taking of me, and could speak some English. Though he spoke but bad English, yet I found him to be a man of considerable understanding. I asked him if I had done any thing that had offended the Indians, which caused them to treat me so unmercifully? He said no, it was only an old custom the Indians had, and it was like how do you do; after that he said I would be well used. I asked him if I should be admitted to remain with the French? He said no — and told me that as soon as I recovered, I must not only go with the Indians, but must be made an Indian myself. I asked him what news from Braddock's army? He said the Indians spied them every day, and he showed me by making marks on the ground with a stick, that Braddock's army was advancing in very close order, and that the Indians would surround them, take trees, and (as he expressed it) "shoot um down all one pigeon".

Shortly after this, on the 9th of July 1755, in the morning I heard a great stir in the fort. As I could then walk with a staff in my hand, I went out of the door which was just by the wall of the fort, and stood upon the wall and viewed the Indians in a huddle before the gate, where were the barrels of powder, bullets, flints &c. and every one taking what suited; I saw the Indians also march off in rank, intire — likewise the French Canadians, and some regulars, after viewing the Indians and French in different positions, I computed them to be about four hundred, and wondered that they attempted to go out against Braddock with so small a party.

I was then in high hopes that I would soon see them fly before the British troops, and that General Braddock would take the fort and rescue me.

I remained anxious to know the event of this day; and in the afternoon I again observed a great noise and commotion in the fort, and though at that time I could not understand French, yet I found that it was the voice of Joy and triumph, and feared that they had received what I called bad news.

I had observed some of the old country soldiers speak Dutch, as I spoke Dutch I went to one of them, and asked him, what was the news? He told me that a runner had just arrived, who said that Braddock would certainly be defeated; that the Indians and French had surrounded him, and were concealed behind trees and in gullies, and kept a constant fire upon the English, and that they saw the English falling in heaps, and if they did not take the river which was the only gap, and make their escape, there would not be one man left alive before sun down. Some time after this I heard a number of scalp halloo's and saw a company of Indians and French coming in. I observed they had a great many bloody scalps, grenadiers' caps, British canteens, bayonets &c. with them. They brought the news that Braddock was defeated. After that, another company came in, which appeared to be about one hundred, and chiefly Indians, and it seemed to me that almost every one of this company was carrying scalps; after this came another company with a number of waggon-horses, and also a great many scalps. Those that were coming in, and those that had arrived, kept a constant firing of small arms, and also the great guns in the fort, which were accompanied with the most hedious shouts and yells from all quarters; so that it appeared to me as if the infernal regions had broke loose.

About sun down I beheld a small party coming in with about a dozen prisoners, stripped naked, with their hands tied behind their backs, and their faces and part of their bodies blacked — these prisoners they burned to death on the bank of Alegheny River opposite to the fort. I stood on the fort wall until I beheld them begin to burn one of these men, they had him tied to a stake, and kept touching him with fire-brands, red-hot irons &c. and he screeming in a most doleful manner, — the Indians in the mean time yelling like infernal spirits. As this scene appeared too shocking for me to behold I retired to my lodgings both sore and sorry.

When I came into my lodgings I saw Russel's Seven Sermons, which they had brought from the field of battle, which a Frenchman made a present of to me. From the best information I could receive there were only seven Indians and four French killed in this battle, and five hundred British lay dead in the field; besides what were killed in the river on their retreat.

The morning after the battle I saw Braddock's artillery brought into the fort, the same day I also saw several Indians in British-officers' dress with sash, half-moon, laced hats &c. which the British then wore.

A few days after this the Indians demanded me and I was obliged to go with them. I was not yet well able to march, but they took me in a canoe, up the Alegheny River to an Indian town that was on the north side of the river, about forty miles above Fort DuQuesne. Here I remained about three weeks, and was then taken to an Indian town on the west branch of the Muskingum, about twenty miles above the forks, which was called Tullihas, inhabited by Delawares, Caughnewagos and Mohicans. — On our rout betwixt the aforesaid towns, the country was chiefly black-oak and white-oak land, which appeared generally to be good wheat land, chiefly second and third rate, intermixed with some rich bottoms.

The day after my arrival at the aforesaid town, a number of Indians collected about me, and one of them began to pull the hair out of my head. He had some ashes on a piece of bark, in which he frequently dipped his fingers in order to take firmer hold, and so he went on, as if he had been plucking a turkey, until he had all the hair clean out of my head, except a small spot about three or four inches square on my crown; this they cut off with a pair of scissors, excepting three locks, which they dressed up in their own mode. Two of these they wraped around with a narrow beaded garter made by themselves for that purpose, and the other they platted at full length, and then stuck it full of silver broches. After this they bored my nose and ears, and fixed me off with ear rings and nose jewels, then they ordered me to strip off my clothes and put on a

breech-clout, which I did; they then painted my head, face and body in various colours. They put a large belt of wampom on my neck, and silver bands on my hands and right arm; and so an old chief led me out in the street and gave the alarm halloo, "coo-wigh", several times repeated quick, and on this all that were in the town came running and stood round the old chief, who held me by the hand in the midst. — As I at that time knew nothing of their mode of adoption, and had seen them put to death all they had taken, and as I never could find that they saved a man alive at Braddock's defeat, I made no doubt but they were about putting me to death in some cruel manner. The old chief holding me by the hand, made a long speech very loud, and when he had done he handed me to three young squaws, who led me by the hand down the bank into the river until the water was up to our middle. The squaws then made signs to me to plunge myself into the water, but I did not understand them; I thought that the result of the council was that I should be drowned, and that these young ladies were to be the executioners. They all three laid violent hold of me, and I for some time opposed them with all my might, which occasioned loud laughter by the multitude that were on the bank of the river. At length one of the squaws made out to speak a little English (for I believe they began to be afraid of me) and said, "no hurt you"; on this I gave myself up to their ladyships, who were as good as their word; for though they plunged me under water, and washed and rubbed me severely, yet I could not say they hurt me much.

These young women then led me up to the council house, where some of the tribe were ready with new cloths for me. They gave me a new ruffled shirt, which I put on, also a pair of leggins done off with ribbons and beads, likewise a pair of mockasons, and garters dressed with beads, Porcupine-quills, and redhair — also a tinsel laced cappo. They again painted my head and face with various colors, and tied a bunch of red feathers to one of these locks they had left on the crown of my head, which stood up five or six inches. They seated me on a bear skin, and gave me a pipe, tomahawk, and polecat skin pouch, which had been skinned pocket fashion, and contained tobacco, killegenico, or dry sumach leaves, which they mix with their tobacco, also spunk, flint and steel. When I was thus seated, the Indians came in dressed and painted in their grandest manner. As they came in they took their seats and for a considerable time there was a profound silence, everyone was smoking, — but not a word was spoken among them. — At length one of the chiefs made a speech, which was delivered to me by an interpreter, — and was as followeth: — "My son, you are now flesh of our flesh, and bone of our bone. By the ceremony which was performed this day, every drop of white blood was washed out of your veins; you are taken into the Caughnewago nation, and initiated into a warlike tribe; you are adopted into a great family, and now received with great seriousness and solemnity in the room and place of a great man; after what has passed this day, you are now one of us by an old strong law and custom — My son, you have now nothing to fear, we are now under the same obligations to love, support and defend you, that we are to love and to defend one another, therefore you are to consider yourself as one of our people." — At this time I did not believe this fine speech, especially that of the white blood being washed out of me; but since that time I have found that there was much sincerity in said speech, — for, from that day I never knew them to make any distinction between me and themselves in any respect whatever until I left them. — If they had plenty of cloathing I had plenty, if we were scarce we all shared one fate.

After this ceremony was over, I was introduced to my new kin, and told that I was to attend a feast that evening, which I did. And as the custom was, they gave me also a bowl and wooden spoon, which I carried with me to the place, where there was a number of large brass kettles full of boiled venison and green corn; every one advanced with his bowl and spoon and had his share given him. — After this, one of the chiefs made a short speech, and then we began to eat.

The name of one of the chiefs in this town was Tecanyaterighto, alias Pluggy, and the other Asallecoa, alias Mohawk Solomon. — As Pluggy and his party were to start the next day to war, to the frontiers of Virginia, the next thing to be performed was the war dance, and their war songs. At their war dance they had both vocal and instrumental music. They has a short

hollow gum close in one end, with water in it, and parchment stretched over the open end thereof, which they beat with one stick, and made a sound nearly like a muffled drum, — all those who were going on this expedition collected together and formed. An old Indian then began to sing, and timed the music by beating on this drum, as the ancients formerly timed their music by beating the tabor. On this the warriors began to advance, or move forward in concert, like well disciplined troops would march to the fife and drum. Each warrior had a tomahawk, spear or warmallet in his hand, and they all moved regularly towards the east, or the way they intended to go to war. At length they all stretched their tomahawks towards the Potomack, and giving a hideous shout or yell, they wheeled quick about, and danced in the same manner back. The next was the war song. In performing this, only one sung at a time, in a moving posture, with a tomahawk in his hand, while all the other wariors were engaged in calling aloud "he-uh, he-uh", which they constantly repeated, while the war song was going on. When the warior that was singing had ended his song, he struck a war-post with his tomahawk, and with a loud voice told what warlike exploits he had done, and what he now intended to do: which were answered by the other wariors with loud shouts of applause. Some who had not before intended to go to war, at this time were so animated by this performance, that they took up the tomahawk and sung the war song which was answered with shouts of joy, as they were then initiated into the present marching company. The next morning this company all collected at one place, with their heads and faces painted with various colors, and packs upon their backs: they marched off, all silent, except the commander, who, in the front, sung the travelling song, which began in this manner: "hoo caugh-tainte heegana". Just as the rear passed the end of the town, they began to fire in their slow manner, from the front to the rear, which was accompanied with shouts and yells from all quarters.

This evening I was invited to another sort of dance, which was a kind of promiscuos dance. The young men stood in one rank, and the young women in another, about one rod apart, facing each other. The one that raised the tune, or started the song, held a small gourd or dry shell of a squash, in his hand, which contained beads or small stones, which rattled. When he began to sing, he timed the tune with his rattle; both men and women danced and sung together, advancing towards each other, stooping until their heads would be touching together, and then ceased from dancing, with loud shouts, and retreated and formed again, and so repeated the same thing over and over, for three or four hours, without intermission. This exercise appeared to me at first, irrational and insipid; but I found that in singing their tunes, they used "ya ne no hoo wa ne", &c. like our "fa sol la", and

though they have no such thing as jingling verse, yet they can intermix sentences with their notes, and say what they please to each other, and carry on the tune in concert. I found that this was a kind of wooing or courting dance, and as they advanced stooping with their heads together, they could say what they pleased in each others ear, without disconcerting their rough music, and the others, or those near, not hear what they say.

Source: Smith, *An Account of the Remarkable Occurences...*, pp. 18–35

Indian Remedies

The *Materia Medica* of the Indians consists of various roots and plants known to themselves, the properties of which they are not fond of disclosing to strangers. They make considerable use of the barks of trees, such as the white and black oak, the white walnut of which they make pills, the cherry, dogwood, maple, birch and several others. They prepare and compound these medicines in different ways, which they keep a profound secret. Those preparations are frequently mixed with superstitious practices, calculated to guard against the powers of witchcraft, in which, unfortunately, they have a strong fixed belief. Indeed, they are too apt to attribute the most natural deaths to the arts and incantations of sorcerers, and their medicine is, in most cases, as much directed against those as against the disease itself. There are, however, practitioners among them who are free from these prejudices, or at least do not introduce them into their practice of the medical art. Still there is a superstitious notion, in which all their physicians participate, which is, that when an emetic is to be administered, the water in which the potion is mixed must be drawn up a stream, and if for a cathartic downwards. This is, at least, innocent, and not more whimsical perhaps, nor more calculated to excite a smile, than some theories of grave and learned men in civilised countries.

Source: Heckewelder's *History...*, p. 224

Charles Stuart
1755

Little is known of Charles Stuart except that he was living in Cumberland County, Pennsylvania when he was captured by Indians on October 29, 1755, that he was taken to Fort DuQuesne, then to Sandusky (via the Tuscarawas and Walhonding valleys), and on to Detroit. From there he was sent to Montreal and forwarded, in an exchange of prisoners, to England, returning to New York later in 1757.

It was November of 1755 when he passed through the Tuscarawas Valley, seven months after DeLery had been there. The two houses at Conchake mentioned by Delery were deserted by then. Since Stuart specifically says that one of the houses was where an English trader had formerly lived, that was probably the one referred to in the Gist journal of 1750 as belonging to George Croghan. The other house was, perhaps, the "King's House", also mentioned by Gist. This, of course, is speculation on my part, but since those houses were probably the most substantial houses in the town of Muskingum when Gist was there in 1750, it seem likely that those houses would have been the ones that continued to be used by whoever was still living at Muskingum in 1755.

Especially poignant in this journal is Stuart's parting with his son at these houses, the son not realizing that they would never see each other again.

This journal is particularly important to the Indian history of the Tuscarawas Valley, for it helps to positively identify the location of the town of Muskingum, or Conchake. Stuart tells of two springs at the site of the two cabins mentioned by DeLery, earlier that same year, being all that was left of Conchake. The Original Survey of 1797, made by the government surveyors when the land was opened up for settlement, also mentions these same two springs, and even shows their locations on their map of the river. Thus, the site of Muskingum is positively established.

Further confirmation of this location is furnished by the Finley field notes of the Bouquet Expedition, mentioned in the separate articles about the Locations of Muskingum and of Bouquet's 16th Encampment.

Fort DuQuesne Inclines to a Square but is Something Rounding on the Front Side next the Land. It is Made of Loggs Laid at Some distance from one another and Fill[d] in with Earth Between & Stockades that raises ab[t] 5 or 5½ feet above the Earth — the French had cleard ab[t] 25 Acres of Land about the Fort from the Fork at the Confluence of the Two Rivers up towards the Land But the Stumps of the Trees remaind, the Cleard Land reach^d a little better than Muskett Shot from the Fort and the Trees seem^d to be Kill^d for some distance Farther than where they were Cut down —

{November 17, 1755} We set off from our Encamping Place the 3^d day after our Arrival there and Proceeded towards Loggs Town, keeping near the River in gen^l — the Land to Loggs Town appeard very hilly and many of the Hills was Steep and some Considerable ridges — But even the Hilly Land appeard to Be rich good Land and Fit for Tillage and in the Bottoms in gen^l Both on the Ohio River & its Branches were exceeding rich and very fit for Indian Corn or other Grain. We Cross^d 3 Considerable Creeks between Du Quesne & Loggs Town, when we came to Loggs town we found all the Cabbins waste but Three, we Pass^d on ab^t 3 miles Farther to a small Creek where was Rich Bottom Land and there we Encamp^d that Night, Being the Second Night from the Camp opposite Fort Du Quesne — The next Day {November 19th} we cross^d Beaver Creek where we Encamp^d a little before night, we forded it. S^d Beaver Creek is not navigable for loaded Battoes without a Fresh is in it. We proceeded on From Beaver Creek Towards Muskingom and Travell^d but a Few Miles that day & the next day {November 20th} Capt John Peter with my Son and Two More Prisoners and 7 Indians overtook Us. we had Left my daughter at the Small Shawnee Town By wch I pass^d ab^t 10 Miles above Fort Du Quesne where I saw my Children But ab^t 20 [rods?] distant and Desired Leave to Bid them Farewell But was not Permitted to do it or to speak [to] them. We Travell^d in Company 3 days till we Cross^d Muskingom, {November 23rd} the Place we Cross^d was ab^t 20 miles nearer Ohio River than the Old Traders Road. {NOTE: I believe that it was the Stillwater rather than the Muskingum he crossed for his description of the terrain through which he passed as he went down the Muskingum much better describes the south side rather than the north side of the river.} After Leaveing Beaver Creek ab^t 10 miles we Found the Land less hilly Till we Cross^d Muskingom and the greater Part of it very good Land. I dont remember that we cross^d any large Creek between Beaver Creek and Musking[um] tho' we Cross^d severall small Creeks and rivers

But none fit for Navigation for Battoes — Muskingom is Very much of the Sise of Swetara at the Pine Ford as To Breadth But not so deep But a Fine Clean Sand Bottom without Rocks or Stones and might be usefull for Battoe Navigation —

We Turn^d down the Side of Muskingom Towards Ohio and Travell^d 2 or 3 Hours along the Bank of Muskingom under a High Steep Ridge wch was within a Few Rods of the River. After Passing s^d ridge we came to Level Rich Land Well Timbered with the Same Kinds of Timber as Pensylvania Land wch continued for ab^t 5 miles and appeard the Same Sort of Land Towards the Norwest as far as I cou^d well see —we Continued Travelling near the river for ab^t 10 miles thro' Land Cover'd with the ground Oaks of Barrens But yet the Soil Seem^d pretty good — the s^d barrens seem^d ab^t 1½ Miles bro^d at the Broadest part and ended at the House where an Eng: Indian Trader had Formerly Lived and where was an Indians House Both of wch were deserted, {Conchake?} S^d Two Houses stood Close on the Bank of Muskingom where was 2 small Springs Under s^d Bank Containing Exceeding Good Water — Muskingom Seem^d deeper here than where we Cross^d it But not much Broader, the place where we Cross^d Muskingom I Judge was ab^t 25 miles Above these Cabbins — We Encamp^d here one Night and that Night my Son was Permitted to Sleep with me — In the Morning Capt John Peter Told me To Take Leave of my Son for that I wou'd never see him again — he said he expected to be at my Sons Home that Night Before Sun down and Told me the distance to it was 21 miles Being a pretty large Shawnee Town on one of the Branches of Scioto — here I parted with my Son and a Sorrowfull parting it was to me But my Poor Son did not know he was then To Take his Final Leave of me, But Expected me to Follow him — he Rode from Fort Du Quesne To the Shawnee Town and was Tied from his Hips down to the Girt of the Saddle To Prevent his Falling off, After Parting wth him we Set off for the Wondot Town, Takeing their Hunting Camps in the way wch Lay Between Their Town & Scioto —

After we had Left the Traders House on Muskingom where I parted with my Son we Travell^d ab^t 5 or 6 miles Thro Hasel Bushes & Small Plumb Bushes or Shrubs, To the Edge of a Long Savannah — we Travell[d] along the Edge of it ab[t] 12 miles Leaving it on our Left hand, after w[ch] we went Slanting across it where it was ab[t] 4 miles Broad, we still Continued up the Savannah about 7 miles Leaving it on the right hand Till we came to a great Buffaloe Lick where we met a Wondot Indian who Had Kill[d] a Buffaloe there the day Before, I saw the Meat w[ch] I judged to be ab[t] 5 or 6 Hundred Weight, they said it was but a Small Buffaloe. It was a Bull and But young and not got to its Full Growth, The Meat appeared Exactly Like Beef and as Fat as Cattle w[ch] had been Fatted For Killing in the Usual Manner That Country Planters generally Fats their Beef — From what I Saw of the Savannah, and what Informations the Indians gave about it I judged it To Be ab[t] 50 miles in Length and in general ab[t] 4 or 5 miles in Bread[th] — In this Savannah there are Some Small Islands or Riseing Grounds tho' not many, & perhaps not above one in 5 miles, these islands Contain from ab[t] 3 acres to ab[t] 5 or 6 Acres of Land and are generally well Timbered with red & white oak &c. and appear'd Very Rich Ground and were Cheifly Covered over with Pidgeon Dung, and a great many Large Limbs of Trees had been Broken down by the great Quantitys of Pidgeons that roosted on them — The greatest Part by Far of the Savannah Land appeard Very Fit For Indian Corn or Hemp and required no other Clearing than Burning the Grass and Weeds — the other Parts of Said Savannah Had Hassocks in it But did not appear wet and swampy — a small Creek or Brook {the Walhonding?}— w[ch] Empty[d] into Muskingom at the above Two Houses or Cabbins Run along down the Savannah, the water of s[d] Creek was very good Water for drinking —

From the Savannah we set off in the Morning and Travell[d] a Norwest Course very hard and reach[d] the first Hunting Camp of the Wondot Nation that Night by dark, which was in the Fork of a Creek. At said Camp was Three Cabbins of the Hunters and ab[t] 8 Hunters Belonging to them & here we got a refreshment of Indian Hominy without Salt w[ch] was very acceptable to Us for we had Eat no Bread Since Leaving Fort Du Quesne But the Two Small Loaves or Roles of Bread of ab[t] 1½ [lbs.] each w[ch] the French Gov[r] gave Us & haveing Lived only on Meat without Salt and Frequently very scarce even at that — After Tarrying here one day we Proceeded to the next Wondot Hunting Came [camp] w[ch] we reach[d] in a days hard Travel and Lay pretty near north from the other, here we found 3 Large Hunting Cabbins and a Pretty Large Creek w[ch] seem[d] to Run ab[t] a South West Course and was Probably some of the Branches of Sioto.

Source: Stuart, "The Captivity of Charles Stuart", pp. 67–70

The Devil

They seem to have had no idea of the devil until in modern times preachers arose among them who proclaimed that there was such a being, having secured their knowledge from the whites. They have no very definite conception of him but consider him to be a very powerful spirit, able to work much harm and unable to do any good.

Source: Zeisberger's *History...*, p. 130

Marie Le Roy and Barbara Leininger
1758–9

Marie Le Roy and Barbara Leininger were captured in October of 1755 near the Susquehanna River in eastern Pennsylvania. The early portion of their narrative is included in this book to show just what could happen to prisoners who attempted to escape from the Indians, which explains why so few even tried.

These girls, however, did escape. Brought into the Tuscarawas Valley after the capture of Fort DuQuesne by the English in 1758, they lived in the vicinity of Muskingum, near the forks of the Walhonding and Tuscarawas rivers. Whether this was on the exact site of the earlier Muskingum and Conchake of Gist's and DeLery's time cannot now be determined with certainty, but it could have been. In March of 1759, they, along with two other persons, made their escape and arrived back at Pittsburgh on March 31st.

Marie Le Roy was born at Brondrut, in Switzerland. About five years ago she arrived, with her parents, in this country. They settled fifteen miles from Fort Schamockin. Half a mile from their plantation lived Barbara Leininger with her parents, who came to Pennsylvania from Reutlingen, about ten years ago.

Early in the morning of the 16th of October, 1755, while Le Roy's hired man went out to fetch the cows, he heard the Indians shooting six times. Soon after, eight of them came to the house, and killed Marie Le Roy's father with tomahawks. Her brother defended himself desperately, for a time, but was, at last, overpowered. The Indians did not kill him, but took him prisoner, together with Marie Le Roy and a little girl, who was staying with the family. Thereupon they plundered the homestead, and set it on fire. Into this fire they laid the body of the murdered father, feet foremost, until it was half consumed. The upper half was left lying on the ground, with the two tomahawks, with which they had killed him, sticking in his head. Then they kindled another fire, not far from the house.

While sitting around it, a neighbour of Le Roy, named Bastian, happened to pass by on horseback. He was immediately shot down and scalped.

Two of the Indians now went to the house of Barbara Leininger, where they found her father, her brother, and her sister Regina. Her mother had gone to the mill. They demanded rum; but there was none in the house. Then they called for tobacco, which was given them. Having filled and smoked a pipe, they said: "We are Alleghany Indians, and your enemies. You must all die!" Thereupon they shot her father, tomahawked her brother, who was twenty years of age, took Barbara and her sister Regina prisoners, and conveyed them into the forest for about a mile. There they were soon joined by other Indians, with Marie Le Roy and the little girl.

Not long after several of the Indians led the prisoners to the top of a high hill, near the two plantations. Toward evening the rest of the savages returned with six fresh and bloody scalps, which they threw at the feet of the poor

26

captives, saying that they had a good hunt that day.

The next morning we were taken about two miles further into the forest, while the most of the Indians again went out to kill and plunder. Toward evening they returned with nine scalps and five prisoners.

On the third day the whole band came together and divided the spoils. In addition to large quantities of provisions, they had taken fourteen horses and ten prisoners, namely: One man, one woman, five girls, and three boys. We two girls, as also two of the horses, fell to the share of an Indian named Galasko.

We traveled with our new master for two days. He was tolerably kind, and allowed us to ride all the way, while he and the rest of the Indians walked. Of this circumstance Barbara Leininger took advantage, and tried to escape. But she was almost immediately recaptured, and condemned to be burned alive. The savages gave her a French Bible, which they had taken from Le Roy's house, in order that she might prepare for death; and, when she told them that she could not understand it, they gave her a German Bible. Thereupon they made a large pile of wood and set it on fire, intending to put her into the midst of it. But a young Indian begged so earnestly for her life that she was pardoned, after having promised not to attempt to escape again, and to stop her crying.

The next day the whole troop was divided into two bands, the one marching in the direction of the Ohio, the other, in which we were with Galasko, to Jenkiklamuhs, a Delaware town on the West branch of the Susquehanna. There we staid ten days, and then proceeded to Puncksotonay, or Eschentown. Marie Le Roy's brother was forced to remain at Jenkiklamuhs.

After having rested for five days at Puncksotonay, we took our way to Kittanny. As this was to be the place of our permanent abode, we here received our welcome, according to Indian custom. It consisted of three blows each, on the back. They were, however, administered with great mercy. Indeed, we concluded that we were beaten merely in order to keep up an ancient usage, and not with the intention of injuring us. The month of December was the time of our arrival, and we remained at Kittanny until the month of September, 1756.

The Indians gave us enough to do. We had to tan leather, to make shoes (mocasins), to clear land, to plant corn, to cut down trees and build huts, to wash and cook. The want of provisions, however, caused us the greatest sufferings. During all the time that we were at Kittanny we had neither lard nor salt; and, sometimes, we were forced to live on acorns, roots, grass, and bark. There was nothing in the world to make this new sort of food palatable, excepting hunger itself.

In the month of September Col. Armstrong arrived with his men, and attacked Kittanny Town. Both of us happened to be in that part of it which lies on the other (right) side of the river (Alleghany). We were immediately conveyed ten miles farther into the interior, in order that we might have no chance of trying, on this occasion, to escape. The savages threatened to kill us. If the English had advanced, this might have happened. For, at that time, the Indians were greatly in dread of Col. Armstrong's corps. After the English had withdrawn, we were again brought back to Kittanny, which town had been burned to the ground.

There we had the mournful opportunity of witnessing the cruel end of an English woman, who had attempted to flee out of her captivity and to return to the settlements with Col. Armstrong. Having been recaptured by the savages, and brought back to Kittanny, she was put to death in an unheard of way. First, they scalped her; next, they laid burning splinters of wood, here and there, upon her body, and then they cut off her ears and fingers, forcing them into her mouth so that she had to swallow them. Amidst such torments, this woman lived from nine o'clock in the morning until toward sunset, when a French officer took compassion on her, and put her out of her misery. An English soldier, on the contrary, named John ———, who escaped from prison at Lancaster, and joined the French, had a piece of flesh cut from her body, and ate it. When she was dead, the Indians chopped her in two, through the middle, and let her lie until the dogs came and devoured her.

Three days later an Englishman was brought in, who had, likewise, attempted to escape with Col. Armstrong, and burned alive in the same village. His torments, however, continued only about three hours; but his screams were frightful to listen to. It rained that day very hard, so that the Indians could not keep up the fire. Hence they began to discharge gunpowder into his body. At last, amidst his worst pains, when the poor man called for a drink of water, they brought him melted lead, and poured it down his throat. This draught at once helped him out of the hands of the barbarians, for he died on the instant.

It is easy to imagine what an impression such fearful instances of cruelty make upon the mind of a poor captive. Does he attempt to escape from the savages, he knows in advance that, if retaken, he will be roasted alive. Hence he must compare two evils, namely, either to remain among them a prisoner forever, or to die a cruel death. Is he fully resolved to endure the latter, then he may run away with a brave heart.

Soon after these occurrences we were brought to Fort Duquesne, where we remained for about two months. We worked for the French, and our Indian master drew our wages. In this place, thank God, we could again eat bread. Half a pound was given us daily. We might have had bacon, too, but we took none of it, for it was not good. In some respects we were better off than in the Indian towns; we could not, however abide the French. They tried hard to induce us to forsake the Indians and stay with them, making us various favourable offers. But we believed that it would be better for us to remain among the Indians, in as much as they would be more likely to make peace with the English than the French, and in as much as there would be more ways open for flight in the forest than in a fort. Consequently we declined the offers of the French, and accompanied our Indian master to Sackum, where we spent the winter, keeping house for the savages, who were continually on the hunt. In the spring we were taken to Kaschkaschkung, an Indian town on the Beaver Creek. There we again had to clear the plantations of the Indian nobles, after the German fashion, to plant corn, and to do other hard work of every kind. We remained at this place for about one year and a half.

After having, in the past three years, seen no one of our own flesh and blood, except those unhappy beings who, like ourselves, were bearing the yoke of the heaviest slavery, we had the unexpected pleasure of meeting with a German, who was not a captive, but free, and who, as we heard, had been sent into this neighbourhood to negotiate a peace between the English and the natives. His name was Frederick Post. We and all the other prisoners heartily wished him success and God's blessing upon his undertaking. We were, however, not allowed to speak with him. The Indians gave us plainly to understand that any attempt to do this would be taken amiss. He himself, by the reserve with which he treated us, let us see that this was not the time to talk over our afflictions. But we were greatly alarmed on his account. For the French told us that, if they caught him, they would roast him alive for five days, and many Indians declared that it was impossible for him to get safely through, that he was destined for death.

Last summer the French and Indians were defeated by the English in a battle fought at Loyal-Hannon, or Fort Ligonier. This caused the utmost consternation among the natives. They brought their wives and children from Lockstown, Sackum, Schomingo, Mamalty, Kaschkaschkung, and other places in that neighbourhood, to Moschkingo, about one hundred and fifty miles farther west. Before leaving, however, they destroyed their crops, and burned everything which they could not carry with them. We had to go along and staid at Moschkingo the whole winter.

In February, Barbara Leininger agreed with an Englishman, named David Breckenreach [Breckenridge], to escape, and gave her conrade, Marie Le Roy, notice of their intentions. On account of the severe season of the year, and the long journey which lay before them, Marie strongly advised her to relinquish the project, suggesting that it should be postponed until spring, when the weather would be milder, and promising to accompany her at that time.

On the last day of February nearly all the Indians left Moschkingo, and proceeded to Pittsburg to sell pelts. Meanwhile, their women traveled ten miles up the country to gather roots, and we accompanied them. Two men went along as a guard. It was our earnest hope that the opportunity for flight, so long desired, had now come. Accordingly, Barbara Leininger pretended to be sick, so that she might be allowed to put up a hut for herself alone. On the fourteenth of March, Marie Le Roy was sent back to the town, in order to fetch two young dogs which had been left there; and, on the same day, Barbara Leininger came out of her hut and visited a German woman, ten miles from Moschkingo. This woman's name is Mary ———— , and she is the wife of a miller from the South Branch. She had made every preparation to accompany us on our flight; but Barbara found that she had meanwhile become lame, and could not think of going along. She, however, gave Barbara the provisions which she had stored, namely two pounds of dried meat, a quart of corn, and four pounds of sugar. Besides, she presented her with pelts for mocasins. Moreover, she advised a young Englishman, Owen Gibson, to flee with us two girls.

On the sixteenth of March, in the evening, Gibson reached Barbara Leininger's hut, and, at ten o'clock, our whole party, consisting of us two girls, Gibson, and David Breckenreach, left Moschkingo. This town lies on a river, in the country of the Dellamottinoes. We had to pass many huts inhabited by the savages, and knew that there were at least sixteen dogs with them. In the merciful providence of God not a single one of these dogs barked. Their barking would at once have betrayed us, and frustrated our design.

It is hard to describe the anxious fears of a poor woman under such circumstances. The extreme probability that the Indians would pursue, and recapture us, was as two to one compared with the dim hope that, perhaps, we would get through in safety. But, even if we escaped the Indians, how would we ever succeed in passing through the wilderness, unacquainted with a single path or trail, without a guide, and helpless, half naked, broken down by more than three years of hard slavery, hungry and scarcely any food, the season wet and cold, and many rivers and streams to cross? Under such circumstances, to depend upon one's own sagacity would be the worst of follies. If one could not believe that there is a God, who helps and saves from death, one had better let running away alone.

We safely reached the river [Muskingum]. Here the first thought in all our minds was: O! that we were safely across! And Barbara Leininger, in particular, recalling ejaculatory prayers from an old hymn, which she had learned in her youth, put them together, to suit our present circumstances, something in the following style:

O bring us safely across this river!
In fear I cry, yea my soul doth quiver.
The worst afflictions are now before me
Where'er I turn nought but death do I see.
Alas, what great hardships are yet in store
In the wilderness wide, beyond that shore!
It has neither water, nor meat, nor bread,
But each new morning something new to dread.
Yet little sorrow would hunger me cost
If but I could flee from the savage host,
Which murders and fights and burns far and wide,
While Satan himself is array'd on its side.
Should on us fall one of its cruel bands,
Then help us, Great God, and stretch out Thy hands!
In Thee will we trust, be Thou ever near,
Art Thou our Joshua, we need not fear.

Presently we found a raft, left by the Indians. Thanking God that He had himself prepared a way for us across these first waters, we got on board and pushed off. But we were carried almost a mile down the river before we could reach the other side. There our journey began in good earnest. Full of anxiety and fear, we fairly ran that whole night and all the next day, when we lay down to rest without venturing to kindle a fire. Early the next morning, Owen Gibson fired at a bear. The animal fell, but, when he ran with his tomahawk to kill it, it jumped up and hit him in the feet, leaving three wounds. We all hastened to his assistance. The bear escaped into narrow holes among the rocks, where we could not follow. On the third day, however, Owen Gibson shot a deer. We cut off the hind-quarters, and roasted them at night. The next morning he again shot a deer, which furnished us with food for that day. In the evening we got to the Ohio at last, having made a circuit of over one hundred miles in order to reach it.

About midnight the two Englishmen rose and began to work at a raft, which was finished by morning. We got on board and safely crossed the river. From the signs which the Indians had there put up we saw that we were about one hundred and fifty miles from Fort Duquesne. After a brief consultation we resolved, heedless of path or trail, to travel straight toward the rising of the sun. This we did for seven days. On the seventh we found that we had reached the Little Beaver Creek, and were about fifty miles from Pittsburgh. And now, that we imagined ourselves so near the end of all our troubles and misery, a whole host of mishaps came upon us. Our provisions were at an end; Barbara Leininger fell into the water and was nearly drowned; and, worst misfortune of all! Owen Gibson lost his flint and steel. Hence we had to spend four nights without fire, amidst rain and snow.

On the last day of March we came to a river, Allequopy, about three miles below Pittsburg. Here we made a raft, which, however, proved to be too light to carry us across. It threatened to sink, and Marie Le Roy fell off, and narrowly escaped drowning. We had to put back, and let one of our men convey one of us across at a time. In this way we reached the Monongahella River, on the other side of Pittsburg, the same evening.

Upon our calling for help, Col. [Hugh] Mercer immediately sent out a boat to bring us to the Fort. At first, however, the crew created many difficulties about taking us on board. They thought we were Indians, and wanted us to spend the night where we were, saying they would fetch us in the morning. When we had succeeded in convincing them that we were English prisoners, who had escaped from the Indians, and that we were wet and cold and hungry, they brought us over. There was an Indian with the soldiers in the boat. He asked us whether we could speak good Indian? Marie Le Roy said she could speak it. Thereupon he inquired, why she had run away? She replied, that her Indian mother had been so cross and had scolded her so constantly, that she could not stay with her any longer.

This answer did not please him; nevertheless, doing as courtiers do, he said; He was very glad we had safely reached the Fort.

It was in the night from the last of March to the first of April {1759} that we came to Pittsburg.

Source: Le Roy, "The Narrative of Marie Le Roy...", pp. 407–16

Indian Infirmities of Old Age

The Indians do not appear to be more or less exempt than the whites from the common infirmities of old age. I have known old men among them who had lost their memory, their sight, and their teeth. I have also seen them at eighty in their second childhood and not able to help themselves.

Source: Heckewelder's *History...*, p. 221

Hugh Gibson
1758–9

Hugh Gibson was living near Carlisle, Pennsylvania when he was captured in 1756. He was fifteen years old at the time.

It appears that he witnessed the same terrible execution of an English woman that Marie Le Roy and Barbara Leininger had witnessed, and his subsequent story is intertwined with theirs. He, too, was taken to the Forks of the Muskingum in the fall of 1758 and it was he, and another young English lad, who escaped with Marie and Barbara in March of 1759.

His narrative establishes that the town at Muskingum, in 1758, was a Delaware town and that Bisquetam (often spelled Pisquetomen), a brother of "Kings" Beaver and Shingas, was one of the principal chiefs of the town at that time. He also names several other brothers of Bisquetam, Beaver, and Shingas.

Several times he refers to a Ft. McIntosh. This was a fort that was erected at the mouth of the Beaver during the Revolutionary War, but was obviously not there in the 1750s. It seems, therefore, that when he refers to Ft. McIntosh, he simply means the location where the fort was later established, rather than the fort itself.

Hugh Gibson, an account of whose trials and sufferings among the Indians is now, for the first time, submitted to the public, was the eldest son of David Gibson and his wife, originally Mary M'Clelland. His parents lived at the Six Miles' Cross, near Stewart's Town, in the north of Ireland, till about the year 1740, when they crossed the Atlantic and settled on a plantation of their purchase in Lancaster county, Pennsylvania, two miles and a half below Peach Bottom Ferry, on the Susquehannah; where the subject of this Narrative was born in February, 1741.

Mr. Gibson at the age of five years was deprived of his father. His mother, in her widowed state, removed to a place in the vicinity of Robinson's Fort, nearly twenty miles from Carlisle, and at length, in consequence of danger apprehended, with others, in 1756, resided in the Fort. On a certain morning in the latter part of July, he and his mother, with Elizabeth Henry, went out in search of their cattle. They were unexpectedly beset by a party of Indians. His mother was shot at some distance from him, and Sarah Wilson, who had joined her, was tomahawked.

Mr. Gibson heard the gun, which had proved instantly fatal to his mother, and was immediately after pursued by three Indians, from whom he attempted to escape; but soon finding it impossible to outrun them, stopped, and entreated them not to take his life. One of them had already aimed his rifle at him, but the powder merely flashing in the pan, the contents of the deadly weapon were not discharged. He was taken by one of the Indians, who was a son of King Beaver, and was afterwards presented by him to Bisquittam, another Delaware chief, and an uncle of the captor. Elizabeth Henry was also captured at the same time. The party of Indians, to whom the three above-mentioned belonged, consisting of about twenty, had killed a number of hogs two or three miles off, and, having breakfasted upon the swine's flesh, took their two young captives through the trackless desert over the mountains, to Kittanning on the Alleghany river, now the site of the pleasant village of Armstrong.

From this place Gibson and two Indians rode to Fort du Quesne, standing near the extremity of the point of land formed by the junction of the Alleghany and the Monongahela, about sixty miles from Kittanning. Here he was first introduced to the before-named Bisquittam. Elizabeth Henry was conducted to some distant region, and her fellow captive never saw her again.

Bisquittam was one of seven brethren, all high in authority among the Delawares of the West. One of these had been killed by the Cherokees, and Gibson was adopted, according to aboriginal usage, to supply his place in the Royal family (to use the phraseology of the narrator), and of course ever after, while residing with his savage associates, bore his name, which was Mun-hut´-ta-kis-wil-lux-is-soh´-pon, — a compound long enough for the cognomen of an eastern prince, yet of somewhat an uncourtly signification, as it is, literally interpreted — Big-rope-gut-hominy.

At the first interview, Bisquittam, addressing himself to Gibson, said, "I am your brother," and, pointing to one after another in the company, added, "This is your brother, that is your brother, this is your cousin, that is your cousin, and all these are your friends." He then painted his adopted brother and told him that the Indians would take him to the river, wash away all his white blood, and make him an Indian. They accordingly took him to the river, plunged him into the water, thoroughly washed him from head to foot, and conducted him back to his master and brother. He was then furnished, in Indian style, with a breech-cloth, leggins, capo, porcupine moccasins, and a shirt. After this ceremony he returned with his new friends to Kittanning. He was at the Middle Kittaning at the time the Upper Kittaning was destroyed ty Colonel Armstrong, and heard the deadly firing. As the Indians were about to pass

over to the east side of the river and to the scene of carnage, Gibson asked Bisquittam what he should do. He said, "Go to the squaws, and keep with them;" which he did. At that encounter, well known in Indian warfare, Armstrong lost forty men, and the enemy but fourteen, as reported by the Indians. Captain Jacobs, a noted warrior in those days of terror, killed, while under the covert of the house in which he was posted (his squaw assisting him in loading his guns), no less than fourteen, and refused to surrender, though repeatedly urged. At length some of Armstrong's men threatened to burn the house over his head. He replied, that "they might if they would; he could eat fire." He and his wife were burnt with the house. In the contest Jacobs had received seven balls before he was brought upon his knees. At this time, besides Jacobs, his brother and another great warrior were among the slain. The Indians told Gibson that they had rather have lost a hundred of their men than those three chiefs.

Gibson was now compelled to witness a painful specimen of savage barbarity — the torturing and burning of an inoffensive female, who had fallen into the hands of the merciless foe. The wife of Alexander M'Allister, who had been taken at Tuscarora valley, was the unhappy victim. The same Indian who had killed Gibson's mother, tied her to a sapling, where she was long made to writhe in the flames. He knew the Indian to have been the murderer of his mother, from her scalp, which hung as a trophy from his belt. Before these unfeeling wretches had satisfied theselves with the slow but excruciating tortures they caused this woman to endure, a heavy thunder-gust with a torrent of rain came on, which greatly incommoded the Indians. Mrs. M'Allister most earnestly prayed for deliverance, but cruel are the tender mercies of the poor unenlightened savages. They however, sooner no doubt than they intended, when they saw that their fire must be shortly extinguished, shot her, and threw her remains upon the embers.

They told Gibson that they had brought him to behold this sight, on purpose to show him how they would deal with him, in case he should ever attempt to run away.

Soon after these events, he went with his companions to Fort du Quesne, where he remained a number of days, and ascertained that the French and Indians daily drew fifteen hundred rations.

His next remove was to Kuskuskin [Hog-Town] on the Mahoning, a considerable distance above its confluence with the Big Beaver, where he stayed till the following spring. At this place his life was, for a period, in great jeopardy. He had inadvertently said that he had heard that the white people were coming against the Indians. Bisquittam's brother, by name Mi-us´-kil-la-mize, was at the place, and his squaw had heard Gibson state the rumor he had heard. She had conceived a violent prejudice against him, and was determined that he should be burnt. A little white girl, about twelve years old, who had been taken in Tuscarora valley, was instructed by the enraged squaw to tell Bisquittam, on his return from Shenango, wither he had gone to tarry a little while, that Gibson said, that he hoped the white men would come against the Indians, and that he wished to run away — adding that, if she did not say all this to Bisquittam, she should be burnt. The little girl told Gibson what a lesson she had received from the squaw. He told the young captive to say no such thing, but to say that he loved Bisquittam, his brothers, cousins, and friends, and that he had no intention to run away.

Miuskillamize ordered Gibson to go into the woods and hunt for his horse, which he might know from others by his large bell; and he should ride him to Shenango, there to be burnt by Bisquittam, to whom he had previously sent word, impeaching his white brother. Gibson spent three days, with a sorrowful heart, hunting for the beast, but did not find him. In the meantime Bisquittam caused information to be given that he would return to Kuskuskin, to burn him at that place.

He accordingly came, and Gibson was standing at the door as he rode up, his face painted black, and vengeance sparkling in his eyes. His first salutation in English, which he well understood, was, "G—d d—n you; you want to run away, do you? The white girl will tell me all about it."

She was called, and Gibson went into the house; but was in a situation to hear all that passed, yet unknown to Bisquittam. The little captive was faithful in stating what Gibson had told her. Upon this, Bisquittam called to him to come out. He made no reply. The call, in a louder tone of voice, was repeated once or twice. At length Gibson answered, and made his appearance.

Bisquittam, speaking with great mildness and affection, said, "Brother, I find the Indians want to kill you. We will go away from them — we will not live with them any more." They then withdrew some distance, to a common, and erected their tent and kindled their fire, living by themselves. Thus he providentially escaped the most horrible kind of death ever inflicted by the savages.

In the spring of 1757 Gibson went to Soh´-koon, at the mouth of the Big Beaver, where he and his brother Bisquittam spent almost a year. At this place Bisquittam took a Dutch captive for his wife.

Gibson, and Hezekiah Wright, another captive, here cherished many serious thoughts of attempting an escape. Wright, to encourage Gibson in the enterprise, told him that he would teach him the millwright's trade, and would give him forty dollars. In pursuance of their object, Gibson took a horse, saddle and bridle, belonging to the Indians, and set out, intending to cross the Ohio river, Wright on the horse, and Gibson by Swimming. This was in the autumn of 1757. They had not proceeded far before Wright began to rue the undertaking, well knowing the dreadful consequence if they should fail to accomplish their purpose. They soon came to the conclusion that it was prudent to abandon their hazardous project; and so they returned to their companions before any suspicions had been excited.

Some Indians came to Fort McIntosh (now Beaver), and said in council, that a white man had run away, followed by two dogs; adding, that they supposed he would kill one of them and eat it, and afterwards the other.

It having been noticed that Gibson and Wright were often in close conversation, they were suspected of an intention to abscond. Bisquittam had no doubts on the subject, and gave vent to his indignation by English oaths and curses, which he had learned of his white fellow creatures; for the Indians have no words in any of their dialects for cursing and swearing. He then gave orders to the Indians to take Gibson away, and burn him. They accordingly took him and led him to the common, where they whipped him with a hickory stick till his body was perfectly livid. One of the Indians told another to go and get some fire, and they would burn him. Gibson now thought it proper to attempt an apology, which he hoped would be satisfactory, for his associating so much with Wright. He told the Indians that the reason why he was so frequently with Wright was, that he was a very ingenious man, and they were mutually contriving how to make a plough, like those used by white men, in order to plough in the rich bottom land, and to raise a great crop of corn. Upon this representation, the Indians told him that he must not be angry with them for what they had done; that Bisquittam was a great man; and that they must do whatever he commanded. They then, to make some amends for the flagellation they had given Gibson, and to secure his future friendship, presented him a new shirt and a pair of new leggins.

On a certain time, Bisquittam came to him, where he was busy making clapboards, and said, "You good-for-nothing devil, why do you not work?" and kicked him down, and trampled him under his feet. At length Gibson, after having borne his abusive treatment for some time, looking up with an unruffled countenance, and in a soft and gentle manner, merely saying, "I hear you, brother," his master was instantly disarmed of his rage, and showed him the greatest kindness.

In the fall of the year they went back to Kuskuskin, where they spent the winter. In the ensuing spring, an Indian, called Captain Birds, from the circumstance that he had two birds painted, one on each temple, was making arrangements for going to war at Tulpehokken. Gibson said that he wished to go too, but was opposed by Bisquittam. All contemplating this expedition were volunteers. Gibson attended the war-dance every night with the Indians. One of his cousins, who encouraged him in his purpose of joining the war party, advised him to spend a few days in hunting, stating that Bisquittam would soon be out of the way, as he was about to set out for Koh-Hok-King, in the neighborhood of Painted Post. "Then," said he, "you can go."

Gibson and a little boy, of twelve years of age, went on a hunting excursion, were absent three days, killed two turkeys, and returned; but Bisquittam, whether suspecting the plan or not

is unknown, was still at the place. He, with the little boy again took a tour into the woods. They reached an Indian sugar camp the first evening, stole a horse and a bag of corn, rode seven miles to a cranberry swamp, tarried there seven days, parched and ate their corn, threw away the bag, killed one turkey, and returned to the sugar camp. Here they heard a gun. Gibson discharged his, which led the Indian who had first fired to come to him, as he expected and wished. His first inquiry was, whether Bisquittam had set out for Kohhokking, and, being answered in the negative, he sent the little boy to the Indian town, and the next morning took the nearest course to Fort McIntosh. He went to the warriors, among whom he saw the cousin who had encouraged him to join the war party. Bisquittam, having ascertained that Gibson was at McIntosh, sent word to the Indians that if they took him away so that he should lose him, he would make them pay him a thousand bucks, or return him another prisoner equally good.

Having spent several days with the warriors, till they were about to repair to Fort du Quesne for their equipments, they told him he should not go with them. One of the savages held a tomahawk over his head and said he would kill him on the spot, and then he would not have the trouble of going — and added, that he only wished to go to the war, in order to have a good opportunity to desert from the Indians. The cousin before-mentioned said, in Gibson's behalf, that he should be with him all the time, and that there would be no danger of his escape, even if he wished it. Upon this, he went over the ferry and accompanied them about five miles, where he saw Buffalo Horn, another brother of Bisquittam, who asked the Indians if Gibson was going with them to the war. They replied, that they could not persuade him to go. Buffalo Horn said that, after he had done eating, he would talk to him about it. This chief shortly after took him aside and said, "Hughey, are you going to the war? I tell you not to go. You and I are going into the country in the fall. I shall go to fight the Cherokees, and you shall go with me. Stay with me, your poor old sick brother. Get me some pigeons and squirrels." Gibson replied, "I will do whatever you wish me to do." He then said to Gibson, "Take my negro man and canoe, and fetch me some corn from McIntosh." In fulfilment of this direction, he went to that Fort, where he saw King Shingiss, (giving the title to this chief which Gibson gave him), a brother of King Beaver, and Bisquittam. King Shingiss said to him, "Are you here? You are a bad boy. We are all sick. You must go as an express to Kuskuskin, to tell the people that three Indians have been killed and three wounded by the Cherokees, and you will occupy my tent till I come." Gibson, taking a loaf of bread and two blankets, immediately set out and travelled on foot to the place, a distance of thirty-six miles, in six hours.

The Indians said that they would all come to him to hear the news, that they might have the truth. Here he remained, dwelling in King Shingiss's tent till autumn.

On one occasion King Shingiss and Gibson went into the woods, in pursuit of any wild animals they could find. The latter killed a large bear, much to the mortification of the former, as he killed nothing, and thought it highly derogatory to his character to be outdone by a white fellow hunter. While on this excursion, Gibson told King Shingiss there would shortly be a peace with the white men. "How do you know?" said he. Gibson replied, "I dreamed so." A few days after, Frederick Post, in company with Bisquittam, came to Kuskuskin, with a view to settle the preliminaries of a peace. This was in the latter part of 1758. Ever after, while Gibson continued with the Indians, he was called a prophet.

Gibson was afraid to see Bisquittam, because he had wished to join the Tulpehokken warriors, contrary to his master's will. However, he approached him affectionately, and said, "How do you, brother? I have brought a large bear skin, and make a present of it to you to sleep upon." Bisquittam received him kindly and thanked him for the donation. They both repaired to Fort McIntosh, where they abode till some time in the winter.

It was in the autumn of 1758, that General Forbes, being at Loyal Hanna, sent Captain Grant, with three hundred men and three days' provisions, to view the ground and ascertain the best route to Fort du Quesne. Grant exceeded his orders, being sanquine of success, and rashly urged his way with the expectation of taking the Fort. He was met and pursued by the French and Indians on or near the hill in Pittsburg, which bears his name to the present day. Grant killed many of the enemy, but not a few of his own men were destroyed and taken. He also became a captive and was sent to Canada. The residue of his forces retreated to Fort Ligonier. This is the purport of Gibson's statement.

The Indians, having strong suspicions that their brother intended to desert them, about the middle of October, 1758, took him to Kus-ko-ra´-vis, the western branch, which united with White Woman's Creek, the eastern branch, forms the Muskingum, There was his home till the beginning of the ensuing April, when he found means to make his escape.

At this place was David Brackenridge, recently taken at Loyal Hanna. Here also were two German young women, who had been captured at Mok-ki-noy, near the Juniata, long before Gibson. The name of one was Barbara. The other was called by the Indians Pum-e-ra-moo, but she was from a family by the name of Grove. It was at length determined by the inhabitants of the forest that the latter should marry one of the natives, who had been selected for her. She told Gibson that she would sooner be shot than have him for her husband, and entreated him, as did Barbara likewise, to unite with them in the attempt to run away. They proposed a plan, which they supposed would afford facilities for the desirable object. They were to feign themselves indisposed; when it was expected that they would be ordered to withdraw from the society of Indians, and to live by themselves for a season. The project succeeded according to expectation. On their making the representation, as agreed, the Indians told them to go and kindle their fire at some distance from them.

They selected for their purpose the bank of the Muskingum, just below the confluence of the two branches of the river. The night was appointed for their flight. In the mean time Gibson, returning late one evening to his master, told him that he had seen the track of his horse, which he knew by the impression of his shoes, no other horse in that quarter being shod, and that he had followed the track for some time without being able to overtake him. He then proposed to Bisquittam to go in search of the horse, and, having found him, to spend three days in hunting; to which his master acceded. It was further agreed that Bisquittam should spend some time in a meadow, a little below the fire of the two women, in digging hoppenies [i.e., groundnuts], and that Gibson should return that way with the horse and venison, and take the hoppenies and meat home. Bisquittam furnished him with a gun, a powder-horn well filled, thirteen bullets, a deer skin for making moccasins and sinews to sew them, two blankets, and two shirts, one of which was to be hung up to keep the crows from pillaging the venison.

After breakfast he started, and instead of going in pursuit of the horse, took his course leisurely to the women's camp, seven miles, where he arrived about ten o'clock in the evening, and found Brackenridge with them, according to previous arrangements. As he travelled, in the evening he discovered some of the natives, though they probably did not notice him. He saw the fire, where Bisquittam had been digging hoppenies during a part of the day, perhaps not more than sixty rods from the spot whence they were to attempt their departure. The utmost caution, prudence, and despatch were indispensable in the hazardous enterprise; for, should their object be discovered, nothing could save them from the stake.

It was about the full moon. The Muskingum was very high, and there were two rafts near the women's fire. They unmoored one, and it soon went down the river. They entered the other with their accoutrements, the women taking their kettle, crossed the Muskingum, and let the raft go adrift. They travelled with all possible expedition during the residue of the night in a southerly direction, in order to deceive the Indians, in case they should attempt to follow them. In the morning they steered a due east course.

On the second day they mortally wounded a bear, which, in the contest, bit the leg of Gibson, and got into a hole, whence they could not obtain him. They however killed a buck, the best part of which they carried in a kind of hopper, made of his skin. On the third day, at night, they ventured to make a fire, roasted and feasted upon their venison. On the fourth day they shot a doe, took the saddle, reached the

Ohio river above Wheeling, made a raft with the aid of their tomahawks, passed over, and entered a deep ravine, where the land above them was supposed to be more than three hundred feet in height. Here they kindled a fire, cooked and ate their meat, and spent the night.

In the morning, with much difficulty they ascended the steep eminence, and set their faces for Fort du Quesne, keeping on the ridge not far, in general, from the Ohio. They saw the fresh tracks of Indians, when opposite to Fort McIntosh, but were not molested, and probably were not seen by them.

On the fifteenth day after leaving the Muskingum, in the evening, they arrived in safety on the banks of the Monongahela, directly opposite to the Fort, and called for a boat. The people were suspicious of some Indian plot, having once before been grossly and treacherously deceived. The captives were directed to state their number, their names, whence they had been taken, with other circumstances, for the satisfaction of the garrison, before their wishes could be gratified.

Brackenride told them that he was taken at Loyal Hanna, where he drove a wagon numbered 39. Some of the soldiers knew the statement to be correct. Gibson informed them that he was captured near Robinson's Fort, and that Israel Gibson was his brother. Some present were acquainted with the latter. The females represented that they were from Mokkinoy, and that there were but four of the party.

Upon this, two boats with fifteen men well armed, crossed the Monogahela. Their orders were, in case there should appear to be more than four, to fire upon them. On approaching the western shore, the boatmen directed the captives to stand back upon the rising ground, and to come forward, one at a time, as they should be called. In this way they were all soon received and carried to Fort du Quesne, where their joy was such as may be better conceived than described. It was not long before they were all restored, like persons from the dead, to the arms of their relatives and friends.

Source: Gibson, "An Account of the Captivity ...", pp. 141–52

John McCullough
1763–4

The last of the captivity narratives, that of John McCullough, is perhaps the most important of all as to clarifying some points regarding the history of the Indians of the Tuscarawas Valley.

Eight years old when he was captured in 1756, he spent the next eight years with the Delawares, wandering from place to place as the frontier moved westward—from the Beaver to the Cuyahoga to the Walhonding to the branches of the Scioto, back to the Walhonding and, finally, (I believe) to Newcomerstown in the autumn of 1764. His narrative gives us a unique perspective of Bouquet's Expedition as viewed from the Indian side, just as Smith's narrative enabled us to view Braddock's defeat from the French and Indian side. He was one of the prisoners redeemed by Bouquet in 1764 and finally got back to his family in December of that same year.

If my theories are correct (and they are set forth in a separate section of this book devoted entirely to an analysis of this narrative alone), McCullough establishes when Netawatwees moved from the Cuyahoga to the southward, why Bouquet refers to Newcomer (Netawatwees) as being on the Scioto in 1764, the approximate date when he finally settled at Newcomerstown, and why Netawatwees refused to meet with Bouquet. It also sheds light on the question of whether or not the "Heckewelder's garden" shown on certain maps of the Tuscarawas region near Bolivar was really his garden, or perhaps the trader Calhoun's garden.

In the introduction to his narrative, McCullough states:

His endeavour throughout the whole is to make it Intelligible to the meanest capacity; wherever he has deemed it necessary to retain Indian Words—he has divided them into Syllables and Accented the Syllable on which the stress of the word lies, in order to give the Reader an idea of the pronunciation.

It will be seen in the analysis referred to above that the accent mark on the name "Neep-waugh´-whese" could be of significance as helping to establish that Neep-waugh´-whese and Netawatwees may be the same Indian.

I was born in Newcastle county, in the State of Delaware. When I was five years old my father moved his family from thence to the back parts of then Cumberland (now Franklin) county, to a place well known by the name of Conococheague settlement, where he made a purchase of a tract of land at sheriff's sale, about a year before what has been generally termed

Braddock's war. Shortly after the commencement of the war, he moved his family into York county, where he remained until the Spring of 1756, when we ventured home; we had not been long at home until we were alarmed again; we then fled down to Antietam settlement, where we remained until the beginning of harvest, then ventured home to secure our crops; we stopped about three miles from home, where we got a small cabin to live in until my father went home and secured the grain. On the 26th of July, 1756, my parents and oldest sister went home to pull flax, accompanied by one John Allen, a neighbor, who had business at Fort Loudon, and promised to come that way in the evening to accompany them back. Allen had proceeded but about two miles toward Loudon until he heard the Indians had killed a man that morning, about a mile and a half from where my parents were at work, he then, instead of going back to accompany them home, agreeable to his promise, took a circuitous route of about six or seven miles, for fear of the Indians. When he came home, my brother and me were playing on the great road, a short distance from the house, he told us to go immediately to the house or the Indians would catch us, adding, at the same time, that he supposed they had killed our father and mother by that time.

{The purpose in setting forth the above is to show the approximate area where McCullough lived when he was captured. Fort Loudon was about 13 miles west of Chambersburg, Pennsylvania. The massacre of Brown and the schoolchildren occurred near there in 1764, and will be of some importance in a later article in this book. The remainder of the narrative picks up about seven years later, after the Indians with whom he was living had moved to Mahoning, a branch of the Beaver, just as the uprising of Pontiac was occurring.}

All the Indians in the town immediately collected together, and started off to the salt licks, where the rest of the traders were, and murdered the whole of them, and divided their goods amongst them, and likewise their horses; my adopted brother took two horse loads of beaver skin, and set off with them to *Tus-ca-law'-ways,* where a number of traders resided, and sold the fur to them. There happened to be an old Indian, who was known amongst the traders by the name of Daniel; he cautioned the traders not to purchase the fur from him, assuring them that he had murdered some traders — to convince them, he shewed them that the skins were marked with so many different marks, which convinced him in his opinion; however, either through fear or some other motive, they exchanged goods for the fur; the same evening, old Daniel offered his service to them, assuring them that he would endeavor to conduct them safe into Pittsburg, adding that, if they would not take his advice, he was sure they would be all murdered by daylight the next morning; they took his advice, and, as they lived about a mile out of the town, they had an opportunity of going away without being discovered; they started shortly after dark, as was conjectured by the Indians, leaving all their merchandise behind them; how many there were of them I do not recollect of hearing; however as I heard, they went on safe until they got to *Ksack-hoong,* an old Indian town at the confluence of the Beaver and Ohio, where they came to an Indian camp unawares; probably the Indians had discovered them before they reached the camp, as they were ready for them, as soon as they made their appearance the Indians fired on them — the whole of them fell, excepting old Daniel and one Calhoun, who made his escape into Pittsburgh; old Daniel had a bullet shot into his saddle, close behind him, the mark of which I frequently saw, after he made his escape back to his friends.

We remained in Mahoning till shortly after the memorable battle at Bushy Run; we then moved to *Cay-a-haw'-ge,* a town not far distant from lake Eire, ---

---

We stayed but a short time in *Cay-a-haw'-ge,* then moved across the country to the forks of *Moosh-king'-oong,* [Muskingum], which signifies clear eyes, as the river abounds with a certain kind of fish that has very clear eyes; from thence we took up the west branch to its source, and from thence I know not where.

Nothing remarkable happened during our peregrinations, excepting that we suffered by hunger, it being in the winter; we sometimes had to make use of the stems of turkey quills for food, by running them under hot embers till they would swell and get crisp. We have subsisted on gum bark, and sometimes on white plantain; but the greater part of our time on a certain kind of root that has something of the resemblance of a potatoe.

In the spring we returned to the west branch of *Moosh-king'-oong,* and settled in a new town, which we called *Kta-ho'-ling,* which signifies a place where roots has been dug up for food. We remained there during the summer.

Sometime in the summer, whilst we were living at *Kta-ho'-ling* a great number of Indians collected at the forks of *Moosh-king'-oong;* perhaps there were about three hundred or upwards, their intention was to come to the settlement and make a general massacre of the whole people, without any regard to age or sex; they were out about ten days, when the most of them returned; having held a council, they concluded that it was not safe for them to leave their towns, destitute of defence. However, several small parties went on to different parts of the settlements: it happened that three of them, whom I was well acquainted with, came to the neighborhood of where I was taken from — they were young fellows, perhaps none of them more than twenty years of age, they came to a school house, where they murdered and scalped the master {Brown} and all the scholars, except one, who survived after he was scalped. a boy about ten years old, and a full cousin of mine. I saw the Indians when they returned home with the scalps; some of the old Indians were very much displeased at them for killing so many children, especially *Neep-paugh'-whese,* or night walker, an old chief or half king, he alluded it to cowardice which was the greatest affront he could offer them.[1]

In the fall we were alarmed by a report that the white people were marching out against them, which, in a short time, proved to be true,

Col. Boquett with an army, was then actually marching out against them. As the Delaware nation was always on the frontier (which was the nation I was amongst) they had the first notice of it, and immediately gave the alarm to the other nations adjoining them; a council was called, the result was, that they were scarce of ammunition, and were not able to fight him, that they were then destitute of clothing, and that upon the whole, it was best to come on terms of peace with the white people; accordingly they sent off special messengers to meet the army on their march, in order to let them know that they were disposed to come on terms of peace with them. The messengers met the army at Tuscalaways, they crept up to the camp after dark, and informed the guard that they were sent by their nation to sue for peace; the commander of the army sent for them to come into camp, they went and delivered their mission. The colonel took care to take hostages for their fidelity, the remainder were suffered to return; but he told them he would march his army on to *Moosh-king'-oong,* where he expected to meet their chiefs and warriors, to come on terms of peace with him, assuring them at the same time, that he would not treat with them, but upon condition, that they would deliver up all the prisoners they had in their possession. The messengers returned, and gave a narrative of their mission; the *Sha-a-noo'-wack,* or Shawanese, were not satisfied with the terms; however as the Delawares had left hostages with the commander of the army, the Shawanese acquiesced to come on terms of peace jointly with the other tribes, accordingly the army marched on to *Moosh-king'-oong.* The day they arrived there, an express was sent off to one of their nearest towns, to inform them that they were ready to treat with them. We then lived about ten miles from *Moosh-king'-oong;* accordingly they took all the prisoners to the camp, myself among the rest, and delivered us up to the army; we were immediately put under a guard; a few days after, we were sent under a strong guard to Pittsburgh. On our way two of the prisoners made their escape, to wit; one Rhoda Boyd and Elizabeth Studibaker, and went back to the Indians. I never heard whether they were ever brought back or not; there were about two hundred of us — we were kept a few days in Pittsburg. There was one John Martin, from the big cove, came to Pittsburg, after his family, who had been taken by the Indians the fall before I was taken: he got leave from the Colonel to bring me down along with his family. I got home about the middle of Dec. 1764, being absent (as I heard my parents say) eight years, four months and sixteen days.

NOTE

1. This refers to a horrid massacre in Pennsylvania, of a whole school, in August, '64. The remains of the murdered and mutilated scholars were all interred together, in a large and rudely constructed box, just as they were found. The name of the teacher was Brown. Seventy-nine years after an exhumation took place, and the bones were again committed to earth, and a mound raised to perpetuate the memory of this sad spot. The school house was truly a solitary one, and some of its remains exist to the present day.

{The above Note is taken from the 1876 version of the *McCullough* narrative set forth in McKnight's "Our Western Border", p. 223.}

Source: Loudon: *Narratives of Outrages...*, Vol. 1, pp. 252–85

Respect for the Aged

It is a sacred principle among the Indians, and one of those moral and religious truths which they have always before their eyes, that the Great Spirit who created them, and provided them so abundantly with the means of subsistence, made it the duty of parents to maintain and take care of their children until they should be able to provide for themselves, and that having while weak and helpless received the benefits of maintenance, education, and protection, they are bound to repay them by a similar care of those who are labouring under the infirmities of old age, and are no longer able to supply their own wants.

Thus a strong feeling of gratitude towards their elders, inculcated and cherished from their earliest infancy, is the solid foundation on which rests that respect for old age for which Indians are so remarkable, and it is further supported by the well-founded hope of receiving the like succours and attentions in their turn, when the heavy hand of time shall have reduced them to the same helpless situation which they now commiserate in others, and seek by every means in their power to render more tolerable.

Source: Heckewelder's *History...*, p. 163

George Croghan
1760–1

George Croghan, the well-known Indian trader and negotiator, had been sent from Fort Pitt to assist Major Robert Rogers in securing possession of Detroit and other Western posts included in the capitulation signed at Montreal, ending the French and Indian War. The following is that portion of his journal describing his return to Fort Pitt, beginning at Sandusky. He was traveling over what is now called the Great Trail and passed through the valley of the Tuscarawas just above Bolivar.

Dec. 16, 1760. — We came to the little Lake called Sandusky which we found froze over so as not to be passable for some days.

The 22ᵈ. — We crossed the little Lake on the Ice which is about 6 Miles over to an Indian Village where we found our Horses which we sent from D'Troit, there were but five Indians at home all the rest being gone a hunting.

23ᵈ. — We came to Chenunda an Indian Village 6 miles from Sandusky.

24ᵗʰ. — We stayed to hunt up some Horses.

25ᵗʰ. — We came to the Principal Mans hunting Cabin about 16 miles from Chenunda level Road and clear Woods, several Savannahs.

26ᵗʰ. — We came to Mohicken Village, this day, we crossed several small Creeks all branches of Muskingum, level Road, pretty clear Woods about 30 Miles, the Indians were all out a hunting except one family.

27ᵗʰ. — We halted, it rained all day.

28ᵗʰ. — We set of[f], it snowed all day &

come to another branch of Muskingum, about 9 Miles good Road where we stayed the 29ᵗʰ for a Cannoe to put us over, the Creek being very high.

30ᵗʰ. — We set of[f] and came to another branch of Muskingum about 11 Miles and the 31ˢᵗ we fell a Tree over the Creek and carried over our Baggage and encamped about one Mile up a Run.

January the 1ˢᵗ. — We travelled about 16 Miles clear woods & level Road to a place called the Sugar Cabins.

2ᵈ. — We came about 12 Miles to the Beavers Town clear Woods and good Road.

3ᵈ. — Crossed Muskingum Creek and encamped in a fine bottom on this side the Creek.

4ᵗʰ. — Set of[f] and travelled about 20 Miles up a branch of Muskingum good Road.

5ᵗʰ. — Travelled about 18 Miles and crossed a branch of little Beaver Creek clear Woods & good Road.

6th. — Travelled about Eighteen Miles and crossed two Branches of little Beaver Creek good Road & Clear Woods.

about 25 Miles good Road & Clear Woods.

7th. — Crossed the mouth of big Beaver Creek at an Indian Village and came to Pittsburg

Source: Thwaites, *Early Western Travels,* Vol. 1, pp. 123–25

Indian Political Maneuvers

In the management of their national affairs, the Indians display as much skill and dexterity, perhaps, as any people upon earth. When a political message is sent to them from a neighbouring nation which they do not approve of, they generally contrive to send an answer so ambiguously worded, that it is difficult to come at their real meaning; they conceive this to be the best way of getting rid of a proposal which they do not like, because those who sent them the message are for some time, at least, at a loss to comprehend the meaning, and not knowing whether the answer is favourable or unfavourable, their proceedings are necessarily suspended until they can discover its true sense; in this manner have operations been sometimes entirely prevented, and matters have remained in the same situation that they were in before.

It may be supposed, perhaps, that such an artful manner of treating each other might be thought provoking, and cause jealousies and disputes among the different parties; such is not, however, the case, as nothing insulting is ever contained in those messages; and as offence is not meant, it is not taken. The Indians consider it on all sides as a kind of diplomatic proceeding, an exercise which tends to invigorate the mind, of which they are very fond. It gives them opportunities to reflect and think deeply on matters of importance, and of displaying their genius, when they have found or discovered the secret of an answer sent to them, or hit upon the true meaning of an ambiguous message.

Source: Heckewelder's *History...,* p. 150

Major Robert Rogers
1761

Born in 1731, the leader of the famed Rogers Rangers was only 29 years old when he received the surrender of Detroit as the French and Indian War was drawing to a close. In January of 1761, with 38 men of his command, he was proceeding back to Fort Pitt and crossed the Muskingum at what he called Beaver Town. This is the same town more commonly called Tuscarawas, near Bolivar.

Although rather brief, his journal gives some description of the towns along the way, and also brings out the fact that the Indians possessed "plenty of cows, horses, hogs, etc." While the fact that Indians had horses would come as no surprise, that they also had cows and hogs is something of a revelation. Since we know that the Indians raised corn and other vegetables, it is clear that they did not live by the hunt alone. To a certain extent, they were farmers, just like the white settlers to the eastward.

His was probably the first English military expedition to enter the Tuscarawas Valley.

I delivered the ammunition to Capt. Campbell, and on the 23d set out for Pittsburg, marching along the west end of Lake Erie till the 2d of January 1761, when we arrived at Lake Sandusky.

I have a very good opinion of the soil from Detroit to this place; it is timbered principally with white and black oaks, hickory, locusts, and maple. We found wild apples along the west end of Lake Erie, some rich savannahs of several miles extent without a tree but clothed with jointed grass near six feet high which, rotting there every year, adds to the fertility of the soil. The length of Sandusky is about fifteen miles from east to west and about six miles across it. We came to a town of the Wyandot Indians, where we halted to refresh.

On January 3d, south-east-by-east three miles, east-by-south one mile and a half, southeast a mile through a meadow, crossed a small creek about six yards wide, running east, trav-

eled south-east-by-east one mile, passed thro' Indian houses, south-east three quarters of a mile, and came to a small Indian town of about ten houses. There is a remarkable fine spring at this place, rising out of the side of a small hill with such force that it boils above the ground in a column three feet high. I imagine it discharges ten hogsheads of water in a minute. From this town our course was south-south-east three miles, south two miles, crossed a brook about five yards wide, running east-south-east, travelled south one mile, crossed a brook about four yards wide, running east-south-east, travelled south-south-east two miles, crossed a brook about eight yards wide. This day we killed plenty of deer and turkeys on our march, and encamped.

On the 4th we travelled south-south-east one mile, and came to a river about twenty-five yards wide, crossed the river, where are two Indian houses, from thence south-by-east one mile, south-south-east one mile and a half, south-east two miles, south-south-east one mile, and came to an Indian house, where there was a family of Wyandots hunting, from thence south by east a quarter of a mile, south five miles, came to the river we crossed this morning; the course of the river here is west-north-west. This day killed several deer and other game, and encamped.

On the 5th travelled south-south-west half a mile, south one mile, south-south-west three quarters of a mile, south half a mile, crossed two small brooks running east, went a south-south-west course half a mile, south half a mile, south-east half a mile, south two miles, south-east one mile, south half a mile, crossed a brook running east-by-north, travelled south-by-east half a mile, south-south-east two miles, south-east three quarters of a mile, south-south-east one mile, and came to Muskingum Creek about eight yards wide, crossed the creek, and encamped thirty yards from it. This day killed deer and turkeys in our march.

On the 6th we travelled about fourteen or fifteen miles, our general course being about east-south-east, killed plenty of game, and encamped by a very fine spring.

The 7th our general course about south-east, travelled about six miles, and crossed Muskingum Creek, running south, about twenty yards wide. There is an Indian town about twenty yards from the creek on the east-side, which is called the Mingo Cabins. There were but two or three Indians in the place, the rest were hunting. These Indians have plenty of cows, horses, hogs, &c.

The 8th, halted at this town to mend our moccasins, and kill deer, the provisions I brought from Detroit being entirely expended. I went ahunting with ten of the Rangers, and by ten o'clock got more venison than we had occasion for.

On the 9th travelled about twelve miles, our general course being about south-east, and encamped by the side of a long meadow where there were a number of Indians hunting.

The 10th, about the same course, we travelled eleven miles, and encamped, having killed in our march this day three bears and two elks.

The 11th, continuing near the same course, we travelled thirteen miles and en-camped, where were a number of Wyandot and Six Nation Indians hunting.

The 12th, travelled six miles, bearing rather more to the east, and encamped. This evening we killed several beaver.

The 13th, travelled about north-east six miles, and came to the Delaware's town, called Beaver Town. This Indian town stands on good land on the west side of the Muskingum River; and opposite to the town, on the east side, is a fine river which discharges itself into it. The latter is about thirty yards wide and the Muskingum about forty; so that when they both join, they make a very fine stream with a swift current running to the south-west. There are about 3000 acres of cleared ground round this place. The number of warriors in this town is about 180. All the way from the Lake Sandusky I found level land and a good country. No pine trees of any sort; the timber is white, black and yellow oak, black and white walnut, cypress, chesnut, and locust trees. At this town I staid till the 16th in the morning to refresh my party, and procure some corn of the Indians to boil with our venison.

On the 16th we marched nearly an east course about nine miles, and encamped by the side of a small river.

On the 17th kept much the same course, crossing several rivulets and creeks. We travelled about twenty miles, and encamped by the side of a small river.

On the 18th we travelled about sixteen miles an easterly course, and encamped by a brook.

The 19th, about the same general course, we crossed two considerable streams of water and some large hills timbered with chestnut and oak, and having travelled about twenty miles we encamped by the side of a small river, at which place were a number of Delawares hunting.

On the 20th, keeping still an easterly course, and having much the same travelling as the day before, we advanced on our journey about nineteen miles, which brought us to Beaver Creek, where are two or three Indian houses on the west side of the creek, and in sight of the Ohio.

Bad weather prevented our journeying on the 21st, but the next day we prosecuted our march. Having crossed the creek, we travelled twenty miles, nearly south-east, and encamped with a party of Indian hunters.

On the 23d we came again to the Ohio, opposite to Fort Pitt; from whence I ordered Lieut. M'Cormack to march the party across the country to Albany, and after tarrying there till the 26th, I came the common road to Philadelphia, from thence to New York, where, after this long, fatiguing tour, I arrived February 14, 1761.

Source: Rogers, *Journals of Major Robert Rogers,* pp. 167–71

Indian Face-Painting

As I was once resting in my travels at the home of a trader who lived at some distance from an Indian town, I went in the morning to visit an Indian acquaintance and friend of mine. I found him engaged in plucking out his beard, preparatory to painting himself for a dance which was to take place the ensuing evening. Having finished his head dress, about an hour before sunset, he came up, as he said, to see me, but I and my companions judged that he came *to be seen.* To my utter astonishment, I saw three different paintings or figures on one and the same face. He had, by his great ingenuity and judgment in laying on and shading the different colours, made his nose appear, when we stood directly in front of him, as if it were very long and narrow, with a round knob at the end, much like the upper part of a pair of tongs. On one cheek there was a red round spot, about the size of an apple, and the other was done in the same manner with black. The eye-lids, both the upper and lower ones, were reversed in the colouring. When we viewed him in profile on one side, his nose represented the beak of an eagle, with the bill rounded and brought to a point, precisely as those birds have it, though the mouth was somewhat open. The eye was astonishingly well done, and the head, upon the whole, appeared tolerably well, shewing a great deal of fierceness. When we turned round to the other side, the same nose now resembled the snout of a pike, with the mouth so open, that the teeth could be seen. He seemed much pleased with his execution, and having his looking-glass with him, he contemplated his work, seemingly with great pride and exultation. He asked me how I liked it? I answered that if he had done the work on a piece of board, bark, or anything else, I should like it very well and often look at it. But, asked he, why not so as it is? Because I cannot see the face that is hidden under these colours, so as to know who it is. Well, he replied, I must go now, and as you cannot know me to-day, I will call to-morrow morning before you leave this place. He did so, and when he came back he was washed clean again.

Thus, for a single night's *frolic,* a whole day is spent in what they call dressing, in which each strives to outdo the other.

Source: Heckewelder's *History...,* p. 204

George Croghan
1761

Once again George Croghan's skills as an Indian negotiator were called upon at a conference held at Detroit in the autumn of 1761. The Six Nations, or Iroquois Indians, who resided in the central New York area, were apparently not satisfied with the treatment that they had received from the British government after the French menace was removed with the fall of Canada, and they were sending messengers to the Western tribes telling them of what they perceived the British intentions to be with respect to the Indians and their land. Rumors of an Indian uprising were spreading throughout the Ohio country and the conference was called to try to calm things down.

The following journal is fairly brief as to the Tuscarawas Valley involvement, principally at Beaver's Town, near Bolivar, but it does establish the dates when Croghan passed through the area.

The 28th [July, 1761 {at Pittsburgh}] I set out for D'Troit and arrived at an Indian Village at the mouth of Beaver Creek.

August 2nd [1761] Marched to the Beavers Town on Muskingum where I was met by Several Delaware Chiefs, who accompanied me to D'Troit to attend on the Conference to be held there by Sir William Johnson. I then acquainted them that one of their People was killed near Tuscarora by some White Men, and that two of them were put in Prison for the Murder they had been Guilty of, which they shou'd see Try'd and Punished for the Crime: after which I condoled with them agreeable to their own Custom, which they received much better than I expected.

The 4th [August, 1761] Set out for Sandusky where I arrived the 8th and found but 5 Old Chiefs at home and all their Warriors gone against the Cherokees.

{After the conference at Detroit, Croghan returned to Fort Pitt}

The 23rd [September, 1761] I arrived at Sandusky where the Mohiconders delivered up two Prisoner Women, and the Wyandotts 4 Boys, One Man and a Woman, here a Wyandott Indian arrived with accounts that a party of Warriors from D'Troit, which had been against the Cherokees were on their Return and wou'd be there Next Day with 4 Scalps and two Prisoners.

The 29th [September, 1761] I reached the Beavers Town where the Indians delivered me 16 Prisoners, & Inform'd me that Sence I went to Detroit thire Nation had sent up 19 prisners to Fort Pitt to send home to thire friends.

October 3rd [1761] I arrived at Fort Pitt...

--

Source: Wainwright, "George Croghan's Journal", pp. 412–15

46

James Kenny
1761–2

James Kenny was a Quaker storekeeper at Pittsburgh in the years 1758-9 and 1761-3. While there, he kept a journal that has become one of the most important sources of information that we have today as to the activities at Fort Pitt in those years. Many of the Indians, and whites, that are mentioned in other journals in this book also appear in his journal. While most of the events described by Kenny are outside the scope of this book, those portions that deal with the attempt of Christian Frederick Post to establish a mission at Tuscarawas in 1761 are set forth herein. Apparently Post did not keep a journal of his own in that year and the references to him in the Kenny journal are the main source we have today for learning something of what Post was doing while he was in the Tuscarawas Valley in 1761.

Christian Frederick Post was a most unusual man. He had married an Indian woman, and apparently had at least peripheral connections with the Moravians and their attempts to establish missions in the Indian country. In 1758, while the British under General Forbes were proceeding west across Pennsylvania as they moved against the French at Fort DuQuesne, Post undertook a very dangerous mission. With one other white man and a few friendly Indians who accompanied him, one of whom was the well-known Pisquetomen, a brother of Beaver and Shingas, he went ahead of the British forces and made contact with the Indians who had been allies of the French to try to persuade them to go back to their homes and not assist the French any longer. He told them that the British forces would drive the French out of the fort and that it would be better for them if they did not help the French but, rather, remained neutral in the coming conflict. He met with the Indians in several of their towns, one meeting being just across the Allegheny River from Fort DuQuesne and even in the presence of some French officers. The French tried to get the Indians to turn him over to them, but they refused to do so. Post's mission was a success, the Indians did desert the French, and the French, as the British got closer to the fort, abandoned it and gave up control of Western Pennsylvania to the English. The captivity narrative of Marie Le Roy speaks of seeing Post at the town where she was being held prisoner and points out the extreme danger that he was in. It was a remarkable achievement and one requiring great courage.

His attempt to establish a mission at Tuscarawas a few years later ended in failure, both in 1761 as described in the Kenny journal and in 1762 as described by Heckewelder in the next journal, but these were, at least, the first tentative steps to bring the teachings of Christianity to the Indians of the Tuscarawas Valley. Later attempts by David Zeisberger would be more successful, but Zeisberger's success was achieved not by going into the Indian towns alone and trying to convert the Indians but by bringing into the Indian country many Indians that had already been converted to Christianity, and establishing new Christian Indian towns. The non-Christian Indians could then see the beneficial effects of living as the mission Indians lived, and some of them would become Christian Indians themselves.

Post eventually drifted away from the Moravians and died at Germantown, Pennsylvania in 1785.

{June} 23ᵈ, {1761 at Pittsburgh} —...
Frederick Post came here & stay'd with us about
two Days and then set off to Beaver Creek in
order to Preach to yᵉ Indians and inform them of
yᵉ Principels of Christianity as yᵉ Moravians do
hold yᵉ Same I hear since; he was made Welcom
by yᵉ Indians and is gon to yᵉ Beaver's Town
Tuscorawas.

{August} 6ᵗʰ. — I receiv'd a Letter from
Frederick Post dated yᵉ 27ᵗʰ of last month at
Tuscorawas Town, in which he informs me that
the Indians are not all willing to deliver up yᵉ
Prisoners as yet & that he has hard living
amongst them any Provisions they have being to
dear—a Bushel of Corn being forty Shillings, one
quart Milk two Shillˢ & Six pence, One Pound
Butter Ten Shillˢ & for washing one Shirt Two
Shillˢ & Six Pence, & Venison 7 pence, he also
adds that he hopes of being of Service amongst
them & signifies that he was in fear some time
ago when yᵉ Beaver took Six Ceggs Rum there &
they were Drunke Six Days; that they talk of
going to Philadᵃ soon to hold a treaty there.

{August} 15ᵗʰ. — Receiv'd some Lines
from Frederick Post, in which he says that things
about them at Tuscorawas is Still & quiet, yᵉ
Indians being gone to yᵉ Treaty at Detroit; but
that he is in a Suffering Condition for want of
Provissˢ & requests of me to send him some yᵉ
first opertunity.

{August} 19ᵗʰ. — Ordered Philip Boyle (he
being going to Sanduskey with flour a Suttling)
to supply Frederick Post with what Flour he
wanted.

{October} 9ᵗʰ. — Frederick Post came here
from Tuscorawas & having a meeting with yᵉ
Indians there, before they set off (to yᵉ Treaty) at
Detroit, he let them know that the good Spirit
had sent him amongst them in order to do them
good & inform them in yᵉ Christian Principels, to
which they answer'd that they were very willing
of his living amongst them, but not on them
tearms, as they seen no better fruits or works
amongst Christians than amongst themselves,
but he told them that yᵉ good spirit was with
him, when he came to them in yᵉ War time &
that they had no reason to repent of his coming
amongst them that time, and that now if they
did not receive him on yᵉ tearms he mentioned yᵉ
Good Spirit ordered him to leave them, and go to
some others, having made them as yᵉ head men
of that Nation yᵉ first offer & call'd for his Horse
to be gone, but they would not consent to let him
go, so he is now prepairing materials in order to
build a House to live in, & keep School, & instruct them as far as he can or they will receive,
but tells them that their hearts are not prepair'd
to hear the gosple.

{October} 23ᵈ. — ...I have had no Answer
as yet from yᵉ Commissˢ, which gives Frederick
Post some encouragmenᵗ (if I am set at liberty) to
go to see him to Tuscorawas.

{December} 26ᵗʰ. — Frederick Post came
here on his way to Philadᵃ having a Message
from yᵉ Beaver King & Shingass to yᵉ Governor
signifying that they had confirm'd yᵉ Peace with
yᵉ Western Nations.

{January} 5th {1762}. — This Day Frederick Post gone for Philad[a].

Source: Kenny, "Journal of James Kenny", pp.
8–172

Indian Council Meetings

The council meetings are as quiet and orderly as
if they were acts of devotion. Noises, talking and laughing are
not heard, even though the young may be present. All pay
strict attention to the speaker. The counsellors are called
together by a servant and when they appear, they welcome one
another, shake hands and express their joy at meeting. Each
brings pouch, pipe and they smoke a considerable amount of
tobacco that has been mixed with dried and crushed sumac
leaves. Women are never admitted to the council; in matters of
public interest they may stand about the house and listen, and
they account it an honor when they are admitted, to hand
victuals and keep up the fire. Provisions must always be in
plenty in the council-house, for eating and deliberating alternate.

The principal chief, either himself or through a
speaker, sets forth the subjects that shall engage the attention
of the council in a solemn speech. If the subjects are of great
importance all who take part in the discussion stand as they
speak. Each counsellor has the liberty to utter his sentiments
and having made his speech, sits down. No one interrupts the
speaker but all sit silent and attentive as if engaged in an act
of devotion. The speeches are delivered in a pleasing manner
and the words of the speakers flow as readily as if they were
read from a manuscript. Whoever visits such an assembly,
whether white man or savage Indian, cannot but be profoundly
impressed.

A subject is often very thoroughly and extendedly
discussed. The chiefs and counsellors in turn give their
opinions, and suggestions. When all have spoken, one of them
is called upon to sum up the principal parts of all the speeches
in a concise manner. This is done extempore and the necessary
amendments proposed, every subject being brought into as short
and comprehensive statement as possible. Before deliberations
begin, the strings and belts of wampum must be placed in due
order, for whatever is said without being confirmed by them is
considered vain and without effect. They are so accustomed to
this that when they communicate the contents of a message,
merely in private conversation, they cannot do so without
something in their hands, a strap, a ribbon or a blade of grass.
Holding some such thing in his hand the speaker will recount
the points in proper order as with the strings or belts of
wampum thereto belonging.

Source: Zeisberger's *History...*, p. 96

John Heckewelder
1762

Much of what we know of the Tuscarawas Valley of the 1700s is due to this man, John Heckewelder.

He was born in England in 1743, came to America with his parents in 1754, and attended the Moravian boys' school in Bethlehem, Pennsylvania. While serving as an apprentice to a cooper in 1762, an opportunity came along that would change the course of his life. The missionary, Christian Frederick Post, had visited the Delawares at Tuscarawas in 1761 and was going to return to their town in 1762, taking with him someone who would serve as a teacher to the Indian children. Heckewelder was to be that assistant even though he was only 19 years of age and completely ignorant of the Indian language. Although this attempt to establish a mission at Tuscarawas was a failure, for the rest of his life Heckewelder was actively engaged in missionary work and was also used on many occasions by the United States government in treaty negotiations, and other dealings, with the various tribes of Indians. At times, he was one of the missionaries at the Moravian towns in the Tuscarawas Valley and, in 1778, made the ride known in local history simply as "Heckewelder's Ride".

He wrote two excellent books concerning the Indians and his life with them, a Narrative of the Mission of the United Brethren Among the Delaware and Mohegan Indians *and a* History, Manners and Customs of the Indian Nations Who Once Inhabited Pennsylvania and the Neighbouring States, *both of which will be referred to in this book simply as Heckewelder's* Narrative..., *and Heckewelder's* History..., *respectively.*

This is the first of several of his journals to appear in this book. The year is 1762 and he is proceeding with Post across Pennsylvania to the Ohio country.

Following his journal are entries from the James Kenny journal that relate to Post and Heckewelder in this 1762 missionary effort.

Having crossed the Laurel Hill and the Chesnut Ridge, we reached Bushy Run on the 1st of April, and pushed on rapidly, in order if possible to reach Pittsburgh, distance twenty-five miles, before night. Having approached the Fort within seven or eight miles, we suddenly found ourselves on the field of Braddock's defeat. A dreadful sight was presented to our eyes. Skulls and bones of the unfortunate men slain here on the 9th of July, 1755, lay scattered all around; and the sound of our horses' hoofs continually striking against them, made dismal music, as,

John Heckewelder

Born: March 12, 1743 Bedford, England
Died: January 31, 1823 Bethlehem, Pennsylvania
Age on entering Tuscarawas Valley – 19 years

Inform'd by y^e Pipe Indⁿ from Tuscorawas that Shingass is got well & in about 12 Days they will be here on their way to the Treaty; that ye Beaver King says that he will Deliver Frederick Post to ye Governor & tell him to keep him at home.

James Kenny   June 21st, 1762

with the Monongahela full in view, we rode over this memorable battle-ground.

We felt as if relieved from an insupportable weight, when, on arriving at Fort Pitt, we again found ourselves in the company of the living. The only private dwelling in the neighborhood of the Fort was situated at the junction of the Alleghany and Monongahela. It was owned by two traders, Messrs. Davenport and McKinney; who received us in a very friendly and hospitable manner. Within the Fort, also, we met with kind well-wishers; and the treatment we received at the hands of the gallant commander Col. Bouquet, and all his officers, calls for my lasting gratitude. To a youth far from home and friends, engaged in an enterprize the success of which was more than doubtful, each kind word is as an angel from heaven.

Post had expected to be able to make arrangements at Fort Pitt for a supply of flour, which could easily have been brought to our new home by the travelling traders. But to our great disappointment, the magazine had been overflowed by a tremendous inundation, and no flour was to be had. Neither could any be procured from the surrounding country, as there were no farms within hundreds of miles.

On the 5th of April, we crossed the Alleghany. The heavy rain of the preceding day, had swelled the different streams in our way, so that we could travel only sixteen miles before night. We pitched our tent on a rising ground near a creek. During the night a dreadful thunder storm came on, and we were awakened by the water rushing through our tent. We immediately laid our baggage on the top of the tent, to prevent it from being washed away, and the night being perfectly dark, we heaped wood on the fire, to produce a bright blaze, that we might see our way to a safer resting place. Our companion from Pittsburgh, a Virginian, who seemed accustomed to a life of hardships, and perfectly at home in such scenes as these, led the way with lighted firebrands, and enabled us to find the most shallow places. Here we crossed while the water was running knee deep around us. By dint of great exertion, we managed to save our horses, tents and baggage. There was no time to lose. The last time we crossed from our first encampment, we could scarcely stem the flood; and in the morning the spot where our tent had been

standing was covered by the deep waters. Our baggage had been completely wetted and as we supposed that the creeks we should have to pass must have risen during the night, we resolved to remain where we were till the next morning.

The Virginian kindly offered to go out hunting and procure us food; and Post and myself spent the greater part of the day together, thanking God for his mercy, and reminding each other, that a path like ours could not be strewn with flowers. The next day we continued our journey, and found the smaller streams fordable. The Beaver river we crossed in canoes with the assistance of the Indians who lived there. They also gave us some venison and bear's fat; and one of them, White Eyes, presented us with a few chickens. Four days after, on the 11th of April, we arrived at Tuscarawas on the Muskingum, after a pilgrimage of thirty-three days. We entered our cabin singing a hymn.

The cabin which Post had built the year before, stood on a high bank, on the east side of the Muskingum, about four rods from the stream. No one lived near us on the same side of the river; but on the other, a mile down the stream, resided a trader named Thomas Calhoon, a moral and religious man. Farther south was situated the Indian town called Tuscarawas; consisting of about forty wigwams. A mile still farther down the stream, a few families had settled; and eight miles above our dwelling, there was another Indian village.

The Indians, having been aware of Post's intention, had allowed him to erect his cabin. But during his absence, they had become suspicious; fearing that this missionary scheme might prove a mere pretence, in order to enable the white people to obtain a footing in the Indian country, and that in course of time a fort would be erected, and the original inhabitants of the land be driven from their territory. When they now observed Post marking out three acres of ground for a corn-field, and beginning to cut down trees, they became alarmed, and sent him word to appear before them at the council house on the following day, and meanwhile to desist from doing any further work on the premises. On his appearance before them at the time appointed, the speaker, in the name of the Council, delivered the following address.

"Brother! Last year you asked our leave

to come and live with us; for the purpose of instructing us and our children; to which we consented; and now being come, we are glad to see you.

Brother! It appears to us, that you must since have changed your mind; for instead of instructing us or our children, you are cutting down trees on our land; you have marked out a large spot of ground for a plantation, as the white people do every where; and by and by, another and another may come and do the same, and the next thing will be, that a fort will be built for the protection of these intruders; and thus our country will be claimed by the white people, and we driven further back, as has been the case ever since the white people came into this country. Say, do we not speak the truth?"

In answer to this address, Post delivered himself thus.

"Brothers! What you say I told you, is true, with regard to my coming to live with you, namely for the purpose of instructing you; but it is likewise true, that an instructor must have something to live upon, otherwise he cannot do his duty. Now, not wishing to be a burden to you, so as to ask of you provision for my support, knowing that you already have families to provide for, I thought of raising my own bread; and believed that three acres of ground were little enough for that. You will recollect that I told you last year, that I was a messenger from God, and prompted by him to preach and make known his will to the Indians; that they also by faith might be saved, and become inheritors of his heavenly kingdom. Of your land I do not want a foot; neither will my raising a sufficiency of corn and vegetables on your land for me and my brother to subsist on, give me or any other person a claim to your land."

Post then retired to give the chiefs and council time to deliberate on an answer; this done, they again met, when the speaker thus addressed my companion.

"Brother! Now, as you have spoken more distinctly, we may perhaps be able to give you some advice. You say that you are come at the instigation of the great Spirit, to teach and to preach to us. So also say the priests at Detroit, whom our Father, the French, has sent among his Indian children. Well, this being the case, you, as a preacher, want no more land than

those do; who are content with a garden lot, to plant vegetables and pretty flowers in, such as the French priests also have, and of which the white people are all fond.

Brother! As you are in the same station and employ with those preachers we allude to, and as we never saw any one of those cut down trees and till the ground to get a livelihood, we are inclined to think, especially, as those men without laboring hard, yet look well, that they have to look to another source than that of hard labour for their maintenance. And we think, that if as you say, the great Spirit urges you to preach to the Indians, he will provide for you in the same manner as he provides for those priests we have seen at Detroit. We are agreed to give you a garden spot, even a larger spot of ground than those have at Detroit. It shall measure fifty steps each way; and if it suits you, you are at liberty to plant therein what you please."

To this proposal Post agreed, as there was no remedy; and the lot was measured off, and we were allowed to proceed as we liked. We perceived at once the insurmountable difficulties of our situation. As was mentioned above, there was no flour to be procured at Fort Pitt. Neither was Indian corn to be had, as a famine prevailed at the time among the Indians, and every grain of maize was saved for planting. Potatoes were also very scarce. We were therefore forced to depend, partly on my expertness with the gun and fishing hook, and partly on the few vegetables that were to be found in the surrounding forest. There were wild ducks in abundance; but the river being in some places too deep to ford, and we having no canoe, I often had to wait very long, until they flew so near the bank that I could reach them when shot. The wild geese were still more difficult to get, as these seldom approach the banks, but generally keep in the middle of the river. Pheasants and squirrels are almost worthless in summer; and the larger game of the forest was rapidly shot down by the more expert Indians, whom hunger rendered still more active. Of fish we could procure more than enough; but in the manner in which we were forced to prepare them they became tasteless and even disgusting; and besides, when used exclusively, these are not a food calculated to give strength to the body. We lived mostly on nettles; which grew abundantly in the bottoms, and of which we frequently made two meals a day. We also made use of some other vegetables and greens. Besides, we had brought along some tea and chocolate; which we drank as well as we could without milk or sugar.

Of course such a diet could have no other effect than to weaken us from day to day. Nevertheless, we were obliged to clear the space allotted us for a garden, and which was covered by thick trees. When these were removed, the ground had to be loosened with pickaxes. The wood we chopped very short, so that we could roll and drag it from the enclosure. How often, while engaged in this laborious employment without strengthening food, did I think of the pieces of bread which I had frequently seen given to the hogs; and how gladly would I have shared them!

One day some chiefs came to request my assistance for a few days in making a fence round their land. I gladly accepted the invitation, being desirous of doing anything to secure their good will; and I did my best to be of service to them. At the same time, I was enabled to restore my health and strength; for as long as I staid with them, I could eat enough to satisfy the cravings of hunger. Thus I found myself suddenly transferred as it were to a land of plenty, and where I had opportunities to cultivate the acquaintance of the Indian youth, and to secure the favour of the tribe by my industry. During my stay with them, I received the name of "Piselatulpe," Turtle; by which I am still known among the Delawares.

Hitherto, amidst all my privations, I had still enjoyed the company of a white man; but of this comfort too I was soon to be deprived. Previously to our leaving Philadelphia, Post had promised the Governor of Pennsylvania to do his best to encourage the chiefs of the Western Delawares to come to Lancaster, in the latter part of summer in order to hold a talk with the Government; and had also given his word to accompany them. In view of this arrangement, it had been resolved at Bethlehem by the Elders of the Congregation, that in case of Post's succeeding in this negotiation, he should not leave me in Ohio, but that we should set out together for Lancaster, and then return to our station. The time when Post was to set out being near at hand, he became not a little embarrassed. It was

evident that if we both left the Muskingum, we should not be able to return, and in travelling to Lancaster together, would be virtually abandoning our missionary enterprize. For the Indians were already suspicious; and during our absence, designing men might easily increase their fears, and induce them to destroy our cabin and forbid our return. On the other hand, Post was unwilling to leave me alone in a strange country, surrounded by an unfriendly and savage tribe, of whose very language I was still ignorant. He laid the whole matter before me; and we at last agreed that I should remain.

In order to enable us to bring down cedar wood, for the purpose of making tubs and the like articles for the Indians, and also to procure the game that I might shoot on the river, we resolved to make a canoe. We set about the work without delay; and with the assistance of one of Mr. Calhoon's men, we succeeded in finishing one that answered our purpose very well.

To assist me in passing the time, Post left me a number of old sermons and religious books, requesting me at the same time, never to read or write in presence of the Indians, and even to conceal the books from their sight. "For otherwise," said he, "you will be in great danger. The Indians are very suspicious of those white people whom they see engaged in reading and writing, especially the latter; believing that it concerns them or their territory. They say that they have been robbed of their lands by the writing of the whites." I was therefore compelled to keep my books and papers in the garret, from a window of which I could see whether anyone was approaching the cabin. Here I whiled away many an hour, far from civilization, alone with my books, my thoughts and God.

As long as I had my canoe, I could always procure a plentiful supply of provisions. The wild ducks were so numerous that I frequently brought down five or six at one shot. But by the carelessness or dishonesty of the Indian boys, who often borrowed the canoe in order to spear fish, or to pursue deer on the river by torchlight, it was lost before many days were over. I was often in great distress for food; and indeed, many a day I was entirely destitute of it. The nettles had become too large and hard; and every vegetable that grew in my garden was stolen by the passing traders. Whenever I wished to visit Mr. Calhoon, I had to wade through the Muskingum; in consequence of which I was soon attacked by fever and ague.

{At this point in the journal he talks briefly about the death and funeral of the wife of Shingas. In his *History* he gives a more complete description of those proceedings and the more complete version is set forth at the end of this journal.}

The fever soon prostrated my strength, and the gloom of my situation increased. It would be impossible to give an adequate idea of my sufferings, both in mind and body; alone and sick, and almost famished. More than once, on returning from Mr. Calhoon's, the paroxysm of fever become so violent that I had to lie down on the path till it was over. An Indian once found me in this condition, and kindly led me to my cabin. Mr. Calhoon, a man of open hand and heart, invited me to come and stay with him; and I would gladly have accepted the kind offer, but I had promised Post to remain at the cabin, as otherwise the Indians would have stolen every thing. At last my strength failed to such a degree that I was afraid to venture upon fording the river, and was compelled to stay at home, if such a place might be called a home.

Whilst I was in this miserable condition, I was once visited by an Indian of my acquaintance; and I begged him to make me a little bark canoe; in return for which I promised to give him a knife. He did so, and I soon made my first trial with it, passing down the river to visit Mr. Calhoon. He hardly recognized me, so much had hunger and fatigue changed my appearance. I was received in the most friendly manner, and food was immediately set before me. I told him of my new acquisition, and I told him that I intended to use my canoe to visit him and the Indians in the village, in order to procure some food, until I should be sufficiently recovered to hunt. "Very well;" said he, "never pass me by in your expeditions, I shall cheerfully share with you." I then preferred my first request for a knife to give the Indian as I had promised. The good-natured trader immediately told me to send the man to his store, so that he might have his choice; as he was the best Indian that he had

ever known; and that I need not pay him any thing for it. I had in fact not one cent in my possession, but had permission from Post, in case of necessity, to draw upon the trader for what was absolutely necessary. At this time I was frequently reduced to such distress, that the least morsel of food, if offered, would have been acceptable. But although I could make out to live, I was unable to do any thing towards effecting the object for which I had come. Indeed, it soon became evident that our enterprize was to be a complete failure.

Post had hardly been gone three weeks, when the rumour was spread that he never intended to return; nay more, that even were he to attempt it, he would not be allowed by the tribe to do so; that his sole purpose was to deliver the Indian country into the hands of the white people, and that this was the secret of his pretended missionary efforts. It was also reported that a war would soon break out between the English and Indians, in which the latter would be assisted by their old allies, the French. All this I had written to Post; having found means to send him the information by a Mr. Denison, from Detroit, who was travelling to Philadelphia. He returned answer, that he had already heard the unwelcome news, and that, in the pass things had come to, I could do no better than to return as speedily as possible. Gladly would I have followed his advice, but my horse was lost, or had been stolen, for upwards of three months. I was too weak to travel on foot; and Mr. Calhoon's pack-horse drivers, who had intended to set out for Pittsburg with furs, were all laid up with the fever. I was therefore under the necessity of waiting for their recovery; and in the meantime put my trust in that Lord whom I served.

Meanwhile I was twice warned by friendly Indians to leave their country; and every time I visited Tuscarawas, I saw strangers among the real inhabitants, and perceived that I was the object of their scrutiny. But I remained in happy ignorance of my dangerous situation, until one afternoon, one of Mr. Calhoon's men called from the opposite bank of the Muskingum, requesting me to lock my door and cross the river immediately, as Mr. Calhoon wished to speak with me on business of great importance. Having wrapped up a few articles of dress in my blanket, I paddled across. As soon as I arrived at Mr. C's, he told me privately, that an Indian woman who frequently came to his store, and who made spirits, which he kept for sale, had asked him that day whether the white man who lived above, on the other side of the river, were his friend; and that, on his answering in the affirmative, she had said: "Take him away: don't let him remain one night longer in his cabin: he is in danger there."

The next morning I wished to return, to see whether any thing had taken place at the cabin, and if possible, to fetch a few necessary articles which had been left behind in the hurry of my departure. Mr. Calhoon however would not let me go, but sent two of his strongest men to see how things stood. One of them, James Smith, was a man of such uncommon strength, that the Indians considered him a Manitto, and would hardly be anxious to engage him personally. They reported that the house had been broken open during the night, and that judging from appearances there, two persons had been in. There were signs of a late fire on the hearth, and they had evidently been waiting for me. Of course my return was out of the question; the attempt would have been actual fool-hardiness. I never saw my lonely cabin again, remaining under the hospitable roof of the trader. Meanwhile, as I afterwards heard, emissaries of the Senecas and Northern Indians, were busily engaged in exciting the Delawares to take up the hatchet against the English; and soon after my departure, war broke out, and more than thirty white people of my acquaintance lost their lives.

At Mr. Calhoon's I experienced nothing but the most true-hearted friendship; and under his kind treatment I recovered from the fever.

About this time the Indian chiefs whom Post had accompanied to Lancaster, returned home; and we soon perceived that from some cause or other, their friendship had considerably cooled. One of them, however, King Beaver, remained favorably disposed; but all he could do was to give me several friendly hints to hasten my departure. Fortunately, Mr. Calhoon's men were now restored to health, and determined to set out on their journey to Pittsburgh. My kind host lent me a young horse to ride on; and in return I offered what assistnce I could give his men in loading and unloading at the encampments.

We now took an affectionate leave of each other. His conduct had been that of a Christian indeed; and his kindness will be remembered by me as long as I live. He would have left the country with me; but property of great amount had been entrusted to him, and this he considered himself bound to guard as long as possible. After my return to Bethlehen, I learned through the public papers, that he and his brother, together with their servants, had been ordered by the Delaware chiefs to leave their country; as they were unable any longer to protect them. They set out for Pittsburgh; but were attacked on the road, at the Beaver river, by a party of warriors, and only two saved their lives, Mr. C. himself, who outstripped his pursuers in the race, and James Smith, who had strangled his antagonist.

On the third day after our departure from Muskingum, we met Post and the Indian agent, Captain McKee; who were returning to the Indian country, totally ignorant of the real state of affairs. In spite of our earnest remonstrances, they insisted on proceeding, not considering the danger so imminent. They were soon undeceived on their arrival; and their lives were in danger. The agent was protected by the friendship of the chiefs; but Post, whom the Indians suspected of secret designs against them, as they were at a loss to explain his missionary movements, had to fly for his life, and was conducted to a place of safety, through a secret forest path, by one of his former fellow-travellers to Lancaster.

Having taken leave of Post, I hastened after my companions, who had proceeded in the meantime. At a distance of five miles I expected to find their tents; and seeing the smoke of an encampment curling above the trees, I rode on, but was much surprised to find myself suddenly in the midst of a war-party. The sight of the Indian captives, and of the scalping pole with its savage decorations, was not caculated to encourage me. I was however suffered to pass on; and on riding five miles farther, I found my company, by whom I was informed that I had fallen in with a party of Senecas, who had just returned from an expedition against the Cherokees.

Source: Rondthaler, *Life of John Heckewelder,* pp. 43–58

{The following is the more complete version of the funeral of the wife of Shingas as set forth in Heckewelder's *History...*, pp. 270–75}

At the moment that she died, her death was announced through the village by women specially appointed for that purpose, who went through the streets crying, "She is no more! She is no more!" The place on a sudden exhibited a scene of universal mourning; cries and lamentations were heard from all quarters; it was truly the expression of the general feeling for a general loss.

The day passed in this manner amidst sorrow and desolation. The next morning, between nine and ten o'clock, two counsellors came to announce to Mr. Thomas Calhoon, the Indian trader, and myself, that we were desired to attend and assist at the funeral which was soon to take place. We, in consequence, proceeded to the house of the deceased, where we found her corpse lying in a coffin, (which had been made by Mr. Calhoon's carpenter) dressed and painted in the most superb Indian style. Her garments, all new, were set off with rows of silver broaches, one row joining the other. Over the sleeves of her new ruffled shirt were broad silver arm-spangles from her shoulder down to her wrist, on which were bands, forming a kind of mittens, worked together of wampum, in the same manner as the belts which they use when they deliver speeches. Her long plaited hair was confined by broad bands of silver, one band joining the other, yet not of the same size, but tapering from the head downwards and running at the lower end to a point. On the neck were hanging five broad belts of wampum tied together at the ends, each of a size smaller than the other, the largest of which reached below her breast, the next largest reaching to a few inches of it, and so on, the uppermost one being the smallest. Her scarlet leggings were decorated with different coloured ribands sewed on, the outer edges being finished off with small beads also of various colours. Her mocksens were ornamented with the most striking figures, wrought on the leather with coloured porcupine quills, on the borders of which, round the ankles, were fastened a number

of small round silver bells, of about the size of a musket ball. All these things, together with the vermilion paint, judiciously laid on, so as to set her off in the highest style, decorated her person in such a manner, that perhaps nothing of the kind could exceed it.

The spectators having retired, a number of articles were brought out of the house and placed in the coffin, wherever there was room to put them in, among which were a new shirt, a dressed deer skin for shoes, a pair of scissors, needles, thread, a knife, pewter basin and spoon, pint-cup, and other similar things, with a number of trinkets and other small articles which she was fond of while living. The lid was then fastened on the coffin with three straps, and three handsome round poles, five or six feet long, were laid across it, near each other, and one in the middle, which were also fastened with straps cut up from a tanned elk hide; and a small bag of vermilion paint, with some flannel to lay it on, was then thrust into the coffin through the hole cut out at the head of it. This hole, the Indians say, is for the spirit of the deceased to go in and out at pleasure, until it has found the place of its future residence.

Everything being in order, the bearers of the corpse were desired to take their places. Mr. Calhoon and myself were placed at the foremost pole, two women at the middle, and two men at the pole in the rear. Several women from a house about thirty yards off, now started off, carrying large kettles, dishes, spoons, and dried elk meat in baskets, for the burial place, and the signal being given for us to move with the body, the women who acted as chief mourners made the air resound with their shrill cries. The order of the procession was as follows; first a leader or guide, from the spot where we were to the place of interment. Next followed the corpse, and close to it *Shingask,* the husband of the deceased. He was followed by the principal war-chiefs and counsellors of the nation, after whom came men of all ranks and descriptions. Then followed the women and children, and lastly two stout men carrying loads of European manufactured goods upon their backs. The chief mourners on the women's side, not having joined the ranks, took their own course to the right, at the distance of about fifteen or twenty yards from us, but always opposite to the corpse. As the corpse had to be carried by the strength of our arms to the distance of about two hundred yards, and hung low between the bearers, we had to rest several times by the way, and whenever we stopped, everybody halted until we moved on again.

Being arrived at the grave, we were told to halt, then the lid of the coffin was again taken off, and the body exposed to view. Now the whole train formed themselves into a kind of semi-lunar circle on the south side of the grave, and seated themselves on the ground. Within this circle, at the distance of about fifteen yards from the grave, a common seat was made for Mr. Calhoon and myself to sit on, while the disconsolate Shingask retired by himself to a spot at some distance, where he was soon weeping, with his head bowed to the ground. The female mourners seated themselves promiscuously near to each other, among some low bushes that were at the distance of from twelve to fifteen yards east of the grave.

In this situation we remained for the space of more than two hours; not a sound was heard from any quarter, though the numbers that attended were very great; nor did any person move from his seat to view the body, which had been lightly covered over with a clean white sheet. All appeared to be in profound reflection and solemn mourning. Sighs and sobs were now and then heard from the female mourners, so uttered as not to disturb the assembly; it seemed rather as if intended to keep the feeling of sorrow alive in a manner becoming the occasion. Such was the impression made on us by this long silence.

At length, at about one o'clock in the afternoon, six men stepped forward to put the lid upon the coffin, and let down the body into the grave, when suddenly three of the women mourners rushed from their seats, and forcing themselves between these men and the corpse, loudly called out to the deceased to "arise and go with them and not to forsake them." They even took hold of her arms and legs; at first it seemed as if they were caressing her, afterwards they appeared to pull with more violence, as if they intended to run away with the body, crying out all the while, "Arise, arise! Come with us! Don't leave us! Don't abandon us!" At last they retired, plucking at their garments, pulling their hair, and uttering loud cries and lamentations,

with all the appearance of frantic despair. After they were seated on the ground, they continued in the same manner crying and sobbing and pulling at the grass and shrubs, as if their minds were totally bewildered and they did not know what they were doing.

As soon as these women had gone through their part of the ceremony, which took up about fifteen minutes, the six men whom they had interrupted and who had remained at the distance of about five feet from the corpse, again stepped forward and did their duty. They let down the coffin into the earth, and laid two thin poles of about four inches diameter, from which the bark had been taken off, lengthways and close together over the grave, after which they retired. Then the husband of the decease advanced with a very slow pace, and when he came to the grave, walked over it on these poles, and proceeded forward in the same manner into an extensive adjoining prairie, which commenced at this spot.

When the widowed chief had advanced so far that he could not hear what was doing at the grave, a painted post, on which were drawn various figures, emblematic of the deceased's situation in life and of her having been the wife of a valiant warrior, was brought by two men and delivered to a third, a man of note, who placed it in such a manner that it rested on the coffin at the head of the grave, and took great care that a certain part of the drawings should be exposed to the East, or rising of the sun; then, while he held the post erect and properly situated, some women filled up the grave with hoes, and having placed dry leaves and pieces of bark over it, so that none of the fresh ground was visible, they retired, and some men, with timbers fitted beforehand for the purpose, enclosed the grave about breast-high, so as to secure it from the approach of wild beasts.

The whole work being finished, which took up about an hour's time, Mr. Calhoon and myself expected that we might be permitted to go home, as we wished to do, particularly as we saw a thundergust from the west fast approaching; but the Indians, suspecting our design, soon came forward with poles and blankets, and in a few minutes erected a shelter for us.

The storm, though of short duration, was tremendous; the water produced by the rain, flowing in streams; yet all had found means to secure themselves during its continuance, and being on praire ground, we were out of all danger of trees being torn up or blown down upon us. Our encampment now appeared like a village, or rather like a military camp, such was the number of places of shelter that had been erected.

Fortunately, the husband of the deceased had reached the camp in good time, and now the gust being over, every one was served with victuals that had been cooked at some distance from the spot. After the repast was over, the articles of merchandise which had been brought by the two men in the rear, having been made up in parcels were distributed among all present. No one, from the oldest to the youngest, was excepted, and every one partook of the liberal donation. This difference only was made, that those who had rendered the greatest services received the most valuable presents, and we were much pleased to see the female mourners well rewarded, as they had, indeed, a very hard task to perform. Articles of little value, such as gartering, tape, needles, beads, and the like, were given to the smaller girls; the older ones received a pair of scissors, needles and thread, and a yard or two of riband. The boys had a knife, jews-harp, awl-blades, or something of similar value. Some of the grown persons received a new suit of clothes, consisting of a blanket, shirt, breech-cloth and leggings, of the value in the whole of about eight dollars; and the women, (I mean those who had rendered essential services) a blanket, ruffled shirts, stroud and leggings, the whole worth from ten to twelve dollars. Mr. Calhoon and myself were each presented with a silk cravat and a pair of leggings. The goods contributed on this occasion, were estimated by Mr. Calhoon at two hundred dollars; the greatest part of them had, the same morning, been taken out of his store.

After we had thus remained, in a manner, under confinement, for more than six hours, the procession ended, and Mr. Calhoon and myself retired with the rest to our homes. At dusk a kettle of victuals was carried to the grave and placed upon it, and the same was done every evening for the space of three weeks, at the end of which it was supposed that the traveller had found her place of residence. During that time the lamentations of the women mourners were heard on the evenings of each day, though not so loud nor so violent as before.

James Kenny Entries relating to Post and Heckewelder

{April} 2nd {1762}. — Frederick Post return'd here from Philadª, broᵗ me a Letter & Silk Map from Israel Pemberton, Enjoyning me to use my best Influence with yᵉ Indⁿˢ to bring yᵉ Prisoners down to yᵉ Treaty.

{April} 5th. — Frederick Post set off to Tuscorawas last Night, he & I had some Argument, he having offten been carping a little about Friends Principles Signifying that they are not Always Subject to yᵉ Governmᵗ where they Live, & they that resist yᵉ Power of yᵉ Legislator shall receive Damnation, hinting that when they have suffer'd, (as I took it in New England) they cry out perscuction, which they bring justly on themselves, also as a law was made to pay Tithes they should do it; I object'd & Argued that if he made it his fix'd Principles to Obey all Laws that were made in any Governmᵗ where he might Come, he might be Guilty of Idolatry & of consequence he must think yᵉ Legislators Infallible to fix such a Principel, all one as yᵉ Church of Rome, thinks their Church but this Stall'd him & he gave out.

{May} 15th. — We had a Letter from Frederick Post, wherein he mentions that since he went to Philadelphia, in his absence Shamoken David [Daniel] & another Indian has prejudiced yᵉ Inhabitants of Tuscorawas against him so much, that altho' they had allow'd him to Clear as much Land as he pleas'd, now they have limmited him to about half an Acre.

{May} 21ˢᵗ. — It's Report'd by a Trader that Winter'd at Tuscorawas, that some of yᵉ Indians there Inform'd him, When yᵉ Traders was not allow'd last year to go to yᵉ Shawanas, & they were Limmitted when they came here in buying Powder & Lead to five Pounds Powdʳ a Man, & Ten of Lead, That Nation had concluded to hold a Council in order to put all their Women & Children to Death & yᵉ Men to carry on a War against yᵉ English while one of them remain'd.

{June} 6ᵗʰ. — We hear from Tuscorowas that Shingass is very Sick, which hinders the Indians coming to go to yᵉ Treaty until his recovery; its generally said by yᵉ White people, that he shews them yᵉ Most Kindness & generossity of all yᵉ Indians thereabouts.

{June} 21ˢᵗ. — Inform'd by yᵉ Pipe Indⁿ from Tuscorawas that Chingass is got well & in about 12 Days they will be here on their way to the Treaty; that yᵉ Beaver King says that he will Deliver Frederick Post to yᵉ Governor & tell him to keep him at home.

{July} 2ⁿᵈ. — This Day yᵉ Beaver King & Frederick Post & many Indⁿˢ came from Tuscorawas going to yᵉ Treaty.

{October} 9ᵗʰ. — Frederick Post came here by whom we were Inform'd much of yᵉ state of yᵉ Treaty.

{October} 11ᵗʰ. — This Evening Frederick Post set off to Tuscorawas to see how his Lad {Heckewelder} does that is Sick with yᵉ Ague & to see what receptions he will have amongst yᵉ Indians, being resolved if these Indians do not accept of his Service, he will Travel to yᵉ West as far as yᵉ English Garisons reach.

{October} 12ᵗʰ. — Post Asked my Advice in such a Case as he thought it his duty being Moved by yᵉ Divine Spirit to settle amongst these Indians & so many Enemies Raised amongst them to his Service in yᵉ Gosple, having destroyed his Garden & small hope of being Alowed to Plant anything next Spring, having no help from yᵉ Publick nor from his Brethren could not see how he could subsist. I told him that if yᵉ work was of yᵉ Lord & he intend'd to help yᵉ Indians by his endeavours at this time, that these difficulties would be removed, & yet to try & wait to see the result. I think his residing amongst yᵉ Indians might be of Great Service to yᵉ English Intrest by removing their jealousies, which they are often subject to from Lies raised by yᵉ Mingoes & others to set them against us, such being now busy amongst yᵉ Shawanas.

{October} 22ⁿᵈ. — Frederick Post's Lad {Heckewelder} that came here, Informs us that Shingass was very cross to him & almost starves yᵉ White Children he has Prisoners.

{October} 23ᵈ. — We had a Letter from Post & he says that yᵉ Indians receiv'd him with much seeming kindness.

Source: Kenny, "Journal of James Kenny", pp. 8–172

The Chief and the Council House

In externals a chief has no advantages above others. He must provide for his own maintenance, for no one is under any obligation to supply his wants. His wife, whose duty it is to provide sufficient corn for the year, is usually assisted by other women in her plantations, for much corn is required in such a house. If the chief is young and able to hunt he will, his official duties permitting, occasionally join the chase. He will even secure his own firewood as far as possible. In case he is old his friends, of whom there are usually many, and other Indians will furnish him with game, especially if he be popular.

The council house is either the house of the chief, which is commonly large and roomy, or a building erected for that purpose. Here public councils are held, that is, such where messages which have arrived from whites or other Indians are published. Every one may listen and the messages are also discussed. In case there is something of particular importance to consider, only the chief and the counsellors assemble and determine upon the matter. The old chief Netawatwes used to lay all affairs of state before his council for consideration. When they gave him their opinion, he either approved of it or indicated what was missing or not correct in the speech, upon which they would make the necessary amendments. Thus he kept them active and was held in great esteem.

Source: Zeisberger's *History...*, p. 93

Alexander McKee
1762

Alexander McKee was a Pennsylvanian by birth and an Indian trader by occupation. In the fall of 1762, George Croghan, the Deputy Agent for Indian Affairs at Pittsburgh, heard rumors of a possible Indian uprising and he sent McKee into the Indian country under secret instructions to see what he could learn about it. The ostensible purpose of his trip as far as the Indians were concerned was to try to get them to be more prompt in returning their white prisoners to the settlements, as they were required to do by the Treaty of Lancaster. Apparently, though, there was some concern among the Indians that if all of the prisoners were returned the whites would then attack the Indians and destroy them.

Very few prisoners were returned at this time, and the next spring the Indian uprising did occur. It was not until Bouquet went into the Indian country, in 1764, with a large force of soldiers that the Indians then sued for peace and did return nearly all of their prisoners.

Alexander McKee was later made a Deputy Agent himself and when the Revolutionary War broke out he remained loyal to the crown. He was one of the famous trio of McKee, Girty, and Elliott who deserted to the British at Detroit, in 1778, and for the rest of the war he fought against the Americans. After the war he settled in Canada where he died in 1801.

October the 12th. 1762, This day set out from Fort Pitt, in order to visit the Shawaneze Towns, in pursuance of the following Instructions received of George Croghan Esquire. {Summarized above.}

October the 13th, I met a Party of twenty Warriors of the Six Nations, returning from War, with a Cherokee Prisoner, and a Scalp; and as their principal Warrior was dead, and most of their Party Sick, They requested I wou'd write back, with them, to Fort Pitt, in order to get a Doctor to view their Sick.

14th. Set off from hence, and arrived at Tuskarawas the 16th., where I made the Delawares acquainted with that part of my Instructions relating to them. After which, the Conversation that pass'd before me, between the Beaver, and Shingass, was, that They cou'd give no positive answer to that Message, as most of their People were already gone a Hunting; and that there had not been time to acquaint them all, with what had passed at the Treaty of Lancaster: But They Said They wou'd Send this Message to the rest of their People living at Guiahoga, and then requested, that I wou'd give it to them in writing, which I accordingly did. — The Beaver then informed me that, He was going a Hunting, and wou'd be at Home in Thirty days, at which time He wou'd expect to meet me returning, and be able to give an Answer, when He heard from Guiyahoga.

The 19th. left Tuskarawas, and arrived at Waketummaky. The 21st. Here I informed the Shawanese with the Same Message, by a String of Wampum from the Commanding Oficer, that I had Delivered the Beaver, and the Chiefs of the Delawares. — Their Chief told me, in answer to it, "That for his part, and the People of his Town, they were always ready, and willing, to deliver up the Prisoners amongst them, and that They could not account for the Backwardness of the People of the lower Towns, in coming up with their Prisoners; and desired me to Insist on the Deputies of their Nation, who were at the Treaty of Lancaster, and heard all that passed there, to press the People of the lower Town, to make all possible Dispatch, in coming up, before the Winter Sat in, that He, & his People wou'd then be ready."

The 23ᵈ. after I had finish'd my Business, Sat off for the lower Shawanese Town ...

{McKee remained at the Lower Shawnee Towns for nearly a month, during which time he was trying to arrange for the return of prisoners to Fort Pitt. He also was receiving information of attempts to organize the Indians to rise up against the English. Such an uprising did take place the next spring as subsequent journals will show—the uprising known as Pontiac's War.}

The 23ᵈ, Set out for Tuskarawas, & arrived the 26ᵗʰ.; at wᶜʰ. place, I was informed the Indians were out a Hunting.

The Beaver, a few days before, had been there, & desired them to inform me, that He had sent the Message I deliver'd Him to Guiyahogo; and their answer was, that the Season was so far advanced, They could not possibly comply with it this Fall. I was inform'd here by a Trader from Guiyahoga that, some time before Shingass, & Weindohelas, Delaware Chiefs, had been there, Stirring up the Warriors of that Town, for war, desiring them to prepare themselves against next Spring, to Strike the English.

Novemʳ. 27ᵗʰ. I Set off from Tuskarawas, & arrived at Fort Pitt, the 31ˢᵗ.—

Source: Hamilton, *The Papers of Sir William Johnson*, Vol. X, pp. 576–80

Indian Opinion on the White Man's Avarice

They wonder that the white people are striving so much to get rich, and to heap up treasures in this world which they cannot carry with them to the next. They ascribe this to pride and to the desire of being called rich and great. They say that there is enough in this world to live upon, without laying anything by, and as to the next world, it contains plenty of everything, and they will find all their wants satisfied when they arrive there. They, therefore, do not lay up any stores, but merely take with them when they die as much as is necessary for their journey to the world of spirits.

Source: Heckewelder's *History...*, p. 189

William Trent
1763

After the French and Indian War ended in 1763, an Ottawa chieftain named Pontiac organized a massive uprising among the western tribes. Striking without warning, all of the smaller English forts west of the Alleghenies fell to the Indians and hundreds of people, soldiers, traders, and settlers in western Pennsylvania, were killed. Only the forts at Detroit and Pittsburgh managed to hold out, but even they were beseiged.

The first news of what was happening to the west of Fort Pitt was brought to the fort by William Calhoun and three of his men. It was dramatic in the extreme—a night visit by the Indian chiefs at Tuscarawas warning Calhoun of the uprising and asking that he and his men depart immediately for Fort Pitt, leaving their guns behind (the idea obviously being that since the chiefs were going to send three Indians with them who would be armed, these Indians could say to any hostile Indians that they might meet that the unarmed whites were their prisoners, in that way protecting them from harm by the hostile Indians), and the subsequent ambush at the Beaver, with most of Calhoun's men being killed.

The writer of this journal was the same William Trent whose trip to the Twightwees in 1752 is set forth in an earlier part of this book. He was living in Pittsburgh at the time the uprising occurred.

[EXTRACTS]

May 30th, 1763, All the inhabitants moved in to the fort. {Fort Pitt} About 4 o'clock one Coulson came in who had been a prisoner (at the lower) Shawnese town, and gave the following account. We came to the town with some traders, where an Indian arrived from the Lakes (with a) belt to acquaint the Delawares that Detroit was taken, the post at Sandusky burnt, and all the garrison put to death, except the officer whom they made prisoner. Upon this news, the Beaver and Shingess (the two Chiefs of the Delawares, commonly called King B and King S) came and acquainted Mr. Calhoon (the trader there) with it, and desired him to move away from there as quick as possible, with all his property, and that they sent three Indians to conduct him and the rest of the white people safe

to this post, and yesterday as they were crossing Beaver Creek, being fourteen in number, they were fired on and he believes all were killed except himself.

31st, Two of Mr. Calhoon's men came in and confirmed the above account. A second express was despatched this night to the general.

June 1st, Two men who were sent off express last night to Venango returned, being fired on at Shanipin's Town and one of them wounded in the leg. About 12 o'clock two men came from Redstone and the same night were sent back with orders for the Sergeant to repair to this post and bring the country people with him with 600 lbs. powder that was there belonging to some traders. About 6 o'clock in the afternoon Mr. Calhoon came in and brought the following account which he took in writing from the Indians at Tuskarawas.

63

Tuskarawas, May 27, 1763, 11 o'clock at night, King Beaver with Shingess, Windohala, Wingenum and Daniel and William Anderson came and delivered me the following intelligence (by a string of Wampum).

Brother: out of regard to you and the friendship that formerly subsisted between (our) grandfathers and the English, which has been lately renewed by us, we come to inform you of the news we had heard, which you may depend upon as true.

Brother: All the English that were at Detroit were killed ten days ago, not one left alive. At Sandusky all the white people there were killed 5 days ago, nineteen in number, except the officer who is a prisoner and one boy who made his escape, whom we have not heard of. At the mouth of the Twigtwee River (about 80 miles from Sandusky by water) Hugh Crawford with one boy was taken prisoner and six men killed. At the Salt Licks five days ago 5 white men were killed, we received the account this day; we have seen a number of tracks on the road between this and Sandusky not far off, which we are sure is a party coming to cut you and your people off, but as we have sent a man to watch their motions, request you may think of nothing you have here, but make the best of your way to some place of safety, as we would not desire to see you killed in our town; be careful to avoid the road and every part where Indians resort.

Brother: What goods and other effects you have here you need not be uneasy about them, we assure you that we will take care to keep them safe for six months, perhaps by that time we may see you or send you word what you may expect from us further. We know there is one white man at Gichanga, don't be concerned for him, we will take care to send him safe home.

Brother: We desire you to tell George Croghan and all your great men (that they) must not ask us any thing about this news, or what has happened, as we are not all concerned in it: the nations that have taken up the hatchet against you are the Ottawas and Chipawas and when you first went to speak with these people you did not consult us upon it, therefore we desire you may not expect that we are to account for any mischief they do, what you would know further about this news you must learn by the

same road you just went, but if you will speak with us you must send one or two men only, and we will hear them.

Brother: We thought your king had made peace with us and all the Western Nations of Indians, for our part we joined it heartily and desired to hold it always good, and you may depend upon it we will take care not to be readily cheated or drawn into a war again, but as we are settled between you and these nations who have taken up the hatchet against you we desire you will send no warriors this way till we are removed from this, which we will do as soon as we conveniently can; when we will permit you to pass without taking notice, till then we desire they may go by the first road you went.

Gave a string

The following is what Mr. Calhoon learned on his journey from one of these three Indians who were sent (to conduct him) safe there, viz. Daniel before mentioned as one of their chiefs. That Detroit was not really taken but had been attacked by the Indians four days before the messenger who brought the account left it, which Mr. Calhoon imagines must have been from about the 13th to the 17th of May and that the Indians had not then met with much success, but strongly persisted in carrying on the attack and said they were determined not (to) give over till they took it, and that the English had sent out three Belts of Wampum and the French two, desiring them to desist, which they refused. Mr. Calhoon says that when he and his people left Tuskerawas fourteen in number the Indians refused to let them bring their arms, telling them that the three Indians who were going along with them were sufficient to conduct them safe, and that the next day passing Beaver Creek they were fired upon by a party of Indians, when their guides immediately disappeared without interfering for them, and he is convinced that they were led by their guides knowingly to this party in order to be cut off, from which himself with three of his people only have escaped.

Mr. Calhoon further says that having lost his way and falling in upon the road leading to Venango, about seventy miles above this post he saw a number of Indian tracks, which had gone that way — two men were sent to the General with the intelligence received.

June 16th, Four Shawnees appeared on the opposite side of the Ohio, and desired that Mr. McKee would go over and speak to them, which he did and they made him the following speech:

"Brother, We received the message you sent us on the death of Colonel Clapham, and our chiefs desired us to inform you that they will take care of the traders in our towns. Mr. Baird and Gibson were taken by the Delaware Indian called Sir William Johnson {White Eyes} and his people at the Muskingum town and carried to our town. Our chiefs say they will take care of them until the war is over. We came to enquire news, we have heard none since the time the message with the belt and bloody hatchet came from the Lake Indians to the Delaware and Tuskarawas, acquainting them that they had struck the English and desired that they would join them. The captains and warriors of the Delawares pay no regard to their chiefs, who advised them not to accept the hatchets, but are determined to prosecute the war against you. It was the Six Nations that left this and the Delawares that killed your people at Beaver Creek with Mr. Calhoon."

Source: Darlington, *Fort Pitt and Letters from the Frontier,* pp. 85–91

Former Prisoners Return to Visit Captors

The Lichtenau Diary for August 10, 1776, is of interest in showing that a peculiar relationship can develop between captor and captive. It states:

Seven white people went through here to go to the Shawanese to visit their friends, as they said. Five of them had been prisoners.

In reading the journals of the times, it often appears that persons who had once been held captive by the Indians were not afraid to go back into the Indian country, certainly at times of peace, even visiting their former captors. As shown by the *Bouquet* journal, real affection would often develop between the Indians and their prisoners, especially if the prisoner was young when captured and grew up with the Indians as part of an Indian family. If adopted into the family, the prisoner was treated in all respects as simply another member of the family and shared equally in everything that the family had and did.

Colonel Henry Bouquet
1764

The siege of Fort Pitt in 1763 was relieved by a column of English and American troops commanded by Col. Henry Bouquet. After defeating the Indians in a battle twenty-six miles east of Pittsburgh, near Bushy Run, he then proceeded on to the fort and the Indians fled into the Ohio country.

The next year, in the fall of 1764, Bouquet took 1500 men, including some Royal Americans and the famed Black Watch, along with 400 cattle, 400 sheep, and over a thousand pack horses carrying flour and other supplies, and advanced into the Ohio country for the purpose of "chastising" the Indians, reducing them to submission, and getting back the several hundred prisoners that the Indians had been holding, some held since the early days of the French and Indian War.

There was no fighting on this expedition—there were simply too many soldiers for the Indians to consider attacking. Meeting first with the Indian chiefs at Tuscarawas, he then proceeded farther into the very heart of the Indian towns, camping finally near Coshocton, within about one mile of the Forks of the Muskingum. Here, he proceeded to erect buildings to house the prisoners, redoubts, and a conference house in which to meet with the Indian chiefs.

The Indians were thoroughly subdued and returned over 200 prisoners. Bouquet then proceeded uneventfully back to Fort Pitt.

While at the Forks of the Muskingum, his orderly book for Saturday, October 27, 1764 reads, in part, as follows:

Divine Service will be performed tomorrow at Eleven oClock all the Men off
duty to attend.

This is very probably the first religious service to be conducted by a Protestant minister (either Church of England or Presbyterian, or perhaps both) within what is now the state of Ohio. (Gist, in 1750, had also conducted a service "extracted from the Homilies of the Church of England", but he was not, by profession, a minister.) If all off-duty personnel did attend the service it must have been one of the largest held in this part of the state for many years, for he still had over 1,000 men with him and, on Sunday, not many would have been on duty.

Bouquet's Expedition was a marked success, and for ten years afterward, until 1774, there was relative peace on the border.

About the time of Col. Bouquet's arrival at Fort Pitt, {Sept. 17th} ten Indians appeared on the north side of the Ohio, desiring a conference; which stratagem the savages had made use of before, to obtain intelligence of our numbers and intentions. Three of the party consented, tho' with apparent reluctance, to come over to the Fort; and as they could give no satisfactory reason for their visit, they were detained as spies, and their associates fled back to their towns.

On the 20th of Sept. Col. Bouquet sent one of the above three Indians after them with a message, in substance as follows---"I have received an account from Col. Bradstreet that your nations had begg'd for peace, which he had consented to grant, upon assurance that you had recalled all your warriors from our frontiers; and in consequence thereof, I would not have proceeded against your towns, if I had not heard that, in open violation of your engagements, you have since murdered several of our people."

"As soon as the rest of the army joins me, which I expect immediately, I was therefore determined to have attacked you, as a people whose promises can no more be relied on. But I will put it once more in your power to save yourselves and your families from total destruction, by giving us satisfaction for the hostilities committed against us. And first you are to leave the path open for my expresses from hence to Detroit; and as I am now to send two men with dispatches to Col. Bradstreet who commands on the lakes, I desire to know whether you will send two of your people with them to bring them safe back with an answer? and if they receive any injury either in going or coming, or if the letters are taken from them, I will immediately put the Indians now in my power to death, and will shew no mercy for the future to any of your nations that shall fall into my hands. I allow you ten days to have my letters delivered at Detroit, and ten days to bring me back an answer."---

He added "that he had lately had it in his power, while they remained on the other side of

the river, to have put their whole party to death, which punishment they had deserved by their former treachery; and that if they did not improve the clemency now offered to them, by returning back as soon as possible with all their prisoners, they might expect to feel the full weight of a just vengeance and resentment."---

We have been the more particular in our account of this first transaction with the Indians; because the Colonel's firm and determined conduct in opening the campaign, had happy effects in the prosecution of it, and shews by what methods these faithless savages are to be best reduced to reason.

Things being thus settled, the army decamped from Fort-Pitt on Wednesday October 3d, and marched about one mile and an half over a rich level country, with stately timber, to camp No. 2. a strong piece of ground, pleasantly situated, with plenty of water and food for cattle.

Thursday October 4th, having proceeded about two miles, they came to the Ohio, at the beginning of the narrows, and from thence followed the course of the river along a flat gravelly beech, about six miles and a quarter; with two islands on their left, the lowermost about six miles long, with a rising ground running across, and gently sloping on both sides to its banks, which are high and upright. At the lower end of this island, the army left the river, marching thro' good land, broken with small hollows to camp No. 3; this day's march being nine miles and a quarter.

Friday October 5th. In this day's march, the army pass'd thro' Loggs-town, situated seventeen miles and an half, fifty seven perches, by the path, from Fort-Pitt. This place was noted before the last war for the great trade carried on there by the English and French; but its inhabitants, the Shawanese and Delawares, abandoned it in the year 1750. The lower town extended about sixty perches over a rich bottom to the foot of a low steep ridge, on the summit of which, near the declivity, stood the upper town, commanding a most agreeable prospect over the lower, and quite across the Ohio, which is about five hundred yards wide here, and by its majestic easy current adds much to the beauty of the place. Proceeding beyond Loggs-town, thro' a fine country, interspersed with hills and rich valleys, watered by many rivulets, and covered with stately timber, they came to camp No. 4; on a level piece of ground, with a thicket in the rear, a small precipice round the front, with a run of water at the foot, and good food for cattle. This day's march was nine miles, one half, and fifty three perches.

Saturday October 6th, at about three miles distance from this camp, they came again to the Ohio, pursuing its course half a mile farther, and then turning off, over a steep ridge, they cross'd big Beaver-creek, which is twenty perches wide, the ford stony and pretty deep. It runs thro' a rich vale, with a pretty strong current, its banks high, the upland adjoining it very good, the timber tall and young. — About a mile below its confluence with the Ohio, stood formerly a large town, on a steep bank, built by the French of square logs, with stone chimneys, for some of the Shawanese, Delaware and Mingo tribes, who abandoned it in the year 1758, when the French deserted Fort DuQuesne. Near the fording of Beaver-creek also stood about seven houses, which were deserted and destroyed by the Indians, after their defeat at Bushy-run, when they forsook all their remaining settlements in this part of the country, as has been mentioned above.

About two miles before the army came to Beaver-creek, one of our people who had been made prisoner by six Delawares about a week before, near Fort Bedford, having made his escape from them, came and informed the Colonel that these Indians had the day before fallen in with the army, but kept themselves concealed, being surprized at our numbers. Two miles beyond Beaver-creek, by two small springs, was seen the scull of a child, that had been fixed on a pole by the Indians. The Tracts of 15 Indians were this day discovered. The camp No. 5 is seven miles one quarter and fifty seven perches from big Beaver-creek; the whole march of this day being about twelve miles.

Sunday 7th October, passing a high ridge, they had a fine prospect of an extensive country to the right, which in general appeared level, with abundance of tall timber. The camp No. 6 lies at the foot of a steep descent, in a rich valley, on a strong ground, three sides thereof surrounded by a hollow, and on the fourth side a small hill, which was occupied by a detached guard. This day's march was six miles sixty five perches.

Monday 8th October, the army cross'd little Beaver-creek, and one of its branches. This creek is eight perches wide, with a good ford, the country about it interspersed with hills, rivulets and rich valleys, like that described above. Camp No. 7 lies by a small run on the side of a hill, commanding the ground about it, and is distant eleven miles one quarter and forty nine perches from the last encampment.

Tuesday October 9th. In this day's march, the path divided into two branches, that to the southwest leading to the lower towns upon the Muskingham. In the forks of the path stand several trees painted by the Indians, in a hieroglyphic manner, denoting the number of wars in which they have been engag'd, and the particulars of their success in prisoners and scalps. The camp No. 8. lies on a run, and level piece of ground, with Yellow-creek close on the left, and a rising ground near the rear of the right face. The path after the army left the forks was so brushy and entangled, that they were obliged to cut all the way before them, and also to lay several bridges, in order to make it passable for the horses; so that this day they proceeded only five miles, three quarters and seventy perches.

Wednesday 10th. Marched one mile with Yellow-creek on the left at a small distance all the way, and crossed it at a good ford fifty feet wide; proceeding thro' an alternate succession of small hills and rich vales, finely watered with rivulets, to camp No. 9. seven miles and sixty perches in the whole.

Thursday 11th. Cross'd a branch of Muskingham river about fifty feet wide, the country much the same as that described above, discovering a good deal of free stone. The camp No. 10. had this branch of the river parallel to its left face, and lies ten miles one quarter and forty perches from the former encampment.

Friday 12th. Keeping the aforesaid creek

on their left, they marched thro' much fine land, watered with small rivers and springs; proceeding likewise thro' several savannah's or cleared spots, which are by nature extremely beautiful; the second which they passed being, in particular, one continued plain of near two miles, with a fine rising ground forming a semicircle round the right hand side, and a pleasant stream of water at about a quarter of a mile distant on the left. The camp No. 11. has the abovementioned branch of Muskingham on the left, and is distant ten miles and three quarters from the last encampment.

Saturday 13th. Cross'd Nemenshehelas-creek, about fifty feet wide, a little above where it empties itself into the aforesaid branch of Muskingham, having in their way a pleasant prospect over a large plain, for near two miles on the left. A little further, they came to another small river which they cross'd about fifty perches above where it empties into the said branch of Muskingham. Here a high ridge on the right, and the creek close on the left, form a narrow defile about seventy perches long. Passing afterwards over a very rich bottom, they came to the main branch of Muskingham, about seventy yards wide, with a good ford. A little below and above the forks of this river is Tuscarowas, a place exceedingly beautiful by situation, the lands rich on both sides of the river; the country on the northwest side being an entire level plain, upwards of five miles in circumference. From the ruined houses appearing here, the Indians who inhabited the place and are now with the Delawares, are supposed to have had about one hundred and fifty warriors. This camp No 12. is distant eight miles nineteen perches from the former.

Sunday 14th. The army remained in camp; and two men who had been dispatched by Col. Bouquet from Fort-Pitt, with letters for Col. Bradstreet, returned and reported — "That, within a few miles of this place, they had been made prisoners by the Delawares, and carried to one of their towns sixteen miles from hence, where they were kept, till the savages, knowing of the arrival of the army here, set them at liberty, ordering them to acquaint the Colonel that the head men of the Delawares and Shawanese were coming as soon as possible to treat of peace with him."

Monday 15th. The army moved two miles forty perches further down the Muskingham to camp No. 13, situated on a very high bank, with the river at the foot of it, which is upwards of 100 yards wide at this place, with a fine level country at some distance from its banks, producing stately timber, free from underwood, and plenty of food for cattle.

The day following, six Indians came to inform the Colonel that all their chiefs were assembled about eight miles from the camp, and were ready to treat with him of peace, which they were earnestly desirous of obtaining. He returned for answer that he would meet them the next day in a bower at some distance from the camp. In the meantime, he ordered a small stockaded fort to be built to deposit provisions for the use of the troops on their return; and to lighten the convoy.

As several large bodies of Indians were now within a few miles of the camp, whose former instances of treachery, altho' they now declared they came for peace, made it prudent to trust nothing to their intentions, the strictest orders were repeated to prevent a surprise.

Wednesday 17th. The Colonel, with most of the regular troops, Virginia volunteers and light horse, marched from the camp to the bower erected for the congress. And soon after the troops were stationed, so as to appear to the best advantage, the Indians arrived, and were conducted to the bower. Being seated, they began, in a short time to smoak their pipe or calumet, agreable to their custom. This ceremony being over, their speakers laid down their pipes, and opened their pouches, wherein were strings and belts of wampum. The Indians present were,

Senecas — Kiyashuta, chief with 15 warriors.

Delawares — Custaloga, chief of the Wolfe-tribe,

Beaver, chief of the Turky-tribe, with 20 warriors.

Shawanese — Keissinautchtha, a chief, and 6 warriors.

Kiyashuta, Turtle-Heart, Custaloga and

Beaver, were the speakers.

The general substance of what they had to offer, consisted in excuses for their late treachery and misconduct, throwing the blame on the rashness of their young men and the nations living to the westward of them, suing for peace in the most abject manner, and promising severally to deliver up all their prisoners. After they had concluded, the Colonel promised to give them an answer the next day, and then dismissed them, the army returning to the camp — The badness of the weather, however, prevented his meeting them again till the 20th, when he spoke to them in substance as follows, viz.

"That their pretences to palliate their guilt by throwing the blame on the western nations, and the rashness of their young men were weak and frivolous, as it was in our power to have protected them against all these nations, if they had sollicited our assistance, and that it was their own duty to have chastised their young men when they did wrong and not to suffer themselves to be directed by them."

He recapitulated to them many instances of their former perfidy — "their killing or captivating the traders who had been sent among them at their own request, and plundering their effects; — their attacking Fort Pitt, which had been built with their express consent; their murdering four men that had been sent on a public message to them, thereby violating the customs held sacred among all nations, however barbarous; — their attacking the king's troops last year in the woods, and after being defeated in that attempt, falling upon our frontiers, where they had continued to murder our people to this day, &c."—

He told them how treacherously they had violated even their late engagements with Col. Bradstreet, to whom they had promised to deliver up their prisoners by the 10th of September last, and to recall all their warriors from the frontiers, which thay had been so far from complying with, that the prisoners still remained in their custody, and some of their people were even now continuing their depredations; adding that these things which, he had mentioned, were only "a small part of their numberless murders and breaches of faith; and that their conduct had always been equally perfidious. — You have, said he, promised at every former treaty, as you do now, that you would deliver up all your prisoners, and have received every time, on that account, considerable presents, but have never complied with that or any other engagement. I am now to tell you, therefore, that we will be no longer imposed upon by your promises. This army shall not leave your country till you have fully complied with every condition that is to precede my treaty with you."

"I have brought with me the relations of the people you have massacred, or taken prisoners. They are impatient for revenge; and it is with great difficulty that I can protect you against their just resentment, which is only restrained by the assurances given them, that no peace shall ever be concluded till you have given us full satisfaction."—

"Your former allies, the Ottawas, Chipwas, Wyandots, and others, have made their peace with us. The Six Nations have joined us against you. We now surround you, having possession of all the waters of the Ohio, the Mississippi, the Miamis, and the lakes. All the French living in those parts are now subjects to the king of Great-Britain, and dare no longer assist you. It is therefore in our power totally to extirpate you from being a people — But the English are a merciful and generous nation, averse to shed the blood, even of their most cruel enemies; and if it was possible that you could convince us, that you sincerely repent of your past perfidy, and that we could depend on your good behaviour for the future, you might yet hope for mercy and peace — If I find that you faithfully execute the following preliminary conditions, I will not treat you with the severity you deserve."

"I give you twelve days from this date to deliver into my hands at Wakatamake all the prisoners in your possession, without any exception; Englishmen, Frenchmen, women and children; whether adopted in your tribes, married, or living amongst you under any denomination and pretence whatsoever; together with all negroes. And you are to furnish the said prisoners with cloathing, provisions, and horses, to carry them to Fort Pitt."

"When you have fully complied with these conditions, you shall then know on what terms you may obtain the peace you sue for."

This speech made an impression on the

minds of the savages, which, it is hoped, will not soon be eradicated. The firm and determined spirit with which the Colonel delivered himself, their consciousness of the aggravated injuries they had done us, and the view of the same commander and army that had so severly chastised them at Bushy-Run the preceeding year, now advanced into the very heart of their remote settlements, after penetrating thro' wildernesses which they had deemed impassible by regular troops — all these things contributed to bend the haughty temper of the savages to the lowest degree of abasement; so that even their speeches seem to exhibit but few specimens of that strong and ferocious eloquence, which their inflexible spirit of independency has on former occasions inspired. And tho' it is not to be doubted, if an opportunity had offered, but they would have fallen upon our army with their usual fierceness, yet when they saw the vigilance and spirit of our troops were such, that they could neither be attacked nor surprized with any prospect of success, their spirits seemed to revolt from the one extreme of insolent boldness, to the other of abject timidity. And happy will it be for them and for us, if the instances of our humanity and mercy, which they experienced in that critical situation, shall make as lasting impressions on their savage dispositions, as it is believed the instances of our bravery and power have done; so that they may come to unite, with their fear of the latter, a love of the former; and have their minds gradually opened, by such examples, to the mild dictates of peace and civility.

The reader, it is to be hoped, will readily excuse this digression if it should be thought one. I now resume our narrative. The two Delaware chiefs, at the close of their speech on the 17th delivered 18 white prisoners, and 83 small sticks, expressing the number of other prisoners which they had in their possession, and promised to bring in as soon as possible. None of the Shawanese kings appeared at the congress, and Keissinautchtha their deputy declined speaking until the Colonel had answered the Delawares, and then with a dejected sullenness he promised, in behalf of his nation, that they would submit to the terms prescribed to the other tribes.

The Colonel, however, determined to march farther into their country, knowing that the presence of his army would be the best

security for the performance of their promises and required some of each nation to attend him in his march.

Kiyashuta addressed the several nations, before their departure, "desiring them to be strong in complying with their engagements, that they might wipe away the reproach of their former breach of faith, and convince their brothers the English that they could speak the truth; adding that he would conduct the army to the place appointed for receiving the prisoners."

Monday October 22d. The army attended by the Indian deputies, marched nine miles to camp No. 14. crossing Margaret's creek about fifty feet wide — The day following, they proceeded sixteen miles one quarter and seventy seven perches farther to camp No 15. and halted there one day.

Thursday 25. They marched six miles, one half and sixteen perches to camp No. 16, situated within a mile of the Forks of Muskingham; and this place was fixed upon instead of Wakautamike, as the most central and convenient place to receive the prisoners; for the principal Indian towns now lay round them, distant from seven to twenty miles; excepting only the lower Shawanese town situated on Scioto river, which was about eighty miles; so that from this place the army had it in their power to awe all the enemy's settlements and destroy their towns, if they should not punctually fulfil the engagements they had entered into. — Four redoubts were built here opposite to the four angles of the camp; the ground in the front was cleared, a store-house for the provisions erected, and likewise a house to receive, and treat of peace with, the Indians, when they should return.

On Saturday 27th. A messenger arrived from king Custaloga, informing that he was on his way with his prisoners, and also a messenger from the lower Shawanese towns of the like import. The Colonel however, having reason to suspect the latter nation of backwardness, sent one of their own people, desiring them — "to be punctual as to the time fixed; to provide a sufficient quantity of provisions to subsist the prisoners; to bring the letters wrote to him last winter by the French commandant at Fort Chartres, which some of their people had stopp'd ever since;" adding that, "as their nation had expressed some uneasiness at our not shaking hands with them, they were to know that the English never took their enemies by the hand, before peace was finally concluded."

The day following, the Shawanese messenger returned, saying that when he had proceeded as far as Wakautamike, the chief of that town undertook to proceed with the message himself, and desired the other to return and acquaint the English that all his prisoners were ready, and he was going to the lower towns to hasten theirs.

October 28th. Peter the Caughnawaga chief, and 20 Indians of that nation arrived from Sanduski, with a letter from Colonel Bradstreet, in answer to one which Colonel Bouquet had sent to him from Fort-Pitt, by two of the Indians who first spoke to him in favour of the Shawanese, as hath been already mentioned. The substance of Colonel Bradstreet's letter was "that he had settled nothing with the Shawanese and Delawares, nor received any prisoners from them.— That he had acquainted all the Indian nations, as far as the Illinois, the bay &c. with the instructions he had received from General Gage, respecting the peace he had lately made; that he had been in Sanduski-lake and up the river, as far as navigable for Indian canoes, for near a month; but that he found it impossible to stay longer in these parts; absolute necessity obliging him to turn off the other way, &c."

Col. Bradstreet, without doubt, did all which circumstances would permit, in his department; but his not being able to remain at Sanduski agreeable to the original plan, till matters were finally settled with the Ohio Indians, would have been an unfavourable incident, if Colonel Bouquet had not now had the chiefs of sundry tribes with him, and was so far advanced into the Indian country, that they thought it adviseable to submit to the conditions imposed upon them.

The Caughnawagas reported that the Indians on the lakes had delivered but few of their prisoners; that the Ottawas had killed a great part of theirs, and the other nations had either done the same, or else kept them.

From this time to November 9th, was chiefly spent in sending and receiving messages to and from the Indian towns, relative to the prisoners, who were now coming into the camp one day after another in small parties, as the different nations arrived in whose possession they had been. The Colonel kept so steadfastly to this article of having every prisoner delivered, that when the Delaware kings, Beaver and Custaloga had brought in all their's except twelve which they promised to bring in a few days, he refused to shake hands or have the least talk with them, while a single captive remained among them.

By the 9th of November, most of the prisoners were arrived that could be expected this season, amounting to 206 in the whole; besides about 100 more in possession of the Shawanese, which they promised to deliver the following spring. Mr. Smallman, formerly a Major in the Pennsylvania troops, who had been taken last summer near Detroit by the Wyandots, and delivered to the Shawanese, was among the number of those whom they now brought in, and informed the Colonel that the reason of their not bringing the remainder of their prisoners, was that many of their principal men, to whom they belonged, were gone to trade with the French, and would not return for six weeks; but that every one of their nation who were at home, had either brought or sent theirs. He further said that, on the army's first coming into the country, it had been reported among the Shawanese that our intention was to destroy them all on which they had resolved to kill their prisoners and fight us; that a French trader who was with them, and had many barrels of powder and ball, made them a present of the whole, as soon as they had come to this resolution; but that, happily for the poor captives, just as the Shawanese were preparing to execute this tragedy, they received the Colonel's message, informing them that his intentions were only to receive the prisoners and to make peace with them on the same terms he should give to the Delawares.

On this intelligence they suspended their cruel purpose, and began to collect as many of the prisoners as they had power to deliver; but hearing immediately afterwards that one of our soldiers had been killed near the camp at Muskingham, and that some of their nation were suspected as guilty of the murder, they again imagined they would fall under our resentment, and therefore determined once more to stand out against us. For which purpose, after having brought their prisoners as far as Wakautamike, where they heard this news, they collected them all into a field, and were going to kill them, when a second express providentially arrived from Col. Bouquet, who assured them that their nation was not even suspected of having any concern in the aforesaid murder; upon which they proceeded to the camp to deliver up the captives, who had thus twice so narrowly escaped becoming the victims of their barbarity.

On Friday, November 9th, the Colonel attended by most of the principal officers, went to the conference-house. The Senecas and Delawares were first treated with. Kiyashuta and 10 warriors represented the former. Custaloga and 20 warriors the latter.

Kiyashuta spoke — "With this string of wampum, we wipe the tears from your eyes — we deliver you these 3 prisoners, which are the last of your flesh and blood that remained among the Senecas and Custaloga's tribe of Delawares — we gather together and bury with this belt all the bones of the people that have been killed during this unhappy war, which the Evil Spirit occasioned among us. We cover the bones that have been buried, that they may be never more remembered — We again cover their place with leaves that it may be no more seen. — As we have been long astray, and the path between you and us stopped, we extend this belt that it may be again cleared, and we may travel in peace to see our brethren as our ancestors formerly did."

"While you hold it fast by one end and we by the other, we shall always be able to discover any thing that may disturb our friendship."—

The Colonel answered that "he had heard them with pleasure; that he received these 3 last prisoners they had to deliver, and joined in burying the bones of those who had fallen in the war, so that their place might be no more known. The peace you ask for, you shall now have. The king, my master and your father has appointed me only to make war; but he has other servants who are employed in the work of peace. Sir William Johnson is empowered for that purpose. To him you are to apply; but before I give you leave to go, two things are to be settled."

1. "As peace cannot be finally concluded here, you will deliver me two hostages for the Senecas, and two for Custaloga's tribe, to remain in our hands at Fort Pitt, as a security, that you

shall commit no further hostilities or violence against any of his majesty's subjects; and when the peace is concluded these hostages shall be delivered safe back to you."

2. "The deputies you are to send to Sir William Johnson, must be fully empowered to treat for your tribes, and you shall engage to abide by whatever they stipulate. In that treaty, every thing concerning trade and other matters will be settled by Sir William, to render the peace everlasting; and the deputies you are to send to him, as well as the hostages to be delivered to me, are to be named and presented to me for my approbation."—

The Colonel, after promising to deliver back two of their people, Capt. Pipe, and Capt. John, whom he had detained at Fort-Pitt, took the chiefs by the hand for the first time, which gave them great joy.

The next conference was on November 10th, with the Turkey and Turtle tribes of Delawares, King Beaver their chief and 30 warriors representing the former; and Kelappama brother to their chief with 25 warriors the latter.

The Senecas and Custaloga's tribe of Delawares were also present. Their speech and the answer given, were much the same as above; excepting that the Colonel insisted on their delivering up an Englishman, who had murdered one of our people on the frontiers and brought the scalp to them; and that they should appoint the same number of deputies and deliver the same number of hostages, for each of their tribes as had been stipulated for Custaloga's tribe.

November 11. King Beaver presented six hostages to remain with Col. Bouquet, and five deputies to treat with Sir William Johnson, who were approved of. This day he acquainted the chiefs present that as he had great reason to be dissatisfied with the conduct of Nettowhatways, the chief of the Turtle tribe who had not appeared, he therefore deposed him; and that tribe were to chuse and present another for his approbation. This they did a few days afterwards — Smile not reader at this transaction; for tho' it may not be attended with so many splendid and flattering circumstances to a commander, as the deposing an East Indian Nabob or chief; yet to penetrate into the wildernesses where those stern West Indian Chieftains hold their sway, and to frown them from their throne, tho' but composed of the unhewn log, will be found to require both resolution and firmness; and their submitting to it clearly shews to what degree of humiliation they were reduced.

But to proceed. The Shawnese still remained to be treated with, and tho' this nation saw themselves under the necessity of yielding to the same conditions with the other tribes, yet there had appeared a dilatoriness and sullen haughtiness in all their conduct, which rendered it very suspicious.

The 12th of November was appointed for the conference with them; which was managed on their part by Keissinautchtha and Nimwha their chiefs, with the Red Hawke, Lavissimo, Bensivasica, Eweecunwee, Keigleighque, and 40 warriors; the Caughnawaga, Seneca and Delaware chiefs, with about 60 warriors, being also present.

The Red Hawke was their speaker, and as he delivered himself with a strange mixture of fierce pride, and humble submission, I shall add a passage or two from his speech.

"Brother, You will listen to us your younger brothers; and as we discover something in your eyes that looks dissatisfaction with us, we now wipe away every thing bad between us that you may clearly see — You have heard many bad stories of us — We clean your ears that you may hear — We remove every thing bad from your heart, that it may be like the heart of your ancestors, when they thought of nothing but good." [Here he gave a string.]

"Brother; when we saw you coming this road, you advanced towards us with a Tomahawk in your hand; but we your younger brothers take it out of your hands and throw it up to God to dispose of as he pleases; by which means we hope never to see it more. And now brother, we beg leave that you who are a warrior, will take hold of this chain (giving a string) of friendship, and receive it from us, who are also warriors, and let us think no more of war, in pity to our old men, women and children" — intimating, by this last expression, that it was mere compassion to them, and not inability to fight, that made their nation desire peace.

He then produced a treaty held with the government of Pennsylvania 1701, and three messages or letters from that government of different dates; and concluded thus.—

"Now Brother, I beg We who are warriors may forget our disputes, and renew the friendship which appears by these papers to have subsisted between our fathers." — He promised, in behalf of the rest of their nation, who were gone to a great distance to hunt, and could not have notice to attend the treaty, that they should certainly come to Fort-Pitt in the spring, and bring the remainder of the prisoners with them.

As the season was far advanced, and the Colonel could not stay long in these remote parts, he was obliged to rest satisfied with the prisoners the Shawanese had brought taking hostages, and laying them under the strongest obligations, for the delivery of the rest; knowing that no other effectual method could at present be pursued.

He expostulated with them on account of their past conduct, and told them — "that the speech they had delivered would have been agreeable to him, if their actions had corresponded with their words. You have spoken, said he, much of peace, but have neglected to comply with the only condition, upon which you can obtain it. Keissinautchtha, one of your chiefs, met me a month ago at Tuscarawas, and accepted the same terms of peace for your nation, that were prescribed to the Senecas and Delawares; promising in ten days from that time to meet me here with all your prisoners — After waiting for you till now, you are come at last, only with a part of them, and propose putting off the delivery of the rest till the spring — What right have you to expect different terms from those granted to the Delawares &c. who have give me entire satisfaction by their ready subission to everything required of them? — But I will cut this matter short with you; and before I explain myself further, I insist on your immediate answer to the following questions."—

1st. "Will you forthwith collect and deliver up all the prisoners yet in your possession, and the French living among you, with all the Negroes you have taken from us in this or any other war; and that without any exception or evasion whatsoever?"

2d. "Will you deliver six hostages into my hands as a security for your punctual performance of the above article, and that your nations shall commit no farther hostilities against the persons or property of his majesty's subjects?"

Benevissico replyed that "they agreed to give the hostages required, and said that he himself would immediately return to their lower towns and collect all our flesh and blood that remained among them, and that we should see them at Fort-Pitt as soon as possible. — That, as to the French, they had no power over them. They were subjects to the king of England. We might do with them what we pleased tho' he believed they were all returned before this time to their own country"—

They then delivered their hostages, and the Colonel told them "that tho' he had brought a Tomahawk in his hand, yet as they had now submitted, he would not let it fall on their heads, but let it drop to the ground, no more to be seen. He exhorted them to exercise kindness to the captives, and look upon them now as brothers and no longer prisoners; adding that he intended to send some of their relations along; with the Indians, to see their friends collected and brought to Fort-Pitt. He promised to give them letters to Sir William Johnson, to facilitate a final peace, and desired them to be strong in performing every thing stipulated."

The Caughnawagas, the Delawares and Senecas, severally addressed the Shawanese, as grandchildren and nephews, "to perform their promises, and to be strong in doing good, that this peace might be everlasting."—

And here I am to enter on a scene, reserved on purpose for this place, that the thread of the foregoing narrative might not be interrupted — a scene, which language indeed can but weakly describe; and to which the Poet or Painter might have repaired to enrich their highest colorings of the variety of human passions; the Philosopher to find ample subject for his most serious reflections; and the Man to exercise all the tender and sympathetic feelings of the soul.

The scene, I mean, was the arrival of the prisoners in the camp where were to be seen fathers and mothers recognizing and clasping their once-lost babes; husbands hanging round the necks of their newly-recovered wives; sisters and brothers unexpectedly meeting together after long separation, scarce able to speak the same language, or, for some time, to be sure that they were children of the same parents. In all these interviews, joy and rapture inexpressible were seen, while feelings of a very different nature were painted in the looks of others; — flying from place to place in eager enquiries after relatives not found! trembling to receive an answer to their questions! distracted with doubts, hopes and fears, on obtaining no account of those they sought for! or stiffened into living horror and woe, on learning their unhappy fate!

The Indians too, as if wholly forgetting their usual savageness, bore a capital part in heightning this most affecting scene. They delivered up their beloved captives with the utmost reluctance; shed torrents of tears over them, recommending them to the care and protection of the commanding officer. Their regard to them continued all the time they remained in camp. They visited them from day to day; and brought them what corn, skins, horses and other matters, they had bestowed on them, while in their families; accompanied with other presents, and all the marks of the most sincere and tender affection. Nay, they did not stop here, but, when the army marched, some of the Indians sollicited and obtained leave to accompany their former captives all the way to Fort-Pitt, and employed themselves in hunting and bringing provisions for them on the road. A young Mingo carried this still further, and gave an instance of love which would make a figure even in romance. A young woman of Virginia was among the captives, to whom he had form'd so strong an attachment, as to call her his wife. Against all remonstrances of the imminent danger to which he exposed himself by approaching to the frontiers, he persisted in following her, at the risk of being killed by the surviving relations of many unfortunate persons, who had been captivated or scalped by those of his nation.

Those qualities in savages challenge our just esteem. They should make us charitably consider their barbarities as the effects of wrong education, and false notions of bravery and heroism while we should look on their virtues as sure marks that nature has made them fit subjects of cultivation as well as us; and that we are called by our superior advantages to yield them all the helps we can in this way. Cruel and unmerciful as they are, by habit and long example, in war, yet whenever they come to give way to the native dictates of humanity, they exercise virtues which Christians need not blush to imitate.

When they once determine to give life, they give every thing with it, which in their apprehension, belongs to it. From every enquiry that has been made, it appears — that no woman thus saved is preserved from base motives, or need fear the violation of her honor. No child is otherwise treated by the persons accepting it than the children of their own body. The perpetual slavery of those captivated in war, is a notion which even their barbarity has not yet suggested to them. Every captive whom their affection, their caprice, or whatever else, leads them to save, is soon incorporated with them, and fares alike with themselves.

These instances of Indian tenderness and humanity were thought worthy of particular notice. The like instances among our own people will not seem strange; and therefore I shall only mention one, out of a multitude that might be given on this occasion.

Among the captives a woman was brought in to the camp at Muskingham, with a babe about three months old at her breast. One of the Virginia-volunteers soon knew her to be his wife, who had been taken by the Indians about six months before. She was immediately delivered to her overjoyed husband. He flew with her to his tent, and cloathed her and his child in proper apparel. But their joy, after the first transports, was soon damped by the reflection that another dear child of about two years old, captivated with the mother, and separated from her, was still missing, although many children had been brought in.

A few days afterwards, a number of other prisoners were brought to the camp, among whom were several more children. The woman was sent for, and one, supposed to be hers, was produced to her. At first sight she was uncertain, but viewing the child with great earnestness she soon recollected its features and was so overcome with joy, that literally forgetting her sucking child she dropt it from her arms, and catching up the new found child in an extasy, pressed it to her breast, and bursting into tears carried it off, unable to speak for joy. The father seizing up the babe she had let fall, followed her in no less transport and affection.

Among the children who had been carried off young, and had long lived with the Indians, it is not to be expected that any marks of joy would appear on being restored to their parents or relatives. Having been accustomed to look upon the Indians as the only connexions they had, having been tenderly treated by them, and speaking their language, it is no wonder that they considered their new state in the light of a captivity, and parted from the savages with tears.

But it must not be denied that there were even some grown persons who shewed an unwillingness to return. The Shawanese were obliged to bind several of their prisoners and force them along to the camp; and some women, who had been delivered up, afterwards found means to escape and run back to the Indian towns. Some, who could not make their escape, clung to their savage acquaintance at parting, and continued many days in bitter lamentations, even refusing sustenance.

For the honor of humanity, we would suppose those persons to have been of the lowest rank, either bred up in ignorance and distressing penury, or who had lived so long with the Indians as to forget all their former connexions. For, easy and unconstrained as the savage life is, certainly it could never be put in competition with the blessings of improved life and the light of religion, by any persons who have had the happiness of enjoying, and the capacity of discerning, them.

Every thing being now settled with the Indians, the army decamped on Sunday 18th November, and marched for Fort-Pitt, where it arrived on the 28th. The regular troops were immediately sent to garrison the different posts on the communication, and the provincial troops, with the captives, to their several provinces. Here ended this expedition, in which it is remarkable that, notwithstanding the many difficulties attending it, the troops were never in want of any necessaries; continuing perfectly healthy during the whole campaign; in which no life was lost, except the man mentioned to have been killed at Muskingham.

Source: Smith, *An Historical Account of the Expedition...*, pp. 5–29

Note

The above account of Bouquet's Expedition does not state the name of the successor to Netawatwees, the Chief of the Turtle Tribe who was "deposed" by Bouquet. *The Papers of Sir William Johnson,* Volume XI, enable us to learn who the Delawares chose, however.

On page 460, at a private meeting with the Chiefs of the Delawares, Bouquet stated "The Chief of the *Turtle Tribe* having given me great Reason to be dissatisfied with his Conduct, I Depose him: from this Moment he is no more Chief, The Tribe is therefore to chuse another Chief, and present him to me.—I shall Confirm him, and he shall be King of the Turtle Tribe, and acknowledged as such by the English."

On page 467, the following entry appears in the journal, "Novem^r. 16th.—The Turtle Tribe of the Delawares presented to Col. Bouquet *Tatpiskahoung* the new Chief they had chosen in the room of Nellohaways deposed, & he was confirmed by the Colonel—"

The next year, at a conference held at Johnson Hall in New York as set forth in *Documents relative to the Colonial History of the State of New York,* Volume VII, at page 731, Killbuck, referred to as "the Delaware Chief", spoke as follows, "Brother, I have been sent here as a Deputy from our Chiefs *Costeloga, King Beaver* and Teatapercaum alias Samuel on behalf of all our Nation,..."

It therefore appears that the successor to Netawatwees, at least for a short time, was the *Tepiss-cow-a-hang* of the *Charles Beatty* journal of 1766. I say "for a short time" because when *Beatty* visited Newcomerstown in 1766, he says nothing about *Tepiss-cow-a-hang* being Chief, but rather refers to the Chief as being called *Netat-whel-man*, obviously meaning Netawatwees.

That the Teatapercaum alias Samuel referred to above is the same as the Tepiss-cow-a-hang of the *Beatty* journal appears to be confirmed by the entry of September 21st, in which *Beatty* refers to him as "Samuel, otherwise Tepiss-cow-a-hang".

Query? Could Netawatwees and Tepiss-cow-a-hang have been brothers? Successors to Chiefs are supposed to be either brothers or nephews, or at least in the maternal bloodline in some way.

BOUQUET, HENRY (1719–Sept. 2, 1765), British officer, was born of a good French Protestant family at Rolle, Canton Vaud, Switzerland. In 1736 he entered the service of the States General of Holland as a cadet in the regiment of Constant, and two years later was commissioned as lieutenant. During the war of the Austrian Succession he served the King of Sardinia, and displayed such coolness and resourcefulness in action that the Prince of Orange engaged him as captain-commandant, with the rank of lieutenant-colonel, in a newly-formed regiment of Swiss Guards. In 1748 he accompanied the officers who received from the French the evacuated forts in the Low Countries, and shortly after traveled through France and Italy with Lord Middleton, from whom he acquired the foundations of his excellent knowledge of English, which he wrote with grace and precision. On his return he devoted himself to a thorough study of his chosen profession of arms, especially in the mathematical branches, and throughout his career contined to enjoy scientific discussion.

In the fall of 1755 James Prevost, supported by the urging of Joseph Yorke, British minister at The Hague, succeeded in gaining Bouquet's consent to take the lieutenant-colonelcy of the first battalion in the newly-planned Royal American Regiment (later the King's Royal Rifle Corps), and in the spring of 1756 Bouquet left for North America, where he contributed to the remarkable recruiting success the regiment enjoyed in 1756 among the Germans of Pennsylvania, and had his first experiences of the unwarlike but obstinate temper of the Quakers, which he never ceased to impugn. The center of the quartering dispute in Philadelphia in the winter of 1756, he met greater resistance in quartering regulars in 1757 in Charleston, S. C., where he commanded a small force of provincials, Royal Americans, and, later, Montgomery's Highlanders. This was the only independent command assigned him by a commander-in-chief during the war.

Promoted to be colonel in America only in January 1758, he served as second under Brigadier John Forbes in the weary expedition against Fort Duquesne, and his rare patience and tact were largely responsible for overcoming the delays of provincials and the uncertainties of transportation, for building new forts, and for cutting through western Pennsylvania the great highway known as "Forbes's Road," which resulted in the evacuation of

Fort Duquesne by the French. His foreign birth prevented Amherst from giving him the command in the west at Forbe's death (*Northcliffe Collection*, Ottawa, 1926, p. 114), and he served for the remainder of the war under Stanwix and Monckton, occupied chiefly in the supervision and strengthening of the western forts, Pitt, Venango, and Presqu'isle. He was commissioned colonel by brevet in 1762, and was naturalized by Maryland and by the Supreme Court of Pennsylvania. Neither the attractions of domestic life upon his estate at Long Meadow, Md., nor the importunities of his many warm American friends could lure him from the army during the war (*Pennsylvania Magazine of History and Biography*, III, 121-143), and leave of absence was denied him in 1761. He continued, therefore, to exploit to the full his long experience on the frontier, by adapting the discipline of European armies to the exigencies of wilderness warfare, and by drilling his own first battalion in the principles of open-order combat and extreme mobility of action.

In Pontiac's conspiracy he proved the worth of his methods. In 1763 he marched a small army of Royal Americans and Highlanders towards Fort Pitt, and at Edgehill, within a short distance of Braddock's fatal field, repulsed a considerable number of Delawares and Shawnees. The following day, Aug. 6, the Indians again attacked at Bushy Run, and Bouquet, drawing up his troops in circle to protect his convoy, lured them from cover by the feigned retreat of one segment, and crushed them by a bayonet charge when they rushed into the gap. Henceforth the Indians respected him, perceiving, as not many contemporaries did, that he was the most brilliant leader of light infantry the war produced, and incomparably in advance of the military practise of the day. The following year he commanded the southern of the two expeditions sent to pacify the Indians, led a small force of provincials and regulars to the forks of the Muskingum, and, by an admirable mixture of firmness and justice, forced the surrender of all prisoners in Indian hands and concluded a general peace. Publicly thanked by the king in general orders, and by the assemblies of the southern provinces, he received the unexpected rank of brigadier in 1765, and the command of the southern district. At Pensacola, the same year, fever carried him away prematurely.

Source: *Dictionary of American Biography*

Map 5

Forks of the Muskingum – 1764

This is a portion of the map made by Ens. Thomas Hutchins, showing the route of Bouquet's Expedition to the Forks of the Muskingum in 1764.

In addition to showing the names of some of the Indian towns in the vicinity of the Forks, it is of interest in showing the location of an "Old Wyandots Town". This would be the Muskingum of *Gist*, and the Conchake of *DeLery*. Since the survey point of the 16th Encampment was within about three miles of the Forks, the town was somewhat closer to the junction. It was to the west of a line drawn between the hill and the river at their closest points. This location can be compared with the modern topographic map [Map 13b] to approximately locate the town site.

It also shows that Newcomerstown was at its present site as early as 1764.

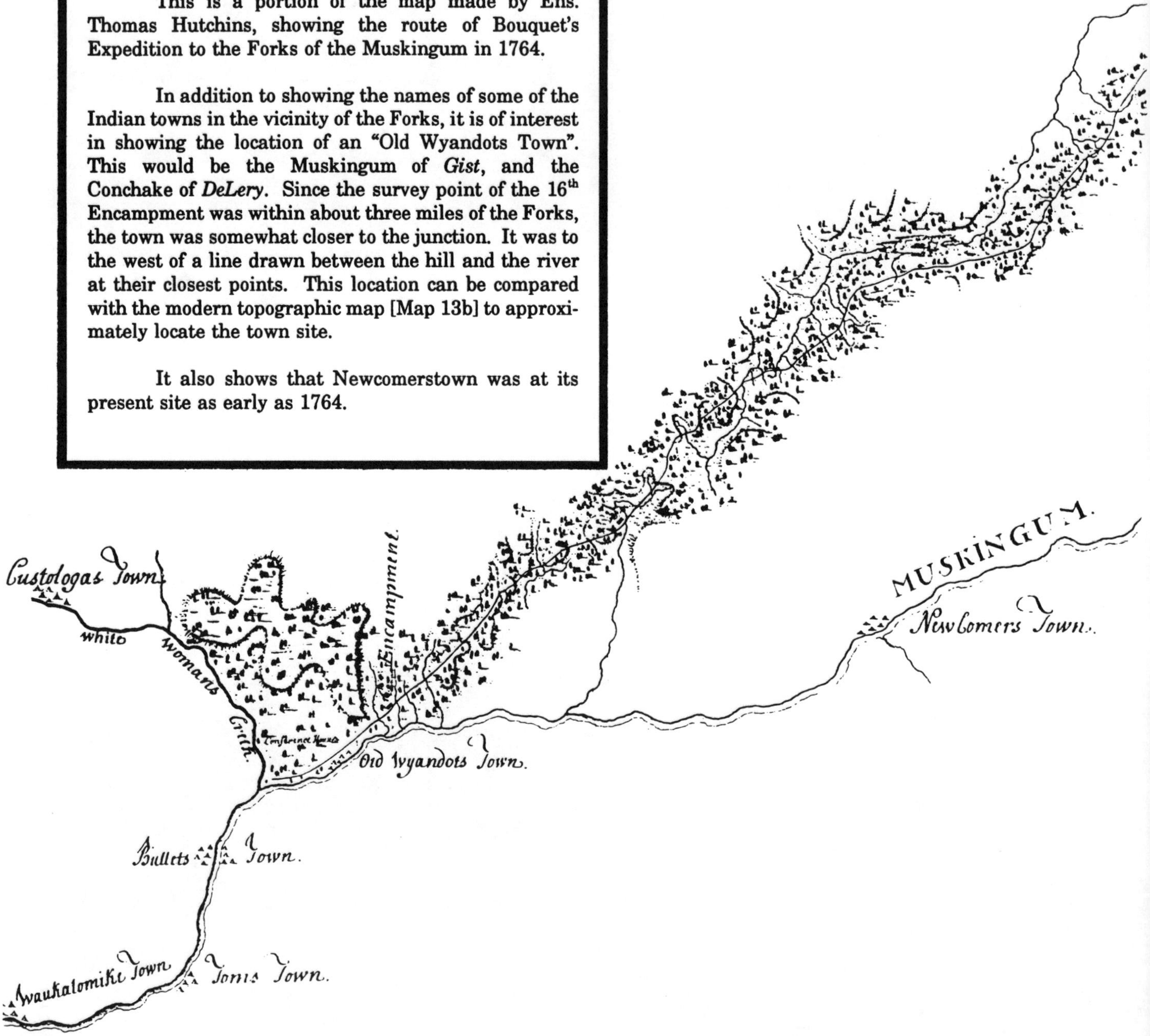

Custologas Town

white

womans Crek

Encampment

MUSKINGUM.

NewComers Town.

Old Wyandots Town.

Bullets Town.

Waukalomike Town.

Tonis Town.

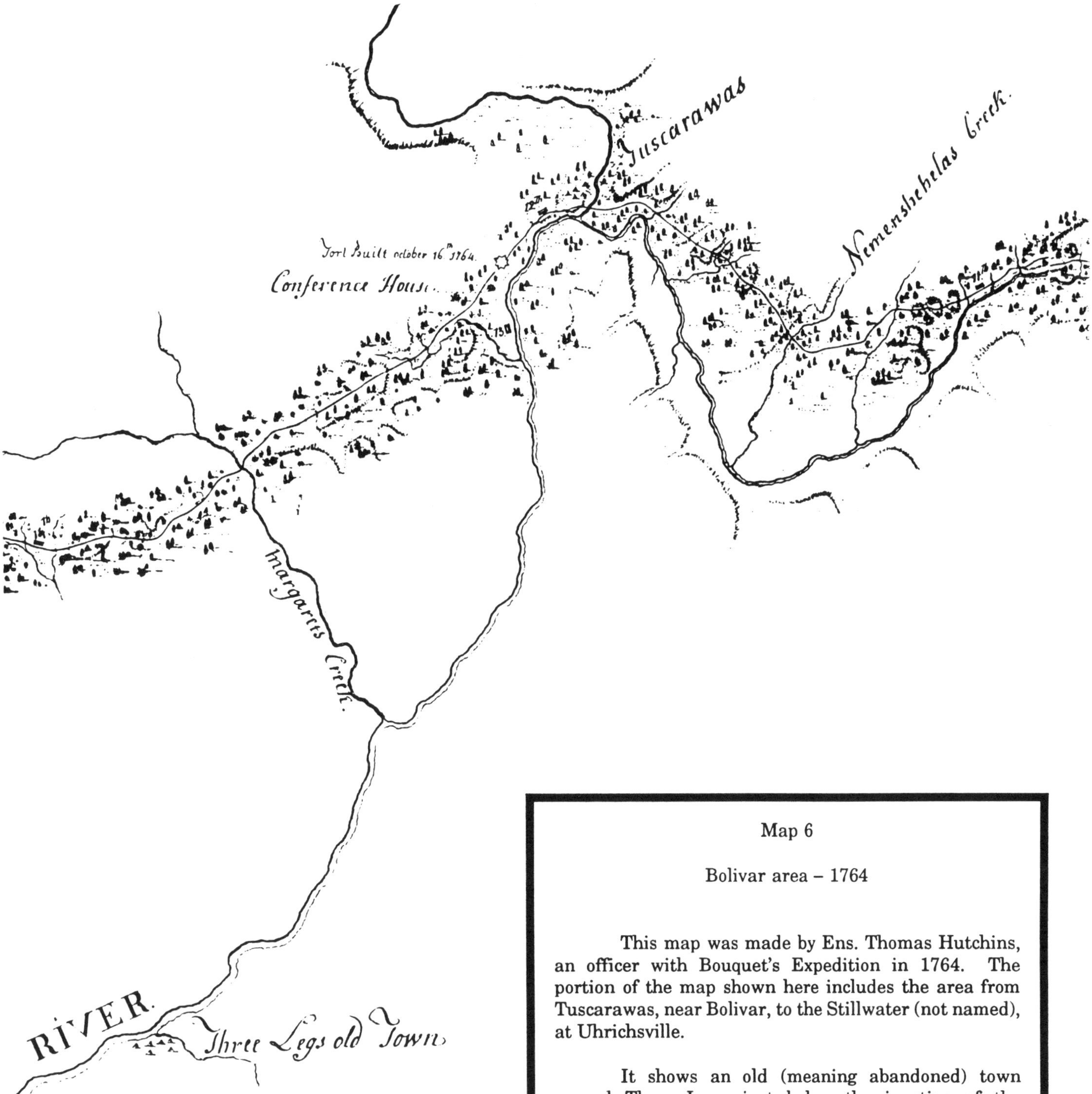

Tuscarawas

Nemenshehelas Creek.

Fort Built october 16ᵗʰ 1764.

Conference House.

Margarets Creek.

RIVER. _Three Legs old Town_

Map 6

Bolivar area – 1764

This map was made by Ens. Thomas Hutchins, an officer with Bouquet's Expedition in 1764. The portion of the map shown here includes the area from Tuscarawas, near Bolivar, to the Stillwater (not named), at Uhrichsville.

It shows an old (meaning abandoned) town named Three Legs, just below the junction of the Stillwater. With respect to the existence of that town, however, see the special article that appears in this book dealing with that subject.

The Margarets Creek shown on the map is now called Sugar Creek.

Charles Beatty

Born: about 1715 Ireland
Died: August 13, 1772 Barbadoes
Age on entering Tuscarawas Valley – 51 years

Charles Beatty
1766

In the fall of 1766 the first of a series of preachers came into the Tuscarawas Valley.

Charles Beatty, in 1756, had been a chaplain with a military expedition led by Benjamin Franklin during the early days of the French and Indian War. The Indians had raided settlements near Bethlehem, Pennsylvania, and Franklin (not a soldier by profession, but a person of much influence in Pennsylvania and then serving as a member of the Assembly) raised a company of volunteers to build some forts for the protection of the inhabitants. The following quotation concerning the chaplain is taken from Franklin's Autobiography, *p. 185:*

> We had for our chaplain a zealous Presbyterian Minister, Mr. Beatty, who complained to me that the men did not generally attend his prayers and exhortations. When they enlisted, they were promised, besides pay and provisions, a gill of rum a day, which was punctually serv'd out to them half in the morning, and the other half in the evening; and I observ'd they were as punctual in attending to receive it; upon which I said to Mr. Beatty, 'It is, perhaps, below the dignity of your profession to act as steward of the rum, but if you were to deal it out and only just after prayers, you would have them all about you.' He liked the tho't, undertook the office, and, with the help of a few hands to measure out the liquor, executed it to satisfaction, and never were prayers more generally and more punctually attended; so that I thought this method preferable to the punishment inflicted by some military laws for non-attendance on divine service.

Beatty also served as chaplain of the First Battalion of the Pennsylvania Regiment on the Forbes Expedition in 1758 that resulted in the capture of Fort DuQuesne.

The George Duffield that accompanied Charles Beatty on his trip to the Ohio country in 1766 later became a chaplain to the Continental Congress during the Revolutionary War and is often mentioned in the letters of John Adams to his wife, Abigail, as well as in the letters of other delegates to the Congress.

The Beatty journal gives us the first really detailed look at Newcomerstown and its people. It also introduces us to Joseph Peepy, a Christian Indian who was to be the interpreter. Joseph Peepy was an elderly man who had attended David Brainerd's Indian school in New Jersey. He was also used as an interpreter by several other preachers who came into the valley. His wife, Hannah, and his daughter-in-law and grandchildren, would die in the Gnadenhutten Massacre in 1782.

August 12th, 1766. {Philadelphia} ...I accordingly set out on my journey, Tuesday the 12th of August, 1766, accompanied with Joseph Peepy, a Christian Indian, who was to serve as an interpreter; and, after traveling 122 miles, we arrived at Carlisle on the 15th instant, where I met Mr. Duffield, who was also appointed to accompany us.

21st. ...After sermon we rode eight miles to Capt. Patersons, where we were kindly received. Here we met with one Levi Hicks, who had been captive with the Indians, from his youth; and we being very desirous to know their present situation and circumstances, he gave us the following relation: {At this point in his original journal he states "that at the Big Beaver Creek about 25 Miles from Fort Pitt there used to be a small Town but now only a tavern is kept by an Indian called white Eyes"}, that about 100 miles westward of Fort Pitt, was an Indian town called Tuskalawas; and at some considerable distance from that was another town named Kighalampegha, where Natatwhelman, the king of the Delawares lived; and from thence, about 10 miles or more, was one called Moghwhiston, i.e., Worm Town, having about 20 houses; that 17 miles thence was another town, named Ogh-hi-taw-mi-kaw, i. e. White-Corn Town; that this was the largest, he supposed in these parts; that about twenty miles farther was a Sha-wa-nagh Town; that there was another at some distance, called Sugh-eha-ungh, that is, the Salt-Lick, of about 20 houses. In this town, he told us, there was an Indian that spoke to the Indians about religion; and 40 miles farther was a town called Migh-chi-laghpiesta, that is, the Big-lick. He told us, that he thought, from some things he observed among the Indians, that they would be desirous of hearing the Gospel. This intelligence, with some other circumstances related to us by an Indian trader, gave us some encouragement to venture out among them.

25th.   Set out from Captain Paterson's this morning, on our journey, accompanied with Joseph the interpreter, and Levi Hicks, mentioned before as being many years a prisoner among the Indians.

Sept. 9th.   Having sought direction of heaven and the divine presence, we resolved to attempt a journey to Kighalampegha, an Indian town about 130 miles from hence. This place we fixed upon because it was most central to the other Indian towns, and because the king of the Delaware nation lived there, whom it was necessary to consult before we attempted anything among his people; and also because we were informed that the Indians there were consulting something about religion. We desired the Indians who were returning home from the fort, where they had been trading, to let their people in their different towns know of our coming and design, and also to meet us at their head town.

We were much engaged this day in preparing for our journey. Mr. Gibson, a trader here, who was taken prisoner last war by the Indians, and was adopted into one of their chief families, and was well respected by them, recommended us to one of the chiefs by a letter, in a string of wampum beads, according to their custom in such cases, and sent by us some wampum as a particular present to one of them.

Mr. Duffield preached in the evening in the town to a considerable congregation, who appeared very attentive. From some things we observed, we have good reason to think our preaching here has not been in vain.

Our interpreter Joseph met with an Indian, who appeared to be a sober man, and expressed great satisfaction and pleasure on hearing of our going out to teach the Indians religion. He told Joseph that the great Spirit above, meaning God, had spoken or told an Indian in his heart last fall, (which is about a year ago) that this summer fall, [sic] two white men (or so they distinguished the English) should come and teaching the Indians religion; and he added, he believed we were the men. — this morning he came to Joseph's lodging, in order to see and, I suppose, to converse further with him. We happening to be there at breakfast, he invited this Indian, who accordingly accepted the invitation. I desired our interpreter, after breakfast, to let him know the meaning of asking a blessing upon our food, and returning thanks for it. He replied, it was very fit that the great Being above should be acknowledged for his goodness to us, and that he and some others did so. — we heard that this man, and about 18 or 19 more Indians, or families, had separated from the rest, and lived in a town by themselves, called Suka Hung, in order to leave a more sober life; and that there they worshiped God, some way or other, as well as they knew how.

18th {10th}. The commanding officer whom we waited upon, being ready to contribute everything in his power to forward our designs, gave us a letter of recommendation, with a string of wampum, to the head man of the Indian Tribes, inviting them likewise to return to their old towns up the Alegh-geny river. After a constant scene of hurry, we got ready and set off about the middle of the afternoon, being accompanied down to the riverside by our good friend Mr. M'Lagan, and several other gentlemen, who have shewn us much kindness, and were greatly assisting to us. We crossed the Alegh-geny river in a canoe, swimming our horses along-side of it. We then proceeded down the river Ohio about five miles, having on our right hand the high hill, and encamped upon the bank of a river about eight or nine o'clock, where we had plenty of herbage for our horses, — the night cloudy and dark.

11th. Set out in the morning, the weather dull and gloomy, and after traveling nine or 10 miles, most part along the riverside, we came to an old Indian town now deserted, called by the traders Log-Town, situated on a fine rich bank, covered with fine grass, commanding a most beautiful prospect up and down the river Ohio.

We halted about noon to let our horses feed, then proceeded to Great Beaver creek about ten miles, which we crossed and made up our fire on the rich high bank on the west side, which afforded our horses exceeding good pasture equal to a meadow. In the night there fell a heavy rain, which wetted us much, notwithstanding all our efforts to screen ourselves.

Here the Indians had once a considerable town, but deserted it the last war, in order to get at a greater distance from the English. — the situation is very pleasant, the land being rich and level for a considerable way up this river, encompassed at a distance by a rising ground, or small hill. A great part of this land that had been cleared, is now grown up again with small brush, or under-wood. The land we passed over yesterday and today, appears in general to be strong and good. The low land on the Ohio, and on the small rivers that empty into it, is very rich, and abounds with walnut timber.

12th. This morning dark and heavy with small rain; — our clothes being wetted last night, made our condition not very comfortable. The clouds after some time beginning to break, we set out, but were advised to travel slow, the road in many places being hilly, and all the way slippery, from the rain that fell last night and today — in the forenoon we had several showers in the hardest of which we endeavored to shelter ourselves under the trees.

After traveling about twelve miles, we came to the second Beaver river which we crossed, and proceeded 6 miles further to the third Beaver river, where we encamped, having but poor food for our horses; however we were advised to put up with it, not being able to reach any better place.

Joseph, our interpreter, who went on before us this morning in order to hunt for us, returned without anything, so that we had poor living for ourselves as well as our horses: However, we had some bread, for which we had reason to be thankful. There fell some rain in the night, but not so much as to wet us through our fence which we had set up at our backs.

13th. The morning cloudy; we set out, but had not traveled far before a heavy shower from the northwest came upon us, from which we sheltered ourselves as well as we could under trees, as there was no thunder. — the weather clearing up after some time, we proceeded, and traveled today as near as we could conjecture, about 16 or 17 miles. We halted upon a rising ground, and kindled up a fire, having a small spring of water on one side and a valley.

14th. Sabbath. We rested and kept the Sabbath as well as we could; and from a supposition that this was the first Sabbath ever kept in this wilderness, we gave the place the name of Sabbath-ridge. It grew very dark and heavy towards evening. A number of Indians that live in Tuskalawa, being on the return from Fort Pitt, where they had been trading, came up to us a little before night, having about a hundred gallons of rum with them. They wondered we did not travel that day — we told them the reason. They encamped by us. Their head man seemed very reserved and distant; — we, however, made ourselves as agreeable to him as we could. We took notice of some of them, particularly those who were sick — we made some tea, and sent it them, and a piece of cheese, (the last we had) with which they were pleased.

Our interpreter conversed with the head man, and some others of them that came to sit a while with us at our fire. A very heavy rain came on in the night, which wetted us, notwithstanding the precaution we had taken to guard against it. The heaviness of the rain drove one of the Indians to take shelter under our fence, to which we made him welcome. Sleeped and waked the night away as well as we could.

15th. The rain continued the forenoon, so that we began to give up hope of being able to travel today.

We visited the Indians who were sick, expecting to find them very bad, as they had been exposed to such a heavy rain; yet, to my surprise, I found a woman who appeared to be the worst last night, sitting up preparing some corn for breakfast, for the family. As they had no meat, two or three of the men went out to hunt in the morning, but returned without killing anything, which was a disappointment to us as well as them, for we expected to have bought some venison of them.

The weather clearing up, about three o'clock in the afternoon, we decamped and set out in company with the Indians. Our interpreter, a little before night, went off from us on one side of the road, to look for a deer, as we wanted

meat; while we proceeded with the Indians, about eight miles further, when we stopt and made up a fire on a branch of Tuskalawa river.

As our interpreter did not come up with us before dark, it gave us some anxiety, lest he should have missed his way, and so have been lost in this vast wilderness, or had met with some unfavorable accident; so that we left caring for the venison, out of greater care for him.

When I was just about lying down, without supper, our interpreter appeared with a young deer on his back to our no small joy. We immediately divided the meat among the Indians who were separated into three parties. We gave to each party a quarter and reserved the other to our own use. This supply came seasonable to them as well as ourselves.

16th. Visited the Indians, our fellow-travellers, this morning; who, after some free conversation about some affairs respecting religion, began to be more open and affable, especially their chief man, whose reservedness and distance hitherto, I understood, was owing to a mistake for he took us to be Moravians; for, whatever influence these people have had hitherto on these savages, yet their conduct (it seems, of late) has been such, as to have given them great umbrage.

As soon as the Indians had got up their horses, we set out in company with them. We crossed several branches, and one river much larger than the rest which were all much swelled by the heavy rains; and, having passed over two or three savannahs, or plains, (some of which are two or three miles broad) we arrived at Tuskalawa town a little before night, having traveled today about twenty miles.

Our fellow traveler, the head man of this town, who was now become very friendly, invited us to tarry at his house. We accepted the favor, and were treated with a great deal of respect by him and his family, in their way. They brought us some green corn in the husk and cucumbers, (the same they themselves lived on) which we thankfully received. — We roasted some of the corn and eat the cucumbers without salt or anything, which would not have been very agreeable at another time. As we had saved a little piece of venison left last night, we made some broth in the evening, and gave part to our host and his family.

17th. Part of the family and some other Indians, being present this morning at worship, we desired our interpreter, after prayer, to explain it, and let them know, particularly, that we had prayed, and would pray to the great Spirit above for them, at which they appeared to be pleased. We took leave of our kind host Apa-ma-legh-on, who sent a young man to bring us seven or eight miles on our way.

In passing through the lower part of this town, we observed Indians drinking, and some drunk, with the rum they had lately brought from Fort Pitt. In these circumstances they generally behave like madmen: It is therefore very dangerous for white people to be with or near them at that time; however we passed by unmolested, and crossed the west branch of Tuskalawa River at the fording place a little below the town where it is about one hundred yards wide.

We traveled about ten miles west, near to a small river called Morgerit {Margaret's} creek; we followed the course of that river, which is near south, about five or six miles, then crossed where it is about fifteen or twenty yards wide. Proceeding about a mile farther, we encamped on the bank of the river Muskingum, which appears to be near one hundred or one hundred and twenty yards broad — this country appears to abound with savannahs or plains, with little or no wood growing on them, and the farther westward the larger they appear to be. We passed over one today, that does not appear to be less than three or four miles in extent.

18th. We set out early this morning, intending, if possible, to reach the Indian town we proposed to visit before night. We traveled therefore without halting, through excessive bad ways; the most part being nothing but swamps or low wet ground, thickets and deep gutters, for eighteen or twenty miles, till we came near the town, our course hitherto being chiefly south, inclining sometimes to the east and sometimes to the west.

We at last came in sight of the town, about three of the clock; ourselves and horses being much fatigued, we were very glad to have reached the place we had so long looked for, and, I trust, thankful to that gracious God who had hitherto preserved and conducted us. We entered the town on one side, and at the first house to which we were providentially directed, lived a widow woman, a near relation of our interpreter's, whom he had not seen for many years nor did he know where she lived. They both seemed very agreeably surprised on seeing each other so unexpectedly, that we could not help looking upon this event as a token for good. The woman very kindly invited us to tarry with her, and we accepted of her kindness. She presently made ready some venison, and baked cakes under the ashes in their way, and set before us, which became very seasonable and acceptable.

As soon as our arrival in town was known, a number of the principal men came to see us, and took us by the hand, to whom our arrival here, so far as we could judge, appeared to be very acceptable.

After some conversation, we opened to them the design of our coming among them, and sent word to Netat-whel-man, the king and head of the Delaware nation, or tribes, that we should be glad to know when we might wait upon him, in order to make him acquainted with our mission, and deliver our message.

We had a little hut assigned us by our land-lady, in which we put our things, and were furnished with some deer-skins, thrown on the floor to sleep on, which was a much better way of lodging than we had hitherto found on our journey.

We understood, that today, about one of the clock, we should have audience of his majesty; we therefore prepared for it as well we could. One of the old Sachems accordingly was sent to inform us, that the king and his council were ready to receive us, and hear what we had to say. — We went accordingly to the council house.

This house is a long bulding, with two fires in it, at a proper distance from each other, without any chimney or partition. The entry into it is by two doors, one at each end. — over the door a turtle was drawn, which is the ensign of their particular tribe. On each door-post was cut out the face of a grave old man, an emblem I suppose of that gravity and wisdom that every senator there ought to be possessed of. On each side the whole length of the house within is a platform, or bed, five feet wide, raised above the floor one foot and a half, made of broad split pieces of wood, which serves equally for a bed on which to sleep, and a place on which to sit down. It is covered with a handsome matt, made of rushes near the end of which the king sat.

As soon as we entered, the king rose from his seat, (which is not usual for him, or any other great men to do, to any person that comes to see them) took us by the hand, and gave thanks to the great Being above, the creator and preserver of all, that we had opportunity of seeing each other in the wilderness and appeared very glad and rejoiced on the occasion. We were then conducted to a seat near his majesty; the council sat some of them near him on the same platform, and others on the opposite side. After sitting a while, according to their custom on the like occasions, I rose up, and delivered our speech, by the interpreter Joseph; then sat down, all being silent for some minutes, and then after some conversation, not at all relating to our speech, we withdrew.

It is an invariable rule with the kings and councils of the Indians, when they receive an address not immediately to return an answer to it, but to take time for mature deliberation, and reserve their reply to some future season.

The substance of what we delivered to the king in council is as follows:

"First, a message from the commanding officer at Fort Pitt, informing them that their fathers, the English, concerned for them, and pitying their state of ignorance, sent now two ministers to ask them, whether they would embrace a Christian religion, that they might see clearly, as we do, and that the evil spirit might not tempt them any more to what is wrong. That he expected they would treat these men sent on such a good errand, well; and send their young men to hunt for them, and bring them back safe to the fort; and that he wished they would put in execution what their agent and he, at the last treaty had invited them to do; namely, to return back to their old towns, and live there, that they might be near their brethren the English, who might more easily send ministers to teach them."

To the above we added, "That in order to explain the matter more fully, and give them an undoubted proof of our sincerity and desire in their welfare, we were further to inform them, that some years ago, our Great Council (for so we called our synod) who met from different provinc-

es once a year to consult about religion had resolved to send to them two men to speak to them about religion: But the war breaking out, stopped the path, and thereby prevented their coming, for which we were very sorry, and therefore prayed earnestly to the great God that the wars so hurtful to them and us might come to an end, and peace again be restored. That now the great God had granted our request.

Our great council, therefore, again at their last meeting thought of their poor brethren the Indians, who were sitting in darkness, and appointed us to come out to our brethren, and to take you by the hand and speak about the things of God; and ask you whether you would be willing to receive the Christian religion, and to have some ministers sent among you, to instruct you in the Gospel, that we might all serve the same great God, and become firmly joined together as one people; that so all anger and strangeness of mind might forever be done away; and that we might be happy together here, and forever happy hereafter; and that if it shall be agreeable to you, our brethren, we should be glad you would return to your old towns, that we mght be near you and so have frequent opportunities of speaking to you of the great things of the Gospel." — We then gave them a string of wampum, according to their custom.

In the evening Tepiss-cow-a-hang, and his sister, both advanced in years, came to our house, who both had formerly been in New Jersey, at the time of the revival of religion among the Indians there, and had received some good impressions under the ministry of Mr. David Brainerd. They went afterwards among the Moravians, and were baptized by some of their teachers; however, for some time past, they seemed to have lost what impressions of religion they had. — They desired us to talk to them about religion which I did some time, by the interpreter, particularly concerning backsliding; and pointed out to them, in the plainest manner I could, how they should come to God again through the Lord Jesus Christ. I then prayed with them. They were both very much affected and took leave of us very affectionately, with tears running down their cheeks.

20th. Five of the principal men came to our hut, about two o'clock in the afternoon: And, after sitting a while according to their usual custom, before they deliver any message, they returned our string of wampum saying they could not understand it. We readily apprehended their meaning, so far as this, that they could not consistently or did not choose to receive it, which made us begin to suspect matters to be taking a more unfavorable turn than we afterwards found there was any real reason for. However, be their design what it would, knowing that the hearts of all men are in the hands of God, we kept a good countenance, determined to do the best we could as to our mission.

We then told them, we were sorry they had not understood, and would again explain it, which we did accordingly, giving them back the string of wampum which they held in their hand a little while and again returned it, saying, "their great man, (meaning their king,) could not understand it." Whereupon we put it up. At the same time, they told us, we must not be discouraged and then taking out a string of wampum of two single threads and one double one they proceeded to speak on the two single strings, one of which was white the other a mixture of black and white and told us as follows:

"Our dear brothers, What you have said, we are very well pleased with, as far as we can understand it. — But dear brothers, when William Johnson spake with us some time ago, and made a peace, which is to be strong and forever he told us, we must not regard what any other might say to us. That though a great many people all round about might be speaking a great many things; yet we must look upon all these things only as when a dog sleeps, and he dreams of something, or something disturbs him and he rises hastily, and gives a bark or two, but does not know anything, or any proper reason why he barks, — and just so the people all around that may be saying, some one thing, and some another, are to be no more regarded, and therefore, they can not understand, or hear in any other way."[1]

On the double string they said,

"Dear Brothers, some time ago, George Croghon spake to us, that no other were to be regarded; but that as William Johnson and he should say, so we should do."

They then brought out and shewed us a large belt of wampum of friendship which Sir William Johnson gave them. This belt they told

us[2] he held by one end, and they by the other; that when they had any thing to say, they must go along that path, (meaning the white streak on the belt) to him; and that when he had any thing to say to them, he must come to that council fire, (referring to the diamond in the middle of the belt) and there speak to them.

To this they added — They believed there was a great God above, and they desired to serve him in the best manner they could, and they thought of him at their rising up and their lying down, and hoped he would look upon them, and be kind to them, and do them good.

After a little pause, some conversation ensued, wherein they told us, we must not at all be discouraged by any thing that had passed in the business we came upon, but wait with patience. We replied, we were not discouraged, as we saw the propriety of what they said, and desired they would consult, and let us know whether it would be agreeable that we should speak to them about religion on the morrow which was a Sabbath. They then withdrew.

About four o'clock, two of the council returned, and gave our interpreter, Joseph, a belt of wampum, with a speech; the purport of which was, to invite the Christian Indians in New Jersey, under the care of the Reverend Mr. John Brainard, to come to Qui-a-ha-ga, a town the king and some of its people here had lived in, about 70 miles northwest of this place, where, as they said, there was good hunting, and where they might have a minister with them, and all the Indians who desired to hear the Gospel as they gave us to understand there was a number of such, might then go and settle with them.

This proposal shewed the good disposition of the Indians to the reception of the Gospel among them, as all Indians from every quarter, who might be desired to be instructed in Christianity, would have a town most conveniently situated, to which they might repair for that purpose. It appeared to be a kind and excellent provision for the free enjoyment of a Gospel-minister, in case some of their great men should themselves reject and discountenance the preaching of it in the towns where they resided.

These men also told us in answer to our request , that they would gladly hear us tomorrow, and be well pleased that their people should attend, again repeating to us, that we should not be discouraged. After some free conversation, wherein they appeared very agreeable and cheerful, they invited us to visit any of them in their houses in town, either now or at any other time we thought proper.

We told them we should be glad if tomorrow was observed as a day of rest among them; and that we should have something more to say to them before we took our leave. Taking us by the hand as a mark of their respect, they withdrew.

We considered matters over this evening, and endeavored to commit the affair to God, and looked to Him for direction and assistance.

21st. Sabbath. This morning, Samuel, otherwise Tepiss-cow-a-hang, who is one of the chief men of the council, went to all the houses in the town, to give them notice that we were to speak to them today, at the council house, about religion — at eleven o'clock, one of the council came to our hut, in order to conduct us to the council house, where his majesty lives. A considerble number both of men and women attended.

I began divine worship by singing part of a psalm, having previously explained the general drift and meaning of it to them. (Psalmody, by the way is exceedingly pleasing to the Indians.) I then prayed, and the interpreter repeated to them my prayer in their own language.

I then preached to them from the parable of the prodigal son, Luke XV, 11. By way of introduction, I gave some short account of man's primitive happy state then of his fall — how all mankind were concerned therein, and affected by it — and that this the Bible taught us, and sad experience and observation abundantly confirmed. I then illustrated our sad condition, particularly by the prodigal son, and shewed what hopes of mercy and encouragement there were for us to return to God the Father, through Christ, from the striking example before them, delivering so much at a time as the interpreter could well retain and deliver exactly again, making things as plain as possible, using such similies as they were well acquainted with, in order to convey a clear idea of the truth to their minds. There was a close attention paid by most of the audience to the truths that were delivered, not only as they might appear to them new and striking, as I hoped, but as matters of the greatest importance, and infinitely interesting. Some, more especially the women, seemed really to lay things to heart.

After sermon was over we sat a-while with them. We then proposed to speak to them again in the afternoon, if it was agreeable. We were told it would. We then withdrew.

About three o'clock, the king was up in town, and told us, he would have his people together as soon as he went home, and would then send us word. Accordingly a messenger was sent to us for that purpose in a little time after, with whom we went to the place of meeting, where Mr. Duffield preached from I Cor. XV, 22, giving just a plain narration of how all became dead in Adam, and how all true believers were made alive, and entitled to life eternal in and through Christ.

The people appeared to be much engaged, and well pleased with the word, as though they desired truly to know these things; and we have great reason to hope, there had been some good impressions made on their minds today. Some of them appeared very solemn and affected. After sermon, we sat a while according to their custom after delivering any speech and then returned to our hut.

Our interpreter, who tarried a-while after us, at his return told us that all their leading men, and especially the king desired we should speak to them again on the morrow, which message we received joyfully, and would bless God for any hope of success.

This day, till evening, had so much the appearance of a sabbath in this town, that it truly surprised us, and made us thankful to God for such a favor; scarce any noise being to be heard, except the women pounding corn for their food, as is their daily custom. Upon the whole, things appeared agreeable; and there is a blessed prospect of these poor benighted Indians receiving the Gospel, had they an opportunity of its being faithfully and prudently preached among them, — in so much as we could not but once and again think on our Lord's remark, that the field appeared white, and ready for the harvest.

God knows what he designs; but surely there is a glorious appearance of an effectual door being opened in these parts, if it be not neglected. A serious thoughtfulness about the great affair of religion, and a diligent attention to the word preached among them, seems to prevail with a number of these poor savages.

In the evening several came to our lodgings, and sat and heard, while I told them about the bible and great things it contains. They appeared very grave and attentive. Among these was Neolin, a young man, who used some time past to speak to his brethren, the Indians, about their wicked ways, who took great pains with them; and so far as we can understand, was a means of reforming a number of them.

I enquired what put him upon this practice; and he told us, that, about 6 years ago, when alone in his hut or cabin, musing by himself, being greatly concerned on account of the evil ways he saw prevailing among the Indians, a man immediately appeared, and stood in his cabin door, while he sat by the fire alone, in the night, and was perfectly awake, and spoke to him in the following manner:

"These things you were thinking of are right, (referring to the miserable condition of the Indians, which he was thinking of) and all who follow evil ways and bad thoughts, shall go to a miserable place after they are dead. — But all they who hate all evil and live agreeable to the mind of God, shall, after death, be taken up to God, and be made happy forever."

Having thus spoken he said the man immediately disappeared but the man's speech made such an impression upon him that he could not help speaking to the Indians, and endeavoured to persuade them to leave their evil ways.[3]

It also deserves our observation that the old man Tepiss-cow-a-hang, before mentioned, was, from our first coming here, greatly assisting in forwarding things respecting religion. The old man's heart seemed much engaged, and he spared no pains.

He told our interpreter, that in case the king did not speak about religion, before we went away, that is, as he supposed he meant, if he did not invite and encourage us to return again to preach to them, that he would himself.

22nd. As we were informed that there was a young woman one Elizabeth Henry, a prisoner yet among the nation; and as we had desired Mr. Gibson, a trader, who is well acquainted and has considerable influence with these Indians, to mention the affair, among other things in his letter to them, which we read to a number of the principal men, who came to our hut in the forenoon; we accordingly desired the king to order the above young woman to be delivered to us, that we might take her to her relations.

The king replied, "He was very well pleased with everything his brother, John Gibson, had said, and would send a prisoner by us, to her relations, (had she been with or near them) but that she was at a considerable distance, at a town upon the Great Bever creek, or river, about a day's journey from Fort Pitt. However, that we should take the string of wampum which Mr. Gibson had sent him, (returning it to us) and give it to the great man of that town, who would instantly deliver her up to us."

About four o'clock in the afternoon, the king, (the headman of this nation) and with him, Tepiss-cow-a-hang, Ke-legh-pa-mahnd, Tuny-e-baw-la-we-hand, and Negh-kaw-leegh-hung, principal men of the council, came to our hut, and addressed us in the following manner:

"Our dear brothers, What you have said to us (referring to our preaching yesterday) we are well pleased with. We believe there is a great God that has made us, the heavens, and the earth, and all things.

Brothers, you have spoken to us against getting drunk — what you have said is very agreeable to our minds — we see it as a thing which is very bad; and is a great grief to us, that rum, or any kind of strong liquor, should be brought among us, as we with a chain of friendship, which now unites us and our brethren, (meaning the English) together, may remain strong, but —

Brothers, the fault is not all with us, but begins with our brothers, the white people; for if they will bring out rum,some of our people will buy it; they must buy it; it is for that purpose it is brought; but, if none was brought, then they could not buy it. And, now,

Brothers, we beseech you, be faithful, and desire our brothers, the white people, bring no more of it us. Shew this belt to them for this purpose, (at the same time holding forth a large belt of wampum) shew it to the great man of the fort (meaning the commanding officer of Fort Pitt) and to our brothers on the way as you return; and to the great men in Philadelphia (meaning the principal men in the government) and in other places, from which rum might be brought, and entreat them to bring no more. And, now,

Brothers, there is another thing we do not like, and complain of very much. There are some (meaning white people) who do at times, hire some of our Squaws (that is their women) to let them lie with them; and give them rum for it. This thing is very bad. The Squaws then sell the rum to our people, and make them drunk.

We beseech you, advise our brothers against this thing, and do what you can to have it stopped."

After having delivered their speech they gave the belt of wampum, and desired us to take down in writing what they had said, that we might not forget any part of it; for that it was a matter about which they were much concerned. After some friendly conversation they withdrew.

In the evening old Tepiss-cow-a-hang came and informed us, that there were a great many here, and at another town called Suk-a-hung, and likewise at other towns, that were desirous to hear the Gospel; and that they intended to go up next Spring to Qui-a-ha-ga, and there make a large town, and then try to get a minister among them. He informed us also, that there were three other nations or tribes, viz. the Chippewas,[4] Puttkotungs, and Wyendots, that lived near the lake, that is Erie, who discovered a great desire to hear the Gospel. I told him I understood that these tribes used to hear the French ministers preach, who worship God in something of a different way from us, and therefore perhaps would not hear us. He replied, that he was persuaded, and that he knew if a minister of our way would go out among them it would be very agreeable to these nations, and that many of them would join us. In short, the old man appeared much engaged in this matter.

This day has been so much taken up, by the chief men in council, about important affairs and doing business, that there was no time for sermon. The king therefore proposed that it should be tomorrow before we set out on our journey.

23rd. The head men met in council this morning. — between eleven and twelve o'th'clock, we attended at the council house for public worship, and found a considerable number convened for that purpose. I spoke from the parable the Gospel-feast; Luke XIV, 16, and in my discourse pursued the following method, namely, that there were rich provisions made in the Gospel for poor sinners. And that opened the nature of these provisions and the reason of their being compared to a marriage and royal feast. — I next shewed that the ministers of the Gospel were sent out to invite poor miserable sinners, the lame, &c. to this feast. — I spoke of the excuses that some made for their not coming. — I then shewed how any were brought to comply with the Gospel call, and then concluded with invitations and arguments to persuade them to come to the Lord Jesus Christ: All which particulars I treated in the most plain and easy way making use of such similies as the Indians were most acquainted with and best adapted, so far as I could judge, to convey a clear idea of the truths on which I discoursed to their minds. A solemn awe appeared on the face of the assembly. Everyone seemed attentive to the things that were spoken and a number were affected. The interpreter was so much affected himself that he could scarcely speak for some time; and indeed, I must own, my own heart was warmed with the truths that I delivered, and the remarkable effects they appeared to have upon the minds of these poor benighted heathens — blessed be God! Let all the praise be to him. We have reason to hope, no one opportunity we have enjoyed here has been in vain; and we trust, that the good impressions that appear to have been made, will remain and issue well with some of them. May the Lord grant, our labors and hopes may not be found vain!

As we had signified to some of the council that we had something to say to them before we departed, four of the principal men came to our hut in the afternoon, in order to hear what we had to communicate. We addressed them in the following manner;

"Dear brethren, as we are soon to set out on our way home, we have a few things to say to you before we go. We are glad, and thank the great God, that brought us out and kept us by the way, that we might visit our brethren in this place, and that we have had an opportunity of spending some time with you, and speaking to you about the great things that concern another world. We are glad that we have had so comfortable a meeting with you; and thank our brethren for all their love and kindness to us.

Brethren, it gives us great pleasure and satisfaction to find our brethren holding so fast that chain of friendship which our good brother, Sir William Johnson, made with you, and we hope and pray it may ever continue to unite us together as one people.

Brethren, we are much rejoiced to see you so earnestly set against those things that are bad, and especially against the drinking of strong liquors, which opens a door to so many evil things. We have carefully attended to what you said to us yesterday concerning that matter: And although as we told you, our council (meaning our synod) does not meddle with civil government, but consults only about the great things of religion; yet we do, by this string (a string of wampum) assure you that we will faithfully deliver the message committed to us. We will tell our great men and our people what you have said and will use our best endeavours to have your desires in this thing fulfilled, as far as lies in our power. And, now,

Brethren, by this string of wampum we bid you farewell; and we pray the great God to be with you, and to bless you, and to lead you in the way which is right: And when we are gone we will pray for you; and when you shall at any time desire it, we will endeavor to have some of our brethren sent out to you again to tell you more about the great and good things of which we have spoken to you."

Here we gave the string of wampum, agreeable to their custom which they accordingly received, and laid up as a mark of friendship, and appeared very well pleased on the occasion.

To one of these men, who had learned in his youth to read a little English, I gave a bible I had with me. He cheerfully accepted this invaluable treasure. To a woman, who could also read, I gave a little book entitled, A compassionate Address to the Christian World, and they proposed to lend their books to one another.

Upon the whole, there really appears a strange, nay a strong desire prevailing in many of these poor heathens after a knowledge of the Gospel, and the things of God, and a door, as we before observed, to be affectionately opening, or rather, already opened for carrying to them the glad tidings of salvation; so that, if proper measures were vigorously pursued, there is much reason to hope, that the blessing of God might attend and crown attempts of this kind with success.

This evening Neolin came to see and sit with us a-while and desired to hear something about the Christian religion. —I desired Mr. Duffield to speak to him, who accordingly told him something concerning the promises of a saviour, Jesus Christ, that had been given of old and recorded in the book of God, and how, according to these promises, Christ came. He then gave him a short summary of the way that a sinner is brought to have an interest in this Saviour , and of the change that is wrought in him, and that by the Spirit of God; and pointed out to him the effects it produces in a person towards God, his laws, his ways, &c., and that these effects are marks and evidences of an interest in Christ, and the promises. He appeared very attentive, and much pleased to hear these things. When we had done he affectionately took us by the hand, and withdrew, and telling us, if he could, he would see us again in the morning.

Some of the Indians observed us consulting a map of the country in order to find out the most direct way to Fort Pitt. One of them went and brought a map of his own drawings, wherein the lakes, rivers, towns, where different tribes or nations lived, council fires, that is, where the different tribes meet, in order to consult about their public affairs, and other remarkable places, seemed pretty justly laid down. On the back of the Lake Superior, I observed a very considerable river running a different course from the rest (its course seemed to be near N.W.) By this it should seem as if there must be some great lake or sea to the north or northwest of these parts which has not yet been discovered, into which this river empties itself. The Indian that pointed out to us these places on his map, said, where this river was, or near it, was very cold, that is, far north. Perhaps by following the course of this river, that passage, which has been long sought for, the south seas by the north west might be found out.

We understand by our good friend, Tepiss-cow-a-hang, that there are about 47 Indians here, who have had some considerable impressions made on their minds by our preaching, the king and Neolin being among the number; the latter, as before mentioned, who had been according to his light, in time past, endeavouring to instruct his brethren the Indians, attended upon us privately as well as publicly, with a desire to know more about religion; and almost all the young Indians, expressed a great desire to learn to read.

The principal men of this town sent an invitation, by our interpreter, Joseph, to the Indians living pretty high up the Susquehannah river, in a town called Wia lusing, to move with their families to Qui-a-ha-ga, where they intend to form the Christian town before mentioned, having heard that these Indians have some knowledge of Christianity, as well as those under the care of Mr. Brainard, that they might see and know how Christians live.

In the evening 20 persons came to the house of Tepiss-cow-a-hang, under religious impressions, who expressed their concern at our leaving them, and wondered we should go away so soon.

We should have been willing and very desirous to have tarried a longer time in this place, as there is such an agreeable prospect to a number of these Indians being brought to embrace the Gospel; but our time appointed by the synod being near expired and we not being provided for continuing longer here, having scarcely as much meal left as would support us till we arrived at Fort Pitt; and the principal design of our visit in order to know what prospect there might be of introducing the Gospel among them, having been answered, we determined to return; and the rather as we had no prospect had we continued longer of assembling many of them together, for it was a time when they begin their fall hunting, upon which their living chiefly depends, a number having already gone out of town with that design; so that upon the whole, it appeared most advisable to return: And accordingly, with the leave of providence, we determined to set out tomorrow.[5]

24th. Neolin came this morning to bring us on our way. — We set out on our journey by a different way to the Fort than that we went, accompanied by an Indian belonging to the town, called by the English Capt. Jacob, a great warrior, who appeared to have some impressions of religion. — After traveling up the bank of the

Muskingum about three miles through rich level land we crossed the river at a fording-place, and traveled with as great expectation as our circumstances would admit, with a view to reach the fort by Saturday night, in order to preach to the people there. We had not traveled many miles before there came on a very heavy rain which continued all the afternoon and wetted us pretty thoroughly, as we had no place of shelter, which obliged us to stop a little before night at a small river, where with some food for our horses, and with difficulty we got a fire kindled. The ground and the blankets we had to lie in being wet, as well as our clothes, made our lodgings not very comfortable. However, we endeavoured to dry them by the fire; and so passed the night as well as we could.

25th. Set out this morning as early as we could and encamped a little before night at the best place we could find for our horses, and made up a fire as usual.

26th. Proceeded on our way. The most of the country we had passed through hitherto has been hilly with high ridges, and some part of it much encumbered with trees fallen down. — It rained in the afternoon, but the night was fair.

27th. We arose before day, as we have done every morning since we set out, on our journey having no great inducement to keep our beds. We set out at daylight, on our way, in order to make as good a day's journey as possible, as we had but little provision. Capt. Jacob went off the road to hunt for us, but returned without anything. Having a little meal, made of Indian corn, parched, I took a spoonful or two of it mixed with water; and was enabled to travel on foot today 25 miles. — We met several Indians from whom we learnt that Elizabeth Henry, the prisoner before mentioned, was married to an Indian, and went some time ago with her husband to hunt, 100 miles distant from the town where she had been prisoner. — In the afternoon we met an Indian with a deer on his back that he had killed, part of which we bought and carried with us. — A little before night we arrived at the Great Beaver Creek, finding our utmost efforts to reach the fort this week in vain, being 25 miles from it. {His original journal states that "here we found King Beavers Brother encamped on the Bank of this Rivr who was very civil to us". This would not have been Shingas, however, for he is believed to have died in the winter of 1763-4. Beaver had five other brothers, (according to the captivity narrative of Hugh Gibson), four of whom were possibly still living, and it was probably one of these that Beatty met.} We made our fire on a pleasant bank of the river, having near half a mile to go for our firewood. We dressed our venison for supper, part of which we gave to an Indian chief and his family, whom we found encamped here. The Indian's wife, seeing us carry our firewood so far on our shoulders, took her hatchet, cut and brought us in a little time, a great burden of wood on her back and threw it down by our fire; She not only pitying us, but thinking it a great scandal, I suppose, to see men doing that which is properly the work of their women.

I signified great desire to be at the fort tomorrow, time enough to preach in the afternoon; but having no horse to carry me there in that time, Capt. Jacob very freely offered his, which was pretty strong, and I thankfully accepted his offer.

28th. Sabbath. I rose before day. Mr. Duffield, by the fatigue of the journey, was taken very ill last night, so that I was afraid to leave him in such a situation; but he insisted on my going to the fort, according to my proposal to preach to the people. — After we had taken the remains of our venison we had dressed last night, I parted with my company at daylight, and arrived at the Ohio, opposite to the fort, between twelve and one o'clock. I crossed the river in a canoe, swimming my horse alongside.

In the afternoon I preached to a considerable number of people, assembled in the little town near the fort. Having made known the distress Mr. Duffield and our company were in for want of food and proper refreshments, a young man went to them with some bread and other necessaries.

29th. Was glad to see Mr. Duffield (considerably recovered from his illness) and the rest of the company safely arrived at the fort. Mr. Duffield preached in the evening.

NOTES {Beatty's}

1. The Indians make great use of similies, particularly, in their public treaties, and some of them very apt and striking, though they may appear uncouth to such as do not understand their language and customs. Sir William Johnson, who perfectly understands their genius and customs, took this similie, it is likely, from them, as most fit to answer his purpose, viz. To guard them against holding treaties with other nations or private persons that might be tampering with them. We begin now to understand that the reason of their returning our string of wampum and refusing to treat with us in that form, was that they looked upon it as inconsistent with the treaty of peace they had entered into with Sir William Johnson, or lest it should give umbrage to him; they not understanding the difference of treating with them about civil and about religious affairs. This difference we took pains to explain to them afterwards.

2. Belts of wampum given on such occasions, as solemn pledges or ratifications of the Treaty, have some emblem or representation of the nature of such treaty in order, it is like, the better to keep them in mind of it. On each edge of this, given to them by Sir William, were several rows of black wampum; and in the middle several rows of white wampum running parallel with the black; the white streak between, they called the path from them to him, and him to them. In the middle of the belt was the figure of a diamond made of white wampum, which they called the council fire.

3. The above is a substance of what he declared to us. We were well informed by a trader, (to whom he related a good deal more, respecting his extraordinary mission) who was taken prisoner in the late war, by the Indians, given to this Neolin, and adopted into his family. — That this man used to boil a quantity of bitter roots, in a large kettle, till the water became very strong — that he himself used to drink plentifully of this bitter liquor, and make his family, and particularly this prisoner do the same — the draughts of this liquor proved a severe emetic — and that dose was taken after dose for

some hours together; the end of which, as Neolin said, was to cleanse them from their inward sins. Poor endeavours of the light of nature! How needful, how salutary the knowledge of the Gospel!

4. The Chippewas are supposed to be 14 or 15 hundred in number; all in one town. The other one there, that Puttkogungs, are considerable as to number in another town. The Wyendots, about 7 hundred persons, are likewise one town, which are about 60 or 70 miles distance from Qui-a-ha-ga, the intended Delaware Christian town.

5. This town (the proper name of which is Negh-ku-unque, that is the Red Bank) is about one mile and a half in length, consisting of 60 or 70 houses, built chiefly on the south side of the river Muskingum, {his original journal states "Some part of the Town lies on the South side of the River but the main body of it on the north"} and contains about six or 700 persons as far as we could learn. In some parts of the town the houses stand pretty close to each other; in other parts at a greater distance, and irregular. — some of the houses are made of broad split pieces of wood, with one end stuck in the ground close to each other standing up like a stockade; others made of logs of wood laid upon one another, notched at the corners into each other; but most of them are made of bark set up on edge, tied to stakes drove in the ground, and all covered with bark; except the king's house, which is covered with broad split pieces of wood, with their ends set to the ridge of the roof, so close together as to keep out the rain, and appears very neat. The houses are in general much longer than they are wide, with a door at each end, which they close or shut by setting up a piece of broad bark. Two or three families live in some houses, and in cold weather have two or three fires in them at proper distances but no chimney. The land on each side of the river is a rich soil but especially the north side where they chiefly plant their Indian corn or maize, beans, pumpkins, &c. The river at the town appears to be considerably more than one hundred yards wide and runs near west; but lower down turns southward, and keeps much that course, as far as we could learn, till it empties itself into the Ohio, and is navigable for canoes or flat-bottom boats. The Indians sometimes go from hence to Fort Pitt in their canoes.

The land the way we came to this place from Fort Pitt, appeared to be very good in general, but uneven, having many high ridges and small, castles, yet abounding with low rich land, usually called bottom; the little streams running through these bottoms are generally very crooked and narrow, with deep and steep banks, owing to the richness of the soil. The nearer we approached to this place, we found the country more level; and to the west and northwest of it, at some distance, the country, we were informed, becomes quite level, and has very great plains, on which there is no wood but fine grass, and therefore plenty of deer. Some of the Indians of this town have just come in from hunting, on one of these plains, which they say is one hundred miles broad, and about four days' journey from hence. Another 10 days' journey from hence, is vastly large, like the sea, the Indians say; I suppose they mean one of the great lakes. The climate here seems to be healthy.

Source: Beatty, *The Journal of a Two Months Tour...*, pp. 3–40

Map 7a – **Original Survey of 1797** – **Newcomerstown**

Map 7b – **Modern Topographic** – **Newcomerstown**

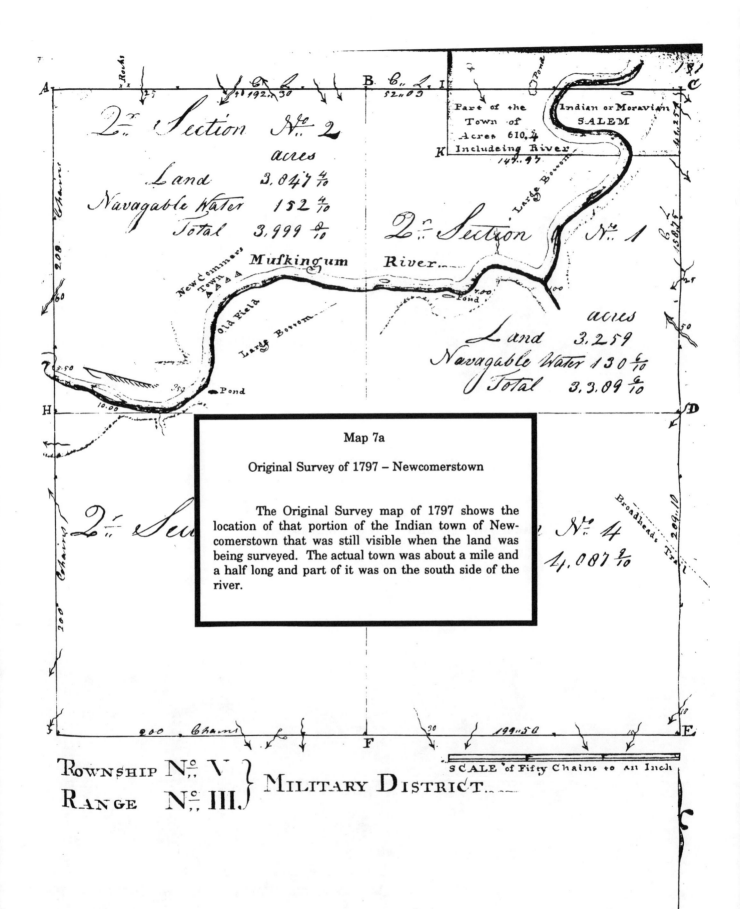

Map 7a

Original Survey of 1797 – Newcomerstown

The Original Survey map of 1797 shows the location of that portion of the Indian town of Newcomerstown that was still visible when the land was being surveyed. The actual town was about a mile and a half long and part of it was on the south side of the river.

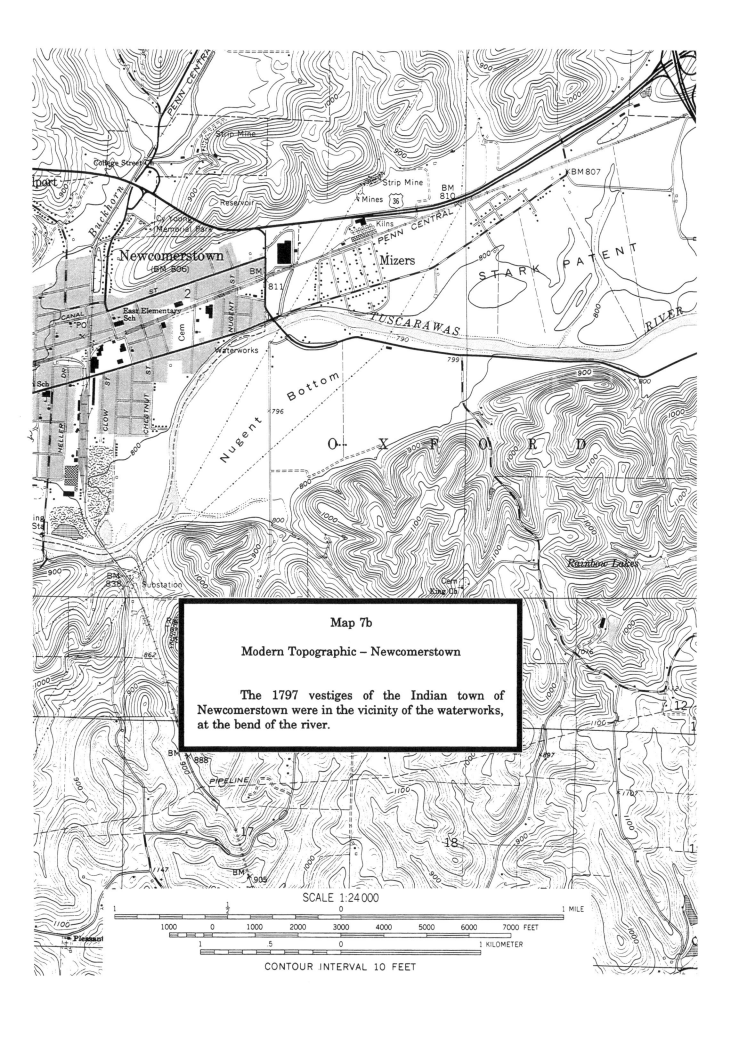

Map 7b

Modern Topographic – Newcomerstown

The 1797 vestiges of the Indian town of Newcomerstown were in the vicinity of the waterworks, at the bend of the river.

SCALE 1:24 000

1   ½   0   1 MILE

1000   0   1000   2000   3000   4000   5000   6000   7000 FEET

1   .5   0   1 KILOMETER

CONTOUR INTERVAL 10 FEET

She presently made ready some venison, and baked cakes under the ashes in their way, and set before us, which became very seasonable and acceptable.

Charles Beatty   September 18th, 1766

George Croghan
1767

Once again, this time in the fall of 1767, George Croghan undertook a mission into the Indian country to try to find out why there was so much restlessness among the tribes. Rumors had reached Fort Pitt that there was to be a large gathering of the Senecas and twelve other tribes the next spring in the Shawnee country. While the purpose of the gathering could only be conjectured, it had only been three years since the last uprising—Pontiac's—was put down, and the English certainly did not want to have another one on their hands.

Apparently his trip was successful. He was able to quiet some of the concerns of the Indians, and the planned meeting of the twelve tribes did not take place.

{October} 24th {1767}. Sett out from Fort Pitt to Detroit.

27th. Came to a large hunting Village of the Delawares, where I met some Chiefs and Warriors of that Nation, who pressed me to stay with them that and the following, which I agreed to.

28th. In the Morning We met at a fire prepared by the Indians for that Purpose. I informed them that I was going to Detroit to restore their Friends the Two Chippawas that had been sent Prisoners to Albany. They Answered, that they were glad to hear it, as the Nations over the Lakes were making a great complaint to their Allies—that every little Crime which any of their People committed in their drink—was taken great Notice of by the English, and their People sent Prisoners to be hanged—When the English at the same time refused to punish their Negroes for Murdering their People before their faces, and that they were not able to obtain Justice from the English for any injuries they did them. The Delawares reply'd We know this to be true; we could never obtain Justice from you, when any of our People were Murdered by Yours; When at the same

time, if any of our People took a Horse from Yours, you always followed us, and insisted for Satisfaction. — They then said, We do not mention this in Anger, tho' We have suffered, only to let you know, that we are sensible when we are ill treated, and do not forget the injuries done us.

In Answer to this, I used every Argument in my Power to convince them, That every step that was in the Power of the General, and Superintendant; were taken to bring such People as committed Offences in the Indian Country, to Justice. To Which they Answered, "We thought you had Laws for that purpose."

I then deliverd them a Belt of Wampum and told them—As I had been some time out of their Country; I should be glad to hear what News was passing among their several Tribes. — They told Me, after taking some time to Consider, that I had come from the Country from whence all the News came, and believed I knew it, as well as they did,—but as I desired to hear it from them, they would tell Me every thing that came to their knowledge. And say'd that a Party of Senecas who came from the Six Nation's Country called the Shawanese, Delawares, and Senecas who lived at the two Creeks, to a Council. At which time they told them, that the English were Robbing them of a Tract of Country lying between the Ohio River, and the Settlements of Virginia, Maryland and Pennsilvania, and had made large Settlements thereon, and had killed several of their Warriors passing to and from War against the Southern Indians, calling their Country which they had unjustly taken Possession of, theirs. They said it was true, they had agreed with Sir William Johnson to give up that Tract of Country to the King for a Consideration, but they never had received any, and had been often cheated by the English in the Sale of Lands, and were now determined to have Justice therein, or bury every Warrior of their Nation, and desired them to consider well what they had said, and prepare themselves to bring the English to a sence of the Injustice they were doing them, and delivered them several Belts. — This Party then sent to Council with the Chipawas and Ottawas. — sometime afterwards, a Party of Chipawas came to the lower Shawanese Town with Messages to the Shawanese and Delawares, informing them that the Chiefs and Principal Warriors of Twelve different Nations, would collect themselves to a Council in the Shawanese Country, (and that the Senecas would likewise attend) in the Fall of the Year. And that since a Second Message was sent them from the Chipewas letting them know, that this Council would not take Place till the Frog Month (which is March) next. This, They said was every thing, that came to their knowledge worth acquainting me with. That they were sorry, things were in such a Situation—for their own parts they wished for Peace, tho' some of their own People had suffered. They then told me I would meet a Number of the Shawanese and some of their People at Muskingham, who would inform Me, that everything they had told me was truth.

30th. I got to Muskingham where I met a large Number of the Shawanese and some Principal Men of the Delawares, who gave me the same Intelligence as I had from the others, and told Me, they longed much to see me, and wished that all the Chiefs of their two Nations were together to speak to me.

After Considering the Situation of Affairs I thought it would be for the good of His Majesty's Service to invite the Chiefs of these Two Nations to meet Me at Fort Pitt on my Return from Detroit. I delivered these Indians Belts for that Purpose to be sent to their several Chiefs.

November 6th. I reached Sandusky...

{Croghan proceeded on to Detroit where he held numerous councils with the Indians, trying to learn the purpose of the large gathering of Twelve Nations that was to take place the next spring in the Shawnee country. He was also trying to learn the cause of dissatisfaction among the Indians, which primarily seemed to be because of a lack of English traders among them.}

24th. I Set out from Detroit and got to Sandusky the first of December, where a number of Indians Settled in that part of the Country Assembled to Meet Me; I informed them of every thing that had been transacted at Detroit, and then Condoled with them for some of their People who had lately Died, for which they returned thanks; And on the Second of December, I took my leave of them, and Set out for Fort Pitt.—

9th. I arrived at Fort Pitt,...

Source: Hamilton, *The Papers of Sir William Johnson,* Vol. XIII, pp. 435–44

There is one thing on which we must insist, namely that when we are in your neighbourhood no other Indians shall settle anywhere near us because we are afraid that they will drink and bother us. We want to live by ourselves.

David Zeisberger   March 18th, 1772

David Zeisberger

Born: April 11, 1721 Zauchtenthal, Moravia
Died: November 17, 1808 Goshen, Ohio
Age on entering Tuscarawas Valley – 49 years

David Zeisberger
1771

Our next diarist would become the most influential of all of the white men who came into the area in Indian days.

David Zeisberger was the leader of the Moravian missionary effort in the Tuscarawas Valley. He was born in Moravia in 1721 and came to America in about 1737, residing first in Georgia, but moving to Pennsylvania in 1740. He was present at the founding of the Moravian settlement at Bethlehem in 1741 and, commencing in 1745, devoted the rest of his life to missionary work among the Indians, first the Iroquois, and then for the last 45 years of his life, the Delawares. He died at Goshen on November 17, 1808, and is buried in the Indian cemetery alongside Chief Gelelemend (Killbuck) and Edwards, another of the Moravian missionaries.

In addition to keeping the mission diary and writing several other books, he wrote a History of the North American Indians, which will simply be referred to in this book as Zeisberger's History.

The Moravians, immediately prior to coming to the Tuscarawas Valley, had three missions in Pennsylvania, two along the Susquehanna (Friedenshütten and Schechschiquanunk), and one on the Beaver in western Pennsylvania. Zeisberger was in charge of the one on the Beaver, called Langunto-Utenünk, or Friedensstadt.

For some time, the Indian Chiefs at Gekelemukpechünk (Newcomerstown) had been intimating to the Moravians that they would be interested in having a mission town established near them, but they had not yet specifically invited the Moravians to do so.

On February 17, 1771, however, Zeisberger received a letter ostensibly from two of the Indians at Gekelemukpechünk which was of a rather menacing nature, demanding that their "sister", a woman of their town named Gertraud who had gone to Langunto-Utenünk voluntarily, be sent back to them, otherwise they would come and "fetch her". The threatening tone of the letter necessitated some kind of response, and Zeisberger decided to go to Gekelemukpechünk personally to discuss the matter with the chiefs, as well as to talk to the Indians about the possibilities of establishing a town in their vicinity.

It was on this trip, in March of 1771, that Zeisberger first preached to the Indians in the Tuscarawas Valley. The claim that some have put forth that this was the first Protestant sermon in what was to become the State of Ohio is obviously erroneous, however, for the Presbyterian ministers Beatty and Duffield preached here in 1766, and Bouquet's chaplain or chaplains had conducted a "divine service" near Coshocton in 1764. Nonetheless, his first sermon deserves its place in the history of the Tuscarawas Valley as being the successful beginning of the Moravian missionary effort in the valley, an effort that was to continue for ten years, reaching its tragic climax with the Gnadenhutten Massacre in 1782.

The following two journals are from the mission diary at Langunto-Utenünk.

{Langunto-Utenünk} On March 5 {1771} we set out for Gekelemukpechünk. Several Indian brethren and sisters accompanied us part of the way, because they were going to cook sugar. The snow was deeper than we had expected, thus travelling was rendered more difficult. On March 6th we met Colonel Bouquet and his army. They were on their way from Pittsburg to the Shawanose in the land of the Indians. We marched with them until March 7 when we separated and we left Tuscarawi way off on the right side. {Note: There would appear to be an error in translation concerning meeting Colonel Bouquet and his army. Bouquet came into the Indian country in 1764. Obviously, Zeisberger was saying that they followed the trail used by Bouquet.} Toward evening there was a terrible thunderstorm with rain and we expected to encounter many floods as we had to cross several big creeks. On March 8 the snow melted almost completely. On March 9 we rode our horses through 2 creeks and when we reached the 3rd creek we could not go any further because for half a mile the land along the creek was flooded. On March 10 it snowed all day long and the following night we had to camp. Meanwhile Jeremies shot a deer. On March 11 it ceased to snow and the snow reached almost up to our knees. We made a long detour through the woods so as to get to the Creek and rode our horses through 2 more creeks. Finally we arrived at the Mushkingum which had also very high water, and there we spent the night. On March 12 we made a raft on which we took our luggage across, then we rode our horses through the creek. We almost lost 2 horses which had gotten into the drift wood and received injuries. They almost drowned. Early in the morning of March 13 we arrived in Gekelemukpechünk, and saw the Chief Netawatwees whom Isaac knows very well. Many of the Indians came to see us during the course of the day. Many of them were glad to see us, because they had hoped for a long time that we would pay them a visit. The Chief offered us to stay in his house. He said that we

should be his guests so that he could hear many things about the brethren. I informed him that if they wanted to hear about the brethren they could, if it so pleased them, have all their people assemble. This however, could not be done today as most of the Indians were out cooking sugar. But the chief sent messengers to them telling them to return the following day. Meanwhile the chief's house was crowded with Indians all day long and I told them many things. In particular I spoke to the Chiefs and Captains about the brethren's mission among the Indians: that they want to show them the way to eternal bliss and to tell them about the Saviour. Similarly the Indian brethren who were with me very bravely gave testimony of the Saviour's life and death saying that if they wanted to know the truth and the right way to happiness they should listen to them very attentively, because they sere going to tell them all about it.

The Chief seems to be a very handsome [or possibly "fine"] man. He loves the good and likes to hear about the Saviour. Several others in his council are like him, they were with us constantly during our sojourn while the others only came from time to time. If only we could open their hearts we would be glad to do it. They hear and are keen to hear, but their minds are clouded with darkness. They will not be able to comprehend our words until the Saviour opens their hearts.

Gekelemukpechünk, which is situated on the Mushkingum River, is rather a big Indian town and is said to consist of 100 houses which I think is quite likely. Most of them are block houses. The Chief's house is a studded house with a floor and stairs of cut wood. It has a brick chimney, a shingle roof and is the biggest one in the whole town. A few other houses have shingle roofs too. The countryside is beautiful and consists of a vast plain. The land on both sides of the river is good. The river "here" is about as wide as the Delaware near Easton, but 6 miles further down a tributary flows into it which is just as wide. Tuscarawi, which is now uninhabited, is situated on a "branch" of this river and approximately 40 miles north of here; from Pittsburg they often come here by water, which however, is a long detour. Many Indians are supposed to live along this river, Delawares, Mohicans, and Shawanose. About 50 miles N W is a town of Delamattanoes.

Most of the Indians here belong to the Unami Nation. There are a few Monsies part of them came here only a year ago, namely from Goschgosching where they had several times attended our services and who were now very friendly to us. On March 14 Captain Kallender of Carlisle who trades here, invited us to breakfast. He told us that many Indians here would like to hear the Gospel. There were about 10-12 white people present.

Towards noon the Indians met in the Chief's house. As there were not enough benches skins were spread on the floor for people to sit on. About as many people as found room inside the house had to stand outside, because very many came. The Chief addressed his people reminding them to sit still and to listen attentively to what was going to be said. I saw many faces and bodies which looked wild and distorted as is to be expected from wild Indians. I spoke to them as follows:

"My dear friends: As I have heard several times that many of you are desirous to hear the word of God, I am glad to have this opportunity to make known unto you the will and word of God. The one and only God is He who came to earth, was incarnate, crucified and shed His blood for the sin of the world. It is He who made Heaven and earth and all therein, and there is no other God beside Him. It is His will that you should renouce to your pagan and sinful life and that, by believing in Him you should obtain forgiveness of your sins, eternal life and salvation. This he will do for each one of you. If you accept His word which I will now make known to you he will bless you in time and eternity etc. Everyone listened attentively and quietly and after I had finished the Chief said to his people: "Now you have heard his speech. Take his words to heart and think about them." I told him that I hoped to have many more opportunities to speak to them while I was here.

After a while I told them that I had some more things to tell them now that they were all assembled. I said that some time ago I had come into possession of a letter which was written to me by 2 Indians of their town, and whose names I gave them. I read to them the letter whose contents were as follows: "We have heard that our sister has gone to you and has accepted your religion and way of living. We, the undersigned, are herewith informing you that we are seriously asking you to send her back to us. If you do not comply with our request we shall come and take her by force which should not be very pleasant for you. We are firmly determined not to let her stay with you and it would be wise of you to send her back to us before we come and fetch her." I told them was not sensible and quite unnecessary to use such harsh words because they had not even asked why the woman was with us. I said "The woman in question, who has been baptized and is now our sister, did not come nor is she now staying with us at our request. She has followed her inclination. and as she wanted to hear about the Saviour, and as we thought the Indians were free people and not obliged to live in one and the same town (as a matter of fact we know that you often change residences) we saw no reason for sending her back." I assured them our sister was not desirous to go back to them, that she did not even want to be reminded of them, and that she thought only or her soul's salvation. I said if they wanted to know more about her they could ask brother Isaac, who is her dearest brother.

Furthermore I said: "There are those of you who accuse us of not letting Indians live with us who want to do so. Those are displeased with us, but when we do allow them to live with us we do not please them either. What are we to do? This woman will not be the only one who will want to live with us. Sooner or later more will come to hear the word of God and to inherit eternal life. If they come for this reason we will allow them to live with us and will not send them away. The best piece of advice that I can give you is the following: Accept the Word of God and have it preached to you so that those who want to hear it, have the opportunity to do so. Then they will not need to leave your town, this is my advice to you. If you follow it you will realize that it is good." Finally I said "This is what I wanted to tell you."

The Chief replied: "We, the old ones, did

not know that this unseemly letter was written. Letters are usually written in my house because we want to be kept informed of current events. But this letter was written secretly and without my knowledge. If any one of us wants to go to you and to hear the word of God I will not prevent him, on the contrary, I shall be pleased because I like to hear it myself. But regarding the matter which you have suggested to us, namely that the word of God should be accepted and preached here, I must inform you that there are not enough of us present at the moment to give an answer. Many of our captains are away, and I have to consult them in so important a matter. As soon as they come home we will discuss it and send you an oral or written answer."

Upon inquiry it turned out that Killbuck, who was present, had dictated the letter without the knowledge of the undersigned who do not even live here. He had to confess his deed and was ashamed of what he had [done]. He had not dreamt, I am sure, that his letter would be read out in public. The meeting was adjourned, and I had the opportunity to discuss my suggestion in greater detail. I said to the Chief: "If you agree to having the Gospel preached here, those who want to hear it, must live by themselves. Here in this town there is nothing but gambling, dancing and drinking and constant noise, therefore it is imperative for us to have a place to ourselves where we are isolated, away from the noise, and unmolested, so that those who want to hear the word of God can come and those who prefer their heathendom, can stay away."

On March 15 we had another sermon. The house was full and surrounded by Indians who could not get in but were listening. Afterwards the Indian brethren talked to a number of Indians who stayed behind because they wanted to hear some more. I spoke to several brethren who had been baptized in Gnadenhütten. {This would be the Gnadenhütten in eastern Pennsylvania, not the one that was later established in the Tuscarawas Valley.} Several of them expressed their desire to come and live with us, whereas others were so taken up with wordly affairs that they could not get out of their obligations, even if they wanted to.

I had long conversations with the chiefs. I also mentioned how we were standing with Packanke [also known as Custaloga] who a year ago promised us to get in touch with the Chiefs here. But we found out that he had not done so and that they did not know anything about our negotiations.

On March 16 the Indians assembled again to hear the sermon. So far the women had not been allowed to come into the house as there was not enough room even for the men. Today they asked whether they could come inside too, so that they could understand everything clearly, and the chief gave them permission. I am positive that there are many Indians here who would like to hear the word of God and if they could do as they pleased most of them would accept it. But we have many bitter enemies here who, although they did not object to my sermons, were very hostile when the Indian brethren talked to them. One of them is particularly base and hostile. He asked Isaac to come to him and said: "Why do you come here with an entirely new religion for our people? I feel like kicking the lot of you out of the house, but if all the Indians accept your religion and believe in your words, I will not do it." Isaac replied saying: "We have come to you solely because we love you. We are sorry for the poor Indians who are utterly blind. Their daily food consists of lies, they are deceived, and I know that many of them would like to know the right way to happiness, and that is what we want to show them. Are you so angry because we are concerned in their well-being and want to show them the way to eternal life? If only you could understand this, how glad you would be and how eagerly you would accept the word of God with all your heart! I feel sorry for you and realize that you are unable to understand and comprehend. Those who do not want to believe us but prefer to live in spiritual darkness and to listen to deceitful preachers can do as they please, but I can assure you that the word of God, which you have heard, is the truth, because I have experienced it in my own heart. That is why I believe in it and if I said it was not true, I would be a liar like all your preachers."

For several years vomiting has been customary here. It is done so much that many Indians are ruining their health, and now the custom has also spread to the Shawanose. The priests are making them believe that vomiting cleanses and frees them from sin. I have talked to them much concerning this matter and told them not to believe such nonsense, because vomiting could cleanse the stomach but not the heart which nothing could cleanse and cure but the blood of Jesus Christ.

As we wanted to be home for the Easter holidays and as we thought we would have to reckon with floods, we made preparations for our return journey today. A Mingo Indian of Onandago who is on his way to a great Council which is going to be held with the Shawanose, came here and called on me. He recognized me at once and said he had been told that a minister of the white people had arrived, but that he had not thought it was I. If he had known it he would have come to see me long ago. He was very friendly, praised my work among the Indians and said that the 6 Nations knew quite well that I was here, but I had already heard that he is supposed to have told the Indians not to listen to me nor to believe my words, because I wanted to lead them off the right path. I learnt from him that the 6 Nations as well as all the Indians living in the N W are peacefully minded, but that the Great Council held with the Shawanose would soon show whether the Indians in the S W were peaceful too or not. All the Indians in this neighbourhood are anxiously awaiting the news and they believe that there will be a war. May the dear Saviour protect us from such an evil, for where could we go with our people to be safe?

The Shawanose call the Monsy Nation their youngest brother, for the following reason: The 6 Nations had annihilated the Shawanose who were at that time living along this river, except for a few survivors, and when their complete annihilation was close at hand the Monsies came to their rescue, settled them at Wajomik-on-Susquehanna, protected them, and saved them from utter destruction. The Shawanose remember this quite well. Would it not be possible for the Gospel to spread to the Shawanose through the Monsies?

After having cordially said good-bye to everybody, and in particular to the Chief Netawatwees who said he was very glad that we had visited him, we told them that we hoped to visit them again in the near future, we departed on March 17. In the evening we reached the Mushkingum where we constructed a raft early in the morning, on March 18, and rode our horses through 3 creeks during the course of the day. After that we made good progress until March 20 when we came to the first branch of the Little Beaver Creek where we were very much delayed. We were equally unfortunate on March 21. But on March 22, when we came to the last branch whose current was so strong that it was not advisable for us to ride our horses through it, we had to make a long detour and seek our way through the forest. There was no road, no path, and in the evening we joined our Indian brethren and sisters in the sugar huts. They were very glad to see us again. That night it rained so hard that the following morning, on March 23, our brethren had to leave their huts because the land along the Creek was being flooded. Isaac and I made a raft which took us a long way through the forest and reached Languntoutanunk in good time, where we were glad to see brother and sister Jungmann and all the other brethren and sisters after such a long time.

This was the report of his journey to Gekelemukpechünk.

Time

In reckoning time they do not count the days but the nights. An Indian says, "I have travelled so many nights." Only if the entire journey has been accomplished in one day, will he speak of a day's journey.

Source: Zeisberger's *History...*, p. 145

David Zeisberger
1772

The Treaty of Ft. Stanwix, in 1768, had opened up for white settlement the lands near the Moravian mission towns along the Susquehanna. This was to have an adverse effect upon the mission, however, for Christian Indians simply could not live close to white settlements. Most whites did not trust any Indian, Christian or otherwise, and the Indians could not resist the temptation of the white man's rum. The Christian Indians would have to move further west.

Things were not going well for the Christian Indians at their town on the Beaver, either, but for a different reason. Here, it was the "wild" Indians of Kuskusky who were causing problems for the mission town, Langunto-Utenünk, located just a few miles away. Parties of drunken Indians would frequently carouse through the town, and there was even open hostility directed towards the missionaries themselves. They finally realized they could not stay there any longer.

By this time, also, it had been explained to Zeisberger why there had been no specific invitation from the chiefs at Gekelemukpechünk to settle near them, even though there had been many indications from them that this is what they desired. It seems that the chiefs felt that if they were the first to make a direct invitation to the Moravians to move to the valley, then if the Moravians should reject their offer, they would feel that they had been insulted. However, if the Moravians were to make the first move, by specifically requesting permission from the chiefs to settle near them, then they would gladly grant the request.

After discussions with the church authorities at Bethlehem, it was decided, therefore, to abandon the Pennsylvania mission towns and accept the "offer" of the chiefs at Gekelemukpechünk to move the mission to the Tuscarawas Valley.

Accordingly, Zeisberger, in March of 1772, made another journey to Gekelemukpechünk to make final arrangements for their relocation and to select a town site. The site chosen was to become Schoenbrunn.

{Langunto-Utenünk} March 26 {1772}: Brother David and his Indians returned from Gekelemukpechünk. They gave the following account of their journey:

We departed on March 11 and the following day we decided to travel via Tuscarawi so as to be able to see the country along the Muschkingum as far as Gekelemukpechünk. On March 14 we came into the neighbourhood of Tuscarawi, but as this place, which is at present uninhabited, has been assigned for settlement to other Indians we did not bother to inspect it but passed by, leaving it on the right hand side. We met the Captain of Kaskaskunk who gave us some information about the country and told us which way to go because none of us had ever been to Gekelemukpechünk. All that day we travelled downstream, along the Tuscarawi. In the morning of March 15 we reached the Muschkingum and travelled down-stream. We had to cross the Muschkingum twice which was very difficult because the water was rather high. Toward evening we came to a nice neighbourhood which we all liked very much. At first we went through an extensive plain, several miles along. The plains here are different from those in Wajomik, they have hedges and [crops?] but no trees. The soil seems to be very good. After having traversed the plain we came to a beautiful forest. It is located on a stretch of land which is rather elevated but even. We camped there and inspected the neighbourhood. We liked it very much, the lowland as well as the highland, but there was a great drawback: we had not yet found any water except river water. On March 16 we inspected the country further down the river which is many miles long, nice and even, and well supplied with wood, which is just what we want, just at the town-place, and because the lowland in between is very wide, so that the town comes to stand rather far from the river, and because it would be a little inconvenient on account of the canoes which we cannot dispense with, this substitutes the spring which is very big and forms a little lake which flows into the river, so that it is possible to take canoes right up to the town and to have a safe harbour for the canoes at the same time. [The translator indicated that the above sentence was a literal translation, and that "this substitutes the spring" might also be read as "the spring substitutes this" or "the spring makes up for this".] The lowland is very rich and good, and the river has plenty of fish, just as the Indians have described it to us. There is also plenty of game, in short the locality offers every thing which the Indians need for their comfort. It is very spacious so that many Indians can live there, because they will not need all the land for plantations. Unfortunatly there are no stones in the river or on the land, but several miles away there are nice stones along the river which can easily be transported in canoes. A long time ago, a hun-

dred years ago or even more, Indians used to live there who must have fortified their town because the walls are still distinctly visible. We found 3 such Forts at distances of several miles as the whole town was fortified where there is now a dense forest in the middle of the place and nobody knows any more what nations lived there. But from all appearances they must have fought great wars. After having inspected this neighbourhood we went down the East bank of the river until we reached the "Fork" where the Gekelemukpechünk empties into the Muskingum. On March 17 we came to a small Indian town where we spent the night. From there we sent a messenger to Gekelemukpechünk to announce our visit to the chief. On the morning of March 18 we reached our destination and were very cordially welcomed by the chief (whose guests we were) and by all those who were at home. As they had already learnt from the messenger that we wanted to speak to them, the members of the Council assembled after a short while and we informed them of the purpose of our journey saying: "We have several times heard from our people as well as from other Indians that you would be pleased if we settled in your neighbourhood. Only the other day you sent us a Belt of Wampum inviting us and our brethren in Friedenshütten. You added that the land along the Beaver Creek was not suitable land on which to settle but that we should come to the neighbourhood of Gekelemukpechünk where we would be able to enjoy peace and quiet and where nobody would molest us, which we were very glad to hear. As we are expecting our friends from Friedenshütten to join us this spring we have discussed the matter at home and thought it advisable to make this journey and speak to you. If you have no objections we will choose a suitable locality and arrange for some of our brethren in Languntoutenünk to go there as soon as we get back. Then they can build some houses and plant, so that our friends from Friedenshütten will have something to live on then they arrive. Perhaps this will not be until the summer because the way from Friedenshütten to here is a long one.

There is one thing on which we must insist, namely that when we are in your neighbourhood no other Indians shall settle anywhere near us because we are afraid that they will drink and bother us. We want to live by ourselves; not that we intend to monopolize the land but we find it impossible to live among drunken Indians. If those Indians did live near us they would corrupt our children and the young people, they would persuade them to drink and dance with them. That is why we have to live alone. We shall not prove troublesome to anybody, on the contrary we will endeavour to be at peace with everyone. We expect the same from you, namely that you will not be hostile to us but let us live our lives the way good Converts should. We also want to inform you that the Indians from Friedenshütten are going to bring their teacher with them. I am going to be here myself for some time, until the end of the summer at any rate." Then we gave him a String of Wampum 2 cords long and said: "These are the words which we have to say to you," adding that we would like to start our return journey as soon as possible. After awhile the chief replied: "I am very pleased to hear that you want to live with us. All of us have often hoped that you would accept our invitation, and not only you but also the Indians in Friedenshütten and Schechschiguanunk. We are very glad that you have now accepted it. We had already thought that the locality at the great spring would be convenient for you. Many Indians can live there, and the site is isolated from other towns. The land from the mouth of the Gekelemukpechünk Creek up to Tuscarawi shall belong to the converted Indians and we will not permit any other Indians to live there. When you establish your residence with us all the Indians will be told to be friendly to you and to be well-behaved. They will also be told that anyone who wants to hear the Gospel and to live the way you do, will be at liberty to do so." The Chief gave the String of Wampum to his Council saying: "Now it is your duty to discuss the ways and means by which to

be of assistance to the converted Indians when they come. You can use horses or canoes to help them carry their possessions." Some of the captains were not at home and we stayed in Gekelemukpechünk for 2 days hoping that they would return so that definite arrangements might be made. At the end of the 2 days we told the Chief that we would send a messenger to inform him and his council of the day of our arrival so that his Indians could meet us and help us carry our belongings. We departed on the afternoon of March 20 after having had long conversations with the Chiefs. This time we reached the site of our future town by way of travelling up the Western bank of the Muschkingum. We arrived there on the afternoon of March 21, the distance from Gekelemukpechünk is about 30 miles. So now we have seen both river banks but we have not found any locality which in beauty and convenience can be compared to ours, although there are many nice ones on either side of the river. We inspected our locality once again and decided on a good place for our fields. We considered this land a present given to us by the Saviour. We thanked him for it and took possession of it in his name. We already made some "improvements" here and there and planted a little corn. We spent the night near the great spring which according to the Indians who know it, never dries up. The Indian brethren shot several Welsh roosters which are here in great numbers. Also there are a good many geese and ducks. On March 22 we chose the nearest way through the forest (there is no straight road between Langundoutenünk and our new locality) and arrived in Langundoutenünk on the morning of March 26. We were very glad and thankful that our journey had been blessed by the Saviour and successful. This is the report of the journey to Gekelemukpechünk.

Eclipses

In case of an eclipse of sun or moon, they say that these bodies have fallen into a swoon.

Source: Zeisberger's *History...,* p. 148

David Zeisberger
1772

Schoenbrunn received its name by chance, literally.

The first Christian Indians reached the area on May 3, 1772, and immediately began to build the town. Several months later their minister, David Zeisberger, went back to Langunto-Utenünk to attend an important conference concerning the future of the mission towns. The minutes of the meeting held on August 12, 1772, are set forth herein as being of interest in seeing how the Moravians decided questions of great importance to the mission. They sought guidance from the Saviour by means of the lot.

Thus it is that the place we now call Schoenbrunn is not called Bethel or Enon or Goshen. The lot chose Welhik Thuppeek, the Indian words for good or beautiful spring. And so it was known, for the first few years of its existence. Several of the journals in this book refer to it as Welhik Thuppeek, or some reasonably close spelling thereof. Only later did the German word for beautiful spring become more common—Schoenbrunn.

Conference Minutes
Langunto-Utenünk, Aug. 12, 1772

Present, Johannes Ettwein, David Zeisberger, Bro. and Sr. Jungmann and Bro. and Sr. Roth.

1. Since Brother David Z. has come hither from Muskingum, in order to consider with us, at once, the further moving of the Indian congregation and since the Brethren who have arrived would like to know soon where they are to remain for the winter, it is necessary that we soon resolve upon something concerning the Holy Communion, concerning the journey to Gekelem:, concerning this place and other matters.

2. It is true that not all our communicants have arrived, but we cannot postpone the Communion longer than till next Saturday,

therefore, a beginning will be made tomorrow with the speaking with the brethren and sisters. Bro. Ettwein and Bro. and Sister Jungmann will do this.

3. Brother Ettwein, David and John Heckewelder will proceed from here to the new place next week, with as many of the Indian brethren as wish to go, from there they will go with five or six brethren to Gekelem: to greet the Chief and speak with him personally. Johannes, Nathanael, Wilhelm, Josua, Cornelius, Joseph, Anton are to be considered in this connection.

4. Since the brethren here, on account of the many intoxicated, are weary of dwelling here and all wish to move away, the brethren have accepted it as known that they would leave the place, as, however, up to this time there have still always been some of this region who have come to the services, and as it would make the

matter very difficult, if we all at the same time wished to begin a new place, especially, where the land must first be cleared, it would be better to hold to this place longer. We cannot, indeed, well help it if no one wishes to remain here, but we will let ourselves be instructed by our dear Lord as to what we are to do, so far as in us lies. Hence, three lots were prepared,

a) The Saviour approves that we propose to leave this place next spring.

b) The Saviour does not approve this.

c) --------

The lot indicated that the Saviour does not approve that we propose to leave this place next spring.

5. Old Joshua has sent messengers and belts to the Chiefs, in the name of the Mohicans and has undertaken separate negotiations with them. We have noted very clearly in course of the journey that the old difference between the Mohicans and the Delawares is still existing and comes to expression on the part of the Mohicans, at least, in the case of Joshua. In Bethlehem the matter has already been considered, whether now, perhaps, there would be an opportunity to separate them. We, therefore, came to an agree-

ment to inquire of the Saviour whether we should propose a separation.

a) The Saviour approves that we now propose a separation of the Mohicans from the Delawares.

b) The Saviour does not approve this.

c) --------

The lot indicated c) --------. We shall, therefore, watch the matter, how it develops.

6. As to the name of the new place, we thought of Bethel, Enon, Goshen and Welik Tuppeck, or good, beautiful Spring, and considered them together by means of the lot.

The lot selected the last, viz. Welik Tuppeck.

7. As we now have two places to care for, circumstances bring it about that Brother and Sister Jungmann and Heckewelder go to Bro. David at Welik Tuppeck, and Brother and Sister Roth remain here in Langunto-Utenünk. The latter would doubtless, have been glad if we had consulted the lot in this matter, but we could not do it.

Source: Zeisberger, "Schoenbrunn Diary"

Election of the Chief

If a chief of the Turtle Tribe is to be elected his own tribe does not choose him but the chiefs of the other two tribes do this. Similarly, if a chief of the Wolf or Turkey Tribe were to be elected, the tribe concerned would have no part in the election.

Source: Zeisberger's *History...*, p. 112

John Ettwein
1772

John Ettwein was a bishop of the Moravian Church and, although not actually living with the Indians as Zeisberger and other missionaries did, he was extremely interested and active in the work being done by the missionaries, especially as it concerned the education of the Indian children. The following journal was kept by Ettwein and describes his trip into the Ohio country just as the first of the mission towns in the Tuscarawas Valley was being established. He was present at the meeting at Langunto-Utenünk when the name of the new town was chosen by lot, and after returning to Langunto-Utenünk, was present when the name of the second mission town, Gnadenhutten, was also chosen by lot. While he was still at Langunto-Utenünk, he met another of our journalists, David McClure, as McClure was about to go into the Indian country.

Ettwein gives us a glimpse of the town in which Beaver died, later to become the site of Gnadenhutten, mentioning that the cornfields of the Indians were on the other side of the river from the townsite. He also is the only diarist to mention that there were apparently "many more" Indian houses or huts for several miles each way from Newcomerstown, all of which, he says, were considered as belonging to that town.

His sense of humor comes through in this journal, in his remarks about Glickihan not much caring for work and suggesting that perhaps the Reverend David McClure's denomination would care to contribute "their mite" to the cause in which the Moravians were then engaged, rather than trying to set up their own missionary effort.

BROTHER ETTWEIN'S AC-COUNT OF HIS VISIT IN LANGUNTO-UTENÜNK, ON THE BEAVER CR., AND WELHIK TUPPEEK, ON THE MUSKINGUM RIVER

The 12th of Aug., 1772. Our dear Br. Dav. Zeisberger arrived in Langunto-Utenünk from Muskingham River, sick and weak in body. So we held the necessary conferences with him; and, because many of the Brethren and Sisters, who had arrived, earnestly desired to journey on to their destination, we resolved to celebrate the Holy Communion with the Indian congregation on the 15th of Aug. We would, indeed, have liked to have waited until all our travellers had gathered; but we could not delay till then, because many had gone to Pitsburg and that region in search of food. Our dear Lord very graciously made His presence felt on this day in the reunited little congregation, both during a general lovefeast service and, particularly, during the Holy Communion, in which 60. participated.

On the 14th of Aug., we first had a conference with the Helpers and, later, with all the married Brethren, concerning 1) a message to be sent to Gekelemuckpechünk, or New Comers Town, as the English call it; 5. Indian Brethren were agreed upon for this purpose, and the words to be addressed to the chiefs were discussed. Concerning 2) the further removal to the new settlement on the Muskingham, and the remaining of certain families in Langunto-Utenünk, where they would more easily find sustenance for themselves and their cattle during this winter, than in the new locality. Concerning 3) the retention, or rather, the introduction of surnames, or family names, because without them church registers cannot be kept plainly; moreover, in daily intercourse, too, many misunderstandings occur if one wishes to use only the baptismal name. The Brethren who have unseemly Indian names, are to adopt their baptismal name as their surname, both for their family and for their descendants. It met with general approval, for example, to say: Salomon Allomewi, Isaac Glikhikan, Jacob Gendaskund, etc.

On the 17th, in a committee appointed for the purpose, a beginning was made with the revision of verses and other matter existing in Delaware translation. Since, for some years, the dear Saviour has given us Indian Brethren who understand English well and since, also, our dear Brethren David Zeisberger, Rothe, Heckewelder and Jungmann are learning the language, it is to be hoped that finally, by this arrangement, accurate and clear translations may be obtained and more of the Word of God rendered into this language. It is sad that, as yet, so little has been translated; it is quite a poverty-stricken language, and for many things, especially things spiritual, no words at all are to be found. And the missionaries have been too hesitant in introducing words from other languages and making them intelligible by means of explanations. The Delawares have, for instance, no word for *"man"*, but say either "Indian" *or* "white man."

"Holy" they cannot express in any other way than "quite clean", "without sin." Through misapprehension, they took the word *"holy"*, when translating it, to mean: "wholly, entirely", or "whole, entire, unbroken," and used it so. It has become an urgent matter of prayer with me, that the Holy Spirit should give our Brethren greater aid in grasping and learning the language, so that the Word of God may be rendered

purely and without adulteration into the Indian language and may not, without our intention, give rise to all kinds of erroneous beliefs. The Lord's prayer, which Br. Rothe translated and which was thoroughly revised by Br. David Zeisberger and the above-mentioned committee: Anton, Johannes, Nathanael, Wilhelm, Samuel, Abraham (Josua and Joseph Pepi being absent), is now to be used in the public services and also to be memorized by the children in school. There is a great lack of public and of family prayer; the prayers and sighs of the heart are know to God alone. On occasion of our gathering, a name was also agreed upon for the new settlement, namely Welhik-Tuppeek (German, Schönbrunn) [English, Beautiful Spring], which name we submitted to [the lot], together with Goshen, Bethel, Enon, and a blank slip.

Johannes Papunham and Nathanael Davis were appointed lay heads of the congregation [Gemein-Diener] in Welhik-Tuppeek for the time being and Anton and Abraham in Langunto-Utenünk; a committee and a helpers' conference were agreed upon for each place, and the Indian congregation was instructed concerning its own duties.

The 19th of Aug, I, with Br. David Z. and John Heckewelder, left for the Muskingham, in company with the Brethren Shebosh, Johannes, Nathanael, Wilhelm, Samuel and Anton, of Tshesheq, and their families. We spent 4. nights en route and reached Welhik-Tuppeek only on [Sunday], the 23rd. It has a very beautiful location in a plain, some 10. miles in length and several miles in breadth, near one very large spring and several other fine small ones. They, together, give rise to a creek, on which one can paddle during most of the year right up to the settlement, in canoes. Between the settlement itself and the Muskingham river is a stretch of very rich bottom land, more than half a mile wide and probably 5. miles long, suitable for Indian corn; it is covered almost entirely by walnut and locust trees. We had left it to the Indian Brethren to choose a suitable and good place; therefore on the 24th of Aug. we inspected a number of sites up river which had been proposed for this purpose. But none of them met the approval of the Brethren, and they elected to remain in Schönbrunn. Therefore the new town was laid out again: 40. lots, each 3. rods wide and 6. rods long, being staked off in the form of a "T", in such a way that the meeting house is to stand about in the center, with the house of the ministers next to it.

On the 26th of Aug., I alone left for Gekelemuchpechünk, or New Comers Town, (because Br. David Z. had become ill again), in company with the Indian Brethren Johannes, Nathanael, Wilhelm, Samuel, and Isaac. Very soon we crossed the river, which is still about half as wide as the Lehigh and has a pretty even depth all over, namely about 2½ feet. We travelled through nothing but the richest bottom land down stream on the west side of the river, until we came close to an old town, where King Beaver resided, toward the end. We inspected it; it lies on the east side of the river, the plantations being on the west side. 4. miles from New Comers Town, we hear that they had received 70. gall. of rum at that place and had already spent 4. days drinking it. We, therefore, sent Isaac Glikhican ahead to reconnoiter; and he returned during the night with the message, that Chief Netawatwes when he heard of our coming, had at once decided to discontinue the boozing; and the chief said, we were to come right on to him, we would find them all sober next morning!

On the 27th, therefore, we finished our journey, going straight to the chief. He has a well built house of nicely squared logs, with a shingle roof. He has received us with great friendliness; and I had to sit down next to him on the floor and the rest in a circle around us. He asked the Brethren several questions and then sent for the other chiefs, who arrived in a couple of hours; but only 3. came: Neskalichen, Killbuk and Welapachtschichen (White Eye was in Pitsburg and Echpalewechund in Langunto-Utenünk.) Johannes Papunham was the speaker With one string of wampum, he wiped their eyes and cleaned their ears, so that they might see and hear us well. With the 2nd, he greeted Chief Netawatwes on behalf of all who had come. With the 3rd, he told him, that they had received his messages, and, in accordance with them, all from Wialusing and Tsheshequannunk had come with their teachers. He expressed thanks with a belt in the name of all, for the piece of land which they had set aside for the believers; and he said, that they had made a beginning with building in Welhik-Tuppeek and would in time, perhaps still build 1 or 2. other places on the land; that they depended upon it that no other Indians should receive permission to settle within the borders of their district, since it was their custom [*i. e.* of the heathen] not to make fences and it would be too bad if others were to harm their cattle, and they had much cattle; that such people loved rum and would, therefore, come into their serttlements when intoxicated, to the hurt of their children, which thing they hated. Thereupon, he said: "Our Brethren have told you already how we are accustomed to live, but we wanted to say this to you again ourselves. We believe in the true and only God and hear His Word gladly; we hear it gladly every day, and therefore we have our teachers to live with us. We love peace with everyone and never want to get involved in any war. Because we know the harm that rum works, therefore we will not tolerate any to be brought upon our land or into our settlements. We do not have any special chiefs in our town, but we are all Brethren. When you wish to send words to us, send them to the Brethren in Welhik-Tuppeek; and call us the Brethren. When you hear anything evil of us, do not believe such lies, but ask us, and we will tell you the truth. Whenever the chiefs have some good undertaking in hand, we will gladly help with it and contribute to it, as others do. Never be concerned about the white Brethren among us; there never will be many among us, and you shall receive word concerning those who do live among us, and be informed why they are with us."

The chief then gave his answer to Killbuk, and he announced it in an impressive tone. It ran thus: "We rejoice greatly to see you and hear your good words. It makes us all rejoice, old and young alike, to see a matter realized which we have desired so long! It will be very fine along the river, should you build a number of towns. At first we planned for you to have land to within 4. miles of this place; but because we heard, that you do not like to live so near to savages, we have placed your boundary further up along the Gekelemuchpechünk creek. However, you may also have the place where King Beaver lived; for this reason we caused the people to move away from there already last spring! When all our people shall be sobered up and the other chiefs shall have returned home, then we will place your words before the whole nation and will thereupon give you a more complete answer, which Killbuk shall bring to Welhik-Tuppeek." All was confirmed by those present with a loud "Kehelle." They asked, if I were one of their teachers. And when they heard that I had merely accompanied them on their journey and would go back, they expressed their joy and gratitude for this; and Killbuk wished that he might be able to bring their words to Welhik-Tuppeek, before I should leave again for Bethlehem! From their private conversation which followed, I gathered that they would ask the Brethren for a teacher too. We received the best that the (royal) kitchen could provide for dinner: beans, that had not been picked over, squashes, with some dried venison, all cooked together without a speck of salt or grease or bread.

Johannes and Wilhelm then spent a long time alone with the two oldest chiefs; and the former was quite inspired with preaching. I asked Wilhelm what Johannes had been so ardent about; and he said, he had related his life and preaching as a heathen to the chiefs, and had told them what he now believes and had experienced as truth. Welapachtschichen, the chief of Assinink on the Hockhoking river, took his friend Isaac aside privately and told him, he, too, sought to please God and therefore prayed and sacrificed according to the best of his understanding; that he had gone to Langunto-Utenünk for that purpose, hoping to hear some good thing from him, but, because he had not met him, he had not tarried there. Isaac then told him of the true God and of the right service of God. We were told that this chief had come from Assinink expressly for the purpose of asking Netawatwes, whether he intended to accept the Christian religion., If he would accept it, he, too, would accept it with his town!

New Comers Town lies on the west side of the Muskingham river. I counted between 40 and 50. houses, very irregularly built. Some miles upstream and some miles down, stand many more houses and huts, which are reckoned as belonging to the town. It is a fine region, but they have no water other than that of the river. Toward evening, we returned to our camp of the night before, where Br. Johannes unexpectedly had found his father's sister; the old folks heard

more about God and His Word on these two evenings than they probably had heard in their life before. Isaac entertained the Brethren with an account of his former ideas, when he had prayed to the Wiperwill and to the serpents, and with the tomfoolery of heathen preachers, causing the Brethren much laughter. In token of the great change which had taken place in Chief Netawatwes, he recounted how just a year ago, this same chief had plagued him much because of his faith and had asked him, how many 6. pence he had given already, in order that one should pray for him. (He had ideas about Catholics.) Isaac replied: "I have never yet paid anything for prayer! But even were it so, why should it seem so strange? I and my friends have paid plenty to the sorcerers for good fortune and protection, when I went on the warpath." The chief said: "You have to pull the cart obediently, don't you?" Reply: "I am building a house and draw up the logs for it" And so the chief did not know what more he could say. This Isaac Glickhican is a very good-humored man and a great orator, was a courageous captain in war, and now likes to preach very much (better than to work.) Some years before his conversion, he had a dream. In it he came to a place, where he saw many Indians in a hall, who had no scalp locks nor nose rings; and a little white man in their midst. They beckoned him to enter; and when he had entered, the white man gave him a book and said: "Read!" He answered: "I cannot read!" The white man said: "When you have spent some time with us, you will learn it all right!" From that day on he told the Indians, that he knew there were people who knew the right way to eternal happiness; he had seen them in a dream, and if he should learn more about this, he would let them know, too! Then, when he was sent with a message to Goshgoshing and came, on that occasion, to Lawunachannek, there he found the Indians and the little white man, Brother David Zeisberger, as he had seen them in his dream; and believed and was baptized.

The 29th of Aug. Certain general rules were agreed upon, which all must promise to observe, who desire to live in Schönbrunn or any other Moravian Indian settlement. Also, we were gladdened by receiving letters from the congregation [*i.e.* Bethlehem]; and the 2. Single Brethren, to their great joy, received the printed festival ode. We met with the Brethren and stayed until near midnight, discussing all manner of words and expressions. The Indian Brethren and Sisters like to hear something out of the Bible; and it was resolved to hold Bible study every Sunday afternoon and sometimes of an evening, during the winter.

[Sunday], the 30th. Nathanael's son, from New Comers Town, a fine fellow, came thence to attend the preaching service. Isaac showed us on the map where the known Indian nations live. He is acquainted far and wide and told us, that Chief Netawatwes had received a map from the Delamattinos, or Wiondots, which they had made, showing the location of 70. towns and as many different dialects of Indians, who are all friendly, that is, live in peace with each other. The Wiondots, or Delamattinos, have given to the Delawares, the land between Beaver creek, the Cajahaga river, Lake Erie, the Sandusky river, thence to the headwaters of the Hockhoking river and then up the Ohio to Shingas Town. And Schönbrunn lies in the middle thereof, 22. miles above New-Comers Town and 16. miles below Tuscerawas, some 50. miles from Lake Erie. The main chief of the Wiondots lives on the Sandusky with a part of the nation; the other part lives with a chief in the region of Detroit. The Wiondots and Shawanosen are pretty nearly of equal strength, but not as numerous as the Delawares. The Shawanose have 4. towns on the headwaters of the Sioto river, about 100. miles from Schönbrunn: Pichuway, Kischkubi, Michenschay, and Chelokraty. In this last place lives Wm. Henry's brother, a gunsmith, with his wife who had been captured by the Shawanose as a child and reared among them. The Chipoways and Tawas together form a strong nation, about as distinct as the Munzys and Unamis Delawares. They live beyond the lakes, as do the Wawijachtanos who are said to be the strongest among the known nations. The Unamiwoas, along the Miamis river, are also said to be pretty strong, and the Okachbaks as well. The Kikabus are not strong, but very savage and no friends of the English. The Unamiwoas and Twichtwis have something of the Schwanosen language and the Wiondots of the Maqua; many of the last named have been baptized by the French.

I and my dear Brother David Zeisberger

rejoiced with grateful tears over the dear Saviour's marvellous and gracious dealing with the Indian congregation, which He now has placed as His candlestick in the midst of the Delawares and in the neighborhood of the Shawanosen and Wiondots. For the congregations have this advantage; wherever they appear, there something substantial results. And, because Brother David wanted to know upon which of the neighboring nations the Brethren should now mainly direct their attention, the Saviour pointed to the Shawanosen, Br. David, with Isaac and one other Brother, will visit them as soon as time and circumstances permit, in order to make their acquaintance. In one of their towns it is a common custom to seek to get rid of sin by means of vomiting; and, after all, this is evidence of some seeking and desire. There is a Sister now in Langunto-Utenünk, who for three years took an emetic each morning in order to get rid of sin; and, because she cherished the fantastic idea that her sin was mounting to her neck, she would have made a complete end of herself, if she had not heard the gospel.

On the 2nd. of Septr. I held the evening service in Schönbrunn on the text: "We entreat also that ye receive not the grace of God in vain." [II Cor. 6:1] In a parting message, I commended their ministers to the love, support, and care of the Indian Brethren and Sisters, under all circumstances.

[Thursday], the 3rd, furnished with the doctrinal text: "Watch ye, stand fast in the faith, quit you like men, be strong," [I Cor. 16:13] I bade my dear Brethren David Zeisberger, John Heckewelder and the Indian Brethren and Sisters a heartfelt and tearful farewell, commended to my dear Lord His work which has been begun here, and journeyed with the Brethren Shebosch and Wilhelm by way of Tuscerawas back to Langunto-Utenünk. Both this route and the one we followed on the journey out, lead through none but good, fertile land; and the further one goes toward the west, the better the land becomes. From Langunto-Utenünk to Schönbrunn is 80. miles and more.

[Saturday], the 5th, we arrived again at our dear Brethren and Sisters Jungmanns and Rothes. There I found a letter addressed to me from a David Maccluer in which he reports to me that he and his companion, Mr. Friesbie, were journeying as missionaries to preach the gospel of our Redeemer to the poor Indians in New Comers Town on the Muskingum; and that Joseph Pepi had promised them to accompany them as interpreter for several weeks, if the Brethren had no objection to this; and, in conclusion, wishes us much blessing from the Head of the Church for our work among the Indians. I wrote him in my reply, that the Indians in New Comers Town desired a witness who belonged to their own nation; and that a Christian congregation had settled within 22. miles of them, which, by the grace of God, should become a light to them; that they should comfort the good people who were concerned about the salvation of the heathen and had sent them out, with this news, even should they not receive the answer they expected in reply to their offer; and, should they like to have a share in the conversion of the Delawares and would make a contribution to that end, their mite would be acceptable to the missionaries now laboring among them. Mr. Macclure came, on the 7th, to visit us in Langunto-Utenünk, and attended an evening and a morning devotion, which were held in the Indian tongue. He lodged with us and could not praise highly enough the reverence shown by old and young, and the beautiful singing. He said they had not known anything of this mission. They had read the history of Greenland in the home of Doctor Wilok in New England, with whom they had lived several years and who had secured them as missionaries among the Indians, the Scottish Society for the Furtherance of the Gospel bearing the costs. Mr. Freisbie remained in Pitsburg because of illness; but Maccluer journeyed with Brother Joseph Pepi to New Comers Town and, no doubt, also visited Welhik Tuppeek, and is thus become a witness to that which the Saviour is doing among the Delawares. Neither the Indians nor existing circumstances will incite him to stay there. This is the 3rd offer made to the Indians of New Comers Town by preachers this summer. They paid no attention to the first 2; how they will take this one, we have yet to hear. The Indians have told us, that King Beaver called his chiefs to him, on his death bed, and said to them: "I know you are seeking something, the one in this direction, the other in that. I will now soon be dead, and therefore I want still to admonish you. Let not

one of you turn to the English Church, the other to the Presbyterians, and the 3rd to the Quakers; but all turn to the same way, to those to whom so many of our nation already belong; otherwise strife and division will come among you, and that is not good."

On the occasion of the Married People's festival, I held an address for the Married People on the texts of these days and gave a hearty admonition particularly to the women, to be subject, and to be cleanly as to their clothing and as to their house-keeping, in which matters I found them lacking considerably.

Because we had found it necessary, after considering all the circumstances, for Brother and Sister Jungmann to join Bro. David in Schönbrunn while Brother and Sister Rothe, on the other hand, would remain in Langunto-Utenünk, it was agreed that Brother and Sister Jungmann should move to their new post before the end of September, thoroughly introducing Brother and Sister Rothe to their work before them. The Brethren and Sisters had proposed leaving Langunto-Utenünk entirely, by next spring, but it did not meet with the Saviour's approval that we should take this step then [the lot negatived the proposal]; therefore plantations are to be made again next year, and we will then see further, what is to be. Apparently, conditions in this neighborhood, also, are improving, and the Saviour has gotten rid of some great enemies of the gospel; and we may say that the Church there, too, enjoys tranquility.

Josua, the elder, had also arrived in Langunto-Utenünk with the Mahikanders and some Delawares who had always kept together, aloof from the others, ever since they were on the great island. We spoke at length, first with Josua alone, and, afterward, with the whole company, concerning the ideas which they had expressed from time to time and concerning a new settlement. We assured them of our satisfaction with and approval of their expressed purpose to start a separate place for themselves. And it was decided, in accordance with our agreement with Br. David, that they should select a suitable place for themselves several miles above or below Schönbrunn, and there, with the approval of Br. David Zeisberger and Br. Jungmann, their ministers, build their houses together. These [Brethren] would visit them in turn from Schönbrunn and conduct services for them, until such time as they could have their own ministers. Josua and John Martin are to be lay heads of the congregation [Gemein-Diener] in that place for the time being; and, if they approve themselves, they shall be authorized to hold a meeting or a service of song from time to time during the week. They are to belong to the Helpers' conference of Schoenbrunn, to which report is to be made of all that concerns their place. They are to go to Schoenbrunn for the Communion. They requested earnestly that ministers of their own be given them at once; but I could not leave Br. David and Heckewaelder alone in Schoenbrunn, nor expect them to live with the Mahikanders. If Brother David does not live with a married couple who can care for him for a time again, he will not be able to hold out long. There are 16. families who will build together at the present time, most of them former inhabitants of Gnadenhütten [the one on the Mahoney river in Pennsylvania, where a massacre had occured in 1755]. They proposed to name their settlement Gnadenhütten or Nain, and *Gnadenhütten* received the Saviour's approval [again, apparently by the lot].

Source: Hamilton, *John Ettwein,* pp. 258–69

Indian Corn

The Indians have a number of manners of preparing their corn. They make an excellent pottage of it, by boiling it with fresh or dried meat (the latter pounded), dried pumpkins, dry beans, and chestnuts. They sometimes sweeten it with sugar or molasses from the sugar-maple tree. Another very good dish is prepared by boiling with their corn or maize, the washed kernels of the shell-bark or hickory nut. They pound the nuts in a block or mortar, pouring a little warm water on them, and gradually a little more as they become dry, until, at last, there is a sufficient quanity of water, so that by stirring up the pounded nuts the broken shells separate from the liquor, which from the pounded kernels assumes the appearance of milk. This being put into the kettle and mixed with the pottage gives it a rich and agreeable flavour. If the broken shells do not all freely separate by swimming on the top or sinking to the bottom, the liquor is strained through a clean cloth, before it is put into the kettle.

Source: Heckewelder's *History...,* p. 194

David McClure
1772

The next preacher to visit the Indians in the Tuscarawas Valley was a Congregationalist from Connecticut, David McClure. He was in the valley from September 20th to October 10th, 1772, and also used Joseph "Pepee" as his interpreter.

His journal is probably the most descriptive of all of the journals of the Tuscarawas Valley in Indian days—not just of the houses and towns, but of the people and what they did. His account of the effect of rum upon the Indians is both extremely graphic and tragic. (Others also speak of the effect of rum upon the Indians: George Croghan's journal of January 1754, while at Logstown—"From the 16th till the 26th we could do nothing—the Indians being constantly drunk", and James Wood in his journal of July 16, 1775—"The Cornstalk Nimwha Wryneck Blue Jacket Silver Heels and about fifteen other Shawanees arrived They immediately got drunk and continued in that situation for two days.")

Also to be noted are the references in his journal to letters sent by a Rev. David Jones to the Indians, he being our next visiting preacher.

From the Schoenbrunn Diary entry of October 7th, immediately following this journal, it is not surprising that the Indians did not particularly like Rev. McClure and asked that he leave their town.

Aug. 23. — ...Providentially, near Pittsburgh, we found a christian Indian, who engaged to be our Interpreter. His name was Joseph Pepee, of the Delaware nation. He had just arrived in the vicinity, with about 50 families who were removing from the Susquehanna to Muskingum, as already mentioned. Pepee was an aged man, & one of the christians of the late pious & laborious David Brainard's Congregation. He proved to be a sincere & faithful & zealous Interpreter. He had officiated in that capacity for Messrs. Beatty & Duffield on their visit a few years past, to the Indians at Muskingum. Mr. John Brainard had recommended him to us, & we esteemed the circumstance which placed him in our way, as a signal smile of providence. He was obliged to go forward with the colony of his countrymen to Kuskuskoong, about 55 miles, to consult upon the place where to settle. Mr. Frisbie has been unwell for several days, & I fear will not be able to encounter the fatigues of the indian Mission. His disorder is the fever & ague.

Sept. 3 & 4. — Preparing for my journey to Muskingum. Engaged Robert McClellan to go with me as a waiter.

5. — Saturday, left Mr. Frisbie, who purposed, God willing, to come forward as soon as his health would permit; & set out with Robert, expecting to meet my Interpreter Joseph returning from Kuskuskoong. Mr. Gibson rode

112

David McClure

Born: November 18, 1748 Newport, Rhode Island
Died: June 25, 1820 East Windsor, Connecticut
Age on entering Tuscarawas Valley – 24 years

On the bank of this stream, which was fordable, we had a wonderful prospect of game. In the midle of the Creek, a small flock of wild geese were swiming, on the bank sat a large flock of Turkies, & the wild pigeons covered one or two trees; & all being within musket shot, we had our choice for a supper. My Interpreter chose the Turkies, & killed three at one shot.

David McClure   September 17, 1772

in company to his house in Logstown, which was the only house there, 18 miles below Pittsburgh.

Tarried at Mr. Gibson's over Sabbath. Spent the day principally in the solitary woods, in meditation & reading. Monday, my interpreter not arriving, I set out with Robert to find him. Mr. Gibson was kind enough to ride with me to a small town of Mingo Indians, on the N. bank of the Ohio, & to send his servant a few miles further to show us the path. The roads through this Indian country are no more than a single horse path, among the trees. For a wilderness the travelling was pleasant, as there was no underbrush & the trees do not grow very closely together. We travelled diligently all day. I was apprehensive that we had missed the path. Robert was a great smoaker of tobacco, & frequently lighted his pipe, by striking fire, as he sat on his horse, & often in the course of the day, exclaimed in his jargon, "Ding me, but this path will take us somewhere." At sun setting we arrived at Kuskuskoong, & found my Interpreter Joseph there. He had been detained by the sickness & death of a Grandchild. It was a neat Moravian village, consisting of one street & houses pretty compact, on each side, with gardens, back. There was a convenient Log church, with a small bell, in which the Indians assembled for morning & evening prayer. The village was full, as their brethren the Susquehanna Indians had arrived with Mr. Etwine. The name of the German Moravian Missionary stationed here is Roth. David Leizburgher is the minister of the Indians going to Muskingum. The Missionaries have their wives & families with them. They received me with great hospitality. At the sound of the bell, the Indians assembled in the church for evening prayer. It was lighted with candles around the walls, on which hung some common paintings of Jesus in the manger of Bethlehem with Joseph & Mary; Jesus on the Cross, & the Resurrection &c. On one side set the elderly men & the boys by themselves, & on the other the women & girls. The evening exercise consisted of devout hymns in the Indian language, & in singing they all, young & old bore a part, & the devotion was solemn & impressive. After singing a number of hymns, the missionary addressed them, in a short exhortation in the Indian language, & they retired with great order & stillness to their houses. Their hymns are

prayers addressed to Jesus Christ, the lamb of God, who died for the sins of men, & exhortations & resolutions to abstain from sin, because sin is most displeasing to him, & to live in love & the practice of good works, as he has given us example.

The same exercise was observed also early in the morning, of the following day. I was agreeably surprised to find so devout & orderly a congregation of christian Indians in the wilderness & pleased with the meek & friendly deportment of the Missionaries.

The moravians appear to have adopted the best mode of christianizing the Indians. They go among them without noise or parade, & by their friendly behaviour conciliate their good will. They join them in the chace, & freely distribute to the helpless & gradually instil into the minds of individuals, the principles of religion. They then invite those who are disposed to hearken to them, to retire to some convenient place, at a distance from the wild Indians, & assist them to build a village, & teach them to plant & sow, & to carry on some coarse manufactures.

Those Indians, thus separated, reverence & love their instructors, as their fathers, & withdraw a connection with the wild or drinking Indians....

Each family has a small well cultivated garden, & a part in a large corn field adjoining the town. The missionaries are remarkably attentive to the cleanliness of the Indians, & have caused necessary houses to be built for the conveniency of the town....

Took leave of the friendly Moravians & set out for Mr. Gibson's, where I had left some baggage.

We came to the mouth of Beaver Creek about sun setting, where was a village of Mingo Indians. Great part of the Indians were drunk: one of the chiefs had sold his horse for 6 cags of rum, & gave a frolic to the people; we avoided the village, & Joseph encamped on the bank of the Ohio, & Robert & I rode on to Mr. Gibson's about 6 Miles.

Sept. 9. — I sent Robert in the morning to Pittsburgh, for a horse for Joseph. The same day Mr. Gibson arrived & informed me that Mr. Frisbie was much better, & no doubt would be able to go with me to Muskingum.

10. — Robert was to have been back to Mr. Gibson's, the last evening; but had not arrived, & Joseph weary of waiting at his encampment, had come to Mr. Gibson's.

12. — Saturday, Robert not coming, I went to Pittsburgh, partly with a view to preach there on the morrow, & principally with the expectation of finding my companion Mr. Frisbie, so far recovered as to accompany me. — Arriving found that Robert, in violation of his engagement, had gone home, up the Monongahala, & I never saw him after. I was also disappointed of seeing Mr. Frisbie, as he had gone to a settlement 24 miles distant....

Monday. I was much at a loss where to find an englishman to go with me, & my Indian interpreter, as an assistant & companion: but providentially, a young man, Joseph Nickels [Nicholson], who was the interpreter for the garrison, & had a salary from the crown, & who had been a captive among the Indians when young, & well acquainted with all their customs, mentioned to me that it would be agreeable to him to go with me, if I could obtain leave of absence. I accordingly waited on the Commandant, & he politely gave him leave of absence, for a month. By the kindness of friends, I was furnished with a horse for him, & one for my interpreter, & another to carry our baggage, which consisted of a markee tent, (lent me by Capt. Gibson;) blankets, some cooking utensils & sundry articles of provisions.

Septr 15, 1772 — Set out with Nickels, & crossing the Allegany River, came on Indian ground. Arrived at Mr. Gibson's, at Logs town about 18 Miles, & found my Interpreter there.

16th — Came to the Mingo village on Bever Creek. On the green lay an old Indian, who, they said, had been a hard drinker; his limbs were contracted by fits. He told me his disorder was brought on him by witchcraft, that he employed several conjurors to cure him, but in vain. I called his attention to his dependence on God, on death & Judgment. He however gave little heed; but in answer told my Interpreter, if he would bring a pint of rum every time he came, he should be glad to see him every day. Awful stupidity! This village is commonly called Logan's town. About half an hour before our arrival, we saw Captn Logan in the woods, & I

was not a little surprised at his appearance. As we were obliged to ride, as it is commonly called in Indian file, the path not admitting two to ride a breast, I had passed beyond Logan without seeing him. He spoke to my interpreter, who was a little distance behind, to desire me to stop. I looked back & saw him a few rods from the path, stand. under a tree, leaning on the muzzle of his gun. A young Indian, with his gun, stood by him.

I turned back & riding up to Logan, asked him how he did, & whether he wished to speak with me? (I had seen him at Pittsburgh). Pointing to his breast, he said, "I feel very bad *here.* Wherever I go the evil monethoes' (Devils) are after me. My house, the trees & the air, are full of Devils, they continually haunt me, & they will kill me. All things tell me how wicked I have been." He stood pale & trembling, apparently in great distress. His eyes were fixed on the ground, & the sweat run down his face like one in agony. It was a strange sight. I had several times seen him at Pittsburgh & thought him the most martial figure of an Indian that I had ever seen. At the conclusion of his awful description of himself, he asked me what he should do? Recollecting to have heard at Pittsburgh, that he had been a bloody enemy against the poor defenseless settlers on the Susquehanna, & the frontiers, in the last french war in 1758, & 9, & it was also reported of him, (though positive proof could not be had) that he had murdered a white man (one Chandler) on the Allegany mountains. I observed to him, perhaps Captn Logan, you have been a wicked man, & greatly offended God, & he now allows these Devils, or evil thoughts which arise in your heart to trouble you, that you may now see yourself to be a great sinner & repent & pray to God to forgive you. If you will repent & ask forgiveness of God from the bottom of your heart, & live a better life, the Great Spirit above will not suffer the Devils to torment you, & he will give you peace.

He attended to what I said, & after conversing a little longer, in the same strain, We left him, in the same distress, as I found him. After parting from him, various thoughts, but none satisfactory, occured to me, relative to the cause of the distress & agitation of so renowned a warrior. I sometimes thought (such was his ferocious character) that knowing of my journey, he had placed himself in a convenient spot for robbery or murder, but was disappointed, finding us armed. For my interpreter & Nickels had each a loaded piece, the Indian a common musket, & the english man, a rifle always loaded, for the purpose of killing game. Perhaps it was some sudden compunction, arising from reflections on his past guilt.

This same Logan is represented as making a very eloquent speech at the close of the revolutionary war, on the murder of his family by Col. Cressup. [This statement was obviously entered into the diary at a later date for the event described did not occur until 1774.]

We left Logan's town, & proceeded on about one mile & came to a pleasant stream of water, where we encamped. My Interpreter kindled a fire & prepared a trammel supported by stakes drove in the ground, on which our kettle was suspended to boil, & assisted me to pitch the Tent. Nickels performed the office of cook, with which he was well acquainted. I spread a Bear skin & blanket for a bed, & my portmantau was the pillow. We supped very comfortably on chocolate & roast venison, & committing ourselves in prayer, to the protecting care of heaven, we lay down to rest.

The Indian chose to sleep in the open air, the englishman in the tent. I slept but little this night, being kept awake by the howling of Wolves. It was the first time I had ever heard their nightly dolorous yells. They came near our encampment; but the sight of the fire kept them off, had they been disposed to attack us. Our horses we let go, each having a bell suspended to his neck. The feed in the woods was good & in plenty.

17. — *Thursday*. We breakfasted, got up our horses, & about 9 O'Clock set out from our encampment. We travelled leisurely, on account of the baggage horse, who was heavily loaded, & moved slowly.

The woods were clear from underbrush, & the oaks & black walnut & other timber do not grow very compact, & there is scarcely anything to incommode a traveler in riding, almost in any direction, in the woods of the Ohio. The Indians have been in the practice of burning over the ground, that they may have the advantage of seeing game at a distance among the trees. We

saw this day several deer & flocks of Turkies. About an hour before sun setting we arrived at Little Beaver Creek.

On the bank of this stream, which was fordable, we had a wonderful prospect of game. In the midle of the Creek, a small flock of wild geese were swiming, on the bank sat a large flock of Turkies, & the wild pigeons covered one or two trees; & all being within musket shot, we had our choice for a supper. My Interpreter chose the Turkies, & killed three at one shot.

We went about 3 miles further & pitched our tent, like the patriarchs, by a small stream, & our evening & night was passed like the preceeding.

Friday morning we were ready to leave our encampment about 8 O'Clock, & travelled through an excellent country of land, about 18 miles & coming to a small & pleasant river, we pitched our tent about an hour before sun setting.

Saturday 19. — Our path had led us along the North bank of the pleasant river Ohio, almost the whole way from Pittsburgh, & frequently within sight of the river. The soil is luxurient, the growth principally white & black oak, Chesnut, Black Walnut, Hickory &c. The sweetest red plums grow in great abundance in this country, & were then in great perfection. Grapes grow spontaneous here & wind around the trees. We have been favored with delightful weather. It would add unspeakably to the pleasantness of this solitary wilderness had I the company & christian conversation of my friend Frisbie. My Indian Interpreter Joseph Pepee, appears to be a sincere christian, but the poor man is ignorant, his ideas contracted & his english broken. Nickels is very good natured & obliging, & his knowledge of men & things no more than we can reasonably expect of one, whose condition in life has been like his.

Lord's Day 20. — We attended to the exercises of prayer & reading the scriptures this morning, & about 11 O'Clock proceeded on our journey. As the season was approaching when the Indians go out on their fall hunting, I thought it most advisable to go on, & we were in hopes of reaching the town before night. We journeyed about 13 miles to a small run of water where we encamped, & the next day reached the town.

Sept. 21, 1772 — This town is called New Comers town by the english, & stands on the West bank of the Muskingum, containing about 60 houses, some of logs, & others the bark of trees, fastened by elm bark to poles stuck in the ground & bent over at the top. There are nearly 100 families. It is the principal town of the Delaware Nation, & the residence of the king & the greater part of the Councillors. There are several small villages up & down the river. This place is about 60 Miles above the mouth of the Muskingum. Eight or ten acres around the town are cleared. On the opposite side of the River is a large corn field, in rich low ground; it is inclosed within one common fence, & each family has its division to plant. Some of the houses are well built, with hewed logs, with stone chimnies, chambers & sellers. These I was told were built by the english captives, in the time of the french wars.

On my arrival in the town, we had the unpleasant sight of several drunken Indians & to hear their savage yells. We halted within the skirts of the town & I sent my Interpreter to the king (to whom I had written from Pittsburgh) to inform him of my arrival. He sent a messenger to invite me to his house. On our way, several Indians asked my interpreter whether we had brought rum.

The king, whose name is *Nettautwaleman*, received me with hospitality. He is an old man, tall & active. His house is the largest, & built of small square logs. Around the walls, for beds & seats, were planks raised from the ground & covered with the hides of Buffaloes & Bears.

He sent a messenger to call his Councillors & 7 or 8 aged men came in. They sat down to smoak their pipes & converse with my interpreter Joseph, & asked him a variety of questions. The king asked me, Whether his brother king George, or Sir William Johnson had sent me? I told him, that some Great men, whom the King had appointed for the business on which I came, had sent me.

He said, "as some of my people are drunk, & not fit to attend to business, I will hear your business tomorrow."

One of the Councillors, Captn Killbuck, well known for his depredations on the frontiers the last war, came in, & taking me by the hand,

very politely requested me not to give myself any concern for accommodations, for he should provide a house for me & my company: he accordingly conducted me to a log house, which was convenient. He mentioned that they were about to be much engaged in consultations, on public concerns, but that they should attend on the morrow to my business. He ordered one of his sons to wait on me: & we attended to putting our things in order in the house, in the best manner we could. I was pleased with the hospitable reception, & was ready to promise myself a successful issue to my errand.

22. — Tuesday, afternoon, a messenger informed me that the King was ready to hear what I had to say, & conducted me to the Council House. It was a long building covered with hemlock bark, with a swinging door at each end. Within the door & fronting the entrance, was the face of an aged man, carved in wood, signifying that wisdom should preside there. There was something impressive in the wild & novel appearences before me.

The King & his Council, in number about 12, sat on Buffalo skins, on one side at the entrance, the warriors on the opposite, & young men & women & children occupied the rest of the house. The men were smoaking their pipes & conversing. The warriors were painted, & their heads & necks ornamented with feathers & strings of wampum; & several of the men & women with silver & ivory or bone bracelets over their arms.

Two council fires were burning, & a bench placed between them, on which the King's Speaker desired us to sit.

After a few minutes, the Speaker spoke a word or two, & there was instantly an universal silence.

The Speaker then said to me, "Brother, the King is ready to hear what you will say."

I then expressed the satisfaction which I felt to see the King & his people, & that the Great Spirit above had kept me on a long & dangerous journey, & given us opportunity to meet them in peace & health. I informed them in a summary manner the nature & design of my errand—from whence I came, & by whom sent— read our commission, passport, & letters recommendatory from sundry respectable characters. Gave some account of pains taken to instruct the

Indians our brethren, in the wilderness in useful science & the knowledge of the true God & Saviour of men. I proposed to continue with them a considerable time, without expence to them, if agreeable to them, to teach them the way to happiness & to heaven. I conversed with them about 40 minutes, during which time, there was great attention. At the conclusion of each sentence they gave a shout of applause, crying *ka-ha-lah,* or *Ah-nan.*

The Speaker said, "The King will consider what you have spoken, & will give you an answer."

The exemplary decorum, (particularly their patient & uninterrupted attention to the speaker) of an Indian Council, has been often mentioned, by those who have been spectators. One circumstance however I do not recollect to have seen noticed by writers of the history of indian manners, which is, that they give shouts of applause to what they dislike, as uttered by the speaker, as freely as they do to what they approve. They say that it signifies no more than that they *attend* & mean to treat the speaker with civility. Their approbation or dislike, is shown by their answer, which is not obtained from an indian council, until after long & tiresome waiting. They have no pressing business to engage attention, & can afford to throw away time on trifles; & small matters are important in their apprehension, as their knowledge is very limited. In the evening some of them came to see me & I conversed with them on the things of religion. They seemed to be more inquisitive for news, & appeared to have no relish for serious information.

My family consisted of Pepee, Nickels & two sons of my host Captn Killbuck. I had sundry of the smaller articles of provisions, & the Indians supplied us with wild meat.

I expected an answer from the Council, the next day, but was obliged to wait several days for it.

Some of the Council mentioned that they were forming a Speech to send to Sir William Johnson, to inform him that they had complied with his advice, & received the Susquehanna Indians to live in their neighbourhood. {The Moravians had established Welhik Thuppeek (Schoenbrunn) in May of that year and had been given permission for the Christian Indians coming from the Susquehannah to establish a second mission town, at Gnadenhütten.}

Sept. 23 — Wednesday the Council met. They sent for me to read a letter, which they had some time previously received from some Quakers in Philadelphia, dated 18th of the 5th Month 1771, respecting teachers of religion coming among them. It promises that when such shall come they will send a Certificate with them, that they may know that they are true men. It was remarkable that the Letter had no signature. If it was genuine, it looked as if the Quakers of Philadelphia, were ashamed to appear openly in opposition to christians of other denominations engaged in the benevolent work of spreading the gospel among the heathen. It also mentions, that if they are inclined to receive School Masters, they will assist to support them. This Letter was written soon after the Synod concluded to send missionaries to those Indians.

The Quakers, I was credibly assured, sent a present of 100 Dollars to the Susquehanna Indians, removing to Muskingum. This was charitable, but to exclude, as far as their influence extends, from access to the Savages, all who do not carry with them, a testimonial of *their* approbation, is worse than uncharitable.

In said Letter the Quakers call themselves the children of the Great *Onas* (a Quill or pen) the indian name of Wm. Penn, for whose memory the Indians have a great veneration; & "hope that the same friendship which existed between their fathers & him, will allways exist between the children."

If this letter was genuine, as the Indians asserted, the policy of it, had its effect, for the Indians appeared to offer it as an objection to the reception of our proposal. No people on the continent have such unbounded influence over the Indians as this denomination, especially as their pacific principles, while they had the ascendency in the government, prevented the raising even a necessary defensive force to stop the progress of their savage & murderous depredations on the frontiers, in the french wars.

The king sent to me again to attend at the Council House. The speaker presented me a long letter which he had received not long since, from one David Jones, a baptist preacher of New Jersey, acquainting him that he was coming among them to instruct them, to learn their language & translate the Bible. He directs them to choose some of their great men to go with him to England next spring, & proposes a plan of government &c. &c.

The big words of this Letter writer were resented by the Council, altho' as I was afterwards informed some of them wished to go to England. The indian Chiefs who have visited there, have commonly returned loaded with presents.

In the evening the King's Chief Councillor came, & spent an hour or two with me. He said I must have patience; that they were engaged in other important business, & would, as soon as possible, give an answer to my proposal.

One of the aged Indians, who appeared well disposed, told me the following story. "Last spring, as we have heard, an Island belonging to the English, was sunk by an earthquake. The night before the dreadful catastrophy, a person appeared to a young man, who was a minister, informing him, that destruction was coming on the Island; & as he had been faithful to warn the wicked, he should be preserved, because the Great Spirit above had more work for him to do; & therefore he must immediately get on board of a vessell, which he did, & saw the Island sink. And when we received your letter from Pittsburgh, informing that you were coming, we believed that you was that young man, & that God has sent you to teach us the way to heaven."

25. — *Friday*. The Council still setting, & no answer. I seem to be loosing precious time; but shall patiently wait their delitory forms of business. In the afternoon, got up my horse to ride to a neighbouring village, but was prevented by one of the Council, who seemed with a degree of earnestness to expostulate against my riding anywhere, as they were, he said, consulting on my business. He said, they should send for me tomorrow, for they did not fully understand my speech. I rode only to the old *conjuring* place, where they were wont to hold their pow-wows over the sick. It was about half a mile from town, & by the side of a branch of the Muskingum. There were half a dozen cage-like things, formed by sticking poles in the earth & bending & fastening the tops, in the conical form of a Sugar loaf. When a sick person is to be operated upon, he is put into one of them, together with large stones heated hot; the cage is then

covered with blankets or skins, & the conjuror pours water upon the red hot stones, & raises such a suffocating steam or vapour as brings on a profuse sweat upon the patient. In the meantime, the conjuror, is in & out, as he can bear it, yelling & capering & making a thousand odd gesticulations, & calling upon the Evil Monetho (the Devil) to help. From the hot house, he is plunged into the water, & from the water again to the hot house, as his strength can bear the operation. It is said that this summary method is efficacious to heal those disorders which arise from obstructed perspiration, & to diseases of this kind, Indians are most subject, owing to frequent exposure to cold & heat, lodging on the ground & the like. To pulmonary disorders it is fatal, as also in the small pox. This latter scourge of the human race has swept off multitudes of Indians from this continent.

A little before my arrival, the grand Conjuror of this town was banished on pain of death. His crime was a failure of success in healing several who were sick. Their opinion of him was, that he had so much influence with the Devil, that he could obtain of him skill to heal those whom he wished to heal. The Evil Spirit, according to the Manechean doctrine, they believe to be the author of all natural evil. They also believe that their conjurors have the power of inflicting diseases, as well as healing. It was this opinion respecting the conjuror of this place, that excited the town to punish him with perpetual banishment.

I was in the Conjuror's house, it was the best built in town except the king's. A celler with stone wall — a stare case, a convenient stone chimney & fire place & closets & apartments, gave it the appearance of an english dwelling. Between the house & the bank of the River was a regular & thrifty peach orchard. The house was for sale, but no one would purchase it. The price was fixed as low as one dollar. Such dread have they of the secret & invisible power of the Conjurors.

26. — *Saturday Morning*. There was a white frost on the ground. The Indians here do but little labour on the soil. One large corn field supplies the town, & in that, the women do all the labour. The savage state has always been unfavorable to the female. The superior strength of the man is used, not in protecting & lightening

the burdens of the weaker sex, but in depressing them. The men are ashamed of all kinds of labour, except war & hunting, to these we may add, the building of their miserable houses.

If an Indian sails in his Canoe, his wife and daughter, if he has one, paddle him, where he chooses to go. When he inclines to take a wife, it is said, the female makes the advances towards courtship. Such is the pride of these lazy lords of the wilderness! There is an air of dignity, however, and a politeness of manners among them, which is surprising to one who has seen no more of Indian manners than what is found among those who live among or bordering on the english settlement. They appear conscious of their uncontrouled independence & almost unbounded liberty.

Their government is simple & democratic. The King and Council administer just so much of it, as the people, especially the warriors, approve. They pay great deference to the aged & to their opinion. The penalties of crimes are few, & such as have received the sanction of custom. Murder is almost the only crime that is punishable, and that the government have nothing to do with. It is avenged by one of the near kindred of the dead, who puts to death the murtherer, and sometimes it goes round, and a friend of the murderer takes up the hatchet. O deplorable state of nature, where men are left without the restraints of government or religion & guided, only by their passions & lusts!

I saw the unhappy effects in some instances of this insecure state of nature. A principle of fear and distrust of each other universally prevails, for every man is the avenger of his own real or imaginary wrongs.

A little before we arrived at Pittsburgh, Eneas McKay Esq., at whose house I afterwards lodged, related the following revenge of Indian murder having taken place there. In a drunken frolic, on an Island a few miles below Pittsburgh, one murdered another. The son of the person murdered became the avenger; and happened, accidentally, to find the murderer of his father at Pittsburgh. He applied to the commander of the Fort for justice to be executed on the murderer; as he was, within the jurisdiction of the english. The commander declined any interference. The Indian then said that if he would not execute justice, *he* would. With an Indian companion he

returned to the murderer and told him to prepare for death. He retired into the house yard of a Mr. Hart, and after smoking his pipe, began to sing his own death song, in a strain of dolorous and mournful melody. The avenger and his companion walked to the Piazza of Esq. McKay's house where they sat in silence, smoking their pipes, about 20 minutes, when suddenly rising, they entered the yard, the murderer was still singing the death song, resting his head upon his hand and his arms upon his knees, when the avenger, without speaking, dispatched him with his tomahawk, and threw his body into the Monongehala. Although a murderer endeavors to keep out of the way of the avenger of blood, yet when he is found by him, he makes no efforts to resist, or even to escape, but peaceably submits to execution.

The frequency of murders, the sad effects of strong drink, and the sanguinary pursuits of the avengers of blood, and in some instances avengers of the death, of the murderers, is one great cause among many, of the rapid decrease of Indians, especially those nations to whom our English traders convey rum. So sensible are they of this being to them the besom of destruction, that they have passed a law or decree that no trader shall bring rum into their towns; but the cuning policy of the traders has evaded the law, by committing it to the squaws that resort to Pittsburgh to carry & barter, and such is the ardent thirst which they have for this destructive liquid, that they connive at this practice.

It is not easy for a white man, used to the warm comforts of civilized life to conceive how delicious & exhilerating rum is, to the taste & stomach of an Indian. Living principally in the shade and damps of forests and sleeping on the moist ground, exposed to rain and cold, with slight covering to their bodies at all seasons, their constitutions are remarkably phlegmatic, their blood cold & slow, and their animal spirits, of consequence, in an habitual state of depression, bordering on melancholy. The powerful stimulus of ardent spirits to this indolent & miserable race of men, is, therefore, most acceptable and wonderfully exhilerating. An aged physician of my acquaintane, who lived in Connecticut, and died many years ago, in younger life, went with a party of Indian hunters, far northward on a hunting expedition, and fared in all respects, in the excursion, as the Indians; on his return home he felt an unsatiable thirst for rum, and drank such a quantity as would at another time have laid him by, yet without any unfavorable effects. The old gentleman used to relate the adventure, and add that he could never blame an Indian for loving rum. He condemned them, however for the excessive use of it, as the poor creatures do themselves after they have recovered from what they call a drunken frolic. For the consequence of such frolics, not unfrequently, are wounds & death.

FIRST SABBATH AT KEKALEMAHPEHOONG

These savages are ignorant of the institution of this sacred day of Rest.

I sent my Interpreter to the King, to inform him, that this day is the Sabbath of the white people, which they spent in the worship of the Great God and the instruction of religion; and that if it was agreeable to him, I would speak to the people on religion. He sent me word, that it was agreeable. A messenger went through the town & summoned the people to the Council House.

There was much the same assembly as I found there, and the same formality as the day after my arrival. I discoursed to them on the nature and duty of prayer, recapitulated in a summary manner the things which I was about to pray for, and then prayed. In this exercise they all stood and attended with decency. I then discoursed to them, on the advent of Jesus Christ into the world, & the atonement which he made for the sins of men, by his obedience, sufferings and death. It was a brief history of the life of our Saviour & of the necessity of repentence and faith. Some were attentive and appeared affected at the representation of the passion of J.X. As the Apostles preached Jesus Christ, at their first access to the Gentiles, I thought the divinely directed example was a warrant for me to attempt the same. The greater part of the audience appeared stupid and insensible of the inportance of what was spoken. They smoaked their pipes in time of sermon, and at the conclusion of each sentence uttered a shout of applause, according to their custom.

They gave me opportunity again in the afternoon to preach to them. My subject was the parable of the prodigal, Luke 15, chapter. After sermon & prayer some of them asked questions, relative to what had been said. I sat down and conversed with them. My Interpreter, who appeared deeply impressed at the melancholy condition of his countrymen, conversed with great freedom, fluency & feeling on their spiritual state. With tears flowing from his eyes, he told them many solemn truths, and made an affectionate and serious application of the discourse to them. He enlarged upon what I had endeavoured to impress on them, that they were that prodigal son, and had wandered from God, and earnestly called upon them to consider their danger and their duty. I was pleased with his pious zeal & thought myself favored by having so faithful an Interpreter. After meeting he explained to me the substance of what he had said.

The Indians here appear to be sunk deep in wickedness. Every night they have held a dance. It begins about 9 O'Clock & continues almost through the night; and after the dance, it is said, there is a promiscuous cohabition among the young people. They are called to the dance by loud yells. The leader of the dance rattles a goad, in which are dried beans, and chants wild notes, beginning low & rising to a kind of scream or yell, in which all join, and keep exact time, with jumping back & forward, to the sound. The ground on which I slept trembled with their frantic mirth.

28. *Monday.* Mr. Freeman, a trader, arrived from Pittsburgh, by him I received a Letter from Mr. Frisbie, and have the satisfaction to find that he has recovered his health. Wrote to him a few days past, informing him of the uncertainty of my continuing here, on account of the hostile appearence of the Indians.

29. *Tuesday.* I informed Capt. Killbuck, that if any difficulties existed in the Council, respecting my proposal, which it was in my power to remove, I should be glad of an interview. He replied that they understood my speech to them well enough, and that when they could agree among themselves, they would give me an answer.

This day some females brought about 18 Gallons of rum from Pittsburgh, employed by the traders there, to sell for them. The head men endeavoured to restrain the sale of it, but in vain. Pepee informed me that some of the head men, wished I would preach on sin, and tell them what it is. They observed that I had said, they must repent and forsake their sins. They should be glad to know what they must forsake. I informed them that I would speak on *sin*, on the morrow, as it was then the close of the day.

But in the evening the fatal liquid, *rum*, began to circulate through the town; not all the authority of the King & Council, nor their former positive law to restrain it, could stop the raging thirst of appetite. It was a dark and dreadful night. May that Almighty Guardian God, who has mercifully guided me hitherto, protect me through this night!

AN INDIAN DRUNKEN FROLIC

If to exhibit the vice of drunkenness in its odious deformities, that their children might see & detest it, the Grecians made their slaves drink to excess and then exposed them to the sight of their children; much more detestable and dreadful does that ruinous vice appear, in the intoxication of a town of savages, who have no dread of a master, or any government or law to restrain the most unbounded indulgence of this beastly vice.

By midnight the body of the inhabitants, of both sexes, were drunk. Myself and my two companions committed ourselves to God in prayer, & I lay down upon my couch, which was composed of a Buffalo and Bear skin. We left the door upon the latch, concluding, that if any of the drunken rout should attempt to enter, to bar the door would make them more violent. The ground trembled with the trampling of feet; hooping, yells, singing, laughter, and the voice of rage & madness, were blended in dreadful discord, adding horror to the darkness of midnight.

Some companies of them came successively to the door, and I expected them in every moment; they were at times very boisterous. My Interpreter, who lay near the door, could hear their conversation. There providentially happened, in every instance, to be some one among them, who dissuaded the rest from entering. This horrid scene gave some idea of the infernal regions, where sin & misery hold a universal sway.

I rose with the appearance of light, & with an Indian trader, whom I met at the door,

walked through the village. The noise and uproar continued. In one place sat several on the ground drinking rum, from wooden bowls — others lay stretched out in profound sleep — some were reeling and tumbling over the green, & one or two companies were fighting, and yelling in the most frightful manner. They fought like dogs, biting, scratching and the like. I stood a few minutes near one of these fighting companies, consisting of 5 or 6.

It was a horrid spectacle. They seemed to use the most insulting language, but it is remarkable that their language is destitute of profane oaths. In the paroxisms of their rage, they broke out and swore in english, some horrid oaths & curses, using most profanely the name of God. This infernal language they, no doubt had learned from the unprincipled traders. It is said that the worst word that they can call each other in their own language is dog or wolf, or the name of some ferocious animal.

In our walk, a fierce Indian, mad with rage came up, and shaking his fist at me, used high & threatening words, as the trader informed me, although he did not well understand him. I was a little alarmed at his threatening gestures & wrathful voice and looks, as well as the angry looks of some others of their warriors.

The men and women this morning were naked, except a piece of blue cloth, about their loins, to cover their shame. It is the nature of this shameless vice, to obliterate all sense of modesty. It is an invariable custom in their drunken frolics, for some to keep sober to prevent mischief, if possible. The duty of these wakeful guardians, is to disarm, and take the clothes of those who are beginning to drink. The arms, such as tomahawks knives &c., they secrete. They make no resistance. These watchmen however do not lose their share. They awaken some of the first drinkers who have slept away their drink, & these take their place, and then they go to drinking.

I returned to my house, & hearing that the king and Capt. Killbuck were sober, I sent a request that they would take breakfast with me. I wished for their company for personal security. They accordingly came. We sat around our table, which was a piece of plank resting on two kegs. My royal guest and his Councillor, regaled themselves with Chocolate and biscuit; but I could not prevail with them to stay after they had finished their repast. The king expressed his sorrow at the state of the town. Killbuck went and joined the rout.

Finding my situation in these scenes of drunkenness and madness, unsafe, I concluded to ride with my interpreter to a village 5 miles down the river. We went to look up our horses. In my absence, the warrior who threatened me, in the morning, had procured a club, and rushing into the house, in which was only the son of Killbuck, asked for the white man, and flourishing the club said, *he came to kill him*. The young Indian, to divert him from the way I had gone, directed him to pursue me in an opposite direction. Turning from the door, eager to find me, he was stopped by another Indian, a stout young man, called young Beaver, who wrested the club from him, which was soon also taken from him & secreted.

They were engaged in a bloody fight, at the time that I returned with my horse. The fight was in the house next to mine. By the noise and confusion within, one would imagine that a number were engaged in bloody conflict. I was ignorant of the cause until, in about 15 minutes, my interpreter arrived, and explained it.

Before he arrived, I stood attending to the noise of the affray, and young Killbuck, just mentioned, ran out of the house to me with a long bloody lock of hair, and smiling and talking presented it to me. Not knowing what it meant, I declined receiving it, he then stuck it on the outside of my house. This, I found by my interpreter was a trophy of victory, for my friend young Beaver had just torn it from the middle of the scalp of my enemy. I then thought it advisable to stay no longer; but with Pepee rode expeditiously out of town.

We were in hopes of finding peace & security at the village below, but in this we were disappointed. When we came in sight of it, we heard

"The sound of riot and ill manage'd merriment."

Part of the rum had been sent to this village, and they were in the height of their frolic. We debated some time whether to go in, reluctant &

"Loath to meet their rudeness and swill'd insolence."

– Milton's *Comus*.

My interpreter Pepee, had a cousin living there, whom he had not seen many years, it happened while we lingered at the entrance of the village, he came up to us. He was sober, very glad to see Pepee, and we followed him to his house. He shewed me great hospitality. Stakes of excellent venison roasted, and some sweet squashes which he baked in the embers, wrapped in large leaves were given us. After this repast, I slept soundly on his bear skin couch. When I awoke my interpreter only was present. He said his Cousin had been absent some time. I walked about the village. About one half of the inhabitants were intoxicated. They did not offer me any injury. Pepee who was respected universally by his countrymen, was a protection. Such is the fondness of Indians for dissipation, that they are building a dancing house in this small village, which will cost them more labour, than one half of the houses in it.

It was now an unfavorable time to say any thing on religion to the poor creatures of this place. A few days past, I was about to make them a visit, but was detained by the Councillors. They had manifested from my first coming an unwillingness that I should visit any of their villages, or see the country.

The Muskingum is a beautiful country. The soil is rich and deep. The land gradually rises from the river & forms extensive meadows and plains. Some places are covered with luxuriant grass, & neither tree or bush growing upon them for some miles in length and breadth, & in a state of immediate preperation for the plow. I sometimes paused to enjoy the prospect, and was ready to anticipate the speedy approach of the time, when, there would be another race of people there, who would properly estimate the advantages which that country will give to its future inhabitants. When populous town & cultivated fields shall arise; and Schools and Colleges & Churches, erected for the advancement of Science and the honor of the Saviour be seen through that extensive & now howling wilderness.

On our departure from the village, a little distance from the path, sat a number of Indians, drinking. One of them was the host who invited us to his house. Seeing me, he came hastily with a bowl of rum, of which he had drank so much as to make him feel sprightly, and said, "here, englishman, drink rum." I said my friend, I do not drink rum, and I hope you won't drink any more. It will get into your head & make you behave bad. He replied, in broken english, "little's good, too much, bad. Come, drink, drink." My interpreter told me it would give offence if I did not. I tasted it, he bowed, & joined his company.

We arrived at Kekalemehpehoong, a little before sun setting. The Indians had nearly exhausted the quantity of rum. I found the king sober. He had ordered the remainder of the rum to be carried out of town, to a house about 2 miles up the river. A number were fast bound in sleep. Those who were able to walk, went along the bank of the river, following the keg of rum, which was carried in front. They made a long file, staggering and singing as they went. I was glad to see them depart. Among these poor savages, the Devil seems to hold an uncontrouled power. They appear to be given over to all manner of vice. To venture back among them, before they had finished the rum, especially considering what had taken place in the morning, was somewhat hazardous, and I should have tarried at the village, had I not apprehended that the night there might be similar to that which I had already passed. Seeing the drunkards go out of town, on our entrance, I persuaded myself that we should find rest.

Accordingly the night following, the town was still, and I slept in peace. My companions were alarmed for my safety in the evening, for I had retired into the woods, partly to avoid being seen by the Indians, and for contemplation. It was to me a consoling consideration, that God rules in the moral as well as the natural world; and that he will permit the wrath of the heathen to rage no further than shall be for his glory, and the best good of those who humbly confide in his almighty & fatherly protection. Under the omnipotent protection of his providence, who moves the planetary worlds, and all the stars in their regular order, beauty & harmony, I felt a humble confidence, that in the way of my duty, and feeble attempts to spread the knowledge of Christ among the heathen, I was most safe; & to

God endeavoured to commit myself.

Thursday. The Indians, about 50 met in the Council House, and I preached to them with freedom, on *Sin.* My subject was drawn from the first chapter of the epistle to the Romans, in which the Apostle gives a dreadful catalogue of the vices, to which the Gentiles were addicted. I dwelt particularly on the vices of drunkenness & fornication, which were shockingly common among those pagans. Some seemed affected with conscious guilt. One observed to my Interpreter, after Sermon, "that if all the things which I had mentioned were *sins*, he believed that all were sinners, and no one was free from sin." Another asked him, how the white man knew what he had done, and who told him? for said he, he mentioned all the bad things I have ever done, and he talked to none but me? Thus the Divine Spirit is pleased in some instances, to make application of the word even to a heathen, who only occasionally hears it. But this Indian shunned me; and his temporary conviction served to make him my enemy.

They gave me liberty to preach again to them the next day. I preached to them to-day (Friday) on the depravity of our nature, and sins of the heart. The audience was small and attentive. At the close, I mentioned that I would preach again the next day, *Saturday, Sept.* {*Oct.*} 3. Having shown them, in preceding discourses the Apostacy and pollution of our nature by sin, and the condemnation of sin on all men, to-day I gave them an historical account of the coming of Jesus Christ into the world, his Obedience & satisfaction for sin, and the terms of pardon & life through him.

SECOND SABBATH

Oct. 4. This day they seemed more disposed to noise & merriment, and to ramble about, than usual. With taking pains, I got about 40 to assemble in the afternoon, and spake with freedom and great plainness on some of the most important truths of the gospel, particularly on a new heart, repentence, faith and a life of religion, as necessary to happiness after death.

Some were affected and wept. In my discourse yesterday, I mentioned the necessity of their receiving the word of God, to their present and future happiness. After I had done preaching today, the Speaker, who appears to be a very sensible and thoughtful person, said to me, "you have told us that we must receive what is in the book (meaning the bible). We believe there is one Almighty *Monetho*, who made all things; he is the father of the Indians and of the White People. He loves one as well as the other. You say, he sent you that book a great while ago. He has not sent it to us. If he intended it for us, he would have let us know it, at the same time that he let you know it. We don't deny that the book is good and intended for you, and no doubt, when you want to know what you should do, you must look into that book; but the Great Monetho has given us knowledge here, (pointing to his forehead) & when we are at a loss what to do, we must *think*." The king was present and all seemed waiting for an answer. It was a deistical objection, founded in the pride of erring reason, and more than I expected from an uncultivated heathen. I spoke to him of the sovereignty of God in his gifts to nations, and to individuals. That he was under no obligations to shew favor to any of his offending creatures. That the will of God revealed in the bible, teaching men their duty and the way to endless happiness, was a favor that none could claim: but in his great mercy to lost sinners, he had been pleased to communicate it to one nation in former ages, and commanded them to make it known to others. That the English were one of the last of the nations, to whom it was communicated; and that we now knowing and rejoicing in the light which that holy book, let into our minds, in all our duty, and guiding us to heaven, were desirous that our brethren in the wilderness, should know the good news which it reveals. And God had commanded us, to convey to them the knowledge of it. To this he made no reply, but immediately started another objection, as follows,

"If we take your religion, we must leave off war, and become as women, and then we shall be easily subdued by our enemies." Having answered him, that we who embraced this religion were not subdued by our enemies, but were free and powerful; and that by embracing & practicing the duties which the bible commands, they would be the same &c.

He again objected, "The white people, with whom we are acquainted, are worse, or more wicked than we are, and we think it better to be such as we are than such as they are."

I gave Pepee some directions in answer, knowing him capable of it. He enlarged with great zeal and ability. Among other observations, he said, "the white people, whom you are acquainted with, (meaning the traders) are no Christians; they do not know or do the things which God has told them in the Bible. No, Christians will not receive them into their society. If you want to see christians you must go to Philadelphia. There you will see good people, who love the word of the Great God, and mind it."

He then spake very solemnly & affectionately, on their deplorable state, and told them, unless they reformed, their ruin would speedily come.

"We remember, said he, that our fathers told us, how numerous the Indians were in their days, & in the days of their fathers. Great towns of Indians were all along the sea shore, and on the Rivers, and now, if you travel through that country, you will scarcely see an Indian; but you will see great and flourishing towns of white people who possess the land of our fathers. And we are cut off, and fall back upon these distant rivers, and are reduced to a small number. The white people increase, and we Indians decrease. I can tell you, my countrymen, the reason of this. The white people worship the true God, and please him, and God blesses and prospers them. We and our fathers worshiped Devils, or them that are no Gods, and therefore God frowns upon us. And if you continue ignorant of him, when you have opportunity to know God and worship him, he will cut you off, & give this good country to a people that shall serve him. And if it shall be asked what has become of the Indians that lived here? none will be able to tell. You will be cut off, and your children as a great many powerful Indian nations have been, and none of them are left." The above is the substance of a lengthy prophetic kind of speech of good Joseph. I observed that it took hold of them. King, Councillors & Warriors, who were present, hung down their heads and made no reply. A similar conversation he held yesterday after sermon. Yesterday one of the Chiefs returned from the neighboring towns, where he had gone to collect their minds, relative to my continuing among them, & this evening a Council was held on the subject.

Oct. 6. Monday After breakfast, was about to ride a few miles, to an Indian family, the friends of my Interpreter, but was desired by one of the Chiefs not to go. I perceived that my movements were watched, and that it was their intention, that I should not visit other Indians.

Today the King sent for me to his house. I found him with 6 or 7 of his Council. The Speaker, in the name of the King, delivered the following Laconic answer.

"My brother, I am glad you have come among us, from such a great distance, & that we see each other, and rejoice that we have had an opportunity to hear you preach. Brother, you will now return home & when you get there give my love to them that sent you. I have done speaking."

The prospect of being instrumental of much good to these poor & perishing heathen, was no more. I asked him, if this short answer was the result of their long consideration on the disinterested and benevolent errand on which I had come? And that I was very sorry that they had rejected an offer intended for their greatest good.

I conversed with them some time, & asked them what reasons, in particular, I should give to the great & good men who had sent me, for their rejection of the offer now made to them. One of them, with expressions of anger, said they did not like that the white people should settle upon the Ohio. They destroyed their hunting. That it was necessary that the friendship between King George and them, should be made more firm and strong, before they could receive the english so much into favor, as to take their religion. That when they were ready they would let us know it. I mentioned that it was our intention to have procured a school master to instruct their children, and also to furnish them some utensils for husbandry, and a grist mill, (as our worthy patron Dr. Wheelock had authorizd us so to do, and for that purpose had given us blanks, for bills of Exchange, on the School's funds in Scotland,) for the pious and benevolent, among the english, were greatly desirous to promote their comfort in this world, as well as their happiness after death; and that they expected and desired no reward from them; that the labour and expence would all be ours, and the benefits all their own. But that I was sorry

that they had now excluded themselves from these kind offers of their brethren, the white people. An aged Councillor & warrior, who had never come to hear me preach, but was violently opposed to my continuance with them, was present, and appeared to scoff at these proposals. I thanked them for their civilities, and mentioned my satisfaction that I had had opportunity to speak to them, on the great things of religion, and prayed that God would make what they had heard, of lasting good to some souls. I rose and bid them farewell. Capt. Killbuck came out with me, & said he would accompany me to Fort Pitt. He, and others, appeared a little surprised at the offer of implements of husbandry. "He said, perhaps, the Council will change their minds; and that they had prepared a lengthy speech to deliver to me, but that one who was violently opposed, spoiled it all."

From the hostile appearance of things, I had, for several days, entertained apprehensions of my personal safety, and that I should not, after a while, be indulged the liberty of leaving them. The following circumstances were the ground of my apprehensions.

1. My interpreter, one of their countrymen, was admitted to their confidence, & from them he received information that a *War Belt* had been sent to them and the Indians of neighboring tribes, informing them, that the english Colonists refused to obey the Great King of England; and if he should send an army to chastize them, his allies and friends, the Indians, were invited to join them. The information of this early hostile intention of the agents of the british government, I received also from others. The rumor had also spread among the people of the new settlements, as I found on my return to Pittsburgh, and some inquired of me concerning it. The person suspected of sending it, was Col. George Croghern, Deputy Superintendent of Indian Affairs.

Thus early commenced the plan of subjugating the Colonies, and of calling in the infernal aid of the savages, to accomplish the work.

2. While at Muskingum, news arrived that the british troops were dismantling Fort Pitt, and were about to leave the country. The warriors could not conceal their joy at this event. The Fort had been a bridle upon them hitherto, to restrain their murders & depredations on the

frontiers.

3. Some of the warriors had expressed to me their extreme resentment at the encroachments of the white people, on their hunting ground, and extending their settlements to the Ohio. I asked one of them, "Have not the white people bought the land and paid you?" — "Yes." — "Well, then they have a right to use it." "No; not so," he replied "for when you white men buy a farm, you buy only the land. You don't buy the horses and cows & sheep. The Elks are our horses, the Buffaloes are our cows, the deer are our sheep, & the whites shan't have them."

This is a short specimen of indian reasoning on property.

4. Thirteen days, King and Council met, and as they pretended, on the business on which, I had come, but I found their consultations were on the subject of hostility against the frontiers. At the King's house I saw an uncommonly large Belt of Wampum, about 5 feet in length. The ground work was grey wampum. 9 diamond figures of white wampum, and a line of the same colour, running through them, from one end to the other.

I asked the King, the meaning & use of it. "He said, Sir William Johnson, has advised the nations to unite and live in peace, and this is a Belt of Union. Eight nations have taken hold of it, & I am going to send it to the Chipewas, who live near Lake Huron."

Several circumstances at that time persuaded me that the proposed Union was for a bad purpose as afterwards appeared.

Such being my apprehensions, I wrote to Captn Arthur St. Clair, with whom I had the honor of some acquaintance, and mentioned the circumstances that appeared to indicate the hostile disposition of the Indians. He afterwards informed me that he communicated the information to Gen. Gage, then at New York.

Tuesday 7.   About to visit Waukataumaka, an Indian town about 24 miles distant; but finding that it was disapproved of by one of the Chiefs, I gave it up, and prepared for my return to Pittsburgh. Joseph Pepee set out with his Wife, who had come for him, to go to the new moravian town, {Welhik Thuppeek} and I bid him, who had been my faithful Interpreter a long farewell. He was an Indian of good principles, temperate, and of unblemished morals.

Nickels had been absent part of the time, visiting his indian acquaintance, for whom he had a friendship, from his early days of captivity among them.

CAPTIVES AMONG THE INDIANS

In the town were two captives, one a female, captivated in infancy, from Path Valley, of the name of Eliot. She appeared perfectly naturalized, and conformed to the Indian customs and dress. I saw her frequently at work with the squaws, pounding corn. She appeared to be a stout & healthy young woman. I believe she could not speak the english language, and knowing no condition other than savage life, probably was as contented as her indian companions. It is not unlikely that the family were slain when she was taken, and no friends have appeared to reclaim her.

The other was a well built young man, of the name of Hamilton, who was captivated from some part of Maryland, on the river Potomac, at the age of 9 years. He was conformed to indian manners. His head shaved & painted and his dress ornamented with beads, broaches &c. His countenance was manly and ingenious. I had frequent oppportunities of conversation with him, and although he could talk common english, yet such was his pride of indian dignity and independence, that he would not converse, except by my interpreter. I advised him to leave the Indians and return to his kindred & friends, for he said, he believed he had a brother and an Uncle in Maryland. I conversed usually with him, in the absence of the Indians, for fear of offence. He told me, he should be glad to see his brother, & desired me to write to him, to come & see him.

I set before him the advantages of his returning to the english; and the deplorable condition in which he would live & die, should he continue there, as to the knowledge of God, and the way to happiness. He told me he was very happy, and innumerated the little articles of his property, such as 4 or 5 horse loads of peltry, blankets &c. "And here, says he, I go and come as I please, and the King is my Uncle; (he was adopted into the Royal family) but if I go among the white people they will make me a Slave." I assured him to the contrary, and engaged, that if he should not like to continue with his kindred, he might return. I felt unwilling that so promising a youth should be lost; but I despaired of success, until the morning of my departure, when he came to me, looking thoughtful, and said, "my friend, you have often advised me to return to my english friends, and now I have concluded to go." I encouraged him in the good resolution; but we both thought it not advisable for him to set out until a day or two after my departure, lest the Indians, who were very fond of him, should be alarmed. He said, "I will see you at Fort Pitt," and bade me farewell for a little while. To finish the story here. A few days after my arrival there, I had the pleasure to see him. He followed me after two days. Providentially, his brother, happened to be in the frontiers of Pennsylvania, and heard of his arrival and hastened to Pittsburgh. He took him to a store, and clothed him in english dress; but he still retained so much of the Indian as to paint his face & head with vermillion and black. I told him, I hoped he would now go and live with his friends, who loved him, & would always be kind to him. He said he should not go to live with the Indians, but thought it was likely he should go & trade with them.

There is an unknown charm in the Indian life, which surprisingly attaches white people; those especially who have been captivated in early life. Whether it is, that uncontrouled liberty, which is found among savages, — or that freedom from all anxiety and care for futurity, which they appear to enjoy, or that love of ease, which is so agreeable to the indolence of human nature, or all these combined, the fact is established by numerous instances of english & french captives, who have resisted the most affectionate and inviting alurements to draw them, and chose to spend their days among their adopted Indian friends.

RELIGION OF THE INDIANS

The most savage nations of the world, have some idea of a being or existances superior to man; and generally believe in the existance of the soul after death.

The Indian tribes, bordering on European settlements, have probably fewer impressions of a religious nature, than those who have little or no intercourse with us, because the former have

their minds habitually stupified by intemperence. Of the religious principles & practices of the Delawares, and other indian tribes on our borders, little can be said.

They have no special season, or day consecrated to religious worship. No temples, priests or religious rites. The religious notions and practices of individuals are such as are the effect of imperfect reasoning — of their fears & hopes, or the traditions handed down from their fathers.

They absurdly believe in two principles who made & govern the world between them. One they call the Good Monetho, the other the Evil Monetho. In this respect they adopt the ancient opinion of the disciples of Manes, or Plato's principle of Light and Darkness. They believe that all good in the natural and moral world is from the Good, & all evil and misery, from the Evil Monetho. To the Evil principle they pray when sick, or in trouble; and it is by pretended power from him alone, that their Conjurors or Powwows, derive all their skill to heal the sick, or to inflict evil on their enemies.

On my return from Muskingum, I visited an aged sick Indian, at a Village on the Ohio. His limbs were contracted by paralytic or convulsive fits. He told me he had been hurt by witches, meaning I conclude Conjurors, 30 years ago; but he had been cured by a friendly Conjuror. "And the Conjuror, said he, of this place, is trying his skill upon me, & I believe will cure me; for the Devil (Evil Monetho), keeps him alive to cure such as he chuses should be healed; and he is a little Devil himself. For they can't kill him. They have tomahawked him, and thrown him into the river, but the great Devil keeps him alive." I told him that he must pray to the Good Monetho. That there was but one God, and the Devil was subject to his government, and could do nothing without his permission. He replied I have always believed otherwise, & *shall pray to the Evil Monetho.*

I was informed that the Delawares, as well as other tribes, have annually, what is called, a *Fall Hunt,* when they all turn out in pursuit of game, & hold a grand feast, of which all partake. That at this feast, the Chief of the Nation publickly offers up a short solemn prayer to the Good Spirit, thanking him for life and health, and success in hunting, and praying for the continuence of those favors through the ensuing Year. They present the skins of the animals, and a considerble part of the meat to the widows and the aged. Some of the flesh they burn, as an offering to their gods.

FUNERALS

They enrap the corpse in bark, & bury it about three feet. They then raise a covering of bark over it, leaving a little space between the body and the upper covering, to prevent the earth pressing upon it, and lay earth upon the covering. This they do, from the idea that the soul, after death, remains hovering about the corpse, & holds some connection with it, until it putrifies. On the same principle, they carry, for some time, every evening, some provisions, and lay it by the side of the grave. The hungry dogs which abound in all their towns, devour it; but they profess to believe that the departed friend eats it. They sometimes bury bows and arrows, wampum, spoons &c. with the dead. They explain this by believing that everything animate and inanimate has a spirit: that the Spirit of the deceased, in the other world makes use of the spirit of the bow & arrow, to kill the spirit of game. A great number of high posts stand at the graves of the chiefs & warriors, & poles at the graves of others. The posts are painted with rough hyroglifics, descriptive of their war expeditions &c.

MARRIAGES

The Indians, formerly, were more chaste & continent than they have been since their connection with the english, & their free use of rum.

The first marriage is attended with some formality. The connection is, sometimes, brought about by the agreement of the parents of the parties. The young man presents to the object of his choice, some cakes of indian bread; if she accepts them, they cohabit; but if she rejects them, he must look somewhere else for a partner. They seperate for trivial causes, and marry or cohabit, without much ceremony with others. If they have children, it is said they are left with the mother.

Several of the aged Councillors had lived with one wife from their youth; but a great part of husbands & wives at Kekalemahpehoong, had seperated and taken others. I was astonished at the profligate description which young Killbuck (whose father had directed him to lodge in my house, and to wait on me), gave me of himself. He slept in a loft which was ascended by a ladder, at the further end of the house. He conducted a squaw up the ladder every night. I asked him, one day, if it was his Wife? He said, No. I admonished him for his conduct. He said, he was 19 years old, and had had several wives, and that he wanted one more, and he should be happy. It is natural to expect that but few children, can be the fruit of such unbounded licenciousness. On an average they are about 2 or 3 to a family.

RETURN FROM MUSKINGUM

1772. Friday, Oct. 9. Set out in company with a Mr. Freeman, an Indian trader, & his servant, and friend Nickels, to return to Pittsburgh. We had fine weather, and killed plenty of wild game, particularly Turkies, with which the woods abounded.

At the Mingo town, about 70 miles below Pittsburgh, I found a sick Indian, with whom I had a conversation. The Conjuror who was to hold a powwow over him at night, came into the Indian house, where I entered. His face and body were frightfully painted with different colours. He looked upon me with severe attention, without speaking a word. Disliking his appearence, as well as that of some others in the village, I concluded it would be most advisable to cross the River Ohio, although it was dark; and encamp on the opposite side. Accordingly we crossed in a Canoe, swimming our horses, kindled a fire and pitched our tent on english ground. About 10 O'Clock, the noise of the powwow sounded across the river, & the doleful echoes resounded through the woods. I thought it prudent to leave the town, partly because it was probable that the conjuror, in case of the failure of success in his infernal incantations to heal the sick man, might be disposed to attribute it, to my presence, & because the village consisted of a banditti of plundering drinking wretches. They permitted us to rest undisturbed.

On my arrival at Pittsburgh, found Mr.

Frisbie in comfortable health. In my absence he had frequently preached to the people there, and in neighboring settlements....

Nov. 11. — {While still at Pittsburgh.} Heard that my Interpreter Joseph Pepee, had gone on to Philadª, to request the Governor and the Quakers, to provide a ship for King Nettautwalemen, and some of his Chiefs, to go to England. Joseph mentioned on the road, that the Indians would have Mr. F. and myself return next spring. That they were not yet ready; but wished to consult other tribes. Good Joseph was deceived by the subtlety of his countrymen.

Source: McClure, *Diary of David McClure,* pp. 46–103

Schoenbrunn Diary – McClure Entries

Sept. 13, 1772. ...a letter had arrived there {Gekelemukpechünk} from two ministers, who are now in Pittsburg and are expected in Gekelemukp. very soon, who have offered to preach to the Indians there.

Sept. 16. Several of our Indian brethren and sisters arrived from Langundoutenünk to remain here. With them came, also, Echpalawehund from Gekelemukp. with whom our Isaac again had extended conversation, especially, concerning the two ministers whom they are expecting, that they should not think that they would teach in the same manner as the Brethren, and should, therefore, well consider the matter before they sent a reply, as to what they would do.

Sept. 26. From Gekelemukp. we heard that the English minister had arrived there several days ago with Joseph Pepi, had addressed a speech to the Indians and was now awaiting an answer.

Oct. 7. ...Jos. Pepi arrived here from Gekelemukpechünk, where he had been the interpreter of the English minister who had been there for a time and had preached several times. Thereupon, he had been called into the Council and was told that they were pleased that he had come and had preached during the time of his stay, but now enough had been preached and he should stop and it would be good for him, if he would return to his home. In consequence, he had been very much wrought up and had said to them that because they would not accept the Gospel, they would have no more fortune nor star (i.e. would be unfortunate), but God would bring judgment upon this city and destroy it from the face of the earth. As we have heard from Jos. Pepi ourselves, he was very incautious in his talk and is, for example, said to have remarked frequently, that the Indians had so much beautiful and good land which lay waste, because they did not use it, as they were lazy people and did not wish to work and begrudged the use of the land on the part of the whites; that in a few years the land would be taken from the Indians by the whites, who would build cities and villages upon it and drive away or destroy the Indians, and more of the same sort of talk, so that it is no matter of surprise that they should send him away.

David Zeisberger
1772

In October of 1772, only a few months after he had come to the valley and while the congregation at the second mission town was constructing their chapel, Zeisberger pushed on to the Shawnee towns, collectively known as Wakatomika, near Dresden. He was anxious to preach to them to see if they seemed receptive to the Gospel and was obviously very pleased with the results of his trip. However, when he returned to these towns the next year, his reception was decidely hostile and it was apparent that nothing could be done with these Indians.

His journal is of interest in pointing out that some of the Delawares who had been living at Newcomerstown had moved west, closer to the Coshocton area, to get farther away from the Christian Indians and their ministers. Obviously, not all of the Delawares liked the idea that the Moravians had been invited to the valley.

Also of interest is the fact that upon his return he conducted the first service in the new chapel at Gnadenhutten. From his diary you could get the impression that it was his decision to call the new town Gnadenhutten, but as is evident from the Ettwein journal, that matter had already been decided at Langunto-Utenünk by means of the lot, and the people of the town were aware of this. Joseph "Pepi" was one of the Indians who accompanied Zeisberger. The following narrative of his trip is set forth in the Schoenbrunn Diary for October 17, 1772.

Oct. 17, {1772}. In the evening, late, Br. David returned from his visit among the Shawanose, concerning the journey he reports the following: — We arrived on the 10th huj. at Gekelemukpechünk, where we were received in a friendly manner, and because there were a number of us we were lodged in a house by ourselves. On the 11th, I conducted a service in the morning, attended by a number of people, also, from the Town. In the afternoon we were summoned to the Council, in order that they might learn what our people had to say. Isaac Senr. addressed a speech to the Chief, thanking him that he had appointed them the right place, where they might dwell, and declared that when they had come, they had not known wither to go, had, therefore, hunted out a place and had been about to erect houses for themselves, when his message had arrived, whereupon, they had immediately resolved to go to that place; they were now actually at the place and he should now take good care of his grandchildren (the Mohicans), since they had them living nearby. The road to them should remain open, so that whoever might wish to hear the Gospel should be at liberty to come. That was the brief content of his speech. Then he gave two strings of Wampum. They approved and confirmed all that he said, but there was no formal answer. As token of gratitude that our people had received their message and obeyed it, they collected a quantity of corn, which was pointed out and handed over to them.

Although I had here learned that the Shawanose had already gone out on the chase, it seemed to me wise to undertake this journey, at any rate, and to risk whether I should find any of them at home or not. I inquired, therefore, of the Chief whether he had ever given his grand-children, the Shananose any information con-cerning us, that we had come into this region and were now dwelling here. To this he an-swered that it had been done long ago. I in-formed him then, that I wished to pay them a visit, which he approved, saying, yes, that would be good and pleasing to him. Accordingly, I started thither, on the morning of the 12th, with the two Brn., Isaac and Joseph Pepi. We passed two Delaware Towns, lying to the right, and crossed two great, open flats, extending for several miles, where there is nothing but tall grass. Within the one we saw the place where Col. Boquet encamped with his army and from which he had returned. Toward evening we came into a Delaware Town, where we stopped for a while. Here dwell those who, during the past spring, fled before us when they heard that we were coming into the region of Gekelemukp., because they do not wish to hear anything of the Gospel. Neverthelss, Isaac proclaimed the Saviour with great joy to the Indian whom we visited, who, at last, answered; You certainly speak truth. Then, we proceeded a little further, and, in the evening, came to the first Shawano Town, where there were, however, only three huts. Here we spent the night. Here, also, we learned, to our joy, that the Shawanose of the town we wished to visit had, indeed started for the chase three weeks ago but had all returned a few days before to their homes. It so happened that without our knowing it we had turned in at the hut of the son of Paxenoos, who recognized me immediately, welcomed me in a friendly manner and was glad to see me. All three of us proclaimed the Saviour to him, through half the night, and the message seemed to find entrance. After he had listened for a time, he said that he certainly believed that our teaching was the right teaching and that we preached the true way of salvation, that they had for a long time busied themselves to find the way to eternal life, that they realized now, however, that everything they had undertaken and all their action and working had been in vain, hence they had well nigh given up everything, because they did not know what else good they might do. He offered, on the morning of the 13th, to go with us, in order that

he might hear more, which was agreeable to us, for he understands and speaks the Delaware language very well. We passed through two more small Shawano Towns, of which each had only from four to five huts, in which we an-nounced while passing, that whoever wished to hear us should follow, for we had priceless words to communicate. Those who were at home came. Toward noon, we arrived at the Town we wished to reach, which is the principal place where the Chief has his home. We turned in at the home of the preacher, as the son of Paxenoos had advised us, because his word counts the most and, as it were, rules everything. The Chief, on the other hand, deals only with Chief-affairs. We were well received and when we made it known that we had come to visit them and that we had something to say to them the preacher asked of what nature that might be? When we told him that we had the words of eternal life to tell them, he replied, well that is agreeable to us and we shall be glad to hear. They made arrangements, at once, that a house should be cleared and prepared for the purpose, as, however, very many, and especially, the women, were busy on their plantations, harvesting their corn, it be-came too late for an open meeting today. Mean-time, we did not wait, but preached, turn about, in the house where we were lodged, for our house was always full and the people listened attentive-ly. And thus we continued until midnight, when the cocks began to crow, after which we lay down to rest for a while. With the break of day it began anew. Up to this time the preacher had answered nothing but had only and continually listened intently. Now he began to speak and told us that he had not been able to sleep the whole night but had thought and meditated upon that which he had heard and he was now minded to tell us what was in his heart. He believed that all which we preached was the truth. A year ago it had become clear to him and he had seen that they were all together poor, sinful people and that, despite all their efforts, they were perishing. They had not known what they should do or undertake in order to be saved. He had, in consequence, ever comforted his people by say-ing, that some one would come to declare to them the right way of salvation, for they were not on the right way. Even on the day previous to our arrival he had said to them that they should have patience a little longer, for some one surely would soon come. And since we have arrived, he believe that God has sent us to make known to them His Word.

These Shawanose have, for several years, practiced vomiting earnestly, in order that they might thereby be freed and cleansed from sin, but have, for a year, desisted from the practice, for they realized that sin continued to rule over them. In lieu thereof, they have begun to lead a good and, according to their standards, pious life. For this their preacher had given them direction, as well as he knew, as, for example, that they should not drink, dance, fornicate, steal, lie and cheat, etc., In this, he said, they expected to continue until God should reveal to us something other and better, in one or another manner. He is a preacher of the kind our Isaac had been, who does not persist in his opinion but only so long until he learns something better and understands it. He told Isaac, out of his own experience, how it had been with him and what he had felt when he first heard the Brethren and how the message concerning Jesus' death and suffering had affected his heart, so that he immediately confessed that it was the word of truth. This morning, they all gathered in the house that had been prepared for the purpose. My heart was open and the Saviour granted me grace to commend to them the Saviour's death and merits through his blood as the ground of our salvation. I had made clear to them in advance that it would not be necessary for them to reply while the sermon was in progress and, also, that they should not raise questions as they had done before in the house where we had spoken to them but simply listen until the address was at an end, when they might say as much as they wished. This was done, and the whole proceeding was very quiet and orderly. The Chief and Captain were among those present, the former appears to be a fine man, and is quite old. The Indian Brethren spoke to them next, and explained my sermon further, they, in turn, asked various questions, which we answered to their satisfaction. In the afternoon, we noticed that they intended to have a council among themselves, we, therefore, left them alone. In the evening, they summoned Isaac and Joseph Pepi, at which time they first notified them of what they had decided and determined upon and

desired of them an expression of opinion on the matter. When these gave expression to their joy and pleasure about it, they asked them further what they ought to do, in order to attain to their purpose. The Brethren answered them, that they should acquaint me with their purpose, and I would answer and counsel them. As it was too late this evening, this was done on the following morning in our house. The preacher, who was the spokesman, addressed me and said: Brother we rejoice very much that you have come to visit us and to bring God's Word which we hear with joy. We will now let you know what we have unanimously decided, yesterday, at our Council. The women were, indeed, not present, as they have much to do with the harvesting of their fields, but that makes no difference for what we men determine upon, therein they agree with us. We have come to an agreement that from this day on, we shall accept God's Word, and will live in accordance with it, this we say not only with our mouths but out of our hearts. Our request and desire, therefore, is that not only Christian Indians but white Brethren, also, shall come to us, dwell with us and instruct us how we may be saved. We are planning now, in a few days, to go out for the fall hunting, when we shall have returned to our homes, which will be in a little over two months, we shall be very glad to see that, at that time, some one will come to us to remain with us. We put our proposition before you, we are, indeed, poor, bad people, but do not despise us because we are so bad and do not deny our petition. The speech of this Shawanose affected my heart so that I could not do otherwise than promise to help in one way or in another, though I see in advance that it will be very difficult for us, as there are so few of us. I, therefore, replied that I was delighted to hear that they would not only receive the Word of God but, also, live in accordance with it. We Brethren always rejoiced when we perceived that Indians, of whatsoever nation, were longing for the Saviour and His Word, and would serve them gladly. There were, however, so few of us, and one place, even now, unoccupied, that I could not promise that some one would come as soon as they wished and desired it. This, at the same time, I would promise, that we would help them as soon as possible and would not neglect them any more. I would not only consult my brethren, when I reached home, but I would, also, write to my brethren in Bethlehem, that they should send more assistants. In the meantime, there would perhaps be opportunity, this winter, that we should hear from them and that they should hear from us, and perhaps some one of us would visit them this winter. They should hold to what they had decided and should allow nothing to disturb them, but they should from this time on firmly believe that they were well thought of by the Brethren. I had to tell them, further, in case we should dwell among them, how their Town would have to appear and how they would have to conduct themselves; there could be no dancing, piping, drinking, gambling, carousing, nor anything of that nature, as is common in other Indian Towns, otherwise we could not dwell among them, there would have to be quiet and order. They answered that they had, some time ago, done away with all that sort of thing, that we should not be troubled with any such evil practices, for they themselves did not care for them. For that reason they should like to have Brethren, who would tell them what they ought to do, for they should like to live as beseems Christians. He, further, said, that since they were not living at a suitable place where many Indians might dwell together, they had, already, considered and discussed the matter of leaving the place and looking for a better so that those of their nation who were likeminded with themselves but lived scattered about might come and dwell with them. When they had, therefore, returned to their homes from the chase, this should be the first matter of concern, to find a suitable place for such a Town, where all those who are believers might dwell, or, at least, those who were minded to become believers. I was greatly pleased to hear this, only it would be good and desirable that we might be present at the beginning of such a settlement, so that nothing might be overlooked and that nothing might be spoiled that could not later be made good. It would, also, be desirable thus from the viewpoint of our ever keeping a free hand to do as we would and should. This Town is commonly known among the Indians as the Vomiting-Town, it will, for that reason, too, be good that a new one be established. We have now come to the border of the Shawanose, for here their district begins, but it is probably nearly a hundred miles

from here to their principal place, and between here and there, there are a number of Towns, all Shawanose, and continues from Gekelemukpechünk toward the west. This Town consists of 17 houses and is the largest in this region. Four small Towns, also, belong it, each consisting of but a few huts which are, at the most, three or four miles away. Most of the people understand the Delaware tongue, and a few speak it very well, so that in the matter of the language it will be quite easy for us, and it will be a good beginning to have an entrance to this Nation. It is, also, in view of the whole matter of the cause of the Saviour among the Indians good and necessary that the Saviour with His Gospel come into this Nation, for if there is entrance among them, it may be counted upon that peace will continue, for this nation is always ready for war, should hostilities break out, and I have here been told for certain that the Lower Shawanose always have a great quantity of ammunition in store and, in addition to this, every hunter, in this as well as in other Towns, has a keg of powder and lead in proportion in stock.

After I had discussed all this with them, we bade them farewell, admonishing them not to forget what they had heard, and started at about noon, examining, on the way, in company with the son of Paxenoos, a strip of fine land, lying along the River, and suitable for a settlement. I had always wished, when our brethren and sisters among the Indians came from Friedenshütten, that we might have a settlement, also, in about this region, which would mean more for the Saviour's cause then if they all lived together, and now the matter is settling itself and the Saviour is opening the way and assigning the place. We advanced about ten miles today and spent the night with a Shawanose who received us very kindly and entertained us most hospitably. Isaac, who can speak the language of the Shawanose quite well, preached the Saviour to him with great enthusiasm. On the evening of the 16th, we arrived again in Gekelemukp. and spent the night with Notawatwees, who rejoiced to hear good news concerning his grandchildren. The Delawares call the Shawanose their grandchildren, and the latter call the former their grandfather. The Monsys call the Shawanose their youngest brother, and the latter call the former their older brother. We met here many of our sisters who are helping to harvest the corn for wages. On the 17th, toward noon, we came to our Mohicans, where I conducted the first service for them and, at the same time, informed them that this place shall be known as Gnadenhütten, for which they were all very glad. They had, in the meantime, already built several houses and were very busy with further building. In the evening we arrived at Welhik Thuppeck, glad and thankful that the Saviour had been with us and had blessed our journey. So far the report of this journey.

Source: Zeisberger, "Schoenbrunn Diary"

The Indian Council Bag and Wampum

The chief has the council bag in his possession, as also the treaties that have been made with the governors of the provinces and other documents, although they are not able to read. These constitute the archives, where all messages and reports are kept. With each message or speech there are one or more strings or belts of wampum. These, with the message or speech after the latter have been properly considered and answered, are deposited in the archives. In connection with such a message there may be a string or belt to each point, for as soon as the deliverer of a message has finished with a point he gives over a string or belt to the chief, gets out another and continues to speak until his message has been fully delivered when he announces that he has done. If the strings and belts are handed about from one to another in the council this is an indication that the message is being favorably received. It may happen, however, that the chief does not take the belt into his hands but pushes it to one side with a stick, in which case no one will touch it. The messenger who has brought it must in this case take it back. This signifies that his message does not find approbation and it is accounted a disgrace. Such a rejected belt may be a war belt summoning the people to war, or it may be a belt admonishing them to maintain peace, or something else that is not agreeable may be required.

Source: Zeisberger's *History...*, p. 93

Map 8a – Original Survey of 1797 – Wakatomika.

Map 8b – Modern Topgraphic – Wakatomika.

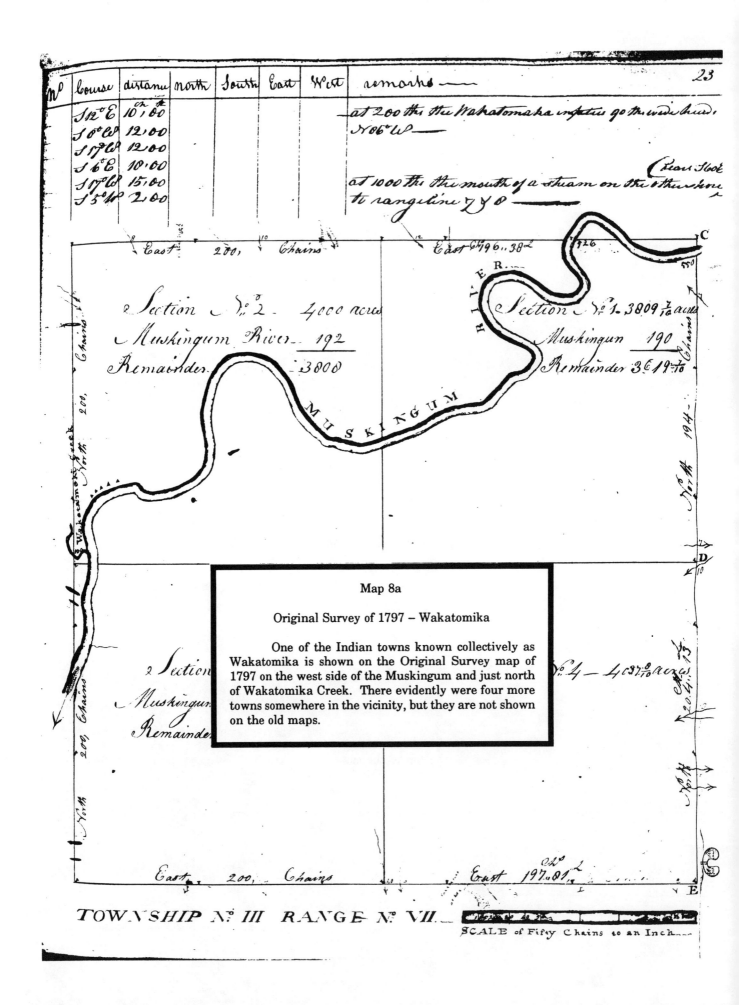

Map 8a

Original Survey of 1797 – Wakatomika

One of the Indian towns known collectively as Wakatomika is shown on the Original Survey map of 1797 on the west side of the Muskingum and just north of Wakatomika Creek. There evidently were four more towns somewhere in the vicinity, but they are not shown on the old maps.

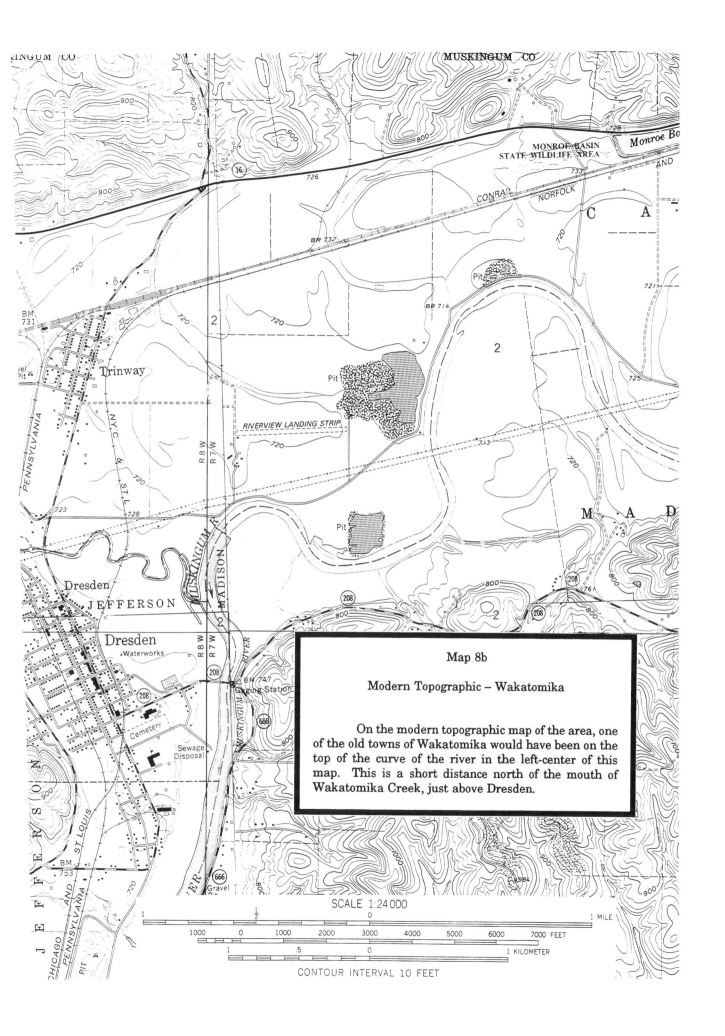

Map 8b

Modern Topographic – Wakatomika

On the modern topographic map of the area, one of the old towns of Wakatomika would have been on the top of the curve of the river in the left-center of this map. This is a short distance north of the mouth of Wakatomika Creek, just above Dresden.

SCALE 1:24 000

1 MILE

1000   0   1000   2000   3000   4000   5000   6000   7000 FEET

1   .5   0   1 KILOMETER

CONTOUR INTERVAL 10 FEET

We, therefore, sent Isaac Glikhican ahead to reconnoiter; and he returned during the night with the message, that Chief Netawatwes when he heard of our coming, had at once decided to discontinue the boozing; and the chief said, we were to come right on to him, we would find them all sober next morning!

John Ettwein   August 26th, 1772

Joseph Peepy
1772

In the fall of 1772, shortly after returning from the trip to the Shawnee towns with Zeisberger, Joseph Peepy and a companion, not otherwise identified, set off for Philadelphia carrying a message from Newcomer, asking that the Governor of Pennsylvania furnish him (Newcomer) with a ship to go to England to see the King. The Governor responded that the chief would have to make such a request to Sir William Johnson, that he himself could do nothing in the matter. Whether this was just a classic case of buck-passing or a legitimate excuse is difficult to determine at this time, but it may very well have been that Sir William Johnson, as the Superintendent of Indian Affairs, was the proper person with whom the Indians should deal. The fact that Johnson lived in the Mohawk Valley not far from Albany, New York, and that it was much more difficult to travel that far to see him was apparently considered irrelevant by the Governor of Pennsylvania.

While what follows is not, precisely speaking, the journal of a traveler into the Tuscarawas Valley, it is, nevertheless, included in this book since it concerns the Indians mentioned so often in other journals, and shows to us, today, some of the things that concerned them at the time. It also illustrates how councils were held with the Indians, how things were stated, etc.

From the Schoenbrunn Diary entries immediately following, it appears that in addition to asking for a ship to England for the Indian chief, Peepy was also to contact the Quakers regarding sending a minister and teacher to their town. I assume that it was this matter, coupled with the fact that he apparently did not tell the ministers that he was going on a journey (which was a violation of Rule 15 of the Mission as set forth in the Appendix herein), that caused Peepy to consider himself a sinner, at least in the eyes of the Moravians, and to later be repentant, for it does not appear that the Moravians knew anything about his trip until he had already left. The next year, some Quakers did come to Gekelemukpechünk, but whether or not this had anything to do with Peepy's message is not clear.

At a Council held at Philadelphia on Thursday 26th November, 1772.

PRESENT:

The Honorable RICHARD PENN, Esquire, Lieutenant Governor, &c.
William Logan, James Tilghman, Richard Peters; Esquires.

Joseph Peepy, and another Delaware Indian came to Town last week, from the Ohio, with a Message from Netattwallaman, or new Comer, Chief of the Delawares on the Ohio, which Jo Peepy delivered to the Governor with a String and Belt of Wampum, on the 19th Instant, in the following words, Viz:

"Brothers and Friends:

"I have been often told that there is a great King over the Great Waters.

"Brothers and Friends:

"I am ready to go over the Great Waters to see that Great King. Now Brother Governor and Friends, I desire you to prepare a Ship for me next Spring. I am your Brother and I am your friend, and I hope we shall soon be united together."

The Governor having since taken the said Message into Consideration, returned the following answer thereto, by the advice of the Council, Viz:

"Brother Netattawalaman:

"I received Your Message by Jos. Peepy, and have considered it well. I have been looking over what past between us last Spring was twelve Months. You then mentioned to me the same business you have now repeated by Jos. Peepy; You may remember I then told you that Sir William Johnson was appointed by the Great King, my Master, to confer with and advise all our Brethren, the Indians, in any matters of Importance; all Indians know this Well. I then recommended you to go to him and Inform him of your Intentions of going over to England to see the Great King, and tell him what you had particularly to say to him. You have not informed me by Jo. Peepy, whether you follow'd my advice in going to Sir William, and if you did, what passed between him and you. When I hear this I shall be better able to Judge of this Important Matter, and give you my Sentiments and advice thereon; at present I can only once more request, if you have not already been to Sir William Johnson, that you would go to him and lay this matter before him to consider of, and know his mind thereon, before you determine to go over Sea. When you have done this, I shall be ready to hear what you may have further to say to me, and do every thing in my power to please and Serve you in this or any other affair."

Delivered a String of Wampum.

"Dear Brother Governor:

"I have considered very well at my Council Fire of what you said in your answer to the Message I sent you by Killbuck, respecting my design of going over the Great Waters to see the Great King, and I cannot agree to what you then recommended to me of going to Sir William Johnson to consult him upon that Business. You know there was formerly a Council Fire established at Philadelphia & by our forefathers, where we have always been since used to do all our Business with our Brethren the English; and I do not think it necessary at this time for me to give myself the Trouble of going to Sir William Johnson to talk with him about my going to England; for I can much better step on Board of a Ship here at Philadelphia."

"Brother Netattawallaman:

"Since I delivered my Message to Jo. Peepy in answer to yours by him, Jo. tells me that you have not followed the advice I gave you last Spring was twelve months, to go to Sir William Johnson and consult him on your Intention of going over Sea to see the Great King.

"Brother:

"You and all the Indians know well it has been told you at all the late Treaties, that the Great King has appointed Sir William Johnson Superintendant of all Indian Affairs, and that all business of any Importance between the King and the Indians, was to be laid before him; I am, therefore, much surprized you have not followed my advice in going to Sir William, and informing him of your Inclination to go over Sea to visit the Great King and talk with him.

"Brother:

"It is long since I gave you this advice; You have had sufficient time to go there and hear his Sentiments, and know his mind; I cannot think what reasons you can have for not going to him.

"Brother:

"I know very well that our Brother Onas [Sir William Johnson] and all our United Brethren the Indians, kindled a Great Council Fire at this Place, where all Business was to be transacted between us. I know also, and you should remember, that when any Business was to be done, it was to be by all the tribes of Indians united with the six Nations, and with their Approbation and Consent; They were all linked in one Chain of Friendship, and Brother Onas with them. Nothing was to be done without the Knowledge of the General Indian Council. You cannot, therefore, my Brother, expect that I can comply with your request in providing a Ship to carry you to England to see and talk with our Great King 'till Sir William has been informed of it, and has Consulted your Uncles, the Six Nations, at their Great Council Fire. If I did so, I should break one of the Strongest links of the Chain of Friendship, and the Solemn treaties entered into between me and all the Indians, they would be very angry with me, and blame me much for doing so.

"Brother:

"I must further inform you that I have lately received a letter from Sir William Johnson, informing me that he has instructions and orders from the Great King, his and my Master, to Transact all Business of Importance with the Indians, excepting that of fixing and regulating the Trade, which is left to me to manage; that he expects when any Indians apply to me on any other Business, I shall send them to him.

"Brother:

"As this is the true state of the Case, I cannot, I dare not, interfere with the Great King my Master's Orders. I cannot Provide a Ship to carry you and your Companions to England to see and talk with the Great King without Sir William's being first informed of your intentions; It would not only be a breach of trust in me to my King and Master, but as I have said, it would be a Breach of That faith and Friendship entered into between me, the good people of this Province, and the Indians of all the six united Nations. Let me therefore, my Brother, recommend it to you in the strongest terms, to go to Sir William Johnson and lay your intentions before him and know his mind thereon."

Delivered a Belt of Wampum.

The Governor, as a token of his affection for New Comer, sent him the following articles by Jos. Peepy, viz:

	£.	s.	d.
2 yards of Scarlet Broad Cloth for a Stroud, at 16s. per yard	1	12	0
2 yards of Blue Strouds at 10s per do.	1	0	0
7 yards of Fine Linnen, at 2s. 9p. per do.	0	19	3
16 yards of Broad Silk ferretting, at 4d. per do.	0	5	4
2 Scarlet Caps, at 2s. 3p.	0	4	6
and 2 pair leggins which were got at the State House			
	4	1	1

And to Joseph Peepy and his Companion, the Governor gave as follows, Viz: to Jos. Peepy:

	£.	s.	d.
1 Indian Blanket, [cost]	0	11	6
1 Striped Cap, do.	0	1	6
3½ yards of fine linnen, at 2s. 6d. p. yrd	0	8	9
And one oznabrigs shirt, 1 pair of Shoes, and			
one pair of Leggins, which were got at the State House			
	1	1	9

To Jos. Peepy's Companion:

	£.	s.	d.
1 Indian Blanket, [cost]	0	11	6
1 Striped Cap, do.	0	1	6
3½ yards of fine linnen, at 2s. 6d. p. yrd	0	8	9
And 1 Oznabrigs Shirt, 1 pair of Shoes, and			
one pair of Leggins, which were got at the State House			
	1	1	9

MEMORANDUM

The Governor sent to New Comer by Jos. Peepy, a Copy of both his answers to the foregoing Messages delivered by Jos. Peepy.

Source: *Pennsylvania Colonial Records,* Vol. X, pp. 61–64

Schoenbrunn Diary – Peepy Entries

Dec. 18 {1772} – Br. David spoke with Killbuck, who had come here three days ago, making clear his views, as we had already heard all manner of things concerning Jos. Pepi's undertaking to Philadelphia, which pleased him.

Dec. 26. ...Today, also, Joseph Pepi returned from his negotiation with the Governor in Philadelphia and brought along most welcome letters from Bethlehem and Lititz, as well copies of the Daily Words and Doctrinal Texts, as far as they were out of the press. He had taken upon himself this message of the Chief in Gekelemukpechünk and, as we had heard, engaged himself, while we were anxious on his account, lest he might suffer harm or, indeed, be separated from us altogether. But the Saviour caused us to rejoice, since he returned as a truly repentant sinner and lamented his wrong-doing with many tears. As to the matter of his negotiations in Philadelphia, he had been charged by the Chiefs to secure from the Governor transportation for several Indians from their midst to England, and, secondly, that he should ask of the Quakers that they should send them a minister and a teacher, as they had made similar application a year before but without success. The Governor had given answer that this matter of securing transport for Indians to England did not come under his authority but under that of Sir William Johnson, to whom they should make application. To the second point he replied, that he could not understand why they should want another minister and another teacher, as they already had ministers of the Brethren and so many Indian brethren dwelling with them, they should, therefore, be satisfied and do as the Brethren told them to do. The Quakers likewise informed them that they did not see how anyone could dwell among them and instruct their children, except it be that they should live in an orderly manner. The elders should make the beginning, then the children would follow them.

Wampum

The wampum which Europeans make and barter to the Indians is made of sea-mussel shells. One variety is quite white, the other dark violet, a quarter of an inch in length, an eighth of an inch in thickness and round. A hole is bored lengthwise through each shell, large enough to admit a heavy cord. They are strung like beads. Wampum constitues the money of the Indians. Two hundred shells cost a buck hide, or a Spanish dollar. Before the white people came they had no such wampum for want of proper instruments to make it. The white are a little less in value then the dark.

Strings are made of the beads that have been strung as described. Two, four or six placed side by side and properly fastened form a string. A string is usually half a yard long, sometimes longer. Upon delivery of a string a long speech may be made and much said upon the subject under consideration. But when a belt is given few words are spoken, and they must be words of great importance, frequently requiring an explanation. Belts are of pure wampum worked in all manner of clever forms by the Indian women, they being informed in each case what the figures must be, inasmuch as the figures must correspond with the message. A belt is three or four inches broad and about a yard long.

Source: Zeisberger's *History...*, p. 94

David Jones
1773

Finally getting to the valley in February of 1773, a Baptist minister named David Jones came here not directly from Fort Pitt, but instead from the Scioto valley where he had been visiting with the Shawnees.

He didn't have much success in preaching to the Indians due, in part, to not having an interpreter. Nevertheless his journal is very interesting in its descriptions of Newcomerstown and Gnadenhutten. The Moravian towns of Welhik Thuppeek (Schoenbrunn) and Gnadenhutten had been founded in May and October, respectively, of the year before (1772), and the visit of Jones to Gnadenhutten is the first eyewitness description of this town that we have, other than from the Moravian diaries themselves. Also, once again, the name of Joseph "Peappi" appears as being a person who would possibly interpret for Rev. Jones, but apparently Killbuck, one of the principal captains at Newcomerstown, did not feel that he should be used in that capacity, stating that "I might as well not speak as to have him for instead of saying what I said, Joseph would say what his own heart thought."

Rev. Jones had a very long, colorful and active life. Not always successful as a preacher, even aggravating at times, his enthusiasm nevertheless carried him from one adventure to another, especially if Indians, or the military, were involved.

Before arriving in the Tuscarawas Valley, while at the Shawnee town of Chillicothe, he had to hide under a blanket in the cabin-loft of a gunsmith and trader named Moses Henry to avoid the wrath of one of the Indians. This incident is mentioned by our prior diarist, David McClure, under date of March 16, 1773, while he was still at Pittsburgh. McClure states:

Saw a Mr. Douglas, a trader, from the Shawanese country, who informs that Mr. Jones, a baptist preacher before mentioned, had been among them, and attempted to preach to them, but the Indians were enraged, and would have killed him, had he not been protected by a Moses Henry, a trader, who secreted him, until he found means to escape. Jones's object was the settlement, it is said, of a township, by people from New Jersey, opposite the mouth of the Sciota.

A few years later, Heckewelder met him at Marietta, Ohio, and on November 20th, 1788, had this to say about him:

Many more boats bound for Kentucke arrived. With them came a certain Doct. Jones, a Baptist minister. He at once offered to preach here on Sunday. He was offered lodging where I was staying. This man, who has decidedly peculiar principles, bothered me often with his questions and discourse. It was not long before the people got tired of his sermons, and so he left this place again after a few weeks.

Wallace, *Thirty Thousand Miles with Heckewelder*, p. 230.

According to the Dictionary of American Biography, he served as a chaplain in the Revolutionary War from 1776 to 1783. Again, during Wayne's Campaigns from 1794 to 1796, he served as a chaplain and is even depicted in Howard Chandler Christy's portrait, "Signing the Treaty of Greene Ville", that hangs in the Ohio State Capitol. And finally, almost incredibly, even though he was seventy-six years of age, "he volunteered and served as chaplain throughout the war [of 1812]."

He died on February 5, 1820, at the age of 85 years.

Tuesday, Feb. 9, 1773 {at Kiskapookee, one of the Lower Shawnee Towns, near Circleville.} ...My course to-day was about northeast. As I passed a certain place called the *Great Lick*, saw the last flock of parrots. These birds are in great abundance about Siota in winter, and in summer 'tis probable they may be seen much further towards the north. Having set out very late, night came on before I arrived to the next town. My road was very small, and the night dark in this wide wilderness, made my travelling more disagreeable than can be easily expressed: but before nine o'clock, came safe to Mr. McCormick's at the Standing Stone. This town consists chiefly of Delaware Indians. It is situated on a creek called Hockhockin. The soil about this is equal to the highest wishes, but the creek appears muddy. Though it is not wide, yet it soon admits large canoes, and from hence peltry is transmitted to Fort Pitt. Overtook here Mr. David Duncan, a trader from Shippen's town, who was going to Fort Pitt.

Wednesday 10, intending to travel forty miles, set out early in the morning—our course more northerly than northeast—the land chiefly low and level—and where our horses broke thro' the frost, it might be called bad road and good land. There were no inhabitants by the way. Before night, came to the designed town, called Dan. Elleot's wife's; a man of that name was said to have here a squaa for his pretended wife. This is a small town consisting of Delawares and Shawannees. The chief is a Shawannee woman, who is esteemed very rich—she entertains travellers—there were four of us in company, and for our use, her negro quarter was evacuated this night, which had a fire in the middle without any chimney. This woman has a large stock, and supplied us with milk. Here also we got corn for our horses at a very expensive price: but Mr. Duncan paid for me here, and in our journey till we parted. About a mile before we came to this town, we crossed a clear large stream, called Salt Lick Creek, which empties into Muskingum, on which the chief Delaware town is situated. The country here appeared calculated for health, fertile and beautiful.

Thursday 11, set out for a small town called Conner's, a man of that name residing there.

Our course was near northeast—the distance was less than the preceding day's journey, so that we arrived to town some time before sunset. Travelled this day over a good country, only wanting inhabitants. This town is situated near no creek, a good spring supplying them with water—the land about it is level and good, the timber being chiefly blackoak, indicates it will produce good wheat, if a trial was made. Mr. Conner, who is a white man, a native of Maryland, told me that he intended to sow wheat in the fall following, and was resolved to proceed to farming at all events. 'Tis probable that he will be as good as his word, for he is a man that seems not to fear God, and it is likely that he will not regard man. His connections will favour his attempts, for according to their way, he and the chief Indian of this town are married to two sisters. These women were captives, and it is likely from childhood, for they have the very actions of Indians, and speak broken English. It seemed strange to me to see the captives have the exact gestures of Indians. Might we not infer from hence, that if Indians were educated as we are, they would be like us? This town consists of Shawannees and Delawares; and some of them dwell in pretty good log houses well shingled with nails. Mr. Conner keeps a sort of a tavern, and has moderate accommodations, and though he is not what he should be, yet he was kind to me.

Friday 12, here we parted with some of our company, whose absence was very agreeable, and in company with Mr. Duncan, set out for New-Comer's Town, which is the chief town of the Delawares. Had gone but a few miles till we came to the Little Shawannee Woman's Town. This is situated on the west side of Muskingum, and chiefly consists of Shawannees. Here we crossed the river in a canoe, our horses swimming by its side. The country began to be hilly, interspersed with some barren plains. We passed Captain White Eye's Town, but this noted Indian was down Ohio, perhaps with my old interpreter, so that I could not have the satisfaction of seeing him this time, but I saw him several times the first visit. He was the only Indian I met with in all my travels, that seemed to have a design of accomplishing something future. He told me that he intended to be religious and have his children educated. He saw that their way of living would not answer much longer—game grew scarce—they could not much longer pretend to live by hunting, but must farm, &c.— But said, he could not attend to matters of religion now, for he intended to make a great *hunt* down Ohio, and take the skins himself to Philadelphia. I was informed that he accomplished this, and went round by the gulf of Florida to Philadelphia. On this occasion, could not but think of that text of scripture, which says, "one went to his farm and another to his merchandise." And it may be said, the Indian went to his hunting. This was the case last year, and perhaps something as important may employ

the next year, and so the life of man is spent, few remembring that one thing is *needful.*

A few miles north {east} of White Eye's town, there is a small town, where we obliged our horses to take the river, following them in a small canoe belonging to the Indians. Thence travelled over very hilly land till we came within two or three miles of New-Comer's Town, and from that to town the land is agreeable and appears good for wheat. Came to town before night, and found it was a great triennial feast, consequently little could be done till that ended. From the great town Chillicaathee to this chief town of the Delawares, is called one hundred and thirty miles. The course may be estimated near northeast, but as the path goes, it varies in many places. This town is situated on the west side of the river Muskingum, which is a pretty large stream. The proper pronunciation in Indian is *Mooskingung*, i. e. Elk Eye River. In their language an elk being called *moos*. This town takes its name from the name of the king, who is called *Neetotwhealemon*, i. e. New-Comer.

Saturday 13, was so happy as to meet Joseph Peappi, a Moravian Indian here, who is a good interpreter. Made application to him for his assistance in speaking to the king. He engaged and spoke very kindly on the occasion. He went and informed the king that I was in town, and would wait on him presently, and was to remain till I came. After proper time for information, went in, desiring Joseph to let the king know, that I was the man that he expected: upon which he met me with some complaisance, and seemed to receive me affectionately, inviting me to sit down. Told him that I was the man that wrote two letters to him last year, one from Monongehela, and the other from Fort Pitt. Asked if he received them with a belt of wampum. He replied that he received all, which he would produce if required. I informed him it was not necessary, if he received them it was enough. Proceeded to let him know that my design in coming now, was the same that was specified in the letters—that I was a minister desirous to instruct them into the knowledge of that God who made us all. That now I was ready to speak to him and his people, if he would only grant me liberty. Replied that in these matters he could do nothing without the advice of his council; that he would inform them of it, and an answer should be given as soon as the great feast was ended. This was not only what they call a feast, but also a time of great dancing and gaming, so that nothing else could be attended to till that was finished. To improve the present time, concluded to visit the Moravian towns.

Sabbath 14, in company with Mr. Duncan, set out, but by reason of ice, arrived not to it till afternoon. When we came, worship was finishing; the minister continued but a few sentences, which were spoken by him in the English tongue, an interpreter giving the meaning to the Indians. This town is situated on high level land east side of Muskingum, about ten miles up the stream from New-Comer's Town. It is laid out in regular form—houses are built on each side of the street. These Indians moved here about August 1772, and have used such frugality, that they have built neat log houses to dwell in, and a good house for divine worship, about twenty-two feet by eighteen, well seated, and a good floor and chimney. They are a mixture of Stock-Bridge, Mingo, and Delaware Indians. Since the last war their chief residence has been about Wioming. Their conduct in time of worship is praise-worthy. Their grave and solemn countenances exceed what is commonly seen among us at such times. Their minister, the Reverend David Siezberger seems an honest man, a native of Moravia, nor has he been many years in this country. He has been successful among these poor heathens, condescending for their sake to endure hardships. While I was present he used no kind of prayer, which was not pleasing to me, therefore asked him if that was their uniform practice. He replied that some times prayer was used. Their worship began and ended with singing an hymn in the Indian language, which was performed melodiously. In the evening they met again for worship, but their minister, inadvertently or by design, spoke in the German language, so that by me nothing was understood. Mr. Seizberger told me that near eighty families belong to their two towns, and there were two ministers besides himself. I was informed that one of them, whose name is Youngman, is a person of good abilities. By what appeared, must say, that the conduct of the Moravian society towards the heathen is commendable. These have behaved like christians indeed, while most of other societies have alto-gether neglected, or in general made but faint attempts. Indeed by what I have heard of the Reverend David Braynard, he was sincerely engaged, but his time was short. In the evening, informed Mr. Seizberger that it would gratify me to preach to his Indians. He replied with some appearance of indifference, that an opportunity might be had in the morning. 'Tis probable he was a little afraid to countenance me, lest some disciples might be made; than which, nothing was more foreign from my intention. Or his reservedness may be ascribed to his natural disposition.

Monday 15, parted here with my kind fellow-traveller Mr. Duncan, who went on his way towards Fort Pitt. At the appointed time the Indians convened—Joseph Peappi was interpreter. Introduced my discourse by observing that it was not my design in coming from home to preach to them, not being informed of their removal; but seeing Providence gave an opportunity, had a desire to speak to them. Proceeded to observe that all the disciples of our Saviour Jesus Christ separated themselves from the course of *this* world, no longer to live as the world lived. As other people were bad, they might expect some difficulties, and perhaps some persecutions; but that they should be strong in heart, for God; in due time would give them rest. That they should be watchful, and beware of backsliding, to live like other Indians; but as God had opened their eyes, to keep on their way till they came to eternal rest with Christ in heaven, &c. &c. The discourse continued about half an hour. On this occasion was very sensible of divine assistance; and from the great and apparent solemnity, it was thought that the word of God was felt with power. Such was the spiritual delight enjoyed, that it seemed no small compensation for my troubles and hardships endured. The next town was situated about ten miles up the same stream, where the ministers chiefly reside. Was informed that the other house of worship was more splendid, adorned with a steeple and bell, but the ice prevented me from seeing it. These Indians are tradesmen, understanding farming and carpenter work; and being already furnished with stock, intend to live as we do and 'tis probable in a few years will live richly; for the land appears good for wheat. While I was here one of the Indians asked the minister, when Easter Sunday was?   Mr. Seizberger seemed to evade any discourse about it, and only told him that it was not for some time, and that he should have notice before it came.   Perhaps had this question been asked among us, should have thought little about it. But here the case was the *reverse*; for while I ruminated on it, my soul was filled with horror to think that *mortal* man should *presume* to teach a heathen religiously to observe what God Almighty never taught him as any part of his will.   'Tis granted, that according to ecclesiastical history, this festival claims antiquity; but the hoary head is a crown of honour only when found in the way of righteousness.

{At this point in the journal, there is a lengthy digression into certain religious practices and beliefs that have nothing to do with the Indians.}

But to proceed, I returned to New-Comer's Town in the afternoon, and went to see Captain Killbuck, who is a sensible Indian, and uses us with part of the complaisance of a gentleman.   He speaks good English, so that I conversed on the subject of preaching, and he was to meet me next morning to converse further.   He invited me to make free in coming to see him. Soon perceived that he bore the chief sway in all their affairs and could do more than the king himself in many things.

Tuesday 16, met Captain Killbuck, spoke on many subjects.   In our discourse he told me, that some years since, two Presbyterian ministers visited them—that they did not incline to encourage their continuance, yet their visit had such effect that they had been thinking of it ever since.   He said, that they intended to have both a minister and schoolmaster, but would not have Presbyterians, because their ministers went to war against them, and therefore did not like to be taught by them now, who were before for killing them.   It was plain that Indian prejudice was very great and unreasonable.   Replied that the Moravians never fought against them, therefore they might receive them.   His reply was, that Moravians did not belong to our kingdom, being from Germany, and could not save their people alive in time of war.   Upon this he related the distresses and dangers of the Moravian Indians last war, and how they were preserved at Philadelphia.   Adding, that for all the assistance that the Moravians could give, their Indians might have been killed.   Hence argued, that it did not signify to be of that religion, that could not protect them in war time.   He said, they intended to go to England and see our king, and tell him that they would be of the same religion that he is and would desire a minister and schoolmaster of his own choosing.   Told him that his speech pleased me, but thought they were too poor to accomplish it, and feared they would get little assistance.   He said, that they had near forty pounds already, and intended to make an early hunt, which would enable them to go in the fall.   To effect this, Captain Killbuck and Swallowhead were chosen messengers to *Sir William Johnson* while I was there.   Encouraged their designs, willing to resign the civilizing them to his majesty's directions: but am persuaded, that the service of the church of England, as it now stands, will never be prescribed for Indians; for nothing would disgust them more than to have a religion, which would consume the greater part of life, only to learn its ceremonies.

Thursday 18, Afternoon, conversing with Killbuck, he told me that the young men were desirous to hear me preach, consequently concluded to preach next day.   In the evening, had an opportunity to converse with Joseph Peappi, who would interpret for me; but I told him that I would give only five pounds for a month; he said, he used to have seven pounds.   Indians, from the greatest to the least, seem mercenary and excessively greedy of gain.   Indeed they are so lazy, that they are commonly needy, and must be more so if they do not cultivate their lands; deer grow so scarce, that, great part of the year, many of them rather starve than live.   Mr. Evans, who is a trader in this town, told me that last summer some were supported by sucking the juice of green cornstalks.

Friday 19,   expected to preach, but Killbuck told me that they were not yet fully united in the point—Had reason to think that the king was not much for it, though he said little—Neither do I conclude that Joseph was very desirous of it, for the traders often told me that the Moravians taught their Indians to disrespect other societies, and I could wish that there were not grounds for the report. Asked Killbuck if he knew the reason why they were not united for my preaching? He seemed to intimate, it would have been otherwise, if I had come last fall, while they were in the notion of it: but found, by conversing with him, there is a jealousy in them, lest we should have some design of enslaving them, or something of that nature. He told me that an highland officer took one of their women as his wife, and went with her into Maryland about Joppa: and they heard there he sold her a slave like a negro. This he said, a gentleman in Philadelphia told him: and as they never saw the squaa afterwards, they were ready to believe that the report was true. If this case is so, and this gentleman could only see that by his means he has prejudiced the heathens against us, am persuaded he would mentally retract his intelligence with a degree of sorrow. Replied, that I never heard it before, yet was persuaded that it could not be true, that she continued a slave; for if the officer was guilty of such a crime, the law of our land allowed no Indians of our country to be slaves, and the magistrates would surely set her free. But he said, their people did not know our law therefore such reports made them afraid of us. He further said, "What is become of the woman, she never came back to us again?" Replied, that I could not tell, maybe she did not choose to come, or she might be dead. By this time, was much discouraged, and by hardships and want of provisions my health and strength were greatly impaired. No meat could be had here for love or money. Bought milk at nine-pence a quart, and butter at two shillings a pound, but not near sufficient could be had. From the king, had bought the rump of a deer dried, after their custom, in the smoke to preserve it without salt, which made it so disagreeable that little could be used. Desires called for a land, where famine doth not raise her baleful head, therefore on Saturday 20, inquired for a pilate to accompany me towards Ohio. The season was severly cold, so that the king and Captain Killbuck would not suffer me to go, for they said the weather was so cold, that it would kill even an Indian. Indeed the season was so intensely cold, that attempts to travel were impracticable. My continuance here was very disagreeable; for though the traders of this town were civil, yet they had no taste for reli-

gion, so that I was alone without suitable sustenance, waiting the permission of Providence to depart homewards.

Sabbath 21, this was a remarkable cold day—Some part of it was spent conversing with Killbuck on several particulars, concerning the belief of the Delaware Indians. 'Twas asked, whether they believed that there is a God who created all things? He replied, that this was their common belief. The second question was, whether they believed that when any person died, their soul went to a happy state, or to a state of misery? Replied, this they also believed. The third was, whether they knew that God would by his great power raise up all the dead to life again at the end of this world? His reply was, that this they knew nothing of, 'till lately they had heard it among the Moravian Indians. These Indians have been so long acquainted with us, that it is not easy to determine what they have learned of us.

This day liberty was granted to preach as often as I pleased but not having my interpreter, could do little; for Killbuck would not accept of Joseph, for, he said, I might as well not speak as to have him for instead of saying what I said, Joseph would say what his own heart thought. Though I had better thoughts of Joseph, soon perceived that Killbuck had such an aversion to him, that if he was used for an interpreter, nothing could be done. This was the only time that opened for doing good, and this opportunity was chiefly lost for want of Mr. Owens my old interpreter; therefore all that was said as preaching, was in the council, using Killbuck as an interpreter, who was capable in common affairs, but knew little concerning religion. To day the king and council concluded, that no more rum should be drank in this town or nation, and that there should be no more gaming or dancing only at their triennial feast. This made me think of the laws of New-Jersey about *horseracing*, in which there were such reserves, as evidently deonstrated that some of the assembly loved the *sport*.

Monday 22, Killbuck told me that they were making up a speech to governor Penn who had wrote to them last fall, and I must wait to write and carry it. He said they would provide me a pilate.

Tuesday 23, the same message was sent,

informing me that for six dollars, should have a pilate to see me over Ohio. This news was not the most agreeable as the wages were unreasonable, and my daily expences similar. 'Twas impossible to purchase one pound of bear's flesh, or one venison ham.—This people live truly poor. The land is indeed good, but at present the price is in the hand of fools. In the afternoon a messenger came for me to wait on the king and council—Their number might be about twenty convened in their council-house, which may be sixty feet by twenty-four. It had one post in the middle, and two fires. Most of them had long pipes in almost constant use—they set round the fires on skins—a stool was prepared for me—then presented a bowl of hommany, of which they were eating. Spoons they had none, but a small ladle serves four or five Indians. After our repast, a sheet of paper was brought, and Killbuck being interpreter, informed me, that it was their desire that I should write to governor Penn from them, desiring that he would inform his people, that if any brought rum their side of Allegini river or Ohio, they had appointed six men, on pain of death, to stave every keg—And that he would let governor Franklin know, that they desired all the Jersey Indians to move into their country, as it is large enough, &c. Accordingly a letter was written, and every word interpreted by Captain Killbuck and an assistant. This was delivered to his honour Richard Penn, esq. 'Tis to be hoped the contents thereof will merit his honour's attention; for as the Indians seemed resolute in the point, 'tis possible that neglects might be attended with undesirable consequences.

Wednesday 24, was called to the council, and desired to deliver a speech to the Quakers at Philadelphia; but as there was nothing worthy of writing in the message, therefore delivered it verbally to Mr. Thomas Wharton in Philadelphia.

As next day I was to begin my journey towards Ohio, therefore it may be said, that at this meeting, I took my leave of them, giving them all the advice that was thought expedient, which they seemed to receive very friendly—so we parted in love and peace.

These Indians are not defective in natural abilities, and their long acquaintance with us, has given some of them better notions than many other savages. They are as void of civil govern-ment as the Shawannees. Their virtues are but few, their vices near the same with other Indians. Their customs are resembling the Shawannees, only they have a great feast once in three years. Asked Killbuck the meaning of it? he said, it might have had some meaning at first, but now was observed only as an old custom. The language of these Indians in general differs very much from the Shawannees, being still more guttural. Shall give you a specimen of their manner of counting to ten, viz. *guitta, nusha, nucha, neah, pelenah, cootash, neeshash, chaash, peshcung, telen.* These Indians at present have no way of worshipping or acknowledging God; but they seem to incline to learn to read—and have begun to farm, to which they are much assisted by a Jersey Indian, who is not only their smith, but also makes their ploughs. Indeed it appears that both a minister and schoolmaster may go among them with safety and success, if they keep their conclusion to suffer no rum to be brought into their country. On this subject I spoke much, shewing the advantages that would arise from the constant observance of this conclusion and exhorted them to be *strong.* To which they answered with loud voices *kehellah,* which is the most emphatical way of saying yes. They shew some honour to a minister; but are so extortionate in the price of their provisions, that a man must expend much more money in preaching among them than he can get by preaching among us. They increase much faster than the Shawannees, poligamy not being so common. Their town is in no regular form. Neither these nor the Shawannees clain any distinct property in lands, looking on it that God made it free for all. Nor could I understand that they have any fixed bounds to a nation, esteeming it chiefly useful for hunting. Providence seems to point out the civilizing of these Indians; for a farming life will lead to laws, learning and government, to secure property. Captain Killbuck told me, he saw the necessity of a magistrate to recover debts, and said, that by and by, he expected that they would have one; but as yet their people did not understand matters. 'Tis a little surprising that *Protestants* should be so neglectful of the Indians; and in common there is no concern appears among them, about civilizing the many nations, that are yet rude savages; while on the other hand, the *French Papists* have been very industrious to instil their principles into the minds of such as were contiguous to them, and with some success. The Waindots are a little tainted, but might, 'tis probable, be easily better informed, and especially as the French are in a manner expelled. This I can say, that though my body and estate suffered by this journey, yet I do not repent my visit but rejoice that some attempts have been made, though not with the success that could be wished. Would have stayed longer, but being destitute of my old interpreter, and scarcity of provisions, rendered it impracticable.

Thursday 25, having a pilate, which cost six dollars, though I paid Mr. Thompson the trader only one guinea, yet he made it up in goods, set out about eleven o'clock from New-Comer's Town on Muskingum, intending the nearest course for the river Ohio. My pilate was a Jersey Indian, whose name is Pontus Newtemus; he spoke English intelligibly, but was almost as great a stranger to the woods as myself—and we had a path only the first part of the way. Our course should be a little south of east. This day travelled only about fifteen miles, and encamped by a brook, where we were surrounded with abundance of howling wolves. Spent the evening conversing on many subjects; found Pontus with little more knowledge than other Indians.—Assisted by a good fire, we slept

well, considering that our frigid curtains were the circumambient air.

Friday 26, set out about eight o'clock. This day we left our little path, and went according to my directions, for Pontus knew not the course, only he was informed from a rough sketch of the new map which I had by me. Some part of the way the land was charming—looked extraordinary for wheat, covered with the finest blackoak trees and goosberry-bushes; at last encamped at a creek about five yards wide, running southeast, neither of us knew into what larger creek it emptied. Surrounded with the protection of him, whose tender mercies are over the works of his hands, we slept safe in the midst of a doleful wilderness.—This day's journey was at least thirty miles.

Saturday 27, set out, and soon left the creek, steered our course near east, till at last we came to a creek which we followed and a little before sunset, came to the river Ohio, opposite to Weeling. This creek empties into Ohio opposite to an island, and as it is common to pass down Ohio the east side of this island, by that means it escaped the notice of Mr. Hutchins, and also of Mr. Hooper, consequently it was not in my map.

Source: Jones, *A Journal of Two Visits...*, pp. 86–109

Schoenbrunn Diary – Jones Entry

Feb. 13 {1773}. Br. David went to Gnadenhütten and, on the 14th, conducted there the Sunday services, taking the opportunity, also, to speak to several of the members. An English Baptist minister, who has several times sent letters to Gekelemukpechünk and offered to preach for them, had heard about us and came to that place (Gnadenhütten) on a visit. As he related, he had spent the winter among the Shawanose with the intention of preaching the Gospel to them, but he had not found one who asked after God, not even one in whom he had observed that he questioned whether there is a God in heaven. He had been in five of their towns, but they had not allowed him to speak privately with Indians, much less, to preach a single time, and he had been obliged, in the end, to flee in order to save his life and to get away secretly. Even so they had pursued him but he had escaped their hands. He said that he would probably never again come into this region, for he had not represented to himself conditions as he found them. Now he wished to learn whether they would give him a favorable answer in Gekelemukpechünk, where he had, also, made application, and if that should prove to be the case, he would remain there for a time. Soon after, we heard that they had not accepted his offer and had not permitted him to preach a single sermon. He made much of praising and extolling the work of the Brethren among the Indians, declaring that we had accomplished more than they themselves should be able to do in all their lives. From his certificate of the Baptist Society of Philadelphia, which he showed the Indians wherever he stopped, though to no purpose, it was to be seen that he was an ordained minister. He appeared to be a pleasant man, telling us, moreover, that he had preached in Br. Gambold's church. At his own request and with Br. David's permission, he delivered a brief and quite appropriate exhortation to our Indians, declaring them happy and blessed and commending them to the protecting care of God which they needed as they were dwelling in the midst of those who were enemies of the kingdom of Christ. He had wished to come, also, to Welhik Thuppeck with Br. David and to see the place, but because the ice in the River had been stopped up and the waters had risen, he gave up the idea and returned to Gekelemukpechünk. He had, as he told us, on his journey hither, last November, received a package of letters for us from Bro. Bill Henry, in Lancaster, since, however, he had taken another course than he had, at first, intended, he had given it to a white man along the Ohio, below Pittsburg, for delivery to us, but we have not as yet received it. Br. David asked him, if he should succeed in securing the letters on his return, he send them to Pittsburg.

Indian Bread

Their bread is of two kinds; one made up of green corn while in the milk, and another of the same grain when fully ripe and quite dry. This last is pounded as fine as possible, then sifted and kneaded into dough, and afterwards made up into cakes of six inches in diameter and about an inch in thickness, rounded off on the edge. In baking these cakes, they are extremely particular; the ashes must be clean and hot, and if possible come out of good dry oak barks, which they say gives a brisk and durable heat. In the dough of this kind of bread, they frequently mix boiled pumpkins, green or dried, dry beans, or well pared chestnuts, boiled in the same manner, dried venison well pounded, whortleberries, green or dry, but not boiled, sugar and other palatable ingredients. For the other kind of bread, the green corn is either pounded or mashed, is put in broad green corn blades, generally filled in with a ladle, well wrapped up, and baked in the ashes, like the other. They consider this as a very delicate morsel, but to me it is too sweet.

Source: Heckewelder's *History...*, p. 195

John Heckewelder
1773

This next journal of John Heckewelder is of a canoe journey down the Ohio and up the Muskingum to Gnadenhutten and Welhik Thuppeek (Schoenbrunn) in the Spring of 1773. He was bringing some more of the Christian Indians from their towns in Pennsylvania to the new towns in the Tuscarawas Valley.

His journal is noteworthy for showing the large number of Indian villages, most of them very small, along the Muskingum and Tuscarawas rivers.

April 22 {1773}. At noon we left the Ohio and entered the Muskingum. This river is very deep a few miles from its mouth, and paddles and oars have to be used there; afterwards it is not so deep any more, and a little wider than the Lehigh at Bethlehem. Today again a bear was shot.

The 23d. We left the lovely countryside; the terrain became very mountainous and the bottoms very swampy and were almost completely covered with beech trees. At evening time our Brethren went on a little hunt and again shot a bear.

The 24th. We met an Indian from Gekelemukpechünk who was acquainted with us. He was on his way home from the hunt after he had shot a buffalo, many of which are found around here.

The 25th. We traveled on till noon, and since many complained of fatigue, we resolved to make camp near a huge rock. Some of the Brethren at once built a sweating oven to sweat out their fatigue; others went out hunting a little and encountered buffaloes, at which they shot, but without success. This night we did not find much rest because of the enormous number of toads, which greatly annoyed us. The Indians, therefore, call this place Tsquallutene, that

means, town of the toads. About midnight we had a terrible thunderstorm accompanied by a heavy rain. A part of our people sought shelter beneath a rock which was standing beside the huge one. This big rock is 70 feet long, 25 high, and 22 wide, and is solid rock.

The 26th and 27th. The channel was pretty good, and we advanced quite a bit. But when we noticed that our grain had been wetted by the last rain and had started sprouting, we resolved to travel on the 28th only as far as Sikhewünk {Duncan Falls} and dry our grain there. Together with some of our Brethren I went about ten miles up this creek to see the famous salt spring {at Chandlersville}, which is imbedded in a sandbank, wells heavily, and has no visible outlet; evidently, it has an outlet underground, because after having been emptied it soon fills up again. We saw quite a few contraptions there for boiling salt. At the mouth of this creek there is a very fine amount of anthracite coal; it lies there like a wall of bricks, and not mixed with soil or other stones, as I have seen it in other places on the Ohio. This wall was 500 ells [1050 feet] long. Here another kind of scenery begins, while up to this point it had continued as previously described. Now rich bottoms and good land presented themselves, and the farther we journeyed the more pleasant did it become. The river here took a different course, which gave us hope to meet our Brethren soon, because previously we seemed to have traveled farther away from them all the time.

The 29th. We had to pass three bad rapids, which gave us much trouble because we had to tow up our canoes.

The 30th. At noon we arrived at the Shawnee Town which had been visited by Brother David last fall. (Wakatomika, near Dresden) Some of our Brethren went into the town, but they found only a few people at home, who received them with kindness; most of them had already moved away. Thereafter we passed another [Shawnee] town (probably another of the Wakatomika towns), and made camp. Today we had a stretch of bad channel, and most of the men became very much fagged out.

The 1st of May, at noon, we rested again close to a Shawnee town (Tom's Town, near Conesville?). The inhabitants of this town moved about among our people and showed friendly feelings for us. Meanwhile I visited a white man (probably Richard Conner) who is living there and who has a white wife; she had been a prisoner and cannot talk anything but Shawnee. After that we journeyed on and were received very kindly in a town where Delaware and Monsey are living (probably Mowheysinck, two miles below Coshocton); they showed us great hospitality and were not satisfied until we all had eaten enough. They would have liked us to stay with them for the night, but as we did not want to lose any time, we traveled on for a few more miles.

The 2d. We had to wade again in the water a great deal, towing our canoes over rapids and shallow places. We met an Indian Brother from Gnadenhütten, who lent us considerable help.

The 3d. We again passed different towns (among them would have been White Eyes Town and the town near the Old Stone Fort), stopped at some and talked with the inhabitants, who showed themselves friendly towards us, and in the afternoon we passed Gekelemukpechünk and

made camp at the upper end of the town. Passing by, I counted 106 spectators. They greeted us with their usual shout of joy, but we were not able to thank them in the same way. No sooner had we gone ashore than we had visitors, some of whom brought food for the hungry. Meanwhile I went with a few Brethren to visit Chief Netawatwes. He, as well as others who were with him, was very friendly toward us, and when we parted I had this feeling about him: "You, too, will be of the Savior's, some day." Then I and another Brother went to see Killbuck, who, among other things, asked the Brother who was with me: "Does this man really like the Indians?" — "Yes," he answered, "not only does he like them, but all the other Brethren who are with us like them, too. It would not be necessary for them to live as poorly as they do; I have seen with my own eyes how well they live at Bethlehem; but because they like the Indians, and want to acquaint them with the Savior, they are content with their poor mode of life and are happy when the Indians become believers in the Saviour. There is nothing else they ask or demand of us." — He replied: "Well, well, now I know it."

The 4th. In the morning we again had many visitors, and our Brethren every once in a while said a word or two about the Savior. Then we parted again. A few Brethren from Gnadenhütten and Welhik Thuppeek, who met us halfway, were very welcome to us, because by now we were all entirely spent. In the afternoon we arrived at Gnadenhütten, where everybody had been looking forward to our arrival and had been busy preparing food in order that the hungry and weak might restore themselves. Three families at once stayed there to live, and the rest of us, on the 5th, arrived happily and safely at Welhik Thuppeek, where we were received by our Brethren and Sisters in the most affectionate and loving fashion.

Source: Heckewelder, "A Canoe Journey from the Big Beaver...", pp. 283–98

John Lacey
1773

For two weeks in the summer of 1773, three Quakers were in the valley and two of them left journals of their visit.

While brief, they add the information that an Indian named Thomas McKee was the brother of Newcomer and lived a few miles below Newcomerstown. (Later, according to the Salem Diary for November 12, 1780, he was killed at Coshocton by a drunken relative.)

Query? If McKee lived in a town, was this the same town that Rev. McClure fled to during the rum frolic mentioned in his journal? I think that it probably was and that it was located in the vicinity of the Old Stone Fort north of Isleta, for McClure states that the village was about 5 miles down the river from Newcomerstown, and that would be just about the right distance to the Isleta area.

Second Query? Was Thomas McKee the same Indian as the Kelappama who met with Bouquet in 1764 and who was stated in the Bouquet journal as being a brother of Newcomer? I have not been able to verify this, one way or the other.

{July} 18th {1773}. We travelled a hilly and swampy road, but the land very good. We arrived at Pittsburgh, before dark, and put up at Sample's.

19th. Concluded to rest ourselves and horses. The people here treated us very kindly.

We had a conference with Captain White Eyes, a Delaware Chief, who was on his return from Philadelphia. He expressed much satisfaction at our arrival, and said he would go with us; but that he was under the necessity of waiting for Joseph Simmons, from Lancaster, who was to bring his goods from there. He informed us that John Gibson, an Indian trader, had set out that morning for Newcomer's Town, the place we were going to; and advised us to endeavor to overtake him; as he would be a very suitable person to accompany us.

20th. We had made preparations to set out early this morning, in order to overtake the Indian trader; but, upon inquiry, learned that he

had returned, and said that John Logan, a Mingo Indian, was lying in wait to kill him. He had returned to town, among the Indians, for protection. He got Gayashuta, a Mingo Chief, and Captain White Eyes to agree to go and see what was the matter with Logan, and endeavor to pacify him. White Eyes said he would attend us all the way to Newcomer's Town: he thought the behavior of Logan would make us afraid as he should be were he in our place.

They set out in a canoe; and we, with a Delaware Indian, by land. We crossed the Alleghany branch [*of the Ohio*] in a canoe; and our horses swam by the side. When we came near to a place called Logtown, where Logan lay, our guide stopped and hearkened very attentively, though we could not tell what he was listening at; but, before we had proceeded much further, we heard a great noise. Our guide, who could not speak one word of English, made motions to us to stop and retire. He took us up

151

a hollow, to some water, where we staid while he went to the camp from whence the noise proceeded. He, for our safety, secretly informed George Girty, a trader, where we were. He immediately came to us and conducted us around the camp, to the river side. He told us that an Indian had got drunk, and fell in the river, and was drowned; and that Logan suspected Gibson of making him drunk, and killing him. Soon after we came to the river, Captain White Eyes and our Indian guide came with canoes; and we again swam our horses by the side, over the river, to the house of John Gibson. Gayashuta was left to pacify Logan, who was very drunk. White Eyes and our two guides returned to Logan's camp, where they staid all night, leaving us at Gibson's.

21st. In the morning, White Eyes came over to us, and wanted us to proceed on our journey, as he was ready to go with us and Logan had become somewhat quieted; but, uncle Zebulon being a little unwell and White Eyes pretty merry, we thought it best, as Gibson was to go the next day, to remain where we were. White Eyes soon fell asleep. About eleven o'clock, Logan, Gayashuta, and several more Indians, came over to Gibson's. They soon began to talk very loud; while all the others stood around them, with their tomahawks in their hands. However, their differences were soon made up.

22d. We set out; crossed the Ohio with Gibson and White Eyes; came to a Mingo town, where they had Logan shut up in a house. An old Indian advised us to go on; but before we could get off, Logan broke down the door, and came to us in a very good humor, expressing a great deal of sorrow for what he had said yesterday. We came to Beaver creek, a very fine stream, about fifteen perches wide, with a fine gravelly bottom. We came to Little Beaver creek about sunset; crossed it; and encamped in a swamp. We were obliged to gather fern and bushes to lie on; yet we slept very well.

23d. This morning, it rained quite hard. We got very wet, as we received a double portion, one from the clouds and one from the bushes. We put up, after travelling all day, at an old Indian cabin.

24th. In the morning, our guide left us, in order to inform the Indians of our coming. We travelled on and came to a Moravian town, {Gnadenhutten} on Muskingum-river, where we staid all night. The Indians treated us very kindly.

25th. Our guides met us, a little out of town: they came to conduct us to the King {Netawatwes}. When we came into the presence of the King, he declared he received us with as great love and friendship as our forefathers and theirs received each other. After giving us a welcome, we were conducted to a house which they had prepared for us, where we were again welcomed. They immediately sent, in the King's name, to the Moravian town, for an interpreter. Gibson followed with his packhorse and goods.

26th. We breakfasted with Freeman, a trader; and, about ten o'clock, Captain Kill Buck came and ordered the women to get us some victuals. In about two hours, they brought us hominy boiled in bear's-grease, boiled squashes, milk and Indian-cake, baked in the ashes. We were visited by the King and his brother. We were told that four white men were traveling through there, a short time before, and had been robbed and murdered by a party of Mingo Indians, at the Scioto-river. Our interpreter, Samuel More, an Indian, came in the evening.

On the *28th*, we had a Meeting. Netow Clemon, King, Meek, Kill Buck, White Eyes, Indian Chiefs, and a number of other Indians, attended. John Parish read our Certificates, from the Monthly Meeting; also an Epistle from the Meeting for Sufferings of Friends, at Philadelphia; which being interpreted to the Indians, by Samuel More, they expressed their satisfaction, and said, "Ka-he-lak" — i. e. "Very well!" after which a Meeting for Divine worship was held; in which the Indians behaved with remarkable sobriety and attention. When the Meeting for worship was over, Captain Kill Buck said, if Friends would retire, they would hold a Council, and consider what answer to make, for Friends to take home; on which we withdrew and went to our house. In about two hours, the Interpreter came and informed us they were ready to give their answer, and desired we would attend; which being complied with, and having taken our seats, Captain White Eyes rose, and, after receiving the Belt from the King, spoke as follows: — "We are glad, and rejoice in our hearts, to see our brothers, the Quakers, speaking before us. What you have said, we believe to be right; and we heartily join in with it. Since our Savior came, a light in the world, there has been a great stir among the people about religion. — some for one way and some for another. We have had offers of religion many times; but would not accept of it, until we had seen our brothers, the Quakers, and heard what they would say to us. And now you have come and opened the road; and we have heard what you have said; and we have felt the grace that was in your hearts conveyed to us — we think the Quakers and Delawares are brothers, brought up together as the children of one man; and that it is our Saviour's will that we should be of one religion. Now you have come and opened the road, we expect to see the way, from town to town, quite over to the Great King, over the water. Then our King will know that the Quakers and Delawares are as one man, and of one religion. We are poor and weak, and not able to judge for ourselves; and when we think of our children, it makes us sorrowful. We hope you will instruct us in the right way, both in things of this life and of the world to come. Now, what we have said, we hope to be strengthened to abide by." He then delivered a Belt to Zebulon Herton.

On the *29th*, we had another Meeting, which was very orderly; the Indians seemed a great deal affected; and attended to what was delivered, with sobriety.

30th. My companions went down to the river, to a blacksmith's, and got their horses shod. When they returned, we went to see Captain Kill Buck's son, who had just returned from hunting. He had been out seventeen days, and had killed thirty deer. He gave us a fresh ham of venison; which was very acceptable.

8th Month, 1st. Last night, another hunter came to town. He had been out thirty days, and had killed forty-seven deer. This day, we had our last Meeting, which was very sober and affecting. After Meeting, we informed them of our intention of returning. They said they could not let us go, until they held a Council and provided a suitable person to accompany us to Pittsburgh. Captain White Eyes sent a messenger for us to come down the river to his house, as he was not well and would be glad to see us. It was agreed to, much to my satisfaction; as I expected something new and curious from the journey.

2d. We set out for White Eyes town; crossed Muskingum-river; came to some glades or plains, of vast extent, which made a beautiful appearance, and are extremely rich; stopped at Thomas McKee's, who soon got ready and accompanied us. White Eyes received us with love and respect. We dined with him upon very good veal, both roasted and boiled, and cabbage. It is a dish rarely to be met with, among the Indians. After dinner, they held a Council, to which we were invited. After discoursing awhile, it was agreed that the King's brother and White Eyes should accompany us to Pittsburgh. The Council then broke up. We returned to our house, at Newcomer's Town, and got our things ready to set out, in the morning, on our return.

3d. We took our leave of the King and others, who looked very sorrowful at parting; and stood looking after us, until we got out of their sight. Uncle Zebulon and John Parish went up to the Moravian Upper Town; {Welhik Thuppeek} and I staid at the lower one. {Gnadenhutten}

4th. My uncle and Parish came to me at eleven o'clock; and, just after dinner, McKee and White Eyes joined us, with John Freeman and James Forbes, two traders. We set forward; crossed Kaalamahong about seven perches wide, and encamped in the woods.

5th. Travelled about thirty miles; and, at night, encamped in the woods.

6th. Crossed Little Beaver-creek, and came to John Logan's house, on Big Beaver-creek, where we staid all night. Logan being from home, our guides left us and went to Gibson's, at Logtown.

7th. Set out, with one Delamon, an Indian trader; got to the Ohio; swam our horses over; and staid at Gibson's.

8th. We rested this day.

9th. Pursued our return, in company with a man from John Gibson's. Being rainy, we stopped at Captain McKee's, an Agent, under Sir William Johnson.

10th. We crossed Shutee and when we came to the Monongahela, there was a good boat, in which we were ferried over to our old lodgings, at Pittsburgh. My uncle much fatigued.

Source: Lacey, "Journal of a Mission...", pp. 103–7

John Parrish
1773

The other Quaker who also left a journal of his visit in the summer of 1773 was John Parrish. He visited the Upper Moravian town (Schoenbrunn) as well as the Lower Moravian town (Gnadenhutten).

{July} 18th {1773}. In the Evening reach'd Pittsburgh in good Health, having been treated with remarkable Civility by the People hitherto. Put up at one Sample's. They reached Pittsburgh in 10 days; not being hindered an Hour in the whole Journey.

The 19th they rested, got their Cloaths washed & sent 18 miles down the Ohio for a Guide to New-Comer's Town, one living so far on the way to that place & intending to set out next morning, but to their surprize he came into Pittsburgh that morning, his Life being threatened by an Indian man named John Logan, whom White Eyes & Cohursater went to appease, by water, leaving them to the care of an Indian Guide who took them by Land near to John Logan's Camp, which under conduct of another Indian they avoided by going round thro' the Woods, & swam their Horses over the Ohio to John Gibbons' ye Trader, where they were kindly & freely entertain'd. Here they staid 4th Day 21st and Logan being pacified they set out ye 22d accompanied by White Eyes & John Gibson, the former agreed to go with them least they should be under any apprehensions of Danger. Rode 9 or 10 miles down the Ohio to Beaver Creek's Mouth where John Logan had his Cabbin. Here along the River were several Cottages & a fine Bottom. Cross'd Beaver Creek & twin'd more Westward, thro but indifferent Land & lodg'd in a low Place for the sake of the Water. 23d saw a few Indians on their way (Lands hardly fit for Cultivation) & lodg'd at a Bark Shelter. 24. Gibbons & White Eyes went on & they staid at a Moravian Town {Gnadenhutten} (12 miles short of New Comers Town) where they were kindly entertained. 25, made them full satisfaction & went on, got to the Town {Newcomerstown} about 1 o'clock being met by Capt Kilbuck who seem'd pleas'd, & were conducted to the King's Palace. He express'd Joy in his Countenance & told them by an Interpreter that "He had a sense of that Love which subsisted between our Forefathers," which was evidently to be felt.

Then they were conducted to a House prepar'd for them, & staid ye 26 & 27 waiting for an Interpreter, visited by several particularly Thos McKee the King's Brother who inquir'd kindly after his 2 friends Is: Pemberton & Isaac Zane & gave them a hearty welcome. They were kindly entertained, the Women daily bringing them the best Provisions the Town afforded.

28. The Day appointed for a Council, Capt Kilbuck waited on them & told them they were ready to hear them. John, after a short Introduction, read the Certificates & Epistle from Friends ...when the Meeting ended they withdrew, & left the Indians in Council. After some time they were sent for & Capt. White Eyes spoke by a Belt, & said "That was the Delawares' writing." He express'd much Joy in seeing some of their Brothers, the Quakers, & believed what had been said to be right — that they had receiv'd offers of Religion many Times but would not accept them til they had seen their Brothers

the Quakers & heard what they would say to them...said they were weak & poor and not able to judge for themselves, & when they thought of their Children it made them sorry, hop'd the Friends would instruct them in the right Way for their Good both in this & the World to come, & that they should be strengthened to abide by what they had heard. He then delivered a Belt as a Confirmation of what he had said.

29. Capt White Eyes & J. Gibbons set off for the Shawanee Town. At 12 o'clock a Meeting was appointed...The Indians declared their Intention of going to England &c. After Dinner the King & several of his Council came to see them at their Quarters. One of the Council undertook to read the Belt so that it might be taken in writing, but fell short of what had been said the Day before. 30th They visited several small Settlements & were kindly entertained. 31. They washed their Cloaths & fished a little...

8 mo. 2d dined with White Eyes, where their Speech being read over to them, they pointed out some Omissions, which were added, & it was read over again before the King & 4 Counsellors who approv'd it.

3d Set off homeward, dined at Connodenhead {Gnadenhutten}, went to the Upper Moravian Town, {Schoenbrunn} staid all night, saw the Indians & their Teachers. A Number of them sent their Love to Friends, in Philadelphia. 4th went back to the Lower Town, where White Eyes & Thomas McKee came to accompany us to Pittsburgh. After dinner put forward about 15 miles & rested comfortably at a fine Spring after taking a dish of coffee. 5th Rode about 30 miles thro' a very poor Soil with little Water — slept in the Woods. 6th John's Beast failed, & the others left him — he at length turn'd her loose & follow'd the Company with his Saddle, Bridle, Bags & Blanket on his Back, overtaking them they got to John Logan's on Beaver Creek, the prospect gloomy he being expected home drunk, his Mother & Sister were however civil & got them some supper. 7. John went back 7 miles on a hired Beast & brot in his tired mare to Logan's — got to John Gibson's — (swam their horses over ye Ohio opposite Logstown). 1st Day (the 8th) rested all Day. 9th pass'd along the English Shore to Captain McKee's, it raining hard & they much wet, treated kindly & stay'd all night. John chang'd his Beast. 10th rode on 4 miles to Pittsburgh where 11th they had an appointed Meeting, at which the most reputable People attended & it was favour'd. Afternoon went to see the Coal Quarry. Spent some Time with the Indians, of whom Capt White Eyes, Thomas McKee & Delemson, all men of Note, were then there.

Source: Parrish, "Extracts from the Journal...", pp. 443–48

Schoenbrunn Diary – Quakers

July 27 {1773}. As the Chief in Gekelemukp. had invited Br. Samuel Moor by letter to that place, in order to serve him as interpreter, for a few days, in affairs with the white people, he started for that town today.

July 30. Br. Samuel returned from Gekelemukp. where he had interpreted for the Quakers who had arrived there from Philadelphia. They had addressed a speech to the Indians and reminded them of the friendship they had maintained with the Indians, since they had come into the country. The Chiefs, in turn, addressed a speech to them and said that it would please them if they would not only send them ministers but, also, teach the Indians various kinds of work and trades, that they might become a substantial people, further, they asked of them that they might help them in the matter of sending some of their own people to England for an interview with the King. So far as we have been able to learn, the Quakers were not willing to grant all these proposals and excused themselves on the ground that these were not their affair and did not concern them. The Indians, however, were not satisfied and urged them, almost by force, to promise that they would aid in the matter of the journey to England. The Indians are not so much concerned about hearing the Gospel, as they are by means thereof to secure benefits and under the appearance of a good intention to seek to profit in externals.

Aug. 3. ...Strangers came up the River on a visit, and toward evening the three Quakers, one of whom was a minister, who had visited in Gekelemukp. arrived here, looked over the place, which pleased them very much. In connection with the evening service, they commented on the orderliness and devoutness of our Indian brethren and sisters. On the following day, they returned to Pittsburg.

Gnadenhutten Diary – Quakers

Thursday, July 29 (1773). ...Concerning the purpose of the Quakers, who passed by here several days ago on their way to Kekelamukpechüng, we were in so far informed, that they had renewed their old friendship with the Indians there; had preached, their teaching had been approved and taken up and accepted by the Chiefs, for the purpose of preaching in the future, etc. Their first address was concerning Light.

Monday, August 2. ...A certain Mr. Anderson visited us, who entered into a friendly conversation with me, assured of his high regard for the work of the Brethren among the heathen, among other things that he had marked a notable change in our people, that we put forth efforts in behalf of the people simply for love of their souls, without selfish interest, which, he said, I surely know; and so the Lord will surely be your reward! I see with mine eyes that you have already accomplished something great, for a notable change has come about in your people, and I do not doubt that it will go further. We give the honor to God, and I told him that it is God's work that they believe in his name and not our industry.

Wednesday, August 4. ...Soon after the same (the early service) we received visitors of all sorts of people, who went with the above mentioned Quakers on their way back, in part, as far as Fort Pitt.

Women's Dancing

The women, who always follow the men, dancing in a circle, act with decency and becoming modesty, as if they were engaged in the most serious business. Neither laughing nor levity are to be noticed and they never speak a word to a man, for this would injure their character. They neither jump nor skip, but move one foot after the other slightly forwards then backwards, yet so as to advance gradually.

Source: Zeisberger's *History...*, p. 118

Abraham Thomas
1774

The following "reminiscence" is the only first person account of the McDonald Expedition during Dunmore's War that I have been able to find. There are some contemporary newspaper accounts and "extracts" from letters of participants but these lack the spontaneity of the authentic eyewitness account, expressed in the participant's own words. For that reason, only the account of Abraham Thomas is set forth in this book.

The war itself was between the Shawnee Indians, assisted by some Mingos and a few others, and the Virginians. Dunmore was the Governor of Virginia at that time.

At the Treaty of Ft. Stanwix, in 1768, the Iroquois, who claimed ownership of the lands on both sides of the Ohio River, ceded the land south of the Ohio to the whites. The Shawnee Indians, however, did not participate in that Treaty, and did not want to recognize it insofar as it affected their hunting rights in Kentucky. When surveyors began coming into the region, followed by settlers, trouble developed. Another incident that helped to bring on the war occurred in April of 1774, when several relatives of Logan, a noted Mingo warrior, were treacherously murdered by whites, causing the remaining Mingos along the Ohio River near Steubenville to flee to the Shawnee towns and to also enter into hostilities against the English (epitomized by the Virginians).

The Shawnees were located, primarily, in two collections of towns in Ohio. The larger was called the Lower Shawnee Town, and was located on the Pickaway Plains, between Circleville and Chillicothe. The Upper Shawnee Town, known as Wakatomika (spelled in as many different ways as there were spellers), was located near Dresden, and consisted of about five small towns. Names sometimes given to these towns are Snakes's Town, the Vomit Town (visited by Zeisberger in 1772), and, possibly, the Little Shawnee Woman's Town.

Governor Dunmore planned to attack both towns.

He ordered Major Angus McDonald, a militia officer from Frederick County, to assume the command of a large force of militia that had gathered near Wheeling and to proceed with them to the Upper Shawnee Town at Wakatomika. Dunmore, himself, would lead the other attack against the Lower Shawnee Town.

The Tuscarawas Valley involvement was primarily with the movement against Wakatomika, and appropriate entries from the Schoenbrunn Diary as they relate to this attack are set forth after the eyewitness account. These diary entries also very plainly bring forth just how isolated the Shawnees were in fighting this war against the Virginians. They got no help at all from the other tribes.

As McDonald approached Wakatomika, there was a skirmish with the Indians, and another the next day at the town itself. A few men were killed and wounded on each side and all of the towns were destroyed. The expedition then returned to Wheeling.

157

Thomas' account is of interest in showing the disrespect in which McDonald was held by the frontiersmen he was commanding. They, of course, were accustomed to following their own leaders, who, in their opinion, were far more experienced in Indian fighting than McDonald was.

The other expedition, against the Lower Shawnee Town, consisted of a two-pronged advance. One wing of the approaching army, having come down the Kanawha River to the Ohio, fought a very severe battle against about 1,000 Indians who attacked them at Point Pleasant, West Virginia, while they were awaiting the arrival of the rest of the army. They defeated the Indians but suffered many casualties themselves. The other wing of the army was personally led by Governor Dunmore and had proceeded down the Ohio as far as the mouth of the Hocking by the time the battle at Point Pleasant was fought. As Dunmore was advancing his wing of the army up the Hocking towards the Pickaway Plains, he learned of the hard-fought victory at Point Pleasant and was soon thereafter contacted by the Shawnees to sue for peace. He nevertheless continued on with his army to within about eight miles of the chief Indian village. The Indians then submitted to his terms of peace at the Treaty of Camp Charlotte. The Shawnees had to recognize the claim of the whites to Kentucky.

It was at this treaty that the famous speech of Logan, known as "Logan's Lament" was given to Dunmore.

"Who is there to mourn for Logan? Not one!"

{Below Wheeling} The collected force consisted of four hundred men. I was often at their encampment; and against the positive injunctions of my parents, could not resist my inclination to join them. At this time I was eighteen years of age, owned my own rifle and accoutrements, and had been long familiar with the use of them. Escaping, I made the best possible provision I could from my own resources, and hastened to enter as a volunteer under old Mike, then Captain Cressap.

The plan of the expedition was for every man to cross the Ohio with seven days' provisions in his pack. The object was to attack the Indians in their villages at Wapatomica. Some were on the waters of the Muskingum. On the first or second day's march after crossing the Ohio we were overtaken by a Colonel M'Donald, a British officer, who highly incensed the troops by ordering a halt for three days, during which we were consuming our provisions. While lying here a violent storm through the night had wet our arms and M'Donald ordered the men to discharge them in a hollow log to deaden the report. My rifle would not go off, and I took the barrel out to unbreech it. In doing this I made some noise in beating it with my tomahawk, on which M'Donald came towards me swearing, with an uplifted cane, threatening to strike. I instantly arose on my feet with the rifle-barrel in my hand and stood in an attitude of defence. We looked each other in the eye for some time; at last he dropped his cane and walked off, while the whole troop set up a laugh, crying, 'The boy has scared the colonel.' Cressap heard what was going on and approached to defend me; but seeing how well I could defend myself, stood by, smiling at the fracas. The colonel having no reputation as an Indian fighter was, very naturally disliked as a leader by Cressap and the men.

From this encampment we proceeded toward the Indian villages with the intention of surprising them; but late in the afternoon before we reached them we encountered the Indians laying in ambush on the top of a second bottom. We had just crossed a branch, and were marching along its first bottom, with a view of finding some place to cross a swamp that lay between us and the upper bottom. The men were marching in three parallel, Indian-file columns, some distance apart. On espying a trace across the swamp, the heads of the columns, in passing it, were thrown together, and as soon as they had gained the bank, unexpectedly received the fire of the enemy. The troops immediately deployed to the right and left, under the bank, and commenced ascending it, when the skirmish became general and noisy for about thirty minutes. The Indians then gave way in every direction. In this fight we had four or five killed and many wounded; it was supposed the Indians suffered much more.

During the engagement, while I was ascending the point of a bank formed by a ravine from the second bottom, in company with two men, Martin and Fox, all aiming to gain the cover of some large oak trees on the top, they both fell; the first was killed—the last wounded in the breast, the ball having entered the bone, but was drawn out with the clothes. These men were walking in a line with each other, and an Indian chief, concealed behind the tree for which I was aiming, shot them both with one ball. I took no notice whence the ball came, and hastened to the tree; just as I had gained it, the chief fell dead from the other side and rolled at my feet. It seems a neighbor, who had seen him fire at Martin and Fox and dodge behind the tree, stood ready to give him a shot whenever he should again make his appearance. The Indian had got his ball half down and peeped out to look at me, when Wilson shot him in the head.

The Indians retreated towards Wapatomica, flanked by two companies in hot pursuit; we followed in the rear, and as the last Indian was stepping out of the water, Capt. Teabaugh, a great soldier and a good marksman, brought him to the ground. I was at the time standing near Teabaugh, and shall never forget the thrilling emotion produced by this incident.

During this battle one of the men, Jacob Newbold, saw the colonel lying snug behind a fallen tree, sufficiently remote from danger, had there been no defence. It was immediately noised among the men, who were in high glee at the joke; one would cry out, 'Who got behind the log?' when an hundred voices would reply, 'The colonel! the colonel!' At this M'Donald became outrageous; I heard him inquire for the man who had raised the report, and threatened to punish him. I went round and told Newbold what the colonel had said. "That's your sort" said he; raising on his feet and going towards the colonel, he declared he did see him slink behind the log during the battle; he gave his rifle to a man standing by, cut some hickories, and stood on the defence, at which the whole company roared with laughter, and the colonel took himself off to another part of the line.

Night was now at hand, and the division was ordered by the colonel to encamp in an oak woods, in sight of the Indian villages, Cressap's party laying by themselves. This evening Jack Hayes was spying down the creek, saw an Indian looking at us through the forks of a low tree: he levelled his rifle and shot him directly between the eyes, and brought him into camp.

Just after nightfall Col. M'Donald was hailed from over the creek by an Indian, who implored peace in behalf of his tribe. He was invited over by the colonel, who held a parley with him, but declined entering into terms until more Indians were present. It was then proposed, if two white men would go with the Indian, they would send over two more of their number to us: but none being willing to undertake the visit, two came over and stayed all night in the colonel's tent; but their only object was to watch the troops, and gain time to remove their families and effects from the town. Capt. Cressap was up the whole night among his men, going the rounds, and cautioning them to keep their arms in condition for a morning attack, which he confidently expected; about two hours before daybreak, he silently formed his men, examined each rifle, and led them across the creek into the villages, leaving M'Donald with the other troops, in the encampment. At this time the Indians who had passed the night in the camp escaped. The village was directly surrounded, and the savages fled from it into the adjoining thicket, in the utmost consternation. In this attack none were killed on either side but one Indian by Capt. Cressap.

By this time, the camp was nearly out of provisions, with a three days' march before them. A small quantity of old corn and one cow were the entire spoils of the villages. These were distributed among the men, the villages burned, and the troops immediately commenced their march for the Ohio river, where they expected to meet provisions sent down from Redstone. The men became exceedingly famished on this march, and I myself being young, was so weak that I could no longer carry anything on my person. An older brother and one or two others kept encouraging me. One of them had a good stock of tobacco; I saw him take it and with an earnestness bordering on delirium, I insisted on having some. As I had never used it before, they refused, thinking it would entirely disable me; but as I

was so importunate, they at last gave me a small piece; I directly felt myself relieved; they gave me more, and in a short time my strength and spirits returned. I took my arms and baggage, and was able to travel with the rest of them, and was actually the first to reach the Ohio. Here we met the boats, but nothing in them but corn in the ear. Every man was soon at work with his tomahawk, crushing it on the stones, and mixing it with water in gourds or leaves fashioned in the shape of cups, while some provident ones enjoyed the aristocratic luxury of tin cups; but all seemed alike to relish the repast. A party of us crossed the Ohio that day for the settlement, when we came up with a drove of hogs, in tolerable order. We shot one and eat him on the spot, without criticising with much nicety the mode or manner of preparation. Indeed, the meat of itself was so savory and delicious, we thought of little else. In a few days, I returned to my parents, and after a little domestic storming, and much juvenile vaunting of our exploits, settled down to clearing.

Source: Dodge, *Red Men of the Ohio Valley,* pp. 163–68

Schoenbrunn Diary – Wakatomika Entries

July 2. {1774} All manner of evil reports came in; among the rest, that the Virginians had already come as far as the region of Gekelemukpechünk Creek, and that they would attack Gnadenh. tonight. To this we paid little attention, for there are all manner of false reports about, through which the Indians, particularly, are made to fear. Yet Netawatwees sent us word, both here and in Gnadenh., to be on our guard, and to send out people to reconnoiter the roads and the country, daily, they would do the same in their vicinity and set guards on the roads to the Ohio, in case the white people would undertake anything against the Indians, so that we should be warned betimes.

July 3. From strange Indians who are coming here in great numbers we heard, again, that already eight parties of Shawanose and Minques, in all a hundred warriors, had gone forth with intent to kill and that the women and children from Woaketammeki had fled to the Lower Towns....

July 21. ...We learned, at the same time, that Capt. Crysop, with five hundred men, was on the march against Woaketammeki,...

Aug. 2. From Gekelemukp. we had news that white people had been seen in the woods along the Ohio. Various Indians took refuge here with their goods. White Eye's wife with her children came here as a refugee, as well....

Aug. 3. After the early service, in which the Daily Word, "For he spake, and it was done; he commanded and it stood fast", was considered, a messenger came from Gnadenh. stating that yesterday more than five hundred men of the Virginians had marched into Waoketammeki, where they had fought, for a time, with the Shawanose and Minques who were there, whereupon the latter had fled and the former had taken possession of the town and camped there during the night. In the afternoon another messenger came to announce that, this morning, they had advanced against the upper Shawano Town, where there had, likewise, been a combat, in which several Indians had been killed. He stated, further, that Mr. Gibson had gone down to them with several Indians from Gekelemukp. to tell them that they were not to advance further up to the Delaware Towns, but he did not meet them....

Aug. 4. ...We received further news of the Virginians in Woaketammeki, that they had been in conflict with the Shawanose three times, that after several of the latter had been killed and some wounded, these had all run away and the Virginians had held the place, of whom a few had been wounded but none killed, all this being confirmed later from Pittsburg. After they had burned all the Towns, of which there were four or five, cut down the corn in the fields and destroyed everything, they marched back, yesterday, taking one Minque Indian with them, as a prisoner. They sent a Delaware Indian, who had been with them as long as they were here and had gone in and out among them, to call a number of Indians, in order that they might speak with them. Some Delawares came, to whom they said that they would do them no harm, nor come near their towns, but asked that they tell them where there were any Shawanose or Minques, on whose account they had come out, because they wanted war. From Gekelemukpechünk they had sent out Indians to observe the white people, to send back news constantly as to how far they were marching. These scouts followed them continually on the return march in order to find out what road they would take, for the Indians were ever afraid they might come up into this region.

Aug. 6. Several of the chiefs of Gekelemukp. came here on their way to Pittsburg. They brought another message from the Shawanose, who beg the Delawares to put in a good word for them with the Virginians, that they might declare an armistice and open peace negotiations with them. They yielded themselves to their grandfather, the Chief in Gekelmp. whatever he would agree upon with the Virginians they would accept, so that they might secure peace. They have removed their Chief Gischensatsi and chosen another, whom they begged to act as quickly as possible that peace might be restored, before the Virginians should pursue their plans further against them. The Shawanose had sent the hatchet to the Twichtwees and the Delamattenoos and bespoken their help and assistance. Both, however, had answered, "You alone were the ones who wanted war, not we, all the nations united for peace, you alone stand with the hatchet in your hand and act against the decision of the Great Council; now be brave and show yourselves to be men, for you will have need of that, as you are but a few, and what you have sought and deserved, that you will receive as a reward; we shall be quiet and observe you, but we will not take part in your actions nor help you." This answer, as well as the fact that the Virginians had destroyed Woaketammeki, has brought fear among them, and now they are begging the Delawares to help them obtain peace, whom they had, up to the time they received this answer, continually threatened and endeavored to deceive with false reports, as though they had already won the Delamattenoos, the Twichtwees and the Cherokees to their side, by which means they had tried to frighten them and force them to join them.

Gnadenhutten Diary – Wakatomika Entries

August 1 (1774). ...From Pittsburg there arrived Mr. Gibson and Mr. Wilson with a letter from Mr. McKee. They were under orders to stay at Gekelemukpechünk for a while, in order to forestall trouble: in case that they heard about the Virginians being headed in this direction they were at once to go and tell them not to advance to Gekelemukpechünk so that the Indians there would not become panicky and flee from the place. After having informed our people about this their order, they, Gibson and Wilson, went to the Chief at Gekelemukpechünk....

On the 3(rd), however, received from Gekelemukpechünk the distressing news that the Virginians are not far from Woaktammike and are battling with the Indians. Toward evening there arrived another bit of news: that in the first engagement one Shawnee and two Mingo had been killed, and a few had been wounded.

The 4(th) Brother Johannes Martin went to Gekelemukpechünk in order to learn what news Mr. Gibson had brought, who, two days previously, had gone with a few Indians to Woaktammike but was back again. In the afternoon, he, Johannes Martin returned and told us that a great many Virginians had been down there and had been very friendly to the Delaware who had come to them from across the river. He further told us that the Virginians had fired a few shots among some Indians whom they saw moving in the high grass and who, upon being challenged, had not come forth. One of these had been killed, and three, wounded. The Virginians had not liked that a bit, but these Indians had themselves to blame, for they had neither answered the challenge, nor had they shown themselves and let it be known that they were not Shawnee or Mingo. Thereafter, the Virginians moved into Woaketammike, where they found no Shawnee, burned the huts and houses, and entirely devastated the corn fields. Then they retreated and went back on their way to Pittsburgh again. All this had been told to Mr. Gibson and his Indian companions by the Indians living in the region, who are on good terms with the English, and are treated by the Virginians in a friendly manner.

> ### The War Dance
>
> The War Dance is very wild and dreadful to behold. One dancer carries his hatchet, another a long knife, another a large club, a fourth a cudgel. These they brandish in the air, to signify how they intend to treat or have treated their enemies, affecting all the while an air of anger and fury.
>
> Source: Zeisberger's *History...*, p. 121

William Robinson
1774

When Thomas Jefferson first published his Notes on the State of Virginia in 1785, it contained the speech of Chief Logan relating to the murders of his relations at Yellow Creek, and attributed these murders to Captain Michael Cresap. Although Capt. Cresap had died in the early days of the Revolutionary War, his defenders immediately came forth and established that Cresap was not responsible for the murders at Yellow Creek, but rather, that they had been committed by men led by Daniel Greathouse. In subsequent editions of the Notes, these statements were contained in an Appendix, and it is from this Appendix that the following narrative is taken. Although the Indian town to which Robinson was taken by Logan is not named in this narrative, numerous entries in the Gnadenhutten Diary for the spring and summer of 1774 clearly indicate that Mingos were living at Wakatomika at that time, and that Capt. Logan was one of them. It would probably have been at one of the Wakatomika towns, therefore, that Robinson was tied to the stake and nearly burnt.

William Robinson, of Clarksburg, in the county of Harrison, and State of Virginia, subscriber to these presents, declares that he was, in the year 1774, a resident on the west fork of Monongahela river, in the county then called West Augusta, and being in his field on the 12th of July, with two other men, they were surprised by a party of eight Indians, who shot down one of the others and made himself and the remaining one prisoners; this subscriber's wife and four children having been previously conveyed by him for safety to a fort about twenty-four miles off; that the principal Indian of the party which took them was Captain Logan; that Logan spoke English well, and very soon manifested a friendly disposition to this subscriber, and told him to be of good heart, that he would not be killed, but must go with him to his town, where he would probably be adopted in some of their families; but above all things, that he must not attempt to run away; that in the course of the journey to the Indian town he generally endeavored to keep close to Logan, who had a great deal of conversation with him, always encouraging him to be

cheerful and without fear; for that he would not be killed, but should become one of them; and constantly impressing on him not to attempt to run away; that in these conversations he always charged Capt. Michael Cresap with the murder of his family; that on his arrival in the town, which was on the 18th of July, he was tied to a stake and a great debate arose whether he should not be burnt; Logan insisted on having him adopted, while others contended to burn him; that at length Logan prevailed, tied a belt of wampum round him as the mark of adoption, loosed him from the post and carried him to the cabin of an old squaw, where Logan pointed out a person who he said was this subscriber's cousin; and he afterwards understood that the old woman was his aunt, and two others his brothers, and that he now stood in the place of a warrior of the family who had been killed at Yellow Creek; that about three days after this Logan brought him a piece of paper, and told him he must write a letter for him, which he meant to carry and leave in some house where he should kill somebody; that he made ink with gun powder, and the subscriber proceeded to write the letter by his direction, addressing Captain Michael Cresap in it, and that the purport of it was, to ask "why he had killed his people? That some time before they had killed his people at some place, (the name of which the subscriber forgets,) which he had forgiven; but since that he had killed his people again at Yellow Creek, and taken his cousin, a little girl, prisoner; that therefore he must war against the whites; but that he would exchange the subscriber for his cousin." And signed it with Logan's name, which letter Logan took and set out again to war; and the contents of this letter, as recited by the subscriber, calling to mind that stated by Judge Innes to have been left, tied to a war club, in a house where a family was murdered, and that being read to the subscriber, he recognizes it, and declares he verily believes it to have been the identical letter which he wrote, and supposes he was mistaken in stating as he has done before from memory, that the offer of exchange was proposed in the letter; that it is probable that it was only promised him by Logan, but not put in the letter; while he was with the old woman, she repeatedly endeavored to make him sensible that she had been of the party at Yellow Creek, and, by signs, showed him how they decoyed her friends over the river to drink and when they were reeling and tumbling about, tomahawked them all, and that whenever she entered on this subject she was thrown into the most violent agitations, and that he afterwards understood that, amongst the Indians killed at Yellow Creek, was a sister of Logan, very big with child, whom they ripped open, and stuck on a pole; that he continued with the Indians till the month of November, when he was released in consequence of the peace made by them with Lord Dunmore; that, while he remained with them, the Indians in general were very kind to him; and especially those who were his adopted relations; but above all, the old woman and family in which he lived, who served him with everything in their power, and never asked, or even suffered him to do any labor, seeming in truth to consider and respect him as the friend they had lost. All which several matters and things, so far as they are stated to be of his own knowledge, this subscriber solemnly declares to be true, and so far as they are stated on information from others, he believes them to be true. Given and declared under his hand at Philadelphia, this 28th day of February, 1800.

WILLIAM ROBINSON

Source: Jefferson, *Notes...*, pp. 218–20

Note

The text of the letter written with gunpowder is set forth in the following:

Extract of a letter from the Honorable Judge Innes, of Frankfort in Kentucky, to Thomas Jefferson, dated Kentucky, near Frankfort, March 2d, 1799

I recollect to have seen Logan's speech in 1775, in one of the public prints. That Logan conceived Cresap to be the author of the murder at Yellow Creek, it is in my power to give, perhaps, a more particular information, than any other person you can apply to.

In 1774 I lived in Fincastle county, now divided into Washington, Montgomery and part of Wythe. Being intimate in Col. Preston's family, I happened in July to be at his house, when an express was sent to him as County Lieut. requesting a guard of the militia to be ordered out for the protection of the inhabitants residing low down on the north fork of Holston river. The express brought with him a War Club, and a note which was left tied to it at the house of one Robertson, whose family were cut off by the Indians, and gave rise for the application to Col. Preston, of which the following is a copy, then taken by me in my memorandum book.

"Captain Cresap,—What did you kill my people on Yellow Creek for? The white people killed my kin at Conestoga, a great while ago; and I thought nothing of that. But you killed my kin again, on Yellow Creek, and took my Cousin Prisoner. Then I thought I must kill too; and I have been three times to war since; but the Indians are not angry; only myself.

"July 21st, 1774   Captain JOHN LOGAN."

With great respect, I am, Dear Sir, your most obedient servant,

HARRY INNES

Source: Jefferson, *Notes...*, pp. 211–12

Indian Marriages

Marriages among the Indians are not, as with us, contracted for life; it is understood on both sides that the parties are not to live together any longer than they shall be pleased with each other. The husband may put away his wife whenever he pleases, and the woman may in like manner abandon her husband. Therefore the connexion is not attended with any vows, promises, or ceremonies of any kind. An Indian takes a wife as it were on trial, determined, however, in his own mind not to forsake her if she behaves well, and particularly if he has children by her. The woman, sensible of this, does on her part every thing in her power to please her husband, particularly if he is a good hunter or trapper, capable of maintaining her by his skill and industry, and protecting her by his strength and courage.

Source: Heckewelder's *History...*, p. 154

James Wood
1775

In the summer of 1775, the Virginia House of Burgesses, at their final session before being suspended by Governor Dunmore (who remained loyal to the Crown), took into consideration the necessity of quieting the Indians on the frontier. Commissioners were appointed to treat with the Indians to ratify a peace and James Wood was appointed to give notice of a conference to be held in September at Pittsburgh. (At the beginning of the Revolution it was uncertain whether Pittsburgh was in Pennsylvania or Virginia, for the boundary between the colonies was not settled until 1780. Both colonies claimed it as within their jurisdiction—hence, the calling of a meeting of Virginia Commissioners at a town in what is now Pennsylvania.)

Setting out from Pittsburgh, Wood went first to Gnadenhutten and then on to Coshocton. From Coshocton he proceeded up the Walhonding to the Wyandot towns on the Sandusky. After meeting with the Wyandots, he then went to Pluggy's town (near Delaware) and to the Shawnee towns on the Scioto plains between Circleville and Chillicothe. He returned to the Tuscarawas Valley, apparently crossing the Muskingum south of Coshocton (for he does not mention passing through it on his return trip) and striking the Tuscarawas at White Eyes town. From there he went to Newcomerstown and Gnadenhutten. His description of the church at Gnadenhutten is the best that we have in these journals. The Indian who played the spinet would have been Joshua, whose daughters, Anna and Bathsaba, died in the Gnadenhutten massacre in 1782 and who, himself, was burned to death by the followers of the Shawnee Prophet (Tecumseh's brother) on the White River in 1806.

In later life, Wood became a general in the Continental Army and was Governor of Virginia. He died in 1813.

{July 18th 1775} At 5 o'Clock this afternoon I sett off from Fort Pitt with Simon Girty an Interpreter encamped ten Miles below on the River Bank.

19th July   Sett off before Sunrise Crossed Big Beaver Creek near the Mouth travelled about 45 Miles this day the Course nearly West.

20th   Started very Early   met Garret Pendergrass about 9 °Clock who informed us that he left the Delaware Towns two days before that the Delawares were just returned from the Wiandots Towns where they had been at a Great Council with the French and English Officer and the Wyandots   that Monsuer Baubee and the English Officer told them to be upon their Guard   that the White People intended to strike them very soon   that tho' their fathers the French were thrown down the last War by the English they were now got up again and much Stronger than ever and would Assist their Children (the Indians) as they formerly did   about two days

166

after met two Delaware Squas who upon interrogations gave the same Account travelled about forty Miles this day and encamped on a Small run.

21st July Started very Early in the Morning at one O'Clock arrived at the Moravian Indian Town {Gnadenhutten} Examined the Minister (a Dutchman) concerning the Council lately held with the Indians by the French who confirmed the Accounts before related six Miles from the Moravian Town Passed a Small Delaware Town a Delaware Man rode with us to New Comers Town where we Encamped having travelled about 30 miles.

22d July Set off Early in the Morning for Koshocktin the Cheif Town of the Delawares Passed White Eyes' Town about 10 o'Clock Arrived at Koshocktin at 1 O'Clock taken to the Council House found Many of the Indians drunk and King New Comer a Sleep waked the King at Dark and Delivered the following speech to him in the Presence of Winganum Young Killbuck and a Number of other Warriours

Brothers the Delawares

Your Elder Brothers in Virginia in their Great Council have Appointed me to come to this Place in Order to Assure you that their hearts are good towards you that they are desirous of brightning the Antient Chain of Freindship between you and them and for which they have Appointed Commissioners to meet you and the other Nations in a General Council at Fort Pitt in [blank in MS.] days from this time when they will be glad to meet the Cheifs of your Nation and will use their best Endeavours to give you a hearty Welcome.

Brothers

I have heard with great Concern that you have lately been in Council with the French and Wyandots and that you have received a Speech from the French and a belt and String of Black Wampum as there has long subsisted the Greatest Freindship between you and us I desire and insist that you will make me Acquainted with any thing which may have been said to you by the French or any others to the Prejudice of your Elder Brothers of Virginia

A String of White Wampum.

23d of July The King and Cheifs of the Delawares met in the Council House and delivered the following Answer to my Speech of Yesterday.

Brothers the Bigknife

Your Brothers the Delawares are very thankful to you for your good talk to them Yesterday and are glad to find their Brothers hearts are good towards them and that they will be joyfull in meeting them at the time and place you Mention.

Brother

in Order to Convince our Elder Brothers of Virginia that we desire to live in freindship with them I now deliver you this Belt and String they were sent to us by an English Man and French Man at Fort Detroit with a Message that the People of Virginia were determined to strike us that they would come upon us two different Ways the one by the Way of the Lakes and the other by the Ohio and that the Virginians were determined to drive us off and to take our Lands that we must be constantly on our Gaurd and not to give any Credit to whatever you said as you were a people not to be depended upon that the Virginians would invite Us to a treaty but we must not go at any rate and to take particular Notice of the Advice they gave which proceeded from Motives of real Freindship and nothing else.

Delivers the Belt and String.

I then hired a Man to go with me to the Seneca Towns set off in a hard rain passed thro' a Town of the Muncys and made them Acquainted with my business kept up White Womans Creek Crossing it Six times and Corcosan Creek once lodged at Mohickins old Town now Inhabited by Delawares travelled about 38 miles this day the Course nearly West.

24th July Set off very early in the Morning travelled very Constant till twelve O'Clock when we Arrived at Indian Nicholas's and then Proceeded on till Night and encamped near a Small run rain all Night Travelled about 45 Miles the same Course as Yesterday.

25th Set out very early in the Morning rode Constant till 5 o'clock in the afternoon when we Arrived at the Seneca Town where we found Logan the Snake the Big Appletree with Several of the Mingoes who were lately Prisoners at Fort Pitt they all appeared to be Pretty Much in Liquor and very inquisitive to know my Business called them together and made the same speech to them which I had before made to the

168   The Emissaries

Delawares they made no other Answer but they would Acquaint the rest of their Nation with what I had said and discovered that the Indians were very Angry Many of them Painted themselves black we Encamped near the Town about ten O'Clock at Night one of the Indians came and Stamped upon my head as I lay a Sleep waked and saw several Indians with Knives and Tomahawks a Squaw informed us privately that they intended to kill us advised us to hide ourselves in the Woods which we did till Morning when we returned again into the Town Logan repeated in Plain English the Manner in which the People of Virginia had killed his Mother Sister and all his Relations during which he wept and Sung Alternately and concluded with telling me the Revenge he had taken he then told me that several of the Mingoes who were long Prisoners at Fort Pitt wanted to kill us and asked me whether I was affraid to which I answered I was not   that we were two lone Men where [who were] sent to deliver a message to them which we had done that we were in their Power and had no way to defend ourselves that they must kill us if they thought proper to which he replied that we should not be hurt.

26th July. At 9 O'Clock in the Morning hired two fresh horses and set off for the Wyandot Towns travelled very fast and Constant till 7 O'Clock in the Evening when we Arrived at the Town   sent off Runners for the Cheifs who were distant about twenty Miles.

{Wood proceeded on to Pluggy's Town and the Lower Shawanee Towns below Circleville. He then began his return trip to Fort Pitt.}

2d August ...I then set off from the Shawanese Towns on my return Called at the Kiocopo Town and then proceeded twenty Miles and Encamped.

3d August sett off before sun rise rode hard and Constant till Seven O Clock in the Evening met a Shawanese Man who Informed me that one of their Nation was lately Killed on Kentucke River and that the white People said it was done by the Southern Indians Travelled about Forty Miles and Encamped rains hard all Night.

4th August rains hard set off early Travelled about thirty Eight Miles stopped at a Delaware Womans Cabbin where I staid all night nothing to eat the two days past but Blackberry's.

5th August set off in a hard rain very Early Travelled four Hours when I arrived at Captain White Eye's Purchased some Meat from an Indian set off for New Comers Town at which I staid two Hours proceeded to the Lower Moravian Town {Gnadenhutten} where we Arrived at Dark taken to the Cabbin of an Indian and Hospitably Entertained.

6th August (Sunday) went to Church with the Indians at which were present about One hundred and fifty of them, who all Behaved with the Greatest Decency and Decorum the Minister who resides at this Town is a German of the Moravian Sect has Lived with them several Years has Acquired their Language and taught most of them the English and German he prayed in the Delaware Language Preached in the English and sung Psalms in the German in which the Indians Joined and Performed that part of Divine Service in a Manner really Inimitable the Church is a Decent Square Log Building with Plank floars and Benches Ornamented with Several Pieces of German Scripture Paintings has a Small Cupola with a Bell and a very Indifferent Spinnet on which an Indian played the remaining part of the day employed in Hunting for our Horses Un-successfully.

8th August at two O'Clock in the afternoon found our Horses and Immediately set off Travelled about Twenty Miles and Encamped.

9th August set off early in the Morning travelled about forty five Miles and encamped at dark.

10th August my Horse failed came to an Indian Hunting Camp where I hired an Horse of an Indian Woman and left mine in her Care to be brought to Fort Pitt in Ten Days Travelled about forty five Miles when I arrived at Mr. John Gibsons where I staid all Night.

11th August. sett off after Breakfast and Arrived Fort Pitt about 3 o'Clock in the afternoon.

Source: Thwaites, *The Revolution on the Upper Ohio,* pp. 43–65.

Gnadenhutten Diary – Wood Entries

July 21 {1775}. A Virginian Captain by the name of Wood and one Simon Girty arrived in our house with pleasure, and soon went from here to the Delamatteno {Wyandots} in order to invite them in addition to the Delaware and the Shawnee, to the Treaty in Pittsburgh for the 10th of Sept.

August 5. It rained unusually hard the whole day. In the evening, the Virginian Captain Wood and his companion returned from the Delamatteno and Shawnee, and were very wet. Marcus took them immediately into his house where they could dry their clothes, and we gave them food and drink since they were very hungry and had received almost nothing from the Indians to eat other than blueberries.

The 6th. My Sermon about the Daily Word, Isaiah 30, 18: "And therefore will the Lord wait, that he may be gracious unto you, and may have mercy upon you", I delivered in English, in His perceptible nearness, and Johannes Martin acted as Interpreter; Captain Wood, his companion, and various Indian strangers were particularly attentive. Brother Jungmann held the Children's Service; afterwards he took over the Boys; and my wife, the Adolescent Girls, with whom they talked about their state of heart. In the evening, we had an enjoyable Singing Service.

The 7th. After the Early Service, the Captain and Simon Girty departed gratefully from here for Pittsburgh....

Indian Recruiting

Previous to going out on a warlike campaign, the war-dance is always performed round the painted post. It is the Indian mode of recruiting. Whoever joins in the dance is considered as having enlisted for the campaign, and is obliged to go out with the party.

Source: Heckewelder's *History...*, p. 209

Nicholas Cresswell
1775

The outbreak of the Revolution found a young Englishman, Nicholas Cresswell, 24 years of age, at Alexandria, Virginia, alone and nearly penniless in a now hostile land. In order to earn some money, he engaged to go into the Illinois country on behalf of some land speculators of Virginia, and while he did not get that far, he did get into the Ohio region.

He arrived at Pittsburgh at a time when preparations were being made for the conference referred to in the prior journal, as well as another conference, also to be in September but this one at the behest of the Continental Congress. Hundreds were expected to attend and, as his journal later mentions, cattle to provide food for these Indians were being brought to Pittsburgh from places as far away as the Moravian mission towns in Ohio. A few days before he got to Pittsburgh, he met James Wood, our prior diarist, who had just returned from his trip to the Ohio country notifying the Indians about the Treaty, and his comments about this meeting with Wood are included herein.

His journal is one of the most detailed and colorful (not to mention frank) of all of the journals in this book. Traveling with a trader and accompanied by a young Indian girl, he visited Newcomerstown, White Eyes town, the new town of Coshocton, some smaller Indian towns, and the Moravian towns of Gnadenhutten and Welhik Thuppeek (Schoenbrunn). He also passed by Bouquet's fort and the vestiges of the old town of Tuscarawas. He saw it all and, fortunately for us, told it all. His journal is probably the most memorable in this book.

A few months after his return to the east, he was able to cross between the lines and make his way to New York (then in British hands) and finally back to England.

Saturday, August 12th, 1775 {Southeast of Pittsburgh}. ...This evening Captn. James Wood arrived here from the Indian town. He had been sent to invite the Indians to a Treaty at Fort Pitt to be held on the tenth of September. The Convention of Virginia had employed him. He says that an English Officer and a French man from Detroit had been at all the Indian towns to persuade the Indians not to go to any Treaty held by the Colonists. But tells us his superior eloquence prevailed and all the different nations he has been at will certainly attend the Treaty.

Friday, August 18, 1775 {Pittsburgh}. Never till now did I put any confidence in Dreams. Last night I went to sleep with a mind as much confused as a skein of silk pulled the wrong way. The behaviour of my landlord had been a principal cause. But find I have a good

Nicholas Cresswell

Born: December, 1750 Crowden-le-Booth, Edale, England
Died: July 14, 1804 Idridgehay, England
Age on entering Tuscarawas Valley – 24 years

The jingling of these Bells and Thimbles, the rattling of the Deer's hoofs and gourds, beating of the drum and kettle, with the horrid yells of the Indians, render it the most unharmonious concert, that human idea can possibly conceive.

Nicholas Cresswell   September 1st, 1775

friend in my Landlady, who wears the breeches. Dreamed that there was a friend that would relieve me near at hand. I woke with a gleam of hope and waited on Mr. John Anderson, the only person in town that I had omitted. He generously proffered me any cash I might want, to find me a Horse, and go with me into the Indian Country, serving as an interpreter and guide.

Friday, August 18th, 1775. This Gentleman is an Indian Trader and has business at their Towns. Tells me he had observed my situation for some days and intended to offer me his assistance this day had I not spoke to him. Got some money from him to pay my Landlord. When he found that I had got a Friend his tone altered and it did not signify anything if I did not pay him till the Treaty. I made use of his own words to him, told him as he paid ready money for his provisions consequently he must expect the same from me. His wife abused him a good deal about his meanness, called him a pitiful rascal in abundance.

Saturday, August 19th, 1775. Waiting for Mr. Anderson. Employed an Indian Woman to make me a pair of Mockeysons and Leggings. This evening two of the Pennsylvania Delegates to Treat with the Indians arrived here, escorted by a party of paltry Lighthorses. Colnl. Arthur St. Clair and Colnl. James Wilson. Supped and spent the evening with them. My Landlady remarkably kind to me, owing to my political sentiments agreeing with hers. She is by nature a most horrid Vixen.

Sunday, August 20th, 1775. Waiting for Mr. Anderson. He is detained by the Indians coming to trade.

Monday, August 21st, 1775. Mr. Anderson informs me that the Indians are not well pleased at anyone going into their Country dressed in a Hunting shirt. Got a Calico shirt made in the Indian fashion, trimmed up with Silver Brooches and Armplates so that I scarcely know myself. Crossed the Allegany River and went about two miles and camped at a small run to be ready to start early in the morning. We had forgotten a tin kettle in Town. I went back for it while Mr. Anderson made a fire, returning in the dark lost my way and got to an Indian Camp, where I found two Squaws, but they could not speak English. By signs made them understand what I wanted and they put me right.

Indian Country — Tuesday, August 22nd, 1775. A very heavy fog this morning. We had got two bottles of Rum, two loaves of Bread, and a Bacon Ham along with us. Agreed to take a Dram to prevent us catching the Fever and Ague, but drank rather too much and most stupidly forgot our provisions. Got to Logg's Town about noon, crossed the River and went to Mr. John Gibson's. Lodged there, but would not make our wants known for fear of being laughed at. We crossed the River in a Canoe made of Hickory Bark, stretched open with sticks.

Wednesday, August 23rd, 1775. Proceeded on our journey, but not one morsel of provision. Crossed Great Beaver Creek at Captn. White-Eye's house. This is an Indian Warrior of the Dellawars Nation. Camped at Little Beaver Creek with three Indian Squaws and a man. Nothing to eat but berries such as we found in the woods. Find Mr. Anderson a good hearty companion. One of the Indian Squaws invited me to sleep with her, but I pretended to be sick. She was very kind and brought me some plums she got in the woods.

Thursday, August 24th, 1775. Parted with the Indians. Met Captn. Killbuch, an Indian Warrior. {This would be Killbuck, Sr., for on the same day and in the same vicinity the next journalist, Richard Butler, also met him and referred to him as "Old Killbuck". It therefore appears that Killbuck, Sr. was still being called "Capt. Killbuck" as of 1775.} Camped at White Oak run. Got plenty of Red plums and wild Cherries which is our only food.

Friday, August 25th, 1775. Very heavy rain all day. Lost our horses, but an Indian brought them to us in the evening for which we gave him a pair of leggings. Breakfasted, dined and supped on Plums and Wild Cherries. Here are wild Plums in great abundance, about the size of our common white plums in England, some Red, others White and very well flavoured. The Cherries are small and black, very sweet, and grow in Bunches like Currants.

Saturday, August 26th, 1775. Set out early this morning, travelled very hard till noon, when we passed through the largest Plum Tree Thicket I ever saw. I believe it was a mile long, nothing but the Plum and Cherry Trees. Killed a Rattlesnake. Just as the Sun went down we stopped to get our Supper on some Dewberries (a small berry something like a Gooseberry). Mr. Anderson had gone before me and said he would ride on about two miles to a small run where he intended to camp, as soon as I had got sufficient. I mounted my Horse and followed him till I came to a place where the road forked. I took the path that I supposed he had gone and rode till it began to be dark, when I imagined myself to be wrong, and there was not a possibility of me finding my way back in the night. Determined to stay where I was till morning, I had no sooner alighted from my horse, but I discovered the glimmering of a fire about four hundred yards from me. This rejoiced me exceedingly, supposing it was Mr. Anderson. When I got there, to my great disappointment and surprise found three Indian women and a little boy. I believe they were as much surprised as I was. None of them could speak English and I could not speak Indian. I alighted and marked the path I had come and that I had left, on the ground with the end of my stick, made a small channel in the earth which I poured full of water, laid some fire by the side of it, and then laid myself down by the side of the fire, repeating the name of Anderson which I soon understood they knew.

The youngest Girl immediately unsaddled my Horse, unstrapped the Belt, Hoppled him, and turned him out, then spread my Blankets at the fire and made signs for me to sit down. The Oldest made me a little hash of dried Venison and Bear's Oil, which eat very well, but neither Bread or Salt. After supper they made signs I must go to sleep. Then they held a consultation for some time which made me very uneasy, the two eldest women and the boy laid down on the opposite side of the fire and some distance away. The youngest (she had taken so much pains with my horse) came and placed herself very near me. I began to think she had some amorous design upon me. In about half an hour she began to creep nearer me and pulled my Blanket. I found what she wanted and lifted it up. She was young, handsome, and healthy. Fine regular features and fine eyes, had she not painted them with Red before she came to bed.

Sunday, August 27th, 1775. This morning my Bedfellow went into the woods and caught her horse and mine, saddled them, put my Blanket on the saddle, and prepared everything ready, seemingly with a great deal of good

nature. Absolutely refused my assistance. The old Woman got me some dried venison for Breakfast. When I took my leave returned the thanks as well as I could by signs. My Bedfellow was my guide and conducted me through the woods, where there were no signs of a road or without my knowing with certainty wither I was going. She often mentioned John Anderson and talked a great deal in Indian. I attempted to speak Indian, which diverted her exceedingly. In about an hour she brought me to Mr. Anderson's camp, who had been very uneasy at my absence and employed an Indian to seek me. I gave my Dulcinea a match coat, with which she seemed very well pleased. Proceeded on our journey and about noon got to an Indian Town called Walehack-tap-poke, or the Town with a good Spring, {Schoenbrunn} on the Banks of the Muskingham and inhabited by Dellawar Indians. Christianized under the Moravian Sect, it is a pretty town consisting of about sixty houses, and is built of logs and covered with Clapboards. It is regularly laid out in three spacious streets which meet in the centre, where there is a large meeting house built of logs sixty foot square covered with Shingles, Glass in the windows and a Bell, a good plank floor with two rows of forms. Adorned with some few pieces of Scripture painting, but very indifferently executed. All about the meeting house is kept very clean.

In the evening went to the meeting. But never was I more astonished in my life. I expected to have seen nothing but anarchy and confusion, as I have been taught to look upon these beings with contempt. Instead of that, here is the greatest regularity, order, and decorum, I ever saw in any place of Worship, in my life. With that solemnity of behaviour and modest, religious deportment would do honour to the first religious society on earth, and put a bigot or enthusiast out of countenance. The parson was a Dutchman, but preached in English. He had an Indian interpreter, who explained it to the Indians by sentences. They sung in the Indian language. The men sit on one row of forms and the women on the other with the children in the front. Each sex comes in and goes out of their own side of the house. The old men sit on each side the parson. Treated with Tea, Coffee, and Boiled Bacon at supper. The Sugar they make themselves out of the sap of a certain tree.

Lodged at Whiteman's house, married to an Indian woman.

Monday, August 28th, 1775. Left Wale-hack-tap-poke. Crossed the Muskingham and went to Kanantohead {Gnadenhutten}, another pretty Moravian Town, but not so large as Wale-hack-tap-poke. About eight miles asunder. Crossed Muskingham again and a large plain about 3 miles over without tree or shrub and very level. Saw several Indian Cabins built of bark. Got to Newcomer Town about noon. This has been a large town, but now is almost deserted. It is on the Muskingham, built without any order or regularity. I suppose there is not twenty houses inhabited now. Crossed the Muskingham again, and another large plain. Met several Indians coming from a Feast dressed and painted in the grandest manner. Lodged at White-Eye's Town only three houses in it. Kindly treated at a Dutch Blacksmith's, who lives with an Indian Squaw. Got a very hearty supper of a sort of Dumplings made of Indian Meal and dried Huckleberries which serves instead of currants. Dirty people, find it impossible to keep myself free from lice. Very disagreeable companions.

Tuesday, August 29th, 1775. Left White-Eye's town. Saw the bones of one Mr. Cammel, a White man, that had been killed by the Indians. Got to Co-a-shoking {Coshocton} about noon. It is at the forks of the Muskingham. The Indians have removed from Newcomer Town to this place. King Newcomer lives here. Sold part of my goods here to good advantage. Crossed a branch of Muskingham and went to Old Hundy, this is a scattering Indian settlement. Lodged at a Mohawk Indian's house, who offered me his Sister and Mr. Anderson his Daughter to sleep with us, which we were obliged to accept.

Wednesday, August 30th, 1775. My bedfellow very fond of me this morning and wants to go with me. Find I must often meet with such encounters as these if I do not take a Squaw to myself. She is young and sprightly, tolerably handsome, and can speak a little English. Agreed to take her. She saddled her horse and went with us to New Hundy about 3 miles off, where she had several relations who made me very welcome to such as they had. From there to Coashoskis, where we lodged in my squaw's Brother's, made me a compliment of a

young wolf but I could not take it with me.

Thursday, August 31st, 1775. At Coashoskis {Coshocton}. Mr. Anderson could not find his horse. Sold all my goods for Furs. In the afternoon rambled about the Town, smoking Tobacco with the Indians and did everything in my power to make myself agreeable to them. Went to see the King. {Newcomer} He lives in a poor house, and he is as poor in dress as any of them, no emblem of Royalty or Majesty about him. He is an old man, treated me very kindly, called me his good friend, and hoped I would be kind to my Squaw. Gave me a small string of Wampum as a token of friendship. My Squaw uneasy to see me write so much.

Friday, September 1st, 1775. At Coashoskin Mr. Anderson found his horse. Saw an Indian Dance in which I bore a part. Painted by my Squaw in the most elegant manner. Divested of all my clothes, except my Calico short breech-clout, leggings, and Mockesons. A fire was made which we danced round with little order, whooping and hallooing in a most frightful manner. I was but a novice at the diversion and by endeavouring to act as they did made them a great deal of sport and ingratiated me much in their esteem. This is the most violent exercise to the adepts in the art I ever saw. No regular figure, but violent distortion of features, writhing and twisting the body in the most uncouth and antic postures imaginable. Their music is an old Keg with one head knocked out and covered with a skin and beat with sticks which regulates their times. The men have strings of Deer's hoofs tied round their ankles and knees, and gourds with shot or pebblestones in them in their hands which they continually rattle. The women have Morris bells or Thimbles with holes in the bottom and strung upon a leather thong tied round their ankles, knees and waists. The jingling of these Bells and Thimbles, the rattling of the Deer's hoofs and gourds, beating of the drum and kettle, with the horrid yells of the Indians, render it the most unharmonious concert, that human idea can possibly conceive. It is a favourite diversion, in which I am informed they spend a great part of their time in Winter. Saw an Indian Conjuror dressed in a Coat of Bearskin with a Visor mask made of wood, frightful enough to scare the Devil. The Indians believe in conjuration and Witchcraft. Left the Town, went about two miles. Camped by the side of a run. A young Indian boy, son of one Baubee a Frenchman, came after us and insists on going with us to Fort Pitt. Find myself very unwell this evening, pains in my head and back. Nancy seems very uneasy about my welfare. Afraid of the Ague.

Saturday, September 2nd, 1775. Got to White-Eyes's Town to breakfast. Saw the Indian Warmarks made by Captn. Wingimund, a Dellawar Warrior which Mr. Anderson and

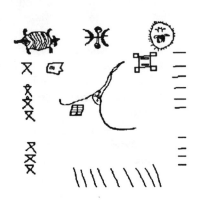

Capt. White-Eyes explained to me. These hieroglyphic marks are the history of his whole warfare. The rude resemblance of a Turtle on the left hand is the emblem by which his Tribe or Nation is known. The Cross and the two Halfmoons are the Characters by which he is personally distinguished among his nation. That figure on the right hand is the Sun. Those strokes under it signify the number of men he had with him when he made this mark, their leaning to the left signifies that they have their backs towards the Sun and are bound to the Northward. Those marks on the Left hand under the Turtle signify the number of scalps and prisoners he has taken and of what sex. Those marked thus X are scalps, those X̂ men prisoners and those marked thus X̊ women prisoners. The rough sketches of Forts in the middle are what he has helped to attack, but what their names were I cannot learn. Called at several Indian Villages. Crossed the River and got to Newcomers Town. Very sick. Nancy is gone to fetch an old Indian woman to cure me as she says, therefore I must lay by my pen.

Sunday, September 3rd, 1775. Last night, Nancy brought an Indian Squaw which called me her Nilum. i.e. Nephew, as Mr. Anderson told me, and behaved very kindly to me, She put her hand on my head for some time, then took a small brown root out of her pocket and with her knife chopped part of it small, then mixed it with water which she gave me to drink, or rather swallow, being about a spoonful, but this I evaded by keeping it in my mouth till I found an opportunity to spit it out. She then took some in her mouth and chewed it and spit on the top of my head, rubbing my head well at the same time. Then she unbuttoned my shirt collar and spat another mouthful down my back. This was uncomfortable but I bore it with patience. She lent me her Matchcoat and told me to go to sleep. Nancy was ordered not to give me any water till morning, however, I prevailed on the good-natured creature to let me take a vomit that Mr. Anderson had with him as soon as the old woman was gone, which has cured me, tho' the old woman believes that her nostrum did it. Obliged to stay here this day, somebody has stolen one of Mr. A's horses.

Monday, September 4th, 1775. Saw an Indian scalp. Heard an Indian play upon a Tin Violin and make tolerable good music. Went to Kanaughtonhead {Gnadenhutten}, walked all the way, my horse loaded with skins. Camped close by the Town. Nancy's kindness to be remembered.

Tuesday, September 5th, 1775. At Kanaughtonhead. Went to the meeting where Divine service was performed in Dutch and English with great solemnity. This Chapel is much neater than that at Wale-hack-tap-poke. Adorned with basket work in various colours all round, with a spinet made by Mr. Smith the parson, and played by an Indian. Drank Tea with Captn. White-Eyes and Captn. Wingenund at an Indian house in Town. This Tea is made of the tops of Ginsing, and I think it very much like Bohea Tea. The leaves are put into a tin canister made water tight and boiled till it is dry, by this means the juices do not evaporate. N. did not choose to go into the town, but employed herself in making me a pair of Mockesons.

Wednesday, September 6th, 1775. Left Kanaughtonhead. Mr. Anderson brought several cows there which he intends to take to Fort Pitt. Camped within two miles of Walehacktappoke.

Thursday, September 7th, 1775. Got to Walehacktappoke to breakfast. N. refused to go into the Town, knowing that the Moravians will not allow anyone to cohabit with Indians in their town. Saw an Indian child baptized, eight Godfathers and four Godmothers, could not understand the ceremony as it was performed in Indian.

Friday, September 8th, 1775. At Walehacktappoke. Find my body invaded with an army of small animals which will be a little troublesome to dislodge. Saw an Indian sweathouse. It is built of logs about eight feet by five and about two foot high, with a small door and covered all over with earth to keep in the steam. The patient creeps into the house wrapped in his Blanket, when his friends put in large stones red hot and a pail of water, then make up the door as close as possible, the patient throws the water upon the hot stones till the house is filled with hot steam and vapour. He continues in this little hell as long as he is able to bear it, when the door is opened and the patient instantly plunged into the River. This method of treating the Smallpox has been destructive to many of them. Bought a blanket made of a Buffalo skin.

Saturday, September 9th, 1775. Left the town. Mr. Anderson, N. and I went to the Tuscarora town. Then got lost in the Woods and rambled till dark, when we camped by the side of a little run. Very merry this afternoon with our misfortune.

Sunday, September 10th, 1775. Rambled till noon when we found ourselves at Bouquet's old Fort now demolished. Went to an Indian Camp, where Mr. Anderson met with an old wife of his, who would go with him, which he agreed to. We have each of us a Girl. It is an odd way of travelling, but we are obliged to submit to it. Met with Mr. Anderson's people in the evening, camped by the side of Tuscarora Creek. Saw the vestige, the Tuscarora old town, but now deserted.

Monday, September 11th, 1775. Mr. Anderson and I with our Ladies proceeded, and left the people to bring the skins and cattle which he had purchased. Travelled over a great deal of bad land. About sundown Mr. A. called out, "A Panther." I looked about and saw it set in a tree about twenty yards from me. Fired at it on horseback and shot it through the neck. It is of a Brown colour and shaped like a cat, but much larger. It measured five foot nine inches from Nose end to Tail end. Camped and skinned the Panther. This exploit has raised me in N. esteem exceedingly, tho' I claim no merit from it, being merely accidental.

Tuesday, Sept. 12th, 1775. Our Squaws are very necessary, fetching our horses to the Camp and saddling them, making our fire at night and cooking our victuals, and every other thing they think will please us. Travelled over several barren mountains, some of them produce great plenty of wild Grapes. Lodged in an old Indian Camp. Bad water.

Wednesday, Sept. 13th, 1775. Met John Gibson and an Indian going to hasten the Indians to the Treaty. Dined at Mr. Gibson's. Camped at the mouth of a small run, ten miles from Fort Pitt.

Fort Pitt — Thursday, September 14th, 1775. Got to Fort Pitt about noon. Left our Girls amongst the Indians that are coming to the Treaty. Great numbers of people in Town come to the Treaty. Terrible news from the Northward, but so confused I hoped there is little truth in it.

Source: Cresswell, *The Journal of Nicholas Cresswell*, pp. 100–114

Schoenbrunn Diary – Cresswell Entries

Aug. 27 {1775}. ...From Pittsburg we received a package of congregation reports and letters, which had been in Lancaster since spring, awaiting an opportunity.

Sept. 9. With several white people who passed through, we sent letters by way of Pittsburg to Lititz and Bethlehem.

Gnadenhutten Diary – Cresswell Entry

Aug. 28 {1775}. Mr. Anderson came with a gentleman from Pittsburgh, and I received encouraging letters from the beloved Brethren Matthaus, Thrane, and Grube, and also from Europe from the dear Brother Johannes, dated Barby, the 1st of August 1774, containing the printed abridged historical report of the present Evangelical United Brethren under the Augsburg Confession,...

Cresswell's Thoughts Regarding the Indians

I have conceived a great regard for the Indians and really feel a most sensible regret in parting from them, however contemptible opinion others may entertain of these honest poor creatures. If we take an impartial view of an Indian's general conduct with all the disadvantages they labour under, at the same time divest ourselves of prejudice, I believe every honest man's sentiments would be in favour of them....Though they have not the advantages of learning, they by the light of natural reason distinguish right from wrong with the greatest exactness. They never mean deceit themselves and detest it in others, nor ever place confidence a second time where it has been once abused. Indeed those that have conversed much with the whites have learned several things from them, that the natural honesty of their nature would never have thought of.

In all their trades with the Europeans they are imposed on in the greatest manner. Their sensibility is quick and their passions ungoverned, I may say ungovernable, and it is not to be wondered at if they make returns in kind whenever it is in their power. It is said they are cruel and barbarous and I believe they exercise some cruelties, the thought of which makes human nature shudder, but this is to be attributed to their national customs. It is a general opinion with White men that their difference in colour, and advantages of education give them a superiority over those poor people which Heaven and Nature never designed. They are beings endowed with reason and common sense and I make not the least doubt but they are as valuable in the eyes of their Maker as we are, our fellow creatures, and in general above our level in many virtues that give real preeminence, however despicably we think of or injuriously we treat them.

...Their language is soft, copious and expressive....They cannot curse or swear in their own language, are obliged to the Europeans for that vice.

Source: Cresswell, *The Journal of Nicholas Cresswell*, pp. 117–21

Map 9 – The Crevecouer Map of 1782.

Map 10a – Original Survey of 1797 – Walhonding Indian towns.

Map 10b – Modern Topographic – Walhonding Indian towns.

Map 9

The Crevecouer Map of 1782

This map was first published in a book entitled *Letters from an American Farmer,* by Michel-Guillaum Jean de Crevecouer.

It is helpful in locating some of the more obscure towns that are not on any other map.

For instance, the "V de Moughwessing" shown in the left center of the map is apparently the same town as that called "Moghwhiston" by Levi Hicks in the *Beatty* journal and "Mowheysinck" and "Bullet's Town" by Hutchins in his description of the Indian trails set forth in the Appendix and as shown on his map of 1764 [Map 5].

It also clears up the location of *Cresswell's* Old Hundy, a town called Old Hunting set forth in the Bouquet papers (Hanna, *The Wilderness Trail,* Vol. 2, p. 385), and the town mentioned by Heckewelder when he refers to Capt. Pipe's town of Walhanding (Heckewelder's *Narrative...,* p. 143). They are all the same town!

From the *Cresswell* journal, it appeared that Old Hundy and New Hundy were close to Coshocton, but there was no way of telling whether those towns were south of Coshocton, along the Muskingum, or west of Coshocton along the Walhonding. The Crevecouer map answers this question. On the Walhonding, there is a town called "Village de Oldhanting". Old Hundy is Old Hunting is Oldhanting is Walhanding is Walhonding. They're simply the name of the river! Even the Ols Landing of the *McCully* journal was his way of saying Walhonding.

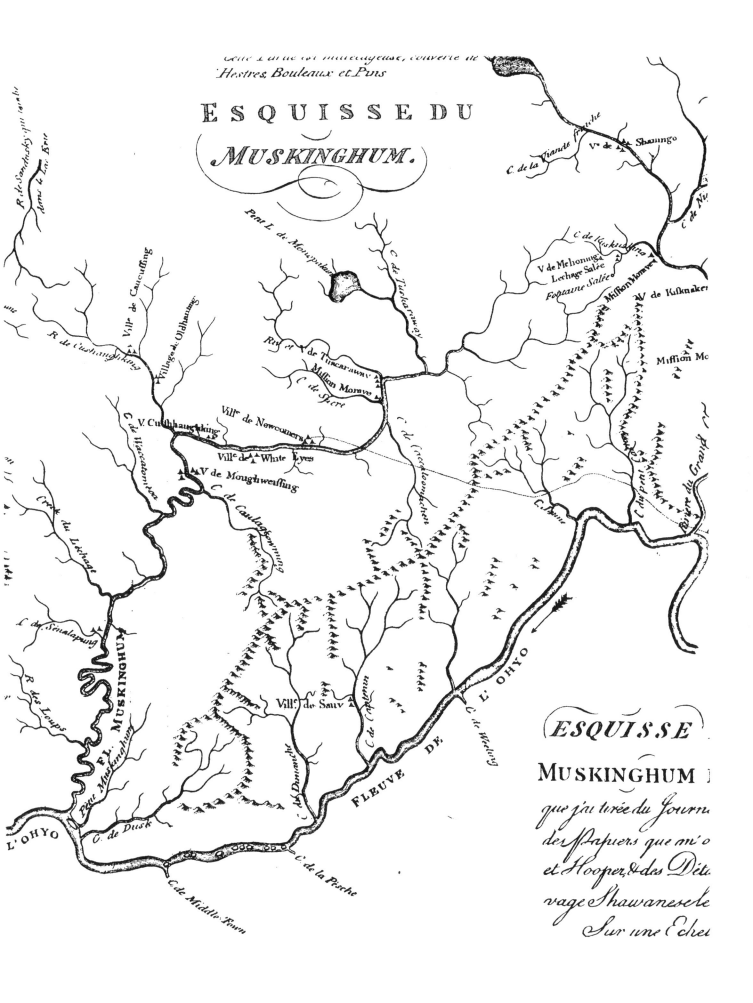

Cette Partie est marécageuse, couverte de
Hestres, Bouleaux et Pins

ESQUISSE DU
MUSKINGHUM.

R. de Sandusky qui tombe
dans le Lac Erié

C. de la Viande Fraiche
V.ᵉ de Shanngo

Petit L. de Monepukan

C. de Tuskarawey

C. de Kiskuchtina
C. de Nu

V. de Mehoning
Lechage Salée
Fontaine Salée

Mission Morave
V. de Kisknakes

Mission Mo

Ville de Caucuting

R. de Cushaughking

Village de Oldhaning

Riv.ᵉ de Tuscarawy

Mission Morave

C. de Shere

C. de Maccalombra

V. Cushhaughking

Vill.ᵉ de Newcomers

Ville d'White Eyes

V. de Moughweissing

C. de Caulaghsomming

C. de Gnadenhutten

C. du pont

Boyau du Grand C.

C. Anne

Creek du Lechage

L. de Senalapung

R. des Loups

FL. MUSKINGHUM

Petit Muskinghum

Vill.ᵉ de Sauv

C. de Captenn

C. de Captenn

C. de Wieling

L'OHYO

FLEUVE DE.

C. du Dimanche

L'OHYO

C. de Dusk

C. de la Pesche

C. de Middle Town

ESQUISSE

MUSKINGHUM

que j'ai tirée du Journ

des Papiers que m'o

et Hooper, & des Déta

vage Shawanese

Sur une Eche

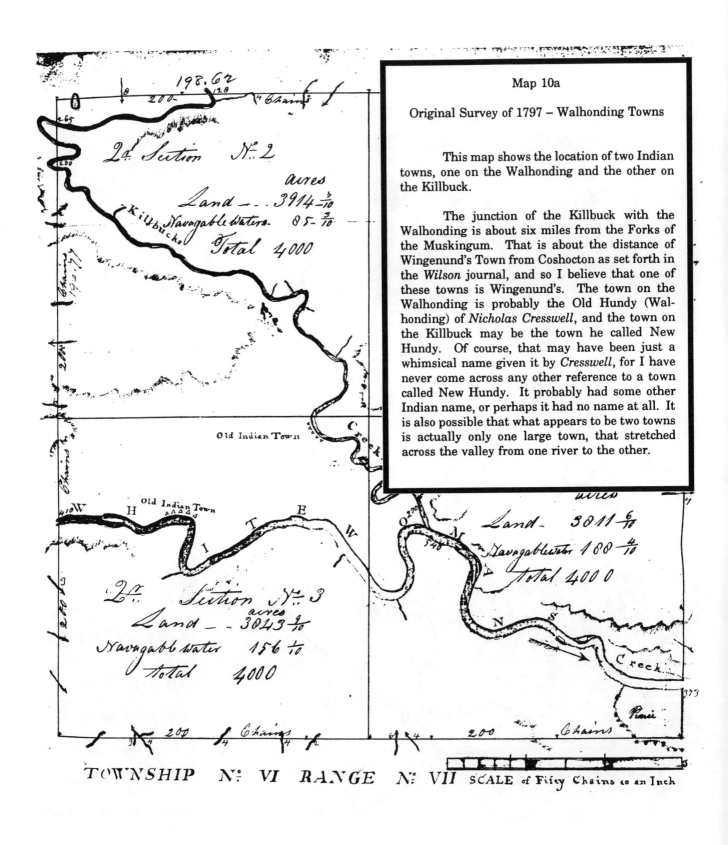

198.62

200   128

2d Section   N: 2

aires

Land ___ 3914 6/10

Navagable Waters ___ 85 3/10

Total 4000

Killbucks

Map 10a

Original Survey of 1797 – Walhonding Towns

This map shows the location of two Indian towns, one on the Walhonding and the other on the Killbuck.

The junction of the Killbuck with the Walhonding is about six miles from the Forks of the Muskingum. That is about the distance of Wingenund's Town from Coshocton as set forth in the *Wilson* journal, and so I believe that one of these towns is Wingenund's. The town on the Walhonding is probably the Old Hundy (Walhonding) of *Nicholas Cresswell*, and the town on the Killbuck may be the town he called New Hundy. Of course, that may have been just a whimsical name given it by *Cresswell*, for I have never come across any other reference to a town called New Hundy. It probably had some other Indian name, or perhaps it had no name at all. It is also possible that what appears to be two towns is actually only one large town, that stretched across the valley from one river to the other.

Old Indian Town

Creek

Old Indian Town

W   H   I   T   E   W

acres

Land ___ 3811 6/10

Navagable Water 188 4/10

Total 4000

2d Section   N: 3

acres

Land ___ 3843 9/10

Navagable Water 156 10/10

Total   4000

Creek

Prairie

200   Chains

200   Chains

TOWNSHIP N: VI RANGE N: VII SCALE of Fifty Chains to an Inch

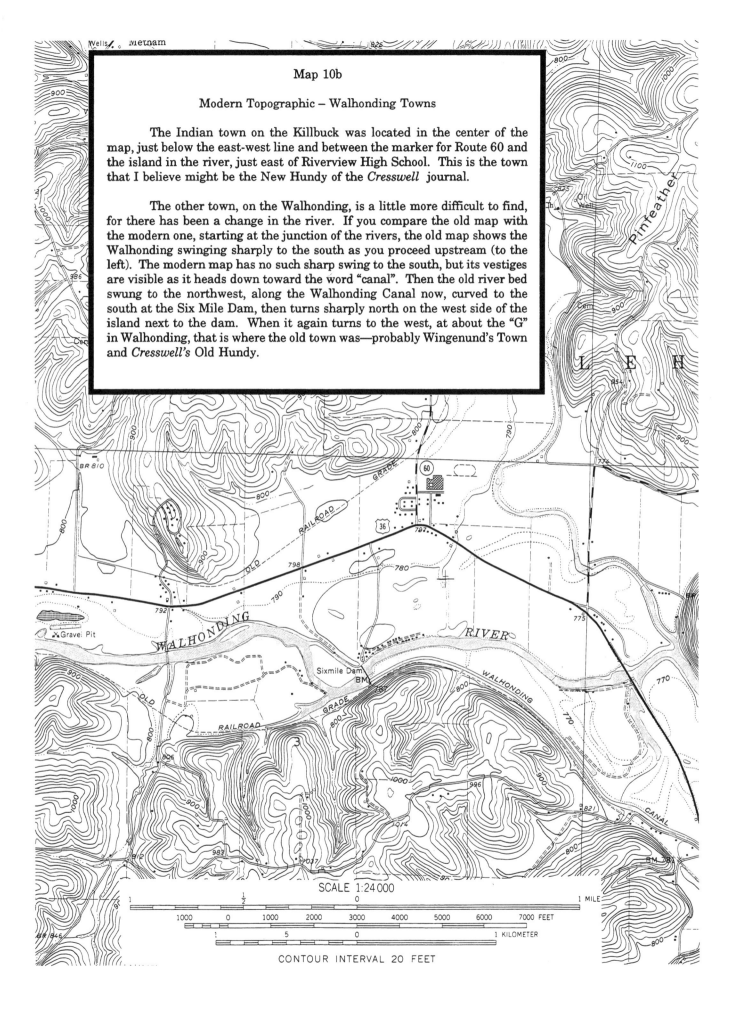

Map 10b

Modern Topographic – Walhonding Towns

The Indian town on the Killbuck was located in the center of the map, just below the east-west line and between the marker for Route 60 and the island in the river, just east of Riverview High School. This is the town that I believe might be the New Hundy of the *Cresswell* journal.

The other town, on the Walhonding, is a little more difficult to find, for there has been a change in the river. If you compare the old map with the modern one, starting at the junction of the rivers, the old map shows the Walhonding swinging sharply to the south as you proceed upstream (to the left). The modern map has no such sharp swing to the south, but its vestiges are visible as it heads down toward the word "canal". Then the old river bed swung to the northwest, along the Walhonding Canal now, curved to the south at the Six Mile Dam, then turns sharply north on the west side of the island next to the dam. When it again turns to the west, at about the "G" in Walhonding, that is where the old town was—probably Wingenund's Town and *Cresswell's* Old Hundy.

SCALE 1:24 000

1000   0   1000   2000   3000   4000   5000   6000   7000 FEET

1   5   0   1 KILOMETER

CONTOUR INTERVAL 20 FEET

Left White Eye's town. Saw the bones of one Mr. Cammel, a White man, that had been killed by the Indians.

Nicholas Cresswell   August 29th, 1775

Richard Butler
1775

The Continental Congress was also concerned about preserving the neutrality of the Ohio Indians and sent Richard Butler to invite the Indians to a conference to be held at Pittsburgh in September of 1775, at the same time as the conference that had been arranged by the Virginia Commissioners referred to in the Wood journal. The result of this joint conference was the Treaty of Pittsburgh, in which the Ohio River was to become the permanent boundary between the Indians and the whites, and the Shawnees were to give up their claim to Kentucky.

The reference, toward the end of the journal, to "the fort being taken possession of by 100 men" is of particular interest. At the outbreak of the Revolution, Dr. John Connolly was the agent at Pittsburgh of Governor Dunmore of Virginia. Dunmore remained loyal to the Crown and , apparently, so did Connolly. In an attempt to weaken the western defenses of the Americans, Connolly disbanded the garrison at Fort Pitt and had intended to proceed to Detroit, raise some troops, and with the aid of the Indians, come back to Pittsburgh and, then, even proceed on to Virginia. Connolly's plans were discovered, however, and he was arrested at Hagerstown, Maryland. The Virginia Provincial Convention then took it upon themselves to order the reoccupation of Fort Pitt. It is to this, then, that Butler is referring. His concern was that the Indians would interpret the actions of the Americans in reoccupying the Fort as being confirmation of what the British at Detroit had been telling them all along—that the Americans intended to stay west of the mountains and, eventually, take all of the Indians' land away from them.

Proceeding from Pittsburgh by the path to Tuscarawas, he first went to Coshocton, then up the Walhonding and on to Pluggy's town (Delaware), from there to the Wyandot town (Upper Sandusky), back to Pluggy's town, and on to the Shawnees at Old Chillicothe (southwest of Circleville), then by way of the Standing Stone (Lancaster) and Wakatomica (Dresden) to Coshocton, and back to Pittsburgh by way of Newcomerstown and the Upper Moravian town (Schoenbrunn).

Butler later was a General in the army of the United States and was killed by the Indians at St. Clair's defeat in 1791.

Left Pittsburgh yᵉ 22ᵈ of August 1775 — on the Tour of the Delawares Yendots — Mingoes & Shawnies —

22:T[uesday] Camp^d at the 2 Mile run Rained All night

23 W[ednesday] Started at 6 OClock met Mr Davison from the Sha.[Shawano] Towns with A letter, & A proclamation Enclosed of Genˡ Carlton for Raising the Quebeck Millitia, which I opened & read & thought fit to push on: Stoped at the Logstown & Dined Saw Old Newcome[r] who Seemed pleased At the Invitation to the

Indian tribes; found one Drunk Indian Lying on the road; More at big beaver Creek   Campd At the big run 2 M from beaver Cr.

24:Th[ursday] Started at 6 OClock Met Some Squas & Old Killbuck Who told me the Principal men of the Delawares was to be that Day at the New Town or Cushohockking which Induced me to go that Road least they might be Scattered before I would See the Head men together, As the other way is Counted the longest Campd Near yellow Cr. fine evening —

25 F'[iday] Started at 7 OClock   Raind all Day Very Heavily, Camp^d at the lower end of the plains Raind Most of the Night Our things being Wet. & it being like to Clear we Stayed to Dry them & —

26 Sa[turday] Started At 10 OClock — Went to Tuskarawas & Dined the Waters rising A little,   it Does not Appear as if the rain was general,   we Campd on the Upper Crossing of the long run, there is very fine Meadow land all Along sam[e] & fine upland —

27 Sunday Started at 6 OClock went to the 10 Mile Camp & dined thence to the 2 Mile run; One horse gave out this Day Near Brush Camp Which Obliged Robt McCully to Stay behind All Night. he Cam[e] up Next Morning at 8 OClock —

28 Mo; Started at 9 OClock & Came to Cushochking & Delivered Our Speech   At 5 OClock we Received An Answer As p^r the Speech Date 28th Ags^t & in it A Message to the windots — The Delawares sends one Man with us to Asure the Windots of their Intentions & to leave A String of wampom with y^m[them] Thos Nicholson Inform^d me that he Read Or in their Way Interpreted A Speech from the Five Nations & Mr Johnston Inviting them to a treaty y^t[that] is to be held at DeTroit but did not Mention the Time; As they are to get Another Message When Mr Johnston is Ready to Meet them but he bids them Sit Still & Do No harm to Any Body till they hear from him Again or See him —

29th Tu; We Set out from Cusshochking at 11 OClock for the Windots The Man from the Delawares having lost his horse Detained us that we got No farther than winginoms who used me very Kindly More So than Common among Savages the Delaware man overtook us just At SunSet Camp^d at Winginoms all Night —

30th Wed Started At 7 OClock went up ye white Womans C^r to the Forks to an old Town, then 2 M: to Windochaloos Town Dined there we Cross^d said C^r 7 times between Cushochking & Said Town there is Very fine land the Whole way & then up Owl C^r About a mile then some small ridges but very fine land up the white Womans branch to the windot road we campd on Owl C^r About 8 M above windochalos Town Crossd Owl C^r Once there is pretty bottoms all along N:B: yesterday morning Kiasota [Guyasuta] told old wingenom that he thought the Sh^o{Shanwano} People had Something bad in their hearts As they Always Cast Up the Selling of the land to him & the Cornstalk had Spoke Very ill of him & of the Delawares who wingenom Said he look^d on or Called Dogs or Serv^ts of the white people; & the Sh^o people Said they Still loved the land & would not part with it; but they both remarked that they Own no land & Kiasota Said that they had Charged him with Acting ill tow^ds them but he was Now determined to See what they mean^d & Defied them to Pronounce One Act of his that was bad; but that he had Still Acted as a Mediator till last Summer & that as they had fell out with the English he Said he was Active in keeping peace between the others & English & let them the Sha^s [the Shawnees] Fight their Own battles & Deside their own quarrels As they Despised being Advised they Should have No Assistance for which the Cornstalk held him at very ill will —

31: Th: Started at 7 OClock   Came to koskosing at 12 OClock; the people there had not heard the Invitation we therefore told them of it & they promised to Attend, left it at 1 OClock & went up A Small branch of the C^r through a Very Rich level Country to An indian Cabbin Near a Deer lick Camp^d All night.

{Butler then proceeded to Pluggy's Town (Delaware) and eventually to the Upper Sandusky area. He then went back to Pluggy's Town and on to the Shawnee towns below Circleville. Cornstalk's sister, known as the Grenadier Squaw because of her size, had a town named for her in this vicinity, and that is where we resume this journal. The Standing Stone mentioned in the early part of the return trip is now Lancaster.}

12 Sept. Tu ...In the Meantime Kiasota went to the Granadiers & got Very Drunk & with Much Ado Got him I got him Away in Coming About A mile he got two falls of[f] his horse which has hurt him Very much

13 We: Started Early Kiasota So bad he Cant ride got only to the Standing Stone About 25 Miles Rained All Day —

14 Th: Still like for rain Started At 8 OClock rained till about 10 OClock the Old man very bad All Day we came to the big lick, about 25 M Camp^d at Sunset Rain All Night in Showers

15th Fr. Started At 7 OClock Still raining: Kiasota Still Very ill Came to the old Delaware Town on Licking C^r at 10 OClock thence to Old waghtomace {Wakatomika} at 6 OClock thence to the beech bank at Dusk Camp^d All Night the Old Man Still poorly.

16th Sa: Started at 6 OClock Kiasota Still bad Arrived at Cushochking about 10 OClock; There was White Eyes & Mohican John who had came from the windot Town he says y^t [that] the windots was not coming Nor the Taways the latter he Says is gone home, They were All stoped by News from Detroit, therefore he set of[f] with 3 other Men & Came to Newcomers Town, the Delawares was Much Surprised at this Sunden [sic] Change As they had Sent them word they were to Set off in three Nights after ye Delaware Messenger left the Wend. Town; The Delawares Imediatly Set of[f] 2 of the Men that had come with John to Desire the wendots & Taways to Attend, that it is Not for them to Attend Alone Therefor they will wait for them till the 20th & No longer; the Messenger had to go to the Taways he Set [sic] of[f] the 13th.

17th Su: This morning I call^d At the Cornstalks Camp As I was Setting off he then told me to write what he had to Say. He Desired me to tell his old Brothers Not to think long or be uneasy that their young Brothers the Shawnoes is this far on their way up; that they will set off this Day & be Still going Lasyly till they are Overtake[n] by their grandfathers the

Delawares & thier brothers the windots Taways & Mingoes that they Expect them that he Expects it will not Exceed 9 Days from this Date as that is the [illegible] of the Delawares he Expects that his brothers will Send Some provisions as far as Mr Gibsons & 5 bags of paint to Distribute Among the young People Again that time the Number of the Shawnios Now on the way is 23 Men & 13 Women & Some Children; they likewise want Some Tobbacco & Salt — (it is Suspected that the Mingoes at the Salt licks is the chief reason of the Stoping the Taways & the windots & that they Dont Mean to Attend after all their fair promises) I met Mr Gibson about 3 OClock yesterday just At white Eyes Town With the Message from the Virginia Commiss^{rs} he tells of the fort being taken possession of by 100 Men & that there is 100 More Raising he Overtook me at the Old Town {Newcomerstown} and says he sent Killbuck with the Speech to the New Town {Coshocton} & he is to wait till Killbuck Comes back with an Ans^r I fear Mr Gibsons News will Not have A good Effect As it Coroborates the Comd^t of Detroits Speech to the Indians that we are Decieving them & will take them prisoner. likewise the reports from Keantucky to the Same purpose; I Arrivd at the upper Moravian Town {Schoenbrunn} About 3 OClock Kiasota being Poorly & our Provision out had to Camp there all night. Mr Gibson Says it is lucky he Came Down As the Shawnies would have hurried back, which by the by is Not So for they were Determined to go On before the[y] Saw him as they gave No Heed to the Messengers Sent After them to Stop them by their Own people but took them Along Also, they was Sent on Account of the News by the Mingo man that the Shawno woman Mentiond to me ye 12th inst.

18th Mo: Mr Gibson Overtook me At the upper Moravian Town Started from that At 8 OClock campd At a little Run about 25 Miles from Said Town —

Source: Butler, "The Journal of Richard Butler", Vol. 46, pp. 390–95; Vol. 47, pp. 149–50

Gnadenhutten Diary – Butler Entries

Sept. 16 {1775}. ...Mr. Gibson came from Pittsburgh with a speech to the Chiefs, which he gave me to read, by which they were requested to come to a Treaty soon to be held there. He told me that the Gentlemen at the Fort had charged them to request that someone from here and from our other Town come to the Treaty in order to hear how the peace with the Delamatteno, Shawnee, the Delaware and the Mingas would be negotiated and concluded. I gave him no positive answer about this,1 but promised to deliberate it with the Brethren.

The 17th. There were the usual Sunday Services concerning the dear Savior; a blessing to our Brethren, Sisters and children. In the afternoon Mr. Gibson returned to Pittsburgh via Schönbrunn....

Schoenbrunn Diary – Butler Entries

Sept. 17 {1775}. ...Mr. Gibson, with another white man {Butler} and a Mingoe Chief, returned from the Shawanose on the way to the Fort. They had gone to bring the latter to a treaty and had left them at Gekelemukp. The first named informed us that the gentlemen at the Fort, who are authorized by the Congress to conduct this treaty negotiation with the Indians, would be glad to see some of our Indians present. We told him, however, that we would rather have our Indians excused, because we knew from experience that on such occasions they suffered harm and were not well treated by the savage Indians, and that our Indians had never had anything to do with the treaties, not having been summoned.

{NOTE: In about the length of time that it would have taken Butler to go to Fort Pitt and send a message back to Schoenbrunn, it appears that the authorities attempted to correct their oversight in having failed to "summon" the Christian Indians to the treaty, for the following entries appear in the Schoenbrunn Diary.}

Sept. 24. By messenger we received a letter from the gentlemen in Pittsburg, who have been authorized by the Congress to conduct this treaty negotiation with the Indians, in which Br. David was cordially invited to attend the same with several of our Indians.

Sept. 29. ...As several of our Indian brethren must go along to the Fort tomorrow, we celebrated the Holy Communion today,...

Sept. 30. ...Because Bro. Jungmann, who has had fever for some time, has become worse and was obliged to take to his bed, Br. David wrote to the Commissioners at the Fort giving them this as reason for his not being able to come.

Oct. 29. The Brn. Wilhelm, Nathanael and Isaac returned from the treaty negotiation at the Fort....

David Zeisberger
1776

In February of 1776, David Zeisberger journeyed to Coshocton at the request of Chief Netawatwees to look for suitable land on which to locate the third mission town. He found such land about two miles below Coshocton, and Lichtenau was later established at that site.

This excerpt from his travel diary is included in this book for the reason that it gives us a glimpse of the appearance of the Indian town of Coshocton, about one year after Netawatwees had moved there. It appears that the chief's house also served as the Council house, and that, although the Indians tried to have some regularity about the placement of their huts in the town, they were not very successful in this regard.

Feb. 8 {1776}. ...After we had, on the 4th huj., again received a message from Chief Netawatwees, who begs of us to start the third Indian brethren's Settlement as soon as possible, reminding us, at the same time that all the heads of this nation had now agreed to accept the Gospel, and asks that we should come to select a place, as they had two places to propose, Br. David left, this afternoon, with Br. Schebosch and five Indian brethren, for Goschachgunk. He reports the following concerning the matter:

We spent the night at Gnadenhütten, from which place three Indian brethren went with us. On the 9th, by way of Gekelemukp., we reached, in the evening, during a heavy rain storm, White Eye's Town, where we spent the night, and were well received. On the 10th, we viewed, first of all, this place and the whole region, which did not fail to please us, then we took our way down the Muskingum, a long circuitous route, viewing the country, which we found, indeed, to be good, but found no suitable place for building a town. Where the land was fine for fields there was no building site, and where a town might be located there was no good land for fields and no wood nor water. Toward evening we came to Goschachgunk, and as we had come quite unexpectedly, because the messengers had received no positive answer in Gnadenhütten whether and when we could come our arrival gave the Chief, his counsellors and all the Indians the greater pleasure. We were very well received and in the Chief's house, which is the largest, a separate fire was assigned to us, where we lodged. The Indians soon came in great numbers and welcomed us in a very friendly manner. Their Town, which lies on the east side of the Muskingum, just across from where the Walhanding, equally large with it, empties into the Muskingum, is quite large but spread out very much, consisting, for the most part, of huts, and although it was laid out and the streets were marked off, I could not find a single street that was built up, in any degree, in regular fashion, each had built according to his fancy, the length of the house or the width toward the street, or obliquely, or even the house in the middle of the street. I preached in the Chief's house to a large number of Indians who had assembled,...

Source: Zeisberger, "Schoenbrunn Diary"

181

William Wilson
1776

In June of 1776, William Wilson had been sent by George Morgan, the Agent for Indian Affairs in what was called the Middle Department, to the Shawnees to try to prevent their going to Detroit to a conference with the British. The Shawnees agreed to stay at their towns until Mr. Morgan himself came to see them. After Morgan got there, Wilson was then sent to the Wyandots to invite them to a treaty to be held at Pittsburgh in September. He got as far as Pluggy's town (Delaware) and then, due to the possibility of being taken captive by some Mingos, left Pluggy's town in the night and went to Coshocton. About two weeks later he proceeded to a Wyandot town near Detroit. After meeting with the Wyandots (and even the British Governor, Hamilton, at Detroit) he returned to Coshocton and then went on to Pittsburgh, where he made his report on September 26th. The following account is taken from his report.

{Pluggy's Town} I advised with the Cornstalk, and Delawares, what was the most prudent step for me to take, and what they thought of the before mentioned speech. The Cornstalk said they only wanted to deceive me; and he and the Delawares recommended to us to make our escape that night, and endeavor to get to Coochocking, a Delaware town. We did so, after engaging a Delaware man to go to the Shawanese towns to hear the news which the before mentioned person brought, and to discover the temper they were in. I thought it expedient to continue at Coochocking, until the return of the messenger I had sent to the Shawanees. He returned in four days, and informed that the party of Shawanees and Cherokees, before mentioned, had killed two men and taken a woman prisoner on the Kentucky; that the white people pursued them, came up with them the next day, and killed two of the Shawanees and rescued the prisoner; that the Cherokees had sent a tomahawk belt, with two scalps tied to it, to the Shawanees, informing them that they had struck the white people; and it was his opinion

that the Shawanees would join, provided the other nations did. He further said that the Hardman intended to proceed to the Wyandots with the messages from Mr. Morgan, and would meet me at Sandusky.

I thought it advisable to engage some of the Delaware Chiefs to go with me to the Wyandot towns. I therefore assembled the Delawares, and desired they would appoint some persons for that purpose. They pitched upon Captain Killbuck and two young men to accompany me. After I had made the necessary preparations for my journey, king Newcomer spoke to me and said, he thought it was dangerous for me to pursue my intended journey, as it was probable the Mingoes might way-lay the road and kill me; that he would send a message of his own to the Wyandots, with Mr. Morgan's, and advised me to continue at Coochocking, and let Captain Killbuck proceed with the messages, and to send Joseph Nicholson to Mr. Morgan to inform him what I had done. I took his advice. Killbuck returned in eleven days, with the messages sent by him, and a message from the Wyandots to me, signifying that those who lived on this side of the lake were not able to give an answer without consulting their chiefs on the other side; that I must come with my message myself; that I need not apprehend any danger from them; that if my heart was good towards them, I would come; if it was not I would stay away.

On receiving this message, I determined to go, and Killbuck and two young men were again appointed to accompany me. We traveled about ten miles from Coochocking, when Killbuck was taken sick, which obliged us to return. I then applied to Captain White Eyes to go with me, who very readily consented. At Winganous town, about six miles from Coochocking, I met with John Montour, whom I employed to go with me, and a Wyandot man, who told me that he imagined that Cornstalk and other Shawanees, and the Wyandot chiefs, had left Sandusky, and that he would pilot me a nearer way, to where the chiefs were. Nothing material happened until we arrrived at a Wyandot village, opposite to Detroit, where the chiefs were assembled.

{Wilson and White Eyes met with the Indians in the vicinity of Detroit at which council even the British Governor Hamilton was present. It was a very stormy meeting on the part of Governor Hamilton, with the Governor tearing to pieces the writing that Wilson had brought, and the wampum belt, strewing the pieces around the council house. They were then ordered to leave the area by the Governor. Judging from the rather laconic conclusion to this report of his mission, the return trip was completely uneventful.}

We set out for Coochocking. Nothing material happened on our journey.

Source: Hildreth, *Pioneer History,* pp. 98–108

Gnadenhutten Diary – Wilson Entries

June 3 {1776}. ...Soon after, Mr. Wilson came from Pittsburg by way of Schönbrunn with a string of wampum and a speech for the Delawares, asking them to stay at home and not to come to the fort since Mr. Morgan intended to come to them himself in the near future, to speak with them at Coschachkung. Jo Peepe was immediately sent with the string of wampum to overtake White Eyes and John Killebock and call them back. Meantime, Mr. Wilson gave me the speech to read; in it, among the rest, the traders were prohibited from bringing any rum either into the Moravian towns or into their neighborhood. I immediately took a copy and made the contents of this speech known to our brethren in the morning service on June 4. Jo Peepe and White Eyes with his people returned at noon; after they had eaten here, they went home.

June 10. In the morning Mr. Morgan and Makie {McKee} arrived here from Pittsburg with six whites and some Shawanoes; the two first-mentioned had dinner with us, inspected our town, and expressed their joy at what they saw. In the afternoon they bade us a friendly goodbye and went to Coschachkung, and I wished them a successful expedition to the Delawares and Shawanoes.

July 15. Toward evening Mr. Morgan arrived with a Shawanos and two white boys whom Mingues had taken from the whites: soon thereafter Mr. Makie also arrived with several Shawanos. The former had fever and we took him into our house for the night; the others remained on the other side of the stream.

July 16. After Mr. Morgan had breakfasted with us, the conversation dealing with the blessed work of the Saviour among the Indians of this place—as it had yesterday evening, he took leave in a very friendly manner and left for Pittsburg by way of Schönbrunn; Mr. Makie and his company followed thither this afternoon.

July 31. ...Today we heard of a white man, Nicholas {Nicholson}, who recently fled from the Shawanos with Mr. Wilson by night to Coschachkung so as not to be captured by the Minques, since they had heard that the Mingues had already begun to murder and that the Indian War would break out soon. This man went to Pittsburg to report this. When we heard this, we could think of no other course than looking to the Saviour and praying: "Have mercy upon us and grant us Thy peace."

August 26. Mr. Anderson, who had come here from Schönbrunn yesterday, went to Coschachkung, where he will remain for a time by order of the commissioners of Congress, so that he may send written copies of all reports or messages reaching the chief to Pittsburg to the commissioners and communicate to the chief and his council, in turn, letters which he shall receive from that place.

September 15. ...An Indian came from Coschachkung with an unpleasant report which Captain White Eyes and Mr. Wilson had brought with them from Detroit, namely, that the commanding officer of that place had listened to the message which White Eyes and Wilson had addressed to the Delamattenoes, had looked at their belts and promptly cut them into pieces, throwing them at their feet and telling them to get away at once or they would lose their heads. They remained there, however, two days longer and then returned.

September 19. Mr. Gibson and Anderson returned from Coschachkung and Mr. Wilson came with them. The latter told us what he had heard while among the Delamattenoes, namely, that not only they but also other nations, such as the Shipawanos,[?] etc., were united with the Five Nations and would carry on war with the Americans. Mr. Gibson said hereupon: "I am directed by the commissioners in Pittsburg to say to the friendly Indians that if hostile Indians commence war with the Americans, Congress plans to summon the peace-loving Indians away and agree upon a quiet place for them, where they shall be protected and supported, otherwise they will run the danger of being slaughtered. I have obeyed these instructions and have communicated and made this known both to the chief and his councillors, as also to the Indians in Lichtenau and especially to Mr. Zeisberger, and now I wish to report it here as well." Some of our people who had heard this from him and Mr. Anderson said that that would be a hard matter for us, to leave houses, cattle, corn, and to lose everything, and I told them the same. May God graciously prevent this; for with many of our people and the savages, if they should live together at the same place, nothing good would result, in such a case we surely would lose some of them who would not want to go with us to live among whites. Finally I said: "Let us not give much thought to this at present; time will counsel us; we put our trust in our dear Lord and Saviour."

September 20. By order of the commissioners Mr. Anderson bought ten head of cattle here for the approaching treaty. Both he and Mr. Gibson ate dinner with us and left in the afternoon for Schönbrunn with an Indian who drove the cattle.

{NOTE: Feeding the hundreds of Indians who were expected to attend the treaty would be a big problem. That is why cattle were being driven all the way from Gnadenhutten to Pittsburgh!}

Lichtenau Diary – Wilson Entries

{June} 5th {1776}. An expresser from Pittsburgh passed through here to the Shawnee from whom we learned that in a few days Mr. Morgan would arrive here. He brought us a proclamation from him, one point of which was this: namely, that the traders or white people should bring no rum or intoxicating liquor to our towns nor should they bring it into our region. We were glad about that because it had happened that the traders had brought rum, not exactly to our towns, but had buried it a few miles away in the forest. Thereby a boozing orgy had started among the wild Indians and we had suffered great inconvenience therefrom.

The 11th. A few of our Indian brethren were summoned to the council to Goschachgunk, because Mr. Morgan had arrived there, whereupon Wilhelm with one brother left for that place. The main point was that they were informed that, as soon as it would be possible to assemble the nations, a treaty should be made with them at Pittsburgh, for which purpose Mr. Morgan asked the assistance of the heads of the Delaware nation in the sending of messages to all the nations as far down as the Wabash in order to invite them. They promised to do that. Finally he reminded them that they had asked for a preacher. Congress, he had told them, was willing to help them; therefore they should think about it and consider the matter well.

The 13th. He arrived here, stayed for a few hours, and then continued his journey to the Shawnees.

{July} 13th. Mr. Morgan stopped here on his return from the Shawanese and stayed the night. He brought two prisoners along which a party of Mingoes brought in while he was there and whom he took away from them again. It does not look at all favorable among the Nations so that we could believe that we will have quiet and peaceful times, for something is working among them that we cannot quite understand at the moment. But it is generally believed that if an Indian war breaks out it will be more fierce than ever has been which Mr. Morgan also believes. Therefore, since the times are so oppressive, Bro. David proposed to him to share with the Delawares the communication from Pittsburgh, so the lies would be stopped and the Indians would know where they were at. Mr. Morgan approved this idea and next day talked to the Council in Goschachgunk and they approved what he said, that every fourteen days or so, or as often as it seemed good, to send a courier to the Fort. This was begun immediately and continued as long as necessary. At the same time he requested of Bro. David that when the Chiefs had anything to report to the Fort, he would do it for them and this he promised.

{July} 23rd. Several white people came, sent by Mr. Morgan, with a party of Shawanese as couriers to the Wyondots. However, since they came into a Mingo town on the way and there were pushed, they thought it safest to leave secretly in the night if they didn't want to be taken prisoner and sent to Detroit or even be killed.

{August} 27th. Mr. Anderson came here. He is ordered by the head of the Commissioners to spend some time in Goschachgunk to strive for what is best for the land in Indian affairs and to assist the Chiefs when necessary by sending couriers to other nations.

{September} 14th.   White Eye returned from Detroit from where he had been awaited for a long time. He went to learn how things are with the Wyondots and other Indian Nations. He was with a white man {Wilson} sent from Pittsburgh; both gave their message to the Wyondots which could not be given other than in the presence of the Governor who cut their belt, tramped it under foot and gave no answer than this: They should not be seen there more than an hour. To White Eye he said: He was a Virginian, whom he had given a beating and he had gone with them against the Shawanese; if he valued his head he should leave the Fort hurriedly, which they did. From that one can clearly see that things don't look good. The Governor has the Wyondots in his power and does what he wants with them and they can do nothing without him. Everyone believes now that there will be an all-out Indian war. It is said the Senecas have taken the hatchet, so it seems that events will break loose from all sides. Mr. Gibson, who came from the Fort yesterday was ordered by the Commissioners to sound out the leading Delawares to see if they are willing to return to the white people where they would be safe and kept should a general Indian war break out....

Indian Pride

The Indians are proud but not vain; they consider vanity as degrading and unworthy the character of a man. The hunter never boasts of his skill or strength, nor the warrior of his prowess. It is not right, they say, that one should value himself too much for an action which another may perform as well as himself, and when a man extols his own deeds, it seems as if he doubted his own capability to do the like again when he pleased. Therefore, they prefer in all cases to let their actions speak for themselves. The skins and peltry which the hunter brings home, the deer's horns on the roof of his cabin, the horses, furniture and other property that he possesses, his apparel and that of his family, the visits with which he is honored by the first and best men among his nation; all these things show what he is and what he has done, and with this he rests satisfied.

Source: Heckewelder's *History...*, p. 170

John Heckewelder
1778

Taken from Heckwelder's Narrative, *this is his version of the dangerous "ride" from Pittsburgh to Coshocton in April of 1778, at a critical period of the Revolution on the frontier.*

The Narrative *was written more than forty years after the event and is somewhat flawed as to certain details. (These flaws are discussed in a later section of this book.)*

Nevertheless, the ride was a very courageous thing to have done at such a dangerous time and he deserves great credit for undertaking it.

The chiefs and council of Goshochking, as the protectors of the Christian Indians, would frequently consult the missionaries on matters necessary for the preservation of peace. They had repeatedly declared that nothing should withdraw their confidence from their American brethren; who, together with them, had sprung up from the same soil. — That their brethren had told them, at the treaty at Pittsburg, not to join either side with a hostile intention — not to go to war against the English, no more than against them, and which language their American brethren still held forth to them, while on the other hand the English, who called themselves their fathers, were continually teazing them to take up the hatchet, and kill the Americans, their brethren. — They (the chiefs and council) called now again on the Christian Indians, to go hand in hand with them towards peace measures, and in saving lives, not in destroying them; adding, "you Christians are in possession of the great book; (the bible) do therefore in all matters as that book tells you!"

Until of late, the missionaries would not give credit to any reports, (and many there were from time to time,) which stated, "that the governor of Detroit was determined to compel all the Indians, be they who they might, the Christian Indians not excepted, to turn out and fight the American People, (or rebels, as he termed them,) and that he would even punish all such as did not obey his orders;" but they were sorry to see by a letter, which bore the signature of the governor, that not only what they had heard on the subject proved to be true, but that, if the threats contained in his letter were carried into execution, all missions amongst the Indians would at once be at an end. This letter was of such a nature, that the missionary Zeisberger, after perusal, thought proper to commit it at once to the flames, and fervently to pray to Almighty God, to avert such disasters from his people. One hope however remained, which was, that the letter, though having the signature of the governor, perhaps might be a forged one, and written by one of the agents or subalterns in the Indian country.

Added to the above, an occurrence had taken place, which, of itself, was enough to break the hearts of the missionaries, and especially that of the faithful and pious servant of God, David Zeisberger. It was the unexpected arrival at Goschochking, of a number of disaffected persons from Pittsburg, led on by Alexander

McKee, Matthew Elliot, and Simon Girty, all three, very suspicious and dangerous characters: the first of whom had been an Indian agent of the British government, but permitted by the United States to go at large, on parole. — The second was the same person who, as noticed before, came into Lichtenau, in 1776, with a cargo of goods, and was taken prisoner at Waketameki, and subsequently brought to Detroit; and had afterwards been heard to boast of the clandestine manner in which he had procured his liberation from the British, though at the same time he had a British Captain's commission in his pocket. The third, Simon Girty, was a depraved wretch, who formerly had been employed as an Indian interpreter. These men, well known to the Indian nations, had, wherever they passed through Indian villages, but particularly at Goshochking, propagated abominable falsehoods respecting the war, and the situation the people were in beyond the mountains, (in the Atlantic States); adding: "That it was the determination of the American people, to kill and destroy the whole Indian race, be they friends or foes, and possess themselves of their country; and that, at this time, while they were embodying themselves for the purpose, they were preparing fine sounding speeches to deceive them, that they might with the more safety fall upon and murder them. That now was the time, and the only time, for all nations to rise, and turn out to a man against these intruders, and not even suffer them to cross the Ohio, but fall upon them where they should find them; which if not done without delay, their country would be lost to them forever!"

The consternation caused among the Delawares on hearing these reports, was, as might be expected, very great, although captain White Eyes, and other chiefs would not give credit to reports of this kind, especially coming from such characters; yet, as the nation had been roused to commence war immediately against the people of the United States, and he (White Eyes) well knew that his conduct in this affair would be closely watched by his rival, captain Pipe, on the Walhanding, he called a general council of the nation, in which he proposed to delay committing hostilities against the American people for ten days, during which time they might obtain more certain information as to the truth

of the assertions of these men; either, from Tamenend (col. Morgan,) or col. Gibson, or some other friend of theirs, who would give them notice. Pipe, considering this a proper time for placing White Eyes in the back ground, construed this wise and prudent advice of his, as though he was in the secret, and now proposed to his own council, "to declare every man an enemy to the nation, that should throw an obstacle in the way, that might tend to prevent the taking up arms immediately against the American people." White Eyes, seeing the blow aimed against himself, once more assembled his men, and told them: "That if they meant in earnest to go out, (as he observed some of them were preparing to do,) they should not go without him. He had taken peace measures, in order to save the nation from utter destruction. But if they believed that he was in the wrong, and gave more credit to vagabond fugitives, whom he knew to be such, than to himself, who was best acquainted with the real state of things, — if they had determined to follow their advice, and go out against the Americans, he would go out with them; but not like the bear hunter, who sets the dogs on the animal to be beaten about with his paws, while he keeps at a safe distance — no! he would himself lead them on, place himself in the front, and be the *first* who should fall. They only had to determine on what they meant to do, for his own mind was fully made up not to survive his nation; and he would not spend the remainder of a miserable life, in bewailing the total destruction of a brave people, who deserved a better fate."

This spirited address of White Eyes had the desired effect: all declared that they would wait until the ten days were expired, and many added, that they never would go to war against the American people, unless they had him for their leader.

It so happened that the Brethren in Bethlehem, towards the latter end of February, of this year, (1778,) feeling an uncommon anxiety for the fate of the missionaries and Christian Indians on Muskingum, they not having received a letter, or obtained any account of them for the last six months, they applied to the writer of this narrative, who in the last summer had come to Bethlehem on a visit, to proceed to Pittsburg for the purpose; and if, when there, it was believed to be practicable and safe, even to repair to his post at Lichtenau, to which he readily agreed: brother John Shabosh, who had been prevented from returning to his family at Gnadenhütten, since August last, would cheerfully accompany him.

Some circumstances at that time making it necessary for us to be furnished with a passport from the highest authority, we waited on the president of congress, Henry Laurens, esq. and also on the secretary of war, Horatio Gates, who at that time were at Yorktown, Pennsylvania, both which gentlemen spoke very highly of the laudable undertaking the Brethren were engaged in, of propagating the gospel among the Indians, for the purpose of bringing them to embrace Christianity and become a civilized people; assuring us, that nothing should be wanting on their part in lending aid, whenever in their power, towards such a good work, and in granting us protection when required; adding, "that it had been the wish of congress, from the beginning of the war between Great Britain and the colonies, that the Indian nations could be brought to see it their interest to remain neutral during the contest, and not join either side, as the only way for them to escape being censured and hurt by either, and finally become a happy people and united with the white Christians."

Being supplied with a passport to Pittsburg, we pursued our journey, meeting with no difficulties by the way, to that place, except the sight of so many deserted houses along the glades, on the doors of which was written, either with chalk or coal, "good people, avoid this road, for the Indians are out murdering us;" and again, as we drew nearer to Pittsburg, the unfavourable account of the elopement of McKee, Elliot, Girty, and others, from the latter place to the Indian country, for the purpose of instigating the Indians to murder, as was generally expected. Indeed the gloomy countenances of all men, women and children, that we passed, bespoke fear — nay, some families even spoke of leaving their farms and moving off.

Far greater was the consternation of the people at Pittsburg, and especially that of the commandant of the place, col. Edward Hand, and col. John Gibson; on whom all eyes were fixed with regard to future safety. Of those men who had eloped but a few days since, the worst might

reasonably be expected: their disaffection to the United States — their disposition to act hostile — the influence they would have over the minds, at least of many of the poor Indians, and the means they would have at command for the purpose of enforcing their evil designs, might be calculated on with certainty. In vain had the commandant sought for a trusty runner, to carry out pacific speeches to the peaceable Delawares: the risk of going out at a time when it was known that the war parties were out, and probably every path beset by them, being thought too great. Even the above named gentlemen, with many others of the place, however anxious they were that something might be done to prevent the Delawares from being deceived, would not venture to advise us to go at this time; declaring that if we should go, and escape, it must be considered a miracle.

However, the matter appearing to us of the greatest importance, we had given it a due consideration during the night; the result of which was, that in our view it appeared clear, that the preservation of the Delaware nation, and the existence of our mission, depended on the nation being at peace, and that a contrary course would tend to the total ruin of the whole mission; — that were we at this time to neglect, or withdraw ourselves from performing a service, nay a duty, in exposing the vile intentions of a depraved set of beings, whose evil designs were but too well known, we must become accountable to our God. Therefore, with entire reliance on the strong hand of Providence, we determined to go at the hazard of our lives, or at least make the attempt.

Accordingly in the morning we made our resolution known to cols. Hand and Gibson, whose best wishes for our success, we were assured of; and leaving our baggage behind, and turning a deaf ear to all entreaties of well meaning friends, who considered us as lost, if we went, we crossed the Alleghany river, and on the third day, at eleven o'clock at night, reached Gnadenhütten, after having at several times narrowly escaped falling in with war parties; and indeed, in one instance, while encamped on the Big Beaver, near the mouth, where a party of warriors on that night were murdering people on Rackoon creek, not many miles distant from where we were, though at that time not known to us. We had travelled day and night, only leaving our horses time to feed; crossed the Big Beaver, which overflowed its banks, on a raft we had made of poles, other large creeks on the way we swam with our horses, and never attempted to kindle a fire, apprehensive of being discovered by the warriors smelling the smoke.

When arrived within a few miles of Gnadenhütten, we distinctly heard the beat of a drum, and on drawing near, the war song sung to the beat of the drum, all which being in the direction the town lay, we naturally concluded that the Christian Indians must have moved off, wherefore we proceeded with caution, lest we should fall into the warriors's hands. However, the people being yet there, informed us, that those warriors we had heard, were Wyandots from Sandusky, who arrived that evening, and were encamped on the Bluff, two miles below the town, on the opposite side of the river, and who probably would the next morning, travel along the path we had just come.

Fatigued as we were, after our journey, and without one hour of sound sleep, I was now requested by the inhabitants of the place, men and women, not to delay any time, but to proceed on to Goschochking (near thirty miles distant,) where all was bustle and confusion, and many preparing to go off to fight the American people in consequence of the advice given them by those deserters, before named, who had told them, that the American people were embodying themelves at this time, for the purpose of killing every Indian they should meet with, be such, friend or foe, and further we were told, that captain White Eyes had been threatened to be killed if he persisted in vindicating the character of the American people; many believing the stories told them by McKee and his associates, and had in consequence already shaved their heads, ready to lay the plume on, and turn out to war, as soon as the ten days which White Eyes had desired them to wait should be expired, and to-morrow being the ninth day, and no message having yet arrived from their friends at Pittsburg, they now were preparing to go — and further, that this place, Gnadenhütten, was now breaking up for its inhabitants to join the congregation at Lichtenau, those deserters having assured them, that they were not a day safe from an attack by the Americans, while they remained here.

Finding the matter so *very* pressing, and even not admitting of a day's delay, I consented, that after a few hours rest and sleep, and furnished with a trusty companion and fresh horse, I would proceed on, when between three and four o'clock in the morning, the national assistant, John Martin, having called on me for the purpose, we set out, swimming our horses across the Muskingum river, and taking a circuit through the woods in order to avoid the encampment of the war party which was close to our path. Arriving by ten o'clock in the forenoon within sight of the town, a few yells were given by a person who had discovered us, intended to notify the inhabitants, that a white man was coming, and which immediately drew the whole body of Indians into the street; but although I saluted them in passing them, not a single person returned the compliment, which, as my conductor observed, was no good omen. Even captain White Eyes, and the other chiefs, who always had befriended me, now stepped back when I reached out my hand to them, which strange conduct however did not dismay me, as I observed among the crowd some men well known to me as spies of captain Pipe's, watching the actions of these peace chiefs, wherefore I was satisfied that the act of refusing me the hand, had been done from policy, and not from any ill will towards my person. Indeed in looking around, I thought I could read joy in the countenances of many of them, in seeing me among them at so critical a juncture, when they, but a few days before had been told by those deserters, that nothing short of their total destruction, had been resolved upon by the "long knives" (the Virginians, or *new* American people). Yet as no one would reach out his hand to me, I inquired into the cause, when captain White Eyes boldly stepping forward, replied; "that by what had been told them by those men (McKee and party) they no longer had a single friend among the American people; if therefore this be so, they must consider every white man who came to them from that side, as an enemy, who only came to them to deceive them, and put them off their guard for the purpose of giving the enemy an opportunity of taking them by surprise." I replied, that the imputation was unfounded, and that, were I not their friend, they never would have seen me here. "Then, (continued captain

White Eyes) you will tell us the truth with regard to what I state to you!" — assuring him of this, he in a strong tone asked me: "are the American armies all cut to pieces by the English troops? Is general Washington killed? Is there no more a congress, and have the English hung some of them, and taken the remainder to England to hang them there? Is the whole country beyond the mountains in the possession of the English; and are the few thousand Americans who have escaped them, now embodying themselves on this side of the mountains for the purpose of killing all the Indians in this country, even our women and children? Now do not deceive us, but speak the truth" (added he); "is this all true what I have said to you?" I declared before the whole assembly, that not one word of what he had just now told me was true, and holding out to him, as I had done before, the friendly speeches sent by me for them, which he however as yet refused to accept, I thought by the countenances of most of the bystanders, that I could perceive that the monent bid fair for their listening at least to the contents of those speeches, and accidentally catching the eye of the drummer, I called to him to beat the drum for the Assembly to meet for the purpose of hearing what their American Brethren had to say to them! A general smile having taken place, White Eyes thought the favourable moment arrived to put the question, and having addressed the assembly in these words: "shall we my friends and relatives listen once more to those who call us their brethren?" which question being loudly and as with one voice answered in the affirmative, the drum was beat, and the whole body

quickly repaired to the spacious council house; the speeches, all of which were of the most pacific nature were read and interpreted to them, when captain White Eyes rose, and in an elaborate address to the assembly took particular notice of the good disposition of the American people towards the Indians, observing, that they had never as yet, called on them to fight the English, knowing that wars were destructive to nations, that those had from the beginning of the war, to the present time always advised them (the Indians) to remain quiet, and not take up the hatchet against either side. A newspaper, containing the capitulation of general Burgoyne's army, being found enclosed in the packet, Captain White Eyes once more rose up and holding this paper unfolded with both his hands, so that all could have a view of it, said "see my friends and relatives, this document containeth great events, not the song of a bird, but the truth!" — then stepping up to me, he gave me his hand, saying: "you are welcome with us Brother;" when everyone present, followed his example; after which I proceeded with my conductor John Martin to Lichtenau, where, to the inexpressible joy of the venerable missionary Zeisberger, and his congregation, we related what had taken place, while they on the other hand assured us, that nothing could have at that time come more seasonable to save the nation, and with it the mission, from utter destruction, than our arrival.

Source: Heckewelder, *A Narrative of the Mission...*, pp. 168–82

Language

The Indians are very proud of a white man's endeavouring to learn their language; they help him in everything that they can, and it is not their fault if he does not succeed.

Source: Heckewelder's *History...*, p. 230

Robert McCready
1778

On June 11, 1778, the Continental Congress authorized an expedition to be undertaken against the British at Detroit. Washington appointed General Lachlan McIntosh as its commander.

McIntosh, just the year before, had killed one of the signers of the Declaration of Independence in a duel, Button Gwinnett of Georgia, but apparently that did not diminish Washington's opinion of him as a military commander. (It did, however, make Gwinnett's signature the rarest and most sought-after of all of the signers, since he lived for such a short time thereafter.)

After many delays, the expedition finally got under way from Fort Pitt on October 23rd and proceeded to the mouth of the Beaver, about twenty miles from Pittsburgh, where they constructed Fort McIntosh, to store the provisions and supplies for the march.

Further delays were incurred while supplies for the expedition were being collected, and it was not until November 4th that the army actually set out for the passage across Ohio. By that time, Detroit was no longer the objective, because it was too late in the season and supplies were still insufficient. Instead, they were now intending to simply attack the Sandusky towns and "chastize" the Indians.

McIntosh had about 1,200 men with him at the commencement of the march, consisting of elements of the Eighth Pennsylvania Regiment and the Thirteenth Virginia, or West Augusta, Regiment, forty North Carolina Dragoons, some French officers, and about 900–1,000 militia.

Robert McCready, a young Scotsman, kept the Orderly Book for the expedition and also a journal of his own, which journal however, unfortunately for us, ends just two days after their arrival at Tuscarawas. Nevertheless, since it is the only journal of the campaign that I am aware of, it is included in this book for the information that it contains pertaining to the march to the Tuscarawas Valley, and their reception by the friendly Indians.

After arriving at the Tuscarawas, the supply problems were so acute that the expedition went no farther toward the Sandusky towns, but, instead, built a stockade which they called Fort Laurens, in honor of the President of the Continental Congress, Henry Laurens. Laurens was a friend of McIntosh and had been instrumental in getting this command for McIntosh. By December 9th, with winter setting in, McIntosh had given up all plans to even attack the Sandusky towns and, leaving only 150 men at Fort Laurens, marched back to Fort McIntosh through six inches of snow.

For the 150 men left behind, it was a terrible winter. In addition to lack of supplies, the British and hostile Indians on several occasions attacked the fort, once killing several men who had just left it, heading for Fort McIntosh (capturing a mail bag containing incriminating evidence that the Moravian missionaries were aiding the American cause with information of British and Indian intentions), and on another occasion surprising and killing 16 men *within sight of the fort.*

By the next year, circumstances of the war had caused a change in objectives and the use to which the Western troops could be put, and the plans to assault Detroit or the Sandusky towns were abandoned. The Fort was finally evacuated on August 2, 1779.

Novembr 4th 1778   Brigadier General Lachlan M[c]Intosh with the Body of his Army marched from Fort M[c]Intosh at 4°Clock in the afternoon and arrived at Camp [   ] N°1 distant from Fort M Intosh Six miles three Quarters and eight perches—this camp is Situate on A small branch of big Beaver Creek running nearly north. on our march this day we crossed no water only a small [spring] run that empties into the Ohio a little below the Fort. The land in general of good quality and well Timbered.

5th The march of the army was detained until Twelve O Clock occasioned by the Negligence of the Centinels in suffering a number of horses and Cattle to pass the lines . . . Arrived at Camp difficulty N°2 later in the evening. this camp is Situate on a small Branch of little beaver creek running S. W. a beautifil Plain and not [an] improper place to erect a Block house. distant from Camp N°1 Six Miles three quarters and forty perches. from Fort M'Intosh thirteen miles and a half and forty Eight Perches ————

6th The Army marched about twelve O Clock and descended a steep hill and Crossed little Beaver Creek which is about four perches wide ———— The Situation of this place renders the passage of an Army difficult as well as dangerous ———— as the Army ascended the hill on the other side an Alarm happened owing to some of the Militia Imprudently fireing at Deer, the Army Arrived at Camp N°3 with an hour of up Sum this is called Camp Pleasent. situate on a

small branch Branch (sic) of little Beaver Creek the lines commanding all the hills around the camp a fine day and the night warm for the season ————

7th The [Army] detained as usual by the horses and Cattle squandring out of the lines until the day was far spent ———— About one mile from Camp on their march Cap[t] Steel of the Thirteenth Virginia Regiment who had Advanced somewhat in the front of the Army was alarmed by the fireing of Two Guns in his front and Advanceing forwards found A Soldier Viz- Ross of said Regiment ———— killed and Scalped by the Indians ————. the Army proceeded on to the Second fork of little Beaver running nearly South about four perches wide Advancing forwards about a mile further found Lieu[t] Parks killed and Scalped likewise. they having both gone out to hunt in opposition to General orders fell a dishonorable and in Some measure unlamented prey to the Enemy The Army Proceeding arriv.d at Camp N°4 an hour by sun in the evening ———— this camp is likewise Situate on a small Branch of little Beaver running S. E. this is call.d Camp cruelty taken from the Instances of cruelty Aforementiond Distant from the former Camp five miles One Quarter and Sixty Eight Perches. from Fort M Intosh Twenty three miles three Quarters and twelve perches

8th The army marched at the usual hour and Arrived at Camp N°5 by an hour of Sun called Camp Beaver ———— This is Situate on the Third Branch of little Beaver On Arising Ground

A proper Situation for a Block house. this day we marched over Shruby Ridges with intervening flats of good White Oak land and Small Rivulets. the Bottoms brushy And and Grassy and in this place Very extensive. on this days march we passed the forks of the road. The left Fork leading to New-comerstown At said forks Are many Trees marked to us unintelligebly —————

9th The army marched by the midle of the day up the Creek About Two miles and crossed at a Good ford ————— Passed over dry Ridges & arrived at Camp N°6 called brushy camp Distant from Camp Beaver Six miles and One Chain. this Camp is Situate on A branch of little Beaver that Runs S E and falls into the Other a little below the ford. which Affords a large Bottom of Good land but somewhat Cold and Swampy. Arising hill on front and Rear —————

10th The army marched about 12 O Clock chiefly through barren dry Ridges untill we Arrived at Camp N 7 alias Smoaky Camp Situate on a small Branch of Sandy Creek a little to the right of the path leading to Tuskarawas Distant from the former 6 miles and Three Quarters and Ten Chains. from Fort M Intosh Forty Miles three Quarters and ten Chains. the latter part of the day proved bad. the Night also and Continued

11th The General thought proper to continue the Army and Ordered out a party from each line to Reconnoiter with permission to hunt under certain Regulations. Amongst which report was to be made to the General of Discoveries. &c this morning — Lieu^t Coll° Bowyers Arived from Fort M'Intosh with Sixty Nine men a small Brigade of Pack-horses And some Stragling Bullocks —————

12th The army Marched from Smoaky Camp about 12°Clock several Barren ridges That divide the waters of little Beaver from those of Sandy Creek spent the day. and Oblig.d us to pitch at N°8 which is called cam[p] delight distant from Smoaky Camp Seven Miles and Forty two perches. Situate on a large Bottom on the Bank of Sandy Creek a main branch of Miskingdom ————— On our march this day we passed a large Spring on the Road side where there was a tree marked with a war Pole two Scalps and the

Resemblance of a moonack or Ground hog denoteing the Wyandot Tribe supposed to have been the Same party who had killed Lieu^t Parks and Ross a fiew Days before —————

13th The Army march.d about 1°Clock passed A large plain About A mile in length and half a mile in Breadth. cross.d A branch of Sandy creek About a perch wide ————— Running nearly S. E. and falling into the main creek About Thirty perches below where the army crossed it. the day continued Cloudy and About Sun set began to Snow. the Army Encamped in their usual Form including the mouth of the aforemention'd Creek and Extending up the Bottom. this place is well Situate for A Block house Afording A beautiful Prospect and Abounding in pasture ————— distant from the Former Two miles and One Quarter and Sixty Eight Perches and from Fort M Intosh 50 miles One fourth and Forty Perches —————

14th It continued to Snow which Occasioned the Army to Remain that day. About 12°Clock two delawar runners came to camp and Informed the Gemeral that the Delawar warriors were on there way to Join our Army and that they Designed to stay at Tuskarawas untill they got there And likewise Declared that the Indians who had Killed Lieu^t Parks and Ross had Came the Sandusky path for they had not Seen or heard of them traveling through their Neighbourhood —————

15th The army marched by 2°Clock and Arrived at Camp N°10th by Sun sett. this camp is Situate on a small Branch of Sandy Creek Six miles and Six perches distant from the Former & Distant from Fort M'Intosh Sixteen miles one Quarter and Forty Six Perches on this days march we Passed Two Extensive plains. the first of which is One mile Three Quarters and Seventy Perches in length and three Quarters of A mile in Breadth near the lower end of which is a little rising on which being posted you had A View of the whole Army in their Order of marching. 120 Perches from thence there beginneth Another one mile and 24 Perches in length and little inferior to the other in Breadth each Yielding a beautiful Prospect —————

16th The army march.d About 10ºClock and arrived at Camp Nº11 by an hour and an half of up Sun. distant from the Former Six miles and 42 Perches. from Fort M'Intosh Sixty Two miles an half and Eight perches. Situate on the east Branch of a Creek call.d [ ] creek About an half mile Above the mouth a fording. a beautiful prospect and a very good Situation for defence being Sarounded with plains descending from the Encampment on either Side

17th Continued to Rain which confined the Army to their Tents and prevented marching ————

18th The Army march.d about twelve OClock and Arriv.d at the banks of Tuskarawas by two hours of up Sun. as soon as Our Stock and Baggage had passed the River the Army was form^d in their usual Order of marching and continued passing through an Extensive plain into a Scattering wood where Ordred to halt for the Reception of the Indians &c who were fully apprised of Our Coming and held themselves in Readiness to receive us in great taste. they Formed themselves with great regularity. And when Our front Advanced near theirs they began the Salute with Three Indian Cheirs. from thence A Regular fire which was Returned By A hasty Running Fire round Our whole lines which being done we Encamped round our Brethren and Included the place where Colº Boqueat had Formerly erected a Block house ————19th Nothing material. Other than Employing Fatigues and Artificers to carry on the work of the Fort ————

20th The Indians made A present to the General of A Quantity of Venison And Skins. and Expressed their great Grief for the loss of White Eyes their Chief but assurd the General there was Yet many Among them that Would render him as much Service as White Eyes Could Do was he then Alive. And keep the Chain as Bright. they likewise Insisted much on the Generals going down to their Town to Build A fort for their Defence And Safety ————

Source: McCready, "A Revolutionary Journal...", pp. 11–17

Indian War Parties

On drawing near to an enemy's country, they endeavour as much as possible to conceal their tracks; sometimes they scatter themselves, marching at proper distances from each other for a whole day and more, meeting, however, again at night, when they keep a watch; at other times they march in what is called *Indian file,* one man behind the other, treading carefully in each other's steps, so that their number may not be ascertained by the prints of their feet. The nearer they suppose themselves to be to the enemy, the more attentive they are to choosing hard, stony, and rocky ground, on which human footsteps leave no impression; soft, marshy and grassy soils are particularly avoided, as in the former the prints of the feet would be easily discovered, and in the latter the appearance of the grass having been trodden upon might lead to detection; for if the grass or weeds are only bent, and have the least mark of having been walked upon, it will be almost certainly perceived, in which the sharpness and quickness of the Indians' sight is truly astonishing.

Source: Heckewelder's *History...,* p. 177

James Thacher
1779

While not a journal of events in the Tuscarawas Valley, the following is nevertheless included in this book since it is the only contemporary description, that I am aware of, of the personal appearance of six of the Delaware chiefs, including their principal chief at that time, Gelelemend or Killbuck.

In the spring of 1779, several Indian chiefs had gone to Philadelphia to meet with the Continental Congress. While there, on May 14th, General Washington held a review of a portion of his army for their benefit, and the description of these chiefs was written by Dr. James Thacher, a surgeon with Washington's army. While it is rather unflattering to the Indians, nevertheless it is presumably an accurate description of their personal appearance as viewed from the perspective of someone who was probably not accustomed to seeing Indians at all.

{Middle Brook, New Jersey} May 14, 1779. Our brigade was paraded for the purpose of being reviewed by General Washington and a number of Indian chiefs. His excellency, with his usual dignity, followed by his mulatto servant Bill, riding a beautiful gray steed, passed in front of the line, and received the salute. He was accompanied by a singular group of savages, whose appearance was beyond description ludicrous. Their horses were of the meanest kind, some of them destitute of saddles, and old lines were used for bridles. Their personal decorations were equally farcical, having their faces painted of various colors, jewels suspended from their ears and nose, their heads without covering, except tufts of hair on the crown, and some of them wore dirty blankets over their shoulders waving in the wind. In short, they exhibited a novel and truly disgusting spectacle. But his excellency deems it good policy to pay some attention to this tribe of the wilderness, and to convince them of the strength and discipline of our army, that they may be encouraged, if disposed to be friendly, or deterred from aggression if they should become hostile to our country.

Source: Thacher, *Military Journal of the American Revolution*, p. 163

{**Note**: In *Letters of Delegates*, Vol. 12, page 536, it appears that the names of the Indians were as follows:

Gelelemend
Welepachtschiechen (Captain Johnny)
Peykeling, a councilor

Tetepachksit, a councilor
John Lewis
John Thompson}

Colonel Daniel Brodhead
1781

By 1781, the Delawares at Coshocton had come into the war on the side of the British. (Some who did not side with the British had settled at Newcomerstown.)

At Pittsburgh a military expedition was organized to proceed to Coshocton and destroy the town. They did this and then returned to Fort Pitt. The following is Colonel Brodhead's report of the expedition. The fifteen Indians that he says were killed were apparently executed after they had been captured. (The letter of Simon Girty following this account would seem to bear this out, for Brodhead attempts to blame the militia for the killing of the Indians.) The town he calls Indaochaie was actually Lichtenau, just below Coshocton, on the site of the earlier Mowheysinck. (Either he misspelled it, or a later scribe misread his handwriting.) The Christian Indians had abandoned Lichtenau the year before, moving to Salem, and some Delawares now occupied the site.

COLONEL BRODHEAD'S REPORT OF THE EXPEDITION TO PRESIDENT REED OF THE EXECUTIVE COUNCIL OF PENNSYLVANIA

"Philadelphia, May 22d, 1781."

"Sir: In the last letter I had the honor to address to your Excellency, I mentioned my intention to carry an expedition against the revolted Delaware towns. I have now the pleasure to inform you, that with about three hundred men (nearly half the number volunteers from the country), I surprised the towns of Cooshasking and Indaochaie, killed fifteen warriors and took upwards of twenty old men, women and children. About four miles above the town, I detached a party to cross the river Muskingum and destroy a party of about forty warriors, who had just before (as I learned by an Indian whom the advance guard took prisoner), crossed over with some prisoners and scalps, and were drunk, but excessive hard rains having

swelled the river bank high it was found impracticable. After destroying the towns, with great quantities of poultry and other stores, and killing about forty head of cattle, I marched up the river, about seven miles, with a view to send for some craft from the Moravian towns, and cross the river to pursue the Indians; but when I proposed my plan to the volunteers, I found they conceived they had done enough, and were determined to return, wherefore I marched to Newcomerstown, where a few Indians, who remain in our interest, had withdrawn themselves, not exceeding thirty men. The troops experienced great kindness from the Moravian Indians and those at Newcomerstown, and obtained a sufficient supply of meat and corn to subsist the men and horses to the Ohio river. Captain Killbuck and Captain Luzerne, upon hearing of our troops being on the Muskingum, immediately pursued the warriors, killed one of their greatest villains and brought his scalp to me. The plunder brought in by the troops, sold for about eighty pounds at Fort Henry. I had

197

upon this expedition Captain Mantour and Wilson and three other faithful Indians who contributed greatly to the success.

The troops behaved with great spirit and although there was considerable firing between them and the Indians I had not a man killed or wounded, and only one horse shot.

I have the honor to be, with great respect and attachment, your Excellency's most obedient most humble servant."

"Daniel Brodhead"

Source: *Pennsylvania Archives,* First Series, Vol. IX, pp. 161–62

Salem Diary – Brodhead Entries

{April} 19ᵗʰ {1781}. – This afternoon we had word that Col. Brodhead with his army was seen at White Eyes Town (ten miles from here) and was marching right to Goschachking. This put us in a great predicament because of the Brothers & Sisters we believed to be in the village. Before evening we had some refugees here, who had been captured by the army but immediately set free.

20ᵗʰ. – Early had this word: The army that had encircled the two towns, Goschachking and Lichtenau unnoticed the evening before had taken everyone prisoner among them our Brethren and Sisters. Some who roamed around wanted us to believe that all Indians found in the two towns had been killed.

21ˢᵗ. – Early in the morning through a courier I received a friendly letter from Col. Brodhead, wherein he invited me to his campsite. I went then that evening along with the Brethren Jung and Shabosch to his camp four miles from here. He was very friendly and spoke much with me regarding the safety of our congregation.

22ᵈ. – Went with Brother Sensemann and others to the camp where we were asked to come again. Col. Brodhead declared himself favorably for our sakes. The military colonels, yes, all officers were friendly and look upon our Indians with amazement. Since we, through Christian and his wife (who to our great joy returned safely yesterday) had the message that a military party after gaining their freedom in Lichtenau, stole away and shot at them wounding our Samuel in the leg, so immediately we sent some Brethren to find them. I complained about this incident to the Colonel and the other officers, who expressed great dissatisfaction and regret over it. This evening Joseph came safely and unharmed just after those were fired on....

23ᵈ. – ...The army left early for Pittsburgh which made us all happy.

British Version of Brodhead's Expedition

"We sent to Coshocton twenty of our men [Wyandots] some time ago, and this day they have returned with the following news:"

"20th April. Colonel Brodhead, with five hundred men, burned the town and killed fifteen men. He left six houses on this [west] side of the creek that he did not see. He likewise took the women and children prisoners, and afterward let them go. He let four men [Delawares] go that were prisoners who showed him a paper that they had from Congress. Brodhead told them that it was none of his fault that their people [the Delawares slain] were killed, but the fault of the militia that would not be under his command....The Christian ["Moravian"] Indians have applied to us to move them off before the rebels come to their town...."

Source: Letter of Simon Girty to Maj. DePeyster, commandant at Detroit, dated May 4, 1781, set forth in Butterfield, *History of the Girty's,* p. 128

David Zeisberger
1781

After nine years in the Tuscarawas Valley, the end came swiftly for the Moravian mission towns.

Suspected by the British of helping the Americans, distrusted by the frontiersmen because they were Indians, and located as they were between the contending parties, the Christian Indians were, quite literally, caught between two fires.

Finally, in August of 1781, a few British and about 300 of their Indian allies, "with British colours flying", came to the mission towns and forcibly caused them to be taken to the Upper Sandusky area, into what the Moravians referred to as "captivity".

The following is David Zeisberger's account of their removal.

Somewhere about August 13th, we heard that a strong party of warriors was on the march for our towns, on which account also we could not have the Lord's Supper, although we had prepared ourselves therefor, for on their account we could no longer be easy, they having already begun to assemble in Salem and Gnadenhütten. Up to the 16th and 17th about 300 warriors had assembled. Their chief men were, first, an English captain (Elliot), with several others, among whom were also Frenchmen, the Wyandot Half-King (Pomoacan), from Sandusky, with his warriors, Pipe, with the Delawares, some Shawanese, Chippewas, and Tawas. The Half-King, in his usual pretended friendly way, sent out messengers announcing his approach, and let it be told our Indians they should not be afraid, not the least harm would happen to them, for on this account was he himself come to protect us, so that no one should do us wrong; that he had something to say to us, and we should therefore let him know at which of our three places this should occur. Since Salem was but a new place,

and they could not support the warriors from want of corn, Gnadenhütten was appointed for them, for we could come also from Schönbrunn to the help of our brethren, so that it might not go too hard with them. We thought also that they would not remain long with us, for the whites who were with them, informed us that they had a great undertaking in hand, either against Wilunk (Wheeling), McIntosh (Beaver, Pa.), or Pittsburg, or against all three places, but they said this only to make us easy. We entertained the Eng. captain and his company the best we could and showed them all kindness so far as lay in our power; they likewise behaved in a friendly way toward us, but had secret guile and we could trust them not in the least.

Aug. 20. After the warriors had taken quarters, and at the west end of Gnadenhütten had put huts and tents, Pomoacan, the Wyandot Half-King, spoke to us and to our Indians as follows: My cousins, ye believing Indians, in Gnadenhütten, Schönbrunn, and Salem, I am no little troubled about you, for I see you live in a dangerous place.   Two powerful and mighty spirits or gods are standing and opening wide their jaws toward each other to swallow, and between the two angry spirits, who thus open their jaws, are you placed; you are in danger, from one or from the other, or even from both of being bruised and mangled by their teeth; therefore it is not advisable for you to remain here longer, but bethink you to keep alive your wives, and children and young people, for here must you all die.   Therefore I take you by the hand, raise you up and settle you there where I dwell, or at least near by me, where you will be safe and will live in quiet.   Make not here your plantations and settlements, but arise and come with me, take with you also your teachers, and hold there, wither you shall come, your worship of God forever, as has been your wont.   You will at once find food there, and will suffer no want, for on this account am I come to say this to you, and to bring you to safety [whereupon he gave a string of wampum].   The Scripture-verse of the day read; Take counsel together, and it shall come to nought; speak the word, and it shall not stand: for God is with us; for here is Immanuel.

Is God for me, what is it — That man can do for me?

This word of the Lord gave us consolation and hope that all would go well.   Brs. David (Zeisberger) and Heckewelder had come together from their respective stations to Gnadenhütten, where we with the national assistants considered about this, and on the 21st answered the Half-King, as follows:

"Uncle, and you, Captains of the Delawares and Monseys, who are our friends and one nation with us, we have heard your words in which you say to us that we are placed between two evil, mighty spirits who open their jaws toward each other, and you admonish us that we should think of our young and old people, our wives and children, seek to keep them alive, and about them we are most concerned.   Your words and exhortations are therefore pleasant for us to hear, and we wish to do as you have pointed out to us, bear the same in mind, and consider them, and we wish, Uncle even before next spring to send you an answer, thereupon can you depend."

We gave this answer without a string of wampum, since this should follow after a time, and it appeared to us as if the Half-King were

content therewith: we believed also that he would have been satisfied with it, had not the English captain concealed himself behind Pipe and other Delawares, and urged them on to excite Pomoacan to carry on the matter farther with us.   Then we soon heard that our given answer was not satisfactory to them.   On the 25th again, Pomoacan made an address to our Indian brethren in Gnadenhütten that our answer was not yet enough, we had appointed too remote a time, and he wished to have something in his hands to show the nations from whom we had orders about this, that he had really made negotiations with us.   Br. David went therefore again to Gnadenhütten, and, Aug. 27 [when the beautiful fitting Scripture-verse was: Thou shalt know that I am the Lord: for they shall not be ashamed that wait for me. My times are in thy hand — I'll always trust in thee], we gave to them through a string of wampum the following answer, and said to them that it was impossible for us to do for them what they required.   We could not by any means bring our wives and children into such need that they must suffer hunger and perish, while hitherto they had had plenty, and in nothing felt any want. We bade them leave us time enough to harvest our fields, so that we, with our wives and children, might have something to live on; for we saw that we put ourselves in extreme need and misery, if so blindly, without consideration, we went away from our towns where we had enough to live upon, into the bush, where there was nothing to be found; they should at least leave us time enough to prepare for our departure.   The Half-King seemed to be well content with the answer, for he said he had now in his hands something from us, namely a string of wampum, which he could show to the nations, and by which they could see that we were willing to gratify their wishes.   Thus the matter passed by, and we hoped always that the Saviour would bring about our release.   We prayed earnestly day and night to him that he would help us also out of this need, and not suffer that his Indian church should come to harm and be dispersed, since once they had tasted of his blood.   Opinions and thoughts over the matter among our Indian brethren were also various, as likewise among the assistants.   Sone thought we should at once arise and go with the warriors without considering the results therefrom. On the contrary, others were against this, and said they would rather die on the spot, for in the bush must they all perish. It was impossible to convince all of the propriety of what we held it best to do. Herein, also, we had ourselves taught by the Saviour what we should do, [by means of the Lot] and he let us know that we should do nothing farther than we had done, and that the answer we had given was enough. We wished to do nothing to the harm of our churches in the land. We were also unwilling to take upon our necks the charge of having brought our Indian Brethren into such need as they afterward felt, since they could have reproached us with being guilty therein because we had acceded thereto. We wished rather it come to the worst, so that we might be without fault. Meanwhile, the daily services were held, and we ceased not to exhort the brethren, to encourage them, to comfort them, and to point out to them the Saviour. Among other things, especially were they reminded that the Saviour had intrusted to them his word of atonement, which they should look upon as a great treasure, and which should be their daily food. If they became indifferent thereto, and should be disobedient to God's word, he would again take it away from them. In Gnadenhütten there were many disorders among our people; not only of late, but already for some time, many had begun to take up again the old heathenish customs and usages, and when they were reminded of this and talked to, not only did they not suffer this, but they waxed wicked and stubborn, and especially by these circumstances bad people made the occasion useful, since the town was full of warriors and rough, wild men, who became the worse the longer they were there, who at first indeed were quiet and modest, but afterward began to dance, to play, and to carry out their own devices. Yes, it went so far that some wicked people spoke and gave us to understand that while there was now war, they could prescribe us rules, and that our remaining and our getting through, in short, our life and maintenance, depended upon them, and that we had reason to be silent, and they would let us do only what they wished. In Schönbrunn and Salem the brethren were reasonably quiet, and if warriors visited them now and then, yet there was little disturbance. From both places we had

to give them provisions, slaughter swine and cattle for them, so long as they were there, and this we did still cheerfully, if only they had left us longer in peace. Meanwhile, parties of warriors made excursions, and they brought some captives to Gnadenhütten, and the place became a theatre of war. [Elliott's camp displayed the English flag, which at last the Wyandots took possession of, and it was then thrown into the fire.] In this matter they were themselves not without fear of being fallen upon, and upon every side they sent out spies.

Aug. 30. Sister Anna Sensemann was delivered of a son, who was baptized into Jesus' death in Schönbrunn, Sept. 1st, by the name, Christian David. Eight days before she had been brought here from Gnadenhütten, since there, on account of the warriors, who committed many excesses, it was very unquiet, and here it was yet tolerable, for the warriors came here in no great number. Meanwhile, we well saw that our hard circumstances were not over; we had tokens enough that the worst was still before us. We could do nothing, however, but give ourselves up to the will of the Saviour as he should find it good and permit. We might think, as we would, upon ways and means to escape our calamity; on every side we were fastened in, and there was no outcome to be seen. We had indeed reason to believe that the Half-King and the captains had already as good as given up their purpose to use force against us; it was said even that they would withdraw and give us time first to harvest our fields so that we could prepare for our departure. But the English, who were with them, left nothing undone to excite the captains and warriors, and to spur them on to drive us out by force. In addition, the warriors found out that our Indians were not of one mind, for had they been so, had they held together, and sustained one another, the warriors would have accomplished nothing; but there were faithless, wretched men among us, who gave them information, and proposed schemes to them for reaching their ends. They gave them plainly to understand, that if they would only take us white brethren prisoners away with them, then the Indians would all follow them. To our pain and mortification, we had to hear and see this on the part of our own people, and be silent about it, at least, for the time. We had also to see harlotry openly carried on, and could not prevent it. Since we afterward found out everything in detail, I will here introduce what we learned from trustworthy sources. The captains had a plan to kill us whites, and when this was not thought enough, to kill the assistants also. [Here ends this note abruptly, but the Bethlehem manuscript says that the warriors imparted their plan to a leading chief, who advised them against it, seeing therein no advantage for them. They then held another council, with the same result; but there the chief spoke more plainly, threatening vengeance if the missionaries were harmed, and thus their schemes came to naught.]

Sept. 1. We had a message that all the white brethren from Schönbrunn and Salem, with the assistants, should come to Gnadenhütten. Br. David, with some helpers, went there from the first place, but left Br. Jungmann with the other two brethren there, and Br. Heckewelder came from Salem, where he left his wife and Br. Mich. Jung. We soon heard here all sorts of rumors of what awaited us, for there were among the warriors some people who rather wished us well than ill, and who said to us what they heard. Thus we awaited our fate in great perplexity and tribulation until, Sept. 3d, it came to an outbreak. The warrior folk became steadily more wanton, and gave free play to their wildness. We felt the power of darkness, as if the air were filled with evil spirits. When they first came here they were starving, and were glad to get something to eat, and herein we let them suffer no want. After they were sated and become wanton, each one acted after the bent of his own wildness. They shot dead our cattle and swine, although we refused them nothing, and if they demanded swine or cattle for slaughter, gave them. This they did not only from hunger, but from caprice, for they left the swine lying dead round about in such numbers that the place stunk with them; still the daily services were held as usually.

On the above-named day, Sept. 3d, the Half-King and the warrior captains again beset us, among whom the Delawares made themselves the most forward, and urged upon us we should once more plainly declare ourselves, whether we would give in to their wish and at once go with them or not. We answered them briefly that we stood by what we had already answered them,

and we could give them no other answer. Then we heard a murmur among our Indians that they had heard we white brethren should be taken captive, but in all this we were quite comforted, though we could not say in contradiction it might not happen. In the afternoon we went together a little back of the town, where a Monsey captain spoke with Br. David, and asked him whether he had heard what he had said in Schönbrunn to Br. Luke, and what Br. David thought about it, for he would like to know at once his opinion about it. This captain had already some days before in Schönbrunn said to Luke, since probably he knew what was going on, that the Monsey nation had adopted Br. David, and looked upon him as their own flesh and blood, he knew that this was accomplished in his nation. If Br. David would accede to this and appeal to it, he would bring it about that no one should lay hand upon him; they, the Monseys, wished to own him as one of their nation, but he would have to go with them where they dwelt. This was also well considered, for thus they thought to get our Monsey brethren, who were the greater part.

The Monsey captain probably meant well; his people, the warriors, had also before all others shown themselves good to us, and had done us no harm; they often showed their discontent with the conduct of the Wyandots towards us, and said they had experience how they had done with them, and so would they do with us if we went with them. But Br. David had purposely taken little notice of the proposition, for he saw that it only had to do with his own person, and perhaps with Br. Jungmann, who lived with him, but that the other brethren in Gnadenhütten and Salem would be shut out; therefore he gave no positive answer, but did not altogether decline the proposition, and would have been glad of further information about it.

But while he was still speaking with him, there came three Wyandots to us, laid hands on Brs. David, Heckewelder, and Sensemann, led them away captive, and brought them first to the Delaware camp, and yelled out over us the Death Hallow. They stripped us and took away all our clothes, hastily loaded their guns, for in all this they were not without fear they would find opposition on the part of our Indians. While this was going on, the whole swarm of the other warriors rushed into the Brothers' house and plundered it, each man taking what he could lay hands on and snatching it away. Some of our young men had stationed themselves in front of the house-door with tomahawks, and would not let them in, but they had to give way to the stronger party.

They showed no desire to touch Br. Edwards, who was in the house, for they were too much set on plundering, and each wished to have the most booty. Finally he went out to the house and to Br. John Martin, where an Englishman met him and brought him into camp to us, where he saw we were all yet living, for as they were bringing us into camp, he heard several muskets fired one after the other, from which he concluded that already we were all dead, and so it would have happened, for they had it in mind, as we afterwards heard, unless a higher hand had ruled over us. The Delaware chiefs and captains, while this was going on, had drawn aside, probably from fear it might not come out well: but they were the same who had allowed themselves to be used to take us prisoners, for the Wyandots would not have dared to do it. Our Scripture-verse was wonderful, it read: Though thou wast angry with me, thine anger is turned away and thou comfortedst me; and the day after it was: God will come and save you.

After they had stripped us we were brought into the Englishman's tent, who, indeed, as he gave out, wished to show us compassion, and said it had not been intended that we should be thus treated, although there were express orders from the commandant in Detroit to bring us away by force, could it not be done by gentler means. And this was the first mention that they relied upon the governor in Detroit, hitherto they had not said so, and yet they had no such orders. But we well knew that he was the originator and prime mover of the whole business. He brought it about, however, with the Indians, that they gave us back some old clothes, so that we were not quite naked, and Br. David got an old night-gown to put on, which had belonged to Sister Sensemann; after this we were brought into the huts of the Wyandots for safekeeping, but we were not put in bonds, as were the other captives. We had now neither blanket nor any thing else to lie upon save the bare ground, unless our Indian brethren had lent us some blankets.

After this one party of warriors went to Salem, another to Schönbrunn. To the first place went thirty warriors; they arrived there in the night, took prisoners Br. Michael Jung and Br. Heckewelder and his wife with her child, led them out of the house and placed them in the street: they plundered the house, took away with them every thing they fancied, likewise also Br. Michael Jung, and came early in the night to Gnadenhütten crying the Death Hallow. Sister Heckewelder, however, with her child, got leave to remain till the next day, whom the Indian brethren then brought in. In Schönbrunn, to which place only two Wyandots with a couple of women came, they took prisoners Br. Jungmann and Sisters Susanna (Zeisberger) and Sensemann: then they said many warriors would come afterward and undo them; that they should put themselves in their hands, so that they might remain alive, they would bring them to Gnadenhütten with all their things, which they would pack up, and all of which they would give back to them. The sisters helped them pack until they saw that the beds were cut open and the feathers thrown about the street, and found themselves deceived in their intentions, just as had also happened in Gnadenhütten and Salem. But some Indian brethren, as well in Salem as here, who were more kindly disposed, took away secretly from the hands of the warriors some of our things and gave them to us afterward, so that we again got some little.

The Indian brethren stood quite amazed, wept aloud, and knew not what to do; some wished to make defense, others deemed this inadvisable and prevented them. They plundered not only our things, but also what belonged to the church, as for instance, the love-feast and the communion utensils were all taken away, and they brought the brethren together with their plunder in a canoe to Gnadenhütten. Sister Anna Sensemann, who had been delivered of a child only three days before, had to go by night and in the mist, so that it would have been no wonder had mother and child perished, but the Saviour, to whom all is possible, let not the least harm happen either to her or to her child.

They were brought into Gnadenhütten early before daylight, likewise with the Death Hallow. From our camp we saw their reception, and how we felt thereby can not be described. But when it became day we got leave to see them, and then we bade one another welcome in our captivity, and comforted one another, and each party had hearty compassion upon the other. What in these sad circumstances was comforting to us and cheered us up, was the fact that the sisters were so resigned and cheerful and bore all with patience. Br. Jungmann and the sisters were set free when it was day, but remained awhile by Br. Schebosh and his wife, for in the brethren's house every thing was wasted and scattered, and there we visited them also often and they us. We saw the warriors going about in our clothes and making a display, while we had nothing upon our bodies, except perhaps some old rags, and though we were again and again promised we should have some of our clothes again, yet this did not happen, for those who had them were unwilling to give them up.

Our Indian brethren who came to visit us in camp bought some trifles from the warriors, and gave them to us again. Out of our own linen, of which they had been robbed, the sisters had to make shirts for them. Also we had nothing to eat except what our Indian brethren and the warriors gave us. Among these there were many not at all content with our treatment, in particular among the Delawares and Monseys, and they said that certainly they never would have gone upon this expedition, had they known it was aimed at us. Many of them came immediately after we were taken prisoners and gave us their hands and showed their compassion. After the five brethren, David, Edwards, Heckewelder, Sensemann. amd Michael Jung had been captives three days in the Wyandot camp, and the captains saw very well that so long as they held us fast, nothing would be done about our departure, and if they wished to have all our Indians with them, they must first let us go, they let us go, and this happened Sept. 6th. Before this, however, a singular thing occurred the second day after we were made captive. An Indian woman, who had come with the warriors, and had nothing further to do with us, had seen with the others how we fared, and said to an Indian sister she could not forget how we had been handled; she could not sleep the whole night on this account, and this gave her much to think about. She took Capt. Pipe's horse, the best in the whole company, and hurried away to

Pittsburg. This was straightway made known, and she was followed and overtaken, but she got away again and brought news of our captivity to the Fort. The warriors were angry at this, and laid the blame upon us and our Indians, and gave out we had sent letters by her to the Fort, and called upon the Americans to free us from their hands, and since this woman was a friend of our Isaac Glikkikan, to whom besides they were very hostile, they seized the occasion to wreak their vengeance on him, saying he had sent her. On this account they sent a war party to Salem, brought him bound to Gnadenhütten, yelled out over him the Death Hallow, and there was great uproar among the warriors, and it was a common saying among them that he ought to be tomahawked. The Delawares, who were the movers of this, would have struck him dead if the Half-King had not interfered and warded them off. They examined him, beset him with many reproaches and threats, but then let him go. It is worthy of note that this Indian brother, who formerly had been a captain of warriors and counsellor of chiefs and a very prominent man among the Indians, as soon as he came to the Lord, had to suffer ignominy and persecutions almost to the end for the Saviour's sake.

After they had again set us free, that we might be among our Indian brethren, they, at the same time, ordered us to encourage our Indian brethren to make ready for departure, and promised us also that upon the journey we should always be with our Indian brethren, and that they, the warriors, would always encamp behind us, in order that, if we were attacked, they might fight for us. The first was agreeable to us for this reason, that the warriors might not overpower our sisters and separate us from them, which we had reason enough to fear.

It is also to be observed that the Half-King, as soon as he came, made quite another speech than he had made to us at Lichtenau, in August, 1777, when he established with us, as it were, a bond of friendship, and had declared us, white brethren, his fathers, of which he now made no mention, but named us cousins, and our Indian brethren likewise. We made ready for departure, ordering our Indian brethren from Schönbrunn to come hither. Thus, on the 8th we made a beginning, and we white brethren went by water, and in the evening got to Salem, where we waited two days for our brethren until they all followed, and since we could be alone there and in quiet, we white brethren strengthened ourselves with the body and blood of our Saviour in the holy sacrament, and realized our Scripture-verse of to-day (Is. lxv. 13,14), of which, in our present circumstances, we stood in pressing need. The Saviour comforted us also in our trouble, and let his friendly face shine over us.

On the 9th, the sermon was upon the Scripture-verse of the day, and the little son of Brother Abel and Sister Johanette, born on the 3d Inst., in the night when we were captured, was baptized into the death of Jesus by the name of Jonas. We were thankful to the Saviour, and it did us much good that we could be among our people, for it is a hellish life to be among murderers and robbers, and in their power.

On the 10th, early service was from the Scripture-verse: Behold, the Lord's hand is not shortened, etc. Especially at this time we had beautiful, comforting, and hopeful Scripture-verses, only we wished them to be at once fulfilled; thus we should have been helped at once, yet we must still content ourselves in hope and faith.

Now came also 100 warriors here from Gnadenhütten, and the wild life went on with them as before. Our brethren from Schönbrunn and Salem came together, and encamped by the river. One can easily imagine that all the brethren were bewildered, and, as it were, in a dream, so that they could hardly trust their senses. We knew now that the warriors would not be got rid of until we should be forth with them, and they had left our towns to go to war; there was thus nothing better than to go.

On the 11th, we broke up, and thus turned our backs upon our homesteads and places where we had enjoyed so much that was good and blessed from the hands of the Saviour, and where he had really been among us and with us. Before us we saw indeed nothing wherein to rejoice, yes, we could imagine nothing but need, misery, and danger, and otherwise had we nothing to look forward to. We must possess our souls in patience, and go where certainly we were unwilling to go, for we saw no other result from our actions, but we went towards more misery and hardship; thus also were our Indian brethren minded, but they must go against their

will. Could they have acted according to their inclination, or secretly brought it about, many of them would have got away, and we should have been scattered, but it could not be, for the warriors not only did not let us whites out of their sight, but also not the Indian brethren either, and had such careful oversight of us that none could escape; they dared not remain behind, they must go forth with us. Indeed, many of our Indian brethren, who always had an inclination for the savages, and were of the opinion we should all go off to them, felt now they had nothing good to expect, and began to perceive that they had wished and sought what was bad for themselves, and began now to regret it, but too late.

We came on September 14th, to Goschachgunk (Coshocton), encamping on the Walhonding, from which place we broke up on the 16th, and followed up this creek northwards. Many brethren went by land, others again by water, just as they could get on. It was a good thing for our sisters with the children that they could go by water, for by land it would have been hard indeed for them to travel such a long, bad, unbroken way, for here one must expect no such travelled and good road as to Pittsburg. We continued our services, and had them nearly every evening, even if the brethren could not always come together for night-quarters, and the warriors, who went with us, commonly lay a little distance from us.

The 18th. Since it rained very hard last night, and the creek was swollen, we had to go, huts and all, away from the creek to higher ground, since we were in danger of overflow. Two canoes with their whole lading were swept away by the stream, and the brethren lost all they had, for they sank to the bottom. This concerned us too, for in one of the canoes were many of our things, all of which we lost, and before this not much was left us. A child, two years old that died yesterday, was here buried.

On the 19th, came to us the Half-King with the Wyandots from Salem, where they had passed the time, and not only completed the plundering of our towns, but had also seized upon the things which our brethren had buried or hidden in the woods, as many as they could find.

The same day a war-party came back

from the settlements with two prisoners, from whom we heard that when the news of our being taken captives reached Pittsburg, they wished at first to follow after us and rescue us from the hands of the warriors, but that they afterwards gave this up. This had hitherto been our greatest concern, that if this should happen, we should be placed in the greatest danger, and with our Indian brethren come between two fires, for the first thing would have been to kill us whites. This also the Saviour turned away from us.

On the 20th, a sister was brought to bed with a daughter, and on the 21st was another born. Then a couple of our young people took away from the Wyandots one of our horses, which they had in their hands, together with the saddle. And two of our sisters took away from them a great kettle which they had appropriated and which belonged to us, and gave it to us again.

After we had lain quiet four days, on account of high water, on the 21st we moved on, and encamped on the 22d at the second fork of this creek where is an old Indian town, and a pleasant beautiful country, as indeed all along the creek so far as we have come.

The 23d we lay still. Pomoacan came to us with his council, and told us to hasten on to Sandusky and to leave behind those who could not go forward. Some women were brought in prisoners. The Monseys, who had thus far journeyed with us, left us and went home another way. Their captain spoke with us, and showed his displeasure at the conduct of the Wyandots towards us.

On the 24th we went on both by land and by water. The creek forked here, and our Indians wished to go up the greatest and strongest fork, which would have been easier and better to follow, but the Wyandots would not permit it, and we must go up the other creek, which was hard to follow it was so small.

We passed Memekasink, an old Indian town, and several such places, and they who went by land always took their course as nearly as possible towards those who went by water, so that we might have night-quarters together. Brs. Michael Jung and Edwards, who went by water with the Indians, found wild honey. On the 26th we came to Gokhosing, the last old town on this creek, and here our journeying by water ended, and from there on we had to go by land. We had hard work to come so far with canoes, for very often they had to be dragged over shallow places. Here we stayed till the 28th, until all those came up who were behind. The Wyandots, who always urged us on, had to borrow some horses for us, since we had not enough and our Indian brethren found all theirs needful for their own use. The Delawares left us here also, and went home, as the Shawanese had already done the day before yesterday, and the Wyandots, whose number was now small, remained with us. With these then we set out, and while our Indian brethren were still packing up when we went away, we white brethren were quite alone with the warriors, who drove us on like cattle, without having the least compassion for the children and sisters, for they left them no time to give the children drink once. Besides the way was very bad, for it went through a swamp and many marshes, where at times the horses stuck fast. Susanna (Zeisberger's wife) fell twice in quick succession from her horse, and it was a wonder she got off with little harm. Some Indian brethren hurried after us with all their might, as they could easily conjecture that the Wyandots would hurry us on, heels over head: they overtook us as we were about to get our night-quarters ready, which we should have done near the warriors, had not our brethren come, but now we encamped somewhat away from them.

The 29th. Early before we broke up, several brethren came to us, which gave us joy, and took us again out of the hands of the warriors, and told them, if they were in such haste, they could go their way and would not find it necessary to wait for us. We came at noon of the 30th through the swamp at the head of the Scioto, and into a country altogether different from what we had thus far passed through.

Source: Zeisberger, *Diary of David Zeisberger,* pp. 3–19

Map 11a – Original Survey of 1797 – Junction of the Mohican.

Map 11b – Modern Topographic Map – Junction of the Mohican.

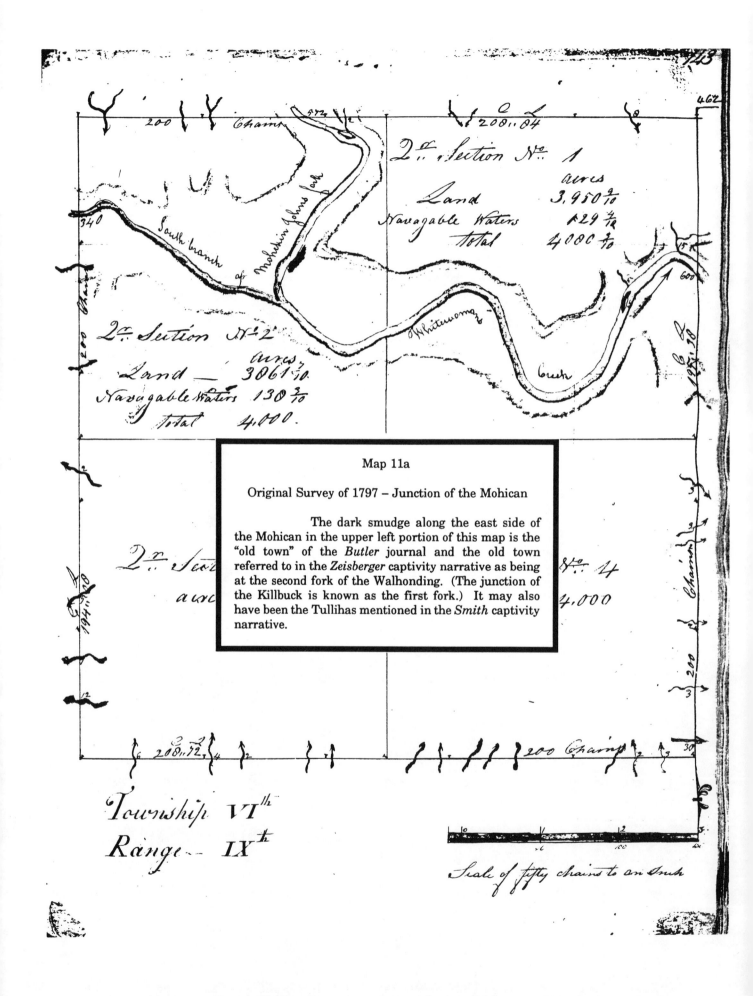

200 Chains

208..04

2ᵈ Section Nᵒ 1

Land   acres   3,950 9/10
Navagable Waters   129 7/12
Total   4000 7/10

340

South branch of Mohikin Johns fork

600

Whitewoman

Creek

2ᵈ Section Nᵒ 2

Land   acres   3061 7/10
Navagable Waters 130 3/10
Total   4,000.

Map 11a

Original Survey of 1797 – Junction of the Mohican

The dark smudge along the east side of the Mohican in the upper left portion of this map is the "old town" of the *Butler* journal and the old town referred to in the *Zeisberger* captivity narrative as being at the second fork of the Walhonding. (The junction of the Killbuck is known as the first fork.) It may also have been the Tullihas mentioned in the *Smith* captivity narrative.

2ʳ Sec...

a cre

8ᵗᵒ 14

4,000

208..72

200 Chains

30

Township VI ᵗʰ
Range IX ᵗʰ

Scale of fifty chains to an Inch

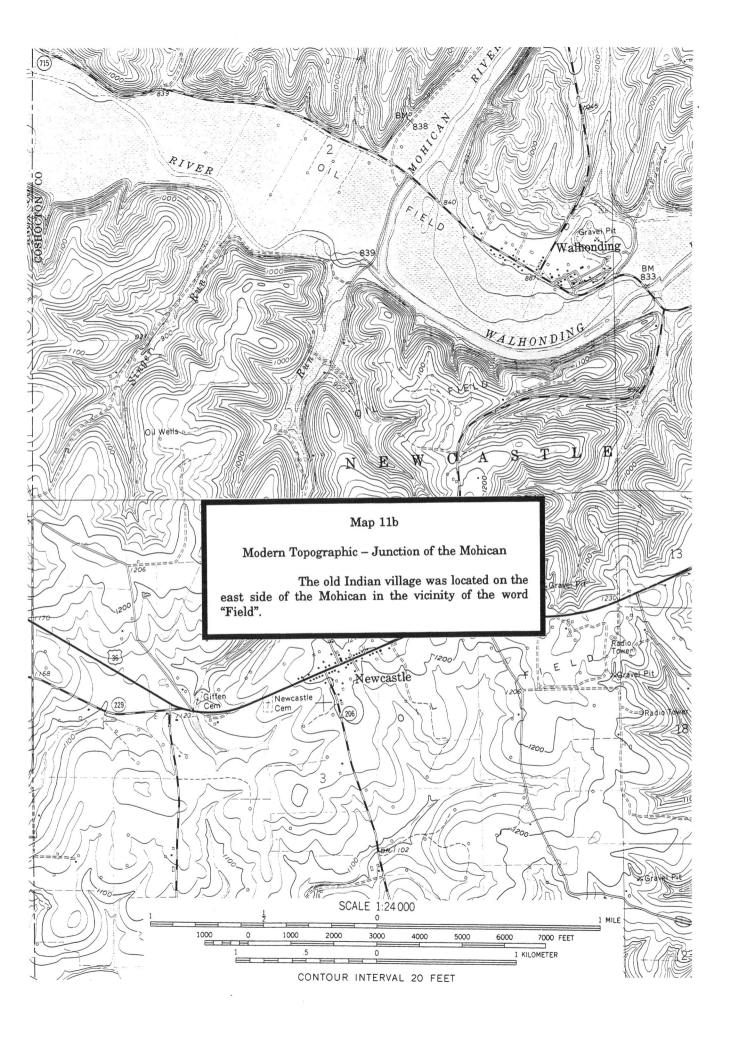

Map 11b

Modern Topographic – Junction of the Mohican

The old Indian village was located on the east side of the Mohican in the vicinity of the word "Field".

SCALE 1:24 000

1 MILE

1000   0   1000   2000   3000   4000   5000   6000   7000 FEET

1   5   0   1 KILOMETER

CONTOUR INTERVAL 20 FEET

On the 11th we broke up, and thus turned our backs upon our homesteads and places where we had enjoyed so much that was good and blessed from the hands of the Saviour, and where he had really been among us and with us.

David Zeisberger   September 11th, 1781

David Zeisberger
1782

The only eyewitnesses to the Gnadenhutten Massacre, from the Indian side, were two boys who survived and got back to the Upper Sandusky area.

It would have been from them, then, that David Zeisberger learned the details of what had happened. The following is taken from his diary written at the time the news was first received by him.

{Lower Sandusky} Thursday, March 14. Very early the Indian, George, came with the frightful news that all our brethren who went to Schönbrunn, Gnadenhütten, and Salem had been captured by the Americans and taken to Pittsburg; the messenger related many unpleasant things that occurred, for example, that they were bound and some killed, but all of this we could not believe. But that our Indian brethren are taken to Pittsburg is the more pleasing to us, were it only all of them there, and had they again a brother with them. We shall be glad to bear our captivity if only our brethren are rescued.

March 23. ...By Joshua and Jacob, Rachel's son, who brought our baggage by water as far as the falls, we have to-day the first trustworthy and very affecting news of the horrible murder, March 7th, of our Indian brethren in Gnadenhütten, and March 8th, of our brethren in Salem.

See our Scripture-verse for March 7th and 8th, which are worthy of note. Our brethren at home numbered 86 missing, but they could not certainly say whether all were killed or some taken prisoners: we hoped the latter, and that

some few, though not the greater part, are yet alive. Our Indian brethren during the whole winter had to make shift to live and suffered great hunger, for among the Wyandots and Delawares, living in this neighborhood, nothing was to be had, for they themselves not only now, but every year, suffer want, for they are lazy and plant little, and although they got some corn from the Shawanese, yet it was not enough. Since now they heard from those who in the autumn had been taken to Pittsburg and had again come back, that in our towns there was corn enough and that they had nothing to fear in going there to get it, they made ready and went away, for they saw nothing else before them if they remained, than that they and their children must starve. We advised them at Christmas and on New Year's day to go there, for as long as the snow remained there was least danger, but they did not go until the snow melted and then it was too late and dangerous: when they were there they used not the least forethought, for they believed themselves quite secure. Instead of hastening to get away again, they stayed several weeks in the towns and fields, having then enough to eat. The most wonderful thing is that while hitherto our Indians had always been careful and distrustful and fearful, and if they thought themselves at all insecure, had fled into the bush, and at least would not pass the night in the towns, now when they really saw danger and the white people before their eyes, they were not at all suspicious and went straight into danger.

The militia, some 200 in number, as we hear, came first to Gnadenhütten. A mile from town they met young Schebosh in the bush, whom they at once killed and scalped, and near by the houses, two friendly Indians, not belonging to us, but who had gone there with our people from Sandusky, among whom there were several other friends who perished likewise. Our Indians were mostly on the plantations and saw the militia come, but no one thought of fleeing, for they suspected no ill. The militia came to them and bade them come into town, telling them no harm should befall them. They trusted and went, but were all bound, the men being put into one house, the women into another. The Mohican, Abraham, who for some time had been bad in heart, when he saw that his end was near, made an open confession before his brethren, and said: "Dear brethren, according to appearances we shall all very soon come to the Saviour, for as it seems they have so resolved about us. You know I am a bad man, that I have much troubled the Saviour and the brethren, and have not behaved as becomes a believer, yet to him I belong, bad as I am; he will forgive us all and not reject me; to the end I shall hold fast to him and not leave him." Then they began to sing hymns and spoke words of encouragement and consolation one to another until they were all slain, and the above mentioned Abraham was the first to be led out, but the others were killed in the house. The sisters also afterwards met the same fate, who also sang hymns together. Christina, the Mohican, who well understood German and English, fell upon her knees before the captain, begging for life, but got for answer that he could not help her. Two well-grown boys, who saw the whole thing and escaped, gave this information. One of these lay under the heaps of slain and was scalped, but finally came to himself and found opportunity to escape — The same did Jacob, who was wonderfully rescued. For they came close upon him suddenly outside the town, so that he thought they must have seen him, but he crept into a thicket and escaped their hands. They knew his horses, which in the

autumn they had seen at his home, and inquired for him, for he was one of those taken prisoners, probably therefore by the very men who were now there. He went a long way about, and observed what went on.

John Martin went at once to Salem when the militia came, and thus knew nothing about how the brethren in Gnadenhütten fared. He told them there, the militia were in Gnadenhütten, whereupon they all resolved not to flee, but John Martin took with himself two brethren and turned back to Gnadenhütten and told them, there were still more Indians in Salem, but he did not know how it had gone with them in Gnadenhütten. A part of the militia went there on the 8th with a couple of Indians, who had come there to Salem and brought the brethren away, after they had first taken away their arms, and when they came to Gnadenhütten, before they led them over the stream, they bound them, took even their knives from them. The brethren and the sisters alike were bound, led into town, and slain. They made our Indians bring all their hidden goods out of the bush, and then they took them away; they had to tell them where in the bush the bees were, help get the honey out; other things also they had to do for them before they were killed. Prisoners said that the militia themselves acknowledged and confessed they had been good Indians. They prayed and sang until the tomahawks struck into their heads. The boy who was scalped and got away, said the blood flowed in streams in the house. They burned the dead bodies, together with the houses, which they set on fire.

In regard to the brethren in Schönbrunn, when we learned we were to be taken to Detroit, we sent at once a messenger to the Muskingum, for a very short time was given us for getting away, that they should come with the horses and help get us to Lower Sandusky. This messenger came to Schönbrunn on the very 7th of March when the militia reached Gnadenhütten and delivered his message. They sent at once the same day a messenger to Gnadenhütten to let them there and in Salem know what was happening here. Before the messenger got quite to Gnadenhütten, he found young Schebosh lying dead by the wayside and scalped, and when he looked about he saw that many white people had gone to Gnadenhütten. He at once turned back to Schönbrunn and brought them this news, whereupon they at once retired. The militia separated the next day, one part going to Salem, the other to Schönbrunn, where, however, they found no one, although our Indians saw them in the town; and of these, six perished who were in Gnadenhütten and Salem, but no one of the others perished, and they all came back to Sandusky after we had already set out. This news sank deep in our hearts, so that these our brethren, who, as martyrs, had all at once gone to the Saviour, were always, day and night, before our eyes, and in our thoughts, and we could not forget them, but this in some measure comforted us, that they had passed to the Saviour's arms and bosom in such resigned disposition of heart, where they will forever rest, protected from the sins and all the wants of the world.

The Wyandot and Delaware warriors, not only while we still lived on the Muskingum, but also now, when pressing hunger drove our Indians there, have always labored to bring upon us the whites, and whenever they came back from murdering they came through our towns, in order that, if they were pursued, the white people might fall upon us, and so they now also did, for as soon as our Indians went there, the warriors went too and did harm to the settlements beyond the river. It happened then that a war party came to Gnadenhütten with a prisoner, whose wife and child they killed near Gnadenhütten, and had impaled. The prisoner

talked with our Indians and warned them to be off, for the whites were already assembled, would follow up the warriors, and fall upon them if they did not go away. When the warriors moved away he perceived that two of them remained behind. In the first night-camp afterwards, however, the prisoner escaped, and had the good luck to get off, and soon after this the militia came and made very sharp inquiries what they had done with the wife and child, but this they could not answer them. From this it can be concluded that the prisoner had betrayed to them that our Indians were there.

April 7. Warriors came in, bringing a prisoner, from whom we now get the certain news that all our Indians in Gnadenhütten and Salem were put to death, and that none were spared; he said the militia had 96 scalps, but our Indians numbered only 86, who went away from us. The rest then must have been friends, who did not belong to us. The prisoner said farther that two men alone had accomplished the whole murder after the Indians had been bound, and they had killed them one after the other with a wooden mallet.

Source: Zeisberger, *Diary of David Zeisberger,* pp. 73–85

Men's Dancing

The men shout and leap and stamp with such violence that the ground trembles under their feet. Whatever man acts in the oddest and most ridiculous manner is the most regarded. They dance in a circle around the fire.

Source: Zeisberger's *History...,* p. 118

John Rose
1782

The Gnadenhutten Massacre occurred on March 8, 1782. Later that year, another military expedition passed through the area on its way to the Sandusky towns, led by Colonel William Crawford. With them, as third in command, was a man named John Rose. This is his account of the appearance of Gnadenhutten about two and a half months after the massacre.

The expedition was a failure and Colonel Crawford was captured and burned at the stake by the Indians.

{On an Indian trail southwest of Steubenville} May 27th {1782} Monday. — At 7 we took up our line of march. Our course was W. a point to the Southward. The woods more open — some hills very steep — and several Defiles. the country very indifferent. On the top of a long ridge running W.S.W. our march was much impeded by fallen timber and thickets. Here we struck upon a path to the moravian Towns. This led us S. W. through a better country; and Fort Tuscarawos bore N.W. A path led S. our proper course, but we declined taking it, for fear of being discovered. Besides, this path leads through several bad swamps, though it is considerably nearer. We halted after a march of 8 miles along a Creek (about 12 miles from Tuscarawos) in a Swampy Bottom, which was unknown to our pilots. After marching 2 miles S.S.W. through low grounds, we discovered several Sugar Camps and crossed Two Legs, [sic] Here we might again have taken a path leading off for the upper Morav. Town, but the former reasons prevailed. After crossing another Creek (name unknown) we encamped about 3 miles from it.

I suppose this day's march at 16 Miles; and we were thought to be 8 miles from Gnadenhutten, to which place a command of 112 Men was ordered to march next Morning —

May 28th Tuesday. — I accompanied Col. Williamson on this command at 8'Oclock A. M. 200 Men turned out to go, and it was merely impossible to detain what was above the number ordered. A short distance from our Camp we entered a fine Bottom for about 2 miles to Still Water Creek, which extended the same distance on the other side. It is a pretty even flowing water about 2½ feet high. Out of the Bottom we ascended a high ridge, from which a most beautiful prospect was occasioned by the Water encircling it allmost. An extensive bottom accompanies this Creek for a considerable distance.

Our course was due W. to the midle Morav. Town or Gnadenhutten.

The Command halted half a mile from the Town, whilst Col. W^mson, our Brigade Major & myself went on foot to reconnoitre the town, whether we could discover any indian Warriors at it. We took a round for near 2 miles up the river across a perspective to the lower town — traversed a level open piece of wood to a pond, at the upper end of which we found a fenced in glade. We struck the fording place just above the town, where we discovered the tracks of a horse & cows, and came to the Town along the Banks of the river. the town was burnt Some time last winter and the ruins of the lowest house in town were mixed with the calcined bones of the burnt bodies of the Indians. A fine plain of considerable extent is enclosed by a ridge of Mountains below the Town. the fording is here very good, which we crossed as soon as the main Body came up. Opposite the Town along the river is a large corn field in which we halted for a refreshment.

At 2 O'clock we were preceded by Col. Williamson with a small party of Sixty, and the whole Body followed upon his heels — pushing forward.

Our course to the upper Town was allmost due N. and the distance 8 miles.

This town called Nazareth lies upon the banks of the Muskingham. At the lower end of her, in an obtuse curve of the river is a pond in which the moravians have hid several things.

After we had fixed our encampment here, we were alarmed by the firing of two Guns and an Indian halloo. Major Brenton and Capt. Bean discovered two Indians about a mile from Town. They fired at them but miss'd them.

This occasioned the assigning of alarm posts and rising & standing to Arms an hour before Day. The result of a formal Council of Officers.

May 29th. — From the upper Morav. Town we took up our Line of march in four Columns agreeable to the first plan proposed and kept an easterly course to the mouth of a Creek which empties into Musk. Riv. the fording of the Creek was deep & muddy & we passed near it a dangerous Defile with the River on our right & a high Ridge on our Left. the passage very narrow. We marched from here N.W. through a Bottom for several miles, ascended the long Ridge allmost N. & struck upon Bouquet's Road to White Woman's Creek, where he treated with the Indians W.B.S. We were led to this path by following a fresh indian track coming down.

In the middle of the afternoon we came to a fork of the Roads. We followed this path to our right running W. In these forks stood a painted Tree, on which an Indian of the Wolf Tribe marck'd 1 prisoner & 3 Scalps. Signs of an old indian encampment & several fresh tracks were visible. In the evening the mountains begun to look less high, fine Bottoms appeared more frequent and the tops of the Ridges seemed covered with a rich soil. We crossed this day different bad narrow Swamps.

May 30th. — We march'd early this day steering N. 75 West along this path called after Bouquet.

A number of horses being lost — 2 Companies were left on the ground.

A short distance from our encampment we saw a large Deer Lick, and 2 miles farther on we struck a path crossing ours in a rectangle allmost. this is the strait path from Sandusky to Wheeling and crosses the Muskingham about 10 Miles from the upper Morav. Town.

"One of our pilots (Zaines) proposed striking this path in a strait direction from the Mingoe Bottom — and the other a path to the N.E. of us, about 8 miles from our first encamping ground, between the 3 forks of Yellow Creek."

Here we left Bouquet's road & followed this Warrior's path running N.W. towards Mohickin John's Town, where the fort Laurens road joins it.

Source: Rose, *Journal of a Volunteer Expedition..., pp. 140–42*

Dancing

If the young are at home and not on the chase hardly a night passes without a dance.

Source: Zeisberger's *History...,* p. 118

Captain George McCully
1783

After the Revolutionary War had ended, Congress directed the Secretary of War to take measures to inform the Indians of the declaration of peace. Ephraim Douglass was appointed as a commissioner to carry the news of peace to the Indians and, if necessary, to go as far as Detroit for this purpose. Douglass chose Capt. George McCully to accompany him and they, along with one servant, set out from Fort Pitt on their perilous trip on July 7, 1783.

Capt. McCully kept a journal of this trip and, while fairly brief, it is of interest in its description of the various Indian trails they used, or crossed. They traveled the customary path to Tuscarawas and then on to Sandusky and, eventually, Detroit. Of special interest is the effect of several years of war upon the trails themselves. They were becoming so overgrown with brush, through nonuse, as to become almost indistinguishable in some places. Of course, the Indian trails from the Sandusky area to Detroit would still have been in good shape, for those trails would have had continual use. Since the Indians could not trade with the Americans at Fort Pitt, they had to turn to the British at Detroit for the white man's goods that they had become so dependent upon, and the travel upon those trails would have been even heavier than before the war, with all of the Ohio Indians heading that way.

{Pittsburgh} Saturday July 7th, 1783. Crossed the Allegany River at 9 O'clock and proceeded Down—found the road intricate as the Bushes were lofty and in many places enterlocked in each other, so that it was impossible to follow the old path. After passing the Narrows we came to many improvements about ½ of an Acre planted with Corn, and three or four rounds of Cabben logs laid up, these continued at a regular distance till we passed logs Town one Mile, where we halted to refresh, after one hour's stay we moved on and found the improvements continued until we arrived at Big Beaver Creek, which we crossed and encamped at Fort McIntosh for the Night—The land which we traveled through today is good, the hills as well as low land—the timber good, and good Water, the General Course of this day west in all 30ᵗ⁷ miles.

Sunday 8ᵗʰ left Fort McIntosh at 2 O'clock, passed the road leading to Newcomers' Town, crossed the first Branch of little Beaver Creek where we halted to refresh; the land Between big and little Beaver Creek is in General good; near little B. Creek the land is but thin, though appears kindly, the Timber is good, in most part white and Black Oak. After two hours' halt, moved on, the road very intricate, the land poor until we passed the second branch of little Beaver, and came on the waters of Yellow Creek where it was much better, the timber good; we halted on a small branch of Yellow Creek for the night, our course this day south of west; in all 24 miles.

Monday 9ᵗʰ we found ourselves this morning in a very disagreeable situation as it rained almost all night on us, our Clothing wet, at 7 O'clock we started and with some difficulty passed Yellow Creek, came on to the Deviding Ridge between yellow and sandy Creek, where are two fine springs the one a branch of Yellow and the Other, of sandy Creek, here we halted to refresh for one hour, and then moved on came to three springs (the waters of Sandy Creek) where we made an other pause—distance from the other 5 miles,—moved on and crossed sandy Creek, kept down it for several miles until we came to two large plains, between which we encamped for the night, our course this day south of west in all 29 miles.

Tuesday 10th from the great quantity of rain last night we were much wetted, yet moved at 7 O'clock, and crossed many small branches of sandy creek—and one large, known to the traders by the Name of Namahshulin Creek and in five miles Gained Tuscorarrie River which we found to be very high and rising very fast. Though by carrying our provisions and Baggage on our Backs we, on our horses got everything over safe. Halted on the west bank to refresh.

After an hours halt, moved on passed Fort Lawrence and came to the fork of the road leading one to Ols Landing, {Walhonding}, and the other to Sandusky. Here we were at a loss, the roads entirely disappearing, and it was some time before we could determine what to do. At length, agreed to keep up Sugar Creek with a view of falling into the road that leads from the Moravian Town, and accordingly moved on, crossed Sugar Creek and passed through a large plain, which was followed by a long swamp, at the end of which we ascended a steep hill and continued along a ridge of fallen timber which was very difficult to pass. In 3 or 4 miles we came to Black Water Creek, which we crossed, and soon fell in on the Beech Run where we found traces of the road and encamped for the night. Our general course today West, the land, water and timber good, in all 27 miles.

Source: Abbatt, "The Journal of George McCully", pp. 253–54

Indian Longevity

Those Indians who have not adopted the vices of the white people live to a good age, from 70 to 90. Few arrive at the age of one hundred years. The women, in general, live longer than the men.

Source: Heckewelder's *History...*, p. 221

Abraham Steiner
1789

In April of 1789, Heckewelder set off once again for the Ohio country, this time to look into the feasibility of the surveying of the lands that Congress was giving to the Moravians. His companion on this trip was Abraham Steiner. The journal kept by Steiner furnishes to us the precise location of the cabin used by Post and Heckewelder in 1762. Steiner says it was 1½ miles above "Tuscarawi" (meaning the junction of the Sandy with the Muskingum). It will be noted that they were still on the north side of the river as they proceeded from the junction to the westward, for they observed the site of Fort Laurens "from a distance", and it was not until later in the day that they actually crossed the Muskingum, some time after they had stopped at noon at the old cabin site. This is the only account that indicates that the cabin had a cellar, and it puts to rest once and for all the erroneous indication found on the old maps of this area, that Heckewelder's Garden was on the south side of the river. Steiner's journal specifically mentions seeing the "corn hills", obviously close to the cabin site, and they were still on the north side of the river. Since Heckewelder was with him on this journey, this is the best evidence that could possibly be obtained as to the location of the cabin, and the garden.

Also of interest in this journal is the meeting with Anton. It will be remembered that he was the son of Joseph Peepy and that his wife, his children, and even his mother, Hannah (Joseph Peepy's wife), had all been killed in the Gnadenhutten Massacre.

The 8th, {April, 1789} On towards noon we set off {from Fort Pitt}. There were six persons: besides us two, there was Isaac Williams, our guide; Geo. Folk (a son of Wm. Folk who used to live in Bethlehem), the Indians took him & his sister prisoner during the last war, & he still lives in Sandusky; David Hill, & Mrs. Girdi [Girty], wife of the brother of the bad Girdi among the Indians. We went straight over hills & across narrow valleys, and came at night to Logtown [Logstown, near present Ambridge] & camped on this side.

Early on the 9th we came through Logtown. Where old Logtown stood there are many plums & large wild apples & beneath them good tame [cultivated] grass. The place is 18 miles from Pittsburg, & seems well situated for a town. One sees here and there the remains of Indian houses & graves, the latter are round, from 60 to more than 100 feet in circumference, & still from 5 to 10 feet high, like a little round hill. We also saw wild turkeys here. After we had ridden 2 miles down along the Ohio, through beautiful bottoms & lowlands, we came to Crowstown [Conway], where there was formerly another Indian town, the fields of which are now full of thickets & old 16-feet-high weeds.

From here we turned away from the Ohio on a good dry path over the mountains, really only hills, which are intersected by narrow valleys in which there are usually good springs. Big Beaver Creek, 9 miles from Crowstown, was too high to ford, so we went 3 miles higher up to the falls. Lieut. Spear, commandant of the blockhouse here, & his 17 soldiers were very friendly, and he invited us to lunch. Meanwhile our horses grazed on the pleasant bottom across the stream. The soldiers brought our things over in canoes, & we went on for another 4 miles.

On the 10th it rained. We met a number of Indians who were going with skins to Beaver Creek, where General Gibson had directed them to come for trading because many of them were afraid to go to Pittsburg. After them came Anton (Wellochalent), formerly one of the Brethren, but he had reverted. He had just now shot a bear. He gave us a ham from it. We let our party go on ahead. Br. Heckewelder reminded him of the grace he had once experienced. He replied that he had never intended to leave the Moravians, but, when his whole family was murdered, that not only grieved him but also so infuriated him that he resolved to go to war, & he had been weak enough to do so. Now he had avenged himself & had no longer any hatred of the white people. He often thought of going back to the Moravians, but believed he was too wicked. Br. Heckewelder said: "The thought of returning to the congregation comes from the Saviour, he has taken hold of you & will not easily let you go. He will forgive you everything if you turn to him." Anton said: "You speak words of comfort to me. I will soon return." And so we parted. Anton was once a very good man. He did much for the white people, saved their lives & during the war brought them himself to safety, often at risk of his life. He had a good wife & lovely, promising children. These were all killed in the great massacre on the Muskingum. 12 miles farther on we came to Little Beaver Creek. The water was high & it was difficult to ford. 1½ miles on this side of it is the straight-carved Pennsylvania Line, 2 rods wide. 6 miles from the first branch is another branch of the Beaver to cross.

On the 11th we went 9 miles farther to the 3rd branch of the Beaver, & then 4 miles up along it through pleasant bottoms where we rested a little. An Indian who was camping a short distance below us came to us, talked with Br. Heckewelder, and gave us a deer ham. From here we crossed the creek and went on another 7 miles. It was cold during the night & froze.

The 12th. In the morning 2 young Delaware Indians came to our camp. The father of one of them was a brother-in-law of the woman who was travelling with us. They were friendly & confirmed the report of the horse-stealing at Wheeling. The Delawares are said to have delivered a Speech to these Mingoes, to get them to mend their ways, but to no effect, & the Delawares are said to have gone quietly off because they saw it was no use. These same Mingoes are said to have stolen 11 horses from Mr. Ludlow, a surveyor, & then returned. On the way we saw the grave of an Indian, who, at sugar-making in the spring, ate so much sugar that his stomach swelled and he died. In the afternoon we came to Tuscarawi Creek {Sandy Creek}, 20 miles this side of Tuscarawi. 15 miles this side of Tuscarawi are the two Tuscarawi Plains, the soil of which is a mixture of sand, brown gravel, & lime, & grows centaury, honeysuckle, & other herbs, upland willows, & small oaks which are different from the "ground oaks" of other plains.

On the morning of the 13th we were only 15 miles from the 3 towns on the Muskingum, where the Brethren formerly lived, but we could not go to see them. This was on Tuscarawi Creek. From a distance we saw the place where Fort Lawrence [Laurens, at Tuscarawas (Bolivar)] once stood. We stopped at noon on the Muskingum, 1½ miles above Tuscarawi, where Post & Heckewelder had once lived. We could still see very well where the house and cellar had been, and also the corn hills. The Muskingum, a quiet, beautiful, delightful stream, might be about 20 rods wide here. We could see the fish swimming down the current. They were very restless and rippled the surface of the water. That meant that a storm was brewing. The sky was clear and bright, but when we set out again we heard thunder in the distance. A few miles farther on, while we were crossing a plain, a violent storm hit us with thunder, wind, & rain. The rain beat so on our faces that we could not see what was happening, & in the woods many trees were blown down. The horses did not want to go on, but we drove them until suddenly they all turned and stood stockstill with their hindquarters to the rain & could not be budged till the worst was over. From here we came into wooded country. We could see, beyond the Muskingum, a hill where rich copper ore is supposed to be. At 6 o'clock in the evening, knowing we could not get much wetter, we rode through the Muskingum, carrying our luggage on our shoulders. Williams, who forded it on foot, got in up to this neck. Afterwards we made a fire, though with some difficulty, dried our-

selves, and spent the night there.

Source: Wallace, *Thirty Thousand Miles with John Heckewelder,* pp. 244–46

Hunting

When a whole party goes out to hunt, they govern themselves according to the wishes of the oldest or the most expert, particularly if he be a member of the council. It is not considered good form for one to leave the party before the end of the hunt. If one has wounded a deer and another followed and killed it, the skin belongs to the first and either the half or the whole of the meat to the latter. If several take aim at once and they cannot determine which of them made the best shot, the skin is given to the oldest of the party, or, if he happened to be one of those taking aim, he is said to have killed the animal. Old men, therefore, no longer able to shoot well, generally get their share of the skins, if they only aim now and then with the others though they do not hit the mark.

Such old men, accompanying a hunting party, get both meat and skins, for the good hunters will not let them return empty-handed. They have, in general, and the Unami in particular, the custom that when a huntsman has shot a deer, and another Indian joins him or only looks on at a distance, he immediately gives him the whole animal and goes in pursuit of another.

Source: Zeisberger's *History...,* p. 91

John Brickell
1791

The author of this brief narrative was only nine years old when taken captive near Pittsburgh in 1791. He lived with the family of the Delaware known as Big Cat for 4½ years before being released. It was nearly fifty years later when he wrote his captivity narrative and some of what he says may be suspect after such a long lapse of time. The general statement, however, as to being taken to the Tuscarawas area, and its being a rendezvous for the Indians, at least occasionally, is probably accurate.

{February 9, 1791 on the Tuscarawas Path west of the Big Beaver} – ...We then went to their camp, where were Indians with whom I had been as intimate as with any person, and they had been frequently about our house. They were very glad to see me, and gave me food, the first I had tasted after crossing Beaver. They treated me very kindly. We staid all night with them, and next morning we all took up our march toward the Tuscarawas, which we reached on the second day late in the evening. Here we met the main body of hunting families and warriors from the Allegheny, this being their place of rendesvous. I supposed these Indians all to be Delawares, but at that time I could not distinguish between the different tribes. Here I met with two white prisoners, Thomas Dick and his wife Jane. They had been our nearest neighbors. I was immediately led to the lower end of the encampment and allowed to talk freely with them for about an hour. They informed me of the death of two of our neighbors, Samuel Chapman and William Powers, who were killed by the Indians; one in their house and the other near it. The Indians showed me their scalps. I knew that of Chapman, having red hair on it.

Next day about ten Indians started back to Pittsburgh. Girty [George] told me they went to pass themselves for friendly Indians, and to trade. Among these was the Indian who took me. In about two weeks they returned, well loaded with store goods, whiskey, &c. After my return from captivity, I was informed that a company of Indians had been there trading, professing to be friendly Indians; and that being suspected, were about to be roughly handled, but some person in Pittsburgh informed them of their danger, and they put off with their goods in some haste.

After the traders came back the company divided, and those who came back with us to Tuscarawas, and the Indian who took me, marched on towards Sandusky.

Source: *The American Pioneer,* Vol. 1, pp. 45–46

John Heckewelder
1793

The following is a brief description of the ruined Moravian towns as of the autumn of 1792. It was told to John Heckewelder by a Major McMahon who had come into the Tuscarawas Valley seeking some horses that had been stolen by the Indians. Apparently they caught up with the Indians along the Walhonding, had a brief fight, and recovered their horses.

January 16th, 1793. We passed Wheeling, and arrived in the evening at Charleston [now Wellsburg, W. Va.] on the Buffalo creek. Here we dismissed our boats; and sent for our horses, which we had left with a farmer in this neighborhood last spring. Major McMahon, who resides here, but who is now at the head of his rifle company in Gen. Wayne's army, happened to be here on a visit to his family. Having been at our ruined towns on the Muskingum, he gave the following information. At Gnadenhütten, there were, this fall, [1792] the best apples he had ever tasted. The peach trees at the three places bore an abundance of peaches, but nearly all the branches had been broken down by bears. The site of Gnadenhütten can scarcely be distinguished, the whole town-plot and adjoining land being overgrown with honey locusts, and the prairies or plains are thickly covered with brushwood; a satisfactory proof that these prairies were caused by bush-fires. On his last expedition he found a camp with four Indians near Gockhosing, far up the Walhalding, (otherwise called White Woman's creek,) whom he attacked. Two of them he killed; and another, who was exceedingly fair and handsome, received a severe wound and uttered a loud cry, but succeeded, together with the fourth of their number, in throwing himself over the high bank into the Walhalding, and swam to the opposite side. The night being very dark, favoured their flight. The party however took their stolen horses, guns and every thing they could find.

Source: Rondthaler, *Life of John Heckewelder,* pp. 124–25

Note: Several months earlier, on June 10th, 1792, while proceeding down the Ohio on this same journey, Heckewelder had first met Major McMahan at Wheeling, after he had just returned from a "Scout" in the Indian country. Heckewelder stated:

[The Major] gave me a very circumstantial description of our towns on the Muskingum, & told me he had found the rendezvous of three hostile nations between Gnadenhütten and Schonbrun, opposite the mouth of Gekelemukpechink [Stillwater] Creek. Three tall painted war-posts had been erected there, and there were 3 large, distinct encampments.

Wallace, *Thirty Thousand Miles with John Heckewelder,* p. 261

John Heckewelder
1797

In 1797, Heckewelder returned to the Tuscarawas Valley to help with the surveying of the three Moravian tracts of land that the United States government was giving to them for their services and sacrifices during the Revolutionary War. By then the Indian menace in the Tuscarawas Valley had passed, and white settlers were starting to move in. A few Indians remained—some the children of more famous chiefs of the earlier days—but the frontier itself had moved westward again. Peace, that state for which Zeisberger, Heckewelder, Edwards, and the others had labored so long in the 1770s, had finally come to the Tuscarawas Valley.

{Portions only of this journal are included in this book. Much of the journal consists of efforts to obtain food and get it cooked, and most of the remainder of the journal details the work being done by the Government surveyors in platting the land for future sale. Those portions of the journal that speak of the Indians still in the valley are included, however. Of note is the fact that there still is a White Eyes Town, although it cannot now be determined if it is on the exact site of the town of the 1770s or not.}

{May 11, 1797, at the site of Gnadenhütten} Our Indian companions, Capt. Bull, Joseph White Eyes, & his brother-in-law who had joined us, lived here in camp on the Western bank of the Muskingum river. Bull has two children, twins, about 2 years old; White Eye's brother-in-law also had two children. The older boy was about 6 years of age, and appeared rather comical in his Indian dress. The mother, Capt. White Eye's daughter, also came with her husband (whose name was Herd) to visit us. Her Indian costume was quite stylish. Her head was bare, hair arranged without ornament; her dress was of black silk, & the cloak which reached to her knees of blue cloth & was trimmed with white. The leggins, or stockings, were also of blue cloth & she wore the usual mocasins or shoes. A dark ash colored blanket hung from her shoulders in a graceful manner.

{May 12th} We took a look at the ruined village {Gnadenhütten} & were surprized at the fine situation which it had upon the banks of the stream. But yet alas! with what sorrow were we filled, when we looked back & remembered that this heretofore flourishing town—where the death of Christ was so faithfully preached to blind & ignorant heathen, & where a band of Christian Indians lived under the blessing of God,—should have been burned to the ground & everything destroyed, & even the greater part of the defenceless inhabitants murdered in cold blood by ruthless savages! The whole situation of the town could be easily traced from the ruined chimneys which were still visible. Every-thing, however, is overgrown with heavy grass, & as this becomes matted down during the winter, we soon perceived that this would serve as a good shelter for numberless snakes. Besides this, the ground was so thickly overgrown with plum trees, hazel-bushes, and black-berries, that there was no getting through them except by means of the paths made by the bears, deer & wolves. This wild mass we set on fire, & obtained thereby considerable more air. Then only did we obtain a correct view of the ruins of the village. Every-where bones could be seen, & in the cellars of the houses, where some of the Brethren had been massacred & burnt, they were also to be found. The majority of our party spent the 12th, around this place. In the evening Mr. Carr, who had gone with Br. Heckewelder to White Eye's town, returned with the news that Bro. Heckewelder had made an arrangement with an Indian to join us next day, to hunt for us.

{May 15th} This evening the Indian, Capt. {George} White Eyes, accompanied by his wife & a white man named Schmidt, came from the western bank of the stream to visit us. White Eyes & the white man, crossed the river on horseback; the horses being obliged to swim but a short distance. They pitched their tent near ours & we presented them with some flour & White Eyes sent us half a bear. The rest of the time they conducted themselves in a quiet & orderly manner. Bro. Henry entered into conver-sation with White Eyes & discussed the object of our journey hither. He seemed to be already acquainted with the fact that his family was entitled to a share in the possession of this land, & named his Uncle, Mother, (whose second husband, Penmaholen by name, was an intimate friend of Bro. Heckewelder,) his brother Joseph, & his brother-in-law. Bro. Henry gave him an opportunity to decide whether he & his friends would take possession of certain parts; he was undecided, however, & promised to give all the aid & advice he could when it came to actual measurements, & also to come then to a decision. To day Bro. Kamp shot a Turkey.

Early on the 16th, Capt. White Eyes with

his squaw, proceeded farther. She is a Wyandot, & a strong, well built person. White Eyes seemed rather dubious as to whether some opposition would not be made to his claim, as he had fought against the States in the last Indian war. This fact we obtained from the white man who accom-panied him.

{May 19th} In the evening Capt. White Eyes returned, & pitched his tent near ours. He had gone in search of & had brought back with him some stray horses. It is wonderful how expert these people are in finding a track upon the ground, and are able to follow it for many miles day after day.

{May 20th} At 9 o'clock Capt. White Eyes & his squaw descended the stream in all the rain. He lives about 10 miles from here, & belongs to the so-called Turtle tribe.

On the 5th {25th of May} Schmick, Clewell & Rothrock went out in search of Salem. Bro. Henry was indisposed & could not go along; they did not however, after a hard day's work arrive at the town, as the woods were so thick with undergrowth that the old path could not be found. On the 6th the above named three breth-ren, together with Bro. Henry, started out on horseback, on the same errand, & towards noon arrived at the site where Salem had formerly stood. They found, however, fewer relics or traces of the village than here in Gnadenhuetten. There is a large bleak flat east of the town which must be very cold, as there is nothing to be found growing upon it but a small species of oak, unknown in our region, but which according to Bro. Kamp's statement, is called Red Jack in Carolina.

{June 27th} About one mile above the Still Water, on the east side of Grindstone Hill, we met with remarkably fine layers of sand stone, which lie upon the surface & are from a few inches to 18 inches in thickness....Towards evening three canoes full of Indians came to visit us. The chief Penmaholen, Capt. Freth & five other males, six females & five children formed the party. Bro. Heckewelder had remained with Genl. Putnam in order to accompany him to Tuscarawas, after the survey of the Schoenbrunn land and as Penmaholen had come with the sole object of visiting him, & amongst us none could be found that was able to speak the Indian language with him we were in a quandry. Among the Indians however was a woman who could speak some English, & as they sat down quietly beside us & smoked their Gilickinik, we regarded each other as silent guests. Penmaholen was dresed in a very respectable manner. He wore a hat, and an undershirt made of silk, over which he wore a shirt made of light satin, & otherwise appeared very cleanly. There were some friendly Indians among them. The majority of them were stoutly built & the men were of middle height, while the females were still smaller. These people differ from the Europeans in this respect, that they are very straight-backed.

{July 1st,} ...In the afternoon the Indians left us. To Penmaholen we presented some chocolate, sugar &c. He was very friendly, & with two families left for White Eye's town, while the others ascended the stream.

Source: Heckewelder, "Notes of Travel of William Henry,...", pp. 140–51

NOTE: Heckewelder's journal of this trip as set forth in Wallace, *Thirty Thousand Miles with John Heckewelder,* p. 336 contains the following interesting passage:

During my journeys by land & water and during my stay in Marietta, I have seen and talked with many Indians, some of whom I knew while others were strangers to me, and they all seemed peacefully disposed; indeed, some of them have moved back from the Miami to the Wahlhanding, where they have built cabins for themselves and planted Indian corn, as White Eyes & Peemaholand (his father-in-law) have done, they having settled ten miles below Salem, built good houses, cleared land, and ploughed and cultivated it on shares with a white man.

The transition from the Indian culture to that of the white man was thus, peacefully, taking place.

Houses Not Locked

Few houses are locked when the people go out. A stick is placed against the door on the outside and the passerby sees that no one is at home and does not enter. Each one is free to do as he pleases without let or hindrance, yet he will rarely do another injury.

Source: Zeisberger's *History...,* p. 123

EPILOGUE

By 1797, most of the Delawares had long since left the valley and were living in north-western Ohio or Indiana. Eventually they would be pushed farther west and finally end up on reservations in Kansas and Oklahoma. Some went to Canada.

The Moravian missionary effort in the Tuscarawas Valley resumed on October 7th, 1798, when Zeisberger and thirty-one Indian converts arrived at Goshen. Their travels after leaving the valley in 1781 had taken them to northern Ohio, Michigan, Canada, and finally back to Ohio. It would be at the Goshen mission that Zeisberger ended his long missionary life, on November 17th, 1808. Heckewelder had returned to the Gnadenhutten area as the Agent for the Society for the Propagation of the Gospel and was active in local political affairs as well until his retirement in 1810. He then returned to Bethlehem and died there in 1823. The Goshen mission gradually declined until the last of the Delawares left the valley on November 5th, 1821, at which time it came to an end.

For those who would like to feel a closer kinship to the "glory days" of the valley, the 1770s, a visit to the old Indian cemetery at Goshen will be well worth while. There, side by side, lie David Zeisberger, the greatest of the Moravian missionaries, and Gelelemend, the John Killbuck, Jr. of these journals—he for whom General Washington held a review of his army—he who tried to keep the Delawares from entering the war on the side of the British—and finally he who later converted to Christianity and lived the remainder of his life by Zeisberger's side at the Goshen mission.

They're all gone now, but the story of what they did in the valley is preserved in these journals. Through their writings we have been able to see the valley as they saw it, and hear the people speak as they heard them speak.

We have come to know them.

SPECIAL STUDIES

Within quoted portions of journals, brackets [ ]
and parentheses ( ) are as in sources.
Braces { } are my comments.

Otherwise, brackets and parentheses are mine.

The Moravian Mission Towns

There were a total of five different Moravian mission towns in the Tuscarawas Valley between 1772 and 1781, but never more than three in existence at any one time. For one year, in the midst of the Revolutionary War period, there was only one town, Lichtenau, just below Coshocton.

The mission towns were not like other Indian towns. Regularity and order were the predominant features. Travelers were known to have gone many miles out of their way just to see for themselves these towns that they had already heard so much about. Visitors were uniformly impressed with what they saw, as many of the journals in this book have attested. Heckewelder, in his *Narrative,* at page 157, thus describes Schoenbrunn:

> Shonbrun had been the largest and handsomest town the Christian Indians had hitherto built; containing upwards of sixty dwelling houses, most of which were of squared timbers. The street, from east to west, was long, and of a proper width; from the centre, where the chapel stood, another street run off to the north. The inhabitants had, for the greatest part, become husbandmen. They had large fields under good rail fences, well pailed gardens, and fine fruit trees; besides herds of cattle, horses and hogs.

Living at peace with everyone, tending their fields and their animals, and staying away from the deleterious effects of rum, they achieved a standard of living that was the envy of the non-Christian Indians and the marvel of the whites. The one word that would best describe the conditions under which the Christian Indians lived, therefore, would have to be—prosperity.

Circumstances beyond their control, however, would occasionally intervene and interrupt the tranquility of their existence, and then there would be a movement to a new town, and a fresh start at the new place. This happened several times while they resided in the Tuscarawas Valley.

The following pages set forth in somewhat graphical form the configurations of these mission towns, along with the ministers at each town and the historical events in the valley that affected the towns.

May 3, 1772 – October 9, 1772

Schoenbrunn

David Zeisberger, age 51

John Heckewelder, age 29, who arrived from the east on August 23, 1772.

Johann Jungmann, age 52, and his wife, Anna, who arrived from the east on September 29, 1772.

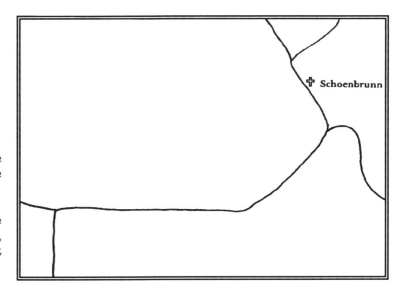

Chief Netawatwees and the Delaware Council at Newcomerstown had invited the Christian Indians to move to the Tuscarawas Valley and had given them land from the mouth of the Stillwater to "Tuscarawi", usually assumed to be the crossing place of the Muskingum above Bolivar, although they may have meant only to the area sometimes referred to as Tuscarawi which seemed to take in everything from the vicinity of Zoarville to Bolivar. Their towns had formerly been along the Beaver and Susquehanna Rivers in Pennsylvania, but due to troubles with the neighboring Indians along the Beaver, and the advancing frontier along the Susquehanna, it was felt that they needed to move further west.

October 9, 1772 – April 12, 1776

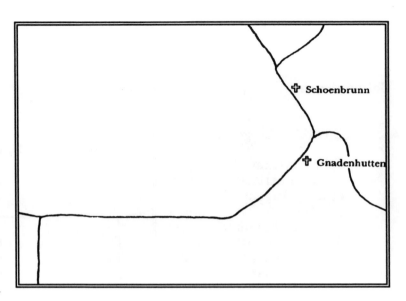

Schoenbrunn

> Zeisberger, until he went back East on June 1, 1775. He returned from the East on August 10, 1775.

> Heckewelder, until he went back East on September 13, 1774. He returned from the East on November 12, 1774.

> Jungmann and wife

Roth and wife, who arrived August 18, 1773, from Gnadenhutten. They departed for the east on May 27, 1774, with their children, due to the dangers caused by Dunmore's War.

Gnadenhutten

> Joshua, a native assistant, until the arrival of John Roth.

> John Roth, age 47, and wife, Maria, who arrived from the east on April 24, 1773. They later moved to Schoenbrunn on August 18, 1773.

> Johann Schmick, age 59, and his wife, Johanna, who arrived from the east on August 16, 1773.

More Christian Indians from the east were being brought to the Tuscarawas Valley. These were Mahicans, and it was felt that it would be better to have them live in a separate town, apart from the Delawares (primarily Munsees) at Schoenbrunn. Accordingly, the Delaware Council at Newcomerstown gave the land from the mouth of the Stillwater to within three miles of Newcomerstown to the Moravians and directed that they establish their new town at the site of a former Delaware town, in which the well-known Indian called King Beaver had died. The name given to this town was Gnadenhutten.

This was probably the best of times for the missionary effort in the Tuscarawas Valley. The two towns prospered and, except for the scare caused by the outbreak of Dunmore's War in 1774 (causing Roth and his family to go back east), there was peace in the valley.

April 12, 1776 – April 19, 1777

Schoenbrunn

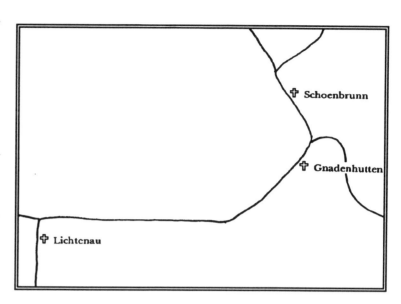

> Jungmann and wife. They fled to Lichtenau on April 1, 1777.

> Heckewelder, from December 13, 1776, until April 19, 1777, when he went to Lichtenau.

Gnadenhutten

> Schmick and wife.

Lichtenau

> Zeisberger

> Heckewelder, until December 13, 1776, when he left to be Jungmann's assistant at Schoenbrunn.

> William Edwards, age 52, who arrived from the east on December 11, 1776.

> Jungmann and wife, who arrived from Schoenbrunn on April 2, 1777.

At the request of Netawatwees, a third mission town was founded, called Lichtenau, about two miles below the Delaware capital at Coshocton. Unfortunately, later that year (on August 31, 1776) Netawatwees died and the mission lost its greatest friend among the Delawares. Border warfare also erupted in the spring of 1777 and Indians hostile to the American cause would frequently pass through the area, heading to the white settlements across the Ohio. The Delawares themselves, however, under the influence of Gelelemend, the successor to Netawatees, and White Eyes, who seems to have become their principal spokesman, maintained a neutral position and did not enter into the war against the Americans.

Many of the Schoenbrunn congregation were Munsees, who were considered cousins of the Delawares. Some of these Indians began to break away from the congregation and return to their former ways. Rumors circulated of hostility to the ministers and finally, on April 1, 1777, it was reported that eighteen warriors were at the forks of the Tuscarawas, about 12 miles north of Schoenbrunn, and were intending to kill the ministers. During that same night, the Jungmann's fled to Gnadenhutten and, the next day, on to Lichtenau. A few days later, the entire remnant of the congregation moved to Lichtenau, and Schoenbrunn was abandoned.

April 19, 1777 – April 25, 1778

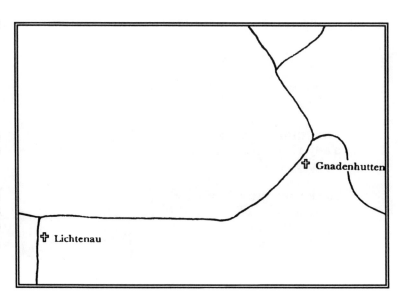

Gnadenhutten

> Schmick and wife, until they went back east on August 10, 1777.
>
> Edwards, who arrived from Lichtenau on August 23, 1777, and returned to Lichtenau on April 25, 1778.

Lichtenau

> Zeisberger
>
> Heckewelder, until he went back east on May 27, 1777. He returned on April 6, 1778. (Heckelder's Ride)
>
> Edwards, until he moved to Gnadenhutten on August 23, 1777. He returned to Lichtenau on April 25, 1778.
>
> Jungmann and wife, until they went back east on August 6, 1777.

It was toward the end of this period that the defectors Alexander McKee, Matthew Elliott, and Simon Girty arrived from Fort Pitt and nearly succeeded in bringing the Delawares at Coshocton into the war on the side of the British. A few days later, Heckewelder arrived, and the news that he brought concerning the events along the Eastern seaboard to the effect that the Americans were not losing the war, and that they had even captured Burgoyne's army, apparently helped to calm things down. Nevertheless, the situation appeared to be so dangerous (it was rumored that American militiamen were coming into the area to destroy the mission towns) that it was finally decided to move the Gnadenhutten congregation to Lichtenau for their better protection. The missionaries with wives had already gone back east, leaving only the unmarried ministers in the valley.

April 25, 1778 – April 6, 1779

Lichtenau

Zeisberger

Heckewelder

Edwards

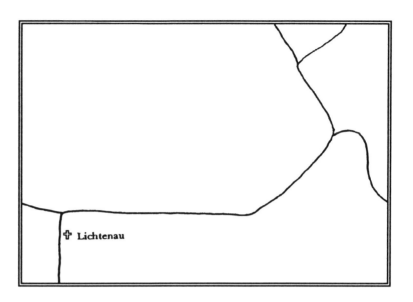

As of April 25, 1778, the remaining congregations of the three former towns were concentrated at Lichtenau. There missionaries, all single men, were with them.

Another blow to the mission was the death of their great friend and supporter, White Eyes, in the fall of 1778. He had been commissioned a Colonel in the American army as it approached the Tuscarawas Valley on the McIntosh Campaign. At the time, it was reported that he died of smallpox, but a number of years later the Indian Agent, George Morgan, claimed that he was murdered by American militiamen.

The loss of White Eyes caused irreparable damage to the future of the mission. Gelelemend, also a supporter of the mission, was just not a strong enough leader to keep his people out of the war, and the British faction of the Delawares, under Captain Pipe, gradually gained the ascendency.

With the Delawares abandoning their neutrality, the proximity of Lichtenau to Coshocton became an embarassment. Hostile Indians from further west would often pass through the town on their way to attacking the white settlements, leading to a disruption in the way of life of the Christian Indians. It was, therefore, decided to move back to their former towns.

April 6, 1779 – December 6, 1779

Lichtenau

    Heckewelder

Gnadenhutten

    Edwards

Schoenbrunn (ruins)

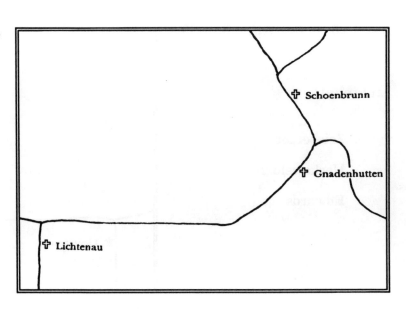

Zeisberger, who left for Pittsburgh on September 22, 1779, and returned on October 3, 1779.

On April 6, 1779, the Gnadenhutten and Schoenbrunn congregations began their moves back to their old towns. The houses at Gnadenhutten were fairly intact, but Schoenbrunn was in ruins, and the Indians of that congregation lived in those ruins while they started the construction of New Schoenbrunn on the other side of the Tuscarawas about one mile west of the old town. Heckewelder remained at Lichtenau.

December 6, 1779 – April 6, 1780

Lichtenau

    Heckewelder

Gnadenhutten

    Edwards

New Schoenbrunn

    Zeisberger

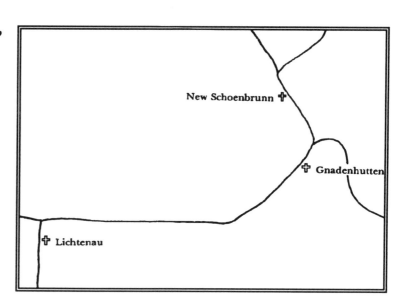

    The Schoenbrunn congregation finally moved to New Schoenbrunn, across the river. The mission towns each had one minister in charge, all of them still single men. That was soon to change, however.

April 6, 1780 – September 11, 1781

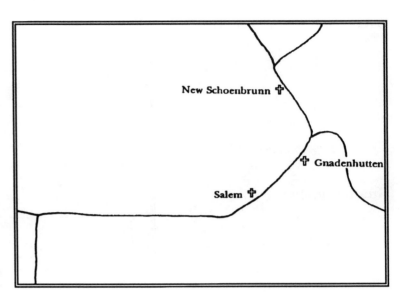

Gnadenhutten

Edwards

Michael Jung, age 37, who arrived from the east on November 6, 1780. Moved to Salem on July 26, 1781.

Senseman and wife, who arrived from New Schoenbrunn on July 15, 1781.

New Schoenbrunn

Zeisberger, until April 1, 1781, when he left for the East. On June 4, 1781, at Lititz, Pennsylvania, he married Susan Lecrone. They arrived back at the mission on July 15, 1781.

Gottlob Senseman, age 35, and wife, Anna, who arrived from the east on June 30, 1780. They moved to Gnadenhutten on July 15, 1781.

Jungmann and wife, who arrived from the east on July 15, 1781.

Salem

Heckewelder. On July 4, 1780, at the chapel at Salem, he married Sarah Ohneburg, who had arrived from the East on July 1, 1780.

Jung, who arrived from Gnadenhutten on July 26, 1781.

The final phase of the Moravian mission in the Tuscarawas Valley during the period covered by this book began with the movement of the Lichtenau congregation to a new town, Salem, about one and a half miles southwest of Port Washington. Lichtenau was now abandoned, and some Delawares moved into the deserted town.

Heckewelder was married in the Salem chapel on July 4, 1780, and Zeisberger, on a trip back east, was married at Lititz on June 4, 1781. He and his wife then rejoined the New

Schoenbrunn congregation, along with Jungmann and his wife. Michael Jung, a single man, and Gottlob Senseman and his wife had previously arrived at the mission towns, and so the towns each had two ministers to serve them, and four of the six ministers had their wives with them.

In the fall of 1781, however, the mission in the Tuscarawas Valley came to an end. Taken into captivity by the Indians in the British interest, and moved to the Upper Sandusky area, on September 11th they began their exodus from the valley.

Since Brodhead had destroyed Coshocton and Lichtenau in the spring of that year, with the departure of the Christian Indians, the valley was now deserted.

The Plight of the Delawares

Thursday, October 18, 1787 ---From Gigeyunk {Ft. Wayne} a couple of Indians came to Thomas, to give him news of the circumstances in which they are, for one of them is a great friend of his. They complained that the Delaware nation was in grievous condition, they knew not whither to go nor where to settle; where they now are they cannot remain, since the nations will not suffer them there; they have made entreaty the whole summer, sending message after message to the Spaniards to make arrangements with them, and to move thither; some indeed have already gone there, who now send them back word to let no one follow, for they are there in very narrow straits, and would gladly come back were it in their power; they were not sure of their lives, the nations there having resolved to root them out; they were hemmed in and could not come free; they would have to be helped; since now the Delawares saw that they had no steadfast place, they first turned to the Six Nations and asked them for land; they answered them they could not help them, for they had themselves not a foot of land they could call their own; they addressed the Wyandots, who told them they had given them leave to dwell on their land, had also told them how far the bounds of their land extended, but that they, the Delawares, had disregarded their request, and had gone over their boundaries to other nations, therefore they would make them no more offers. The Twightwees, whom they then addressed, had pointed out to them a place where they could settle, but where they were surrounded by swamps, and also, as it were, closed in. They suffered hunger, too, all the time, for their corn did not thrive, and was frosted. So it is with the Delaware nation, which a few years ago greatly flourished, but since the old chiefs, Netawatwes and White Eyes, are dead, it goes with hasty steps to ruin.

Source: Zeisberger, *Diary...*, pp. 373–74

Size of the Moravian Mission Towns

The following table sets forth the end-of-year populations of each of the Mission towns for which figures are available. Unless otherwise noted, the figures used are those from the appropriate town diary. Estimated figures are those of Earl Olmstead, a well-known authority on the Moravian Missions in the Tuscarawas Valley.

1772	Schoenbrunn	92
	Gnadenhutten	94
		186
1773	Schoenbrunn	184
	Gnadenhutten	108
		292
1774	Schoenbrunn	220
	Gnadenhutten	139
		359
1775	Schoenbrunn	263
	Gnadenhutten	151
		414
1776	Schoenbrunn	204 (est.)
	Gnadenhutten	136
	Lichtenau	59
		399 (est.)
1777	Gnadenhutten	125 (est.)
	Lichtenau	232
		357 (est.)
1778	Lichtenau	328
1779	New Schoenbrunn	100
	Gnadenhutten	99
	Lichtenau	130 (est.)
		329 (est.)

1780	New Schoenbrunn	143
	Gnadenhutten	135
	Salem	<u>105</u> (est.)
		383 (est.)

The Death of a Trader during Dunmore's War

May 16. (1774) In the afternoon, again two messengers sent by Netawatwees passed through here [Gnadenhütten] on their way to Pittsburg to take notice thither that he was going to the Shaw. Chief to bring them to peace and that the traders Mr. Anderson, Dunken and Jones with two of their people are still alive and in Gekelemuckpechünk are being guarded and cared for by the Indians there in a locked house, further, that, however, one of Mr. Jones' people, by the name of Cammel, had been murdered not far from their Town by some Maqua Indians, who had not gone at once with the Shaw. Capt. but had remained behind and had met this person. They had first talked with him and, then, he was obliged to take off his coat and shirt, then they had given him some Phittamoon (?) (may have been a preparation from parched corn) to eat. Then one who had been standing behind him hacked him to death with the hatchet (tomahawk) and had hastened away. Mr. Jones and another one and this one of his people had always walked in the bush, but this one had no longer wished to walk in the bush but on the foot-path and thus he came into the hands of the enemies and soon lost his life. This deed of murder has stirred up very much the Indians at Gekelemuckpechünk against the Maqua Indians who are and live about here. They went out at once to look these up, because they had missed six of the twenty who had been with them for the night in their town. These messengers related, also, that their people had heard from the Maqua Indians that they would have gladly killed me and my wife, two of them had for that reason gone back from their company on the Sabbath evening, to attempt their evil intention but two Indians from here whom they had seen with weapon had hindered them therein. Praise and thanks to God, said our people, and we when we heard it.

Source: Gnadenhutten Diary for May 16, 1774

This murder took place between White Eyes Town and Coshocton, for the next year, while traveling between these towns, *Nicholas Cresswell*, in his journal, mentions seeing the bones of Cammel.

Locations of Indian Villages

There were many Indian villages in the Tuscarawas Valley, especially if the Walhonding and the Muskingum as far downstream as Dresden are considered. Newcomerstown and Coshocton were, by far, the largest of the towns. For the most part, there are no population figures for the other towns, but since many of them consisted of only a few houses or huts, they could not have been very large. The purpose of this article is to set forth with as much accuracy as possible the locations of such of these towns as are shown on maps or mentioned in the journals. Vestiges of some of these towns were still visible when the land was surveyed in 1797 and in a number of cases, these towns are shown on the surveyor's maps. In some instances the size of the towns is set forth in the surveyor's notes and, occasionally, even Indian trails are shown on the maps. These records are in the office of the Auditor of State at Columbus.

Wakatomika
(near Dresden)

Wakatomika, sometimes spelled Wappatomika, was the name given to a small group of Shawnee towns near Dresden. It was also sometimes called the Upper Shawnee Town or Towns. Vestiges of at least one of the towns were still visible when the land was surveyed in 1797, and it is marked on the surveyor's map. It is on the west side of the Muskingum and the north side of Wakatomika Creek, just north of Dresden. See Maps 8a and 8b.

Hutchins, in his account of the Indian trails set forth in the Appendix, called it Waukautaumeka Town and states:

> About 200 yards above the Town {referring to Tom's Town} the River is Fordable, after crossing of which the Country is very open & mostly Barrens for 8 Miles to Waukautaumeka Town [on or near the site of the present Dresden], Situate on a Very High Bank, about 100 yards from the Muskingum River. There is About 40 Houses in this Town and near the same Number of warriors, and upward of 90 women & Children. Their Cornfields are near ¾ of a Mile from the Town, on the same side, up the [Wakatomika] Creek. From this Town to the Ohio River is 80 Miles.

Levi Hicks, in the *Beatty* journal of 1766, states that it was called "Ogh-hi-taw-mi-kaw, i. e. White-Corn Town; that this was the largest, he supposed in these parts;"

Zeisberger visited the area in 1772, and has this to say about it in the Schoenbrunn Diary for October 17, 1772, "This Town is commonly known among the Indians as the Vomiting-Town...", and later, "This Town consists of 17 houses and is the largest in this region. Four small Towns, also, belong it, each consisting of but a few huts which are, at the most, three or four miles away."

Jones, in 1773, crossed the Muskingum at a place he called the "Little Shawannee Woman's Town", but there is no way of being sure whether this was at one of the Wakatomika towns, or perhaps farther north near Tom's Town, or still farther north near Mowheysinck.

In 1774, McDonald destroyed the towns, and in his account he mentions five towns, including one he called Snake's town.

Tom's Town
(near Conesville)

Hutchins, in his account of the Indian trails, says the following regarding Tom's Town:

5 Miles from Mowheysinck, down the River on this side, is Black Tom's Town. The path between these Towns is through a Level, Rich Bottom, free from Hills or Creeks. Tom's Town has 8 or 10 Houses in it, And consists of about 8 Warriors and 15 or 16 women & Children; their Cornfields are close by the Town. The shortest distance from this Town to the Ohio is 100 Miles.

It is also shown on his map of 1764.

From its distance from the Dresden area, and from the next village upstream (Mowheysinck, which was about two miles below Coshocton), it appears that Tom's Town was near Conesville, on the east side of the river.

Mowheysinck
(two miles below Coshocton)

This town has an interesting history.

It is first mentioned by *Hutchins* in his account of the Indian trails, wherein he says:

13 Miles further is Bullet's Town, or Mow-hey-sinck, on Muskingum River. For the first 5 Miles the Land is Level to a Savannah; the rest of the way is in some places broken with small Hills.
Mowheysinck Town is Situate about 100 yards from the River, on this side, and has upwards of 35 Persons in it, 15 of which are Warriors. Their Cornfields are better than half a Mile below the Town, close on the Opposite side of the River. From the nearest part of the Ohio River to this Town is about 100 Miles.

He also shows it as Bullet's Town on his map of 1764 [Map 5].

Levi Hicks, in the *Beatty* journal, says this about it, "...about 10 miles or more {from Newcomerstown} was one called Moghwhiston, i. e., Worm Town, having about 20 houses;..."

On the Crevecoeur map [Map 9], it is called "Moughwessing" and is shown as being on both sides of the river, just as the Hutchins map shows Bullet's town as being on both sides of the river.

As to the question of how close to Coshocton it was, the Original Survey map of the Muskingum [Map 13a] and the 1872 Atlas of Coshocton [Map 12] are of help, along with the Schoenbrunn Diary and Finley's field notes of the Bouquet Expedition set forth in the separate article on the Location of Bouquet's 16th Encampment.

The Original Survey map of the river shows an "Old Field" on the west side of the river about three miles below the Forks of the Muskingum. The 1872 Atlas of Coshocton County (on facing page) shows a ford across the Muskingum about two miles below the Forks. *Hutchins,* on his map of 1764 [Map 5], shows the town as being on both sides of the river, which would seem to indicate that it was fordable at that point, and that their corn fields were "better than" one-half mile below the town on the west side of the river. All of this would appear to pretty accurately locate the town at the site of the ford. Also, Heckewelder, in his *Narrative,* pp. 143 & 148 indicates that Lichtenau was two miles below Coshocton (presumably at the same ford), and the Schoenbrunn Diary for June 9, 1780, states:

> From Mochessunk (formerly Lichtenau) several members returned who had cattle there which they went to fetch. They declared that it is now a much worse place than Goschachgunk {Coshocton}, that it did not resemble itself any more and that they were very uncomfortable there. {Apparently un-christian-ized Delawares were living there then. Brodhead destroyed it when he destroyed Coshocton in 1781.}

Further evidence that the town was two miles below Coshocton is found in Finley's field notes mentioned above. He states that Bullet's Town was "supposed" to be 5 miles from the survey point of the 16th Encampment of Bouquet's Expedition. Since that point was 3 miles from the Forks of the Muskingum, and Coshocton was later established right at the Forks, the distance of Bullet's Town, or Mowheysinck, below Coshocton would have been two miles.

It therefore appears that the town has been known as Mowheysinck, Moghwhiston, Moughwessing, Bullet's Town, and, finally, Lichtenau (when the Christian Indians occupied the site).

Its location would appear to have been at the ford shown in the 1872 Atlas, approximately two miles below the Forks of the Muskingum.

Coshocton
(at Coshocton)

According to *Zeisberger* in the Schoenbrunn Diary for February 10th, 1776, Coshocton "...lies on the east side of the Muskingum, just across from where the Walhanding, equally large with it, empties into the Muskingum."

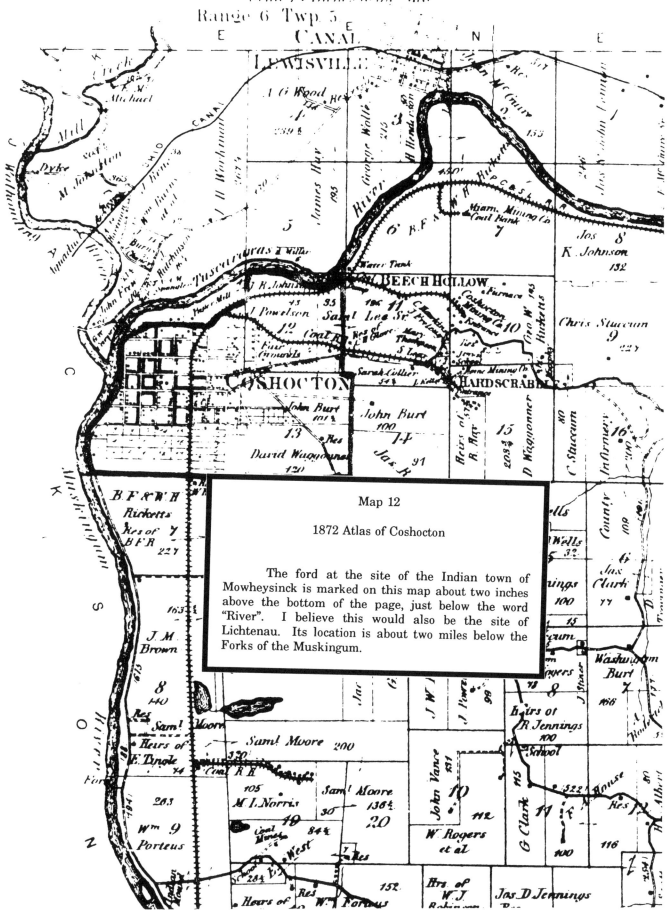

Map 12

1872 Atlas of Coshocton

The ford at the site of the Indian town of Mowheysinck is marked on this map about two inches above the bottom of the page, just below the word "River". I believe this would also be the site of Lichtenau. Its location is about two miles below the Forks of the Muskingum.

We Encamp'd here one Night and that Night my Son was Permitted to Sleep with me.   In the Morning Cap't John Peter Told me To Take Leave of my Son for that I wou'd never see him again.

Charles Stuart   November 24, 1755

He also states that it is "...quite large but spread out very much, consisting, for the most part, of huts, and although it was laid out and the streets were marked off, I could not find a single street that was built up, in any degree, in regular fashion, each had built according to his fancy, the length of the house or the width toward the street, or obliquely, or even the house in the middle of the street."

He says that the chief's house was "the largest" in the town.

Although the Original Survey map of the river does not say anything about the town itself (perhaps because nothing was still visible in 1797, it having been destroyed by Brodhead in 1781), the survey does mention the point along the river where the cornfields at Coshocton began, and where they ended. Coming upstream, they began at a point 1.25 miles below the junction of the Walhonding, and they ended at a point .50 miles above the junction, thus stretching for 1.75 miles along the river. The town itself, of course, would have been between these two points, evidently at the junction with the Walhonding.

The Walhonding Towns

The Original Survey maps of 1797 show two Indian towns along the Walhonding and one along the Killbuck. The mouth of the Killbuck is about 5 miles from Coshocton. Maps 10a and 11a show the locations of these towns. Maps 10b and 11b are the modern maps of these areas.

The distance from Coshocton to the first town along the Walhonding is about 7 miles. The surveyor's notes show the town as being 13.52 chains long. Since a chain is 66 feet, the town was 892 feet, or nearly 300 yards long.

The town on the Killbuck is about 1 mile from the junction of that creek with the Walhonding and distant about 1½ miles from the town on the Walhonding. It was 22.76 chains in length, which is 1499 feet, or about 500 yards long.

The second town shown on the surveyor's maps as being along the Walhonding is at the junction with the Mohican, a total distance from Coshocton of about 18 miles.

Whose towns were these?

The earliest journal, that of *Christopher Gist*, refers to going west 5 miles from Muskingum to the White Woman's Creek on which was a small town in which the white woman lived. Since the town of Muskingum was located about two miles northeast of the Forks of the Muskingum, going west (cross-country) 5 miles from there takes you to a point about one mile east of the mouth of the Killbuck. It is possible, of course, that *Gist* may have been off by about a mile in his estimate of the distance traveled, and the White Woman Town may have been actually at the mouth of the Killbuck, but even so, I do not think it would have been either of the towns shown on the surveyor's map. The Walhonding town would be 8 miles from Muskingum, and the one on the Killbuck would have been 7 miles. I don't think *Gist* would have been that far off. It is therefore my opinion that the White Woman

Town was about one mile east of the Killbuck, or possibly near the junction of the Killbuck, if *Gist* was off by one mile in his estimate of the miles traveled.

James Smith, in his captivity narrative of 1755, states that he was taken "to an Indian town on the west branch of the Muskingum, about twenty miles above the forks, which was called Tullihas, inhabited by Delawares, Caughnewagos and Mohicans." This town may be the one shown at the junction of the Mohican.

Samuel Finley's field notes of the Bouquet Expedition of 1764, described in the separate article on the Location of Bouquet's 16th Encampment, state that Custaloga lived about 8 miles from that encampment. It is likely, therefore, that the first town along the Walhonding, about 2 miles west of the mouth of the Killbuck, was his town.

James Wood, in his journal in 1775, says, as he left Coshocton heading west along the Walhonding:

> ...set off in a hard rain passed thro' a Town of the Muncys and made them Acquainted with my business kept up White Womans Creek Crossing it Six times and Corcosan Creek once lodged at Mohickins old Town now Inhabited by Delawares travelled about 38 miles this day the Course nearly West.

The town of the Muncys is probably the first of the towns along the Walhonding.

Cresswell, also in 1775, speaks of leaving Coshocton and going to Old Hundy, "a scattering settlement". He does not state how far it was from Coshocton, but it is probably the town called "Oldhanting" (Walhonding) on the Crevecoeur map [Map 9], and is possibly the town along the Walhonding shown on the surveyor's map as being about 2 miles above the Killbuck. (Perhaps the same town even extended "cross-country" to the town shown on the Killbuck, if this is what *Cresswell* meant when he said "a scattering settlement".)

As to the location of New Hundy, all that he says is that it was three miles from Old Hundy. It is possible, however, that the town on the Killbuck is *Cresswell's* New Hundy and he was wrong about the distance being three miles, for it's more like a mile and a half. I suspect that *Cresswell's* calling it New Hundy is just a play on words. Perhaps it had no name at all.

Butler, in his 1775 journal, states that he left Coshocton at 11 o'clock but got no farther than "winginoms", where he camped all night. I believe this would be the first town on the Walhonding. Then the next day he went up the White Womans Creek "to the Forks to an old Town". I believe that this is the forks of the Mohican, and the "old Town" is the one shown on the map at the junction of the Walhonding with the Mohican, possibly the Tullihas of the *Smith* narrative. Two miles further along the Walhonding he came to "Windochaloos" town, but that town does not appear to be marked on the surveyor's map.

Wilson, in his 1776 journal, states "At Winganous town, about six miles from Coochocking...". This is very close to the actual distance of the first town on the Walhonding shown on the surveyor's map, and corroborates the *Butler* journal as to that town being Wingenunds.

Heckewelder, in his *Narrative* at page 143, states, "Pipe's place of residence was on Walhanding, about fifteen miles from Goshochking, (forks of the Muskingum.)"

Fifteen miles from Coshocton sounds too far to be the towns at the junction of the Killbuck, but, if Heckewelder is short by a few miles, Pipe's town might be the one shown at the junction of the Mohican.

Finally, *Zeisberger*, in his diary for September 22, 1781, as they were being taken into captivity, says "...we moved on, and encamped on the 22d at the second fork of this creek where is an old Indian town, and a pleasant beautiful country, as indeed all along the creek so far as we have come."

The second fork of the Walhonding was the junction of the Mohican. The junction of the Killbuck was the first fork.

It is clear, therefore, that the Moravians stopped at the old Indian town at the junction of the Mohican, shown on the surveyor's map, as they were being taken to the Sandusky area.

Muskingum
(Near Coshocton)

For the location of this town, see the special article on this subject.

White Eyes Town
(two miles east of West Lafayette)

The first specific mention of White Eyes Town in these journals is the *Jones* journal of 1773. Heading in an easterly direction towards Newcomerstown, he states:

We passed Captain White Eye's Town.... A few miles north {east} of White Eye's town, there is a small town, where we obliged our horses to take the river, following them in a small canoe belonging to the Indians. Thence travelled over very hilly land till we came within two or three miles of New-Comer's Town, and from that to town the land is agreeable and appears good for wheat.

In the *Wood* journal of July 27, 1775, as he was heading west, going from Newcomerstown to Coshocton, he states:

Passed White Eyes' town about 10 o'Clock. Arrived at Koshoctin at 1 O'Clock.

Thus it was about a three-hour ride from White Eyes Town to Coshocton. At 2½ miles per hour that would be about 7½ miles.

The Original Survey notes of 1797 contain this statement concerning the running of the line in a northward direction along the west boundary of Township 5, Range 4 [the east line of Map 3]:

...to River bank at upper point of an island below White Eyes Town.

From this statement, it seems that White Eyes Town was east of this line [which line is also the west line of Map 4], and since the river is running in a generally north-south direction east of this line, it would appear that White Eyes Town was somewhere along the river as it was running in this north-south direction.

Confirmation of this fact is furnished by the following excerpt from a diary entry for March 26, 1801, made by the Reverend Bernard Kluge as he was traveling down the Tuscarawas from Goshen to the Moravian Indian Mission on the White River in Indiana. This diary is set forth in Gipson, *The Moravian Indian Mission on White River*, 68–69.

After making two miles we passed new farms and some miles further we passed the former Indian town, Newcomera {Newcomerstown}, which is a fine level place. Not far from here our Indians shot a number of ducks, of which we saw a great number as well as geese in large flocks. The course of the river is very winding and has many small islands. At noon we landed for a short time, and the Indians made a big fire around which we all encamped and warmed ourselves. Whoever had anything to eat, ate it. Half an hour later we continued our journey and four miles beyond we passed the old Indian town, White Eyes Town. Quite near it old Indian Jacob recognized his old home. Half a mile further we encountered a waterfall and had to disembark, while three Indians safely directed our canoes over the same. It was amusing to see how the swift current bore the canoe along like an arrow. Yet at the same time great attention was necessary, on account of the many large rocks in the water. After all the canoes had passed down safely we got into them again.

An examination of the depths of the river in this region, as shown in the book by Alan F. Gintz entitled *The Tuscarawas Navigator*, at the page designated as Chart 14, reveals that there is an area known as The Orange Rapids at the point in the river where it has turned to the west again at the end of the north-south course. Mr. Gintz states, "The Orange Rapids are the largest set on the river. A cataract at the head has a 1½' drop, avoid the rocks in the middle." Heckewelder, in his *History...*, p. 147, says these rocks were known as "White Eye's falls".

Since the falls were one-half mile beyond White Eyes Town, that places the town at about the halfway point along the north-south stretch of the river. This point is also about 7½ miles from the Forks of the Muskingum, which would agree with the *Wood* journal and would also explain why both *Jones* and *Wood*, in their journals, say "passed" White Eyes Town, rather than actually going through it. Travelers heading in an east-west direction on the south side of the Tuscarawas would have to go out of their way nearly a quarter of a mile to go to the town itself. Also, *Zeisberger*, when he traveled to Wakatomika in 1772, after leaving Newcomerstown, says he "passed two Delaware Towns, lying to the right". I believe that the second of these towns was White Eyes Town, and the first was the town to be discussed next. Note that he also says "passed" these two towns "to the right". He did not actually go through them because they were out of the way of the path itself. The river bends to the south just before coming to each of these places, and keeping below the river, as the path undoubtedly did, means that these towns (which almost certainly were to the north, and along the river itself) were not on the direct east-west route.

Further confirmation, if any were still needed, of the location of White Eyes Town as being as stated above is furnished by the Salem Diary for April 19th, 1781, when Heckewelder says that "This afternoon we had word that Col. Brodhead with his army was seen at White Eyes Town (ten miles from here) and was marching right to Goschachking." The distance from Salem to the above location of White Eyes Town is precisely ten miles.

I therefore believe that White Eyes Town was approximately two miles to the east of West Lafayette, and at about the midpoint of that portion of the river that heads in a north-south direction.

Cresswell, on August 28th, 1775, had this to say about the town:

Lodged at White-Eye's Town only three houses in it. Kindly treated at a Dutch Blacksmith's, who lives with an Indian Squaw. Got a very hearty supper of a sort of Dumplings made of Indian Meal and dried Huckleberries which serves instead of currants. Dirty people, find it impossible to keep myself free from lice. Very disagreeable companions.

Village near Old Stone Fort
(just north of Isleta)

Jones, in his journal, states:

A few miles north {east} of White Eye's town, there is a small town, where we obliged our horses to take the river, following them in a small canoe belonging to the Indians. Thence travelled over very hilly land till we came within two or three miles of New-Comer's Town, and from that to town the land is agreeable and appears good for wheat.

This description of the location of the town and the terrain to Newcomerstown after crossing the river at the town would appear to place it near the Old Stone Fort, north of Isleta.

Also, *McClure*, in his journal, wherein he fled to "a village 5 miles down the river", would appear to be describing this town, for that is exactly its distance from Newcomerstown.

This is also probably the first of the two Delaware towns mentioned by *Zeisberger* as he proceeded west from Newcomerstown and stated he passed two Delaware villages "to the right". (White Eyes Town is probably the second village.)

Newcomerstown
(at Newcomerstown)

Newcomerstown was located on both sides of the river, but chiefly on the north side, according to the *Beatty* journal, at the location of the present-day town of the same name.

The survey map of the river shows it as being at the bend of the river, as it heads to the south, near the present waterworks, and *Beatty,* in his journal, says it is "about one mile and a half in length". See Maps 7a and 7b.

Village at site of Salem
(about 1½ miles southwest of Port Washington)

Wood's journal of July 21, 1775, refers to a small Delaware town "six miles from the Moravian town" enroute to Newcomerstown. There would have been no Delaware town six miles from Schoenbrunn in the direction of Newcomerstown, but this would be precisely the distance to the site of Salem if the Moravian town referred to was Gnadenhutten. The Gnadenhutten Diary confirms the fact that *Wood* was there on that date.

Village at site of Gnadenhutten
(at Gnadenhutten)

There are several references in the Schoenbrunn Diary as to the Moravian town of Gnadenhutten being located at the site of a former Delaware town:

Sept. 13, 1772. The brn. Isaac and Nathan.Davis returned from Gekelemukp., whither they had gone yesterday, and brought us news from the Chief that the place, ten miles below us on the river, where the old Town is located, should be ours for purposes of settlement...

Oct. 2, 1772. ...{the chiefs at Newcomerstown} had determined and arranged a place for you, viz., the old Town below Gekelemukp. Creek, for you to settle...

Ettwein, in his journal for August 27th, 1772, states:

{The chiefs at Newcomerstown said that} you may also have the place where King Beaver lived; for this reason we caused the people to move away from there already last spring

Heckewelder stated that he placed a marker on Beaver's grave at Gnadenhutten in 1797. Wallace, *Thirty Thousand Milles with Heckewelder,* p. 338.

It is thus abundantly clear that there was an earlier town at the site of Gnadenhutten, and that King Beaver died there.

Three Legs Town
(near Midvale)

See special article on this subject for the location of this town.

Town of the Ottaways
(near Zoarville, on the west side of the river)

See note at the end of the *Gist* journal for a discussion of the location of this town.

A second Tuscarawas
(somewhere between Schoenbrunn and Bolivar)

It would appear that the name of Tuscarawas was given to another town besides the well-known one just above Bolivar.

Cresswell, in his journal for Sept. 9th and 10th, 1775, says:

Saturday, September 9th, 1775. Left the town {Schoenbrunn}. Mr. Anderson, N. and I went to the Tuscarora town. Then got lost in the Woods and rambled till dark, when we camped by the side of a little run. Very merry this afternoon with our misfortune.

Sunday, September 10th, 1775. Rambled till noon when we found ourselves at Bouquet's old Fort now demolished. Went to an Indian Camp, where Mr. Anderson met with an old wife of his, who would go with him, which he agreed to. We have each of us a Girl. It is an odd way of travelling, but we are obliged to submit to it. Met with Mr. Anderson's people in the evening, camped by the side of Tuscarora Creek. Saw the vestige, the Tuscarora old town, but now deserted.

Clearly when he speaks of visiting "Bouquet's old Fort" on the 10th, followed that same day by the statement, "Saw the vestige, the Tuscarora old town, but now deserted", he is speaking of the town called Tuscarawas, just two miles above Bouquet's fort, the well-known Tuscarawas, above Bolivar.

Just as clearly, however, when he speaks of visiting, on the day before this, "the Tuscarora town", he must be talking of some other town, perhaps one in which there are still Indians residing, for he does not call it an old town!

That there were two towns called Tuscarawas comes as something of a surprise to those familiar with the journals of the time, but this conclusion seems unavoidable.

Additional support for this theory comes from the Schoenbrunn Diaries as set forth below:

July 20, 1773. From Tuscarawi came a woman, Michael's mother, who, for a whole year has desired to dwell here.

August 13, 1773.   ...From Tuscarawi an Indian came with his family for a visit......

January 1, 1774.   ...impressive baptissmal rite for four people, viz., Jonas, brother of Luke, who came to us right at the beginning in Goschgosching, Stephen, Silas and Debora from Tuscarawi,...

If there was another town called Tuscarawas, where was it located?

I think that it could possibly have been in the vicinity of Zoarville, or perhaps anywhere along the river between Zoarville and Bolivar. *Zeisberger*, in his 1772 journal on his second visit to Newcomerstown, seems to call the river between Bolivar and Zoarville "Tuscarawi", and so perhaps any town in this area could also be thought of as "Tuscarawi". My reason for thinking that Zoarville may be a possibility is because that was where a trail crossed the Tuscarawas, the one used by *Gist* and *DeLery*. *Heckewelder*, in his journal of 1762, mentions another small village "a mile still farther down the stream" from the well-known Tuscarawas, but this site would seem to be too close to Bouquet's Fort to be the town visited by *Cresswell* on September 9th.

Unless further evidence is discovered, the location of the second Tuscarawas, if there actually was one, may simply remain unknown.

Tuscarawas
(near Bolivar)

Little needs to be said about the location of this town, for it is quite well known in the journals of the time. See Maps 6, 16, 18a and 18b.

The surveyor's map for 1797 has its location designated; the Greenville Treaty Line points directly at the ford above the junction with the Sandy, north of Bolivar; and the Indian town was in the vicinity of the ford. It will be noted that the Greenville Treaty Line on the modern topographic map points directly to the junction of the Sandy rather than to the ford which was nearly a third of a mile above it. The explanation for this is that the Sandy has been relocated to the northward and now intersects the Tuscarawas River precisely at the former location of the ford. The Greenville Treaty line has not moved at all. It is the Sandy that has moved.

Since Indian villages come in all sizes, there were probably other very small towns throughout the valley, but their locations are not shown on maps of the period, nor are they specifically mentioned in the journals. It is especially difficult to determine the number and location of the towns between Mowheysinck (two miles below Coshocton) and Wakatomika (near Dresden). Several journals contain references to these towns, but putting a specific name to a particular location is almost a hopeless task.

Coshocton – Good Intentions Gone Awry

Indian towns were notoriously casual in the placement of their huts or houses. When Newcomer decided to move his town to Coshocton, he tried to do something about this. The results were somewhat disappointing, however. The following entries from the Schoenbrunn Diary show us that even the Indians had trouble converting government planning into reality.

"April 7, 1775.   The Brethren Isaac and Wilhelm returned from Goschachgunk, the new town which the people of Gekelemukpechünk are founding,...

Their new town has been laid out and staked off in the form of a cross street, lying along the Mushkingum, the design having been copied from us, for usually the Indians do not build regularly, but each one builds his house, as it seems good to him. Each tribe, clan and nation is to have its own street. One street has been designated for those Indians who are sent away from our town or who leave here of their own volition. As they have much work and there are many people, who, however, hinder each other, because they do not know how to portion out the work and there is no one to assign people to their tasks, our brethren, upon their request, gave them good advice and told them how we proceeded in our Towns, which pleased them so that they declared they would follow our example. They will in externals profit somewhat through us and become more order loving."

That was the plan.

"February 10, 1776. ...Toward evening we came to Goschachgunk, and as we had come quite unexpectedly, because the messengers had received no positive answer in Gnadenhütten whether and when we could come our arrival gave the Chief, his counsellors and all the Indians the greater pleasure. We were very well received and in the Chief's house, whch is the largest, a separate fire was assigned to us, where we lodged. The Indians soon came in great numbers and welcomed us in a very friendly manner. Their Town, which lies on the east side of the Muskingum, just across from where the Walhanding, equally large with it, empties into the Muskingum, is quite large but spread out very much, consisting, for the most part, of huts, and although it was laid out and the streets were marked off, I could not find a single street that was built up, in any degree, in regular fashion, each had built according to his fancy, the length of the house or the width toward the street, or obliquely, or even the house in the middle of the street."

That was the result.

Size of the Indian Villages

Tuscarawas
just above Bolivar

1761 – *Rogers*	about 180 warriors – Delaware
1762 – *Heckewelder*	about 40 wigwams
1764 – *Bouquet*	deserted – estimated 150 warriors
1766 – *Beatty*	reoccupied on east side of river but numbers not given
1775 – *Cresswell*	deserted

Town of the Ottaways
near Zoarville

1750 – *Gist*	not above six or eight families

Newcomerstown
at Newcomerstown

1766 – *Beatty*	600 - 700 persons 60 or 70 houses one mile and a half in length both sides of river but mostly on the north side
1771 – *Zeisberger*	rather a big Indian town said to consist of 100 houses
1772 – *Ettwein*	between 40 and 50 houses, very irregularly built
1772 – *McClure*	about 60 houses – nearly 100 families
1775 – *Cresswell*	not 20 houses inhabited
1781 – *Brodhead*	not exceeding 30 men

White Eyes Town
two miles east of West Lafayette

1775 – *Cresswell*   3 houses in it

Muskingum (Conchake)
near Coshocton

1750 – *Gist*   about one hundred Families – Wyandots

1754 – *Trent*   30 men – Wyandots

1755 – *Delery*   two cabins (as of March 29th)

1755 – *Stuart*   deserted (as of November)

1758 – *Le Roy*   reoccupied by Delawares but no
                                 numbers given

1758 – *Gibson*   reoccupied by Delawares but no
                                 numbers given

1764 – *Bouquet*   deserted

Coshocton
at Coshocton

1775 – *Wood*   no numbers given – July 22nd

1775 – *Butler*   no numbers given – August 28th

1775 – *Cresswell*   no numbers given – August 29th

1776 – *Zeisberger*   quite large

1776 – *Wilson*   no numbers given

Wakatomika
near Dresden

1763 – *Hutchins*   about 40 houses

1772 – *Zeisberger*   principal town – 17 houses
                                 four other small towns within
                                 3 or 4 miles, each consisting
                                 of but few huts

The Location of Muskingum

One of the most puzzling questions concerning the Indian history of the Tuscarawas Valley has been the exact location of the town of Muskingum, mentioned first by *Gist* in 1750, then *Trent* in 1752, *DeLery* (calling it Conchake) in 1755, and many others in succeeding years. It was abandoned, however, by the time Bouquet came into the area in 1764.

But just where was it?

The confusion begins with *Gist*. It is not clear from his journal exactly where he struck the Muskingum after leaving the town of the Ottaways, near Zoarville. Apparently he had proceeded in a southwesterly direction for about 28 miles before arriving at the river, and then west five miles to the town he called Muskingum. When he left the town, on January 15th, he states he "went W 5 M to the White Woman's Creek, on which is a small town;..." referring to the town in which Mary Harris lived.

But what did he mean when he said "went W 5 M to the White Woman's Creek"?

Some writers have concluded from this statement that the town of Muskingum was five miles east of the junction with the Walhonding (called the White Woman in those days). If that is the correct interpretation, then was the town where Mary Harris lived right at that junction (in other words, where Coshocton is now, or perhaps across the river from it), for *Gist* does not say that any additional miles had to be traveled up the Walhonding to get to her town?

Or, did *Gist* mean that he went west five miles to the town in which Mary Harris lived, which was somewhere upon the Walhonding at a distance of five miles in a direct line from the town of Muskingum, but not necessarily that distance by the way the rivers flow. (An examination of the map will show that at the junction of the rivers, both rivers are heading in a southerly direction, but someone heading west from a town on the north side of the Tuscarawas would simply cut "cross-country" from one river to the other, and not follow the first river to the actual junction with the other.)

I believe that this latter interpretation is the more correct one, and virtually all of the writers on the subject do place the White Woman Town somewhere up the Walhonding and not at the junction with the Tuscarawas.

But that still leaves us with the question of the precise location of Muskingum. Was it 5 miles east of the junction with the Walhonding, right at the junction (where Coshocton is now), or somewhere in between? As a compromise, many persons have simply said it was a few miles east of Coshocton, without being any more specific than that.

I believe, however, that its actual location can be precisely determined.

I base this statement upon an analysis of the *DeLery* journal, the *Stuart* captivity narrative, the Hutchins map of the Bouquet Expedition, the early survey map of the river, the modern topographic map of the Coshocton area, and the field notes made by Samuel Finley, an Engineer with Bouquet's Expedition.

DeLery says that on the 29th, while coming down the Conchake (Walhonding) they crossed a "second branch" (this would be Killbuck Creek) at 3 o'clock. By 5 o'clock they came to a small branch "across which we waded". This small creek is marked on the original survey map of the area and is also on the modern topographic map. It is five miles from Killbuck Creek and is now known as Mill Creek. *DeLery* was therefore averaging about two and a half miles per hour. He proceeded down the Conchake for another half hour, then cut "cross-country" to the town of Conchake, arriving at about 6 o'clock. This means that he traveled about one mile further down the Conchake (one-half hour) before cutting across to the town itself on the Tuscarawas (another one-half hour). He would have gone about one mile, or a little more, in this last half hour, so that places Conchake just across the Tuscarawas River and directly north of the easternmost part of Coshocton.

This location also corresponds very closely with the "Old Wyandot Town" shown on the Hutchins map of 1764.

Furthermore, when the river was first surveyed in 1797, there were two islands just opposite the town. This would have indicated fairly shallow water, easily fordable, and the hillside across the river, still there, of course, and still heavily forested, would have provided plenty of firewood close to the town. That would have been a very good reason to have placed the town there in the first place—plenty of flat land around the town for their cornfields, and firewood easily available just across the shallow river. It is even a possibility, indeed I think a probability, that some of their houses may have been on the south side of the river, just as Newcomerstown had some houses on the south side, according to the journals in this book.

These surveys also mention two springs in the immediate vicinity of the lower of the two islands, on the south side of the river. They are even shown on the surveyor's map of the river. *Charles Stuart,* in his captivity narrative, mentions two springs just under the bank of the river at the site of the two cabins (all that was left of Conchake at that time). In my opinion, these are the same springs, and, if that is really the case, this further confirms the fact that the town was at this site.

In this connection, although *Stuart* says he crossed the Muskingum about 25 miles above these two cabins (which would place him on the north side of the Muskingum as he proceeded through the valley to the Forks), I believe it was the Stillwater he crossed, for his description of the terrain through which he passed afterwards much better describes being on the south side of the Muskingum rather than the north. Since he appears to have been on the south side of the Muskingum when he reached the site of Conchake, his statement that the "barrens...ended at the House where an Eng. Indian Trader had formerly lived..." clearly implies that the two cabins were also on the south side of the river, close to the bank, and the two springs were "under s^d bank". I believe, therefore, that the town was on both sides of the river.

After having already arrived at my opinion as to the location of Muskingum from piecing together the above journals and maps, confirmation of its location is further furnished by the Finley field notes of the survey of Bouquet's route, discussed more fully in the separate article on Bouquet's 16th Encampment.

The distance, by the river, from its junction with the Walhonding is two miles, but, simply put, it was on both sides of the river at the northeastern corner of the present-day town of Coshocton.

Indian Trading

Trade with Europeans is carried on usually on the basis of fixed price, both as concerns goods and pelts. The Indians trade their deer, beaver, otter, raccoon, fox-skins, wild-cat-skins and others for goods which the traders often take a considerable distance into the Indian country. If they can deceive the whites, they do so with pleasure, for it is not easily done. They are delighted, also, if they succeed in purloining something. They are fond of buying on credit, promising to pay when they return from the chase. The traders may be willing to take the risk, hoping to control all that they catch. But if the Indians, on their return, find other traders in the country, they barter with them and trouble themselves no longer over their creditors. If the latter remind them of their debts, they are offended, for to pay old debts seems to them to be giving goods away for nothng. Usually traders learn from their losses to give nothing or but little on credit. This is the safest course and there is no danger in arousing the enmity of the Indians. When war breaks out the traders are the first in danger, not only of losing their property but also for their lives. When the Indians suspect a war approaching, they keep it secret and take as many goods upon credit as they can get; as soon as the war breaks out all debts are cancelled.

The Indians trade much among themselves, especially the women, who deal in rum, which they sell at exorbitant prices, which occasions much disorder.

Source: Zeisberger's *History...*, p. 117

Meanders of Muskingum River in Town 5 Range 6 — Cont

Course	Dist.	N	S	E	W	Remarks
N 15..30 W	11.. -					
N 17.. 45 W	4..50					Narrows on west side of River
N 26.. - W	17..50					Old field below Cooshekton
N 14.. - W	2..50					
N 20.. - W	5.. -					
N 24.. - W	10.. -					
N 21.. - W	4..50					
N 13.. - W	9.. -					
N 1.. - W	5.. -					Bottom Land begins on west side of River
N 10.. - E	3..50					
N 19.. - E	4.. -					mouth of a small creek bears N 80 W
N 29.. - E	3..50					the mouth of said creek bears S 76 W
N 31..30 E	2..50					
N 47.. - E	9.. -					
N 29..30 E	9.. -					(= 36 W
N 3..30 E	9..50					Mouth of Whitewomans creek bears N 26 E
N 3.. 30 W	11.. -					
N 43.. - E	7..50					mouth of W. Domans Creek bears S 62 W
N 13.. - E	7.. -					
N 71.. - E	12.. -					
S 81.. - E	5.. -					
S 59.. - E	6..50					
S 83..30 E	9.. -					
N 72.. - E	6.. -					leave old field above mentioned
N 56..30 E	6..50					Low Bottom Land begins
N 32.. - E	5.. -					
N 24.. W	5..50					
N 99.. - E	0.. -					

1797 Survey Notes

The "Old field below Coshocton" mentioned at top right begins about 2.1 miles north of the bottom of Map 13a. Heading upstream as noted at the bottom of the notes, the field ends at a point 141 chains (1.7 miles) north of the beginning. Therefore, the field began about 1.25 miles below the junction of the White Woman (Walhonding) and ended about .5 miles above the junction. The town, itself, was right at the junction. These notes give us some idea of the size of Coshocton, including its fields.

116

Meanders of Muskingum River in Town 5 Range 6 — Cont.d

Course	Dist.	N	S	E	W	Remarks
S 00° 30' E	7.50					
S 76.. — E	5.. —					good Bottom Land timber white & black walnut &c
S 66.. — E	15.. —					
S 79.. — E	5.. —					
N 60.. 30 E	4.50					
N 75.. 30 E	5.. —					
N 59.. — E	8.. —					small Island middle of River aros which River is 10 ch° wide
N 45.. — E	4.50					
N 40.. — E	3.50					
N 31.. — E	4.50					at 1 ch. a spring & at 2 ch. another proceeding to River
N 46.. 30 E	16.. —					to lower point of an Island — Narrows East side began at the 2 springs last mentioned
N 60.. 30 E	5.. —					
N 49.. — E	12.. —					at 5.50 upper point of the Island water East side 80 links wide
N 01.. — E	4.. —					
N 64.. 30 E	3.50					the hill recedes from the River the narrows timberd with bush spanish Oak & hickory Land Rich but broken & steep
N 32.. 30 E	5.50					
N 21.. — E	5.. —					
N 6.. — W	26.. —					
N 19.. 30 W	12.50					Plain Land on west side of River nearly destitute of timber the bank high —

This survey is a continuation of the preceding page and mentions, at about the middle of the page, the two springs referred to in the *Stuart* captivity narrative. They were about 1 chain, or 66 feet, apart. *Stuart* says that the two cabins were located at these two springs. These springs, therefore, provide a definite, surveyed, location of the site of at least two of the houses at Muskingum. A surveyor, today, could locate this site with precision. The town itself, though, was also on the north side of the river as shown by Map 5 and Finley's survey notes set forth on page 281.

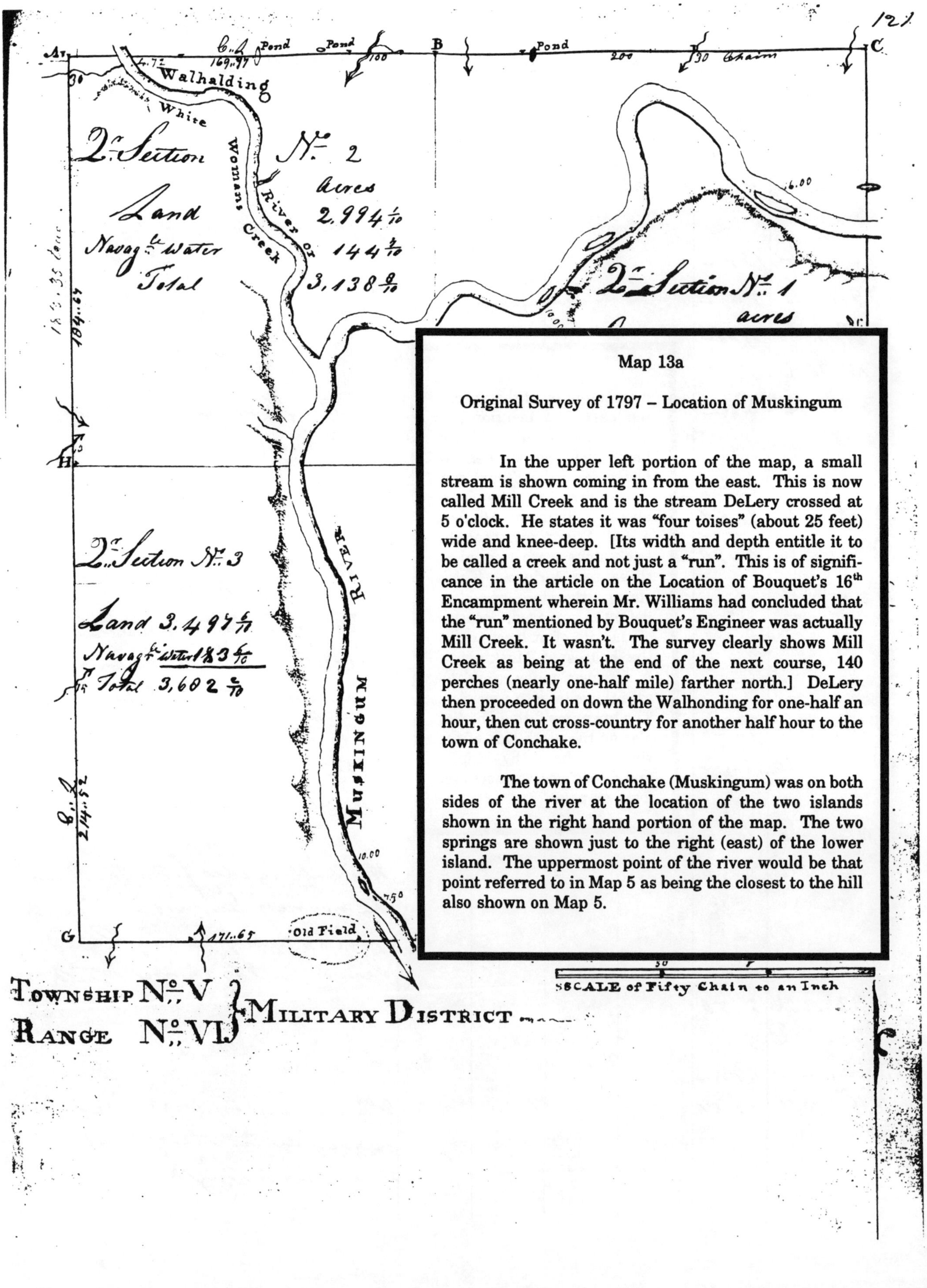

(map with handwritten annotations)

A B C
Walhalding

White

Woman's Creek

Walhonding River

2ᵈ Section Nᵒ 2
acres
2,994 ⁴/₁₀
or 144 ⁴/₁₀
Total 3,138 ⁸/₁₀

Navag⁺ Water

2ᵈ Section Nᵒ 1
acres

H

2ᵈ Section Nᵒ 3

Land 3,497 ⁵/₁₀
Navag⁺ water 183 ⁴/₁₀
Total 3,682 ²/₁₀

MUSKINGUM RIVER

10.00
7.50

G 171.65 Old Field

Map 13a

Original Survey of 1797 – Location of Muskingum

In the upper left portion of the map, a small stream is shown coming in from the east. This is now called Mill Creek and is the stream DeLery crossed at 5 o'clock. He states it was "four toises" (about 25 feet) wide and knee-deep. [Its width and depth entitle it to be called a creek and not just a "run". This is of significance in the article on the Location of Bouquet's 16th Encampment wherein Mr. Williams had concluded that the "run" mentioned by Bouquet's Engineer was actually Mill Creek. It wasn't. The survey clearly shows Mill Creek as being at the end of the next course, 140 perches (nearly one-half mile) farther north.] DeLery then proceeded on down the Walhonding for one-half an hour, then cut cross-country for another half hour to the town of Conchake.

The town of Conchake (Muskingum) was on both sides of the river at the location of the two islands shown in the right hand portion of the map. The two springs are shown just to the right (east) of the lower island. The uppermost point of the river would be that point referred to in Map 5 as being the closest to the hill also shown on Map 5.

SCALE of Fifty Chain to an Inch

TOWNSHIP Nᵒ V
RANGE Nᵒ VI
MILITARY DISTRICT

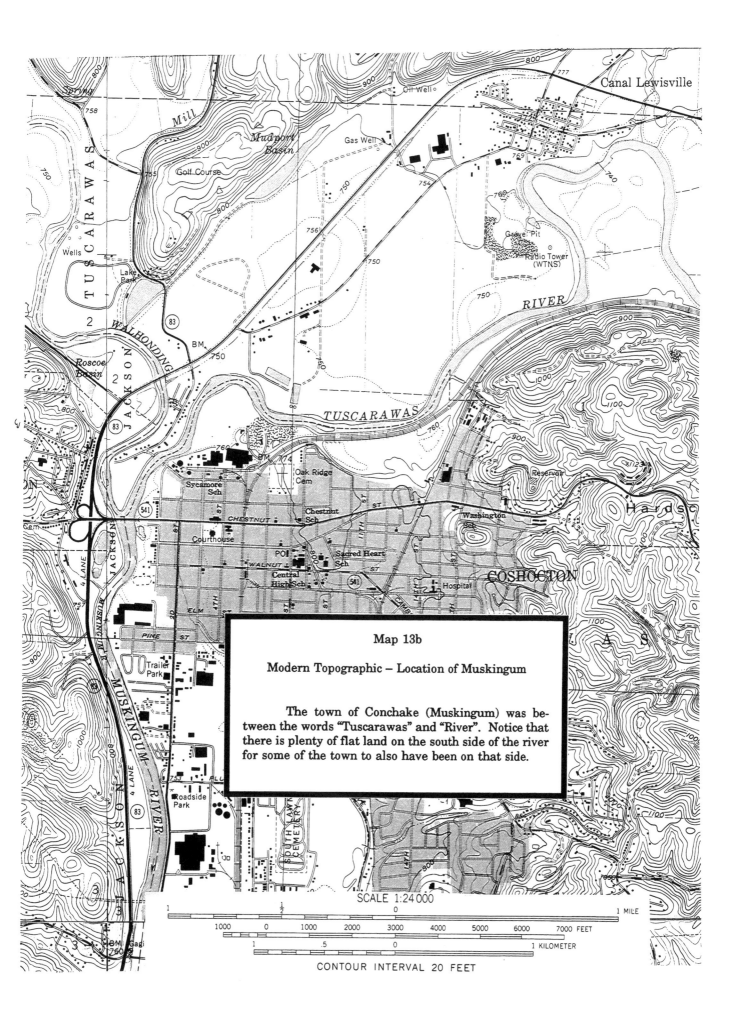

Map 13b

Modern Topographic – Location of Muskingum

The town of Conchake (Muskingum) was between the words "Tuscarawas" and "River". Notice that there is plenty of flat land on the south side of the river for some of the town to also have been on that side.

SCALE 1:24 000

CONTOUR INTERVAL 20 FEET

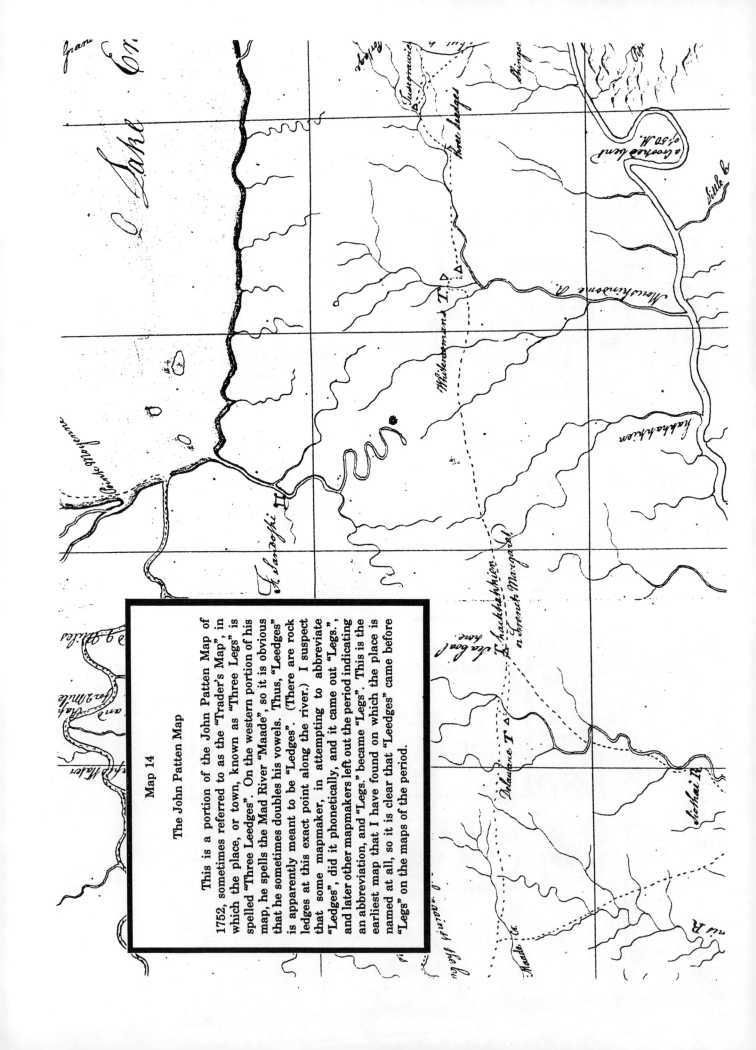

Map 14

The John Patten Map

This is a portion of the John Patten Map of 1752, sometimes referred to as the "Trader's Map", in which the place, or town, known as "Three Legs" is spelled "Three Leedges". On the western portion of his map, he spells the Mad River "Maade", so it is obvious that he sometimes doubles his vowels. Thus, "Leedges" is apparently meant to be "Ledges". (There are rock ledges at this exact point along the river.) I suspect that some mapmaker, in attempting to abbreviate "Ledges", did it phonetically, and it came out "Legs.", and later other mapmakers left out the period indicating an abbreviation, and "Legs." became "Legs". This is the earliest map that I have found on which the place is named at all, so it is clear that "Leedges" came before "Legs" on the maps of the period.

Three Legs

Another of the enigmas of the Indian history of the Tuscarawas Valley is the location, and even the existence, of an Indian town named Three Legs Town.

Most maps of the period show such a town on the south or east side of the Tuscarawas somewhere in the vicinity of Uhrichsville or Midvale. But nothing at all is known about who inhabited this town—it's just a name on the maps—nothing else.

I think there never was such a town known as Three Legs.

I think the name was originally "Three Ledges", or perhaps just "The Ledges", and it simply referred to a place along the river where there were rock ledges close to the river. There may very well, at some time or other, have been an Indian town in the vicinity, for apparently traders passed through this area and the presence of an Indian town at this place would have been a good reason to go there, but the name itself referred to the place on the river, not the town.

I first started to question the existence of a town known as Three Legs Town when reading the *American Gazetter*, by Jedidiah Morse, published in 1797. He has this to say about the Muskingum River, "...it is navigable by large batteaux and barges to the Three Legs, 110 miles from its mouth,..."

It sounds like he is talking more about a place along the river than a town.

Then, in trying to find the earliest map on which the name Three Legs appeared it was noted that the map attributed to John Patten, a trader, in about 1752, appears to be that map. But he does not call it Three Legs, but rather "Three Leedges"—apparently meaning Three Ledges. (He also spells the Mad River "Maade", indicating that sometimes he doubles his vowels.)

The discovery on the map that perhaps the original name was Three Ledges, rather than Three Legs, certainly reinforced my suspicions that it was just a place along the river where there were rock outcroppings, and that the word "Legs" had probably come about as the result of an attempted abbreviation of the word Ledges — "Legs." Later, the period was dropped and Ledges became Legs from then on.

This was still supposition, however, but a search of the original survey notes of the river, made in 1797, looking for any evidence of rock ledges noted by these surveyors furnished the physical proof that there were, indeed, rock ledges in the vicinity.

These notes, contained in the survey books kept by the State Auditor's Office in Columbus, yield the following information for a point along the river 77.5 chains (just under one mile) above the mouth of the Stillwater—"shelving rocks close on the river."

"Shelving rocks" could certainly mean ledges.

Also, Heckewelder, in his 1797 journal states in the entry for the 26th of June, "About one mile above the Still Water, on the east side of Grindstone Hill, we met with remarkably fine layers of sand stone, which lie upon the surface & are from a few inches to 18 inches in thickness."

Thus he, too, noted the rock layers or ledges on a hill which, even then, had been given the name of Grindstone Hill.

Are these ledges still there?

Yes, but, perhaps not as noticeable now as they were then, for a railroad cuts through the easternmost part of the hill and may have altered the original rock outcroppings.

The modern topographic map, when compared with the original map made by the first surveyors and their notes as to the distance of the "shelving rocks" from the mouth of the Stillwater, shows that there is a hill immediately adjacent to the old river bed at exactly the place where these rocks were noted by the surveyors. The same railroad that cut off a part of the hill also cut off part of the river, and that part of the river that was cut off is now just a large pond. The rock outcroppings, however, are still there, and the hill is right at the water's edge.

I believe, therefore, that there never was a Three Legs Town, but that there probably was a place on the river originally known as The Ledges, or perhaps Three Ledges. If any Indian town did exist at this place, its historic name, if it had one, has not come down to us at all.

Indian Character

Every person who is well acquainted with the true character of the Indians will admit that they are peaceable, sociable, obliging, charitable, and hospitable among themselves, and that those virtues are, as it were, a part of their nature. In their ordinary intercourse, they are studious to oblige each other. They neither wrangle nor fight; they live, I believe, as peaceably together as any people on earth, and treat one another with the greatest respect. That they are not devoid of tender feelings has been sufficiently shewn in the course of this work. I do not mean to speak of those whose manners have been corrupted by a long intercourse with the worst class of white men; they are a degenerate race, very different from the true genuine Indians whom I have attempted to describe.

Source: Heckewelder's *History...*, p. 330

Map 15a – Original Survey – Three Legs.

Map 15b – Modern Topographic – Three Legs.

Surveyor's Field Notes relating to Three Legs.

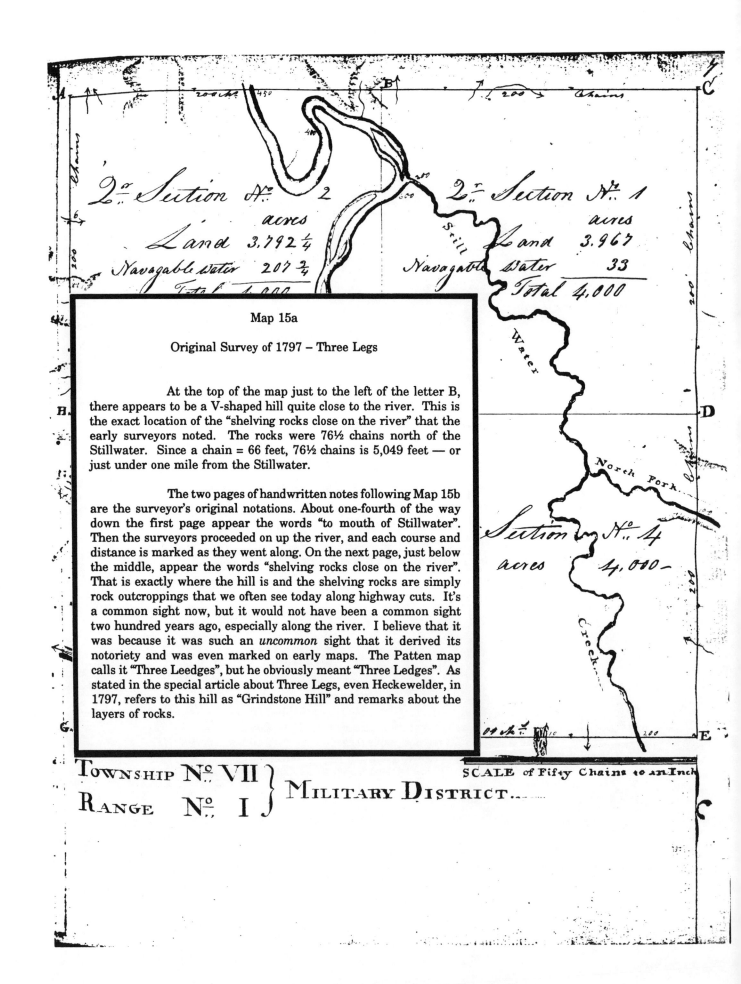

2ᵈ Section Nᵒ 2
acres
Land 3.792 ¼
Navagable water 207 ¾
Total 4,000

2ᵈ Section Nᵒ 1
acres
Land 3.967
Navagable Water 33
Total 4,000

Still

Water

North Fork

Section Nᵒ 4
acres 4,000

Creek

Map 15a

Original Survey of 1797 – Three Legs

At the top of the map just to the left of the letter B, there appears to be a V-shaped hill quite close to the river. This is the exact location of the "shelving rocks close on the river" that the early surveyors noted. The rocks were 76½ chains north of the Stillwater. Since a chain = 66 feet, 76½ chains is 5,049 feet — or just under one mile from the Stillwater.

The two pages of handwritten notes following Map 15b are the surveyor's original notations. About one-fourth of the way down the first page appear the words "to mouth of Stillwater". Then the surveyors proceeded on up the river, and each course and distance is marked as they went along. On the next page, just below the middle, appear the words "shelving rocks close on the river". That is exactly where the hill is and the shelving rocks are simply rock outcroppings that we often see today along highway cuts. It's a common sight now, but it would not have been a common sight two hundred years ago, especially along the river. I believe that it was because it was such an *uncommon* sight that it derived its notoriety and was even marked on early maps. The Patten map calls it "Three Leedges", but he obviously meant "Three Ledges". As stated in the special article about Three Legs, even Heckewelder, in 1797, refers to this hill as "Grindstone Hill" and remarks about the layers of rocks.

TOWNSHIP Nᵒ VII
RANGE Nᵒ I
} MILITARY DISTRICT

SCALE of Fifty Chains to an Inch

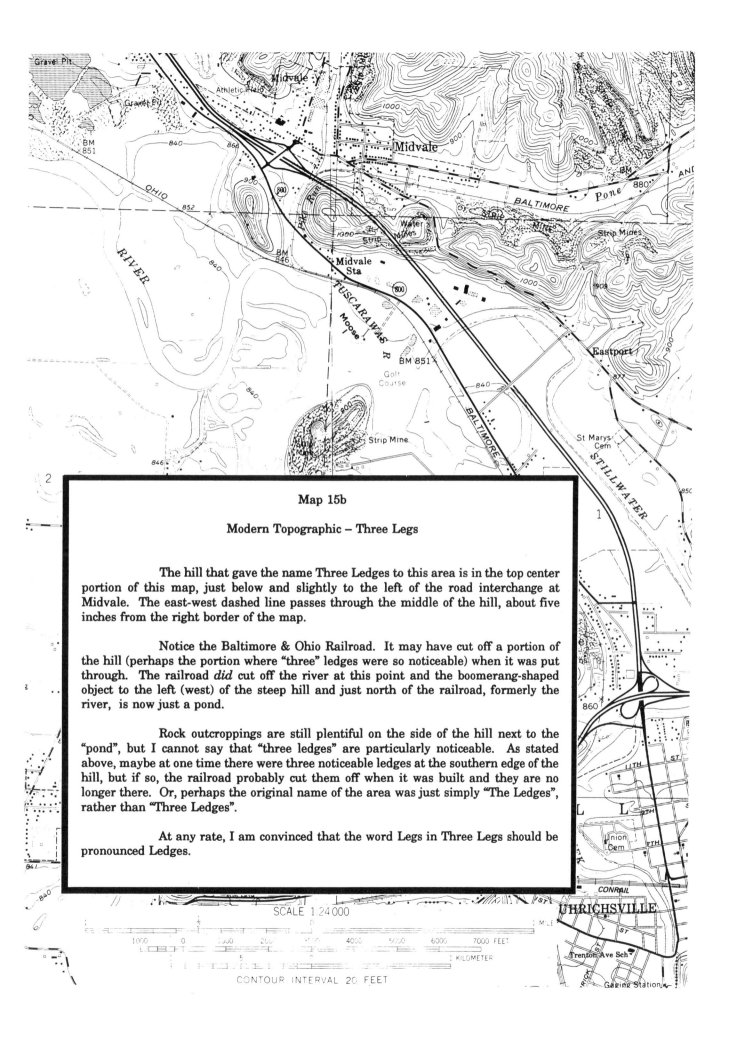

Map 15b

Modern Topographic – Three Legs

The hill that gave the name Three Ledges to this area is in the top center portion of this map, just below and slightly to the left of the road interchange at Midvale. The east-west dashed line passes through the middle of the hill, about five inches from the right border of the map.

Notice the Baltimore & Ohio Railroad. It may have cut off a portion of the hill (perhaps the portion where "three" ledges were so noticeable) when it was put through. The railroad *did* cut off the river at this point and the boomerang-shaped object to the left (west) of the steep hill and just north of the railroad, formerly the river, is now just a pond.

Rock outcroppings are still plentiful on the side of the hill next to the "pond", but I cannot say that "three ledges" are particularly noticeable. As stated above, maybe at one time there were three noticeable ledges at the southern edge of the hill, but if so, the railroad probably cut them off when it was built and they are no longer there. Or, perhaps the original name of the area was just simply "The Ledges", rather than "Three Ledges".

At any rate, I am convinced that the word Legs in Three Legs should be pronounced Ledges.

Course	Distan	N	S	E	W	Remarks
N62..30 E	1.. 83					object N21E over River
N64. — E	2.. 50					
N48 — E	3.. 35					object N22.. 30 W
N48 — E	1.. 65					high Land W.O. B.O. spice Hick beech
N60.. — E	3.. 50					
N59.. E	1.. 50					River narrow at this place
N72.. E	2.. —					
N62.30 E	1. 50					to mouth of Still Water —
N37.. E	2.. —					sighted back S37 W then S59½E Then Back S48 W
N40.. E	2.. —					pt of Island begins middle River
N41.. E	1.. 50					
N30 E	4.. —					Rich Bottom Land from mouth of Creek
N9. — E	2.. —					
N2 — E	2.. 50					W Walnut B Walnut sugar tree
N25..30 W	3.. 50					Hickory beech Elm &c
N42.30 W	2.. 50					
N44. W	3.. —					
N60 W	2.. —					
N62. W	2.. 50					
N51 W	2.. —					
N35 W	2.. 50					
N30..30 W	2.. 50					
N23.. W	2.. —					
N45..15 W	2.. 50					
N60 W	2. 50					
N68.30 W	4. 50					upper pt Island still in the middle of River —

Course	Dist	N	S	E	W	Remarks —
N 67..30 W	3 .. —					
N 65.. W	5 .. —					Bottom excelent
N 01.. W	2 .. —					
N 62 W	2 .. —					mouth of a run 40 lks wide
West	2.50					
N 77 W	1..50					
N 74 W	1..50					
N 72.30 W	2 .. —					foot of hill 66 lks distant N of course
N 83.. W	1..50					
N 67..30 W	1.. 50					
N 58 W	1..50					
N 50 W	1.. —					
N 53.31 W	2.. —					
N 38 W	3..50					shelveing rocks close on the River
N 22. W	7.. —					object bears S 67 W
S 65.. W	4.. —					object bears S 13 E narrows end
West	3.. —					Good Bottom Land
S 70 W	2..50					
S 57 W	1.. —					
S 45 W	3.. —					Good Bottom Land
S 31 W	2..50					
S 03..36 W	3.. —					
S 37.. E	14.. —					
S 35.. E	3..50					
S 9.. E	3.. 50					
S 6..30 W	5.. —					Bottom still first rate timber as usual —
S 9..30 W	2..50					

The Minister who resides at this Town is a German of the Moravian Sect   has Lived with them several years   has Acquired their Language and taught most of them the English and German he prayed in the Delaware Language Preached in the English and sung Psalms in the German in which the Indians Joined and Performed that part of Divine Service in a Manner really Inimitable

James Wood   August 6th, 1775

The Princeton Experiment

In 1779, when several Indian chiefs journeyed to Philadelphia to visit the Congress, they took with them three boys for the purpose of receiving an education at Princeton, New Jersey. (The Indian Agent, George Morgan, lived at Princeton and had offered to look after them while they were attending school.) The boys were John Killbuck, age sixteen, son of Captain Killbuck (Gelelemend); Thomas Killbuck, age eighteen, the Captain's half-brother, and George M. White Eyes, age eight, their cousin and the son of the famous Captain White Eyes, by then deceased.

The boys attended the grammar school in the basement of Nassau Hall for several years. The oldest, Thomas Killbuck, apparently did not take to the educational process and obtained work on a farm. Colonel Morgan stated that he was addicted to "Liquor & to Lying", and that his services as a farmhand were not very valuable. He wanted to go back to the Ohio country, but it was not until October of 1785 that he was allowed to return to his tribe. The other Killbuck, John, was a better student and by the summer of 1783 had advanced to geography, mathematics, and Latin. Unfortunately, however, he became romantically involved with one of Colonel Morgan's serving maids, and she became pregnant. They were married and he continued his studies for a few more years. Then he, too, returned to his tribe at the same time as his uncle, Thomas, taking with him his wife and child.

The third boy, George M. White Eyes, did the best of all. By May of 1784, he was reading Virgil and had begun Greek. He was at the head of his class in grammar school and was expected to enter college in the Fall. Presumably he did, for there are records showing that he was living in one of the upper rooms at Nassau Hall in 1788. He apparently did not graduate, however. In September of 1788, George Morgan had to give up his "guardianship" of White Eyes for the reason that his business was going to require his absence for several months. He therefore sent White Eyes to New York, to the residence of a Mr. R. Cox, to await the pleasure of Congress which was sitting in New York at that time. They, apparently, did nothing for him, and in August of 1789, he seems to have headed back to the Ohio country.

Colonel Morgan's assessment of the "experiment" was that the Killbucks had been too old at the time their educational process was begun, and for that reason had not done very well, but that White Eyes, being only eight years of age when he began his schooling, had been able to do much better.

For additional information, see Collins, V. L., "Indian Wards at Princeton", cited in Bibliography.

Heckewelder's Garden

With respect to the matter of the "Heckewelder's Garden" of 1762, early maps of the area near Bolivar designate it as being on the south side of the Tuscarawas, about a half mile above the mouth of the Sandy.

But was that really the location of his garden, or was it, perhaps, the garden of the Indian trader, Calhoun?

I believe the latter to be the case.

The most obvious problem with stating that Heckewelder's garden was on the *south* side of the Tuscarawas is that his cabin was on the *north* side!

Why would he put his garden across the river from his house? It makes no sense at all.

In his diary for 1762, set forth in this book, he makes many statements that show that crossing the river was a real problem for him:

> there were wild duck in abundance; but the river being in some places too deep to ford, and we having no canoe, I often had to wait very long, until they flew so near the bank that I could reach them when shot.

...we resolved to make a canoe...

[The first canoe was lost, or stolen, and then he says:]

I was often in great distress for food...

Every vegetable that grew in my garden was stolen by the passing traders...

When I wished to visit Mr. Calhoon, I had to wade through the Muskingum...

At last my strength failed to such a degree that I was afraid to venture upon fording the river, and was compelled to stay at home...

Then an Indian made another canoe for him. Finally, when one of Mr. Calhoun's men called to him from across the river to leave immediately, he states "...I paddled across...".

It seems that he hesitated to venture across the river without the canoe.

Why, then, would the garden be put across the river from the house, where he would have to be constantly crossing the river to tend it and collect its produce?

Also, if it really was where the map shows it to be, no trader would have been passing near that spot, for the paths to Sandusky and Cuyahoga do not go by it.

256

The Sandusky path cuts straight across from Tuscarawas to the west, crossing the Muskingum two more times in just a mile or two, making three crossings in all. It was at least a half mile south of the location of "Heckewelder's Garden" as shown on the map.

The Cuyahoga path passed along the *north* side of the Tuscarawas and would have been across the river from the garden as shown on the map. This path also forks, though, and joins the Sandusky path, thus permitting travelers heading that way to cross the Muskingum only once.   *Steiner* proceeded that way.

For these reasons, I believe the garden would have been closer to these paths, either on the north (or west) side of the river near the Sandusky path, or on the north side of the river near the Cuyahoga path, (probably the latter since *Steiner* was using this path when he passed the cabin).

But there is another good reason to doubt that the garden was actually at the location shown on the map. It's too close to the Indian town.

Heckewelder, in his journal of 1762, states:

The cabin which Post had built the year before, stood on a high bank, on the east side of the Muskingum, about four rods from the stream. No one lived near us on the same side of the river; but on the other, a mile down the stream, resided a trader named Thomas Calhoon, a moral and religious man. Farther south was situated the Indian town called Tuscarawas; consisting of about forty wigwams.

This means that Heckewelder's cabin would have been over a mile from the Indian town, for Calhoun was a mile below him, and the Indian town was still farther down the river.

How much farther?

This is where the *McCullough* narrative is of help.

It had been a question in my mind as to whether or not Calhoun's trading establishment would have been quite close to the Indian town, or perhaps some distance from it.

The map shows the garden to be about a half mile from the Sandy, and the Indian town was located just above this junction.

Could Calhoun have been this far from the town? I think so.

McCullough says that when Daniel warned the traders at Tuscarawas to leave in the night, "as they lived about a mile out of town, they had an opportunity of going away without being discovered."

It therefore appears that the garden on the map could very well be Calhoun's garden, for it is about the right distance from the Indian town. Heckewelder lived a mile still farther up the river.

Confirmation of all that has been said above can be found in the Abraham Steiner journal. He was traveling in company with Heckewelder himself, and says that 1½ miles above the junction of the rivers they came to the site of Heckewelder's cabin, and they could "see very well where the house and cellar had been, and also the corn hills." They had not yet crossed the Muskingum at this time, so, clearly, the garden was close to the house and on the *north* side of the river, at a distance of 1½ miles from the junction with the Sandy. Since the "Heckewelder's Garden" shown on the old map is only ½ mile from the junction and on the *south* side of the river, it cannot possibly be Heckewelder's garden. If it actually dates from 1762, it was probably Calhoun's garden, for Heckewelder states his cabin was about a mile above Calhoun's, and since the garden site on the map is ½ mile from the junction, that would come out exactly to the 1½ miles above the junction mentioned by Steiner (with Heckewelder present) as to the site of Heckewelder's cabin.

Considering all of the matters set forth above, I am convinced that the garden shown on the map is not Heckewelder's but could very possibly be Calhoun's garden.

Indian Food

The principal food of the Indians consists of the game which they take or kill in the woods, the fish out of the waters, and the maize, potatoes, beans, pumpkins, squashes, cucumbers, melons, and occasionally cabbages and turnips, which they raise in their fields; they make use also of various roots of plants, fruits, nuts, and berries out of the woods, by way of relish or as a seasoning to their victuals, sometimes also from necessity.

They commonly make two meals every day, which, they say, is enough. If any one should feel hungry between meal-times, there is generally something in the house ready for him.

Source: Heckewelder's *History...*, p. 193

/

Map 16

Map Showing Location of Heckewelder's Garden

The original of this map is in the Land Office of the Auditor of State at Columbus. Near the right edge, it shows the location of Heckewelder's Garden as being on the south side of the river and just about one-half mile above the ford at the crossing place of the Muskingum. According to the *Steiner* journal, however, the garden was on the north side of the river and about one and one-half miles above the junction of the Sandy, which junction was about one-third of a mile below the ford. The Greenville Treaty Line intersects the Muskingum at the crossing place, or ford. The surveyor's notes state that the ford was 24 chains, or about 1/3 mile, above the Sandy. The vestiges of the Indian town began 4 chains, or 264 feet, above the ford and the location of Heckewelder's Garden was 42.68 chains, or about one-half mile above the ford.

Scale of Forty Chains to an Inch.

Surveyed by Joseph H Larwell 1807.

Range Nº IX *West of the Muskingum River.*

stern part of this Township see Book Nº I page 168.

uality of the land on the interior sectional lines.

Between
Sections.

6 . 7 . Good soil; timber W r Pt Oak, Hickory)
7 . 13 . Rich and level; timber W r Pt Oak Hickory), Ash &c
8 . 17 . Good soil, exceeding) brushy with Thorn, Hazle-bush &c
16 . 21 . Thin soil, mostly scrubby, brushy barrens: Oak Thorn &c

it

est ¾ brushy barrens &c.

&, Hickory) &.

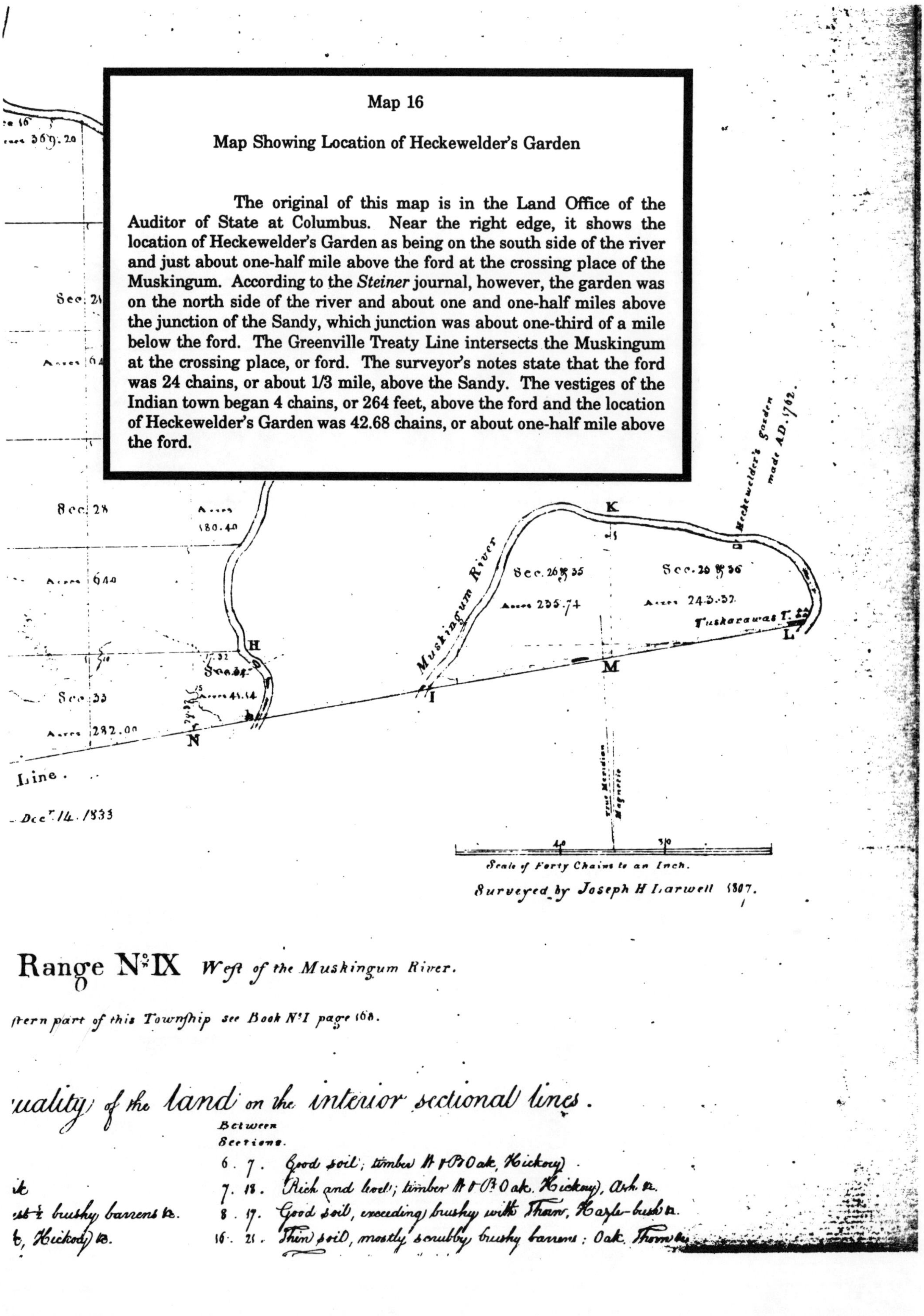

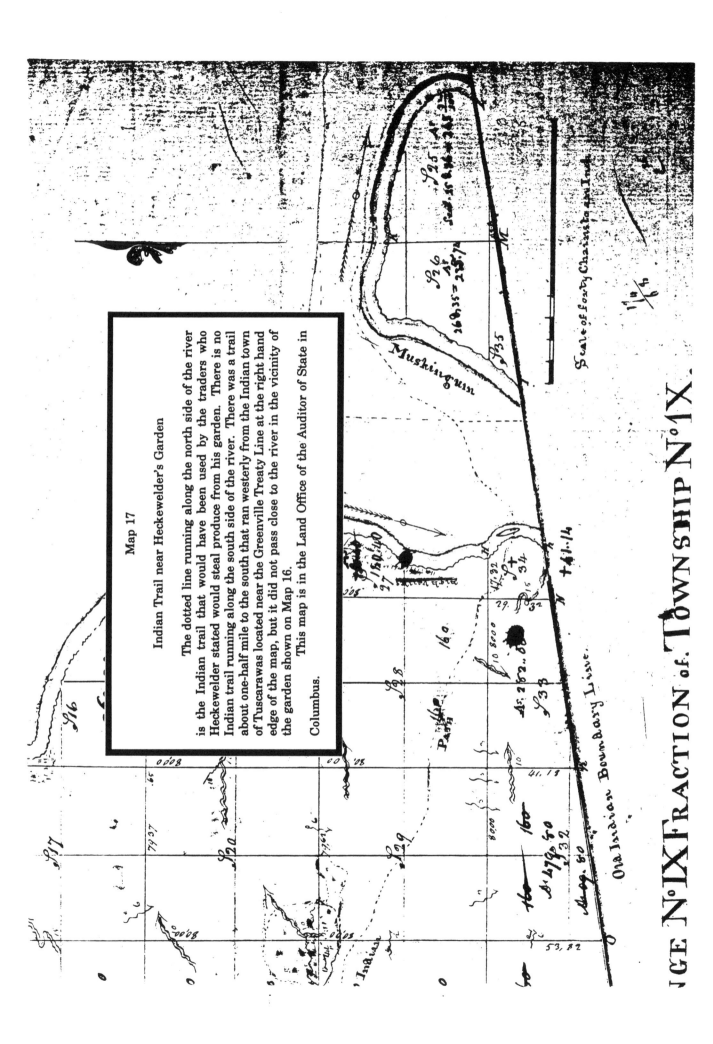

Map 17

Indian Trail near Heckewelder's Garden

The dotted line running along the north side of the river is the Indian trail that would have been used by the traders who Heckewelder stated would steal produce from his garden. There is no Indian trail running along the south side of the river. There was a trail about one-half mile to the south that ran westerly from the Indian town of Tuscarawas located near the Greenville Treaty Line at the right hand edge of the map, but it did not pass close to the river in the vicinity of the garden shown on Map 16.

This map is in the Land Office of the Auditor of State in Columbus.

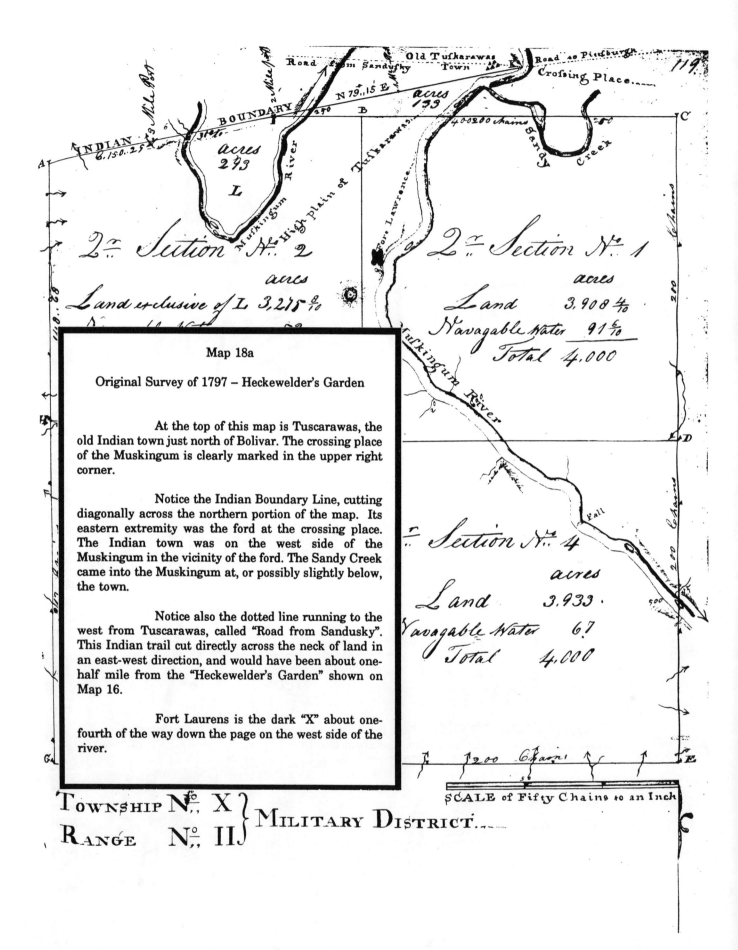

Map 18a

Original Survey of 1797 – Heckewelder's Garden

At the top of this map is Tuscarawas, the old Indian town just north of Bolivar. The crossing place of the Muskingum is clearly marked in the upper right corner.

Notice the Indian Boundary Line, cutting diagonally across the northern portion of the map. Its eastern extremity was the ford at the crossing place. The Indian town was on the west side of the Muskingum in the vicinity of the ford. The Sandy Creek came into the Muskingum at, or possibly slightly below, the town.

Notice also the dotted line running to the west from Tuscarawas, called "Road from Sandusky". This Indian trail cut directly across the neck of land in an east-west direction, and would have been about one-half mile from the "Heckewelder's Garden" shown on Map 16.

Fort Laurens is the dark "X" about one-fourth of the way down the page on the west side of the river.

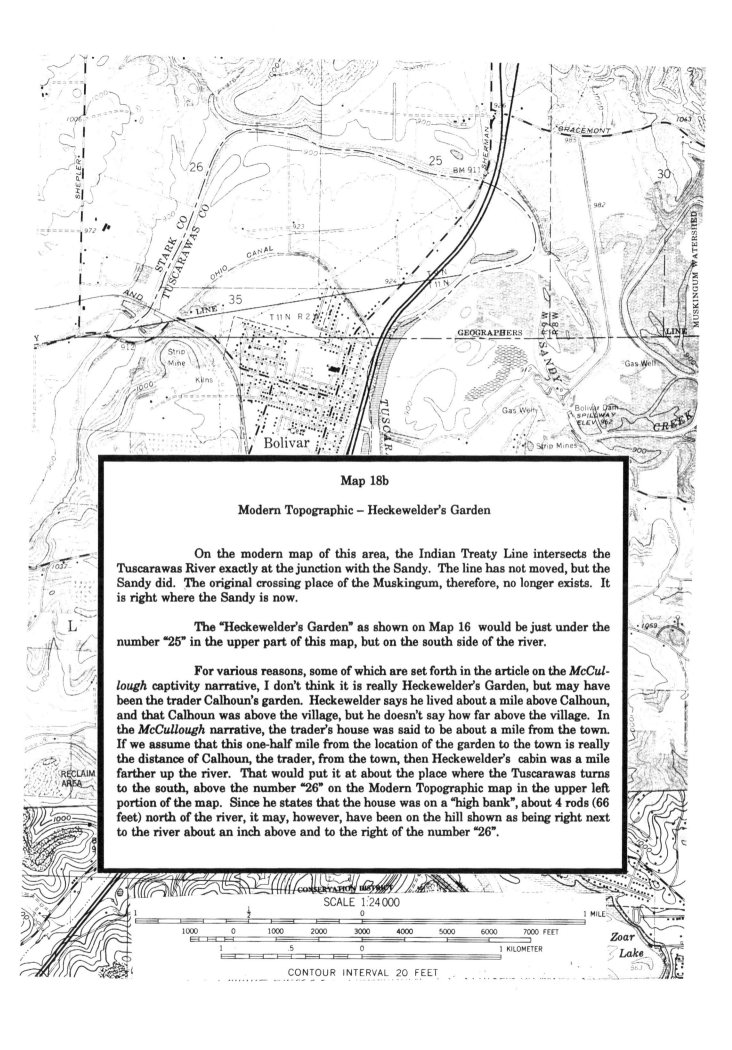

Map 18b

Modern Topographic – Heckewelder's Garden

On the modern map of this area, the Indian Treaty Line intersects the Tuscarawas River exactly at the junction with the Sandy. The line has not moved, but the Sandy did. The original crossing place of the Muskingum, therefore, no longer exists. It is right where the Sandy is now.

The "Heckewelder's Garden" as shown on Map 16 would be just under the number "25" in the upper part of this map, but on the south side of the river.

For various reasons, some of which are set forth in the article on the *McCullough* captivity narrative, I don't think it is really Heckewelder's Garden, but may have been the trader Calhoun's garden. Heckewelder says he lived about a mile above Calhoun, and that Calhoun was above the village, but he doesn't say how far above the village. In the *McCullough* narrative, the trader's house was said to be about a mile from the town. If we assume that this one-half mile from the location of the garden to the town is really the distance of Calhoun, the trader, from the town, then Heckewelder's cabin was a mile farther up the river. That would put it at about the place where the Tuscarawas turns to the south, above the number "26" on the Modern Topographic map in the upper left portion of the map. Since he states that the house was on a "high bank", about 4 rods (66 feet) north of the river, it may, however, have been on the hill shown as being right next to the river about an inch above and to the right of the number "26".

SCALE 1:24 000

1   ½   0   1 MILE

1000 0 1000 2000 3000 4000 5000 6000 7000 FEET

1   .5   0   1 KILOMETER

CONTOUR INTERVAL 20 FEET

It is not easy for a white man, used to the warm comforts of civilized life to conceive how delicious & exhilerating rum is, to the taste & stomach of an Indian.

David McClure   September 26, 1772

The John McCullough Captivity Narrative

As was mentioned in the introduction to the captivity narrative of *John McCullough*, it may be that this one narrative provides answers to several questions concerning the history of events in the Tuscarawas Valley, some of which would appear to have no connection at all with any of the others.

The questions to be considered are the following:

A. When did Newcomer move away from the Cuyahoga?

B. When did he move to Newcomerstown?

C. Why does Bouquet, in his papers, state that Newcomer was on the Scioto?

D. Why did Newcomer refuse to meet with Bouquet in 1764?

E. Is the "Heckewelder's Garden" that is labelled as such on early maps of the area near Bolivar really his garden, or perhaps the trader Calhoun's garden?

In trying to find answers to the above questions, we will start with the known fact that Newcomer was on the Cuyahoga as late as February of 1763. *James Kenny,* at Fort Pitt, in his diary entry for February 21st of that year, states:

> Frederick Post came here last Night from Cyahaga & informs that ye Delawars had Except'd ye War Belt & Tomhock, which came from ye Six Nations last Summer, that they held War dances & Sung of bringing in more White Prisoners, & of hearing of ye Peace being made & ye French to quit this side ye Missisipi. Their head King Neetotwhelemy, i-e Newcomer was Struck dumb for a considerable time & at last sd he did not know whether ye News was true but if they could hear it from their fathers, i. e. ye French he would believe it,...

By the time Bouquet came into the valley in October and November of 1764, he was where Newcomerstown is now located, for Hutchins' map shows a town called Newcomerstown at its present location.

The question, then, is when did he move there?

The key to the answer to that question depends upon whether or not McCullough was being held captive by Indians of Newcomer's band. I believe he was.

First, he mentions moving from the Cuyahoga to the forks of the Muskingum (this would be at Coshocton), and "from thence we took up the west branch (the Walhonding) to its source, and from thence I know not where."

259

It is apparent that they went beyond the source of the Walhonding. This would place them in the headwaters, at least, of the Scioto, if not all the way to the river itself.

He then mentions the very hard time they had getting through the winter, subsisting on roots, bark, and even turkey quills.

Then, "In the Spring we returned to the west branch…" of the Muskingum {meaning the Walhonding} "…and settled in a new town, which we called Kta-ho´-ling." Could this, perhaps, be the town better known as Kokosing, near Mount Vernon? He states that "We remained there during the Summer". This implies that, after the summer, they moved again.

While there, the massacre of Brown, the schoolmaster, and the children occurred, committed by three Indians of the band, as stated in his narrative.

Then, a short time later, when Bouquet's army came into the area, McCullough stated he was living about ten miles from where the army camped (near Coshocton). He could have been living at Newcomerstown at this time, for that is only about 12-13 miles from Bouquet's encampment near the forks of the Muskingum. With respect to McCullough's estimate of ten miles, it is to be noted that Finley's original field notes of the Bouquet Expedition, set forth in the separate article dealing with the Location of Bouquet's 16th Encampment also uses the estimate of ten miles as the distance to Newcomerstown from Bouquet's Encampment.

The above "timetable" would indicate the move from the Cuyahoga took place sometime in the year 1763, for the next year he was redeemed by Bouquet, and that happened in 1764.

The move from the Cuyahoga was apparently a sudden thing, for it was made without adequate preparation for having enough food to get through the winter. This would be consistent with the message sent by the Indians at Tuscarawas to Fort Pitt, quoted in the *Trent* journal of 1763, stating that they were going to move away from the area as soon as they conveniently could. That message was sent in May of 1763.

I think that they left soon after that, either sometime in the summer, or perhaps autumn, of 1763. Because they had not been able to harvest their crops, they had a very hard time finding food to get them through the winter, just as McCullough states.

And if they did, indeed, go as far as the waters of the Scioto, that would explain why Bouquet states that Newcomer was on the Scioto. Perhaps he was there at the time Bouquet had been given that information, or perhaps he had already been there and had moved back to the Walhonding by that time, without Bouquet realizing this. In this regard it is to be noted that among the questions asked of the Indian deputies who had come to Fort Pitt before the expedition got underway was "Where do you live now?" (See Attachment B at the end of this article.) If Newcomer was still on the Scioto, or one of its branches, at the time the Indians had left his town, that could be the explanation for Bouquet's belief in this regard.

The statement that Newcomer was on the Scioto is contained in Attachment A at the end of this article.

Second, is there anything in the *McCullough* narrative that names Newcomer as being the head of the band he was living with?

I think that there is.

In referring to the massacre of the school children, he states that "some of the old Indians were very much displeased at them for killing so many children, especially Neep-paugh´-whese, or night-walker, an old chief or half-king."

Notice the similarity in the sounds of Neep-paugh´-whese and Netawatwees. The last two syllables are nearly identical, and even the first syllable starts with the "N" sound. In fact, the *Kenny* journal quoted above refers to Newcomer as "Neetohwhelemy", and the *David Jones* journal calls him "Neetotwhealemon"—both indicating a "Nee" sound, rather than a "Net" sound at the beginning of his name. McCullough also seemed to hear the "Nee" sound—"Neep-paugh´-whese". And McCullough placed the accent on the "waugh" syllable, just as in Netawatwees the accent is on the "wat" syllable. Putting all of this together, then, it seems that there is a great deal of similarity in the two names.

Also, Netawatwees, or Newcomer, was old and was often referred to as King Newcomer. (McCullough calls Neep-paugh´-whese "an old chief or half-king".) Heckewelder, in his article on Indian Names which appeared in the *Transactions of the American Philosophical Society,* New Series, IV, (1833), at pages 351-396, states on page 389 that when Netawatwees died in the autumn of 1776, he was "near ninety years of age". That would place him in his 70s in 1764, certainly old by the standards of those times.

I think it highly possible that Neep-paugh´-whese and Netawatwees were the same Indian. Even night-walker and Newcomer could, perhaps, sound somewhat similar, both three syllables, the last ending in "er" and the first starting with an "N".

With regard to Newcomer's failure to meet with Bouquet, if Neep-paugh´-whese really was the same Indian as Newcomer, and if members of his band were the ones who killed the schoolchildren in August of 1764, it is possible he was afraid to meet Bouquet, who came into the area just a few months after this happened, for fear of reprisals for the killings.

In an attempt to see if there would have been anything said by Bouquet to the Indians, either before he left Fort Pitt, or at the conference held at Tuscarawas, that would cause the Indians to believe that he was looking for the killers of the schoolchildren, I examined the Bouquet papers, page by page, to see what I could find in this regard. And there it was.

During a meeting with the three Indians who had come across the river to Fort Pitt shortly after Bouquet had arrived there on September 17th, he apparently asked certain questions of them, some of which are set forth on the page entitled Attachment B at the end of this article, and he specifically asked "Who are the people who have killed Brown, so long after the Peace?" and two more times at that same meeting he refers to the "murder of Brown".

Keeping in mind that Brown was the name of the schoolmaster, any Indian hearing these questions asked of them by the leader of an army of 1500 men intending to come into their territory just a few months after the massacre had occurred would certainly have cause for concern for his safety if he was the leader of those Indians, even if he was not directly involved. It is also to be noted that the two Indians who were detained as hostages were Captain Pipe and Captain Johnny. Pipe was one of the principal captains of the Wolf Tribe and Johnny was one of the principal captains of the Turkey Tribe. I think it highly probable that the third Indian would have been of the Turtle Tribe, thus completing the representation of the entire Delaware Nation at that meeting. Perhaps he was even Captain Killbuck, himself, although I have no proof of this. At any rate, whoever he was, he probably was of the Turtle Tribe and would have certainly taken Bouquet's message back to his chief, Netawatwees. It would make sense for Bouquet to have sent as the messenger the Indian who had the farthest to travel to get to his tribe, for he could also deliver the message to the other tribes as he passed by. That is another reason supporting the belief that the Turtle Tribe really was on the Scioto at that time.

I think, therefore, that Netawatwees stayed away from Bouquet because he *was* the leader of the band of Indians, three of whom killed Brown and the schoolchildren, and feared what Bouquet might do to him if he got his hands on him. Adding to his fears would have been Bouquet's statement at the conference with the chiefs at Tuscarawas that "I have brought with me the relations of the people you have massacred, or taken prisoners. They are impatient for revenge;..."

There must have been some good reason for Newcomer to have stayed away from Bouquet, and this could very well have been that reason.

For the discussion as to the importance of the McCullough captivity narrative to the location of Heckewelder's Garden, see the special article on that subject.

Journeys

If the chiefs have a journey to make, they usually take some of the younger men along, who supply the larder during the journey by engaging in the chase. A journey is rarely hurried for usually it makes little difference whether they arrive at their destination a day late or not, and they are everywhere at home in the woods. They rarely leave camp early in the morning, wishing always to have a good meal before starting and sometimes they delay to mend their shoes.

Source: Zeisberger's *History...*, p. 119

ATTACHMENT A

ACCOUNT OF PRISONERS IN THE SHAWNEE TOWNS

[B. M., Add. MSS. 21655, f. 251, D.]

A List of the Prisoners supposed to be at the different Shanoes Towns on Scioto.

The New comers Town 50

The Kiew Town 15

at the Old Town 7

Salt Lick Town 5

Bull Heads Town 1

At the Grenadeers a Woman 6

————

84

[Endorsed in Col. Bouquet's handwriting] Prisoners lefft amongst the Shawanese the 15th Novr 1764

ATTACHMENT B

QUESTIONS ASKED OF THE INDIAN DEPUTIES

[B. M., Add. MSS. 21655, f. 268, D.]

What is your Intention in coming here?

Of what Nations are the men who sued for Peace at Presqu' Isle?

Did the Delawares & Shawanese authorize them to ask it for them?

Have all your and their Chiefs consented to the Peace, and upon what terms?

How many Prisoners have you already delivered?

How many more have you?

Is Colonel Bradstreet at Sandusky and what time has he given you to deliver the Prisoners?

What has passed between him & you since Presqu' Isle?

Where do you live now?

Who wrote the Letter sent to Niagara by the Shawanese & you?

Where is Lowry?

Who are the People who have killed Brown, so long after the Peace?

I will know whether what you have told me is true, and send a Letter to Col. Bradstreet, by Mr. McKee, and to me of my men formerly you were honest but now you are corrupted & have been guilty of so many Treacheries that I can no more trust you particularly after the murder of Brown and as I can not trust you after your repeated Treacheries, and the murder of Brown you must remain with me as hostages till Mr. McKee brings me a Letter from Col. Bradstreet, and if you have Said the Truth, you will then be released, and be well used.

You will Send one of your men with him, who is to return with him, and all my People.

I need not tell you that if any of those men is killed by any of yours, You will all be put to death.

Heckewelder's Ride

The story of the ride of John Heckewelder from Fort Pitt to Coshocton originates in his own *Narrative of the Mission,* written more than forty years after the event. As stated, it was a very dramatic event, climaxing on the ninth day of the ten day waiting period proclaimed by White Eyes before the Delawares would go to war against the Americans.

But was there the ten day waiting period as described in the *Narrative,* commencing with the arrival of the defectors from Fort Pitt, and did White Eyes give the speech quoted in the *Narrative* at the commencement of the waiting period?

Heckewelder, in his *History of the Manners & Customs,* at page 153, after describing the same speech as set forth in his *Narrative of the Mission,* states "I was present when he made the speech which I have related, and never shall forget the impression it made upon me."

If the speech was made shortly after the defectors from Fort Pitt arrived and at the beginning of the ten day waiting period, how could Heckewelder have heard it? He was not even there! He was still in Pennsylvania at that time!

This inconsistency prompted a further search into the "timetable" of events concerning the ride and raised questions about the matter of the ten day wait—one of the most dramatic parts of the whole story.

There is ample authority that the defectors left Fort Pitt on the night of Saturday, March 28, 1778.

Thwaites, *Frontier Defense on the Upper Ohio* contains the following letters:

p. 249 – Letter of General Hand to Jasper Yeates.

"Fort Pitt 30th March 1778
Dear Yeates – I am in such Distress on being Satisfied that Mr. McKee has made his escape from here the night before last, Accompanied by Mat. Elliott, Simon Girty, two others I am not Acquainted with & two negroes, that I can Say very little to you at this time..."

p. 250 – Letter of General Hand to General Horatio Gates.

"Fort Pitt, 30th March, 1778

Sir – I have the mortification to inform you that last Saturday night, Alexander McKee made his escape from this place, as also Mathew Elliott, a person lately from Quebec on parole, Simon Girty, Robt. Surplus, and one Higgins...."

p. 253 – Letter of Maj. Jasper Ewing to Jasper Yeates.

"Fort Pitt, Mar. 30, 1778

Hond. Sir – Last Saturday Night Mr. McKee, Matt. Elliott and Simon Girty, together with one Higgans ran off...."

[NOTE: Alexander McKee had been a Deputy-Agent for Indian Affairs under Sir William Johnson and at the beginning of the Revolution was suspected of favoring the royalist side. He was placed on parole, however, and allowed his liberty, but was not to leave the neighborhood of Fort Pitt. It is for this reason that his defection to the British is referred to as an "escape".]

Leaving on the night of March 28th and traveling as rapidly as they could, it probably would have taken at least three, but more likely four, days to reach Coshocton, a distance of about 120 miles. (Heckewelder says it took him three days to reach Gnadenhutten, and Coshocton is about 28 miles farther.) This means that they would have reached Coshocton the evening of March 31st at the very earliest, but more probably sometime on April 1st.

If the speech of White Eyes was given on the same day, April 1st, and the ten days started to run at that point, the ninth day would have either been on April 9th or 10th, depending upon how the days are counted.

The defectors were still at Coshocton on April 4th, for in a letter from Governor Henry Hamilton, at Detroit, to Sir Guy Carleton, set forth in Thwaites, *Frontier Defense of the Upper Ohio*, p. 285, he states, concerning Alexander McKee, "In his letter to me dated Kushayking April 4th,...".

Heckewelder does not say in his *Narrative* exactly when he left Fort Pitt, or when he arrived at Coshocton at the end of his ride. If his statement is correct as to the ten day waiting period commencing *after* the defectors had arrived at Coshocton, and if he arrived at Coshocton on the ninth day of the waiting period, his arrival would have been on the 9th or 10th of April.

However, independent evidence places the date of his arrival at Coshocton as being on April 6th!

His date of arrival can be determined from two different sources. The Fliegel *Index to the Moravian Archives* states that he arrived at Lichtenau, the Moravian town just below Coshocton, on April 6th, and on that same date, presumably as a result of the news that he brought from the east, the Delaware Council wrote a letter to George Morgan, the Indian Agent at Fort Pitt, expressing friendship to the United States. The reference to the letter is found in Thwaites, *Frontier Defense of the Upper Ohio*, at page 269, in a letter of George Morgan to the Delaware Council, dated April 13th, 1778:

THE UNITED AMERICAN STATES to the wise DELAWARE COUNCIL

Brothers – We have received your Letter dated the 6th inst. we have considered the Contents and are well pleased with your repeated professions of Friendship to the United States....

It thus appears clear that Heckewelder arrived on April 6th, several days before the end of the ten day waiting period, *if the period began with the arrival of the defectors at Coshocton,* as Heckewelder states in his *Narrative.* It is possible, of course, that the ten days began *before* the defectors had arrived from Fort Pitt and if Heckewelder did arrive on the ninth day, then the waiting period must have begun on March 28th, the day the defectors left the fort. Just exactly what precipitated the commencement of the waiting period, if it was not the arrival of the defectors at Coshocton, cannot be determined from the *Narrative* alone.

Zeisberger's Lichtenau Diary, however, provides what may be the answer to this question.

The entry for March 27th, 1778 reads as follows:

27th.—Brother David was called to Goschachgunk {Coshocton} by a messenger who had come from the Fort. The reason we had not heard from there for so long was that they could not get anyone to come out in these times and Mr. Morgan by chance found a Wyondot Indian to come here. With this opportunity, to my great joy, came letters from Bro. Mattheo from Lititz. Since White Eye and the Chiefs were called to the Fort, Bro. David had a talk with White Eye asking that he do his best to see to it that our and the Delaware towns should be secure, to which he consented....

Several things should be noted in this entry. First, it confirms Heckewelder's statement as to the difficulty that the authorities at Fort Pitt had in finding anyone to carry messages into the Indian country. It evidently really was an exceedingly dangerous time on the border. Second, White Eyes and some of the other chiefs were asked to come to the Fort to make arrangements for a Treaty to be held later in the spring or summer. Copies of the letters sent to White Eyes are attached to this article as Letter 1 and Letter 2. Zeisberger then talked to White Eyes about protecting the interests of the mission towns in his dealings with the authorities at the Fort, showing concern on his part about the survivability of the mission itself. Third, in response to these letters, White Eyes did set off for Fort Pitt, probably on either the 27th or 28th of March. My guess, and I have to admit that I have no direct proof of this, is that it was at this time that White Eyes asked the Indians not to make any decision as to whether they would go to war until he returned from his trip to the Fort. Since it normally took four days to get there and another four days to return, that would leave him two days at the Fort itself to find out the true state of affairs as to the war in the east. If he left on the 28th, April 6th would be the ninth day of the ten day waiting period. I believe, therefore, that Heckewelder was right about there being a ten day waiting period. He was wrong, however, as to how, and when, it started. It did not start *after* the defectors reached Coshocton, but several days before they got there. Heckewelder states that it was at White Eyes' request that there be a ten day waiting period. I believe that is an accurate statement, but not for the reason put forth in his *Narrative.* In the *Narrative* the reason seems to be just to see if there might be any other news received at Coshocton during those ten days that would either prove or disprove the things that the defectors were telling the Indians about the situation of the War in the East and the intentions of the Americans towards the Indians. It is almost as though White Eyes is saying, "Let's just wait for ten more days to see if we hear anything else during that time." That doesn't make a whole lot of sense. Probably nothing at all would be heard during those ten days if they just waited for chance, alone, to bring them some news. It makes much more sense to believe that, just as Heckewelder said, it was White Eyes who asked for the ten day wait, but for the reason that it would take him that long to get to Pittsburgh and back, thus finding out for himself just exactly what the situation was at the Fort, and in the East. That was the reason for the ten day wait, to have time to travel to the Fort and return to Coshocton.

If there really was a ten day waiting period, and it is the ninth day already, is there any contemporary evidence as to the sense of urgency in getting the news brought by Heckewelder to Coshocton, thus lending support to the ten day wait story? I believe that there is and, again, the Lichtenau Diary is very helpful in this regard.

The entry for April 6th, 1778 reads as follows:

6th.—Before noon a messenger came from Gnadenhütten with the unexpected but very joyful news that the Brethren Heckewelder and Schebosch arrived there safely last evening. At the same time, to my exceeding joy, I received many letters from Bethlehem and Lititz. At the same time, because I got also a letter from two congressmen who were in the Fort, I went with it soon to Goschachgunk, read it to the Council and made a speech which caused White Eyes to get up and to express his doubts and objections, that we could hope that everything would be brought into order. In the evening Bro. Heckewelder himself came with Anton to the joy of everyone, for we received the news that all the Brothers and Sisters in Gnadenhütten had decided to come here.

Consider the above timetable in conjunction with the statements of Heckewelder in his *Narrative*. Heckewelder stated that he reached Gnadenhutten at eleven o'clock at night, rested until about three or four o'clock in the morning, and then went on to Coshocton with Anton. He then proceeds to tell about the cool reception that he received, but that after showing the Indians the documents that he had brought from the east, the Indians finally believed him, and White Eyes "gave me his hand". He gives the impression in his *Narrative* that it was his unexpected appearance and the news that he brought that "saved the day" for the mission.

Yet Zeisberger says that even before Heckewelder himself had arrived, he had received word that Heckewelder was at Gnadenhutten and he had also received letters that were so important that he took them directly to the Indian Council at Coshocton and read one of them to the assembled Indians. Only later in the day did Heckewelder finally arrive.

Without passing judgment upon these discrepancies, one thing stands out very clearly. It evidently was felt to be so important to get the news brought by Heckewelder to the Indians at Coshocton at the earliest possible moment that, even while Heckewelder slept for a few hours, someone was sent on through the night to Zeisberger at Lichtenau with the documents. And Zeisberger felt that they were so important that he immediately took them to the Indians and informed them of their contents. To me, this is very strong evidence that perhaps there was, indeed, a ten day waiting period that was about to expire, or at least was believed to be about to expire. The Lichtenau Diary entry for April 1st will explain my last sentence:

> April 1—Today we had word from Goschachgunk that the messengers mentioned 18 March had returned from the Fort and 6 white people, deserters that they overtook on the way had come with them. Among them was Mr. McKee, the King's Agent of Indian Affairs whom the Wyandots had immediately taken prisoner and tied up but soon released after they heard the connection of the affairs. White Eyes met them on the way to the Fort and heard much bad news from the deserters and went back again with them. Afterwards this caused difficulties because the Chiefs were quite influenced by bad news from the deserters.

The reason for the ten day wait no longer existed. White Eyes had not actually reached the Fort, but had returned with the deserters. Now, however, the *only* news that the Indians had at all was the bad news brought by these deserters, and the crisis was becoming even more serious. It may be that the Christian Indians at Gnadenhutten did not know about the return of White Eyes, or, even if they did, the only way that good news was going to get to the Coshocton Indians, to counteract the bad news brought by the deserters, was if the documents brought by Heckewelder were taken to Coshocton as quickly as possible. Only if there really was a serious crisis could the nighttime trip to Coshocton be justified.

Finally, is there anything in the Lichtenau Diary that indicates that Zeisberger felt the seriousness of the situation? Yes, I believe there is. In my opinion, the entry of April 1st, set forth above, wherein he stated "this caused difficulties because the Chiefs were quite influenced by bad news from the deserters" and the following entry for April 4th show that he was very much worried about the future of the mission:

> 4th.—*Today and yesterday were two difficult days.* We were about to hand over to the Council a speech about which they should speak their opinion and then give us an answer, wherefore most of the Brethren left the Conference for Goschachgunk. However, we didn't find the Chiefs inclined to do that and they did not listen; they were all very disturbed and confused and not united among themselves, so *now at this stage it was in doubt and came to the point whether they would decide for peace or war. This was an anxious and distressing time for us* and if they had not feared separation from us, with which we had threatened them plainly enough, they would long since have split away. *We pray the Saviour to graciously keep us through this predicament* and to take our hand and show us the best way to be of help in this matter. Meanwhile, we were glad that the Deserters had decided that some of them would go to Detroit and some to the Shawanosen on the Alnami River.[Emphasis added]

Did the news that Heckewelder brought have any influence upon the Delawares?

It would certainly appear so from the fact that they immediately sent a message back to Pittsburgh expressing "Friendship to the United States", as set forth in the above-quoted correspondence of April 6th. The uncertainty as to whether or not they were going to go to war was apparently rather quickly resolved after the documents brought by Heckewelder had reached Coshocton. They decided to maintain their neutrality.

As to Heckewelder's having heard the speech of White Eyes set forth in his *Narrative* and which he says was given just after the defectors arrived and at the start of the ten day wait, I think it more likely that, since he states so positively that he did hear it, it was given *after* he had arrived at Coshocton at the end of his ride, rather than before, when he was not even there and could not possibly have heard it.

These discrepancies aside, however, it appears that Heckewelder did journey into the Indian country just shortly after the defectors had fled from Fort Pitt and at an extremely dangerous time on the frontier, so dangerous that the authorities at the Fort could not find people who were willing to go into the Indian country, and that perhaps the news he carried as to the true state of affairs in the colonies did have an effect upon the Delawares, causing them to decide not to actively enter the war on the side of the British at that time.

His ride deserves its place in Tuscarawas Valley history.

Indian Opinions of the White Man's Meetings

They sometimes amuse themselves by passing in review those customs of the white people which appear to them most striking. They observe, amongst other things, that when the whites meet together, many of them, and sometimes all, speak at the same time, and they wonder how they can thus hear and understand each other. "Among us," they say "only one person speaks at a time, and the others listen to him until he has done, after which, and not before, another begins to speak." They say also that the whites speak too much, and that much talk disgraces a man and is fit only for women. On this subject they shrewdly observe, that it is well for the whites that they have the art of writing, and can write down their words and speeches; for had they, like themselves, to transmit them to posterity by means of strings and belts of wampum, they would want for their own use all the wampum that could be made, and none would be left for the Indians.

Source: Heckewelder's *History...*, p. 189

Letter 1

Fort Pitt March 20, 1778

Brother Capt White Eyes—Agreeable to the letters I sent you some days ago I flatter'd myself with seeing you and some others of your Wisemen here very soon but unhappily the Messenger took sick and returned to this Place. He is now recovered and I send him to you and to call on Capt Pipe in his Way with Micheykapeecci the old Delaware Woman who was taken at Beaver Creek and also the Young Munsey Woman. I hope you will use your Interest to bring Capt Pipe and other Wisemen here that we may renew and strengthen our Ancient Friendship.

Two Wisemen are arrived from Virginia tho not the same I mentioned to you as they were detained by unavoidable Bussiness. Be strong Brother and let us bear down the evil Spirit. I shall now be stronger than ever and I desire you be so too.

George Morgan

Source: Thwaites, *Frontier Defense on the Upper Ohio,* p. 228

Letter 2

Pittsburgh March [blank in MS.] 1778

Captain White Eyes—The Messenger sent by M^r: Clymer & Colonel Morgan about [blank in MS.} days ago falling sick upon the Road was obliged to return here, by which Accident you were unhappily prevented from hearing sooner of the good disposition of Congress towards the Delaware Nation, but as he is now well again, We who are all the Commissioners appointed by Congress send him back to your Nation with a confirmation of every thing that is said in the former Message. And to give further assurance of the good intentions of Congress he takes with him [blank in MS.] the Delaware Woman taken by our People that she may be restored to her Friends. The other Woman taken with her being a Munsey is in our possession & is well treated. We shall stay here long enough to give an opportunity for you & the other wise Men to visit us at Pittsburgh, in consequence of the invitation already given, to lay the foundation of a Treaty of Peace with your Nation & all other Indians who incline to have our Friendship & good Will, but as we wish to go home to our Wives and Children who are a great way off, we hope you will lose no time in coming with the Messenger. We are Your Friends & Serv^{ts}:

Samp. Mathews
Geo. Clymer
Saml: M^c:Dowell

Source: Thwaites, *Frontier Defense on the Upper Ohio,* pp. 228–29

The Death of White Eyes

Did White Eyes die of smallpox, or was he murdered by the Americans?

In the fall of 1778, White Eyes had received a commission as Colonel in the American army and was to accompany General McIntosh's army as it headed towards Tuscarawas. Near Pittsburgh, however, he died, and it was reported at the time that he died of smallpox. A number of years later, however, George Morgan, the former Indian Agent, wrote two letters in which he stated that White Eyes had been murdered.

The Lichtenau Diary contains some interesting entries on this matter:

November 20th, 1778. Heard that the advance party of the army came to Tuscarawi night before last; likewise that Col. White Eye died not far from Pittsburgh from an old illness plus smallpox.

November 23rd. ...Through an Indian from Tuscarawi we heard that Bro. Daniel had smallpox.

November 29th. ...Joh. Martin returned from Tuscarawi where he had gone to visit his sick brother Daniel, who however, was already buried when Joh. Came.

It does appear, therefore, that there really was some smallpox with the army at Tuscarawas. If so, the story of White Eyes having died from smallpox could be true.

On the other hand, as stated above, several years later George Morgan had occasion to write two letters, copies of which are set forth below, in which he states that White Eyes was murdered. These letters were written, however, to attempt to get Congress to furnish more money for the use of one of White Eyes' sons who was being educated at Princeton, under the care of Morgan, and could, perhaps, have been an attempt to influence Congress to come forth with the funds he was seeking. It seems difficult to imagine that if White Eyes was actually murdered by the Americans, such a secret could have been so successfully kept for all those years. We have only Morgan's word for it that it happened that way.

Probably what really happened will never be known for certain.

The First Letter

"Princeton, May 12th 1784

Sir

Last Month I received the inclosed Letter from one of the chief Men of the Delaware Indians—at least he was so until the active-part he took in favour of the United States divided the Nation. This has reduced him & his few surviving Adherents to the lamentable Situation of Refugees. His Son & his half Brother are two of the Boys whom Congress have been pleased to keep at School here, in some Measure in the light of Hostages. His Son who is now married, is well disposed & sober—but is very anxious to go to his Parents, & to take his Wife with him—The other young Man, lives with a Mr. Lukens in Bucks County—He goes to School, & occasionally assists Mr. Lukens on his Farm, more by way of receiving Instruction, than for the benefit of his Labour—This Lad is ill disposed, given to Liquor & to Lying. He is also very anxious to return to his Friends, And I see no Reason for detaining him longer. Yet I beg leave to recommend the sober one, who is disposed to turn his Attention to a Farm, to the Generosity of Congress—His Wish, is to have his Expenses paid from here to Muskingham, & to have a Grant of necessary Farming Implements, Kitchen Furniture, some Cloathing & the proper Materials given to him, such as Nails Locks, Hinges &c to build himself a House & a Barn—

In regard to the young Man, Thomas, who is given to Liquor, every thing more than cloathing, will be thrown away upon him.—

These two Lads were 16 or 18 Years old when their Parents brought them here, which was at too advanced an age to expect they would derive much benefit from a common Schooling but the third, who was then in his eighth Year, is [in] every way worthy the further Patronage of Congress—Having now enter'd Virgil, & began the Greek, & being the first Scholar of his class, he will be prepared to enter College next Fall—His mildness of Disposition is equal to his capacity; & I cannot but take the Liberty to entreat a continuation of the Patronage of Congress, to this worthy Orphan, whose Father was treacherously put to Death, at the moment of his greatest Exertions to serve the United States; in whose Service he held the Commission of a Colonel—The Son is now in his thirteenth Year—His Father had settled a Tract of Land, of about thirty thousand Acres, on Muskingham, had built several good Shingled Houses on the Tract, mowed Meadow, planted large Fields of Corn, kept a considerable Stock of Horses & Cattle, used Ploughs, & hired white Men to work his Farm— Would it not be worthy of Congress to appropriate this Tract of Land to this Lad, & give such Orders to prevent Incroachments on it, as may secure it to his Heirs forever?

Key ley lamond {Gelelemend, or Killbuck, Jr.} also wishes something of this Kind to be done for himself, & his Adherents, who followed the Fortunes of America during the late War— A Tract of twenty Miles square including his old Village at Cochocking will satisfie them.

I have carefully concealed, & shall continue to conceal from young White Eyes, the Manner of his Fathers Death, wch I have never mentioned to any one but Mr. Thomson, & two or three Members of Congress—

I am with Respect

Your Excellencys

most obt. hum Servant

To
His Excellency   Geo: Morgan
The President of Congress.

The Six Nations, & the Western Tribes are now busy in forming a League to defend their Country—They will however <u>sell</u> a Part. This I have by a late verbal Message from Key Ley lamond."

The Second Letter

"A Letter from Geo. Morgan respecting Geo. White Eyes to the Board of Treasury"

"Prospect, Sept. 25th, 1788

Sir

As I am about to leave New Jersey for two or three Months, and it will consequently be out of my power to continue my Charge over the Son of Col° White Eyes, I propose to send him herewith to New York and to give him a letter to the Commissioners of the Treasury recommending him to their Care until Congress may be pleased to give further Directions.

The Murder of Colonel White Eyes as mentioned in my letter to Congress of the 12th of May 1784 will no doubt recommend the Son to their further protection, notwithstanding, he has lately been much deranged in his Studies & Conduct which I impute to my Absence & to the News of the Murder of his Mother, said to be by a party of White men painted like Indians for the Sake of Peltries she was bringing to Market; which some officious person has told her Son of.

He has neglected his Studies several Months past, & associated with other Lads in College, who have been expelled; & has been induced to sell all his Clothes, Books, Maps, Instruments with an Intention to go off to the Western Country, but as he really is or pretends to be conscious of his Error & promises future Attention, I (suspect) Mistakes and Misconduct have been far surpassed (by) White Boys of his Age, who have had the superior Advantage of enlightened & tender parents to guard over them(.) I presume to solicit Congress on his behalf that he may compleat his Education for which his Abilities, Sprightling (?) yet Mildness of temper is every way equal.

It may not be improper to inform Congress that young White Eyes is descended from Taimenend the Indian Chief who received Wm. Penn on his first landing in Pennsylvania and extended Hospitality & Protection to the first English Settlers of that State in a commendable manner.

A kind treatment of this Lad with a liberal Education under the Patronage of Congress may render him capable of considerable service to his Nation, as well as to the United States.

I took the Liberty to recommend the resumption of his Studies at New Haven or elsewhere in preference to Princeton that there may be no temptation to error from former bad connections.

Or if he was employed as a writer in the War Office, Treasury Board or other public Department under a kind Superintendence I am satisfied he would soon work satisfaction and acquire much useful knowledge.

But should Congress think it advisable to restore him to his Nation I will undertake to do it & in company with him proceed to the interior Towns to know & to report to Congress the true Disposition & Views of the Indian Nations.

As I propose to visit my Farm in the Neighborhood of Fort Pitt in a few days, I will wait the answer of Congress should any be necessary until the 6th of October.

Should Congress resolve to dispose of him otherwise I beg leave to observe that I have addressed him to the present care of Mr. R. Cox, No. 4 William Street, New York who has my orders to supply him with Necessaries & with Lodging & to call on the Treasury Board for payment.

> I have the honor to be
> With the greatest Respect
>
> Your Excellency's
> Most Ob[t] hum[ble] Serv[t]
>
> George Morgan"

The exact date of White Eyes' death is not known, but it was evidently before November 9th, 1778, for that is the date on which an Inventory of his effects was done in Pittsburgh, as shown in the Appendix of this book, entitled "Estate of White Eyes". Especially touching in this list of personal effects is the last item–"1 P spectacles".

Sources of the Letters: *First Letter*   National Archives Record Group 360
M 247, r 180, i 163, p 365

Second Letter   National Archives Record Group 360
M 247, r 104, i 78, v 24, p 619

Warriors

The warriors consist of the young men, among whom, however, are those of fifty years and over. The warriors are under the command of the captains, especially in times of war, and do nothing without their consent.

Zeisberger's *History*, p. 102

Journalists Whose Paths Crossed

The first journalists in this book whose paths crossed were Heckewelder and McKee in October of 1762. Heckewelder, at page 55 in this book, on his return to Pittsburgh from "Muskingum" mentions meeting "Post and the Indian agent, Captain McKee" as they were coming into the Indian country. This was three days after he had left the Bolivar area. Later that same day he ran into "a party of Senecas, who had just returned from an expedition against the Cherokees." McKee, in his journal for October 13th, on page 61 of this book, mentions meeting "a Party of twenty Warriors of the Six Nations, returning from War, with a Cherokee Prisoner, and a Scalp". The Senecas were one of the Six Nations. This meeting with the Indians was probably near the Beaver, for there would have been an Indian trail heading in a north–south direction along the Beaver, and at the point where it meets the east–west Tuscarawas path that Heckewelder and McKee were using would probably have been where they met.

The other journalists whose paths crossed were Cresswell, Wood, and Butler. Nicholas Cresswell first met Captain James Wood on August 12th, 1775, somewhere southeast of Pittsburgh, as described on page 170 in this book. Wood was returning from his trip to the Indian country and Cresswell was just going into it. The paths of Cresswell and Richard Butler later crossed, or nearly crossed, as both went into the Indian country, leaving Pittsburgh one day apart and going by different paths after crossing the Beaver. The following chart describes their routes:

Date	Cresswell	Butler
Aug. 21st	Left Pittsburgh	
22nd	Stayed at Gibsons	Left Pittsburgh
23rd	Camped at Little Beaver	Camped 2 miles from Beaver
24th	Met "Capt. Killbuck"	Met "Old Killbuck"
	Camped at White Oak run	Camped near Yellow Creek

Their routes are diverging now, with Cresswell heading southwest towards Gnadenhutten, while Butler was heading westerly on the Tuscarawas path, considered the shorter route to his destination of Coshocton.

Date	Cresswell	Butler
25th	"very heavy rain" stayed at camp	"Rained all day very heavily". Camped at the plains.

28th	At White Eyes Town	Arrived at Coshocton
29th	Got to Coshocton "about noon"	Left Coshocton "at 11 OClock"

From the above it appears that when Butler left Coshocton, heading west, Cresswell was approaching it from the east and was only a mile or two away. They missed each other by about an hour. Later that day, however, Cresswell went on to Old Hundy and Butler stayed at Winginoms. Since those towns were both along the Walhonding, and may have been the same place, it is possible that both journalists were staying in the same town that night. Neither mentions the other, however. The next day, Butler went on to the west and Cresswell returned to Coshocton.

The Location of Bouquet's 16th Encampment

Considerable uncertainty has existed for many years as to the location of Bouquet's 16th Encampment. Smith's account of the Bouquet Expedition says it was within one mile of the Forks of the Muskingum, but the Hutchins map of the same expedition places it closer to three miles from the Forks. Both are correct. The Hutchins map shows the survey point of the 16th Encampment, but, as discussed below, the camp would probably have stretched for nearly two miles to the southwest of that point, so that the end of the Encampment was just over one mile from the forks.

A few years ago, the original survey field notes of the entire expedition from Fort Pitt to the Forks of the Muskingum were discovered by Edward G. Williams, and he wrote an excellent series of articles on the subject which appeared in the Western Pennsylvania Historical Magazine for 1983 and 1984. His articles included the verbatim field notes kept by one of the Engineers on the expedition, Samuel Finley.

These notes conclusively establish that there was a Light Horse camp just above Canal Lewisville, which would presumably be on one flank of the army, and another camp of Light Horse at the junction of Mill Creek with the Walhonding, also presumably on the other flank of the army and just over one mile from the Forks of the Muskingum.

A further comparison of the field notes with the Original Survey of 1797 for this region enables us to virtually pinpoint the precise location of the survey point of the 16th Encampment. Such precision, standing alone, is a case of overkill, however, for nearly 1,500 men, 1,000 horses, and what was left of 400 oxen and 400 sheep are going to take up a lot of room, and the actual encampment, as stated above, would have stretched for nearly two miles between the two Light Horse Camps.

Nevertheless, there is something to be learned by establishing its precise location, for having done that, the exact location of the Forks of the Muskingum as it existed at that time can be determined, and the question as to whether or not the Forks have moved in the nearly 230 years since Bouquet was there can be answered. Some people have felt that the location of the Forks has changed to a considerable extent in these intervening years. Indeed, even Mr. Williams, in his article on this subject, concludes that the Forks in Bouquet's time was about 3/4 of a mile to the north of where it is today.

I don't believe that this is the case. however.

After arriving at the 16th Encampment, a few days later, the survey was continued on down the Tuscarawas to the Forks and then up the Walhonding for a few miles. By plotting the survey to the scale of the Original Survey of 1797 and superimposing it on the Original Survey map of 1797, the 16th Encampment survey point can be precisely located, and this location can be expressed as a certain distance east, and then north, of the midpoint of the north line of Township V, Range VI, of the Original Survey, for those lines (the Township and Range lines) are, of course, on the Original Survey.

Those same Township and Range lines are on the modern topographic map.

By redrawing the survey to the scale of the modern topographic map and placing the point of beginning at the precise location of the 16ᵗʰ Encampment survey point as determined above, using the Township and Range lines on the modern topogaphic map, it can then be seen that the Forks of the Muskingum has not moved at all, or, if there has been some movement, it has been very slight—certainly not 3/4 of a mile. Other portions of the river, of course, have changed their location, curves have become larger, etc., but the point of intersection of the two rivers, with respect to its distance and bearing from the 16ᵗʰ Encampment survey point, is still where it was at that time.

Maps 19a and 19b following this article show the survey as superimposed on the 1797 Survey and as superimposed on the modern topographic map. It can readily be seen that the Forks have not moved in the nearly 230 years since Bouquet was here, but that many other parts of the river have moved rather substantially.

These field notes of the Bouquet Expedition also refer to passing through the "Old Muskingum Town" at precisely the same location as set forth in the separate article on that subject in this book, providing conclusive evidence that it was, in fact, located near the northeast corner of Coshocton, and not several miles to the east of Coshocton. These notes are set forth in full as Attachment A at the end of this article.

At the end of Finley's field notes, on page 149 of the April 1984 issue of the Western Pennsylvania Historical Magazine, several entries of significance are also noted. These concern the distances to certain Indian villages from the 16ᵗʰ Encampment survey point.

The entries read as follows:

"the Bearing of Newcombers town on the North Side of muskingum Creek supposed to be N 73 E about 10 miles Taken from the end of Course N:°601: this Course N 65 W: 34 p:ˢ to Camp N:°16:"

"then the Bearing Taken at same Camp to Bullets Town below the fork of the white Womans Creek on the south side of moskingum Creek: Bears S 35 W supposed 5 miles"

"the Bearing of Cusoa Logus {Custaloga's} Town on the North East side of the White womans Creek on the West Branch. N 86 W — supposed to be about — 8 miles."

The distances to each of the Indian villages mentioned above are estimates, for in each instance he uses the word "supposed".

The estimate of 10 miles to Newcomerstown is also exactly the same figure used by McCullough in his captivity narrative, thus lending support to the theory that he was, in fact, residing in Newcomerstown when Bouquet came into the area.

The distance to Bullet's Town, estimated at 5 miles, also corresponds with other evidence to the effect that Bullet's Town, also known as Mowheysinck, Mogwhiston, Moughwessing, and Lichtenau, was 2 miles below Coshocton. Since the Forks of the

Muskingum was about 3 miles from the 16th Encampment survey point, and Coshocton was later located right at the Forks, the total distance to Bullet's Town would have been exactly the 5 miles that was estimated by Finley in his field notes.

And finally, the estimated distance of 8 miles to Custaloga's Town gives to us strong evidence that his town was the one shown on the 1797 Original Survey maps as being about 7 miles west of the Forks of the Muskingum, for that would make it very close to the 8 miles from the 16th Encampment survey point. It is not necessary to go, first, all the way to the Forks of the Muskingum and then west on the Walhonding to Custaloga's Town, making 10 miles altogether. Rather, a person wanting to go west along the Walhonding would immediately proceed in a westerly direction from the 16th Encampment until striking the Walhonding, thereby saving at least 2 miles of unnecessary travel.

In the Remarks for Course 602?, the engineers passed a Light Horse Camp to their left. This would be just above the word "Lewisville". At the end of course 616 (at the junction of Mill Creek with the Walhonding) they mention another Light Horse Camp. Bouquet did have two companies of Light Horse with him and it would make sense to place them on each flank of the army. I believe, therefore, that the rest of his army was between the Light Horse camps, and was probably also upon the hill to the north of the line connecting them.

The distances from the 16th Encampment survey point to the Indian towns referred to above would appear to be correctly shown on the 1764 map. Since we know Bullet's Town was two miles below the Forks of the Muskingum, the 16th Encampment survey point does measure about three miles from the Forks. If the location of the Conference House is accurately shown on the 1764 map, it's distance from the survey point was approximately a mile and a half. This places it about midway between the Drive-in Theater and the Radio Tower on the modern map.

Indian Vegetables

They also prepare a variety of dishes from the pumpkin, the squash, and the green French or kidney beans; they are very particular in their choice of pumpkins and squashes, and in their manner of cooking them. The women say that the less water is put to them, the better dish they make, and that it would be still better if they were stewed without any water, merely in the steam of the sap which they contain. They cover up the pots in which they cook them with large leaves of the pumpkin vine, cabbages, or other leaves of the larger kind. They make an excellent preserve from the cranberry and crab-apple, to which, after it has been well stewed, they add a proper quantity of sugar or molasses.

Source: Heckewelder's *History...*, p. 194

Attachment A

The following are the courses and distances of the Finley survey from Camp No. 16 to the Forks of the Muskingum and up the Walhonding for a few miles. Course No. 600 ended at the uppermost right corner of this survey. Then Course No. 601 headed in a westerly direction to the 16th Encampment. When he began his survey to the Forks, however, he started it back at the end of Course No. 600 and then headed southwesterly, probably following the same Indian trail leading to the town of Muskingum that they had been following as they approached the Forks. The 16th Encampment survey point, therefore, is at the end of the line on the right-hand side of this survey, even though that line is heading in a westerly direction when it ends. A Perch is 16½ feet.

N:°	Cour:ˢ	Per:ˢ	Remarks
601	N65W	34	all Thro: Level rich Land into Camp N:° 16. The Distance from Fort Pitt = 127½ miles and 53 p:ˢ to the Camp Near Moskingum old Town lay By at Camp N:° 16: from the Munday the 25:ᵗʰ of Oct:ʳ 1764: Till the 5:ᵗʰ of Nov:ʳ 1764 then started at the end of Course 600 on the Bank of a Small run below the Camp from thence Down thro: the old Town of Muskingum to the Great Forks————————
602?	S28W	64	all a Long Level Ground below the Camp on the Right [on, written over] the Left a small Low ridge where the Light Horse Camp
602	S43W	105	a Low Bottom to the Left & to the right a Low ridge neigh [sic] and at a bout 160 p:ˢ on S:ᵈ hand a High Hill
603	S27W	110	at the end of 60 p:ˢ moskingum Creek on the Left about 60 p:ˢ a Hill on the right a bout ¾ mile Dist: at the end of this Course the Creek about 4:ˢ Dist: all this Course on Clear Sevanna to the Old Town
604	S40W	238	all thro; rich Low rich Bottom all thro: the Old moskingum Town Hill on the right a bout one mile Distan:ᵗ. & a Creek about 50 p:ˢ Dist: at the end of 60 p:ˢ Came into the Low Bottom & the Creek about 100 p:ˢ Dist:ᵗ to the Left
605	S43W	68	all a Long a Low rich Bottom the Creek to the Left 90 p:ˢ the Hill to the right one mile
606	S45W	65	all Thro. a Low very rich Bottom, the Creek to the Left about 80 p:ˢ to the right a very Low rich Bottom & very wide
607	S70W	22	all Thro. D:° the Creek to the Left about 40 p:ˢ

608	S47W	106	at the end of 20 p:ˢ Came on the Creek Bank on the Left the remainder Down D.° & a Large rich Bottom on the right
609	N85W	32	all Thro. D:° the Creek about 20 p:ˢ to the Left
610	S48W	28	all Thro. D:° the Creek to the Left 5 p:ˢ thence Down d:° on the opposite side of the Creek very good up Land
611	S72W	157	at the end of 80 p:ˢ Cross:ᵈ a gutt on the side of the Creek & a small Island in the Creek all Down D:° at the end 6 p:ˢ the Creek to the Left
612	S39W	52	To the Large Fork of muskgum Creek where the white womans Creek Emp:ˢ the right hand Branch about 8 p:ˢ wide; at the end of 26 p:ˢ Came to a Low Bottom on the side of the right hand Branch from thence up said Branch all overs flows.
613	N35W	62	the Creek on the Left & a Large Bottom on the right a Hill on the opposite side of the Creek in this Course the Creek Circular in the middle about 5 p:ˢ off
614	N30E	86	up the Creek side: Bottom Land on Both sides of the Ck. & on the opposite side of the Creek a Hill about 100 p:ˢ Dist:ᵗ
615	N20W	90	Just Cross:ᵈ the mouth of a run runing at the end of this Course into the Creek on the Left. a Large Bottom on Each side of sd. Creek & a Hill on the opposite side about ¾ of a mile Distant at [sic]
616	N47W	140	up D:° a Large Bottom on Each side in the midle of this Course the Creek to the Left about 6 p:ˢ at end of this Courˢ Light Horse Camp
617	N2W	58	up D:° the same on Each side of this Creek.
618	N28W	100	up D:° a Large Low rich Bottom on Each side of this Creek. But overflows by the Creek.
619	N75W	158	at end of 20 p:ˢ the Indian Path ——— up D:° the Same on Each Side; at the end of this Course on the opposite of the Creek a Hill about 50 p:ˢ off
620	N41W	400	up D:° & a Large Bottom on Each side at the end of this Course a Low ridge on the right all these Bottoms subject to overflow

Source: Finley, "A Survey of Bouquet's Road", pp. 143–49

Map 19a – Original Survey of 1797 – Location of 16th Encampment

Map 19b – Modern Topographic – Location of 16th Encampment

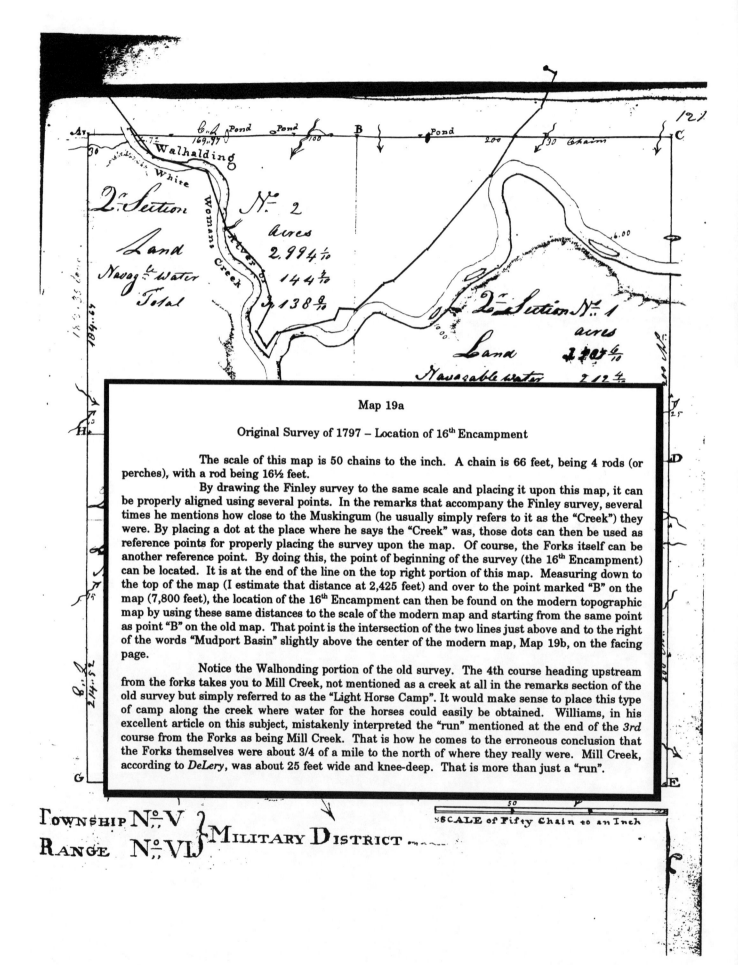

Map 19a

Original Survey of 1797 – Location of 16th Encampment

The scale of this map is 50 chains to the inch. A chain is 66 feet, being 4 rods (or perches), with a rod being 16½ feet.

By drawing the Finley survey to the same scale and placing it upon this map, it can be properly aligned using several points. In the remarks that accompany the Finley survey, several times he mentions how close to the Muskingum (he usually simply refers to it as the "Creek") they were. By placing a dot at the place where he says the "Creek" was, those dots can then be used as reference points for properly placing the survey upon the map. Of course, the Forks itself can be another reference point. By doing this, the point of beginning of the survey (the 16th Encampment) can be located. It is at the end of the line on the top right portion of this map. Measuring down to the top of the map (I estimate that distance at 2,425 feet) and over to the point marked "B" on the map (7,800 feet), the location of the 16th Encampment can then be found on the modern topographic map by using these same distances to the scale of the modern map and starting from the same point as point "B" on the old map. That point is the intersection of the two lines just above and to the right of the words "Mudport Basin" slightly above the center of the modern map, Map 19b, on the facing page.

Notice the Walhonding portion of the old survey. The 4th course heading upstream from the forks takes you to Mill Creek, not mentioned as a creek at all in the remarks section of the old survey but simply referred to as the "Light Horse Camp". It would make sense to place this type of camp along the creek where water for the horses could easily be obtained. Williams, in his excellent article on this subject, mistakenly interpreted the "run" mentioned at the end of the *3rd* course from the Forks as being Mill Creek. That is how he comes to the erroneous conclusion that the Forks themselves were about 3/4 of a mile to the north of where they really were. Mill Creek, according to *DeLery*, was about 25 feet wide and knee-deep. That is more than just a "run".

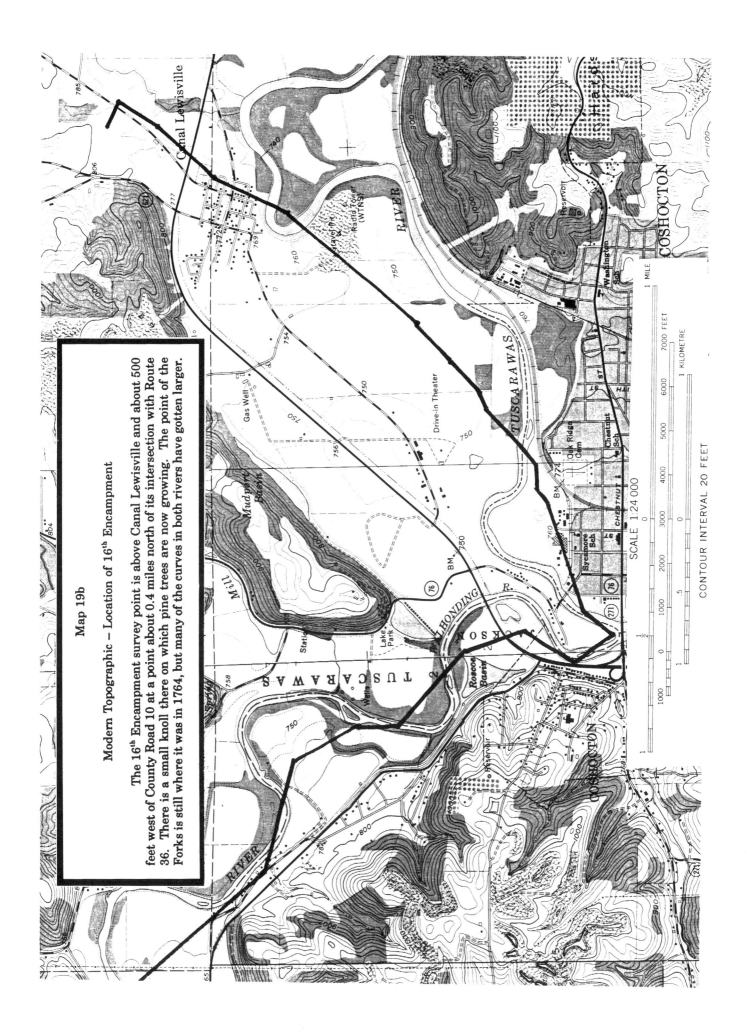

Map 19b

Modern Topographic – Location of 16th Encampment

The 16th Encampment survey point is above Canal Lewisville and about 500 feet west of County Road 10 at a point about 0.4 miles north of its intersection with Route 36. There is a small knoll there on which pine trees are now growing. The point of the Forks is still where it was in 1764, but many of the curves in both rivers have gotten larger.

SCALE 1:24 000

CONTOUR INTERVAL 20 FEET

1 MILE
7000 FEET
1 KILOMETRE

There is an unknown charm in the Indian life, which surprisingly attaches white people; those especially who have been captivated in early life.

David McClure   October 7, 1772

The Killbucks

This discussion concerns two matters relating to the Killbucks:

1. How can you tell which Killbuck a person is talking about if no other words are used to identify him?

2. Was Gelelemend (John Killbuck, Jr.) the grandson of Netawatwees, or was he his nephew?

As to the first question set forth above, certain facts concerning the Killbucks are well documented:

A. Killbuck Sr. was a well-known warrior of the Wolf lineage during the French and Indian War and was one of Netawatwees' principal counsellors at Newcomerstown and Coshocton.

B. He was originally hostile to the Moravians but toward the end of his life began to modify his position in this regard.

C. According to the Schoenbrunn Diary of January 25, 1777, when he returned from a trip to Philadelphia he was "quite blind".

D. He traveled to Pittsburgh on April 28, 1779. *Frontier Advance,* p. 296.

E. The Schoenbrunn Diary for November 10, 1780, refers to him as the "late, blind chief".

F. He therefore died sometime between April 28, 1779 and November 10, 1780.

G. He is sometimes called old Killbuck, Killbuck, Sr., and, more rarely, Capt. Killbuck, the elder.

H. According to Heckewelder, he spoke good English.

John Killbuck, Jr. was born in 1737 and so would have been 20 years old in 1757 and 40 years old in 1777. Sometimes the age of the person is a clue as to which Killbuck is meant. Killbuck, Jr. would have been a very young warrior during the French and Indian War, and would probably not have achieved the degree of fame or the leadership position that his father had gained by that time in his life.

Based upon the above facts, references to Killbuck in the journals of the 1750s to the mid-1770s are probably to Killbuck, Sr. unless it is clear that Killbuck, Jr. is the one they are talking about.

After the mid-1770s, it is more difficult to tell which is meant. Since Killbuck, Sr. was blind as of January 25, 1777, probably references after that date would be to Killbuck,

Jr., especially if the activities in which Killbuck is engaged at that time would not be those of a blind man. After November 10, 1780, references to Killbuck would be to Killbuck, Jr. There were, of course, other Indians named Killbuck, but the probabilities are that one or the other of the two we have been discussing are the persons meant in these journals.

Coming now to the second question set forth above, virtually all of the modern authorities state that Gelelemend was the grandson of Netawatwees. Even De Schweinitz, in the 1870s, says that Killbuck, Sr. was the son of Netawatwees.

I don't believe that this is correct, however. I think Gelelemend was the nephew of Netawatwees.

I have never found a contemporary statement to the effect that Killbuck, Sr. was the son of Netawatwees.

The only contemporary statement that I have found as to Gelelemend being the grandson of Netawatwees is that set forth in Zeisberger's Lichtenau Diary for April 16, 1776, wherein he states "John Killbock, Netawatwees' grandson (he is something of a headman at Goschachgunk) came with quite a number of Indians and they offered to help us in our work."

And that's it. To my knowledge, there is no other evidence to the effect that he was the grandson of Netawatwees, based on the statements of the people who were living at the time.

Of course, that statement, *standing alone*, would seem to be conclusive of the point.

But there is a wealth of contemporary evidence that he was the *nephew* of Netawatwees—much more evidence along that line than just the one statement of Zeisberger set forth above. And most of the evidence comes from the statements of Gelelemend himself, wherein he consistently refers to Netawatwees as his uncle!

First, from the Lichtenau Diary for April 21, 1776, just five days after the Zeisberger entry stating that he was a grandson—"...Another one, of the name of Gelelemend, or John Killbuck, who after Netawatwees has been destined to be the Chief asked Brother David among other things to what extent a believer or one who wished to accept the faith could busy himself with a Chief's affairs? ...He further said, that is Killbuck, that as early as last fall, he had a notion in his heart to move to us. He also said that some time ago before we had come here he had spoken with his uncle, the Chief about it, namely that he would like to move to Gnadenhütten. At that time he, the Chief had had no objection...".

And later, on May 30, 1776, "...from Goschachgunk John Killbuck with his wife as visitors and they spent the night here. He revealed to us the state of his heart, stating that he was tired of living any longer among the infidels and to have to do with the Chief Affairs. He said that he was entirely tired of it and therefore his desire to live with us was becoming ever greater. He said that only a few days ago he had spoken with his uncle Netawatwees about this and had revealed to him his desire to be with the Brethren."

And still later, on June 17, 1776, "John Killbuck...told us that his uncle Netawatwees had advised him to build a house in Goschachgunk even if he would decide to live with us."

Even earlier, in the Gnadenhutten Diary for January 3–4, 1776, "...Killebock's son said to them: 'I am very glad that I came hither;...It is true that my uncle, the chief, desires that I should take his place (already when the last treaty was being negotiated he was declared to be in line for the office of chief as Netawatwees' successor). But I do not wish this; I want to have the Saviour and gladly live in your midst; and I will speak with my uncle regarding this and make my wish known to him.'"

And later, on February 2, 1776, "...in the evening Jo Peepe from chief Netawatwees in company of two of the latter's councilors, one being the son of old Killebock. After the service the latter informed our conference brethren that he had talked with his uncle, the chief, and had told him the following: 'My uncle: I will now tell you what I intend to do ....' His uncle thereupon had replied to him:...Thereupon John Killebock said to the chief..."

Thus, from John Killbuck himself, we have these five statements that Netawatwees was his uncle. I can think of no better evidence of the truth of that fact.

Further evidence that he was a nephew is derived from the manner in which the successor to a chief is chosen.

William Penn, in his book entitled *William Penn's Own Account of the Lenni Lenape or Delaware Indians* at page 35 states:

Their Government is by Kings, which they call *Sachema,* and those by Succession, but always of the Mothers side; for Instance, the Children of him that is now King, will not succeed, but his Brother by the Mother, or the Children of his Sister, whose Sons (and after them the Children of her Daughters) will reign; for no Woman inherits; the Reason they render for this way of Descent, is, that their Issue may not be spurious."

Thus, the brother of a chief could succeed him, or a nephew who was the son of a sister of the chief, or a son of a daughter of a sister of the chief (in other words, a great-nephew) could succeed him. But not his own son or grandson.

That is how the matter of descent was to work when a new chief was to be chosen.

Gelelemend's obituary, when he died on February 17, 1811, is set forth in the Goshen Diary for February 19, 1811, and reads, in part, as follows:

In his youth he moved with his family and friends to this side of the Allegheny mountains, where he first had an opportunity of hearing the gospel, when he was about 35 years old. {Since he was born in 1737, that would have been in about 1772, when Netawatwees was chief of the tribe.} *As he was by birth entitled to the chief office among his nation* who were at that time very numerous, compared to what they are at present, he was even then active in all their public affairs. *[Emphasis added.]*

From this obituary it appears that he would have been a nephew of Netawatwees.

And lastly, the Indians at Coshocton themselves can add the final point in this discussion as recorded in the Lichtenau Diary entry of December 9, 1776, "...A certain Indian from Goschachgunk came forth again to bring heathenism,...He preaches openly and clearly that the teaching of the Brethren is not for Indians,...To reach his goal easier, *he is working to have the office of the Chief descendent line changed to another* who is an enemy of the Brethren. To this end he stirred up the Indians to vote for this one." *[Emphasis added.]*

The Indians who did not approve of Gelelemend's favorable attitude toward the Moravians did not want him as their chief and were even talking about changing the line of descent! If he was a grandson of Netawatwees, he would not be in that line anyway, so there would be no need to change it.

Considering all of the above, I believe the overwhelming weight of the evidence, much of it in Gelelemend's own words, is to the effect that Netawatwees was his uncle, not his grandfather.

King Beaver's House

Not all Indian houses were simply huts made of bark, etc. Some could get pretty elaborate, especially the house of a chief. The following quotation is from a letter written on September 24, 1761 by Lieutenant Elias Meyer at Lake Sandusky, and addressed to Lt. Col. Bouquet at Fort Pitt.

"A carpenter, who has worked on a house for the Beaver King at Tuscarawa, came here today. I kept him here for the King's service, as I needed him badly."

King Beaver must have been building a pretty substantial structure to have had a real carpenter working on it.

Source: Bouquet, *The Papers of Henry Bouquet*, Vol. V, p. 779

APPENDIX

Names of Captives Released by Bouquet

The following is an alphabetical listing of the captives released as a result of the Bouquet Expedition. They had been held by the Delaware and Shawnee Indians in their towns along the Muskingum and the Scioto. Most of them were delivered to Bouquet at his camp at the Forks of the Muskingum. Some, however, were brought to Pittsburgh weeks later by their captors. Virtually all of them, therefore, would have either been living in the Tuscarawas Valley during their captivity, or were brought through it on their way to the Shawnee towns or on their way back to Pittsburgh. This list is found in Ewing, William S., "Indian Captives Released by Colonel Bouquet", *The Western Pennsylvania Historical Magazine,* Volume 39, (1956) pp. 199–202. The reader is referred to that article for more details in connection with these prisoners, such as where they had been captured, what articles of clothing were given to them after they were brought in by the Indians, and to whom they were turned over after reaching Pittsburgh. This information is not available for all of the prisoners, but is set forth for some of them.

Anna Catharina
Babson, Mordicai
Bacon, Catherine
Baskin, Peggy
Beaty, James
Bell, James
Betty
Betty-black eyes
Bird, Margaret
Bird, Molly
Bittikanety
Blankenship, Stephen
Bonnet, Henry
Boyd, Sarah
Boyd, Thomas
Bridgets Son
Bryan, Rebeca
Burd, John
Butler, James
  (or Jemmy Buttler)
Campbell, James
Campbell, Mary
Carpenter, Jerry
Carpenter, Solomon
Cartmill, Molly
Cartmill, Peggy
Castle, Mary
Cawacawachi
Christina
Clandinnon, Jean
Clark, And^w

Clausser, Betty
Clausser, Magdalen
Clausser, Mary
Clem
Clam, Felty
Clem, Ludovich
Cobble, Micheal
Cochran, John
Colley, Peggy
Collins, Thomas
Conogoniony
Coon, Elizabeth
  & two children
Counsman, Elizabeth
Craven, Mary
Crooked Legs
Crow, Jane
Crow, Polly
Cuningham, Marg^t
David bighead
Davis, Willm
Davison, Agnus
Davison, Molly
Davison, Nancy
Devine, Morice
Diver, Hans
Diver, John
Donohoo, John
  (or John Donehoo)
Dorothy's Son
Ebenezer

Ewins, John
Fincher, Rachell
Finley, Ann
Fishback, Margaret
Fishback, Susan
  (or Susannah Fishback)
Fisher, John
Flat nose
Flaugherty, Esther
Forsyth, John
Franse, Elizabeth
Freeling, John
Freeling, Peggy
Fulkison, Elizabeth
Gibson, Sarah
Gilmore, Elizabeth
Gilmore, Elizabeth, Jr.
Gilmore, Jane
Gilmore, John
Gore, Rose
Greenwood, Mary
Haig, John
Hamilton, Arch^d
Hamilton, Mary
Hamilton, Miriam
Hannah
Hannel, Mary
Hans
Harmantrout, Charl^s
  (or Hormontrout)
Harmantrout,Christopher

(or Hormontrout)
Harper, Eve
Harper, Thomas
Harris, James
Heat, Catherine
Henry
Henry, Elizabeth
Hormontrout, see
 Harmantrout
House, Christina
 (or Christiana House)
Huntsman, see
 Huntzman
Huntzman, Adam
Huntzman, Barbara
 (or Barbara Huntsman)
Huntzman, John
 (or John Huntsman)
Hutchinson, Florence
Hutchison, David
Hyerd, Leonard
Ice, Catherine
Ice, Christian
Ice, Elizabeth
Ice, Eve
Ice, John
Ice, Lewis
Ice, Thomas
Ice, William
Innis, Francis
Innis, Jenny
Irena
Jacob
James (or Jemmy)
Jean or Ketakatwitche
Johnson, David
Joseph or Pechyloothamo
Ketty
Kincake, Eleonard,
 & two children
Kitty
Knox, Jane
Knox, Mary
Knox, Robert
Knox, Susan
Knox, Susan, Jr.
Lansisco, Mary & child

(or Mary Lanssisco &
child)
Leake, Hans
Leake, William
Lengenfield, Mary Cath.
Le Roy, John Jacob
Linenger, Margareta
Linenger, Rachel
Lingerfield, Catherine
 (or Lengenfield)
Louaveska
Lowry, Jane
Lowry, Mary
Lowry, Susan
McCord, Mary
McCullough
McIlroy, Elizabeth
 & Child
McIlroy, Mary
McQueen, Jane
Magdalen, or Pagothow
Mansel, Dorothy
Mansel, Margarite
Martin, James
Martin, Martha
Martin, William
Mekethiva, sister to
 Jacob
Metch, Molly (or Mitch)
Miller, Beverly
Miller, Margaret
Mitch, see Metch
Molly
Mouse, Elizabeth
Myers, Frederick
Nalupua, sister to
 Molly Bird
Neculissika
Neicheumata
Netumpsico
Nosewelamah
Palmer, John
Pampadour
Paquwesee
Peggy
Peggy, a Mullato
Peter
Petro, Nicholas

Petro, Phillip
Petterson, Micheal
Pheby
Polly
Polly (not her
 real name)
Pouter, or Wynima
Price, Hannah
Price, James
Price, Sarah
Punnel, Henry
Punnel, Peggy
Rachel
Red Jacket, Joseph
Rennox, Geor.
Reyneck, Peggy
Rhoads, Daniel
Rhoads, Micheal
Riddle, John
Rigar, Barbara
Rigar, Dorothy
Ross, Taverner
Sally
Schlyer, Magdalen
Sea, John
Sea, Mary
Sea, Peggy
Sea, Sally
See, Catherine
See, George
See, Mary
See, Micheal
Sheaver, Ebenezer
Sheaver, John
Silkspiner, Joseph
Simon
Sims, Andrew
Sivers, Catherine
Sivers, Elizabeth
Sivers, Margarite
Slover, Elizabeth
Slover, Elizabeth, Jr.
Smallman, Thomas
Smeltzer, Hans Adam
Smeltzer, Jacob
Smith, Elizabeth
Smith, Hannah, & child
Snodgrass, Elizabeth

Sore mouth
Sourbach, Hannah Maria
Sour Plumbs
Stettler, Alice
Stewart, Mary
Stintson, Elizabeth
Stroudman, Catherine
  (or Kitty Stroudman)
Stroudman, Uly
Studebaker, Joseph
Tamer - Mulato
Tanner, Christopher
Tewanima
Theecheapei
Tosher, Elizabeth

Vila, Mary
Wallace, Samuel
Walter, John
Walters, Ephraim
Wampler, Christina
Wapatenequa
Wechquessinah
Westbrook, Catherine
  (or Kitty Westbrook)
Wheat, Thomas
Whitehead
Wig, Tommy
Wilkins, Elizabeth
Wilkins, Mary
Williams, Catherine

Williams, David
Williams, Jeany
Williams, Mary
Wiseman, John
Wood, Experience
Yoakim, Elizabeth
Yokeham, George
Yokeham, Margaret
Yokim, Sally
Young, Betty
Young, William W
girl with a Sore Knee

Total .. . . . . 260 captives.

Warmarks

If a party of Indians have spent a night in the woods, it may be easily known, not only by the structure of their sleeping huts but also by their marks on the trees, to what tribe they belong. For they always leave a mark behind made either with red pigment or charcoal. Such marks are understood by the Indians who know how to read their meaning. Some markings point out the places where a company of Indians have been hunting, showing the number of nights they spent there, the number of deer, bears and other game killed during the hunt. The warriors sometimes paint their own deeds and adventures, the number of prisoners or scalps taken, the number of troops they commanded and how many fell in battle.

Source: Zeisberger's *History...*, p. 114

Rules of the Mission

The following Statutes were adopted at a missionary conference held at Schoenbrunn in August of 1772. They are as set forth by Heckewelder in his *Narrative....* A similar set of rules is set forth in the DeSchweinitz biography of Zeisberger, and wherein there is a material difference in the two copies of the rules, the DeSchweinitz portion is placed in brackets. Comments after Rules 18 and 20 are Heckewelder's.

1. We will know of no other God, nor worship any other but him who has created us, and redeemed us with his most precious blood.

2. We will rest from all labour on Sundays, and attend the usual meetings on that day for divine service.

3. We will honour father and mother, and support them in age and distress.

4. No one shall be permitted to dwell with us, without the consent of our teachers. [and the helpers have examined him.]

5. No thieves, murderers, drunkards, adulterers, and whoremongers, shall be suffered among us.

6. No one that attendeth [games], dances, sacrifices, or heathenish festivals, can live among us.

7. No one using *Trchappich* (or witchcraft) in hunting, shall be suffered among us.

8. We will renounce all juggles [tricks], lies, and deceits of Satan.

9. We will be obedient to our teachers, and to the helpers, (national assistants,) who are appointed to see that good order be kept, both in and out of the town.

10. We will not be idle and lazy [nor scold]—nor tell lies of one another—nor strike each other—we will live peaceably together.

11. Whosoever does any harm to another's cattle, goods or effects, &c. shall pay the damage.

12. A man shall have only one wife—love her and provide for her, and the children. Likewise a woman shall have but one husband, and be obedient unto him; she shall also take care of the children, and be cleanly in all things.

13. We will not permit any rum, or spirituous liquor, to be brought into our towns. If strangers or traders happen to bring any, the helpers (national assistants) are to take it into their possession, and take care not to deliver it to them until they set off again.

291

14.   None of the inhabitants shall run in debt with traders, nor receive goods on commission for traders, without the consent of the national assistants.

15.   No one is to go on a journey or long hunt, without informing the minister or stewards of it.

16.   Young people are not to marry without the consent of their parents, [and the minister] and taking their advice.

17.   If the stewards or helpers apply to the inhabitants for assistance, in doing work for the benefit of the place, such as building meetings and school houses, clearing and fencing lands, &c. they are to be obedient.

18.   All necessary contributions for the public, ought cheerfully to be attended to.

The above rules were made, and adopted at a time [1772] when there was a profound peace; when however, six years afterwards, (during the revolutionary war,) individuals of the Delaware Nation took up the hatchet to join in the conflict, the national assistants proposed and insisted on having the following additional rules added: namely,

19.   No man inclining to go to war—which is the shedding of blood, can remain among us.

20.   Whosover purchases goods or articles of warriors, *knowing* at the time that such have been stolen or plundered, must leave us. We look upon this as giving encouragement to murder and theft.

According to custom, these rules were, at the commencement of every year, read in public meeting; and no new member, or applicant, could be permitted to live in the congregation, without making a solemn promise that he or she would strictly conform to them. When any person residing in the congregation gave offence, or caused disturbance, it was the duty of the national assistants, first to admonish such person or persons in a friendly manner; but where such admonition proved ineffectual, then to consult together for the purpose of publicly putting him, her, or them, out of the society, and dismissing such altogether from the place. Next to these rules, other necessary and proper regulations were made and adopted; for instance, respecting the daily meetings and the duty of church wardens, schools, attending to visitors, and the attention to be paid to the poor, sick and needy, or distressed—and also with regard to contributions to be made from time to time for the benefit of the congregation at large, as also individuals in the same, unable to support themselves, or furnish the necessary attire for the deceased, so that the corpse of the poorest person in the community was dressed as decent as the wealthy, &c.

Source: Heckewelder's *Narrative...*, pp. 122–25

Estate of White Eyes

The following is set forth simply to show the types of personal effects that were owned by White Eyes at the time of his death. Of special interest is the last entry on the list, indicating that he wore glasses.

Pittsburgh 9 Novʳ 1778

Inventory of Sundry Moveables the Property of the Late Col. White Eyes of the Delewar Nation Deceased now in the Possession of Thomas Nicholas [Nicholson] of Pittsburgh Viz.

1 Breech Clout fully trim'd
1 Bundle of blue & Red Ferreting. Qᵗʸ 31½ Red D° 33½ blu D°
1 Paint Bag with some paint in it.
1 Silver Medal Effigee of Geo. the 3ᵈ of Great Britain.
1 Large be[l]t Wampum 11 Rows
1 Quill Back'd Comb 1 pr. Scissars 3 yards Gartering
1 Printed Linen Jacket, 1 Bundle Sundry Papers
1 Pʳ Saddle Bags
1 Green Coat fac'd with Red with an Apatch
1 Old D° D° Cotawy [Cuttaway] 1 Crib & Bridle
1 P Old Buck Skin Leggons. 1 plain Scarlet Jacket new
1 D° Old, 1 P Scarlet Breeches. 1 P of Buck Skin d°
1 Scarlet Silk Jacket Trim'd with Gold Lace
1 small Red Pocket Book with some papers & needles
1 Fur Cap 1 pair plated Buckles 3 p Shoes viz 1 new & 2 Old
1 Old blue Breech Clout 1 P of white Legons bound
1 Knife Case, & belt 1 Match Coat
1 New Saddle & Saddle Cloth
1 Beaver Hat 1 Rifle, Pouch & Horn
1 Broach & Ear Ring 1 pipe Tomahawk 1 P Knee buckles
1 P Spectacles

I do Certify that the within Inventory was taken by me at the Request of Thomas Nicholas & by order of Col. Archib'd Steel and that the within Articles were Produced by him which are now in his Custoday.

Dᵈ Moore

Witness Present at the Taking of the within Inventory.

John Handlyn

Pittsburgh Novʳ 10ᵗʰ 1778

Received of Thomas Nicholas the Contents of the within Inventory being the

Property of the Late Col. White Eyes of the Deleware Nations Deceaˢ which articles I promise to be Accountable for to any Person having Authority to Call upon me for the same.

Dan¹ Sullivan

Tesᵗ David Moore

Source: Kellogg, Frontier Advance on the Upper Ohio, pp. 168–69

Minutes of Court of Yohogania County
March 24th. 1779

Admn. of the Est. of the late Colo. White Eyes is granted to Thos. Smallman he having complied with the Law.

Jos. Skelton David Duncan Wm. Christie & Saml. Ewalt appointed appraisers to said Est.

Source: Crumrine, Virginia Court Records in Southwestern Pennsylvania, p. 305

Pouch and Pipe

An Indian carries pouch and pipe with him wherever he goes, for they are indispensable. For state occasions they may have an otter skin pouch or a beaver-pouch or one decorated with coral, made by the women. Sometimes they have a buffalo horn, from which a pouch, made possibly of tanned deer-skin, depends. In the pouches they carry tobacco, fire materials, knife and pipe. Sumac is generally mixed with tobacco or sumac smoked without tobacco, for but few can stand smoking pure tobacco. Their common conversation turns upon hunting or the news of the day. Matter that has no foundation in fact may be drawn into conversation, and even though all may be aware of this, the narration continues uninterrupted. They may laugh now and again but they will listen attentively. No one interrupts another. When one has finished another begins. They never put any one publicly to blush; they are polite to each other and enjoy being politely treated.

Source: Zeisberger's History..., p. 115

Regulations for Traders

Throughout the period covered by the journals in this book, there were traders living in, or near, the large towns in the valley, and other traders were constantly coming and going between the valley and Fort Pitt. Sometimes even Indian women were used for the purpose of bringing rum to the Indians, something that the licensed traders were forbidden to do. This prohibition against bringing rum to the Indian towns may not have been in effect throughout the entire period covered by these journals, for I have seen Regulations governing the amount of furs to be traded for so many kegs of rum. However, it apparently was in effect in 1772 when the Rev. David McClure was there, for he specifically mentions it in his journal and says that women brought the rum to Newcomerstown. Also, the Instructions to Lieut. Hutchins set forth herein state quite clearly that he is not to allow any trader to sell spiritous liquors to the Indians.

The following documents, therefore, are illustrative of the attempt to regulate the trade with the Indians on the part of the government. They are taken from Hanna's *Wilderness Trail*, Vol. 2, pp.164–66. Brackets and parentheses are Hanna's.

(September 18, 1761)

REGULATIONS FOR INDIAN TRADE AT FORT PITT

[B. M., Add. MSS. 21655, f. 284, D.]

BY THE HONOURABLE SR. WM. JOHNSON BARONET His Majestys Sole Agent Superintendant & Coll[n]. of the Six United Nations, their Allies &cc, &cc,.

As Nothing can contribute more to the Strengthening and extending his Majestys Indian Interest in this Country, than a free open Trade on the fairest, and most reasonable terms with the Indian Inhabitants thereof, I have, with the approbation of his Excellency General Amherst, Judged it adviseable for the preventing of any extorsion or abuses therein, to make following Regulations with Regard to the prices of Indian Goods, Hereby ordering all Traders, &cc, strictly to adhere to the same on pain of being banished from the Post at which they Trade by the Commanding Officer thereof, their Lycence to be taken from them, and they rendered incapable to trade at any of his Majestys Garrisons, or Posts for the future and Each of the Comm[dg]. Officers of his Majestys Garrisons, are required not to allow any Person or Persons whatsoever to carry on any Trade with the Indians; who do not first produce him their Pass Signed & Sealed by Sr. Wm. Johnson or George Croghon Esqr his Deputy.

Regulations for the Trade at Fort Pitt

Indian Goods	To be Sold for
A Stroud of two y[ds] Long	2 Good Beaver or three Bucks
Penniston Stockings of 1 1/4 yds:	1 Medlin Beaver or Buckskin
Mens Plain Shirts	1 Beaver or Buck & a Doe
Mens Ruffeld Ditto	2 Beavers or 3 Buck Skins

Childrens Shirts	1 Small Beaver or Doe Skin
Mens Large Blankets	2 good Beavers or 3 Bucks
Mens Single Stript Ditto	2 Medlin Beavers or 2 Buck Sk^s
30 in a piec for Children Ditto	1 Medlin Beaver or 1 Buck
Mens Penniston Coats bound	2 Beaver or three Bucks
Boyes Ditto Ditto of 16 years old	1 Good Beaver or Buck & Doe
Womens Wosted Stocks P: P^r.	1 Buck Skin
Womans Yarn Ditto	1 Doe Skin
Child^s: Ditto	1 Racoon
Black Wampum p Hundred	1 Buck
White D^o. Ditto	4 Racoons
Gun Powder P. Pound	1 Buck Skin
4 bars Lead	4 Bucks
12 flents	1 Racoon
one fathem Calico	1 Buck & a Doe or Good Beav^r.
one Ditto Calamanco	1 Buck
Large Silk Handk^s	1 Buck & a Doe
Vermillion P. P^d.	2 Good Beavers or 3 Bucks
Cutteau Knives	2 Raccoons
Small Ditto	1 Racoon
1 piec of Role Gartring	1 Buck
2 fathem of Ribbon	1 Buck
1 Brass Kettle by Weight	1 Pound of Beav^r.
Tin Kettles of a Gallon	2 Bucks
Large Silver Arm Bands	4 Beaver or 5 Bucks
Small Ditto Ditto	3 Beaver or 4 Bucks
Wrist Bands	2 Bucks
Womens Hair Plates	3 Beaver or 4 Bucks
Silver Brochess	1 Racoon
Large Croses	1 Small Beaver or Medlin Buck
Ear Bobs	1 Doe

[Endorsed in Col. Bouquet's handwriting] Sir William Johnson
        His Regulation for Indian Trade.

(October 25, 1761)

CAPT. GEORGE CROGHAN TO LIEUT. THOMAS HUTCHINS

[B. M., Add. MSS. 21655, f. 172, C.]

[Fort Pitt, Oct. 25, 1761.]

Instructions for Thomas Hutchins Esqr. Assistant
Agent for Indian Affairs in the Western Division at
Fort Pitt 25th October 1761.

Sir,

You are to Remain here and Transact the Business of your Department with all Indians that may come here of any Nation whatsoever that is in Friendship with his Britanick Majesty and his Subjects to see Strict Justice done them in Trade Agreeable to the late Regulations made by Sir William Johnson.

You are to use your Utmost endeavours with the Indians of all Nations to get them to Deliver up all our Prisoners Agreeable to their Engagements to us.

You will apply to the Commanding Officer for such Provisions as may be wanting to give such Indians as come here on Publick Business or to Trade being as frugal as Possible in that Article and Dispatching the Indians as soon as their Business is done to save Expence of Provisions.

You are not to suffer any Trader Licenced by me or otherwise to sell or give any Spirituous Liquors to any Indian whatsoever, But in Case any Indian should bring in any of our Prisoners you may if you see it necessary give such from One Gallon to three or the Value thereof in Goods as a token that we are well pleased with their Conduct in bringing in our Prisoners agreeable to their Repeated Promises.

When ever any Indians come here on any Publick Business when you know it you are to acquaint the Commanding Officer thereof, and brake that Custom they have of going to see the Commanding Officer as they have no Business to give him any trouble, and their View is only to get a Dram or beg some Presents from him. But, if the Commanding Officer desire you to bring any Indians to him, You are to follow his Orders.

You are to make no Presents to any Indians unless as above Mentioned, except a Twist of Tobacco or the like when they first come and apply for Provisions, which you will always do as it is an Old Custom. I wish you Success and am

            Sir,
               Your Most Humble Servt
               [no signature]
For Thomas Hutchins Esqr

[Endorsed in Col. Bouquet's handwriting] Mr. Croghan's Instructions to Mr. Hutchins   25th October 1761

Government

Although the Indians have no code of laws for their government, their chiefs find little or no diffficulty in governing them. They are supported by able experienced counsellors; men who study the welfare of the nation, and are equally interested with themselves in its prosperity. On them the people rely entirely, believing that what they do, or determine upon, must be right and for the public good.

Source: Heckewelder's *History...*, p. 107

Hutchins' Account of the Ohio Indian Trails

In Volume I of the Thomas Hutchins Manuscripts, preserved in the Library of the Pennsylvania Historical Society, is the following account of the Land Trails and Water Routes from Fort Pitt to the Ohio Indian towns, written by Lieutenant Hutchins himself. The exact date of the writing of this account is not certain, but internal evidence [the movement of Beaver from Tuscarawas to the Hocking] would suggest the autumn of 1763. The following is that account as set forth in Hanna's *Wilderness Trail*, Volume II, pp. 192–202. The bracketed material and footnotes are Hanna's. The New Note at the end is my contribution. Also, for easier identification of the trails, I have separated them by bracketed headings giving approximate beginning and ending points.

"A Description of part of the Country Westward of the River Ohio, with the Distances Computed from Fort Pitt to the several Indian Towns by Land & Water:—

[Fort Pitt to Painted Post (Dungannon)]

"From Fort Pitt to big Beaver Creek by Land, is 28 Miles; the Path is mostly along the Riverside, and crosses a Number of small Ridges that Border on the River.

"Little Beaver Creek is 16 Miles further; for the first two Miles, the Woods is very Levell, at the End of which is a Run [Two Mile Run] and A very Steep & Difficult Ridge, which may be Avoided by inclining about half A Mile to the Right of the Path; the Country then is made up of small broken Hills, all the way to Little Beaver Creek, the Descent to which is steep.

"This Creek is 60 yards wide and has A very good Fording. After crossing it [the North Fork], there is A very steep Ascent to the top of A Ridge, which the path continues on for some Miles, and then takes over many Little Hills till it reaches another Creek [Middle Fork of Little Beaver] 12 [?] Miles from the preceding one. This Creek is 70 yards wide, has A good Fording and Runs through level Land that has Abundance of underwood & thickets.

"12 [?] Miles further is Yellow Creek [probably not the present Yellow Creek, which flows into the Ohio below the mouth of the Little Beaver; but apparently the stream now called the West Fork of Little Beaver Creek. Both it and the present Yellow Creek head in Franklin Township, Columbiana County], 60 yards wide; for the first Seven Miles the Country is Level & pretty, free from Underwood; the other 5 Miles is much broken with small Hills.

"About three Quarters of A Mile from [north of] Yellow Creek, the Path forks. The Right hand Crosses Yellow Creek and leads to Tuscarawas, about 70 Miles further; And the Left hand Path crosses the Creek lower down and Leads to the Delaware Towns on Muskingum River.

[Painted Post (Dungannon) to Mowheysinck (below Coshocton)]

"After passing the [Yellow] Creek the Muskingum [or lower] path continues for 9 Miles on A Ridge, which has then an easy descent to A large Run, where, after Ascending A Steep Hill and traversing A number of little Hills for 6 Miles further, the Path reaches A Creek 8 yards wide; two Miles on this side of the Creek is an Easy descent to an Extensive, Shrubby bottom, which continues to the Creek.

"About 8 Miles further is another Creek, near the same width of the former one, the first 5 Miles to which is Along A Ridge, the other 3 Miles over swampy Ground, full of Thickets.

"4 Miles further is Another small Creek, about 10 yards wide; the first two Miles, over Level, Shrubby, Swampy Land; the path then Crosses the end of A small Ridge into A Draught between two low Hills and Continues to the Creek.

"12 Miles Further, after Crossing A number of small Ridges, is Another Creek, 12 yards wide;

"Then the path takes over broken Land for 7 Miles, to A Creek 30 yards wide, with A Stony Ford.

"10 Miles further is Another Creek, 70 yards wide [Will's Creek?], the Descent to which is steep. Most part of the way between these Creeks is a number of little Hills.

"Then 7 Miles further, over several small Ridges, the Path leads to the same Creek, at which is A good Ford.

"13 Miles further is Bullet's Town, or *Mow-hey-sinck,* on Muskingum River[1] [two or three miles below what is now Coshocton]. For the first 5 Miles the Land is Level to a Savannah; the rest of the way is in some places broken with small Hills.

"Mowheysinck Town is Situate about 100 yards from the River, on this side, and has upwards of 35 Persons in it, 15 of which are Warriors. Their Cornfields are better than half A Mile below the Town, close on the Opposite side of the River. From the nearest part of the Ohio River to this Town is about 100 Miles.

[Mowheysinck (below Coshocton) to Wakatomika (Dresden)]

"5 Miles from Mowheysinck, down the River on this side, is Black Tom's Town. The path between these Towns is through a Level, Rich Bottom, free from Hills or Creeks. Tom's Town has 8 or 10 Houses in it, And consists of about 8 Warriors and 15 or 16 women & Children; their Cornfields Are close by the Town. The shortest distance from this Town to the Ohio is 100 Miles.

"About 200 yards above the Town the River is Fordable, after crossing of which the Country is very open & mostly Barrens for 8 Miles to *Waukautaumeka* Town [on or near the site of the present Dresden], Situate on A very high Bank, about 100 yards from the Muskingum River. There is About 40 Houses in this Town and near the same Number of warriors, and upward of 90 women & Children. Their Cornfields are near ¾ of a Mile from the Town, on the same side, up the [Wakatomika] Creek. From this Town to the Ohio River is 80 Miles.

[Wakatomika (Dresden) to Lower Shawnee Town (below Circleville)]

"From Waukautaumike, the Path that leads to the Lower Shawanoe Town takes over A number of small Hills for 9 Miles, to A Creek [Wakatomika Creek?] 15 yards wide, at which is A good ford.

"6 Miles further, over broken Land, is A small Creek [a branch of Licking], the Descent to which is Steep, and A Swamp at the bottom of the Descent.

"The path then leads through Level, Rich Land for 3 Miles, to Licking Creek, 30 yards wide, at which is A good Ford.[2] Then through Level, wet Land, but Not Swampy, and Shrubby only in some places, 28 Miles to the Beaver's New Town, on A branch of Hockhocking River, about half A Mile above the Ford. This Town had, last Spring [1763?], about 15 Houses in it, and Consisted of thirty Warriors and near 80 women & Children; but as the Indians some distance from it purposed Moveing to it immediately, it's very probable the Warriors there now are more Numerous then they were then. Their Houses are close to each other, and their Cornfields are between the Town and the Path.

"From the Beaver's Town, the Path takes over level Land, and in some places Shrubby, 15 Miles, to A Creek 10 yards wide, then through Level Land and, for 50 Miles [the distance was much less], to the Lower Shawanoe Town. This Town is Situate in A very large Savannah [the Pickaway Plains]; part of the Town is on the [east] Bank of the Sioto River and part about A Mile from it, but Opposite sides [on and opposite the site of Westfall, Wayne Township, Pickaway County]. Near 80 Houses Compose these Towns, and Consist of 130 Warriors and 200 women & Children. Their Cornfields are in Sight of the Towns. There is A Ford opposite the Town nearest the River. From this Place to the Ohio is 100 Miles.

[Wakatomika (Dresden) to Will's Town (Duncan Falls)]

"Now, set out from Waukautaumeke again, & proceed 12 Miles through A Level Country down the [Muskingum] River side to a small Delaware Town, the path to which in some places touches near A few Ridges which Are not Steep or Difficult. This Town is Situate in A fork Where A Creek [Licking Creek?] Empties into the Muskingum, and has 8 Houses in it, and about 12 Warriors and 30 women & Children. Their Cornfields are close to the Town. Muskingum & the Creek that Runs into it are both Fordable here. From this Place to the Ohio is 70 Miles.

"The Path continues down the Muskingum through level Land for 3 Miles to the Mouth of A Creek [Moxahala?], then up the Creek 3 Miles further to A Small Town of 7 Houses, 15 Warriors, and upwards of 20 women & Children. Their Cornfields are on the Opposite side of the Creek, which has A good Ford [at mouth of Shawnee Run?], about 15 yards wide. This Town is about 60 or 70 Miles from the Ohio.

"After Crossing the Creek, the Path leads through level Land, 3 Miles, to A fording at Muskingum; for 2 Miles of the way the Path is Commanded on the Right by A very high, Steep Ridge. The Ford is 200 yards wide, with a good Bottom. The Path still Continues through level Land, free from underwood, 3 Miles, to Will's Town, *Se-key-unck,* or the Salt Licks [now Duncan's Falls], 50 Miles from the Ohio. Will's Town has 35 Houses in it and About 45 Warriors, & 80 Women & Children. The Houses are close together, and their Cornfields in sight of the Town. The Muskingum is not Fordable opposite the Town.

[Will's Town (Duncan Falls) to Crow's Town (below Steubenville)]

"The Path, then Leading to the Crow's Town,[3] takes over several little Ridges for 6 Miles to A Creek 8 yards wide.

"21 Miles further, through A very Shrubby Country, is A small Delaware Town, at a Creek [Will's Creek, near Cambridge], 30 yards wide. There is about a Dozen Houses, 20 Warriors, and 30 women & Children;

"About 75 Miles further[4] is the Crow's Town on the Ohio River, which is now Evacuated.

"The Indians have not any Forts at the aforementioned Towns.

[Ohio River from Fort Pitt to mouth of Scioto (Portsmouth)]

"From Fort Pitt by Water to big Beaver Creek is 30 Miles; the Current is gentle. 3 Miles below the Fort is an Island [Brunot's] & a Creek [Chartier's], on the Left. 9 Miles further is Another Creek [Montour's] on the Left; then 15 Miles further, to A Creek [Elkhorn Run], on the Left, 3 Miles above Beaver Creek. Most part of the way A Number of Short Hills border on each side of the River.

"Then 7 Miles lower down is A small Creek [Raccoon Creek], on the Left.

"About 11 Miles further, to little Beaver Creek, on the Right.

"28 [11] Miles further is Yellow Creek[5] on the Right.

"Then 25 Miles to the Crow's Town on the Right [now Mingo, Jefferson County, Ohio], at which A Creek empties into the Ohio, and Another on the Left, almost opposite each other [the two Cross creeks].

"From big Beaver Creek to this Town is A number of Hills & Ridges on both sides of the River, but none of them so close but Loaded Horses may pass between them & the water, or with some Difficulty March over them. There is also on the Right hand side of the River A small Path which has been so little frequented of late that it's Scarce perceivable in some places.

"8 Miles below the Crow's Town, on the Left hand side, is A Creek [Buffalo Creek?], 8 yards wide.

"9 Miles further to Button Wood Creek [Short Creek], on the Right, 12 yards wide.

"Then 8 Miles, to A Creek on the Left, 16 yards wide, and Another on the Right [the two Wheeling creeks], 12 yards wide.

"12 Miles further, A Creek [Pipe Creek] on the Left, 16 yards over.

"Then 6 Miles, to A Creek on the Right, near 100 yards wide, called Captain's [now Captina] Creek.

"30 [7] Miles further, to *Paugh-chase-wey's*, or Sun Fish Creek [still so called] on the Right, 16 yards wide,

"Then 7 Miles, to the upper end of A large Bent, which continues in the form of A Horseshoe 7 Miles further. This Bent is in the narrowest place 3 Miles A cross by Land; At the beginning of this Bent is a Very high, steep Hill, close on the Left of the River; but on the Right hand side the Land is Level some distance from the Water [this is a description of the Great Bend, one hundred miles below Sunfish Creek.]

"Then, 9 Miles below the Bent is A very large Creek [Fishing Creek, ten miles below Sunfish?] on the Left,

"9 Miles further is Another [Middle Island Creek is twenty-six miles below Fishing Creek] on the same side, 8 yards wide.

"It is 88 Miles from this Creek [seventeen miles from Middle Island Creek] to the next [Little Muskingum, fifty-two miles below Sunfish Creek] which is on the Right hand side of the River, about 6 Miles above the Mouth of the Muskingum, which comes in on the same side.

"There is between the Crow's Town & the Mouth of Muskingum on both sides of the Ohio, in several places, many fine pieces of Bottom Land and A great Number of Hills &

Ridges, some of which are pretty high, but none of them so near as to prevent loaded Horses passing by the River side, except in time of a Fresh, And then they may be Avoided by going some small distance from the River.

"8 Miles below Muskingum, on the Left, is *Lacomie*, or Sandy Creek [Little Kanawha, twelve miles below Muskingum; the present Sandy Creek is 45 miles below Muskingum], 30 yards over.

"2 Miles further is A Creek on the same side, 12 yards over.

"Then 35 Miles, to Hockhocking River on the Right, This River is Navigable for Canoes about 80 Miles. Between Muskingum & this River the Country is very much broken with small Hills.

"Then about 8 Miles down the Ohio to little Hockhocking [Little Hocking is six miles *above* the Big Hocking], on the Right, 100 yards wide, Navigable 30 Miles up.

"12 Miles further down the Ohio is A Creek on the Left, 10 yards wide.

"8 Miles further, to A Creek on the same side, 10 yards wide.

"Then about 4 Miles, to the beginning of Another big Bent [at Old Town Creek, just below the Horse Shoe Bend], which is about 10 Miles round to the End of the Bent; from which, to the Mouth of Sioto on the Right of the Ohio, is 12 Miles [113 miles].

"This River [the Scioto] is not Navigable when the waters are Low, And with great Difficulty when they are high. The Country hereabouts is much freer from Hills & Broken Land then near Muskingum or Hockhocking.[6]

[Mouth of Muskingum (Marietta) to Will's Town (Duncan Falls)]

"Now, Return to Muskingum and Proceed up that River, which is seldom Navigable with Loaded Canoes but in time of a Fresh, And then Scarce further than to the white Womans Creek, 120 Miles.

"About 30 Miles up Muskingum [from its mouth] is A Creek on the left [Wolf Creek], 15 yards wide.

"At 3 Miles further on the same side is another Creek, 12 yards wide.

"Then 20 Miles, to the Canoe place [Big Rock at Roxbury, in what is now Morgan County?], on the Left of the River, where the Traders formerly Landed their Goods for the Lower Shawanoe Town.

"From the mouth of Muskingum to this place the Country is in several places Hilly, but many of them are more than Gunshott from the River and none of them so near but Loaded Horses may pass Between them & the water. The Right hand Shore is the best for Horses, as the Hills are Scarcest on that side, The Stream is pretty Gentle to A Rift, about 43 Miles from the Mouth [Luke's Chute?].

"8 Miles further up [above the Canoe Place] is Another Rift [SilverHills Riffle at Stockport?]. After that, the Current is something stronger. There is about 100 yards below Will's Town, A Ledge of Rocks A Cross the River [Duncan's Falls] which Occasions the Water to Run very Rapid and shallow over them. 5 Miles above the Town there is much such another place.

[Canoe Place (Roxbury) to Lower Shawnee Town (below Circleville)]

"Now, to Return to the Landing or Canoe place & proceed for the Lower Shawanoes Town by Land.

"15 Miles from the Canoe place is A Shelving Rock, under which Neal McCollen, a Delawre Indian, Built a Cabbin.

"20 Miles further is Hockhocking River, 100 yards over and A good Fording.

"10 Miles further, to a Branch of the same River, 10 yards wide.

"Then 35 Miles, to the Lower Shawanoe Town.

"The Country all the way from the Canoe place is well watered and free from large hills or Swamps.

[Lower Shawnee Town (near Circleville) to Salt Lick Town (Columbus)]

"From the Lower Shawanoe Town to the Salt Lick Town [on the west bank of the Scioto, near Columbus, and about opposite the Ohio Penitentiary], up Sioto, is 25 Miles; The Path takes Along the River through several Savannahs and A Rich Level Country. This Town is about 60 Miles from Waukautaumike.

[Lower Shawnee Town (near Circleville) to another trail near Mt. Gilead]

"Now, from the Lower Shawanoe Town again [on the east side of Scioto[7]], Along the Path that Leads to Sandusky, through Level Land, Swampy, & Shrubby in some places, 8 Miles, to A Branch of Scioto River [Little Walnut Creek?], 12 yards wide, at which is A good Fording.

"5 Miles further is Another Branch of Scioto [Black Lick Creek?], 12 yards wide, & A good Fording place.

"Between these two Creeks is Abundance of underwood & wet ground but not very Swampy. Then 9 Miles, to A Savannah, better than A Mile wide. Most part of the way to the Savannah is Shrubby, and all the way very Level.

"20 Miles further through Level, wet, low ground, but not Swampy, to Another Savannah, A Mile wide & 5 long.

"Then 20 Miles, to A Creek 20 yards wide, This Creek has A good Ford and Runs into the White Woman's Creek; the Country very shrubby.

"9 Miles further, over little, short Hills, through Timbered Land, to A very steep Descent, leading to a Creek, 17 yards wide, the Main Branch [Owl Creek, in the present Morrow County?] of White Woman's Creek; here is A good Fording.

"Then 5 Miles, through Timbered Land and over short, small Hills, to the partings of the Road.

[Near Mt. Gilead to Owl's Town (Mt. Vernon)]

"The Right hand Path leads over A Number of small Hills, 17 Miles, to the Owl's Town.[8] 9 Miles from the partings of the Road, this path crosses A Creek, 10 yards wide, which has a good Fording.

[Near Mt. Gilead to Sandusky]

"Now, Return to the Partings of the Road and follow the Left Hand Path, which takes over Timbered Land & small Hills 15 miles to A Branch of White Woman's Creek [one of the branches of Black Fork of Mohican?], 8 yards wide.

"Then, through Timbered, level Land, in general very level, and Shrubby in some places, 45 Miles, to Sandusky.

[Sandusky to Tuscarawas (near Bolivar)]

"From Sandusky, the Path leads through several very Extensive Savannahs and A Rich level Country, well watered and Timbered, 110 Miles to Tuscarawas.

"A little below this place the Muskingum forks.

[Tuscarawas (near Bolivar) to Cuyahoga (above Akron)]

"After Crossing the Ford at Tuscarawas to the East side of the Creek, the Path leading to Cayahoga takes up a Branch of Tuscarawas [the main branch], 5 Miles, to where the Path crosses the Creek, about 17 yards wide [probably near the present Navarre].

"Then over Timbered Land, Swampy in some places, but not Hilly, 16 Miles, to the same Creek, 8 yards wide.

"After crossing of which the Path takes up the Creek about 7 Miles, to where the same Creek Runs out of a Lake [Long Lake], 3 Miles broad and about 4 in Length.

"Then, 5 Miles, through Swampy Grounds by the End of this Lake, to another Lake [Summit Lake], on the same side of the Path, near A Mile from the former one, which Conveys itself by A Creek 10 yards wide into Cayahoga River.

"From this Lake to Cayahoga Town is 18 Miles, the Path mostly Along the Creek, through level Timbered Land free from Swamps. At the Town the [Cuyahoga] Creek is 17 yards wide.

[Cuyahoga (above Akron) to the Salt Lick Town (near Niles)]

"After crossing the Creek, the Path Leads [eastward] through level Timbered land, 11 Miles, to a Branch of Cayahoga [the Main Branch] 10 yards wide, at which [probably at Kent] is A good Fording.

"Then, through Swampy Land, for 9 Miles, to A Swamp, two Miles over. This Swamp, the French, sometime ago, Bridged, by laying Logs A Cross the Path; but it is now much out of Repair.

"After Crossing the Swamp, the Path leads [south of Ravenna] by A Savannah on the Left hand and continues for 5 Miles through Thickets, but not Mirey; then [through the present townships of Edinburg, Palmyra, and Paris, Portage County] Along level, Timbered Land, 15 Miles, to Mohoning Town on [the west side of Mahoning Branch of] Beaver Creek [probably at or above the site of the present Newton Falls].

"Half a mile below this Town, the Path crosses Beaver Creek at a good Ford, 8 yards wide. The path then leaves the Creek on the Left hand and takes through Low, wet, Swampy Land [across Newton, Lordstown, and Weathersfield townships, Trumbull County] for 9

Miles, to the Salt Lick Town, situate on the west [south] side of the same Creek [about a mile southwest of Niles].

[Salt Lick Town (near Niles) to Venango (Franklin, Pa.)]

"After crossing the Creek, which is 15 yards over at this Town, the Path to Shaningo takes through Timbered Land, about 4 Miles, to a Branch [Squaw Creek] of the same Creek, 8 yards wide, at which is a Mirey ford.

"15 Miles further, through low Land, Timbered with Beach, is Shaningo Town [below Sharon], on Another [Shenango] branch of Beaver Creek 15 yards wide.

"After crossing the Creek at a good Ford the Path leads through level Land, 6 Miles, to the partings of the Venango Road.

"The left Hand Path goes about 3 Miles to Pemeytuning [at or near the mouth of Pymatuning Creek], situate on the same Creek: After crossing of which, takes through level Land, well Timbered, 8 miles to the same [Shenango] Creek again, 8 yards wide; here is a good Ford and A Number of Indian Graves.

"Then 9 Miles, along Level, Shrubby Land, to A large Run [Otter Creek], 5 yards wide, very Swampy.

"8 Miles further, through wet Land & Swampy in some places, to A Lake on the Right [Sandy Lake, in Mercer County], two Miles Long and half a Mile wide, the Head of Sandy Creek.

"Then 2½ Miles Along A Ridge, to the Crossing of Sandy Creek, 8 yards over.

"Two Miles further, down the Creek and Ascend A steep Hill. The Path then is over short Ridges, 14 Miles, to Venango.

[Salt Lick Town (near Niles) to the mouth of the Beaver]

"Now, return to the Salt Lick Town on [Mahoning Branch of] Beaver Creek, The Path then to the Kishkushes [now Edenburg, Lawrence County] crosses the Creek 2½ Miles below the Town, at A good ford, 10 yards wide.

"6 Miles further, through level Timbered Land [back] to the Main branch of Beaver [Mahoning] Creek 18 yards over, A good Fording with A steep Descent to it.

"The Path then takes down the Creek [west side], 7 Miles, along level, Rich Land, free from Swamps or Thickets, to A large Savannah, two Miles long and half a Mile wide.

"14 Miles further is the Kishkuskee Town on the [west] Bank of Beaver Creek, [Mahoning Branch]. This Town is 12 Miles from Shaningo, and the Country is made up with little Hills of Timbered Land.

"From the Kishkuske to the Mouth of Beaver Creek the path takes down the Creek Along A Bottom 2 Miles, then Ascend A pretty large Hill & proceed Along A Ridge 5 Miles to the Creek again at an Old Town [near Newport].

"Then the Path leaves the Creek and goes over Timbered Land and short Ridges, 7 Miles, to a Steep Hill, which the Path ascends after crossing A large Run,

"Then Along Timbered Land at about a Miles's Distance from the Creek, 14 Miles.

"Then Ascend A very Steep Hill and Continue on it about 2 Miles to A Steep descent, which is about ¾ of A Mile from the mouth of Beaver Creek, to which the Land is level."

NOTES
[Hanna's]

1. Either the distances or streams are not correctly given in this Route. The largest creek between Sandy Creek and the Muskingum on the south side is the Big Stillwater. This enters the Tuscarawas some thirty-five to forty miles above its mouth (which is four or five miles above the site of Bullet's Town). From Little Beaver Creek, the Lower Trail passed southwest diagonally across the present Carroll County, crossing Connotton, or One Leg Creek in that county; thence, in the same direction, to near the Northwest corner of Harrison County, across the southeastern part of Tuscarawas County, crossing Little and Big Stillwater [Three Legs] creeks; thence into the southeastern part of Coshocton County possibly crossing Will's Creek twice before reaching the Muskingum.

2. At the present Clay Lick post-office, Licking County.

3. See map of the Path from Will's Town to Mingo Town on the Ohio (Crow's Town) in Winsor's *Mississippi Basin,* p. 247.

4. The present road from Cambridge to Steubenville, through Cadiz, follows in part the course of this path.

5. This statement, if it was Hutchin's, indicates no confusion of Yellow Creek as at present known, with the West Fork of Little Beaver; which latter seems to have been the stream called Yellow Creek in the preceding itinerary.

6. This description of the Ohio River Route is full of errors, both as to locations and distances. The Horse Shoe Bend of the Ohio is here located more than a hundred miles above the Muskingum, while it is really forty-eight miles below. The Little Hocking is placed below the Big Hocking, instead of above. No mention is made of the Kanawha River. The distance from Fort Pitt to Muskingum is given as 300 miles, instead of 174; and from the Muskingum to Scioto, as 99 miles, instead of 176.

The "Rout Down the Ohio," published as an appendix to Hutchin's and Smith's *Account of Bouquet's Expedition* (Phila., 1765), gives the following distances and landmarks on the River: "From Fort Pitt to the mouth of Big Beaver Creek, 27 miles; to the mouth of Little Beaver Creek, 12; to the mouth of Yellow Creek, 10; to the Two [Cross] Creeks, 18; to Wheeling, 6; to Pipe Hill, 12; to the Long Reach, 30; to the foot of the Reach, 18; to the mouth of Muskingum River, 30; to the Little Canawha River, 12; to the mouth of Hockhocking River, 13; to the mouth of Le Tort's Creek, 40; to Kiskeminetas, 33; to the mouth of Big Canawha, or New River, 8; to the mouth of Big Sandy Creek, 40; to the mouth of Scioto, 40." Total, 349 miles.

The following distances are given in Cumming's *Western Pilot* (Cincinnati, 1834): From Pittsburgh to Big Beaver, 28½ miles; to Little Beaver, 14½; to Yellow Creek, 11; to Mingo Island, 19¾; to Captina Creek, 38¾; to Sunfish Creek, 5½; to Muskingum River, 56; to Big Hockhocking, 25; to Great [Horse Shoe] Bend, 24½; to Great Kanawha, 38; to Scioto, 89; total 350½ miles.

7. Hutchin's map of 1778 shows the path from Scioto to Sandusky as on the west side of the Scioto; but apparently this is a description of a path on the east side.

8. Hutchin's map of 1764 shows Owl's Town to have been located between the forks of Owl Creek and White Woman's River. This point is within the present township of Newcastle, Coshocton County, Ohio.

New Note as to Hanna's Note 1

Hanna, in his Note 1, states that "either the distances or streams are not correctly given in this Route. The largest creek between Sandy Creek and the Muskingum on the south side is the Big Stillwater. This enters the Tuscarawas some thirty-five to forty miles above the mouth (which is four or five miles above the site of Bullet's Town)." He then sets forth what he believes to be the route of the trail and concludes that the trail "possibly [crossed] Will's Creek twice before reaching the Muskingum."

Hanna erred as to several matters in this note. The trail did not cross Will's Creek at all; Bullet's Town is only two miles below the Forks at Coshocton, not four or five miles; and, most importantly of all, Hutchins did not err as to the distances he traveled or the streams he crossed, at least not in the part of most interest to us, the Tuscarawas Valley involvement in the trail.

I will have to admit that, initially, I could not understand Hutchins' description of the trail at all as he approached Bullet's Town. He stated that 13 miles before reaching Bullet's Town he crossed "the same creek" that he had crossed 7 miles before that, and that the creek was "70 yards wide". Ten miles before that he had crossed a creek "30 yards wide" and 7 miles before that a creek "10 yards wide".

What were these creeks, especially the one that was 70 yards wide?

Hanna concluded that the 70 yard wide creek that Hutchins crossed twice may have been Will's Creek, because it does bend to the north and it could be that someone heading west would have to cross it twice.

This did not seem reasonable to me, however, for several reasons. First, Will's Creek is too far south for someone heading to Bullet's Town to have to cross. There's no need to go that far out of the way, for Bullet's Town, as shown in the separate article on the Locations of the Indian Villages, is only two miles below the Forks of the Muskingum at Coshocton, not four or five miles as Hanna states. Also, Will's Creek is not 70 yards wide, and on its loop to the north, it would only be about two miles from one side of the loop to the other, not the seven miles that Hutchins mentioned as being the distance he traveled between the crossings of whatever stream it was.

So, what is the answer? What creek could Hutchins have crossed twice, seven miles apart, and that was 70 yards wide?

After several hours of looking at the topographical map and trying to understand how all of this could be explained, the answer finally came to me. Hutchins was right. He did cross a 70 yard wide stream twice as he approached Bullet's Town. That stream was the

Muskingum River itself! Hutchins did not call it that, but there can be no doubt about the fact that that is what it was.

Thirteen miles east of Bullet's Town, you do come to the Muskingum River (the Tuscarawas now), just west of Newcomerstown, probably at the same ford used by *Zeisberger* in 1772 when he traveled to Wakatomika. Then, the trail passed "over several small ridges" (these would be just north of Newcomerstown) for 7 miles to the Muskingum again just below Port Washington. There was a ford in that vicinity, for several of the journalists in this book crossed the Muskingum at about that point. Then, 10 miles farther, you do come to the Stillwater, and 7 miles beyond that, the Connotton.

It all makes sense when we realize that the 70 yard wide stream was actually the Muskingum River.

Is it possible that Hutchins did not realize that that "creek" was actually the Muskingum River?

Yes, I believe so, for the following reasons.

1. When he struck the Muskingum at Bullet's Town, it was a broad, majestic stream, for the Walhonding had joined the Tuscarawas by this time, thus nearly doubling its size. The 70 yard wide "creek" he had crossed earlier was much smaller and probably did look like an entirely different stream.

2. The map that he drew in 1764 during Bouquet's Expedition, about a year later, clearly reveals a lack of understanding as to the courses of the Muskingum between Coshocton and Bolivar. Hutchins' map shows it curving gracefully in a northeasterly direction toward Bolivar, without any substantial changes of direction. In fact, however, it heads east from Coshocton for about 16 miles, then northeast for 14 miles to Midvale, then northwest for 8 miles to Dover, then northeast 6 miles to Zoarville, and finally northwest another 6 miles to Bolivar. All of these changes of direction were unknown to Hutchins when he made his map in 1764, and, of course, were unknown to him in 1763 when he was describing the Indian trails.

Indian Games

Nine-pins, ball-playing and cards they have learned from the whites. The Indian game of dice is the most popular of amusements. They may devote days in succession to it, always gambling on the throwing.

Zeisberger's *History, p. 118*

Indian Trails at Tuscarawas

The following are excerpts from Thomas Hutchins' manuscript entitled "The Rout from Fort Pitt to Sandusky, and thence to Detroit", written in 1764 and set forth in Hanna's *The Wilderness Trail*, Vol. 2, pp. 204–5. Brackets and parentheses are Hanna's.

"...The path continues from hence over a very rich bottom to the main branch of Muskingum about 70 yards wide, with a good ford, four miles from Nemenshehelas creek and 94 miles a half and 64 perches from fort Pitt.

"A little below [the fording place] and above the forks of this river, [north of Sandy Creek], about a quarter of a mile from the ford, is Tuscarawas, a place exceedingly beautiful by situation, the lands rich on both sides of the river; the country on the N.W. side being one entire, level plain, upwards of five miles in circumference. From the ruined houses appearing here [in 1764], the Indians who inhabited the place, and are now with the Delawares, are supposed to have had about one hundred and fifty warriors.

"Three paths branch out from Tuscarawas; the southermost leads to the Indian towns on the Muskingum and Sioto rivers and to the forks of the Muskingum, where General Bouquet had his sixteenth and last encampment, when he marched against the Ohio Indians in 1764, and where he redeemed from them upwards of 200 white persons who were prisoners amongst them, and also obliged them to give hostages for the punctual performance of their engagements with him.

...

"About two miles below Tuscarawas, on a very high bank, with the Muskingum at the foot of it, which is 100 yards wide at this place, with a fine, level country at some distance from its banks, producing stately timber, free from underwood, and plenty of food for cattle, was erected a small stockaded fort, to deposit provisions for the use of the troops on their return, and to lighten the convoy.

"The path from this place to the forks of the Muskingum leads through a fertile country, interspersed with little hills and vallies, rivulets and springs, and at five miles and 46 perches from the fort, the path crosses a branch of the Muskingum called Margaret's creek [now Sugar Creek] about 30 feet wide, bordered with very rich land, producing a variety of timber.

"The north, or Cayahoga path, from Tuscarawas, takes through level, good land for ten miles, and about two miles further reaches a small branch of the Muskingum; the first half of this distance over level, light soil, as just mentioned, and the remaining 5 (five) miles the land is something superior in quality to that last described. From hence to the sources of Muskingum, the country is fertile, interspersed with swamps and many small Lakes.

...

"The third, or middle path, leading from Tuscarawas to Sandusky, a distance of nearly one hundred miles, in general passes over a level and extremely fertile country, remarkably well watered with rivers, rivulets, brooks, and springs; and, except where extensive Savanahs or natural meadows intervene, well timbered with different kinds of oak, walnut, ash, hickory, mulberry, sassafras, etc.

"The path, within the distance of two miles from Tuscarawas, crosses the Muskingum, twice; and continues over a fertile soil, composed of gradual ascents and descents, free from underwood and very pleasant, six miles and a half further, to Margaret's creek [now Sugar Creek, in the south part of Sugar Creek Township, Stark county], 15 yards wide, with a mirey bottom at the ford. The second crossing of Margaret's creek is six yards wide and distant two miles from the first.

BIBLIOGRAPHY

Abbatt, William. "The Journal of George McCully", *The Magazine of History with Notes and Queries,* Extra Number 10. New York, 1910.

Abbott, W. W., ed., *The Papers of George Washington, Colonial Series,* vol 1. Charlottesville: University Press of Virginia, 1983.

Beatty, Charles. *The Journal of a two months tour; with a view of Promoting Religion among the Frontier Inhabitants of Pennsylvania, and of Introducing Christianity among the Indians to the Westward of the Alegh-geny Mountains.* Edinburgh: T. MacCliesh & Co., 1798.

————*Journals of Charles Beatty, 1762–1769.* Edited by Guy Soulliard Klett. University Park, The Pennsylvania State University Press, 1962.

Bouquet, Henry. *The Papers of Henry Bouquet.* 19 vols. Edited by S. K. Stevens and D. H. Kent. Harrisburg, Pennsylvania Historical Commission, 1940–41.

————.*The Papers of Henry Bouquet.* 5 vols. Edited by Louis M. Waddell, John L. Tottenham, Donald H. Kent. Harrisburg: The Pennsylvania Historical and Museum Commission, 1984.

Brickell, John. "Narrative of John Brickell's Captivity Among the Delaware Indians". *The American Pioneer* 1(1842): 43–56.

Brown, Lloyd Arnold. *Early Maps of the Ohio Valley.* Pittsburgh: Univ. of Pittsburgh Press, 1959.

Butler, Richard. "The Journal of Richard Butler, 1775." ed. by Edward G. Williams. *The Western Pennsylvania Historical Magazine,* 46(1964): 381-95; 47(1964): 31-46, 141-56.

Butterfield, Consul W. *An Historical Account of the Expedition Against Sandusky under Col. William Crawford in 1782.* Cincinnati: Robert Clarke & Co., 1873.

————.*History of the Girtys.* Cincinnati: Robert Clarke & Co., 1890. Reprint. Columbus, Ohio: Long's College Book Co., 1950.

————.*The Washington-Crawford Letters.* Cincinnati: Robert Clarke & Co., 1877.

————.*Washington-Irvine Correspondence.* Madison, Wisconsin: David Atwood, 1882.

Collins, V. L. "Indian Wards at Princeton". *The Princeton University Bulletin,* Vol. XIII, No. 5 (1902): 101–6.

Cresswell, Nicholas. *The Journal of Nicholas Cresswell, 1774–1777.* New York: The Dial Press, 1924.

Croghan, George. "The Journal of George Croghan, 1760–1761." *Massachusetts Historical Collections,* 4th series, IX(1871): 362–79.

Crumrine, Boyd. *Virginia Court Records in Southwestern Pennsylvania, 1775–1780.* Baltimore: Genealogical Publishing Co., Inc., 1981

Darlington, Mary C. *Fort Pitt and Letters from the Frontier.* Pittsburgh: J. R. Weldin & Co., 1892. Reprint. New York: Arno Press, 1971.

————.*History of Col. Henry Bouquet and the Western Frontier of Pennsylvania, 1744–1764.* New York: Arno Press, 1971. (Privately printed in 1920.)

De Hass, Wills. *History of the Early Settlement and Indian Wars of Western Virginia.* Wheeling: H. Hoblitzell, 1851. Reprint. Parsons, West Virginia: McClain Printing Company, 1960.

De Schweinitz, Edmund. *The Life and Times of David Zeisberger.* Philadelphia: J. R. Lippincott, 1870. Reprint. New York: Arno Press, 1971.

Dictionary of American Biography. Eds. Allen Johnson and Dumas Malone. 21 vols. New York: Charles Scribner's Sons, 1937.

Doddridge, Joseph. *Notes on the Settlement and Indian Wars of the Western Parts of Virginia and Pennsylvania from 1763 to 1783, inclusive.* Wellsburg: By the author at the office of the Wellsburg Gazette, 1824. Republished with additional material. Pittsburgh: John S. Ritenour and Wm. T. Lindsey, 1912. Reprint. Parsons, West Virginia: McClain Printing Company, 1960.

Dodge, J. R. *Red Men of the Ohio Valley.* Springfield, O.: Ruralist Publishing Co., 1860.

Downes, Randolph C. *Council Fires on the Upper Ohio.* Pittsburgh: Univ. of Pittsburgh Press, 1940.

Eavenson, Howard N. *Map Maker & Indian Traders.* Pittsburgh: University of Pittsburgh Press, 1949.

Ewing, William S. "Indian Captives Released by Colonel Bouquet", *The Western Pennsylvania Historical Magazine,* Volume 39. Pittsburgh, 1956.

Fliegel, Rev. Carl John. *Index to the Moravian Records of the Moravian Mission among the Indians of North America.* 4 vols. Moravian Archives, Bethlehem, Pennsylvania. Microfilm. Woodbridge, Conn.: Research Publications, Inc., 1970.

Forbes, John. *Writings of General John Forbes Relating to his Service in North America.* Compiled and edited by Alfred Procter James. Menasha, Wisconsin: The Collegiate Press, 1938. Reprint. New York: Arno Press, 1971.

Franklin, Benjamin. *The Autobiography of Benjamin Franklin.* New York: Washington Square Press, 1960.

Gibson, Hugh. "An Account of the Captivity of Hugh Gibson among the Delaware Indians of the Big Beaver and the Muskingum, from the Latter Part of July 1756, to the Beginning of April, 1759" *Collections of the Massachusetts Historical Society,* Vol. VI of the Third Series(1837): 141–53.

Gintz, Alan F. *The Tuscarawas Navigator.* New Philadelphia, 1974.

Gipson, Lawrence Henry. *Lewis Evans.* Philadelphia: The Historical Society of Pennsylvania, 1939.

———.*The Moravian Indian Mission on White River.* Indianapolis: Indiana Historical Bureau, 1938.

Gist, Christopher. *Christopher Gist's Journals.* Edited by William M. Darlington. Pittsburgh: J. R. Weldin & Co., 1893.

Gray, Elma E. *Wilderness Christians: The Moravian Mission to the Delaware Indians.* Ithaca, New York: Cornell University Press, 1956.

Hamilton, Kenneth Gardiner. *John Ettwein and the Moravian Church during the Revolutionary Period.* Bethlehem, Pa.: Times Publishing Company, 1940.

Hamilton, Milton W. *The Papers of Sir William Johnson,* 14 Vols. Albany: The University of the State of New York, 1946–.

Hanna, Charles A. *The Wilderness Trail.* 2 vols. New York: G. P. Putnam's Sons, 1911.

Heckewelder, John. "A Canoe Journey from the Big Beaver to the Tuscarawas in 1773: A Travel Diary of John Heckewaelder." Edited by Dr. August C. Mahr. *Ohio State Archaeological and Historical Quarterly,* Vol. 61, No. 3(July, 1952): 283–98.

———.*A Narrative of the Mission of the United Brethren Among the Delaware and Mohegan Indians, from its Commencement, in the year 1740 to the close of the year 1808.* Philadelphia: McCarty and Davis, 1820. Reprint. New York: Arno Press, 1971.

———.*History, Manners, and Customs of the Indian Nations Who Once Inhabited Pennsylvania and the Neighbouring States.* Philadelphia: Abraham Small, 1819. Reprint. New York: Arno Press, 1971.

———."Notes of Travel of William Henry, John Heckewelder, John Rothrock, and Christian Clewell, to Gnadenhuetten on the Muskingum, in the Early Summer of 1797." *The Pennsylvania Magazine of History and Biography,* Vol. X, No. 2(1886): 125–57.

Hildreth, S. P. *Pioneer History.* Cincinnati: H. W. Derby & Co., 1848. Reprint. New York: Arno Press, 1971.

Hutchins, Thomas. *The Courses of the Ohio River.* Edited by Beverly W. Bond, Jr. Cincinnati: Historical and Philosophical Society of Ohio, 1942.

Jacob, John Jeremiah. *A Biographical Sketch of the Life of the Late Captain Michael Cresap.* Cincinnati, Ohio: William Dodge, 1866. (Originally published in 1826.) Reprint. Parsons, West Virginia: McClain Printing Company, 1971.

Jefferson, Thomas. *Notes on the State of Virginia.* New York: Harper & Row, 1964.

Jones, David. *A Journal of Two Visits Made to Some Nations of Indians on the West Wide of the River Ohio in the Years 1772 and 1773.* Burlington: Isaac Collins, 1774. Reprint. New York: Arno Press, 1971.

Kellogg, Louise Phelps, ed. *Frontier Advance on the Upper Ohio 1778–1779.* Madison: Wisconsin Historical Society, 1916.

————.*Frontier Retreat on the Upper Ohio 1779–1781.* Madison: Wisconsin Historical Society, 1917.

Kenny, James. "Journal of James Kenny, 1761-1763, 1758-1759." *The Pennsylvania Magazine of History and Biography,* Vol. XXXVII, No. 1(1913): 1–47, 152–201, 395–449.

Kopperman, Paul E. *Braddock at the Monongahela.* Pittsburgh: Univ. of Pittsburg Press, 1977.

Kraft, Herbert C. *The Lenape: Archaelogy, History and Ethnography.* Newark: New Jersey Historical Society, 1986.

Lacey, John. "Journal of a Mission to the Indians in Ohio, by Friends from Pennsylvania, July-September, 1773." *The Historical Magazine and Notes and Queries,* Vol. VII, Second Series(1870): 103–7.

Lake, D. J. *Atlas of Coshocton County, Ohio.* Philadelphia: C. O. Titus, 1872.

LeRoy, Marie and Leininger, Barbara. "The Narrative of Marie LeRoy and Barbara Leininger, for Three Years Captives Among the Indians." *The Pennsylvania Magazine of History and Biography,* Vol. XXIX(1905): 407–20.

Letters of Delegates to Congress, 1774–1789. Paul H. Smith, Editor. Washington: Library of Congress, 1976–.

Loskiel, George Henry. *History of the Missions of the United Brethren among the Indians of North America.* Translated by Christian Latrobe. London: Burlinghouse, 1794.

Loudon, Archibald. *A Selection of Some of the Most Interesting Narratives of Outrages, committed by the Indians in Their Wars with the White People.* Carlisle: A. Loudon, 1803. Reprint. New York: Arno Press, 1971.

Mason, A. Hughlett. *The Journal of Charles Mason and Jeremiah Dixon*. Philadelphia: American Philosophical Society, 1969.

McClure, David. *Diary of David McClure*. with notes by Franklin B. Dexter. New York: The Knickerbocker Press, 1899.

McCready, Robert. "A Revolutionary Journal and Orderly Book of General Lachlan McIntosh's Expedition, 1778." Edited by Edward G. Williams. *The Western Pennsylvania Historical Magazine,* Vol. 43, No. 1, March 1960: 11–17.

McKnight, Charles. *Our Western Border*. Philadelphia: J. C. McCurdy & Co., 1876.

Mitchell, John. *The Contest in America between Great Britain and France*. London: A. Millar, 1767. Reprint. New York: Johnson Reprint Corporation, 1965.

Morse, Jedidiah. *The American Gazetter*. Boston: S. Hall, 1797.

Mulkearn, Lois. *George Mercer Papers Relating to the Ohio Company of Virginia*. Pittsburgh: Univ. of Pittsburgh Press, 1954.

O'Callaghan, E. B. *Documents relative to the Colonial History of the State of New York*. Albany: Weed, Parsons and Company, 1856.

Olmstead, Earl P. *Blackcoats among the Delaware*. Kent, Ohio: The Kent State University Press, 1991.

O'Meara, Walter. *Guns at the Forks*. Pittsburgh: Univ. of Pittsburg Press, 1979.

Parkman, Francis. *Montcalm and Wolfe*. 2 vols. Boston: Little, Brown, 1902. Reprint. New York, The Library of America, 1983.

————.*The Conspiracy of Pontiac and the Indian War after the Conquest of Canada*. 2 vols. Boston: Little, Brown, 1893.

Parrish, John. "Extracts from the Journal of John Parrish, 1773." *The Pennsylvania Magazine of History and Biography,* Vol. XVI(1892): 443–48.

Peckham, Howard H. *Pontiac and the Indian Uprising*. Princeton, New Jersey: Princeton University Press, 1947.

————.*The Colonial Wars: 1689–1762*. Chicago: The Univ. of Chicago Press, 1964.

Penn, William. *A Letter from William Penn, Proprietary and Governour of Pennsylvania in America, to the Committee of the Free Society of Traders, etc*. London: The Free Society, 1682. Revised edition edited by Albert Cook Myers. Somerset, New Jersey: The Middle Atlantic Press, 1970.

Pennsylvania Archives, First Series, 12 Vols. Philadelphia, 1852–56.

Pennsylvania Colonial Records, 16 Vols. Harrisburg, 1838–53

Pieper, Thomas I., and Gidney, James B. *Fort Laurens 1778–79.* Kent: Kent State University Press, 1976.

Powell, Allan. *Christopher Gist: Frontier Scout.* Hagerstown, Maryland: Allan Powell, 1992.

Pownell, T[homas]. *A Topographical Description of the Dominions of The United States of America.* Ed. by Lois Mulkearn. Pittsburgh: University of Pittsburgh Press, 1949. Reprint. New York: Arno Press, 1976.

Rogers, Robert. *Journals of Major Robert Rogers.* London: J. Millan, 1765. Reprint. New York: Corinth Books, 1961.

Rondthaler, Edward. *Life of John Heckewelder.* Philadelphia: Townsend Ward, 1847.

Rose, John. "Journal of a Volunteer Expedition to Sandusky, from May 24 to June 13, 1782." *The Pennsylvania Magazine of History and Biography,* Vol. XVIII, No. 2(1894): 129–57, 293–328. Reprint. New York: Arno Press, 1969.

Rupp, Israel Daniel. *Early History of Western Pennsylvania.* Pittsburgh, Pennsylvania: Daniel W. Kauffman, 1847. Reprint. Laughlintown, Pennsylvania: Southwest Pennsylvania Genealogical Service, 1989.

Sargent, Winthrop. *The History of an Expedition against Fort Du Quesne in 1755.* Philadelphia: Lippincott, Grambo & Co., 1855. Reprint. New York: Arno Press, 1971.

Savelle, Max. *George Morgan: Colony Builder.* New York: Columbia University Press, 1932.

Sipe, C. Hale. *Fort Ligonier and its Times.* Harrisburg, Pannsylvania: The Telegraph Press, 1932.

————.*The Indian Chiefs of Pennsylvania.* Butler: Zigler Printing Company, 1927.

————.*The Indian Wars of Pennsylvania.* Harrisburg, Pa.: The Telegraph Press, 1929.

Slick, Sewell E. *William Trent and the West.* Harrisburg, Pennsylvania: Archives Publishing Company of Pennsylvania, Inc., 1947.

Smith, James. *An Account of the Remarkable Occurrences in the Life and Travels of Col. James Smith.* Lexington: John Bradford, 1799. Re-titled, reprinted and annotated by John J. Barsotti under the title *Scoouwa: James Smith's Indian Captivity Narrative.* Columbus, Ohio: Ohio Historical Society, 1978.

Smith, Thomas H. *The Mapping of Ohio.* Kent, Ohio: Kent State University Press, 1977.

Smith, William. *An Historical Account of the Expedition Against the Ohio Indians, in the Year 1764, under the Command of Henry Bouquet, Esq.* Philadelphia: William Bradford, 1765. Reprint. Ann Arbor: University Microfilms, Inc., 1966.

Stevens, Henry N. *Lewis Evans: His Map of the Middle British Colonies in America.* London: Henry Stevens, Son, and Stiles, 1920. Reprint;. New York: Arno Press, 1971.

Stuart, Charles. "The Captivity of Charles Stuart, 1755–57." *The Mississippi Valley Historical Review,* Volume XIII(June 1926–March 1927): 58-81.

Tanner, Helen Hornbeck, ed. *Atlas of Great Lakes Indian History.* Norman, Oklahoma: Univ. of Oklahoma Press, 1987.

Terrell, John Upton. *American Indian Almanac.* New York: Thomas Y. Crowell Company, 1974.

Thacher, James. *Military Journal of the American Revolution.* Hartford, Conn: Hurlbut, Williams & Company, 1862. Reprint. New York: Arno Press, 1969.

Thwaites, Reuben Gold, ed. *Early Western Travels.* Cleveland: Arthur H. Clarke, 1904.

————.*France in America, 1497–1763.* New York: Harpers, 1905. Reprint. New York: Haskell House Publishers Ltd., 1969.

Thwaites, Reuben Gold and Kellogg, Louise Phelps, eds. *Documentary History of Dunmore's War 1774.* Madison: Wisconsin Historical Society, 1905.

————.*Frontier Defense on the Upper Ohio 1777–1778.* Madison: Wisconsin Historical Society, 1912. Reprint. Millwood, New York: Kraus Reprint Co., 1977.

————.*The Revolution on the Upper Ohio 1775–1777.* Madison: Wisconsin Historical Society, 1908.

Thompson, Charles N. *Sons of the Wilderness: John and William Conner.* Indianapolis: Indiana Historical Society, 1937.

Transactions of the American Philosophical Society, New Series, Volume IV, Art. 11. Philadelphia, 1833.

Trent, William. *Journal of Captain William Trent.* edited by Alfred T. Goodman. Cincinnati: Robert Clarke & Co., 1871. Reprint. New York: Arno Press, 1971.

Volwiler, Albert T. *George Croghan and the Westward Movement 1741–1782.* Cleveland: The Arthur H. Clark Company, 1926.

Wainwright, Nicholas B. *George Croghan: Wilderness Diplomat.* Chapel Hill: The University of North Carolina Press, 1959.

————."George Croghan's Journal, 1759–1763", *The Pennsylvania Magazine of History and Biography,* October 1947.

Wallace, Paul A. W. *Indians in Pennsylvania.* Revised Edition. Harrisburg: The Pennsylvania Historical and Museum Commission, 1989.

————.*Indian Paths of Pennsylvania.* Harrisburg: Pennsylvania Historical and Museum Commission, 1987.

————.*Thirty Thousand Miles with John Heckewelder.* Pittsburgh: Univ. of Pittsburgh Press. 1958.

Washington, George. *The Journal of Major George Washington.* Williamsburg: William Hunter, 1754. Reprint. Williamsburg: Colonial Williamsburg, 1959.

Weslager, Conrad A. *The Delaware Indians.* New Brunswick: Rutgers University Press, 1972.

————.*The Delaware Indian Western Migration.* Wallingford, Pennsylvania: The Middle Atlantic Press, 1978.

Wilcox, Frank. *Ohio Indian Trails.* edited by William A. McGill. Kent, Ohio: The Kent State University Press, 1970. (Originally published in 1933.)

Williams, Edward G. *The Orderly Book of Colonel Henry Bouquet's Expedition Against the Ohio Indians, 1764.* Pittsburgh, Pennsylvania: Mayer Press, 1960.

————."A Survey of Bouquet's Road, 1764", *The Western Pennsylvania Historical Magazine,* April 1984: 143–49.

Withers, Alexander Scott. *Chronicles of Border Warfare.* Clarksburg, Virginia: Joseph Israil, 1831. Edited by Reuben Gold Thwaites. Cincinnati: The Robert Clarke Company, 1895. Reprint. Parsons, West Virginia, McClain Printing Company, 1961.

Zeisberger, David. *Diary of David Zeisberger.* 2 vols. ed. by Eugene F. Bliss. Cincinnati: Robert Clarke & Co., 1885. Reprint. St. Clair Shores, Michigan: Scholarly Press, Inc., 1972.

————."The History of the North American Indians," written 1779–1780, translated by Archer Butler Hulbert and William Nathaniel Schwarze. *Ohio Archaeological and Historical Society Publications* 19(1910): 1–173.

INDEX

The names of rivers and Indian tribes are not indexed, for they appear so frequently throughout the book that to list them would be of little value. Also, since nearly all of the journals start and end at Pittsburgh, it is not indexed either. In the Special Studies section of the book, only new matter is indexed.

Neolin, 87, 89–91
Neskalichen, 107
Netatwhelman. *See* Netawatwees
Netawatwees (Natatwhelman, Neepwaughwhese, Neetotwhelemy, Neghkuunque, Netatwhelman, Netowclemon, Nettautwaleman, Nettowhatways, Notawatwees, Newcomer): a chief of tribe holding McCullough, 37, 39; deposed by Bouquet, 73, 77; King of the Delawares, 80; Beatty meets, 84; Zeisberger meets, 96; glad Zeisberger visited, 99; house described, 107; meets McClure, 116; sober during rum frolic, 121; Zeisberger spends night with, 133; wants ship to go to England, 135; presents for, 137; meets Jones, 142; Heckewelder visits, 150; Quakers visit, 152; warns Christian Indians to be on their guard, 160; meets Wood, 167; meets Cresswell, 173; meets Butler at Logstown, 177; asks Moravians to start a third town, 181; trying to make peace during Dunmore's War, 198; at Cuyahoga in 1763, 259; nearly 90 when he died, 261; grandfather of Gelelemend, evidence, 284; uncle of Gelelemend, evidence, 284–86
Newbold, Jacob, 159
Newcastle (Pa.), 307
Newcomerstown (Neghkuunque, Red Bank, Kighalampegha, Gekelemukpechunk): McCullough narrative, 37; Beatty traveling to, 80; council house described, 83; town described, 92; vomiting had been the custom, 98–99; council gives land to the Christian Indians, 102; described, 108; McClure visits, 110, 116, rum frolic at, 121–23; Zeisberger preaches at, 130; Jones arrives at, 142; Quakers arrive at, 154; Wood visits, 166–68; Cresswell visits, 170, 173–74; Butler visits, 177, 179; Brodhead goes to, 197; prisoners at, 263; Finley's notes, 279; Indian paths near, 308. *See also* Gekelemukpechunk.
New Hundy, 173
Newport (Pa.), 305
New Schoenbrunn, 231–32
Newton Township (Trumbull County, Ohio), 305
Nickels, Joseph. *See* Nicholson, Joseph
Nicholas (Indian), 167
Nicholas, Thomas. *See* Nicholson, Thomas
Nicholson, Joseph: interpreter to accompany McClure, 114–15; visits former captors, 126, accompanies Wilson, 182, 184; mentioned, 117, 128
Nicholson, Thomas, 178, 293
Night walker (Neepwaughwhese), 39, 261
Niles (Ohio), 305
Nimwha, 74, 112

North Carolina Dragoons, 192
Oghhitawmikaw. *See* Wakatomika
Ohio Company of Virginia, 3–4
Ohneburg, Sarah, 232
Old age, 30
Old Chillicothe, 177
Old Hundy, 173
Old Stone Fort, 150
Old Town, 263
Old Town (near Newport), 305
Ols Landing (Walhonding), 213
Orange Rapids (White Eyes Falls), 242
Ottaways, Town of, 2, 5–6, 8–10
Owens, ———, 145
Owl's Town, 303, 307
Painted Post, 34, 68
Palmyra Township (Portage County, Ohio), 304
panther, 175
panthers, 15
Paris Township (Portage County, Ohio), 304
Parks, Lieut., 193–94
Parrish, John: journal, 154–56
Paths crossing, of journalists, 277
Patten, John, 253
Paxenoos: son of, 131, 133
peach orchard, 118
Peappi, Joseph. *See* Peepy, Joseph
Peemaholand (Penmaholen), 220–21
Peepe, Jo. *See* Peepy, Joseph
Peepy, Joseph: Delaware translator, 79–81; to be interpreter for McClure, 110, 112; finds him at Kuskuskies, 113; speaks "broken English", 115; stayed with McClure at Newcomerstown, 117; conversed with McClure about religion, 120; goes to village five miles down river, 122; preaches to Indians, 124; goes to Welhik Thuppeek, 126; goes to Philadelphia, 129, 135–38; accompanies Zeisberger to Wakatomika, 130–32; presents for, 138; meets Jones, 142; interprets for Jones at Gnadenhutten, 143; discusses pay with Jones, 144; sent to overtake White Eyes, 183; father of Anton, 214; visits Gnadenhutten with Gelelemend, 285; mentioned, 106
Peepy, Hannah, 214
Pemberton, Israel, 58, 154
Pemeytuning, 305
Pendergrass, Garret, 166
Penmaholen. *See* Peemaholand
Penn, Governor, 145
Penn, Lt. Gov. Richard, 135, 146
Penn, William, 117, 275, 285
Pepee, Joseph. *See* Peepy, Joseph
Pepi, Joseph. *See* Peepy, Joseph
Peter, Capt. John (Indian), 24
Peter (Indian), 72

White Eyes' estate, 293–94
White Eyes' house: at Beaver, 171
Whiteman, 172
White man's meetings, 270
White Womans Creek, town on, 8
Wialusing, 90, 107
Wilhelm: to go to Newcomerstown, 103; on committee to revise the Lord's Prayer, 106; accompanies Ettwein to Newcomerstown, 107–9; returns from treaty at Pittsburgh, 180; goes to Newcomerstown, 185; returns from Coshocton, 247
Williams, Isaac, 214
Williamson, Col. David, 210–11
Will's Town. *See* Sikeyunck
Wilson, ———: kills Indian on Wakatomika Expedition, 159
Wilson, ———, 162
Wilson, Capt. (Indian), 197
Wilson, Col. James, 171
Wilson, Sarah, 31
Wilson, William: journal, 182–84; 186
Windochaloos Town, 178
Windohala, 64
Wingenum (Winginom, Winganous): warns Calhoun, 64; at Coshocton, 167; Cresswell meets, 174; warmarks, 174; Butler visits his town, 178; Wilson passes through, 183
Wingenum's Town, 178, 183
Wolf Tribe, 211
Wolves, 115
Wood, James: sent to invite Indians to treaty, 166–69; threatened by Indians, 168; Cresswell meets, 170; mentioned, 177, 277

Worm-Town. *See* Moyheysinck
Wright, Hezekiah, 33–34
Wryneck, 112
Wyandots: at Muskingum, 6–8, 11–12; Fugitives Camp, 13; deliver prisoners, 46
Wyandot Town, 168
Wyoming. *See* Wajomik
Yaughyaughgany big bottom, 12
Yeates, Jasper, 265–66
Youngman. *See* Jungman
Zaines, 211
Zane, Isaac, 154
Zeisberger, Rev. David: manner in which he brought Christianity to the Indians, 47; biography, 95; first journey to Newcomerstown, 95–99; receives threatening letter, 95; discusses letter about Gertraud, 97–98; his first sermon at Newcomerstown, 97; his second and third sermons at Newcomerstown, 98; second journey to Newcomerstown, 100–102; tells chiefs what they require for their mission town, 101–2; at conference at Languntoutenunk, 103–4; revises Roth's translation of Lord's Prayer, 106; accompanies Ettwein to Muskingum, 106; in Glickhikan's dream, 108; goes to Wakatomika, 130; conducts first church service at Gnadenhutten, 134; meets Jones, 143; visits Coshocton, 181; captivity journal, 199–206; describes Gnadenhutten Massacre, 207–9; mentioned, 138, 180, 184–85, 191, 204
Zeisberger, Susanna, 203, 206
Zoarville (Ohio), 8–10, 16, 246, 308

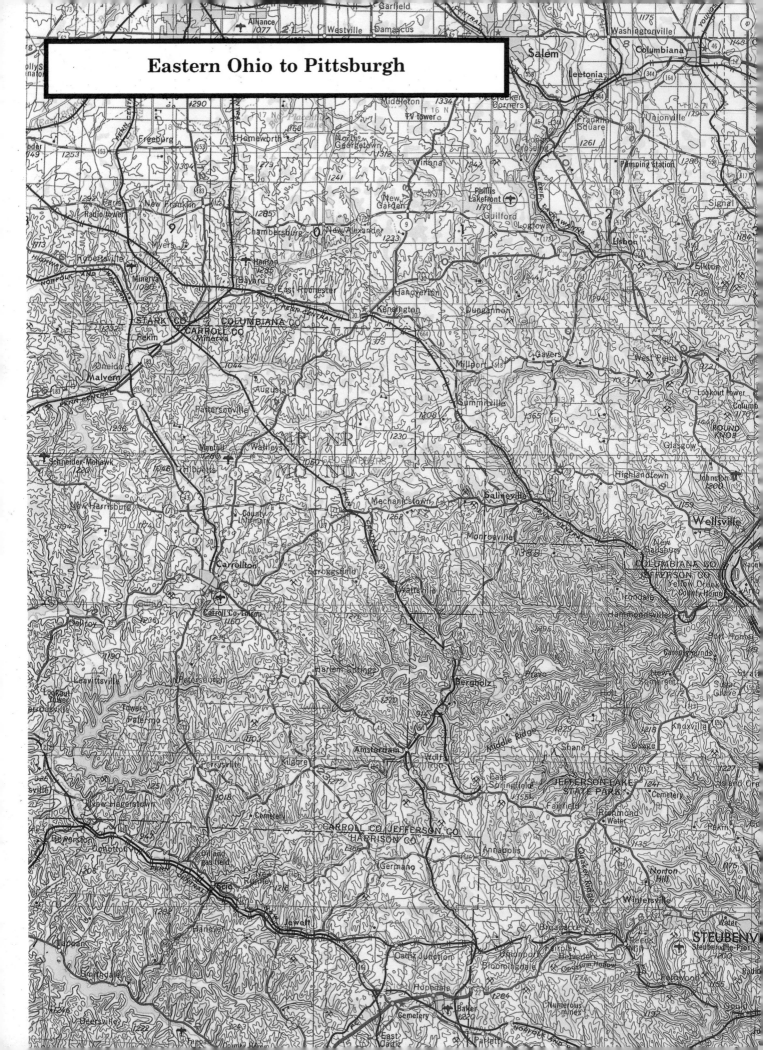

Eastern Ohio to Pittsburgh